# World History

Second Edition

(Revised 1982)

## Irving L. Gordon

*Author of*
*Review Text in American History*
*American Studies: A Conceptual Approach*
*Review Text in World History*

*Dedicated to serving*

**AMSCO**

*our nation's youth*

When ordering this book, please specify:
*either* **R 216 P** *or* WORLD HISTORY, SECOND EDITION, PAPERBACK

**AMSCO SCHOOL PUBLICATIONS, INC.**
**315 Hudson Street   New York, N. Y. 10013**

ISBN 0-87720-624-4

Copyright © 1982, 1980, 1979 by Amsco School Publications, Inc.

No part of this book may be reproduced in any form
without written permission from the publisher.

Printed in the United States of America

# Preface

Americans are increasingly affected by world affairs. In the years since World War II, we have witnessed such great tides of change as independence for almost all African and Asian peoples, the advent of nuclear energy, the growth of Soviet power, and the emergence of the United States as the leader of free nations. Americans, consequently, need an understanding of the peoples and forces that have helped shape our world.

Students are afforded an opportunity to secure such understanding by a course in world history. Because of the vast quantity of historical information, however, students have need of a concise basic text. *World History* has been designed to meet this need. It may be supplemented, as the teacher sees fit and as the interests of the students indicate, by other materials, such as primary sources, readings, and audiovisual aids.

*World History* offers the following features:

1. *Global History.* The text encompasses the history of most of the world. Although European developments predominate, ample attention is paid to the non-European aspects of world history. The major Asian nations—India, China, and Japan—are portrayed from earliest times. The problems facing Africa and Asia today are fully discussed.

2. *Attention to Concepts.* The text organization eliminates nonessential data and focuses attention upon important facts and significant concepts. To enable students to comprehend key concepts and to develop analytical powers, the text discusses such vital questions as these: Why have violent revolutions for democratic change often resulted in dictatorship? Are the major differences in outlook between the Russian people and the West European peoples explicable in terms of Russia's isolation from the main currents of West European historical development? Was Nazism an aberration from or a natural outgrowth of West European civilization?

3. *Present-day Viewpoint.* The text has an up-to-date perspective. Considerable attention has been given to the discussion of recent world affairs, and the past is viewed in terms of current forces and problems.

4. *Language—Graded, Clear, and Unbiased.* The text has been carefully graded to meet the comprehension level of students. Difficult terms and concepts are explained at length. Every effort has been made to achieve fair and equal treatment of men and women and to avoid conscious or unconscious racial bias. The text employs crisp, clear, and varied language so as to facilitate understanding and maintain interest.

5. *Extensive Illustrative Materials.* The text contains much illustrative material—maps, photographs, drawings, charts, and cartoons. The maps help students relate geographic factors to historical events. The photographs and drawings illustrate cultural developments. The charts and cartoons, mostly pertaining to recent times, help encourage critical thinking about world problems.

6. *Abundant Test Questions.* The text contains many test questions, both short-answer and essay types. These are arranged by topic and appear after the text discussion of each topic. Carefully graded, the tests probe significant information and enable students to measure their mastery of the content. Many questions require logical reasoning and mature understanding—major objectives of social studies teaching.

—I. L. G.

# Contents

## SECTION THREE. MODERN HISTORY

# Introduction to the Study of History

## WHAT IS HISTORY?

History is the story of humanity's past. History systematically records and explains what people have thought, said, and done. History deals with political, economic, and social matters.

1. **Political**—pertaining to *government*.

2. **Economic**—relating to *agriculture, industry,* and *trade*.

3. **Social**—referring to *everyday life* and *culture*.

These three aspects of history are interrelated; a development in one phase usually affects the others.

History describes humanity's efforts to improve the world. It recounts the achievements and setbacks in the long, uphill climb toward a high level of civilization.

*Le Pelley in The Christian Science Monitor © 1961 TCSPS*

**"Hello, I don't believe we've met socially."**

What world challenges face students before graduation? After graduation? Are they friendly? Hostile? Formidable?

## WHY STUDY HISTORY?

**1. For Knowledge.** We study history to understand *(a)* our way of life and its development, *(b)* today's world problems by comparing them with relevant past situations, and *(c)* the interdependence of nations.

**2. For Skills.** History helps us sharpen our ability to *(a)* comprehend books, newspapers, and radio and television programs, *(b)* interpret maps and graphs, *(c)* separate fact from opinion, *(d)* analyze problems, gather and evaluate evidence, and arrive at conclusions, and *(e)* discuss current issues.

**3. For Attitudes.** As we study history, we learn that we *(a)* owe a debt to other peoples for their contributions to civilization, *(b)* have an obligation, as civilized persons, to seek peaceful settlement of differences, and *(c)* have the responsibility to protect and preserve our democracy.

## WHY DO AMERICANS STUDY WORLD HISTORY?

**1. To Become Aware of Our Debt to Other Peoples.** Americans follow a way of life founded upon the achievements of many peoples—past and present. Our democratic ideals originated with the ancient Greeks; our belief in a single, all-powerful God stemmed from the ancient Hebrews; our scientific knowledge grew out of the work of European pioneers; our ideas of government derived in part from the writings of European scholars. As the American writer Herman Melville said, "We are the heirs of all time and with all nations we divide our inheritance."

**2. To Learn About Our Racial and Ethnic Backgrounds.** All Americans either have come themselves from other areas of the world or are the descendants of peoples who did. These individuals brought their own cultural heritages here. Many of these ideas, customs, and traditions have become part of our American way of life. We wish to know more about our ancestors—our racial and ethnic origins.

**3. To Learn the Lessons of the Past.** Americans face problems similar to problems faced by past peoples: how to prevent war, how to raise living standards, how to find equality for all. Although history may not repeat itself *exactly*, it provides enough similarity between past and present to enable us to learn from previous failures and successes. As the American philosopher George Santayana said, "Those who do not remember the past are condemned to relive it."

**4. To Understand Our Interdependent World.** Americans do not live in isolation. We are dependent upon the rest of the world: *economically* for markets for our agricultural and manufactured goods and supplies of raw materials and *politically* for allies and military bases. Whatever happens anywhere in the world eventually affects us. For our government to participate successfully in world affairs, we Americans must attain insight into world problems.

# Section One

# Ancient History

## UNIT I.  HUMANITY: FROM PRIMITIVE LIFE TO EARLY CIVILIZATIONS

## Part 1.  Primitive Peoples Emerge

### HUMANS APPEAR AND SURVIVE DURING THE ICE AGE

About a million years ago, the earth entered a period that *geologists* (scientists who study the structure of the earth) call the *Ice Age.* Four times during the Ice Age, tremendous sheets of ice *(glaciers)* advanced southward from the north polar region, covered large portions of the Northern Hemisphere, and then receded. The last retreat of the ice occurred about 15,000 years ago. Today the earth is in its fourth postglacial, or warm, period.

The earliest human or human-like peoples appeared on earth during the Ice Age. Their remains—bones and crude implements—have been found (1) in the colder Northern Hemisphere in northeastern China near Peking and in western Europe and (2) in the warmer Southern Hemisphere in Indonesia on the island of Java and in eastern Africa. The African discoveries in Olduvai Gorge in Tanzania are among the most recent diggings, dating from the 1950's with the work of *Louis and Mary Leakey.*

(Scholars who unearth the remains of earlier peoples and study their origins and cultures may be known as *anthropologists* or *archaeologists.*)

The early peoples survived the intense cold, wild animals, scanty food supply, and other hardships because they had (1) *brains* to reason and learn from experience, (2) the *power of speech* to communicate, (3) *hands* with which to grasp objects and make tools and weapons, and (4) an *upright posture* that enabled them to use their hands freely.

These characteristics enabled humans not only to survive but also to progress and create complex civilizations.

3

## AGES OF HUMANITY: CLASSIFIED BY MATERIALS
## USED IN IMPLEMENTS

**1. The Old Stone Age, or Paleolithic Age (1,000,000–8000 B.C.).** These early peoples shaped *rough* or *chipped stone* into crude tools and weapons, such as fist hatchets, knives, spearheads, arrowheads, and chisels. They also made implements of wood and bone. These peoples were nomads, wandering from place to place in search of food. Humans learned to *(a)* live in small groups and cooperate in hunting and fighting, *(b)* sew clothes of animal skins, *(c)* seek shelter in caves, *(d)* paint pictures on cave walls, and *(e)* make fire.

Late in the Old Stone Age, there existed in Europe and elsewhere—each for many thousands of years—several types of people. Notable were the *Neanderthals*—short, stocky, and low-browed—and later the *Cro-Magnons*— taller and more intelligent. Cro-Magnon people are classified as being of the same species as today's humanity: *Homo sapiens* (knowledgeable people).

**2. The New Stone Age, or Neolithic Age (8000–4000 B.C.).** These early peoples *ground* and *polished stone* into sharper implements. They settled in small communities and secured food by farming. They learned to *(a)* plow the soil and domesticate animals, *(b)* use the wheel and axle for transportation, *(c)* weave plant fibers into cloth, and *(d)* mold clay pottery.

**3. The Copper and Bronze Age (4000–1000 B.C.).** These peoples used metals to form more serviceable implements: daggers, swords, axes, and hammers. At first they worked with *copper*, which is comparatively soft. Later, by adding some tin to copper, they created *bronze*, a harder metal. During this period the first civilizations developed. Peoples *(a)* organized governments, *(b)* built cities, *(c)* developed industry, *(d)* established trade, and *(e)* kept the first written records.

**4. The Iron Age (Starting 1000 B.C.).** Peoples forged *iron*—a harder, more durable metal than bronze—into stronger tools and weapons. Because today's complex industrial civilization depends on iron (and *steel*, an alloy, or mixture, usually of carbon with iron), many scholars consider our own time to be part of the Iron Age.

## AGES OF HUMANITY: CLASSIFIED BY TYPES OF
## HISTORICAL EVIDENCE

**1. The Prehistoric Period (Before 4000 B.C.).** Because they did not know how to write, prehistoric peoples left no written records. Our knowledge of this period comes from *material remains:* bones, tools, weapons, utensils, cave paintings, cloth, pottery, and buildings.

Since prehistoric remains lack inscriptions, they cannot provide an exact *chronology* (measure of fixed time periods). The dating of events in the Prehistoric and early Ancient Periods remains approximate.

**2. The Historic Period (Since 4000 B.C.).** After peoples developed writing, they left, not only material remains, but also *written records*. These include stone inscriptions, tablets, scrolls, letters, diaries, newspapers, and books.

More accurate dating of events began with written records. During the Historic Period, as the use of writing spread, chronology became more nearly precise.

For chronological convenience, the history of Western civilization is usually subdivided as follows:

*a. Ancient History*—4000 B.C. to 500 A.D.

*b. Medieval History*—500 A.D. to 1400 A.D.

*c. Modern History*—1400 A.D. to the present.

The earliest written records describe humanity's first civilizations. These arose in the Middle East—Egypt and the Fertile Crescent.

# Part 2. Ancient Egypt: The First Civilization

## FAVORABLE GEOGRAPHIC CONDITIONS

**1. The Nile.** Ancient Egypt, located in northeast Africa, was a narrow strip of land about 550 miles (880 kilometers) long. It extended 15 miles (24 kilometers) on each side of the Nile River. Each summer the Nile overflowed. The rich soil it deposited on the adjacent fields could produce as many as four crops per year. This fertility encouraged the nomadic people of the region to settle down permanently and secure their livelihood through farming.

Because the land would be a desert without Nile waters, the ancient Greek historian Herodotus called Egypt "the gift of the Nile."

**2. Natural Boundaries.** Egypt was partially protected against invasion by natural barriers: deserts, mountains, and seas. (See map, page 6.) Thus shielded, the early Egyptians devoted themselves chiefly to peaceful pursuits.

## HISTORY OF ANCIENT EGYPT

**1. Early Governments.** Governments evolved in ancient Egypt to control the Nile. The people needed (*a*) *dikes* and *reservoirs* to restrain the annual flooding of the Nile Valley and (*b*) *canals* to irrigate the dry farmlands. These major projects—too large for individuals acting separately—required group effort, which led to local governments, usually chiefdoms.

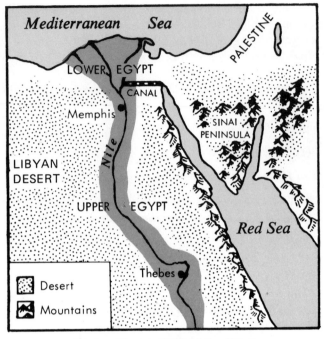

**Ancient Egypt: "Gift of the Nile"**

After the canal was built in 1900 B.C., the Red Sea receded,
and the canal was extended southward.

Through war and marriage these chiefdoms eventually combined into two
large kingdoms: (a) *Lower Egypt*, the northern part of the Nile Valley, including
the river's mouth, or delta, and (b) *Upper Egypt*, the central part of the Nile
Valley. About 3100 B.C. *Menes*, ruler of Upper Egypt, conquered Lower Egypt
and united the country. He became the first *pharaoh*, or king.

**2. The Old Kingdom (3100–2200 B.C.).** The "Old Kingdom," with its capital at
*Memphis*, lasted about 1,000 years. The pharaohs of this period erected huge
stone pyramids to serve as their tombs. *Khufu* (2900 B.C.) kept 100,000 workers
toiling over 20 years to build the famous *Great Pyramid* outside Memphis at
Gizeh. *Khafre* (2850 B.C.) constructed another imposing pyramid at Gizeh and
also carved the *Great Sphinx*, a tremendous statue having a lion's body and a
human face.

**3. The Middle Kingdom (2200–1730 B.C.).** During this period, also called the
"Age of Nobles," the pharaoh's power declined and that of the nobles increased.
Egypt experienced disunity and civil wars. Nevertheless, some pharaohs accomplished great engineering feats, building (a) huge irrigation projects and (b)
a ship canal that, together with the Nile, connected the Mediterranean and Red

The Sphinx and pyramids at Gizeh.

seas. (Thousands of years later, in 1869 A.D., the Suez Canal was completed on approximately the same site and connected the same seas.)

In 1730 B.C. Egypt was almost completely conquered by invaders from western Asia, the *Hyksos*. From these fierce warriors, the Egyptians learned to fight on horseback and use war chariots. Egypt was ruled by the Hyksos for about 160 years.

**4. The Empire (1570–1100 B.C.).** A strong Egyptian leader finally drove out the Hyksos. The "Empire" that arose, with its capital at *Thebes*, lasted about 470 years.

During this period ambitious pharaohs assembled large armies and organized great war fleets. They conquered Nubia (Ethiopia) to the south and Palestine and Syria to the northeast. They built huge stone statues of themselves as well as splendid temples. The most famous, near Thebes, is the *Temple of Karnak*.

The best-known pharaohs of the Empire were the military leaders *Thutmose III* and *Rameses II*, the religious reformer *Amenhotep IV* (see page 8), and *Tut-ankh-amen*, an unimportant ruler whose cliff tomb, discovered intact in 1922, helped give us a picture of Egyptian life during the Empire era.

About 1100 B.C. Egypt began to decline militarily. Ruled for 3,000 years thereafter by successive foreign invaders, Egypt did not regain national independence until the 20th century A.D.

## ASPECTS OF EGYPTIAN LIFE

**1. Absolute Monarchy.** The *pharaoh*, almost always a man, was the absolute ruler, worshipped as the gods' earthly representative. He made laws, maintained courts, waged war, collected taxes, constructed irrigation canals and public buildings, kept written records, and owned the land. The pharaoh was assisted by the *(a) nobles*, who served as advisers, local governors, tax collectors, and military commanders and the *(b) priests*, who gave advice, managed the temples, maintained schools, and conducted religious matters.

**2. Wide Class Distinctions.** The privileged aristocracy consisted of the pharaoh, the royal family, the nobles, and the priests. These dominant classes lived luxuriously.

The unprivileged masses included most of the people—men, women, and children. Work was done by *(a) freemen*, who were scribes (public writers), city merchants, and skilled workers or artisans; *(b) peasants*, who worked the farms; and *(c) slaves*, the manual laborers who dug irrigation ditches and built temples. The unprivileged classes could not participate in government. While the freemen enjoyed some wealth and comfort, the peasants and slaves suffered hardship and poverty.

**3. Economic Activities.** The Egyptians depended chiefly on agriculture. They plowed the land, using oxen and crude wooden plowshares; they grew wheat, barley, and flax; and they raised sheep and cattle. In the cities they developed such industries as construction, glassblowing, metalworking, cloth weaving, and pottery. They also engaged in foreign trade, exporting glassware, linen cloth, and clay vases, and importing ivory, spices, timber, and copper.

To support the pharaoh's government, the Egyptians paid heavy taxes in either labor or products.

**4. Religious Beliefs.** The Egyptians worshipped many gods. A belief in many gods is called *polytheism*. The chief gods of the Egyptians were *Re*, the sun god; *Amen*, god of Thebes; and *Osiris*, judge of the dead. The Egyptians hoped for life after death. Only those who could prove they had led a good life were granted immortality by Osiris. In preparation for judgment, deceased Egyptians were entombed with a collection of religious hymns, magical terms, and moral principles—together called the *Book of the Dead*. Among its moral principles were: "I did not steal, I did not murder, I did not lie, I have given bread to the hungry and drink to the thirsty."

The Egyptians chemically preserved (embalmed) the bodies of important persons to provide their souls with permanent resting places. A body so preserved is called a *mummy*.

In 1375 B.C. Pharaoh Amenhotep IV, known as *Ikhnaton*, introduced the worship of a single god, the new sun god *Aton*. A belief in one god is called *monotheism*. Ikhnaton was opposed by the priests, who feared the loss of their power, and by the people, who feared the wrath of their traditional gods. After Ikhnaton's death, the Egyptians restored polytheism.

## CONTRIBUTIONS TO CIVILIZATION

**1. Architecture and Engineering.** The Egyptians excelled in working with stone (stonemasonry) and constructed gigantic pyramids and temples. The temples featured vast halls lined by massive *colonnades* (rows of columns). Egyptian engineers also built dams and irrigation canals.

**2. Art.** The Egyptians were accomplished sculptors who created huge stone statues. On the stone walls of temples and tombs, artists carved and painted domestic and historical scenes. Egyptian workers skillfully designed delicate metal jewelry, elaborate wood furniture, and beautiful pottery.

A commemorative stone slab with hieroglyphics. It dates from 2475 to 2000 B.C.

*The Metropolitan Museum of Art, Rogers Fund, 1925*

**3. Hieroglyphic Writing.** The Egyptians developed one of the first systems of writing, *hieroglyphics*—a word meaning sacred carvings or priestly writings. Hieroglyphics are picture symbols that represent objects, ideas, or sounds. First inscribed on stone, these symbols were later written in ink on specially prepared plant material called *papyrus* (the origin of our word "paper"). On papyrus scrolls the ancient Egyptians recorded their history, literature, mathematics, scientific knowledge, and government records such as tax lists and treaties. To house their papyrus scrolls, the Egyptians established the first libraries.

The key to the translation of hieroglyphics was the *Rosetta Stone*. This slab was unearthed in the town of Rosetta in the Nile delta in 1799 by one of Napoleon's soldiers. The Rosetta Stone bears the same inscription in both Egyptian hieroglyphics and Greek letters. *Jean Champollion*, a French scholar, in 1822 used his knowledge of Greek to deciper the hieroglyphics.

## 4. Science

*a. Solar-Year Calendar.* The Egyptians, excellent astronomers, devised the first calendar that divided the year into 365 *days.* It was more accurate than the previous *lunar* calendar, based on the revolutions of the moon around the earth. Introduced about 4200 B.C., the Egyptian solar-year calendar is the basis of the calendar we use today.

*b. Other Scientific Achievements.* The Egyptians acquired considerable knowledge of practical science. In their construction projects Egyptian engineers calculated weight by simple arithmetical operations. They surveyed land and computed area by geometrical formulas. In preparing mummies Egyptian embalmers used chemical processes. Egyptian healers, though relying primarily on magic, set broken bones, recognized disease symptoms, and prescribed drugs.

## MULTIPLE–CHOICE QUESTIONS

Select the number preceding the word or expression that best completes the statement.

1. The *least* important reason for studying history is to learn   (1) to avoid mistakes made in the past   (2) to distinguish fact from opinion   (3) historical dates   (4) how our present civilization has developed.
2. The *least* important reason for Americans to study world history is that   (1) we all have immigrant origins   (2) the United States imports large quantities of sugar and coffee   (3) we can learn from past experience   (4) our nation is a world power.
3. Prehistoric peoples had an advantage over animals in that humans had   (1) matchless strength   (2) superior resistance to heart and cold   (3) ability to think and to use their hands freely   (4) power of communication through writing.
4. The first farmers have been traced back to the   (1) Old Stone Age   (2) New Stone Age   (3) Middle Kingdom era of ancient Egypt   (4) Empire era of ancient Egypt.
5. *Homo sapiens,* the biologic species that includes modern human beings, has been traced back to the   (1) beginning of the earth   (2) Old Stone Age   (3) New Stone Age   (4) beginning of the Ice Age.
6. The first metal weapons were made from   (1) tin   (2) copper   (3) iron   (4) silver.
7. The beginning of the Historic Period corresponds to the beginning of the   (1) Old Stone Age   (2) New Stone Age   (3) Copper and Bronze Age   (4) Iron Age.
8. An archaeologist is a specialist in   (1) building stone bridges   (2) painting and sculpting   (3) studying habits of birds   (4) studying remains of past civilizations.
9. A person living about 500 B.C. would consider his or her own times as   (1) prehistoric   (2) ancient   (3) medieval   (4) modern.
10. Egypt is said to be "the gift of the Nile" because the Nile   (1) flows through the center of Egypt   (2) overflows each spring, fertilizing the lowlands   (3) provides a means of transportation   (4) protects the Egyptians against invasions.
11. The delta of the Nile River is located   (1) in the Sinai Peninsula   (2) on the Red Sea   (3) in Lower Egypt   (4) in Upper Egypt.

12. The Egyptians were able to build the pyramids because they (1) had many workers (2) perfected the process of making sun-dried bricks (3) domesticated sheep (4) discovered the process of mixing concrete.

13. The pyramids of ancient Egypt were (1) tombs (2) forts (3) storehouses for treasure (4) temples.

14. The government of ancient Egypt was a (1) democracy (2) dictatorship (3) city-state (4) republic.

15. The ancient Egyptians worshipped (1) many gods (2) only Aton (3) the pyramids (4) fire.

16. *Not* characteristic of farming in ancient Egypt was (1) irrigation (2) the use of artificial fertilizer (3) slave labor (4) cultivation of wheat and barley.

17. A contribution of the ancient Egyptians to architecture was the (1) column (2) arch (3) stained-glass window (4) rounded dome.

18. The Rosetta Stone was (1) a symbol of the pharaoh's authority (2) the keystone in the Great Pyramid at Gizeh (3) an island in the Nile delta (4) the key to translating hieroglyphics.

19. A major contribution of the ancient Egyptians was in the field of (1) law (2) printing (3) the calendar (4) philosophy.

20. Egypt was a major power in the ancient world for about (1) 100 (2) 500 (3) 1,000 (4) 2,000 years.

## MATCHING QUESTIONS

Match the items in column *A* with those in column *B*.

| *Column A* | *Column B* |
|---|---|
| 1. Champollion | *a.* Built the Great Pyramid at Gizeh |
| 2. Menes | *b.* Wrote the *Book of the Dead* |
| 3. Hyksos | *c.* Deciphered hieroglyphics |
| 4. Khufu | *d.* Conquered ancient Egypt |
| 5. Ikhnaton | *e.* United ancient Egypt |
| | *f.* Introduced religious reforms |

## ESSAY QUESTIONS

1. Discuss *three* ways in which the study of world history may be of importance to you.

2. Explain *one* reason why each of the following advances achieved by primitive people was important: (*a*) invention of the wheel (*b*) use of fire (*c*) ability to cooperate in mutually beneficial projects (*d*) domestication of animals.

3. Explain *two* reasons why the use of metals is a measure of humanity's progress toward a more complex civilization.

4. (*a*) Discuss *two* factors that enabled Egypt to become a leading power of the ancient world. (*b*) Why is Egypt *not* considered a leading power in the world today?

5. "Government arises to meet the needs of the people. Once in power, however, government may take advantage of the people." Agree or disagree with each of these two sentences by making specific references to ancient Egypt.

# Part 3.  Other Early Civilizations
## of the Middle East

**THE FERTILE CRESCENT**

While Egyptian civilization was developing in northeastern Africa, other civilizations were evolving in nearby southwestern Asia, chiefly in the *Fertile Crescent*. This region was so named because of its rich soil and half-moon shape. The Fertile Crescent was divided into (1) the eastern portion, consisting of the *Tigris* and *Euphrates* river valleys, called *Mesopotamia* (land between the rivers), and (2) the western, or Mediterranean, portion. (See map below.)

**GEOGRAPHIC FACTORS INFLUENCING THE FERTILE CRESCENT**

**1. The Tigris and Euphrates Rivers.** The waters of these rivers enriched the land in Mesopotamia, thereby encouraging nomads to settle and farm. As in

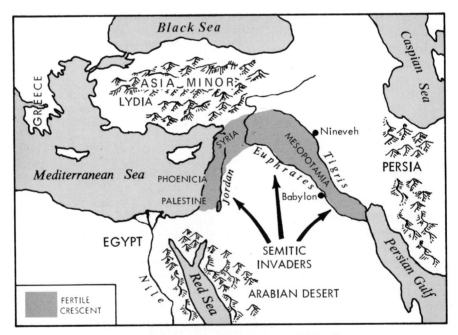

**The Fertile Crescent: The Ancient Middle East**

12

Egypt, the need for dikes to control floods and for canals to irrigate farms led to the establishment of governments.

**2. Mediterranean Coastline.** As seaports developed along the Mediterranean coast, the people became seafarers. They built ships and traded throughout the Mediterranean area.

**3. Lack of Stone.** Lacking stone, the people used sun-dried clay bricks for construction and clay tablets for writing.

**4. Low, Level Plains.** The Mesopotamian plain and the Mediterranean coastal plain afforded no natural barrier against invasion. The inhabitants were therefore conquered repeatedly by invaders from the adjoining mountains and deserts. These newcomers remained in the region, adapting and contributing to its civilization.

## LANGUAGES OF THE MIDDLE EAST

*Linguists*—specialists in the study of language—analyze sounds, interpret their meanings, and compare languages. They classify related languages into distinct families on the assumption that these languages probably evolved from one common (usually unrecorded) parent tongue. Linguists have classified most of the languages of the Middle East as either *Semitic* or *Indo-European*.

**1. The Semitic family** of languages was so named because the ancient peoples speaking these languages supposedly descended from a single biblical ancestor, *Shem*, son of Noah. The chief Semitic languages of the Middle East were *Babylonian*, *Hebrew*, *Phoenician*, *Aramaic*, and *Assyrian*. Among modern Semitic tongues are *Hebrew* and *Arabic*.

**2. The Indo-European family** of languages was so named because these languages were spoken in the vast area from northern India to westernmost Europe. Indo-European languages of the ancient Middle East included *Lydian*, *Hittite*, and *Persian*. The languages of India—*Sanskrit*, *Bengali*, and *Hindi*—are also Indo-European, as are most languages of Europe—*Greek*, *Latin*, *French*, *Spanish*, *Italian*, *Russian*, *German*, and *English*.

## A. Peoples of Early Mesopotamia

### Sumerians

### BRIEF HISTORY

The earliest-known people of the Fertile Crescent were the *Sumerians*. About 4000 B.C. they lived in southern Mesopotamia in a number of independent *city-states*. Each consisted of a small city and its surrounding area. The rulers of these city-states constantly warred with one another.

## CONTRIBUTIONS TO CIVILIZATION

**1. Cuneiform Writing.** The Sumerians developed *cuneiform*, a system of writing about as old as Egyptian hieroglyphics. The Sumerians employed a sharp-pointed instrument—called a *stylus*—to inscribe wedge-shaped characters on soft clay tablets, which were then hardened by baking. Reading and writing in cuneiform were difficult because the Sumerian alphabet consisted of about 550 characters. Nevertheless, cuneiform was widely used in the Middle East for thousands of years.

Cuneiform characters being inscribed on a clay tablet with a stylus.

The key to the deciphering of cuneiform was the *Behistun Rock*, carved on a mountainside near the village of Behistun in western Persia. This rock contains inscriptions in both cuneiform and Persian. The cuneiform was translated in 1846 by an English diplomat and scholar, *Sir Henry Rawlinson*.

**2. System of Numbers.** The Sumerians developed a number system based on the unit 60. Today we use this unit in measuring time.

**3. Architecture.** The Sumerians invented the *arch* and built temple towers, or *ziggurats*. A ziggurat was a pyramid-like structure consisting of progressively set-back floors, the highest of which contained a shrine to the chief god.

## *Babylonians*

### BRIEF HISTORY

Semitic-speaking invaders from the Arabian Desert entered southern Mesopotamia (1900 B.C.) and captured the city-state of Babylon. About 1750 B.C., led by their king, *Hammurabi*, they conquered the other city-states in the Tigris-Euphrates Valley and formed the *Babylonian Empire*. The *Babylonians* adopted and built upon the prevailing Sumerian culture. About 1700 B.C. the Babylonian Empire was overthrown by new invaders.

*The Bettmann Archive, Inc.*

A ziggurat in Babylon.

## CONTRIBUTIONS TO CIVILIZATION

**1. Code of Law.** Guided by Hammurabi, the Babylonians recorded their laws and customs. This *Code of Hammurabi,* the oldest known legal system, reveals *(a)* a *stern sense of justice*—proclaiming the principle of "an eye for an eye" and demanding severe punishment for crimes—bribery, theft, dishonest weights and measures, and damage to another's property, *(b)* a *sharp division of classes*—providing harsher punishment for an offense against a noble or priest than for the same offense against a common person—an artisan, merchant, farmer, or slave, *(c)* a *fair treatment of women*—permitting them to own property and engage in business, and *(d)* an *advanced business society*—establishing regulations for protecting property and business contracts, limiting interest on loans, and setting wages for workers.

**2. Astronomy.** The Babylonians believed in *astrology*—the superstition that the movements of stars, planets, and other heavenly bodies directly affect the lives of human beings. However, by studying the heavens, the Babylonians learned to recognize planets and to foretell eclipses, thereby recording data later essential to *astronomy.*

**3. Religious Literature.** The *Babylonian Epics,* partly based upon the Sumerian *Gilgamesh Legends,* describe the creation of the world, the first man and woman, and the building of an ark before the Great Flood. These stories resemble those in the Old Testament.

# B. Peoples of the Eastern Mediterranean

## Hebrews

**BRIEF HISTORY**

From 1400 to 1200 B.C., Semitic-speaking *Hebrews* from the Arabian Desert gradually invaded and settled Palestine. For about 500 years the Hebrews maintained their independence. In 722 B.C. the Assyrians conquered the *Kingdom of Israel* in northern Palestine. In 586 B.C. the Chaldeans overran the *Kingdom of Judah* to the south and exiled many of the inhabitants to Babylon. In 539 B.C. the Persians captured Babylon and allowed the Hebrew exiles to return to their homeland. Later, Palestine was controlled by the Greeks—except for a 100-year period of independence beginning in the 2nd century B.C. with the victorious revolt of the *Maccabees*. Still later the region was ruled by the Romans. In 70 A.D. the Roman armies under Titus suppressed a Hebrew revolt for independence and drove most of the people from their land. This expulsion partly explains why the Hebrews, or *Jews*, are presently scattered throughout the world. (Many Jews have returned to Palestine in recent years, especially after 1948, when part of the land became the independent Jewish state of *Israel*.)

**CONTRIBUTIONS TO CIVILIZATION**

**1. Monotheism.** The Hebrews were the first people to accept the belief in a single ethical God as the Creator and Supreme Ruler of the Universe.

**2. Old Testament.** The Hebrews recorded their history, moral principles, and religious beliefs in the *Old Testament*, the Hebrew Bible. A great literary masterpiece, the Old Testament constitutes the first part of the Christian Bible.

**3. High Moral Principles.** Judaism, the religion of the Hebrews, embodies precepts of ethical behavior that were far advanced for the ancient world and that are applicable in our own times. It set moral standards for relationships among peoples.

*a.* The *Mosaic Law* is found in the *Torah*, the first five books of the Old Testament. This Law of Moses teaches "Love thy neighbor as thyself." It includes the *Ten Commandments*. Some of these commandments are: "Remember the Sabbath day, to keep it holy"; "Thou shalt not kill"; "Thou shalt not steal"; "Thou shalt not bear false witness"; and "Honor thy father and thy mother."

*b.* The *Hebrew prophets* of the Old Testament cried out for social righteousness and a better world. They denounced evil and oppression, and demanded justice for the poor and weak. The prophet *Isaiah* envisioned a time when nations "shall beat their swords into plowshares" and "shall not learn war any more." The prophet *Micah* asked, "What doth the Lord require of thee, but to do justly, and to love mercy, and to walk humbly with thy God?"

The essence of Judaism, as summed up by the great teacher Hillel, who lived at about the time of Jesus, is the rule of conduct: "What is hateful unto thee do not do unto others."

In its emphasis on monotheism and high moral principles, Judaism influenced Christianity and became part of the Western world's declared code of ethics, known as the *Judeo-Christian heritage* (see pages 141–142).

## FAMOUS HEBREWS (AS RELATED IN THE OLD TESTAMENT)

(1) *Moses* led his people from servitude in Egypt and gave them the Ten Commandments. (2) *Saul* united the 12 Hebrew tribes, led them against the Philistines, and became the first Hebrew king. (3) *David* slew Goliath, the Philistine giant, and later succeeded Saul as king. David wrote many *psalms* (sacred songs). One of the most famous begins, "The Lord is my shepherd; I shall not want." (4) *Solomon,* son of David, was a king renowned for his wisdom. He also built the famous temple in his capital city of Jerusalem.

## *Phoenicians*

### BRIEF HISTORY

From 1200 to 800 B.C. the Semitic-speaking *Phoenicians* lived and prospered on the Mediterranean coast north of Palestine. Their chief cities were *Tyre* and *Sidon.* The Phoenicians, highly skilled shipbuilders and navigators, were seafaring merchants. They traded throughout the Mediterranean and even ventured to the Atlantic coasts of Europe and Africa. They established many overseas colonies; the most important, located in northern Africa, was *Carthage* (see page 56).

From a species of shellfish, the Phoenicians obtained their trademark: a purple dye known as *Tyrian purple.* It became the favorite color of royalty.

### CONTRIBUTIONS TO CIVILIZATION

**1. "Missionaries of Civilization."** The Phoenicians served as "missionaries of civilization," bringing eastern Mediterranean products and culture to less advanced peoples.

**2. The Alphabet.** As merchants, the Phoenicians needed a simple alphabet to ease the burden of keeping records. They therefore replaced the cumbersome cuneiform alphabet of 550 characters with a phonetic alphabet, based on distinct sounds, consisting of 22 letters. After further alterations by the Greeks and Romans, this alphabet became the one we use today.

# Aramaeans

## BRIEF HISTORY

Semitic-speaking *Aramaeans* occupied Syria about 1200 B.C. and established several independent city-states; the most important was *Damascus*. By overland caravans, Aramaean merchants traded throughout the Middle East. In the 8th century B.C., the Aramaean city-states fell to the Assyrians.

## CONTRIBUTION TO CIVILIZATION

**Language.** Spread by Aramaean merchants and diplomats, *Aramaic* became the international language throughout the Middle East for over 1,000 years. It was spoken by Jesus and used in many early Christian and Jewish religious writings.

# Lydians

## BRIEF HISTORY

After 1000 B.C. the Indo-European-speaking *Lydians* lived in *Asia Minor,* a region directly northwest of the Fertile Crescent. In the first half of the 6th century B.C., the Lydians enjoyed great power and prosperity. *Croesus,* their king, was reputed to be the wealthiest person of ancient times.

## CONTRIBUTION TO CIVILIZATION

**Government Coinage of Money.** As a merchant people, the Lydians sought a simple and safe method of payment for goods in place of *barter*—the exchange of goods for goods—and in place of money of uncertain value minted by private individuals. The Lydian government was the first to mint coins and guarantee their value. These government coins facilitated business transactions.

# C. Empire Builders

# Hittites

## BRIEF HISTORY

About 2000 B.C. the Indo-European-speaking *Hittites* appeared in northern Asia Minor, a region rich in iron. In 1650 B.C. the Hittites began building a powerful empire. They extended their control in Asia Minor, seized northern Syria from the Egyptians, and expanded into northern Mesopotamia. Hittite culture was greatly influenced by contacts with the Babylonians. The Hittite Empire lasted to 1200 B.C.—about 450 years.

## CONTRIBUTION TO CIVILIZATION

**Use of Iron.** The Hittites were the first to make tools and weapons of iron—a stronger, sharper, and more durable metal than copper or bronze. Hittite knowledge of ironwork soon spread throughout the Fertile Crescent and Egypt.

# Assyrians

## BRIEF HISTORY

After 800 B.C. the Semitic-speaking *Assyrians* from northern Mesopotamia embarked on a policy of expansion. Having learned about iron from the Hittites, the Assyrians were the first to outfit armies entirely with iron weapons. To besiege cities, they devised new military equipment—movable towers and battering rams. The Assyrians conquered the Fertile Crescent and Egypt and established a great empire with its capital at *Nineveh.*

The Assyrians terrorized their enemies by deliberately employing *cruelty* and *violence.* They also employed terror in ruling their subject peoples— ruthlessly suppressing rebellions and deporting rebellious populations from their homelands. The Assyrian Empire lasted over 150 years—to 612 B.C.— before being destroyed.

## CONTRIBUTIONS TO CIVILIZATION

**1. Government.** The Assyrians *(a)* divided their empire into provinces, each administered by a governor responsible to the all-powerful king, and *(b)* built military roads to move troops quickly to any part of the empire.

**2. The Library.** *Assurbanipal,* an Assyrian king, built a great library at Nineveh containing many thousands of clay tablets. These documents have enabled scholars to accurately reconstruct life in the ancient Middle East.

# Chaldeans

## BRIEF HISTORY

In 616 B.C. the *Chaldeans,* Semitic-speaking nomads from the Arabian Desert, seized Babylon. In 612 B.C. they (in alliance with the Medes, who lived to the northeast of the Fertile Crescent) captured Nineveh and overthrew the Assyrian Empire. The Chaldeans then gained control of the entire Fertile Crescent and established the *Second Babylonian Empire.* In 539 B.C. this empire was overthrown by the Persians.

## CONTRIBUTIONS TO CIVILIZATION

**1. Architecture.** During the reign of *Nebuchadnezzar*, the Chaldeans constructed the famous *Hanging Gardens* of Babylon. These roof gardens were noted as one of the great wonders of the ancient world.

**2. Astronomy.** The Chaldeans continued the Babylonian practice of recording accurate observations of the heavens.

## *Persians*

### BRIEF HISTORY

In the 6th century B.C., the Indo-European-speaking *Persians* lived east of the Fertile Crescent on the Plateau of *Iran*. Under *Cyrus the Great* (who ruled 559–529 B.C.) the Persians overthrew the Medes and ruled the entire Iranian Plateau. Thereafter Cyrus conquered Lydia, Asia Minor, and the Fertile Crescent. Cyrus' son seized Egypt. Under *Darius* (521–486 B.C.) the Persians expanded their empire eastward as far as the Indus River in northern India. (To the west, however, Darius failed to conquer the Greek city-states—see page 45.)

The Persian Empire, the largest yet seen in the ancient world, extended 3,000 miles (4,800 kilometers). (See map below.) The empire flourished for 200 years, finally collapsing about 330 B.C. (see page 46).

### CONTRIBUTIONS TO CIVILIZATION

**1. Government.** The Persians *(a)* divided their empire into provinces, each ruled by a *satrap* (governor) responsible to the all-powerful king, *(b)* appointed

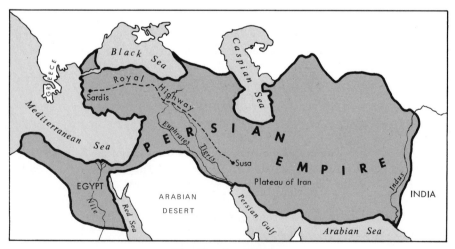

**The Persian Empire**

special agents, the *king's eyes and ears,* to check upon the loyalty of the satraps, *(c)* built numerous roads to speed military movements and trade, and *(d)* treated subject peoples *humanely* to avert revolt.

**2. Spread of Culture.** By maintaining their vast empire, the Persians stimulated cultural interchange among many peoples. The Persians adopted many features of these civilizations. However, they remained faithful to their own religion, *Zoroastrianism.*

**3. Religion.** The Persians accepted the beliefs of their 6th-century-B.C. prophet *Zoroaster.* He preached that: *(a) Ahura-Mazda,* the god of light and goodness, was constantly fighting *Ahriman,* the spirit of darkness and evil. *(b)* Those supporting Ahura-Mazda by living virtuously will reach heaven; those following Ahriman will be punished in hell. *(c)* Goodness will eventually prevail, and the world will achieve eternal peace.

Zoroaster's teachings form the basis of the Persian Bible, the *Avesta* or *Zend-Avesta.*

## MULTIPLE-CHOICE QUESTIONS

1. As the Nile was to Egypt, so were the Tigris and Euphrates to   (1) Asia Minor   (2) Iran   (3) Palestine   (4) Mesopotamia.
2. The chief building material used in the Fertile Crescent was   (1) concrete   (2) stone   (3) clay brick   (4) wood.
3. The stylus was a Middle Eastern implement used for   (1) cutting cloth   (2) writing   (3) farming   (4) besieging cities.
4. A Semitic language in use today is   (1) Greek   (2) Assyrian   (3) Hebrew   (4) French.
5. Which of the following is *not* an Indo-European language?   (1) Sanskrit   (2) English   (3) Persian   (4) Arabic.
6. The Sumerians built ziggurats, which were   (1) irrigation canals   (2) religious shrines   (3) royal palaces   (4) large libraries.
7. The Babylonians are credited with having   (1) possessed considerable legal and business ability   (2) erected the largest buildings of ancient times   (3) built a navy that dominated the Mediterranean   (4) conquered India.
8. The Babylonians studied astrology because they believed that   (1) the fate of human beings was determined by the stars   (2) other worlds existed   (3) science was the basis of military power   (4) the Old Testament required such study.
9. The Hebrew kingdom had a perilous existence because it   (1) was situated between powerful rival states   (2) was peopled by many different races   (3) had valuable deposits of iron ore   (4) lacked a powerful navy.
10. The Hebrew capital and site of the famed Hebrew temple was   (1) Nineveh   (2) Carthage   (3) Damascus   (4) Jerusalem.
11. The ancient conquerors who treated the Hebrews most humanely were the   (1) Assyrians   (2) Babylonians   (3) Persians   (4) Romans.

12. By predicting that nations "shall beat their swords into plowshares," the Hebrew prophet Isaiah was calling for (1) more farming (2) government jobs for the unemployed (3) an era of world peace (4) greater effort to find mineral resources.
13. Micah, the Hebrew prophet, extolled (1) justice, mercy, and humility (2) wars of conquest (3) gaining wealth (4) Persian rule.
14. A Phoenician product particularly desired by monarchs was (1) purple dye (2) royal chariots (3) sundials (4) iron weapons.
15. The Aramaic language spread throughout the Middle East because of Aramaean (1) military conquests (2) religious leaders (3) merchants (4) astrologers.
16. The Assyrian practice of appointing governors to rule separate provinces was adopted later by the (1) Persians (2) Lydians (3) Egyptians (4) Sumerians.
17. The *Zend-Avesta* was the sacred book of the (1) Babylonians (2) Persians (3) Sumerians (4) Hebrews.

## MATCHING QUESTIONS

| *Column A* | *Column B* |
|---|---|
| 1. Cyrus | *a.* Ruler renowned for wisdom |
| 2. Hammurabi | *b.* Founder of Persian Empire |
| 3. Moses | *c.* Persian god of light |
| 4. Nebuchadnezzar | *d.* Translator of cuneiform |
| 5. Rawlinson | *e.* Arranger of oldest known legal code |
| 6. Solomon | *f.* Builder of hanging gardens |
| 7. Zoroaster | *g.* Founder of Carthage |
| | *h.* Prophet of the Persians |
| | *i.* Lawgiver of the Ten Commandments |

## IDENTIFICATION QUESTIONS

For each description below, select the name of the people to whom it best applies, making your selection from the following list:

| Aramaeans | Hebrews | Persians |
|---|---|---|
| Assyrians | Hittites | Phoenicians |
| Babylonians | Lydians | Sumerians |

1. A seafaring merchant people, we devised a simplified alphabet and were known as "missionaries of civilization."
2. Our government was the first to mint coins, which replaced money minted by private individuals.
3. Although we were known for our military, not scholarly, pursuits, our extensive library has enabled modern scholars to reconstruct life in the ancient Middle East.
4. We were the first people to accept monotheism, and our prophets denounced evil and injustice.
5. We developed cuneiform writing and the number system still used in measuring time.
6. We settled in Asia Minor, discovered iron ore deposits, and were the first people to make iron tools and weapons.

## ESSAY QUESTIONS

1. Explain *one* way in which life in the ancient Fertile Crescent was affected by *each* of the following geographic conditions: *(a)* low, level plains *(b)* Tigris and Euphrates rivers *(c)* Mediterranean coastline *(d)* absence of stone and timber.

2. Discuss briefly *one* reason for agreeing or *one* reason for disagreeing with *each* of the following statements: *(a)* The Assyrians are a splendid example of the saying, "Might makes right." *(b)* The *Zend-Avesta* was the only religious writing of the ancient world. *(c)* Trade in ancient times furthered civilization. *(d)* Temperate climates have been most favorable to the development of an advanced civilization. *(e)* Although a superstition, astrology in the ancient Fertile Crescent had value for later astronomers.

3. Of all the inhabitants of the ancient Fertile Crescent, only the Hebrews have been able to survive to this day as a distinct people. *(a)* Discuss *one* factor that enabled the Hebrews to survive. *(b)* Explain *three* ways in which modern Americans are indebted to the ancient Hebrews.

4. Discuss *one* way in which the Persian Empire was similar to *or* different from the Assyrian Empire in each of the following categories: *(a)* territory included in the empire *(b)* treatment of conquered peoples *(c)* method used to assure royal control *(d)* contribution to civilization.

# UNIT II. EARLY CIVILIZATIONS OF THE FAR EAST

## Part 1. Introduction

The previous unit described the culture of the ancient Egyptians and of other ancient Middle Eastern peoples. From them evolved the Mediterranean-centered Greco-Roman civilization. This civilization, which later spread throughout Europe and the Americas, is the basis of our *Western*, or *Occidental*, culture.

This unit will discuss developments in southern and eastern Asia, a region that Europeans called the *Far East* because it is far to the east of Europe. In India and China originated the *Far Eastern*, or *Oriental*, cultures.

Far Eastern history does not conform to the time periods of ancient, medieval, and modern history as used for the West. This book, however, will present the Far East within the framework of Western chronology to enable the reader to compare simultaneous developments in the Occidental and Oriental worlds.

During ancient and medieval times, the Far East and the West had relatively few contacts. Since the year 1500, however, relations between them have gradually expanded. Today they influence each other considerably.

## Part 2. Ancient India: An Advanced Civilization in Southern Asia

### GEOGRAPHIC FACTORS INFLUENCING ANCIENT INDIA

**1. Location and Size.** India (today constituting three nations, India, Pakistan, and Bangladesh) is a landmass located in southern Asia. It extends about 2,000 miles (3,200 kilometers) from north to south. India lies north of the equator, but the lower region falls within the tropical zone and has a warm tropical climate. Mainly a triangular peninsula, India is sometimes termed a *subcontinent* because its geographical features sharply separate it from the rest of Asia. (See map, page 25.)

**2. Boundaries.** Ancient India was geographically isolated and therefore largely protected against invasion (*a*) from the east, west, and south by the extensive waters of the *Bay of Bengal*, the *Arabian Sea*, and the *Indian Ocean* and (*b*) from the north by towering mountain ranges, chiefly the *Himalayas*. Nevertheless, a few mountain passes on the northwest border, such as the *Khyber Pass*, enabled ancient invaders to enter northern India.

**3. Monsoons.** The *monsoons* are winds that blow, with considerable regularity, over India. The summer monsoons—June to October—come from the southwest, absorbing moisture from the Indian Ocean and depositing rain inland. This rainfall is essential throughout most of India for its major economic activity—farming. If the summer monsoons are late or do not contain enough moisture, they can hinder crop growth and even cause famine.

**4. Topography.** India contains two major regions:

*a. In the North: The Plain of the Indus and Ganges.* This fertile region is watered by two great river systems, both originating in the Himalayan Mountains. The *Indus River* flows southwest to the Arabian Sea, and the *Ganges River* flows southeast to the Bay of Bengal. The Indus Plain, directly accessible through

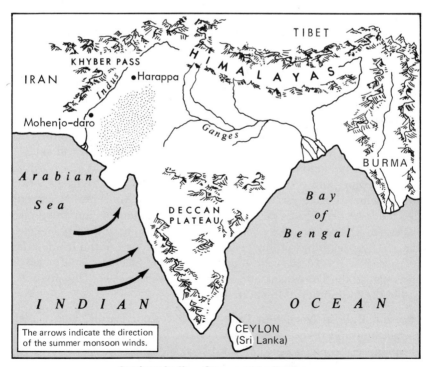

**Ancient India: Geographic Factors**

the northwest mountain passes, attracted many invaders to India. (From the Indus River was derived the name India.)

*b. In the South: The Deccan Plateau.* This relatively inhospitable region, despite some good farmland, includes mountain ranges, tropical forests, and rocky soil. Although the Deccan was not impassable, usually little unity existed between northern and southern India. The numerous mountain ranges also tended to isolate population groups from each other and to foster a feeling of regional loyalty, or regionalism.

## HISTORY OF ANCIENT INDIA

**1. The Early Indus River Valley Civilization (3000–1500 B.C.).** Like the Nile in Egypt and the Tigris and Euphrates in Mesopotamia, the Indus River fostered the development of civilization. Archaeological excavations in the Indus Valley, at the ancient cities of *Harappa* and *Mohenjo-daro*, have disclosed *(a)* well-planned cities containing extensive drainage systems and brick buildings with bathrooms, *(b)* highly productive farms with irrigation canals and domesticated animals, *(c)* pictographic writing (still undeciphered) on clay seals, and *(d)* cloth, jewelry, pottery, and implements of copper and bronze. The resemblance between Indus and Sumerian pottery and implements suggests that these civilizations may have been related.

About 1500 B.C. the Indus River Valley civilization ended abruptly, destroyed (according to some scholars) by the invading *Aryans.*

**2. The Aryan Conquests (2000–600 B.C.).** The Indo-European-speaking *Aryans,* a light-skinned people probably related to the Persians, crossed the northwest mountain passes and invaded the Indus Plain. They conquered the inhabitants, the dark-skinned *Dravidians.* (Many Dravidians fled south, where their descendants still live.) By the 6th century B.C., the Aryans had subjugated the Ganges Valley and occupied the entire northern plain. They formed small states that frequently warred among themselves.

Aryan history and culture are revealed chiefly by their religious writings, *Vedas,* of which the oldest is the *Rig-Veda.* During the Aryan period, sometimes called the *Vedic Age,* India's civilization began to assume its important characteristics. *(a)* The Aryans spoke *Sanskrit,* later the principal literary language of India. *(b)* The teachings of the Vedas later became part of the *Hindu religion* (see page 28). *(c)* To prevent intermarriage and maintain supremacy, the Aryans placed the Dravidians into a separate, inferior class. This division was possibly the forerunner of the *caste system.*

**3. Persian Rule in Northwest India (521–367 B.C.).** Darius, king of Persia, annexed the Indus River region to his empire. Persian rule stimulated cultural and commercial contacts between northwest India and the eastern Mediterranean area, including Greece.

**4. Alexander of Greece Conquers Northwest India (326 B.C.).** Alexander the

Great (see page 46) mastered the Persian Empire and subdued the Indus River region. Although short-lived, Alexander's conquest increased Greek influence on India, particularly in trade, culture, and government.

**5. The Maurya Empire (321–184 B.C.).** The *Maurya*, an Indian family, established the country's first great empire. Its outstanding rulers were Chandragupta (ruled 322–298 B.C.) and Asoka (ruled 273–232 B.C.).

*a. Chandragupta Maurya.* Inspired by Alexander's military feats, Chandragupta drove out the Greek garrisons left by Alexander, won control of the northern plain, and founded the Maurya Empire. He established a highly centralized government modeled after Persian practice.

*b. Asoka.* Asoka, Chandragupta's grandson, continued the Maurya conquest southward until he ruled more than two-thirds of India. Rejecting war thereafter, he became a devout convert to the *Buddhist religion* (see page 29). He then promoted Buddhism within India and sent Buddhist religious teachers as missionaries to convert the people of Ceylon (now Sri Lanka) and Burma.

Asoka's edicts, inscribed on stone pillars and large rocks, furnish considerable information about his activities and beliefs. A benevolent emperor, he emphasized truth, justice, charity, religious tolerance, and nonviolence. Moreover, he restricted the slaughter of animals and urged vegetarianism. Asoka is often regarded as one of the world's noblest rulers.

After Asoka's death the Maurya Empire declined. It was followed by five centuries of invasion, war, and disorder.

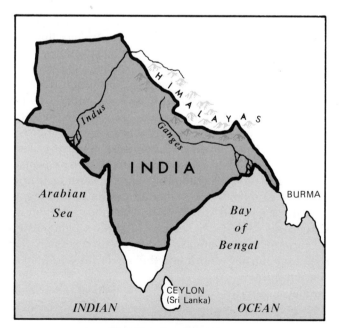

**The Empire of Asoka**

**6. The Gupta Empire (320–535 A.D.).** In the 4th century A.D., the *Gupta*, another native Indian family, established an empire embracing northern India. By restoring law and order, the Guptas revived prosperity. Their reign witnessed great achievements in literature, art, mathematics, and science. India became a center of learning, and its culture spread throughout eastern Asia. The Gupta period is sometimes called India's "golden age."

In the 6th century the Gupta government was overthrown by invaders from central Asia, the *White Huns*.

## ANCIENT INDIA'S CONTRIBUTIONS TO CIVILIZATION

### 1. Religion and Philosophy

#### a. Hinduism (Brahmanism) and the Caste System

(1) *Caste in Daily Living.* About 1500 B.C. India began to develop rigid, increasingly complex social and economic divisions called *castes*. (a) In order of importance the four main castes were scholars and priests (Brahmans), rulers and warriors, landowners and merchants, and peasants and artisans. These castes were further divided into several thousand subcastes. (b) Below the castes were millions of despised persons—menial laborers—the outcasts, or *untouchables*. (c) Each person remained in his or her own hereditary caste, was restricted in occupation, and was forbidden close contact with members of other castes. (d) A violator of caste rules became an outcast.

Thus, the outstanding feature of the caste system was strict segregation.

(2) *Hindu Beliefs and Caste.* Hinduism evolved into a complex religion. (a) The supreme universal soul assumes three forms: *Brahma* the creator, *Vishnu* the preserver, and *Siva* the destroyer. (b) To achieve union with the universal spirit, people must purify their souls by performing religious duties and living righteously. Religious duties include praying, respecting the Brahmans, and making pilgrimages to the sacred Ganges River. Righteous living consists of avoiding untruth and envy, seeking knowledge, granting charity, practicing nonviolence, and observing caste rules. (c) Since soul purification requires many lifetimes, each person's soul experiences rebirths, a process called *transmigration* or *reincarnation.* (d) Persons who disregarded Hindu precepts in a previous existence are punished by reincarnation into either a lower caste or an outcast, or even an animal. (Since animals may contain human souls, they may not be killed. Cows in particular are sacred.) (e) Persons who followed Hindu precepts in a previous existence are rewarded by reincarnation into a higher caste. (f) Through innumerable upward reincarnations, the soul will eventually be completely purified, freed from further rebirth into this sorrowful world, and united with the all-embracing spirit.

Today Hinduism survives chiefly in the Republic of India, where it is practiced by the vast majority of the people. By stressing caste divisions and opposing the slaughter of animals, Hinduism has delayed India's development into a prosperous modern nation.

*b. Buddhism.* In the 6th century B.C., *Gautama,* a noble, left his comfortable life for one of self-denial and meditation. He ultimately developed a philosophy that rejected the Hindu caste system but accepted the Hindu belief of reincarnation. As *Buddha,* the "Enlightened One," Gautama taught: (1) A person's life consists of suffering caused by desire. (2) A person can eliminate desire only by following the *eightfold path* of righteous living: renouncing material pleasure, controlling emotions, meditating selflessly, respecting all living creatures, acquiring knowledge, cultivating goodness, speaking truth, and acting generously. (3) By living righteously a person escapes endless reincarnations, and one's soul enters a spiritual state of peace, *Nirvana.*

Buddhism battled Hinduism and the caste system for over 1,000 years. As certain Buddhist principles were absorbed by Hinduism, Buddhism disappeared in India. Today Buddhism survives mainly in Sri Lanka, Thailand, Burma, China, Japan, and the nations of Indo-China.

**2. Art and Architecture.** Ancient India's art, revolving about Hinduism and Buddhism, stressed symbolic and ornate design. This style predominated in human and animal statues, cave-temple wall paintings, and temple construction. Indian architects used wood, brick, and stone in buildings featuring pointed domes, columns, and conical towers.

**3. Literature.** Ancient India produced an impressive literature, chiefly in Sanskrit. *(a)* The *Vedas* contain hymns, prayers, and religious principles. *(b)* The

A statue of the Hindu god Siva, the destroyer.

*Mahabharata* and the *Ramayana* are great epic poems, often compared with the Homeric epics of Greece (see pages 39–40). *(c)* Hindu storytellers delighted in animal fables illustrating morals. These stories possibly provided the basis for Aesop's fables in Greece. *(d) Kalidasa,* a 5th-century-A.D. poet and playwright, is sometimes called "India's Shakespeare."

**4. Science and Technology.** Indian physicians diagnosed major diseases, prescribed medicinal plants, and placed the sick in hospitals. They observed an ethical code similar to the Greek Hippocratic Oath (see page 50). The Indians applied chemical principles in dyeing cloth, tanning leather, manufacturing soap and glass, and refining iron ore. (Later their process for purifying iron passed to the Arabs and then to Medieval Europe.)

**5. Mathematics.** In mathematics India was the most advanced of the ancient nations. Indian mathematicians devised the concept of zero, employed the decimal system, developed a rudimentary algebra, and created our modern written numbers. (Transmitted by the Arabs to Medieval Europe, these numeric symbols are misleadingly called *Arabic numerals.)*

# Part 3. Ancient China: Development of an Inbred Civilization

## GEOGRAPHIC FACTORS INFLUENCING ANCIENT CHINA

**1. Location and Boundaries.** China, a huge country in eastern Asia, comprises China proper and the outlying regions of Tibet, Sinkiang, Mongolia, and Manchuria. In ancient times China proper was virtually isolated from the surrounding world by such natural barriers as the *Gobi Desert,* the *Tibetan mountain plateau* (sometimes called the "Roof of the World"), and the *Pacific Ocean.* (See map, page 31.) Little affected by outside cultures (except for India's Buddhism), China developed an inbred civilization.

**2. Topography.** Of China's land surface, one-fifth consists of coastal and river plains; the remaining four-fifths of mountains, plateaus, and hills. Not suitable for agriculture, the mountainous terrain contributes little to China's food output. As population growth pressed against food supply, the Chinese endured a *survival economy.*

Despite the mountainous terrain, the ancient Chinese migrated, spread their culture, and maintained a degree of cultural and political unity.

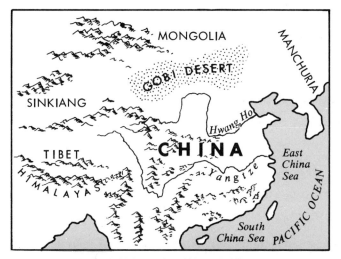

**Ancient China: Geographic Factors**

3. **Important Rivers: Yangtze and Hwang Ho (Yellow River).** Flowing several thousand miles eastward from the Tibetan highlands, the *Yangtze River* in central China and the *Hwang Ho* (Yellow River) in northern China both empty into the Pacific Ocean. These rivers drain China's heavily populated fertile plains. Because of its devastating floods, the Yellow River is often called "China's sorrow."

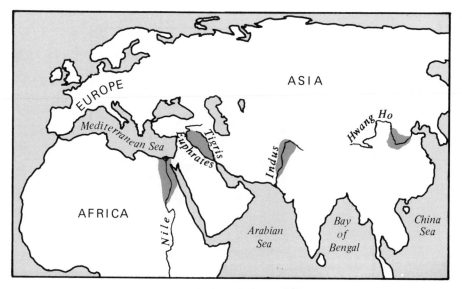

**The Early River Valley Civilizations**

## HISTORY OF ANCIENT CHINA

**1. Early Yellow River Valley Civilization (4000–2000 B.C.).** China's first civilization, like those of Egypt, Mesopotamia, and India, evolved from river valley conditions: fertile soil, uncertain rainfall, and disastrous floods. In the Yellow River region, the people raised agricultural produce, herded animals, used bows and spears, and made crude pottery. They lived in small, self-governing villages.

**2. Hsia Dynasty (2000–1500 B.C.).** According to legend, *Hsia*, China's first *dynasty* (a succession of monarchs from the same family), ruled the eastern Yellow River city-states. During this period the Chinese began casting bronze, cultivating silkworms, and, reputedly, writing.

**3. Shang Dynasty (1500–1000 B.C.).** The Shang Dynasty developed a highly organized state in the Hwang Ho Plain. To protect their domain, Shang warriors frequently fought frontier tribes. During this period the Chinese produced artistic bronze implements and beautiful pottery or ceramics; wrote on shells, metal, and wood; and began to worship their ancestors.

**4. Chou Dynasty (1000–256 B.C.).** The *Chou*, the longest-ruling dynasty, first overran Shang territory and then temporarily occupied part of the Yangtze Valley. Later Chou kings, unable to maintain authority, lost power to provincial nobles.

The Chou Period witnessed the introduction of iron implements, written laws, and metal coins. This era, China's "classical age," produced memorable literature and the renowned philosophers: *Lao-tse* and *Confucius* (see page 34).

**5. Ch'in Dynasty (256–206 B.C.).** The *Ch'in* was a short-lived but significant

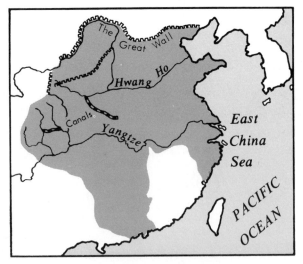

**Ch'in: The First Empire**

dynasty whose outstanding ruler was the self-named *Shih Huang Ti,* meaning the *First Emperor.* To bar northern invaders, he linked existing sectional fortifications into the 1,500-mile (2,400-kilometer) *Great Wall.* He expanded the empire southward by annexing the Yangtze region and gaining nominal control of southern China.

Shih Huang Ti sought vigorously to unify the country *(a) politically*—by creating a strong centralized government, suppressing nobles, appointing provincial governors responsible to him, and enforcing a uniform legal code; *(b) physically*—by building roads, bridges, and canals; and *(c) culturally*—by simplifying and standardizing writing.

Also, to provide unity, he attempted to eradicate knowledge of China's past political and cultural diversity by ordering the burning of most books.

From *Ch'in* was derived the name *China.*

**6. Han Dynasty (206 B.C.–220 A.D.).** Han rulers *(a)* preserved political unity with a tightly centralized administration. *(b)* promoted Confucianism, even selecting government officials by tests on Confucian literature, *(c)* allowed Buddhism to be introduced from India, *(d)* established overland trade routes over which Chinese silks and spices reached the Roman-dominated Mediterranean world, and *(e)* expanded the Chinese Empire to Indo-China, central Asia, southern Manchuria, and northern Korea.

The Han Empire marked the height of ancient China's power, prosperity, and culture. Literature, art, science, and industry flourished as never before. Subsequently the Chinese were so proud of this period that they often called themselves "the sons of Han."

The fall of the Han Dynasty was followed by four centuries of civil war, invasion, and disorder. These turbulent years led many Chinese to accept Buddhism because it promised eternal peace (see page 29).

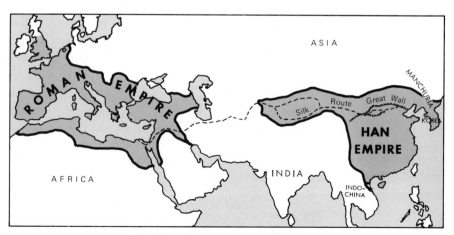

**The Han Empire (1st Century A.D.)**

## ANCIENT CHINA'S CONTRIBUTIONS TO CIVILIZATION

### 1. Religion and Philosophy

*a. Lao-tse (6th Century B.C.).* For individuals to attain happiness, the philosopher Lao-tse taught: (1) Governments should minimize their controls over the people. Since laws cannot improve conditions, people should be permitted to conduct their own affairs. (2) Individuals should passively accept their lot in life. They can achieve peace of mind only by practicing humility and by renouncing wealth and prestige. They should live in a simple manner in harmony with *Tao*, "the way of nature."

Centuries later, Lao-tse's teachings, distorted by magic and combined with ideas of personal immortality, became part of the polytheistic religion *Taoism*.

*b. Confucius (551–479 B.C.).* To improve society and achieve good government, the great philosopher Confucius formulated a code of ethical conduct. He taught that individuals should be guided by the following "virtues": (1) Careful observance of ancient traditions. (2) Reverence for learning. (3) Cherishing of honesty. (4) Devotion to parents, family, and friends. (5) Obedience to the rule "What you do not want done to you, do not do to others."

Whereas Lao-tse advocated a passive life for individuals and urged the least possible government, Confucius urged individuals to participate forcefully in society and recommended vigorous government action. He further believed that a ruler who practiced the Confucian virtues would govern as an influential, parental force. Unlike other Oriental philosophies, Confucianism placed little emphasis on the hereafter.

As *Confucianism* evolved, the original stress on tradition became associated with ancestor worship. For more than 2,000 years, Confucianism dominated Chinese daily life and politics. Confucian writings served as official school textbooks. By emphasizing tradition and ancestor worship, Confucianism stabilized society but retarded progress.

*c. Intermingling Beliefs.* The Chinese did not believe it illogical to live according to principles taken from different philosophies. While universally accepting Confucianism, many Chinese simultaneously practiced Buddhism and Taoism.

### 2. Strong Family Ties.
In keeping with Confucian teachings, the family—not the individual—became the basic unit of Chinese life. The family included all relatives. Living together or near one another, they sometimes constituted an entire village. The oldest person was the honored and obeyed family head. The family assumed responsibility for the livelihood and good conduct of its members. Marriage was not intended for individual happiness but to perpetuate the family.

Intense family loyalty hampered the development of Chinese nationalism.

### 3. Written Language and Literature.
Complex Chinese writing existed by 1500

B.C. Lacking an alphabet, it employed up to 40,000 characters (originally pictures), each representing a distinct idea or sound. The resulting difficulty in reading and writing sharply limited Chinese literacy to a small number of educated persons. (Recently attempts have been made to simplify Chinese writing by using a phonetic alphabet.)

Despite their complex written language, the Chinese created a noteworthy literature of poetry, history, and philosophy. The *Confucian Classics*, outstanding works, consist of *(a)* Confucius' collection of earlier writings, *(b)* Confucius' own sayings, the *Analects*, and *(c)* commentaries by later philosophers. The Imperial Library housed an extensive collection of books and manuscripts.

**4. Art and Architecture.** The ancient Chinese created elaborately decorated bronzes, clay vases, and other ceramics. They fashioned fine jewelry and figurines, using their most prized stone, *jade*. Chinese artists excelled in expressive, symbolic landscape paintings. Chinese musicians developed an advanced music, different from that known in the Western world. Chinese architects, in designing palaces and pagodas, favored wood and stone columns, highly ornamented walls, and gaily colored tiled roofs. The most distinctive Chinese structure was the *pagoda*—a many-storied, tapered temple with a series of upward-curving roofs.

Chinese Architecture: A pagoda built of glazed brick near Peking.

*The Bettmann Archive, Inc.*

**5. Science and Technology.** The Chinese invented the sundial, the water clock, and instruments to detect earthquakes. Their astrologers contributed to the science of astronomy by observing sunspots, studying eclipses, and devising a solar calendar of 365¼ days. Chinese farmers plowed the land, used fertilizer, and rotated crops. The Chinese also wove silk cloth and produced glazed pottery plates (chinaware). About 100 A.D. they discovered how to make paper.

## MULTIPLE–CHOICE QUESTIONS

1. The Indian subcontinent is separated from the rest of Asia by the (1) Gobi Desert (2) Ganges River (3) Himalaya Mountains (4) Deccan Plateau.

2. Ancient invaders entered India from the northwest because the (1) invaders came mainly from Europe (2) northwest of India was unpopulated (3) Khyber Pass provided an invasion route (4) northwest of India consisted of open plains.

3. Two ancient cities, where excavations have revealed much of India's early civilization, were (1) Harappa and Delhi (2) Harappa and Mohenjo-daro (3) Delhi and Bombay (4) Mohenjo-daro and Bombay.

4. "No Behistun Rock has been found for the Indus River cities" means that these cities (1) had fertile soil (2) lacked minerals (3) constructed buildings entirely of wood (4) left writings that remain undeciphered.

5. The Vedas were (1) religious writings (2) priests (3) iron swords (4) Hindu gods.

6. The period of disorder from the end of the Maurya Empire to the beginning of the Gupta Empire lasted approximately (1) 10 (2) 100 (3) 300 (4) 500 years.

7. The Gupta Period is sometimes called India's "golden age" because its (1) skilled workers sculpted many gold statues (2) writers, artists, scientists, and mathematicians brought forth great achievements (3) merchants secured much gold in exchange for exports of Indian goods (4) rulers conquered the gold mines of the Deccan.

8. The Brahmans, the highest Hindu caste, were mainly (1) rulers and warriors (2) merchants (3) priests and scholars (4) farmers.

9. The caste system emphasized (1) national unity (2) local community cooperation (3) racial equality (4) strict segregation.

10. Reincarnation is the Hindu belief that each person (1) should return good for evil (2) has a soul that will experience successive rebirths (3) should make pilgrimages to the river Ganges (4) should give his or her life in defense of "Mother India."

11. Gautama, the 6th-century B.C. philosopher, was called "Buddha," meaning the (1) great nobleman (2) enlightened teacher (3) stone heart (4) fierce warrior.

12. Hinduism and Buddhism both agree that each person's life on earth (1) is one of sorrow (2) is preparation for immediate entrance to heaven (3) must conform to caste rules (4) has the ultimate goal of Nirvana.

13. Today Buddhist influence is *least* evident in (1) India (2) Sri Lanka (3) Japan (4) Burma.

14. Kalidasa, who lived in the 5th century A.D., was a great (1) mathematician (2) ruler (3) playwright (4) religious reformer.

15. One achievement in ancient India *not* paralleled in ancient Greece was in (1)

writing epic poems   (2) relating animal fables   (3) prescribing an ethical code for doctors   (4) developing a simplified way of writing numbers.

16. Ancient China, in its natural boundaries and their effect upon China's civilization, most closely resembles ancient   (1) Egypt   (2) Babylonia   (3) Lydia   (4) Persia.

17. China's topography consists chiefly of   (1) plains   (2) mountainous terrain   (3) river valleys   (4) deserts.

18. Hsia, China's first dynasty, is legendary, meaning that   (1) its rulers were great warriors   (2) its writers wrote imaginative novels   (3) its existence has not been confirmed by archaeological evidence   (4) its people worshipped many gods.

19. The first emperor of the Ch'in Dynasty, Shih Huang Ti, ordered the burning of books because he   (1) feared that an educated people might revolt   (2) feared that knowledge of China's past would hamper his efforts to establish a centralized government   (3) wanted to combat monotheism   (4) wanted scholars to produce original works.

20. While the Han Dynasty ruled in China, the Mediterranean world was dominated by   (1) Egypt   (2) Persia   (3) Greece   (4) Rome.

21. The philosopher Lao-tse taught that individuals could achieve happiness by   (1) relying on the government   (2) accepting, with humility, their lot in life   (3) pursuing wealth and giving it to the poor   (4) reforming the evils of the world.

22. One might expect Lao-tse's attitude toward modern minimum wage laws to be   (1) strong approval   (2) hesitant approval   (3) indifference   (4) disapproval.

23. The chief purpose of the code of conduct Confucius formulated was to   (1) improve society and government   (2) prepare human souls for the hereafter   (3) enable the Chou rulers to retain power   (4) encourage the Chinese to conquer eastern Asia.

24. Confucianism encouraged the Chinese people to   (1) learn from foreigners   (2) experiment with new food crops   (3) respect traditional ways of doing things   (4) seek principles of science.

25. Confucianism encouraged a feeling of intense loyalty to the   (1) family   (2) province   (3) neighboring warlord   (4) nation.

26. Which was *not* an achievement of ancient China?   (1) a solar calendar   (2) glazed pottery   (3) a phonetic alphabet   (4) the making of paper.

## COMPLETION QUESTIONS

Provide the word or expression that completes the statement correctly.

1. The earliest civilization in India developed in the valley of the _____ River.

2. The invaders who brought the Sanskrit language into India were the _____.

3. The European conqueror who in the 4th century B.C. extended his empire into northwest India was _____.

4. The great Maurya ruler who, after renouncing war, governed according to Buddhist ideals was _____.

5. The sacred river of the Hindu religion is the _____.

6. Early civilization in China developed in the valley of the _____ River.

7. A succession of monarchs from the same family is called a(an) _____.

8. Han rulers selected government officials by "civil service" examinations based upon a knowledge of the _____ Classics.

9. A major religious development during the Han Era was the introduction of _____.

10. The most distinctive Chinese structure, typified by a series of upward-curving roofs, is called a(an) _____.

## ESSAY QUESTIONS

1. Select either ancient India *or* ancient China for comparison with the ancient Fertile Crescent. For the two regions selected, discuss *(a)* *two* developments that were similar and *(b)* *two* developments that were different.

2. Asoka (3rd century B.C.), an Indian king of the Maurya family, has been regarded as one of the world's noblest rulers. *(a)* Present *two* arguments to support the statement. *(b)* Which *one* characteristic of Asoka would you most like to see in present-day rulers? Explain.

3. According to some scholars, the key to the understanding of ancient China is *stability*. *(a)* Discuss *two* facts that prove the statement. *(b)* Discuss *one* fact that disproves the statement. *(c)* In a nation's history, is stability a desirable factor? Present *one* argument to support your opinion.

4. Agree or disagree with each of the following statements and present *one* argument in each case to support your opinion: *(a)* Geography played a major role in shaping the history and economy of ancient India *or* ancient China. *(b)* In its overall influence on India, Hinduism has been a force for good. *(c)* In its overall influence on China, Confucianism has been a force for good. *(d)* Our Western, or Occidental, civilization owes a considerable debt to the peoples of the ancient Far East.

# UNIT III. THE CLASSICAL CIVILIZATIONS OF ANCIENT GREECE AND ROME

## Part 1. Ancient Greece: The First Experiment with Democracy

### THE CRETAN CIVILIZATION (3000–1400 B.C.)

On *Crete*, an island near Greece in the eastern Mediterranean, developed an advanced civilization. The Cretans, influenced by poor soil and good harbors, became seafaring merchants. Their rulers, the "Sea Kings of Crete," controlled the prosperous eastern Mediterranean trade. By carrying Egyptian and other Middle Eastern learning to the backward Aegean islands and the Greek mainland, Crete served as a cultural bridge. (See map, page 40.)

Our knowledge of Cretan civilization derives chiefly from excavations of the palace at Crete's leading city, *Knossos*. These ruins were unearthed starting in 1900 by the archaeologist *Sir Arthur Evans*. The Cretans devised excellent plumbing systems, using drains and tiled pipes. They enjoyed such sports as boxing and leaping over bulls. They made superb clay vases; bronze daggers decorated with enamel, gold cups, ivory carvings, and wall paintings. The Cretan civilization collapsed in 1400 B.C. when Knossos was destroyed, possibly by the invading *Hellenes*.

### THE HELLENIC INVASIONS OF GREECE (1500–1000 B.C.)

The *Hellenes*, Indo-European-speaking nomadic tribes of eastern Europe, migrated south to seek richer grasslands. These primitive people conquered Greece, Crete, and many Aegean islands. The Hellenes intermarried with the natives and evolved into a new people, the *Greeks*.

### THE HOMERIC AGE (UNTIL 750 B.C.)

1. **The Poems of Homer.** Our knowledge of the early Greeks derives mainly from two long epic poems, the *Iliad* and the *Odyssey*, both attributed to the blind Greek poet *Homer*. The *Iliad* relates the adventures of a Greek military expedition against the city of Troy on the coast of Asia Minor. The *Odyssey* describes the

39

wanderings of the Greek hero Odysseus returning home from the Trojan War. People doubted the existence of Troy until its ruins were uncovered in the 1870's by the archaeologist *Heinrich Schliemann.*

**2. Life During the Homeric Age.** The Greeks lived primitively. They *(a)* were ruled by tribal chieftains or kings usually advised by councils of elders, *(b)* were farmers growing wheat, olives, and grapes and shepherds herding sheep and cattle, *(c)* warred constantly, using iron weapons and horse-drawn chariots, and *(d)* believed that their gods actively intervened in human affairs.

## GEOGRAPHIC FACTORS INFLUENCING GREEK DEVELOPMENT

**1. Location.** Greece is a peninsula in the northeastern Mediterranean within easy sailing distance of the Fertile Crescent and Egypt. The Greeks learned about writing, navigation, and other achievements of these earlier civilizations mainly from Cretan and Phoenician merchants.

**Crete and Greece in Ancient Times**

**2. Deep Harbors.** Because Greece has numerous good harbors on its irregular coastline, many Greeks turned to the sea. They became merchants and traders who sailed the Black, Aegean, and Mediterranean seas. The Greeks exported wine, olive oil, pottery, cloth, and metal implements; they imported foodstuffs, timber, hides, and metal ores.

**3. Insufficient Farmland.** Since Greece lacks sufficient farmland, many Greeks between 750 and 500 B.C. established colonies on the shores of the Mediterranean and Black seas. (Greeks also emigrated to escape oppression by the nobility. See page 42.)

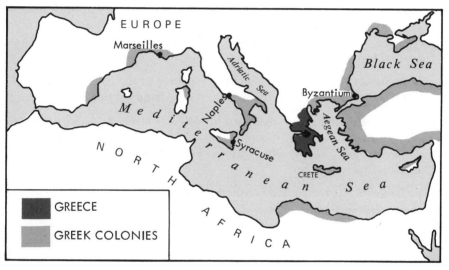

**The Greek World (750–500 B.C.)**

They founded important colonies at *Byzantium* (later called Constantinople) at the mouth of the Black Sea, *Naples* in Italy, *Syracuse* in Sicily, and *Marseilles* in France. These colonies became important as centers of Greek population, trade, and culture.

**4. Mountains.** Greece is a land of high mountain ranges enclosing fertile valleys. These valleys were isolated because transportation over the mountains was hazardous. Such geographic barriers led the Greeks to organize, not a central government, but many independent *city-states*. Because the mountains helped cause political disunity, the first loyalty of the people was not to Greece as a nation but to their own city-state.

## ATHENS: DEVELOPMENT OF A DEMOCRATIC CITY-STATE

*Athens,* in east central Greece on the Attic Peninsula, was the leading Greek city-state. After 750 B.C. Athens slowly progressed from (1) *monarchy—*

rule by one man, the king, who inherited power by family succession; to (2) *aristocracy*—rule by a small group of nobles who wrested power from the king; to (3) *tyranny*—rule by one man, the tyrant, who seized power and generally favored the people; and finally to (4) *democracy*—rule by the people. Athenian democracy encouraged similar reforms in a number of Greek city-states. (These four political terms—monarchy, aristocracy, tyranny, and democracy—are all derived from the Greek language.)

### 1. Discontent in Athens (8th–7th Centuries B.C.)

*a. Economic.* The small farmers, unable to compete with low-priced grain imports, were poverty-stricken. They borrowed money from the wealthy nobles and mortgaged their land as security. When unable to pay their debts, these farmers (1) lost their land and (2) were sometimes sold into slavery.

*b. Political.* The common people had no voice in the government. As the king lost power, control passed entirely into the hands of the aristocracy.

### 2. Leaders and Reforms in Athens (7th–5th Centuries B.C.).

As the nobles gradually responded to the people's demand for reforms, Athens advanced toward democracy. Leadership was provided by the following men, all drawn from the aristocratic class:

*a. Draco* in 621 B.C. *codified* (arranged systematically and set down in writing) the existing Athenian laws. Limited by this code, the judges, who were nobles, could no longer interpret unwritten laws to favor their own class at the expense of the common people. The code provided severe punishment for crimes; death was the penalty for even a minor offense. (From *Draco* comes our word *draconic*, meaning "harsh" or "severe.")

*b. Solon* in 594 B.C. rewrote the laws to (1) cancel mortgages on land, (2) free persons enslaved for debt, (3) limit the amount of land owned by one person, (4) allow all male citizens to serve on juries, and (5) grant male commoners the right to vote in the legislature, the *Assembly*. Thus, for the first time, the common man gained a voice in his government. (Today the word *solon* means "a wise lawmaker.")

Despite Solon's reforms, the wealthy retained control of the government. Only they could gain membership in the policymaking and administrative body, the *Council*. Only they could serve as chief executives.

*c. Clisthenes* in 508 B.C. expanded democracy by extending citizenship to more males and permitting men of all economic classes to serve in the Council. Under Clisthenes' leadership the Assembly adopted the practice of *ostracism*, banishing for 10 years any citizen deemed dangerous to the state. Ostracism was intended to prevent the rise of an Athenian dictator.

*d. Pericles,* from 461 to 429 B.C., headed the Athenian government. This great orator and popular leader (1) removed the remaining restrictions on officeholding, thereby opening government service to all men, and (2) paid salaries to public officials, thus enabling poor male citizens to accept jury duty and other government service. Pericles expressed his democratic ideals in his famed *Funeral Oration*. Honoring the Athenian war dead, Pericles described their receptiveness to new ideas, their love of liberty, and their willingness to sacrifice their lives for freedom. (As an enduring wartime statement of democratic principles, Pericles' Funeral Oration is often compared with Lincoln's Gettysburg Address.)

The years of Pericles' leadership, the *Age of Pericles* or the *Golden Age of Athens,* marked the height of Athenian democracy. Arts and sciences thrived, manufacturing and trade prospered, and the city was beautified as never before. (See pages 47–50 for the Greek contributions to civilization during the Age of Pericles.)

## Two Democracies: Major Differences

| Ancient Athens | Modern America |
| --- | --- |
| 1. *Direct democracy*—citizens themselves were members of the legislature. | 1. *Representative democracy*—the citizens elect legislators to represent them. |
| 2. Citizenship based on Athenian ancestry. Generally denied to aliens. | 2. Citizenship based on American birth. Granted also to immigrants following naturalization. |
| 3. Women denied voting and other rights. | 3. Women and men granted equal rights. |
| 4. Slavery permitted. | 4. Slavery prohibited. |

## SPARTA: AN ARISTOCRACY AND MILITARY CITY-STATE

*Sparta* was situated in southern Greece on the Peloponnesian Peninsula. Sparta's population consisted of (1) a small number of Spartan citizens, the landowning and ruling nobility, and (2) a large number of slaves *(helots)* who worked the land.

Fearing helot rebellions, the Spartans maintained an aristocracy in the belief that such a government could act more effectively than a democracy to suppress uprisings. As an aristocracy, Sparta resisted political change, maintained inflexible institutions, and sought cohesion and stability. Unlike most other Greek city-states, Sparta did not develop trade and industry but remained agricultural.

The Spartans emphasized military might and made Sparta an armed camp. The government regulated all aspects of the people's lives. Spartan boys, taken from their homes at the age of seven, received a strict military education. Spartan girls underwent vigorous physical training to prepare for motherhood. Sparta exemplified the autocratic, or totalitarian, philosophy that the individual exists to serve the state.

The Spartans were the greatest warriors of ancient Greece. Their emphasis on militarism, however, caused them to neglect art, literature, and science. Sparta exemplified a monolithic, or uniform and unvarying, culture.

## BONDS UNITING THE GREEKS

Although divided into several hundred independent city-states, the Greeks were united by a common culture.

**1. Language and Literature.** The people spoke dialects of the Greek language and shared Greek literature, especially the stories of Homer.

**2. Religion.** The Greeks shared a polytheistic religion. Their most important deities were *Zeus*, the chief god; *Apollo*, the sun god; *Athena*, goddess of wisdom; and *Aphrodite*, goddess of love. These divine beings supposedly dwelt in northeastern Greece on top of *Mount Olympus*.

The Greeks attributed human appearance and characteristics to their gods. The gods' personal lives, rivalries, and participation in human affairs are described in ever-popular Greek mythology.

The Greeks believed that priests could receive prophecies from the gods at holy places called *oracles*. People from all Greece sought advice at the famous oracle of Apollo at *Delphi*.

**3. Olympic Games.** The Greeks shared an interest in the Olympic games, held to honor the gods, especially Zeus. These athletic contests, attracting many spectators, were conducted every four years in southern Greece at the city of

*The Bettmann Archive, Inc.*

The *Discus Thrower,* a bronze sculpture by Myron. This statue has survived in a Roman copy.

*Olympia.* The finest Greek athletes competed in racing, jumping, discus throwing, boxing, and wrestling. All Greeks acclaimed the victors, often in songs and poems. (See Pindar, page 48.)

**4. Fear of Persia.** The Greeks feared that the mighty Persian Empire planned to conquer them. When the Persians attacked, most Greek city-states temporarily cooperated to preserve their freedom.

Conscious of these unifying bonds, the Greeks felt superior to non-Greek peoples and referred to them as "barbarians."

## THE WAR AGAINST PERSIA (500–479 B.C.)

**1. Outbreak of the War.** The Persians controlled the entire Middle East (see page 20), including the Greek colonies on the coast of Asia Minor. In 500 B.C. these colonies revolted and received military aid from Athens. After suppressing the revolt, *Darius*, king of Persia, determined to punish Athens and annex all of Greece.

**2. Major Events.** In 490 B.C. Darius' huge army invaded Greece but was defeated by a smaller Athenian force at the *Battle of Marathon.* Carrying the glad news, a Greek messenger ran the 26 miles (41.6 kilometers) from Marathon to Athens. (Today the word *marathon* means "a long-distance race" or "an endurance contest.")

Led by *Themistocles*, Athens prepared to repel further Persian attacks. Themistocles *(a)* rushed the construction of 200 additional warships *(triremes)* for the Athenian navy and *(b)* organized most Greek city-states, including Sparta, into a defensive alliance.

In 480 B.C. King *Xerxes*, the son of Darius, launched another Persian invasion. At the *Pass of Thermopylae* in northern Greece, the Persians overwhelmed a small band of gallant Spartan warriors led by King *Leonidas.* The Persians then marched southward and captured Athens. Although Greece seemed doomed, the Greeks rallied their forces to win two great naval engagements off *Salamis* (480 B.C.) and *Mycale* (479 B.C.) and a land battle at *Plataea* (479 B.C.). The Persians withdrew, and Greece was saved.

**3. Significance.** By repelling the Persian forces, the Greeks preserved their political independence and individual freedom. Unlike Persian despotism, Greek democracy, typified by Athens, permitted individuals to develop their abilities and interests. With the Persian threat removed, the Greeks directed their energies to building a rich and varied civilization.

## THE PERSIAN WAR IS FOLLOWED BY GREEK DISUNITY

After the Persian War Athens and Sparta bitterly vied for control of Greece. Athens dominated a city-state alliance, the *Delian League.* Sparta headed an opposing alliance, the *Peloponnesian League.* Athens and Sparta engaged in a long and costly struggle, the *Peloponnesian War* (431–404 B.C.). Sparta eventually triumphed. (Sparta's victory provides a warning that, in a struggle between autocracy and democracy, democratic peoples cannot assume the triumph of freedom.)

Despite its victory, Sparta was so weakened by the war and so detested for its anti-democratic policies that it was unable to unite Greece.

## PHILIP OF MACEDON UNITES GREECE

The *Macedonians,* living north of Greece, were a less civilized, warlike people related to the Greeks. In 359 B.C. *Philip,* an admirer of Greek culture, became king of Macedonia. He formed a powerful army and resolved to unify the Greek city-states by force. Because he threatened Greek independence, Philip was often denounced by an Athenian orator, *Demosthenes.* However, Demosthenes' warnings to the Greek city-states went unheeded. (Our word *philippic,* derived from these speeches against Philip, means "a bitter verbal attack.")

Philip conquered the city-states at the *Battle of Chaeronea* (338 B.C.), united them militarily (excepting Sparta), and planned to attack Persia. Before Philip could proceed, he was assassinated. His throne, his armies, and his ambitions were inherited by his 20-year-old son, *Alexander.*

## CONQUESTS OF ALEXANDER THE GREAT (336–323 B.C.)

Alexander, leading Macedonian and Greek troops, won great victories at *Granicus River, Issus,* and *Arbela.* He conquered the entire Persian Empire: Asia Minor, Egypt, the Fertile Crescent, and Persia. He then subjugated the Indus River region in India. Alexander's empire, encompassing these territories plus Macedonia and Greece, was the greatest then known. (See the map on page 47.) Suddenly, at age 33, Alexander fell ill and died.

Alexander's achievements—so much in so little time by so young a man— make Alexander one of the most remarkable figures in world history. Within his empire, he opened the way for a fusion of Greek and Middle Eastern cultures (see Hellenistic Period, pages 50–51); he also maintained peace and unity— ideals that later influenced the Romans (see Pax Romana, page 62).

## ALEXANDER'S EMPIRE FALLS APART

After Alexander's death, his empire was divided into three major kingdoms, each ruled by one of his generals. (1) *Macedonia,* including part of Greece, was governed by Antigonus. (2) *Syria,* including most of southwestern Asia, was governed by Seleucus. (3) *Egypt* was governed by Ptolemy.

These kingdoms maintained their independent existences until, in the 2nd and 1st centuries B.C., they fell under the rule of Rome.

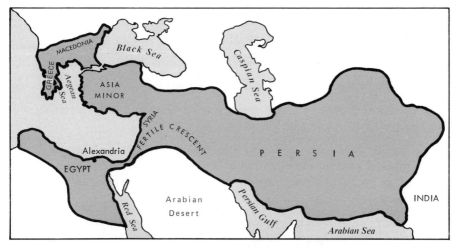

**The Empire of Alexander the Great**

## GREEK CONTRIBUTIONS TO CIVILIZATION: THE HELLENIC PERIOD

The *Hellenic Period* refers approximately to the five centuries preceding the conquests of Alexander the Great. Hellenic culture reached its height in Athens during the Age of Pericles (461–429 B.C.). By its many contributions to civilization, Athens reflected the values of its society: free, individualistic, changing, experimental, and diverse. Athenians boasted that Athens was the educator of Greece, the *school of Hellas.*

1. **Theater.** Greek dramas, produced in outdoor amphitheaters, employed little scenery and used a chorus to help relate the story.

The outstanding Greek playwrights who wove moral themes into tragedies were:

*a. Aeschylus* (525–456 B.C.) wrote *Agamemnon, Prometheus Bound,* and *The Persians.* He argued that the gods ultimately provide human justice.

*b. Sophocles* (495–406 B.C.) wrote *Oedipus Rex, Antigone,* and *Electra,* dramatic plays dealing with the conflict between a person's will and fate.

*c. Euripides* (480–406 B.C.) wrote *Medea* and *Orestes.* He realistically examined social and political ideas and vigorously criticized war, prejudice, hypocrisy, and greed.

The outstanding Greek playwright of comedies was:

*d. Aristophanes* (446–385 B.C.) satirized the political and cultural leadership of Athens in his plays *Lysistrata* and *The Frogs.*

**2. Poetry.** Greek writers of poetry selected themes from Greek history, legend, and heroes and also from the lives and ideals of ordinary persons.

*a. Homer* (9th century B.C.) wrote the *Iliad* and the *Odyssey.*

*b. Hesiod* (750–700 B.C.) wrote poems about farm life and hard labor.

*c. Sappho* (600 B.C.), a woman, wrote beautiful lyric love poems.

*d. Pindar* (522–443 B.C.), the great lyric poet, wrote odes honoring the victorious athletes at the Olympic games.

**3. Philosophy.** Philosophers seek to understand individuals in their relationships with God, nature, and other individuals and to determine the meaning of such human ideals as justice, morals, and success. The outstanding Greek philosophers were:

*a. Socrates* (469–399 B.C.) advocated the maxim "Know thyself." He sought truth through persistent questioning—an approach called the *Socratic Method.* Tried and convicted for corrupting the minds of youth, Socrates was put to death by poison. Socrates left no written works. His philosophy is contained in the writings of his students, especially Plato.

*b. Plato* (427–347 B.C.) wrote many fascinating discussions of ethics, religion, beauty, and logic, called *Dialogues.* In the dialogue *The Republic,* Plato described his ideal government, not democracy, but aristocracy of intelligence trained to rule. His most famous student was Aristotle.

*c. Aristotle* (384–322 B.C.) wrote learned treatises on philosophy, science, government, and literature. His encyclopedic works strongly influenced European thinking for almost 2,000 years. Among his important books were *Logic* and *Politics.* Aristotle served as personal tutor to the young Alexander and stimulated the future leader's interest in Greek culture.

The Greeks held to the ideal of a well-rounded individual, expressed by the philosophy "a sound mind in a sound body." They considered both mental and physical faculties to be essential for a happy and useful life.

**4. Historical Writing**

*a. Herodotus* (484–424 B.C.), the "father of history," described the Persian invasions of Greece. He embellished facts with fable, superstition, and hearsay.

*b. Thucydides* (471–400 B.C.), the "first scientific historian," wrote an accurate and impartial account of the Peloponnesian War.

**5. Architecture.** The Greeks constructed many public buildings, employing marble and featuring slender, well-proportioned columns. The *Parthenon,* the most famous building of ancient Greece, was a magnificent marble temple dedicated to the goddess Athena. Considered one of the world's most beautiful

*Greek National Tourist Office*

Ruins of the Parthenon on the Acropolis in Athens.

structures, the Parthenon was erected during the Age of Pericles on a hilltop in Athens—the *Acropolis*.

Many modern public buildings imitate the three great styles of Greek columns: *Doric*—simple; *Ionic*—more decorative, topped with scrolls or ram's horns; and *Corinthian*—most elaborate, with carvings of large plant leaves.

**DORIC**

**IONIC**

**CORINTHIAN**

The three orders of Greek columns.

**6. Sculpture.** Greek sculptors embodied their city-state ideals in their works, emphasizing simplicity, dignity, restraint, and patriotism. In many statues of gods and athletes, these skillful sculptors realistically depicted the human body. They utilized various materials such as ivory, gold, bronze, and marble. Their works, designed mainly for public exhibition, have served as models and inspirations for subsequent sculptors—even to our day.

*a. Phidias* (500–432 B.C.), the greatest sculptor of ancient Greece, carved the majestic statue of the goddess Athena for the Parthenon and the marble frieze (ornamental band) that extends along the Parthenon's walls.

*b. Myron* (about 450 B.C.) created the *Discus Thrower*, a statue portraying strength and motion. (See illustration, page 44.)

*c. Praxiteles* (364–330 B.C.) carved lifelike statues of gods and goddesses.

**7. Science and Mathematics**

*a. Pythagoras* (582–507 B.C.), a philosopher and mathematician, discovered important mathematical principles still studied in geometry.

*b. Hippocrates* (460–377 B.C.), a physician called the "father of medicine," attributed disease to natural, not supernatural, causes. The "Hippocratic Oath" to uphold medical standards is still taken by medical students upon graduation.

*c. Democritus* (460–362 B.C.), a philosopher and scientist, advanced the theory that all matter is composed of small, indivisible atoms.

## GREEK CONTRIBUTIONS TO CIVILIZATION: THE HELLENISTIC PERIOD

The *Hellenistic Period* starts with the conquests of Alexander the Great and ends late in the 1st century B.C. Hellenistic culture fused Greek with Egyptian, Middle Eastern, and Oriental cultures.

In the lands he conquered, Alexander (1) introduced Greek language, literature, and art and (2) founded many cities to serve as centers of Greek culture. In Egypt he founded *Alexandria*. Famed for its marble buildings, museum, and library, it was the greatest Hellenistic city.

**1. Philosophy.** Discontented with the old ideas and old gods, Hellenistic peoples sought new philosophies to guide them in their daily living.

*a. Diogenes* (412–323 B.C.), the leading *Cynic*, taught that, to achieve contentment, individuals should practice self-control and independence. He rejected society's accepted values—wealth, power, pleasure, social position, and patriotism. (Our word *cynic* describes "one who sneeringly distrusts people's motives, attributing their actions wholly to self-interest.")

*b. Zeno* (342–270 B.C.), the founder of *Stoicism*, urged individuals to live according to reason and be indifferent to pleasure or pain. (Our word *stoic* means "one who calmly accepts pleasure without rejoicing and endures pain without flinching.")

*c. Epicurus* (341–270 B.C.) believed that people should seek pleasure and happiness. However, he emphasized that pleasures should be temperately chosen to attain a balanced, moral life. (Today an *epicure* is "one who displays a highly refined taste in eating, drinking, and other pleasures.")

**2. Sculpture.** Hellenistic sculptors carved realistic statues, including the *Venus de Milo*, the *Death of Laocoön*, the *Dying Gaul*, and the *Winged Victory of Samothrace*. (See illustration, page 51.)

French Government Tourist Office

The *Winged Victory of Samothrace*
was created to honor a Greek naval triumph.
It depicts Nike, the goddess of victory.

## 3. Science and Mathematics

*a. Aristarchus* (310–230 B.C.), an astronomer, concluded that the earth revolves about the sun.

*b. Euclid* (about 300 B.C.), a mathematician, systematized the subject matter of geometry.

*c. Archimedes* (287–212 B.C.), a mathematician and physicist, discovered important principles regarding the lever, the pulley, and specific gravity.

*d. Eratosthenes* (276–195 B.C.), a geographer, believed the earth to be round and accurately estimated its circumference.

## MULTIPLE–CHOICE QUESTIONS

1. As seafaring merchants and transmitters of culture, the Cretans most closely resemble the (1) Phoenicians (2) Persians (3) Aryans (4) Hebrews.

2. In the nature of his work at Knossos, Sir Arthur Evans may be most closely compared to (1) Champollion (2) Rawlinson (3) Euclid (4) Schliemann.

3. Between 1500 and 1000 B.C., Crete, Greece, and many of the Aegean islands were invaded by the (1) Assyrians (2) Hellenes (3) Spartans (4) Persians.

4. A city-state was (1) a city that performed all the functions of an independent nation (2) a city governed by a foreign nation (3) a capital of an empire (4) the fortified section of a city.

5. A city-state in Greece that taught its boys absolute obedience to authority was (1) Thebes (2) Athens (3) Olympia (4) Sparta.

6. Athenian democracy resembled American democracy in that (1) women took no part in the government (2) few foreigners were granted citizenship (3) jury trials were common (4) the states joined to form a strong central government.

7. The Athenian practice of banishing a citizen considered dangerous to the welfare of the state is known as (1) tyranny (2) aristocracy (3) ostracism (4) welfare state.

8. A similarity between Athens and Sparta was that both (1) emphasized military training (2) were city-states (3) produced great art and drama (4) followed monotheism in religion.

9. The Greek war against Persia (500–479 B.C.) (1) was fought chiefly in Asia Minor (2) ended Athenian power (3) destroyed the Persian Empire (4) preserved the independence of the Greeks.

10. In the Peloponnesian War (1) democracy triumphed over aristocracy (2) aristocracy triumphed over democracy (3) Greece triumphed over Persia (4) neither side won a military victory.

11. The intellectual center of Greece about 450 B.C.—the "school of Hellas"—was (1) Sparta (2) Athens (3) Byzantium (4) Syracuse.

12. An achievement of ancient Greece was the (1) introduction of algebra (2) development of philosophy (3) beginning of the alphabet (4) abolition of slavery.

13. The Parthenon was (1) a temple to Athena (2) the city hall of Athens (3) a theater (4) the home of Pericles.

14. In which field did the Athenians make the most lasting contributions to Western civilization? (1) industry (2) literature (3) militarism (4) religion.

15. Alexandria, the famed Hellenistic city, was established in (1) Macedonia (2) Egypt (3) Persia (4) northern India.

## MATCHING QUESTIONS

| Column A | Column B |
|---|---|
| 1. First codified Athenian laws | a. Alexander |
| 2. Expanded the Athenian navy to fight Persia | b. Darius |
| 3. Led Macedonian and Greek troops to conquer Persia | c. Demosthenes |
| 4. First granted male commoners the vote in the Athenian Assembly | d. Draco |
| | e. Leonidas |
| 5. Ordered Persian army to invade Greece | f. Pericles |
| 6. Governed Athens during its "Golden Age" | g. Philip |
| | h. Solon |
| | i. Themistocles |

## IDENTIFICATION QUESTIONS: WHO AM I?

| | | | |
|---|---|---|---|
| Archimedes | Epicurus | Phidias | Socrates |
| Aristophanes | Herodotus | Pindar | Sophocles |
| Aristotle | Hippocrates | Plato | Thucydides |
| Democritus | Homer | Pythagoras | Zeno |

1. Because I taught youths to seek truth through persistent questioning, I was accused of corrupting their minds and was condemned to death.
2. I insisted that disease results from natural, not supernatural, causes and composed an oath of medical ethics.
3. I was the sculptor who carved the statue of the goddess Athena for the Parthenon.
4. A blind poet, I wrote two epics, the *Iliad* and the *Odyssey,* which portrayed the life of the early Greeks.
5. The first "scientific historian," I wrote the history of the Peloponnesian War.
6. I influenced European thinking for many centuries by my encyclopedic works on government, science, and philosophy.
7. A philosopher, I urged people to seek happiness and pleasure within a balanced moral life.
8. A philosopher, I urged not a democracy but an aristocracy of intelligence in my book *The Republic.*
9. As founder of Stoicism, I urged people to be indifferent to pleasure or pain.
10. I theorized that matter is composed of small, indivisible particles called atoms.
11. I portrayed the conflict between the individual and fate in plays of tragedy, such as *Oedipus Rex.*
12. I discovered significant mathematical relationships still studied in geometry.

## MULTIPLE-CHOICE QUESTIONS

Select the number of the item that does *not* belong in the corresponding group.

1. Geographical features of Greece:   (1) sharply indented coastline   (2) high mountain ranges   (3) small arable land areas   (4) numerous navigable rivers.
2. Greek bonds of union:   (1) Olympic games   (2) fear of Persia   (3) common language   (4) loyalty to the central government.
3. Evidences of Athenian democracy:   (1) jury system   (2) election of officials   (3) right of male citizens to vote   (4) representative legislative body.
4. Greek contributions to the theater:   (1) the chorus   (2) seats grouped around a stage   (3) elaborate scenery   (4) tragic plays.
5. Fields of Greek civilization of which much has survived:   (1) sculpture   (2) architecture   (3) drama   (4) painting.

## ESSAY QUESTIONS

1. Provide *two* examples to explain how geography affected the people of ancient Greece.
2. Although Athens was considered a democracy in ancient times, it had features that a citizen of the United States today would consider undemocratic. Explain *(a) two* features of the Athenian government that would be considered *undemocratic* today and *(b) two* features that would be considered *democratic* today.

3. Discuss *one* similarity and *one* difference between the two items in each of the following pairs:
   
   a. Delian League—Peloponnesian League     c. democracy—aristocracy
   
   b. Hellenic Period—Hellenistic Period     d. Herodotus—Thucydides

4. *(a)* What is meant by "an aggressor nation"? *(b)* Using either Persia *or* Macedonia in ancient times as an example, explain *(i)* why it might have been called an aggressor nation *(ii) one* cause for its aggression and *(iii) one* result of its aggression.

5. Ancient Greece was noted for its sculpture, literature, science, and philosophy. For *each* category, name *two* outstanding ancient Greeks and discuss the work of *one*.

6. Discuss *one* fact to prove either the truth or the falsity of *each* of the following statements: *(a)* Crete was a cultural bridge for ancient peoples. *(b)* Inadequate food supplies at home led the Greeks to colonization. *(c)* The great tragedy of ancient Greece was its failure to achieve unity except by force of arms. *(d)* Alexander the Great's effect upon world history was most unfortunate. *(e)* Western peoples owe a great debt—politically and culturally—to the ancient Greeks.

# Part 2. Ancient Rome:
# An Enduring World Empire

## THE FOUNDING OF ROME

The *Latins*, an Indo-European-speaking *Italic* people from central Europe, crossed the Alps about 1500 B.C. and invaded Italy. Attracted by the warm climate and fertile land, the Latins conquered the native peoples and settled in central Italy. On the seven hills overlooking the *Tiber River*, they founded the city of Rome.

(According to Roman legend, the city was founded in 753 B.C. by two descendants of the gods—the twin brothers *Romulus* and *Remus*.)

## LIFE AMONG THE EARLY LATINS

The early Latins, a simple and hardy people, (1) worked chiefly at farming and cattle-raising; (2) maintained close family ties, with the father exercising absolute authority; (3) worshipped tribal gods *(Jupiter*, the chief god; *Mars*, god of war; *Neptune*, god of the sea; and *Venus*, goddess of love), and (4) defended Rome against frequent attacks.

## ROME: FROM ETRUSCAN RULE TO INDEPENDENCE (750–500 B.C.)

Rome was captured about 750 B.C. by its northern neighbors, the *Etruscans*. From these more advanced people, the Latins, or *Romans*, learned to (1) construct buildings, roads, and city walls, (2) make metal weapons, and (3) apply new military tactics. The Romans in 500 B.C. drove out the Etruscans and established an independent republic.

## THE EARLY REPUBLIC: AN ARISTOCRACY

The Roman Republic at first was an *aristocracy*, with power in the hands of the wealthy landowning nobles, the *patricians*. Only they could serve (1) as *consuls* (heads of state) and (2) as members of the hereditary *Senate*, which passed laws, approved appointments, and controlled foreign affairs. Largely excluded from government were the rest of the Roman people, mainly small farmers and city workers, known as *plebeians*.

## THE ROMAN REPUBLIC BECOMES MORE DEMOCRATIC (5TH–3RD CENTURIES B.C.)

The plebeians clamored for democratic reforms. Over the course of two centuries, they gained the right to (1) elect *tribunes* empowered to veto (forbid) actions of the consuls and the Senate, (2) enact laws in the *people's assemblies*, and (3) hold all government offices, including those of consul and senator.

The plebeians' demands also resulted in codification (arranging and writing down) of Roman law into the *Twelve Tables*. This prevented judges—who were nobles—from twisting unwritten laws to favor their own class.

The Romans achieved these reforms rather harmoniously, because both the patricians and the plebeians willingly compromised their differences for the good of the Republic. (Later, when willingness to compromise disappeared, civil wars destroyed the Republic.)

## ROME GAINS CONTROL OF ITALY (340–270 B.C.)

In a series of wars Rome conquered the Italian peninsula. The Romans (1) in central Italy, overwhelmed the other Latins as well as the Samnites and Etruscans, (2) in northern Italy, drove back the Gauls, and (3) in southern Italy, captured the Greek colonies. (See map, page 57.) Rome succeeded in conquering and uniting Italy because of its:

**1. Powerful Armies.** Roman citizen-soldiers felt deeply responsible to their Republic. They fought not for a despot but for their own freedom, land, and government. Well-trained and strictly disciplined, the Roman legions were the ancient world's most effective fighting force.

**2. Ability to Move Troops.** The *Apennine Mountains*, running north and south through Italy, did not obstruct Roman troop movements appreciably.

**3. Wise Treatment of Conquered Peoples.** The Romans secured the friendship and allegiance of the conquered peoples by granting them the privileges of either partial or full Roman citizenship. From these allies Rome received troops and support for its foreign policy.

## ROME CONQUERS THE WESTERN MEDITERRANEAN (264–146 B.C.)

After subjugating the Greek colonies in southern Italy, Rome sought to control western Mediterranean trade. Its chief rival, located across the Mediterranean in northern Africa, was the city-state of *Carthage*. Originally a Phoenician colony, Carthage had become a powerful commercial empire. Rome defeated Carthage in three *Punic* (Phoenician) *Wars* and gained mastery of the western Mediterranean.

1. **The First Punic War (264–241 B.C.).** Fighting chiefly on the island of Sicily and in the Mediterranean Sea, Rome's citizen-soldiers eventually defeated Carthage's mercenaries (hired foreign soldiers). Rome annexed Sicily and then Sardinia and Corsica. Both sides prepared to renew the struggle. Carthage acquired part of Spain and recruited Spanish troops. Rome consolidated its position in Italy by conquering the Gauls, thereby extending its rule northward from the Po River to the Alps.

2. **The Second Punic War (218–201 B.C.).** *Hannibal*, Carthage's great general, led an army from Spain across the Alps and into Italy. At first he won numerous victories, climaxed by the *Battle of Cannae*. However, he was unable to seize the city of Rome. Gradually the tide of battle turned in favor of Rome. The Romans destroyed a Carthaginian army sent to reinforce Hannibal, then conquered Spain, and finally invaded North Africa. Hannibal withdrew his army from Italy to defend Carthage but, in the *Battle of Zama*, was at last defeated. Rome annexed Carthage's Spanish provinces and reduced Carthage to a second-rate power.

*Reasons for Rome's victory:* (a) superior wealth and military power, (b) the loyalty of most of its allies, and (c) the rise of capable generals, notably Fabius and Scipio. *Fabius* was called the *Delayer* because he did not commit his troops to decisive battle in Italy. Believing that time would help Rome, he merely harassed the enemy. *Scipio* was named *Africanus* because he triumphed over Hannibal in North Africa.

3. **The Third Punic War (149–146 B.C.).** Some Romans believed that Carthage remained a threat. *Cato*, a Roman Senator, ended his speeches, regardless of subject, with the statement "Carthage must be destroyed." Rome finally attacked Carthage, destroyed the city, and annexed the territory.

## ROME CONQUERS THE EASTERN MEDITERRANEAN
## (BY THE 1ST CENTURY B.C.)

After the Second Punic War, Rome conquered (1) Macedonia, including Greece, and (2) Syria, including most of southwestern Asia. Egypt, recognizing

**Italy Under Roman Control**

Rome's might, submitted to Roman domination of the eastern Mediterranean. In 30 B.C. Rome annexed Egypt. Rome was now master of the entire Mediterranean world.

## THE MEDITERRANEAN CONQUESTS AFFECT ROME

**1. Conquests Introduce Greek Culture.** The Romans enthusiastically accepted the advanced Hellenistic culture of the eastern Mediterranean (see pages 50–51). They (a) shipped Greek treasures—books, statues, and vases—to Rome, (b) enslaved educated Greeks to serve as tutors, actors, writers, and scientists, and (c) imitated Greek culture extensively. Roman arms conquered Greece, but Greek culture conquered Rome.

**2. Conquests Bring Wealth to Some Romans.** *(a) Nobles* cheaply acquired huge estates in the provinces and in Italy. They often seized public lands illegally. *(b) Merchants and business people* prospered by filling army contracts, buying booty, supplying slaves, and trading with the provinces. *(c) Government officials* in the provinces amassed huge fortunes at the expense of their subject peoples.

These wealthy classes enjoyed lives of ease and luxury. Hard work, discipline, and patriotism—early Roman virtues—disappeared.

**3. Conquests Ruin Small Farmers and Workers.** Small farmers and city workers could not compete with slave labor employed by huge estates and in industry. Unable to pay their debts, farmers abandoned their lands and migrated to the cities; city workers suffered serious unemployment.

To gain the support of landless farmers and unemployed workers, Roman politicians sponsored free government programs of *bread and circuses* (food and entertainment).

**4. Conquests Change the Character of the Army.** The small farmer had been the backbone of the Roman army. As he disappeared, the nature of the army changed. Citizen-soldiers, loyal to the state, were replaced by professional soldiers, fighting for pay and booty, loyal to their own commanders.

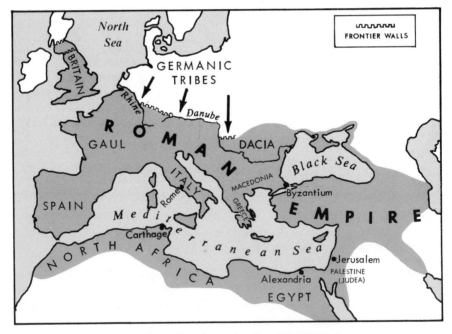

**The Roman Empire at Its Greatest Extent**

## FROM REPUBLIC TO DICTATORSHIP

By the 2nd century B.C., the common people were again demanding economic and political reforms. The aristocracy, controlling the Senate, bitterly opposed measures that threatened their wealth and power. Since the spirit of compromise of the early Republic was dead, peaceful reform failed. In a series of civil wars, rival Roman generals battled for supremacy. The entire conflict, lasting more than 100 years, wrecked the Roman Republic and its many democratic features. In 27 B.C. the Republic was replaced by an absolute monarchy, the Roman Empire.

1. **The Gracchi Brothers Vainly Seek Peaceful Reform (133–121 B.C.).** First, *Tiberius Gracchus* and, later, *Gaius Gracchus,* nobles favoring the common people, were elected tribunes. The Gracchi obtained laws in the people's assembly that would (*a*) recover public lands wrongfully seized by the nobles and (*b*) distribute these lands to landless Romans. Gaius further proposed to weaken the stronghold of aristocratic power, the Senate. Both brothers were killed in riots led by senatorial opponents of reform.

2. **Civil War: Marius vs. Sulla.** Beginning in 88 B.C. two generals—*Marius,* the popular leader, and *Sulla,* the senatorial leader—vied for control of Rome. Their clashes killed thousands of soldiers and civilians. Sulla prevailed and temporarily restored senatorial power.

3. **Civil War: Caesar vs. Pompey.** In 60 B.C. three men—*Julius Caesar,* a popular leader; *Pompey,* a famous general; and *Crassus,* a wealthy noble—formed the *First Triumvirate.* This political alliance enabled the three men to dominate Rome. Caesar became a general and, through military victories in Gaul (France), won his army's loyalty. Caesar spread his fame by his book, *Commentaries on the Gallic War.*

In 49 B.C. the Senate, fearing Caesar's popularity and power, ordered him to disband his army. Caesar refused and, taking an irrevocable step, crossed the *Rubicon River* and invaded the senatorial portion of Italy. Caesar defeated Pompey's senatorial army and became dictator of Rome.

A farsighted leader, Caesar planned to establish stable government, reform provincial rule, provide land for the poor, and beautify the city of Rome. But he lacked time. In 44 B.C. a group of conspirators, some envying his power and others hoping to restore the Republic, assassinated Caesar.

4. **Civil War: Octavian vs. Antony.** After Caesar's death, civil war again erupted. The army of Brutus and Cassius, the chief conspirators, was defeated by forces led by Caesar's friend, *Mark Antony,* and Caesar's grand-nephew, *Octavian.* In the final conflict for power, Octavian defeated Antony at the naval *Battle of Actium* (31 B.C.). This battle off the Greek coast ended the era of civil wars. Octavian then became absolute ruler of the Roman Empire.

## THE ROMAN EMPIRE: A DICTATORSHIP (27 B.C.–476 A.D.)

The Roman Empire, existing about 500 years, was a military dictatorship. Of the many Roman emperors, some dominated the army; others were its puppets. Some devoted themselves to the Empire's welfare; others sought personal advantages. However, only a few were qualified to meet imperial problems.

The outstanding Roman emperors were:

1. **Augustus** (27 B.C.–14 A.D.). From the Senate Octavian accepted the title *Augustus,* meaning "Sacred Majesty." Just and capable, Augustus (*a*) maintained peace, (*b*) provided stable government, (*c*) reformed provincial administration, (*d*) established fair taxation, (*e*) developed trade and industry, (*f*) encouraged science, art, and literature, and (*g*) constructed many roads and buildings. Augustus boasted, according to legend, that he transformed Rome from a city of brick into a city of marble.

During Augustus' reign *Jesus* was born in the Roman province of Judea.

The *Augustan Age* began a 200-year period of peace and progress in the Mediterranean world (see Pax Romana, page 62).

2. **Claudius** (41–54 A.D.) established Roman authority in the southern part of Britain. In Italy he promoted public works.

3. **Vespasian** (69–79 A.D.) dispatched an army, led by his son *Titus,* to Palestine. Titus suppressed a Hebrew revolt, destroyed Jerusalem, and expelled most Jews from Palestine.

4. **Trajan** (98–117 A.D.), through conquest, expanded the Empire to its greatest territorial extent. (See map, page 58.) His most important acquisition was Dacia (modern Rumania).

5. **Hadrian** (117–138 A.D.), to repel barbarian tribes seeking to enter the Empire, built defensive walls in northern Britain and central Europe.

6. **Marcus Aurelius** (161–180 A.D.) was a conscientious and high-minded ruler concerned with the people's welfare. He was also a Stoic philosopher who wrote the famous book, *Meditations.* His death marked the end of the Pax Romana (see page 62).

7. **Diocletian** (284–305 A.D.) became emperor after a period of incompetent rule and internal strife. To simplify government, he divided the Empire into East and West—each portion administered separately. To prevent civil war, he established a system of succession to the throne. Nevertheless, his death led to renewed civil wars.

Diocletian was the last Roman emperor who actively persecuted Christians (see page 77).

8. **Constantine** (312–337 A.D.) reunited the Empire by military force and moved his capital from Rome to *Constantinople* (formerly Byzantium). By the *Edict of Milan* (313 A.D.), he ended the persecution of Christians. Just before his death, Constantine himself was converted to Christianity.

# BARBARIC TRIBES DESTROY THE ROMAN EMPIRE

**1. Germanic (Teutonic) Tribes Exert Pressure (1st–4th Centuries A.D.).** *Germanic,* or *Teutonic,* tribes—primitive, warlike peoples—lived in central and eastern Europe. They were attracted to the Roman Empire by its fertile land, great wealth, and advanced civilization.

Early Germanic efforts to enter the Empire were thwarted by Roman troops. Later, Rome permitted some Germanic peoples to settle within its borders and enlisted Germanic soldiers in its armies.

**2. The Huns Invade Europe (4th and 5th Centuries A.D.).** The *Huns,* savage invaders from central Asia, terrorized Europe, causing many Germanic tribes to flee into the Roman Empire. *Attila,* the "Scourge of God," later led the Huns in ravaging the Empire until turned back by a combined Roman-Germanic force at the *Battle of Châlons* (451 A.D.). The Huns, nevertheless, had weakened Rome militarily and hastened its downfall.

**3. The Germanic Tribes End the Roman Empire (4th and 5th Centuries A.D.).** The full-scale Germanic migrations into Roman territory could not be stemmed by the enfeebled Roman government. Gradually the Germanic tribes established kingdoms within the Empire: the *Visigoths* in Spain, the *Ostrogoths* in Italy, the *Vandals* in North Africa, the *Franks* in Gaul, and the *Angles* and *Saxons* in Britain.

In 476 A.D. Germanic mercenaries overthrew the last emperor in Rome. This event, according to most historians, ended the Western Roman Empire. (For a discussion of the Eastern, or Byzantine, Empire, see pages 86–89.)

# REASONS FOR THE FALL OF THE ROMAN EMPIRE

Why could the Germanic tribes crush Rome, so long the master of the Mediterranean world? The answer lies not in Germanic strength but in Roman weakness. By the 4th and 5th centuries A.D., the Roman Empire had declined because of the following internal conditions:

**1. Political.** *(a)* The dictatorial government was frequently inefficient and corrupt and did not command the people's loyalty. *(b)* The vast Empire, having primitive transportation and communication, could not be governed efficiently from one central city. *(c)* Rivalry over succession to the throne often resulted in destructive civil wars.

**2. Economic.** *(a)* Small farmers had abandoned their lands, and many had become workers on large estates. No longer independent, they lost the incentive to improve farming methods or to increase production. *(b)* The self-sufficiency of the large estates hampered trade and curtailed industry, thus causing an economic decline. *(c)* Heavy, often unjust, taxation burdened the people and destroyed their ambition to work and progress. *(d)* The widespread use of slaves in industry and agriculture caused great unemployment among the plebeians.

3. **Social.** (*a*) People were interested mainly in luxury and survival. The early Roman ideals of patriotism, service, and morality had almost vanished. (*b*) Sharp class distinctions existed. The upper classes were wealthy and educated; the lower classes were poor and ignorant. (*c*) Cities—previously centers of culture and industry—declined as people fled to the rural regions.

4. **Military.** (*a*) The warlike spirit of early pagan Rome was weakened by Christian teachings of peace and universal love. (*b*) The Roman armies included many Germanic mercenaries of uncertain loyalty. (*c*) The armies, considering themselves masters of the state, not its servants, often chose the emperors and determined government policy.

## ROMAN CONTRIBUTIONS TO CIVILIZATION

1. **Pax Romana (27 B.C.–180 A.D.).** For over 200 years Roman military might enforced in the Mediterranean world the *Pax Romana,* or "Roman peace." This was a period of social cohesion on an international scale. Trade and commerce expanded; the arts and sciences thrived; Greco-Roman, or classical, civilization reached everywhere in the Empire. The achievements under the Pax Romana prove that peace means progress.

2. **Roman Law.** The Romans developed bodies of law on business matters, family relationships, individual rights, and international affairs, *Justinian,* Roman emperor at Constantinople (527–565 A.D.), directed jurists to codify these laws. The *Justinian Code* influenced the legal systems of western Europe and, less directly, the United States.

Roman law was intended to be impartial and humane. Two of its principles were: (*a*) All persons are equal before the law. (*b*) Accused persons are guaranteed legal protection. For example, forced confessions are invalid.

3. **Architecture.** The Romans constructed military roads, aqueducts, bridges, and marble buildings—some still in use. Roman architects effectively employed the arch, dome, and column.

During the reign of Emperor Vespasian, the Romans erected the famous stone amphitheater, the *Colosseum.* In its arena gladiators and wild beasts battled to entertain spectators.

4. **Language.** Latin, the Roman language, is (*a*) the root of the *Romance* (or Romanic) languages: French, Italian, Spanish, Portuguese, and Rumanian and (*b*) the source of about one-half of the words in the English language.

5. **Literature**

    *a. Cicero* (106–43 B.C.), an orator and writer, is known as the "father of Latin prose." He wrote extensively on ethical, religious, and political subjects, and delivered famous orations in defense of the Roman Republic.

An air view of the Colosseum in Rome.

*b. Vergil* (70–19 B.C.) wrote the famous epic poem, the *Aeneid*. In relating the adventures of Aeneas, whose descendants supposedly founded Rome, Vergil extolled Rome's greatness.

*c. Horace* (65–8 B.C.) wrote *Odes*, charming poetry about everyday life. A moralist, he praised the early Roman virtues of simplicity, courage, and reverence.

*d. Seneca* (3 B.C.–65 A.D.), a Stoic philosopher, wrote essays on morals.

## 6. Historical Writing

*a. Livy* (59 B.C.–17 A.D.) wrote an encyclopedic history—only part of which has survived—of Rome from its founding to the Augustan Age. Livy deplored the decay of the early Roman virtues and the fall of the Republic.

*b. Plutarch* (100 A.D.) compared Roman and Greek heroes in his book of biographies, *Parallel Lives*.

*c. Tacitus* (55–120 A.D.), in his work *Germania*, vividly described life among the Germanic barbarians.

**7. Science.** The Romans were practical scientists, specializing in sanitation, public health, and engineering. The research scientists of the Empire were generally non-Romans.

*a. Galen* (131–201 A.D.), a Greek physician, wrote books summarizing the ancient world's medical knowledge. He also performed experiments involving the nervous and circulatory systems.

*b. Ptolemy* (2nd century A.D.), a Greek astronomer, taught—erroneously as we now know—that (1) the earth is the center of the universe and (2) the sun revolves about the earth. (This *Ptolemaic theory* was corrected in the 16th century A.D. by the *Copernican theory*, see page 131.)

## MULTIPLE-CHOICE QUESTIONS

1. Rome is situated on the  (1) Po River  (2) Tiber River  (3) Adriatic Sea  (4) Mediterranean Sea.
2. The aristocrats who controlled the Roman Senate in the days of the Republic were called  (1) plebeians  (2) priests  (3) caesars  (4) patricians.
3. Most planets in our solar system are named after Roman  (1) emperors  (2) gods and goddesses  (3) generals  (4) scientists.
4. In gaining control of Italy, the Romans  (1) employed great cruelty  (2) extended citizenship to the conquered peoples  (3) fought only defensive wars  (4) used hired soldiers chiefly.
5. Carthage and Rome became bitter rivals because the Carthaginians  (1) refused to worship Roman gods  (2) drove the Romans out of Gaul  (3) competed with Rome for trade in the Mediterranean  (4) were allied with Alexander the Great.
6. As a result of its Mediterranean conquests, Rome  (1) became a democracy  (2) destroyed Hellenistic culture  (3) adopted Christianity  (4) experienced growing dissatisfaction among its lower classes.
7. Roman politicians offered programs of "bread and circuses" mainly to  (1) keep agricultural prices high  (2) provide work for entertainers  (3) gain the support of the unemployed  (4) encourage enlistments in the army.
8. Soon after the Punic Wars, the redistribution of land in Rome was urged by  (1) Nero  (2) Mark Antony  (3) Tiberius Gracchus  (4) Vespasian.
9. Caesar's great rival for supremacy in Rome was  (1) Pompey  (2) Marius  (3) Octavian  (4) Hadrian.
10. Who ruled Rome at the time of the birth of Jesus?  (1) Augustus Caesar  (2) Sulla  (3) Brutus  (4) Diocletian.
11. French is known as a Romance language because it is  (1) based on Latin  (2) the language of diplomacy  (3) the language of courtship  (4) derived from the Rumanian language.
12. The Roman orator known as the "father of Latin prose" was  (1) Galen  (2) Hadrian  (3) Cicero  (4) Cato.
13. A famous Roman historian was  (1) Livy  (2) Horace  (3) Galen  (4) Claudius.

14. The great expansion of commerce in the Mediterranean area during the first two centuries A.D. is best explained by the (1) adoption of protective tariffs (2) introduction of money (3) invention of the compass (4) maintenance of peace.

15. Roman law upheld the principle that (1) an accused person is entitled to bail (2) possession is nine points of the law (3) forced confessions are not valid (4) a plebeian may not testify against a patrician.

16. The Roman poet who wrote the *Aeneid* was (1) Trajan (2) Horace (3) Vergil (4) Fabius.

17. The *least* important factor explaining the downfall of Rome was the (1) rise of self-sufficient manors (2) widespread use of slaves (3) lack of orderly succession to the throne (4) military strength of the Germanic tribes.

18. Which of the following pairs of modern nations occupy areas that were once included in the Roman Empire? (1) India and Egypt (2) Norway and Denmark (3) Spain and England (4) China and Germany.

19. Two outstanding contributions of Rome to Western civilization were in (1) literature and medicine (2) painting and drama (3) engineering and law (4) music and military tactics.

20. Historian Edward Gibbon described the 2nd century A.D. in Rome as a time when the human race was most happy and prosperous. Historian Arnold Toynbee described the same period as one of stalemate. These statements illustrate that (1) history repeats itself, regardless of the civilization concerned (2) true historians must differ with each other (3) historical evidence is subject to differing interpretations (4) the history of any civilization that lacked a written language will be subject to differing interpretations.

## COMPLETION QUESTIONS

1. The author of *Commentaries on the Gallic War* was _____ .

2. The military leader who defeated Antony and became first ruler of the Roman Empire was _____ .

3. Roman civilization made its greatest progress during the 200-year period known as the _____ .

4. The Roman Empire astronomer who mistakenly taught that the earth is the center of the universe was _____ .

5. Germanic barbarians invaded the Roman Empire in the 4th century A.D. because they were being pushed westward by the _____ .

## TRUE–FALSE QUESTIONS

If the statement is correct, write the word *true*. If the statement is incorrect, substitute a word or phrase for the italicized term to make the statement correct.

1. The lowest class of citizens in Rome was the *plebeian*.

2. *Scipio*, the great Carthaginian general, was unable to capture the city of Rome.

3. The Roman laws were codified during the reign of Emperor *Claudius*.

4. The Huns, who invaded the Roman Empire (5th century A.D.), were led by *Xerxes*.

5. The people who most influenced Roman culture were the *Egyptians*.

6. The Roman amphitheater where gladiatorial combats took place was the *Colosseum*.

7. To fill the ranks of its armies, the declining Roman Empire hired soldiers who worked for pay and were called *consuls*.
8. In the Roman Republic the common people, to protect their interests, elected officials called *tribunes*.
9. The eastern part of the Roman Empire, which existed until the 15th century A.D., was known as the *Byzantine Empire*.

## ESSAY QUESTIONS

1. The history of Rome proves that willingness to compromise by opposing sides is essential to the survival of a democratic state. *(a)* Present *two* examples to prove that the spirit of compromise enabled the Roman Republic to rise and prosper. *(b)* Present *two* examples to prove that the lack of compromise led to the downfall of the Republic.
2. Show how the Roman Republic was either strengthened or weakened by each of the following: *(a)* widespread use of slaves following the Mediterranean conquests *(b)* efforts of the Gracchi brothers *(c)* actions of Julius Caesar *(d)* power of the tribunes to veto Senate laws *(e)* codification of early Roman law into the Twelve Tables.
3. *(a)* Describe briefly how ancient Rome gained control of the Mediterranean. *(b)* Discuss *two* ways in which control of the Mediterranean world affected the Roman way of life.
4. Explain the historical origin and present meaning of each of the following: *(a)* Fabian policy *(b)* plebeians *(c)* All roads lead to Rome *(d)* Carthage must be destroyed *(e)* Cross the Rubicon.
5. The Roman Empire had comparative peace for about 200 years. Explain what this period of peace meant for *(a)* commerce and trade, *(b)* culture, and *(c)* the lives of ordinary people.
6. The Romans were great builders, great governors, and great lawgivers. They left their abiding mark on much of our civilization. Illustrate this statement by referring specifically to the *three* aspects of Roman greatness mentioned above.
7. *(a)* List *four* important causes of the gradual decline of the Roman Empire. *(b)* Explain why each cause listed is like or unlike a problem faced by Western civilization today.

# Section Two

# Medieval History

## UNIT IV. THE MIDDLE AGES: IN EUROPE AND THE MIDDLE EAST

## Part 1. Barbaric Invasions and the Age of Feudalism in Europe

### THE MIDDLE AGES

The *Middle Ages* covers the 900-year period from the political expiration of the Roman Empire in the 5th century to the beginnings of modern times in the 14th century.

This era in the history of western Europe is often divided into (1) the *Early Middle Ages*, also known as the *Dark Ages* (5th to 10th centuries), a period of disorder and decline, and (2) the *Later Middle Ages* (11th to 14th centuries), a period of advance toward a higher level of civilization.

### THE DECLINE OF CIVILIZATION IN THE DARK AGES

The Germanic invasions resulted in the political collapse of the Roman Empire and the ruin of its highly developed economic and social system, thus bringing on the Dark Ages.

1. **Decline of Trade and Industry.** Merchants, fearing the seizure of their goods by highway robbers and pirates, stopped shipping to distant points and confined their trade to the local marketplace. The excellent Roman roads deteriorated. Lacking sufficient markets, industry shut down. Unemployed workers moved to rural areas. As trade and industry dwindled, cities declined in population, and many disappeared; also, money fell into disuse.

2. **Decline of Learning and Culture.** During these unsettled times *(a)* Roman schools, libraries, and museums were destroyed, *(b)* arts and sciences were neglected, and *(c)* reading and writing were forgotten. People were concerned not with learning and culture but with remaining alive.

3. **Decline of Strong Central Government.** Government was now in the hands of weak Germanic kingdoms: the Visigoths in Spain, the Ostrogoths in Italy, the Angles and Saxons in England, and the Franks in Gaul (France). Their rulers generally failed to provide protection, insure justice, and maintain order. Such weaknesses existed because the Germanic kingdoms: *(a) Lacked power* to control their large territories and populations. Only a few hundred thousand Germans governed millions of other peoples. *(b) Lacked large armies* to subdue ambitious nobles. A noble sometimes commanded military forces stronger than those of a monarch. *(c) Lacked roads and bridges* to transport armies to trouble spots. Because the Germans knew little about engineering, they could not maintain the Roman transportation facilities. *(d) Lacked rules of succession to the throne* to prevent civil war after a ruler's death.

The only strong Germanic government was the Frankish kingdom in the 8th and early 9th centuries.

(Some historians criticize the emphasis upon the destructive aspects of the Germanic invasions and argue that the Germanic invaders preserved, at least, a significant portion of the ancient world's classical heritage.)

## THE FRANKISH KINGDOM

1. **Created by Clovis.** Late in the 5th century, invading Frankish warriors completed the defeat of the Roman armies in Gaul. Leading one Frankish group was a capable king, *Clovis.*

Seeking to rule all Gaul, Clovis *(a)* removed possible Frankish rivals, *(b)* subdued other Germanic tribes in Gaul, and *(c)* converted the Franks to Catholic Christianity, thereby gaining support of the pope and of Gaul's large Christian population. By these measures Clovis created a powerful Frankish kingdom.

2. **Ruled by "Do-Nothing" Kings.** Clovis' descendants, who nominally ruled for more than two centuries, were incompetent and became known as "do-nothing" kings. Their reign was marked by recurrent outbreaks of civil war and by a sharp increase in the power of the nobles at the expense of the king. Control of the government eventually passed into the hands of a powerful noble, an official called the *Mayor of the Palace.*

3. **Provided Leadership for Western Europe.** During the 8th and early 9th centuries, the Frankish kingdom dominated western Europe. It was governed successively by three outstanding individuals of the *Carolingian* family:

*a. Charles Martel,* as Mayor of the Palace, led the Frankish army that defeated the invading Moors (Arabs) at the *Battle of Tours* (732). This battle ended the Moslem thrust into Christian Europe (see page 90).

*b. Pepin* in 741 became Mayor of the Palace upon the death of his father, Charles Martel. In 751, with the pope's approval, Pepin removed the last "do-nothing" king and assumed the Frankish throne. Grateful for papal support, Pepin drove the *Lombards,* a Germanic people, out of central Italy and ceded their lands to the pope. This *Donation of Pepin* gave the Catholic Church political control over part of central Italy. For over 1,000 years the Church ruled this area—the *Papal States* (see pages 255–256).

*c. Charlemagne* in 768 succeeded to the Frankish throne upon the death of his father, Pepin.

## CHARLEMAGNE RULES A MEDIEVAL EMPIRE (768–814)

Charlemagne was the outstanding ruler in medieval Europe. During his 46-year reign, he demonstrated extraordinary ability in:

### 1. Warfare

*a. Charlemagne's Conquests.* Charlemagne conquered (1) the *Lombards* in northern Italy, (2) the *Moslems* in the Spanish March, a strip of land just south of the Pyrenees Mountains in Spain, (3) the *Slavs* in Bohemia (now part of Czechoslovakia), and (4) the *Saxons,* a pagan Germanic people in northwestern Germany.

*b. Effects of Charlemagne's Conquests.* Charlemagne increased the power of the Catholic Church by ending the Lombard threat to the Papal States and by converting pagan peoples to Catholicism. He also expanded the Frankish realm into an empire that included most of western Europe. (See map, page 70.)

*c. "Emperor of the Romans."* At Rome in 800 Pope Leo III, recognizing Charlemagne's services to the Church and mastery of western Europe, crowned him "Emperor of the Romans." (For the subsequent political significance of this act, see page 83.)

Charlemagne's "Roman" Empire differed from the original Roman Empire in that (1) it encompassed chiefly central and western Europe; whereas the original Roman Empire had centered about the Mediterranean, and (2) it crumbled upon Charlemagne's death, whereas the original empire had endured many centuries.

### 2. Government.
Charlemagne divided his empire into provinces, each administered by a noble responsible to him. To maintain the authority of the central government in the provinces, Charlemagne sent to them official messengers called *missi dominici.* They reported on the nobles' loyalty and ability. This system of continuous investigation, coupled with Charlemagne's tremendous prestige, temporarily halted the shift of power from the central government to the nobles.

### 3. Education.
Charlemagne, unlike most Germanic rulers, valued education. He *(a)* established schools in monasteries and cathedrals to instruct both the clergy and the common people, *(b)* encouraged the collecting and copying of

Latin manuscripts to preserve ancient learning, and *(c)* maintained a *palace school* at his capital, *Aix-la-Chapelle,* to educate the nobles' children. To head this school, Charlemagne appointed the famous English scholar, *Alcuin.*

## BREAKUP OF CHARLEMAGNE'S EMPIRE

Charlemagne's death (814) was followed by years of incompetent rule and civil war. Charlemagne's successors lacked his ability and were unable to keep the empire intact. By the *Treaty of Verdun* (843), his three grandsons agreed to divide the territory as follows: *Louis* received the eastern part, the basis of modern Germany; *Charles* received the western part, the basis of modern France; and *Lothar* received the central part, which included the basis of modern Italy.

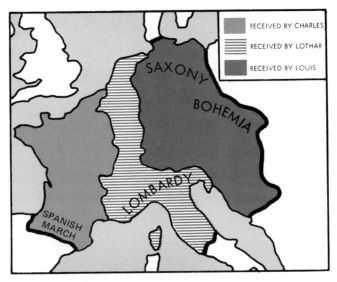

**The Division of Charlemagne's Empire**

Charlemagne's successors proved unable to control the nobles, prevent local warfare, and suppress piracy and highway robbery. Most important, they were unable to repel new invasions of western Europe.

## NEW INVASIONS OF EUROPE (9TH AND 10TH CENTURIES)

1. The **Norse** (people of the north), also known as **Vikings,** were Germanic barbarians from the north European region of Scandinavia (Norway, Sweden, Denmark). Poor soil and a coastline with many natural harbors encouraged them to become sailors. Attracted chiefly by western Europe's wealth, the Norse at first plundered coastal and river cities. Later, faced with overpopulation at

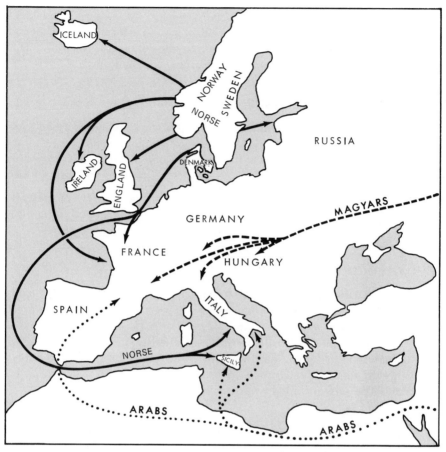

**Invasions of Europe (9th–10th Centuries)**

home, they settled in England, Ireland, France, Italy, and Sicily. They also settled in Russia and Iceland. (From Iceland *Leif Ericson* sailed west and, long before Columbus, reached the New World.)

**2.** The **Magyars,** a people from central Asia, settled in Hungary. From this base, they attacked France, southern Germany, and northern Italy.

**3.** The **Arabs,** or **Moors,** although stopped in 732 at the Battle of Tours, retained control of Spain and North Africa. From these bases they continued to raid southern France and Italy.

Since the governments of western Europe failed to withstand these various invaders, the people were inadequately protected. Their effort to safeguard their lives and property hastened the development of new relationships among people—the system of *feudalism.*

## DEFINITION OF FEUDALISM

Feudalism may be considered (1) a *social* system of rigid class distinctions and a static, or unchanging, way of life, (2) a *political* system of local government and military defense, and (3) an *economic* system of self-sufficient agricultural manors. Feudalism varied in detail according to regional conditions.

## REASONS FOR THE RISE OF FEUDALISM

1. **Weakness of Central Government.** The central government could not protect its subjects from foreign invasions and local warfare. Small farmers consequently surrendered their lands to the powerful local noble in exchange for his promise of protection.

2. **Land Policy of the Germanic Kings.** In return for pledges of military assistance, the Germanic rulers granted landed estates to the important nobles. Possessing these large estates substantially increased the nobles' power.

## FEUDAL SOCIETY

1. **Rigid Class Distinctions.** Feudal society was sharply divided into (*a*) landholding *nobles*—the privileged aristocracy, or upper class—and (*b*) the great mass of peasants, or *serfs*—the unprivileged lower class. Position in feudal society was determined by birth. Regardless of ability or hard work, the serf could not advance to higher social status. (At this time, the rulers and nobles were generally men, although their wives and daughters were also part of the aristocracy. The serfs included women and children as well as men.)

2. **The Feudal Social Pyramid**

   *a.* The *king*, at the apex of feudal society, nominally owned all the land in the kingdom. Actually the king controlled only his own estates, the *royal domain*.

   *b.* The *powerful lords*, few in number, stood immediately below the king as his subordinate *vassals*. These lords received grants of land called *fiefs* from the king and in return pledged him allegiance and military service. The king (or lord) who granted the land was called the *suzerain*. The vassal pledged to fulfill his obligations in a ceremony called *homage*. He was granted his fief in a ceremony called *investiture*.

   *c.* The *lesser lords*, a more numerous group, were vassals of the powerful lords and received fiefs in exchange for pledges of allegiance and military service. The lesser lords could in turn grant fiefs to other nobles. This process, which could be repeated several times, is called *subinfeudation*.

   *d.* The *knights*, the lowest and most numerous group of nobles, constituted the bulk of the feudal armies. (Only men could be knights.)

*e.* The *serfs*, far outnumbering the entire nobility, constituted the broad base of the feudal pyramid.

**3. Complicated Vassal–Lord Relationships.** Feudal relationships of the nobility were quite complicated. When lesser lords and knights received fiefs from different suzerains, they were vassals to several lords. The question of the vassal's primary allegiance led to many bitter disputes.

**4. Feudal Hereditary Relationships.** *(a)* The mutual obligations between lord and vassal or between noble and serf were usually *hereditary*—binding upon the heirs of both parties. *(b)* A noble's title and property could be inherited only by his first-born son. This restriction, awarding to the first-born son a status superior to his younger brothers, is called *primogeniture.*


## FEUDAL GOVERNMENT

**1. Weak Central Government.** Although the central government or king theoretically administered the entire kingdom, the king could not generally exercise authority beyond the royal domain. Supposedly the supreme ruler, he was in reality only one of several powerful lords.

**2. Vigorous Local Government.** Because the king was weak, the local nobles completely controlled their own territories. The nobles made laws, levied taxes, dispensed justice, and waged war, thereby assuming the functions of government. Thus, feudal government was decentralized.


## MILITARY ASPECTS OF FEUDALISM

**1. During Wartime.** When invasion or major war threatened, the powerful lord would summon his vassals to military service. In turn the vassals would enlist their subvassals, and then all the nobles would unite into a single army to repel the invasion or prosecute the war. At other times minor feudal lords fought among themselves for prestige or land.

Invasions and feudal wars destroyed crops and property. Casualties among fighting men and civilians were minimized, however, by such defenses as heavy armor and strong castle walls.

**2. The Castle.** Dominating the lord's estate, or *manor*, was a castle. A cold, dark, damp home, lacking comforts and simple conveniences, it nevertheless constituted an excellent fortress. It was *(a)* located on elevated ground, *(b)* constructed of heavy wood or (after the 11th century) thick stone, and *(c)* surrounded by a deep, wide, water-filled trench, called a *moat*. A drawbridge, lowered across the moat, provided access to the outside. During attacks the families of the lords, vassals, and serfs found protection in the castle.

**3. During Peacetime.** When peace prevailed the lord *(a)* hunted wild animals, *(b)* held mock battles called *jousts* and *tournaments,* and *(c)* trained young nobles for knighthood.

The young noble received extended military schooling at horsemanship, in wearing armor, and in using the sword, lance, and battle-ax. At age 21 he became a warrior on horseback, or *knight.*

The knight was expected to observe a code of honorable conduct called *chivalry.* This code stressed *(a)* loyalty to God and to the knight's lord, *(b)* protection of the oppressed and helpless, *(c)* support of justice, *(d)* defense of Christianity, and *(e)* courage, courtesy, gallantry, and generosity. Unfortunately these chivalrous ideals were frequently violated.

## FEUDAL ECONOMIC CONDITIONS

**1. The Self-sufficient Agricultural Manor.** The manor, or lord's estate, consisted of *(a)* the farm and pasture lands, *(b)* the lord's castle or manor house, and *(c)* the village buildings: church, blacksmith and carpenter shops, serfs' huts, and the lord's winepress, flour mill, and baking oven. The manor was largely self-sufficient economically. Its inhabitants raised crops and livestock for food, spun wool for clothing, tanned leather for shoes, and cut lumber for furniture and buildings. However, some essential items, such as salt for preserving and seasoning food and iron for making tools and weapons, had to be secured from outside sources.

On the manor the lord directed the activities—determining what was to be produced and how; the serfs performed the physical labor.

**2. The Serfs**

*a. Neither Slaves nor Free People.* The serfs were not slaves since they could not be sold apart from the land and could claim the lord's protection. Nonetheless, the serfs were not free since they were "bound to the soil" and could not leave without the lord's permission.

*b. Obligations of the Serfs.* In return for protection and the right to earn a living on the manor, serfs owed the lord (1) *services*—several days of labor each week on the lord's farmlands, and (2) *payment in kind*—a portion of the grain and other crops raised on the serfs' land. The serfs also had to give the lord a share of the goods they prepared in the lord's winepress, flour mill, and baking oven.

*c. An Impoverished Life.* After meeting their obligations to the lord, the serfs had little left for themselves. They lived a hard, tedious life and had little opportunity for recreation and education. Many historians believe that the serfs paid a heavy price for the security they received.

**3. Low Agricultural Output.** In proportion to its size and labor force, the manor raised insufficient crops. *(a)* Each serf family was assigned scattered strips of land rather than a compact farm. Although ensuring a fair distribution of fertile land, this arrangement wasted working time. *(b)* The serfs had only wooden plows and crude sickles and hoes. *(c)* Little was known about crop rotation or fertilizer. To restore soil fertility, the manor followed the inefficient *three-field system.* This meant letting one-third of the land lie fallow, or uncultivated, every year.

**4. Disappearance of Trade.** At the height of feudalism (9th to 11th centuries), trade was at a virtual standstill. As manors became more self-sufficient, the need for outside products declined. In addition feudal wars and inadequate roads and bridges made commerce unsafe and difficult. Moreover, heavy taxes imposed by each feudal lord on goods transported across his domain raised the cost of the goods.

## FACTORS LEADING TO THE DECLINE OF FEUDALISM

**1. The Crusades.** During a 200-year period (1095–1291), western Europe undertook many *Crusades,* religious wars intended to recover the Holy Land from the Moslems. The Crusades weakened the economic basis of feudalism by awakening European demand for Eastern goods. Trade revived, towns grew, the merchant class prospered, serfs fled to the towns, and the self-sufficiency of the manor ended. (For a discussion of the Crusades, see pages 94–96.)

**2. The Rise of National States and Absolute Monarchy.** From the 14th to the 17th centuries, the rise of national states weakened political and military feudalism. As the Crusades and feudal wars decimated the nobility, the monarch or central government gradually regained absolute power. (For a discussion of national states and absolute monarchy, see pages 144–154.)

Long after the feudal period ended, the French Revolution (1789) helped destroy the remaining traces of feudalism in western Europe. Even today, however, parts of Asia, Africa, and Latin America retain certain feudal aspects: rigid class distinctions, landless peasants, and landowning by the wealthy few.

## MULTIPLE–CHOICE QUESTIONS

1. The "Dark Ages" in western Europe refers to the period   (1) before the dawn of history   (2) soon after the assassination of Julius Caesar   (3) following the collapse of the Roman Empire   (4) directly following the end of the Pax Romana.
2. Which was *not* a result of the Germanic invasions of the Roman Empire?   (1) raising the level of civilization   (2) overthrowing the Roman government   (3) curtailing trade   (4) destroying many fine Roman buildings.
3. In the Frankish kingdom the Mayor of the Palace was usually the   (1) do-nothing king   (2) Lord Mayor of Paris   (3) spiritual head of Gaul   (4) powerful noble who controlled the central government.
4. By the Donation of Pepin, the Catholic Church received   (1) money   (2) valuable Greco-Roman manuscripts   (3) land   (4) a monopoly over Mediterranean trade.
5. The Frankish leader who defeated the Moors at the Battle of Tours was   (1) Clovis   (2) Charlemagne   (3) Pepin   (4) Charles Martel.

6. Charlemagne was able to dominate western Europe successfully because he (1) controlled the commerce of this area (2) allied himself with Anglo-Saxon England (3) maintained an efficient military force (4) developed Frankish sea power.

7. In 800 A.D. the pope gave Charlemagne the title of (1) Emperor of the Romans (2) King of the Franks (3) Mayor of the Palace (4) Master of the Royal Domain.

8. Areas that Charlemagne united within his empire are now part of (1) France and Germany (2) England and Spain (3) Spain and Portugal (4) Austria and Russia.

9. An important result of Charlemagne's conquests was the (1) spread of Christianity (2) union of the Eastern and Western Roman empires (3) expulsion of the Moslems from Europe (4) decline of feudalism in central Europe.

10. A basic reason for the rise of the feudal system in Europe was the (1) increase in population (2) influence of the Crusades (3) end of the manorial system (4) lack of effective central governments.

11. Power and position during the feudal period were based on (1) possession of money (2) holding of land (3) success in jousts and tournaments (4) number of slaves on the manor.

12. Which son of a feudal lord inherited the father's estate? (1) the eldest (2) the best fighter (3) the best educated (4) whichever son the lord named in his will.

13. Feudalism served a useful purpose because it (1) encouraged education (2) eliminated warfare (3) gave the people some protection and security (4) encouraged the development of industry.

14. Serfs were (1) bound to their master (2) the property of the state (3) free when they reached the age of 21 (4) bound to the land.

15. A vassal under feudalism owed his lord (1) military service (2) labor on the estate (3) fees for the use of the mill and winepress (4) one-fifth of his income.

16. The medieval manor (1) was economically self-sufficient (2) depended on trade for many of its supplies (3) produced many luxuries (4) continuously cultivated all its arable land.

17. One cause of the decline of feudalism in western Europe was its failure to (1) gain the support of the medieval Church (2) keep pace with economic changes in society (3) provide adequate protection from barbarian invasions (4) provide job security for the serfs.

18. Which characteristic of the feudal period in western Europe made it most *unlike* any other period in European history? (1) the relationships established by the granting of land (2) the misery and backwardness of the peasants (3) the number of wars and combats (4) the existence of a class system.

19. Certain nations today are referred to as *feudal*. What is their outstanding characteristic? (1) ownership of the land by a very small percentage of the population (2) possession of military bases on foreign soil (3) lack of natural resources (4) existence of a large middle class.

## TRUE–FALSE QUESTIONS

If the statement is correct, write the word *true*. If the statement is incorrect, substitute a word or phrase for the italicized term to make the statement correct.

1. During the Early Middle Ages, the number of towns *remained about the same*.

2. Under feudalism the central government was *all-powerful*.

3. The Viking leader who reached the New World long before Columbus was *Lothar*.

4. One characteristic of Scandinavia that encouraged its inhabitants to become sailors was *poor soil.*

5. Feudal class distinctions required the first son of a serf to become *a knight.*

6. In feudal society a vassal could receive land from *only one* superior lord.

7. The feudal restriction requiring an estate to be willed in its entirety to the eldest son was called *investiture.*

8. The medieval manor used the three-field system in order to *provide a variety of crops.*

## ESSAY QUESTIONS

1. Discuss the Germanic invasions of the Roman Empire, explaining *(a) two* causes of the invasions, *(b) two* reasons for the success of the invaders, *(c) two* results of these invasions.

2. Some historians refer to the period 500 A.D.–1000 A.D. in western Europe as the "Dark Ages." Discuss fully *two* reasons why this period does or does *not* deserve the title "Dark Ages."

3. *(a)* Discuss *three* problems that confronted Charlemagne when he became king of the Franks. *(b)* Explain how Charlemagne solved *one* of these problems.

4. Feudalism in western Europe had political, economic, and social features. Show how the feudal system affected *(a)* the form of government, *(b)* the method of making a living, *(c)* the system of social classes.

5. Show *three* ways in which the living conditions of the people in your community today are better than the living conditions of the nobles in Europe during the feudal period.

6. Presenting one argument, prove that each of the following statements *does or does not* describe the feudal period of western Europe: *(a)* The feudal manor was a self-sufficient economic unit. *(b)* The feudal system glamorized military combat. *(c)* Feudalism was a system of mutual obligations between lords and vassals and between nobles and serfs. *(d)* Feudalism contained many democratic aspects. *(e)* An uprising by the underprivileged class of serfs was the main cause for the decline of feudalism.

# Part 2. The Roman Catholic Church: Dominant Institution of the Middle Ages

## JESUS AND THE IDEALS OF CHRISTIANITY

*Jesus* was born in Bethlehem in the Roman province of Judea (part of Palestine) during the reign of Emperor Augustus. Jesus received a thorough Jewish religious education and became a preacher. Emphasizing religious morals and ethics, he taught the following principles:

1. A single God is the Father of all humanity. Therefore, all men are brothers and all women are sisters. (All human beings should be concerned about each other.)

2. Love God above all; love your neighbor as yourself.

3. The life and person of each individual are sacred.

4. The worthy individual practices charity, justice, and the Golden Rule: "Do unto others as you would have others do unto you."

5. All persons may be cleansed of sin and achieve eternal salvation. The meek, the oppressed, and the forgiving will receive special heavenly rewards.

Jesus' disciples (followers) believed that He was the Son of God sent to humankind as the Savior, or *Christ*. His teachings, presented in the *New Testament*, became the basis of a new religion, *Christianity*.

## THE SPREAD OF CHRISTIANITY WITHIN THE ROMAN EMPIRE (1ST TO 4TH CENTURIES A.D.)

### 1. Early Church Leaders

*a. St. Paul* (1st century A.D.) envisioned Christianity, not as merely a Jewish sect, but as a universal religion. He therefore directed Christian missionaries to emphasize the conversion of non-Jewish peoples called *Gentiles*. St. Paul, himself a missionary, is known as the "Apostle to the Gentiles." (Missionaries are men and women who undertake missions to persuade other peoples to accept the beliefs of a certain religion.)

*b. St. Peter* (1st century A.D.), the first Bishop of Rome, began to shape the Church's internal structure (see pages 80–81). As his model he used the administrative organization of the Roman Empire.

*c. St. Jerome* (340–420) translated the Bible from Hebrew and Greek into the first Latin, or *Vulgate*, edition.

*d. St. Augustine* (354–430), a philosopher, related the story of his conversion to Christianity in his autobiographical *Confessions*. He described how Christianity could lead to a world of peace and perfection in his book *The City of God*.

**2. Favorable Factors.** Christianity gained many converts throughout the Roman Empire.

*a.* People were dissatisfied with the old pagan religions, those honoring many gods and goddesses.

*b.* People were attracted by the ideals of Christianity: one God, universal love, and eternal salvation. The concept of equality of individuals appealed especially to the poor and oppressed.

*c.* Christian missionaries could travel and preach with relative ease throughout the Roman Empire, a political and cultural unit.

*d.* Early Church leaders displayed courage, sincerity, and ability.

*e.* People were impressed by many early Christians who, rather than renounce their faith, suffered persecution and in some instances died as *martyrs.*

**3. Opposition and Persecution.** Christianity was opposed within the Roman Empire.

*a.* Pagan priests feared that the success of Christianity would doom their religions.

*b.* The upper classes considered Christianity a "slave religion" because it appealed to the lowly by preaching equality and universal love.

*c.* Roman officials accused the Christians of treason because they (1) refused to worship the Roman emperor, (2) refused to serve in the Roman armies, and (3) disapproved of gladiatorial combats and pagan feasts.

For 300 years Christians were persecuted by the Roman government, most severely under the emperors Nero and Diocletian. The Christians suffered the loss of Roman citizenship, confiscation of property, torture, and death. Nevertheless, Christianity continued to grow stronger and gain converts.

**4. Christianity Triumphs.** In 313 the Christians gained freedom from persecution when the Emperor *Constantine* ordered religious toleration by the *Edict of Milan.* After Constantine later became a Christian, the faith grew in public esteem. In 392 the Emperor *Theodosius* proclaimed it the official state religion. Christianity was then overwhelmingly accepted by the people of the Empire.

## THE SPREAD OF CHRISTIANITY OUTSIDE THE ROMAN EMPIRE (4TH TO 11TH CENTURIES)

**1. Western Europe.** The *Roman Catholic Church,* centered in Rome, gradually converted the Germanic peoples and other west Europeans. Outstanding landmarks of such progress were the conversions of *(a)* Clovis and the Franks in 5th-century France, *(b)* the Irish in the 5th century (by the missionary *St. Patrick), (c)* the Angles and Saxons in England at the end of the 6th century (by the missionary *St. Augustine of Canterbury),* and *(d)* the Saxons in 8th-century Germany after their subjugation by Charlemagne (see page 69). By the 11th century the Roman Catholic branch of Christianity dominated western Europe.

**2. Eastern Europe.** The *Greek Orthodox Church,* centered in Constantinople, gradually converted certain Slavic-speaking peoples (Serbs, Bulgars, and Russians) and other east Europeans. By the 11th century the Greek Orthodox branch of Christianity dominated eastern Europe.

## SPLIT IN THE CHRISTIAN CHURCH

During the early Christian era, Rome and Constantinople vied for religious power. The *Pope,* or Bishop of Rome, claimed supremacy over the whole

Church; the *Patriarch*, or Bishop, of Constantinople asserted authority over Church affairs in the East. They also had conflicting views on Church language, religious beliefs, and rituals. As a result of these disagreements, the Christian Church in 1054 split into two distinct parts: the Roman Catholic Church at Rome and the Greek Orthodox Church at Constantinople. (The Greek Orthodox Church later split into a number of Eastern Orthodox Churches.) The Roman Catholic and Greek Orthodox Churches retain separate identities to this day. The Roman Catholic Church proved to be more influential.

1. It was free from political control, whereas the Greek Orthodox Church was controlled by the Byzantine emperors.
2. It was the dominant factor in western Europe during the Middle Ages, whereas the Greek Orthodox Church was less significant in eastern Europe.
3. After the Middle Ages, as western Europe assumed greater importance in world affairs, the Roman Catholic Church expanded its missionary and other religious activities throughout the world.

## STRUCTURE OF THE ROMAN CATHOLIC CHURCH

1. **Secular Clergy.** These Church officials live and work in the everyday world. They constitute the Church *hierarchy*.

*a.* The *Pope*, who resides at the *Vatican* in Rome, is the supreme leader of the Roman Catholic Church. He is considered to be in direct line of succession from St. Peter, the first Bishop of Rome. Since the 11th century, each pope has been elected for life by the College of Cardinals.

*b.* The *cardinals*, called the Princes of the Church, are clergymen, usually bishops or archbishops, appointed by the pope as his chief advisers.

*c.* The *bishops* head religious districts, or *dioceses*. An important diocese, called an *archdiocese*, is headed by an *archbishop*.

*d.* The *priests* direct local communities, or parishes. They serve and guide their parishioners—men, women, and children of the parish—who are known as the *laity*.

2. **Religious Orders.** The Church structure also includes those men and women who withdraw from ordinary pursuits to enter *religious orders*. Each order lives according to a special set of rules *(regula)*. The members normally take vows of *poverty*—not to possess worldly goods; *chastity*—not to marry; and *obedience*— to their superiors within the Church and to God.

*a.* The men, designated by such names as *monks* and *friars*, live in buildings generally known as *monasteries*. Monks and friars who are also priests comprise the *regular clergy*.

*b.* The women are called *nuns*. Their residences are usually known as *convents*.

## IMPORTANT RELIGIOUS ORDERS FOUNDED DURING THE MIDDLE AGES

**1. Benedictines.** The monks of the Benedictine order, founded in the 6th century, lived according to the *Rule of St. Benedict*. It introduced the vows of poverty, chastity, and obedience. These monks devoted themselves to prayer and hard work. They farmed, provided food and medical care for needy persons, extended hospitality to travelers, and maintained schools chiefly for prospective clergymen. By hand copying ancient manuscripts, they preserved the classical Greek and Roman literature.

**2. Templars and Hospitalers.** Founded during the Crusades, these orders combined the functions of monks and knights. They cared for the sick and injured, and they fought the Moslems to regain the Holy Land.

**3. Franciscans and Dominicans.** Both orders were founded in the 13th century, the first by *St. Francis of Assisi* and the second by *St. Dominic*. These orders consisted of *mendicant* (begging) *friars*, who originally wandered from place to place, living on alms and preaching Christianity. The Franciscans ministered to the lower-class people; the Dominicans concentrated chiefly upon the educated upper class. The Dominicans also combated *heresy* (religious doctrines contrary to Church teachings).

## ACTIVITIES OF THE MEDIEVAL CHURCH

The most powerful institution in medieval western Europe was the Roman Catholic Church. Supreme in religious matters, it also undertook many non-religious functions that were beyond the power of the weak feudal governments.

### 1. Religious Activities

*a.* The Church completely supervised the religious needs of the people, dispensing such *sacraments*, or religious rites, as baptism at birth and final rites at death. Moreover, the Church taught that faith, good works, and Church membership assure eternal salvation.

*b.* The Church used the power of *excommunication* against those persons, including kings and powerful lords, who flagrantly violated Church laws or trampled on its rights. By excommunication the Church expelled a person from its membership and banned that person from taking part in its rites and services.

By being deprived of the sacraments, the excommunicated person ran the risk of eternal damnation. If he was a king or a powerful noble, excommunication freed his subjects from all obligation to him.

*c.* In the 13th century the Church established the *Holy Inquisition* to uncover and try *heretics*—those Christians whose religious views the Church considered false and therefore dangerous. Persons suspected of heresy sometimes were tortured to secure confessions and repentance. Unrepentant heretics were handed over to the civil authorities for punishment—usually death.

## 2. Economic Activities

*a.* The Church derived a considerable income from its lands, gifts, and various assessments, or taxes. The most important tax, amounting to about 10 percent of each person's income, was called the *tithe.*

*b.* The Church maintained hospitals and asylums for the sick, aged, orphaned, and poor.

*c.* The Church encouraged the monks who farmed monastery lands to follow the best agricultural practices and thereby to set a good example for nearby farmers.

*d.* The Church prohibited the charging of interest for a loan of money—a practice then called *usury.* (Today the term usury is understood to apply only to excessively high or unlawful interest rates.)

*e.* By the 13th century the Church owned 30 percent of the land of western Europe. These holdings represented gifts of land for the establishment of monasteries, convents, and cathedrals, as well as land that Church officials had received from powerful lords as feudal fiefs.

## 3. Cultural Activities

*a.* The Church promoted learning by maintaining schools, chiefly to educate young men for the priesthood. (Talented boys, even from the lower class, could thus become priests and rise in the Church hierarchy.) Although the general public was illiterate, the clergy could read and write.

*b.* By copying ancient books and manuscripts, the monks helped preserve Greco-Roman culture.

*c.* The Church influenced literature and architecture. Medieval authors, usually members of the clergy, wrote about religious themes (see page 101). Medieval architects designed magnificent cathedrals (see pages 99–100).

## 4. Political Activities

*a.* The Church governed the Papal States in Italy.

*b.* The Church maintained its own courts for cases involving marriages, wills, contracts, orphans, widows, and the clergy. (The privilege of the clergy to be tried in Church courts rather than civil courts is called *benefit of clergy.*) The legal system developed in Church courts is called *canon law.*

*c.* The Church prohibited feudal warfare during certain days of the week and on special holidays—a prohibition called the *Truce of God.* This truce was often violated by feudal lords.

*d.* The Church claimed supremacy over civil government. This claim led to disputes between medieval popes and civil rulers.

## MEDIEVAL POPES BESTOW CROWNS UPON CIVIL RULERS

In 800 Pope Leo III crowned Charlemagne "Emperor of the Romans." Upon Charlemagne's death, his empire collapsed and his title of emperor remained unused. In 962 Pope John XII crowned Otto I, a ruler in central Europe, as emperor. Thus began the *Holy Roman Empire.*

On the basis of these papal crownings, the medieval Church asserted that (1) popes may dethrone as well as crown emperors and (2) popes are superior to civil rulers, including kings and emperors. These claims led to many disputes between the Church and states (civil authorities).

## STRUGGLES BETWEEN CIVIL RULERS AND POPES

During the Later Middle Ages, a number of civil rulers challenged papal authority. Since the popes often triumphed, these conflicts demonstrated the strength of the medieval Church.

**1. The Investiture Struggle**

*a. The Issue.* For many years both civil rulers and popes claimed the right to appoint major Church officials. Civil rulers claimed this right because they invested Church officials with land as feudal fiefs. The popes also claimed this right because they invested Church officials with religious authority. (*Invest,* used in this sense, means "endow" with power.)

*b. The Papal Triumph at Canossa (1077).* Pope Gregory VII (Hildebrand) ordered civil rulers *not* to appoint Church officials. When Henry IV, King of Germany and Holy Roman Emperor, defied the order, Gregory excommunicated and deposed him (ordered him to give up his throne). This action freed Henry's subjects from allegiance to him and encouraged his feudal lords to revolt. Acknowledging defeat, Henry journeyed to Canossa (in northern Italy) where, reputedly barefoot in the the the snow for three days, he did penance before the papal residence. Pope Gregory then forgave him. This episode is a dramatic illustration of the power of the medieval Church.

*c. The Concordat of Worms (1122).* Despite Canossa, the investiture struggle continued, not only between Henry and Gregory, but also between succeeding emperors and popes. Finally a compromise agreement was reached in the *Concordat of Worms.* (1) The Church alone could appoint Church officials and invest them with religious authority. (2) The civil rulers retained the right to invest these officials with feudal fiefs, thus exercising, for all practical purposes, a veto power over the selections of the Church. This settlement resolved the question of investiture, but it did not end the rivalry between popes and civil rulers.

**2. The Archbishop of Canterbury Struggle.** In 1206 Pope Innocent III appointed Stephen Langton as *Archbishop of Canterbury,* leader of the Catholic Church in England. This papal choice was rejected by King John, who preferred his own candidate. As a result, Innocent first excommunicated John and then ordered him deposed (1212), thereby encouraging John's feudal lords to revolt. These events forced John to *(a)* accept Langton as archbishop and *(b)* acknowledge the pope as his superior lord. Innocent III, who so humbled John, is considered the most powerful medieval pope.

## MULTIPLE–CHOICE QUESTIONS

1. The events described in the New Testament took place in the    (1) Golden Age of Greece    (2) Pyramid Age of Egypt    (3) early Roman Empire    (4) Middle Ages.
2. The word *Christ*, derived from the Greek language, means    (1) Son    (2) Savior    (3) Leader    (4) Prince.
3. Which contributed to the early spread of Christianity?    (1) its adoption by the Roman upper classes    (2) its offer of hope in a world of fear and uncertainty    (3) its spread by Roman conquests    (4) its acceptance of polytheism.
4. The first Bishop of Rome, from whose office evolved the papacy, was    (1) St. Paul    (2) St. Peter    (3) St. Patrick    (4) St. Augustine.
5. Rome persecuted the Christians mainly because they    (1) refused to pay taxes    (2) would not worship the emperor    (3) converted the pagans    (4) persecuted the pagans.
6. Roman persecution of Christianity was ended by    (1) Emperor Nero    (2) the Edict of Milan    (3) the Patriarch at Constantinople    (4) the Holy Inquisition.
7. Roman Catholic missionaries were *least* active in    (1) France    (2) England    (3) Spain    (4) Russia.
8. The Templars, as monks and knights,    (1) took part in the Crusades    (2) copied ancient manuscripts    (3) lived on alms    (4) practiced good farming methods.
9. The monastic order that introduced the vows of poverty, chastity, and obedience was the    (1) Franciscans    (2) Benedictines    (3) Hospitalers    (4) Dominicans.
10. The pope is elevated to office following election by    (1) all Catholic believers    (2) the College of Cardinals    (3) the people of Rome    (4) the residents of the Vatican.
11. The pope's power to deny a person Church sacraments is called    (1) benefit of clergy    (2) hierarchy    (3) excommunication    (4) investiture.
12. The courts of the Inquisition were established to    (1) combat heresy    (2) stamp out corruption    (3) convert Germanic barbarians    (4) punish traitors to the king.
13. The Roman Catholic Church considers heretics to be those Christians who    (1) lead lives of luxury    (2) refuse to pay taxes    (3) disagree with Church doctrine    (4) live in solitude.

14. The Church attempted to limit feudal warfare by means of (1) chivalry (2) the Concordat (3) the Inquisition (4) the Truce of God.
15. During the Middle Ages the Church prohibited the lending of money for interest—a practice then called (1) homage (2) usury (3) donation (4) tithe.
16. The tithe was (1) an asylum for the poor (2) the class of parish priests (3) a tax levied by the Church (4) a monastic order.
17. During the Middle Ages civil rulers and popes most often disagreed over the (1) use of the Latin language (2) establishment of monastic orders (3) appointment of Church officials (4) control of education.
18. Emperor Henry IV of Germany went to the pope at Canossa to (1) enjoy a vacation (2) beg forgiveness (3) secure military aid (4) urge a crusade.
19. A compromise in the investiture struggle was reached by (1) St. Dominic (2) Pope Gregory VII (3) the Benedictine Rule (4) the Concordat of Worms.
20. The best description of the role of the Christian Church in western Europe during the Middle Ages is that the Church (1) acted as a bridge between Roman and Greek cultures (2) maintained a degree of unity in a society that bordered on anarchy (3) played a minor role in economic and political life (4) preserved the culture of the barbarian peoples at the expense of classical civilization.

## ESSAY QUESTIONS

1. (a) Describe *two* factors that enabled Christianity to spread within the Roman Empire. (b) Explain *two* other factors that enabled Christianity to spread elsewhere in western Europe.
2. Show how the medieval Church exerted an important influence in each of the following fields: (a) culture (b) agriculture (c) peace (d) education (e) west European unity.
3. Discuss the work of the religious orders of the Middle Ages, giving *one* specific detail for each of the following kinds of services: (a) economic (b) social (c) missionary (d) cultural.
4. During the Middle Ages the Church provided more than religious services. (a) Describe *two* religious services provided by the medieval Church. (b) Discuss *three* services performed by the medieval Church that are today generally carried on by the government.

# Part 3. The Byzantine and Moslem Empires: Advanced Civilizations

While medieval Europe consisted mainly of small kingdoms and feudal domains, the Middle East contained two large realms: the Byzantine Empire and the Moslem Empire. They brought stable rule to their people and made important contributions to Western culture.

## A. *The Byzantine Empire*

### BRIEF HISTORY OF THE BYZANTINE EMPIRE

**1. Origin.** By the 4th century A.D., the Roman Empire was divided into two parts: the West governed from Rome and the East governed from Constantinople. Although the western Roman Empire fell to the Germanic invaders by 476 (see pages 61–62), the eastern part survived independently until 1453, an additional thousand years. It became known as the *Byzantine Empire*, a name derived from Byzantium, the ancient Greek colony founded on the site that became Constantinople. The Byzantine Empire displayed predominantly Middle Eastern and Greek cultural characteristics.

**2. Greatest Extent.** Under the Emperor *Justinian* (ruled 527–565), the Byzantine Empire expanded westward and reached its greatest extent. Justinian,

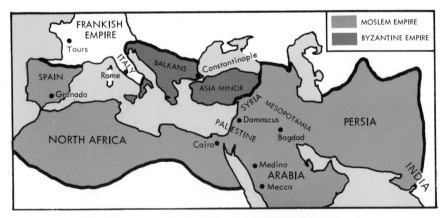

**The Moslem and Byzantine Empires (8th Century)**

ambitious to restore the former Roman Empire, conquered northern Africa, southern Spain, and Italy.

**3. Decline and Fall.** From Justinian's reign to the 15th century, a 900-year period, the Empire battled continuously against various invaders. Despite occasional successes, the Empire gradually yielded the following territories: Italy to the Lombards; southern Spain to the Visigoths; Egypt, the rest of northern Africa, Syria, and Palestine to the Arabs; the Balkan provinces to the Bulgars, Serbs, and other Slavic-speaking peoples; and Asia Minor and some Balkan provinces to the Turks.

The Byzantine Empire ended in 1453 when Constantinople fell to the Ottoman Turks.

## ASPECTS OF BYZANTINE LIFE

**1. Autocratic Government.** The emperor, regarded as God's earthly representative, lived in splendor and maintained a lavish court. He exercised absolute power over all Empire affairs. For defense against invaders, he kept the imperial army and navy at instant readiness. He regulated the economy, derived a large income from taxes, and dominated the Byzantine, or Greek Orthodox, Church.

**2. Eastern Christianity.** The *Patriarch of Constantinople,* usually selected by and subservient to the emperor, headed the Greek Orthodox Church. The Church attended to the religious needs of the Byzantine people and also sent missionaries into eastern Europe, converting the Russians and many Balkan peoples to eastern Christianity. In 1054, after centuries of dispute, the Greek Orthodox and Roman Catholic churches formally separated (see pages 79–80).

**3. Prosperous Trade and Industry.** The Byzantine Empire grew rich through trade and industry. Merchants imported Far Eastern luxuries: raw silk, spices, and precious stones. Skilled workers produced other luxuries: silk cloth, tapestry, gold and silver jewelry, perfumes, and fine glass. Constantinople, the great trade center of the Empire, exported these luxuries to Italian cities and Russia, and imported furs and agricultural products.

Agriculture, within the Empire, was limited by insufficient farmland.

**4. Constantinople, a Magnificent City.** Constantinople contained *(a)* paved streets that were lighted at night; *(b)* beautiful homes, churches, and palaces; *(c)* recreational facilities: parks, playgrounds, and the *Hippodrome,* a famous chariot-racing arena; and *(d)* museums, libraries, and schools. Large, populous, wealthy—Constantinople surpassed any city in medieval western Europe.

## BYZANTINE CONTRIBUTIONS TO CIVILIZATION

**1. Codified Roman Law.** Under Emperor Justinian, Byzantine legal experts collected and arranged Roman law (see page 62).

**2. Preserved Ancient Greek Civilization.** Byzantine culture represented a continuation of classical knowledge, especially its Greek and Hellenistic aspects. The Byzantines spoke Greek. At the University of Constantinople, scholars cherished ancient manuscripts and studied classical literature, philosophy, and science. Thanks to Byzantine scholars, writings of the ancient Greeks were preserved for future generations.

Byzantine culture spread outside the Empire. It fascinated peoples in Russia and in the Balkans, forming the foundation of their civilizations. In western Europe Byzantine classical knowledge helped stimulate the revival of learning during the Later Middle Ages and the Renaissance.

**3. Fostered Architecture and Art.** In construction and decoration the Byzantines made many original contributions. Their architects combined features of Greco-Roman and Persian architecture by devising a new structure—a rectangular building topped by a round dome. Their artists adorned building interiors with brilliant *mosaics*—decorations consisting of small pieces of colored glass, stone, or tile fitted together to form pictures or designs. Great skill and artistry went into the portrayal of biblical stories and historical episodes. *Santa Sophia,* the famous church erected in the 6th century at Constantinople by Emperor Justinian, is a noteworthy example of Byzantine architecture and art. Its plain but massive exterior contrasts with its sparkling and magnificent interior. Byzantine artisans also produced gold, silver, and glass objects that rank as works of art.

*The Turkish Government Tourist and Information Office*

Santa Sophia, once a Byzantine church, is now a mosque.

**4. Shielded Western Europe.** Because of its location, the Byzantine Empire received the first blows of invaders coming from the east, especially the Arabs and Turks. By resisting these invaders, Byzantine forces indirectly were defending western Europe.

# B. The Moslem Empire

## MOHAMMED AND THE IDEALS OF ISLAM

*Mohammed* (570–632) was born in the city of *Mecca*, in Arabia. He became a religious reformer who condemned his people's worship of idols (idolatry) and urged a new, more ethical religion. Because his attacks on idolatry aroused hostility in Mecca, he fled for his life to *Medina*, where the people accepted his religion, *Islam*. Mohammed's flight, or *Hegira*, in 622 marks the first year of the *Moslem* (Islamic) calendar.

Islam embodies the following principles:

1. There is no God but *Allah*, and Mohammed is the Great Prophet. All persons must submit to, praise, and glorify God.
2. Individuals must observe the following religious duties: *(a)* praying daily, *(b)* fasting during the daylight hours of the Moslem month of Ramadan, and *(c)* if possible, making at least one pilgrimage (religious journey) to the Holy City of Mecca.
3. Individuals must follow a code of moral behavior that includes *(a)* giving alms to the poor, *(b)* shunning gambling and alcoholic beverages, *(c)* revering one's parents, and *(d)* treating all Moslems as being within one family.
4. The faithful will be rewarded by luxurious eternal life. Moslems who die fighting for the faith are assured entrance to paradise.

Mohammed's teachings became the basis of the Moslem Bible, the *Koran*. (Some Islamic precepts—monotheism, a high moral code, and life after death —were drawn from Judaism and Christianity.)

## THE ARABS SPREAD ISLAM (7TH AND 8TH CENTURIES)

The Arab tribes rapidly adopted the new Moslem religion, became unified, and prepared for conquest. The promise of paradise made the Arabs courageous warriors. In the 7th and 8th centuries, they carved out a great empire. (See map, page 86.)

**1. Northward.** They annexed Palestine and Syria but were unable to destroy the Byzantine Empire and seize Constantinople.

**2. Eastward.** They subjugated Mesopotamia, Persia, and part of northwestern India.

**3. Westward.** They overwhelmed Egypt, the rest of northern Africa, and most of Spain. The Arabs also invaded France but were defeated by the Franks led by Charles Martel at the Battle of Tours (732). This clash halted Moslem expansion into western Europe.

As the Arabs acquired their empire, they introduced the Moslem religion to their conquered peoples. Although the Arabs generally did not forcibly convert these peoples, many accepted Islam because they *(a)* wanted to avoid special taxes on nonbelievers and *(b)* approved of Islam's ethical code and promise of eternal life. Those conquered peoples who did not adopt Islam were usually allowed to pursue their own religion.

## THE MOSLEM EMPIRE

**1. Extent (in the 8th Century).** The Moslem Empire, the largest and most populous empire of its time, extended from India to Spain. (See map, page 86.) Unified by Islam and the Arabs' military might, it was ruled by a *caliph,* who served as both the religious and political leader. The Empire had its capital first at *Damascus* and later at *Bagdad.* In cleanliness and beauty these large, magnificent cities far surpassed those of western Europe.

**2. Breakup of the Empire (by the 10th Century).** Over a period of 200 years, the Moslem Empire gradually disintegrated as rival chieftains gained absolute control of their own domains. By the 10th century the Empire had been divided into a number of independent Moslem kingdoms.

**3. Moslem Loss of Spain (by the 15th Century).** Over a period of 400 years, the Moslem kingdoms in Spain were attacked and slowly conquered by the Christian states in Spain. In 1492 *Granada,* the last Moslem stronghold in Spain, fell to the Christians (see page 149).

## THE TURKS CREATE A MOSLEM EMPIRE

By the 10th century many Turkish tribes of central Asia had adopted Islam. In the 11th century, the *Seljuk Turks* seized Bagdad and for two centuries dominated the Moslem Middle East. As Seljuk Turkish power waned, the *Ottoman Turks* achieved Moslem leadership. In the 14th century they conquered part of the Balkans. In the 15th century, led by *Mohammed II,* they captured Constantinople (1453), ending the Byzantine Empire. (In the 16th and 17th centuries, the Turks advanced deep into central Europe, twice failing to take Vienna, the capital of Austria. At the naval battle of *Lepanto* in 1571, the Turks were crushed by allied Christian fleets. After the 17th century Turkish power declined, and eventually the Turks were driven almost entirely out of Europe. See pages 261–262).

## MOSLEM CONTRIBUTIONS TO CIVILIZATION

While western Europe declined during the Early Middle Ages, the Moslem world developed a flourishing civilization.

1. **Education.** The Moslems founded great universities, especially at Cairo in Egypt, Bagdad in Mesopotamia, and Cordova in Spain. These universities preserved and taught Greco-Roman culture. Classical learning provided a foundation for further advances by Moslem scholars, who were permitted to study and write with considerable freedom.

2. **Mathematics.** The Moslems *(a)* introduced *Arabic numerals* (which they adopted from India) to replace the clumsy Roman numbering system and *(b)* furthered the studies of algebra, geometry, and trigonometry.

3. **Physical Science.** The Moslems *(a)* prepared chemical compounds such as sulfuric acid and alcohol, *(b)* improved metal refining and cloth dyeing, and *(c)* gained new knowledge about the relationship between light and vision.

4. **Medicine.** The Moslems *(a)* used anesthetics (drugs that ease pain), *(b)* performed difficult surgery, particularly progressing in eye operations, and *(c)* compiled medical textbooks.

5. **Agriculture.** The Moslems improved farming methods by rotating crops and using fertilizer.

6. **Industry.** The Moslems produced Cordovan leather, Damascus steel (especially swords), damask cloth, crystal glass, smooth paper, and exquisite rugs.

7. **Navigation.** The Moslems used the *mariner's compass* (probably adopted from China) to determine direction at sea. They believed the world to be round.

8. **Literature.** The Moslems esteemed books and maintained extensive libraries. Their famous literary works include the collection of adventure stories *The Thousand and One Nights (The Arabian Nights)* and the long poem about life *The Rubaiyat of Omar Khayyam.*

9. **Language.** The Moslems spread the Arabic language, which helped to culturally unify the Moslem world. Arabic is the source of some English words: alcohol, algebra, almanac, cipher, coffee, cotton, syrup, and sofa.

10. **Architecture.** The Moslems designed graceful *mosques* (temples) and palaces typified by rounded domes, tall slender minarets, and delicately carved, lacelike decorative patterns, called *arabesques.* An outstanding example of Moslem architecture, near Granada, Spain, is the *Alhambra* palace. (See illustration, page 92.)

11. **Outstanding Scholars**

   *a. Avicenna* (980–1037), Arabian philosopher and physician, utilized ancient Greek sources for his encyclopedic medical textbook, *Canon of Medicine.*

The "Court of the Lions" in the Alhambra palace.

*b. Averroës* (1126–1198), Spanish-Arabian physician and philosopher, wrote highly regarded commentaries upon the works of Aristotle.

*c. Maimonides* (1135–1204), Jewish philosopher of the Moslem world and court physician to the ruler of Egypt, attempted to reconcile Judaism's faith with Aristotle's reason in his work, *Guide for the Perplexed.*

## MULTIPLE–CHOICE QUESTIONS

1. The word *Byzantine* was derived from the name of (1) an ancient Greek colony (2) a Roman emperor (3) an eastern patriarch (4) a Persian god.

2. Which was true of the Byzantine Empire? (1) It was established during the Augustan Age. (2) It was conquered by Charlemagne. (3) It lasted a thousand years after the "fall" of Rome. (4) It ended with the rise of Islam.

3. The culture of the Byzantine Empire was based chiefly upon the civilization of (1) India (2) Russia (3) Greece (4) China.

4. The wealth of the Byzantine Empire resulted from (1) agriculture (2) rich gold mines (3) trade and industry in luxury products (4) plunder seized in wars.

5. The Byzantine Empire furthered civilization by (1) utilizing ancient Greek democratic practices (2) transmitting Indian mathematical knowledge to Europe (3) shielding western Europe from Arab and Turkish invaders (4) originating the column.

6. The birthplace of Christianity, Judaism, and Islam was in (1) Africa (2) the Middle East (3) Europe (4) North America.

7. In its original teachings, Islam differed from Judaism and Christianity in that Islam (1) lacked a high moral code (2) was not monotheistic (3) appealed strongly to the warrior class (4) did not believe in life after death.

8. Islam—in common with Judaism and Christianity—teaches (1) the importance of Mohammed (2) total abstinence from intoxicating beverages (3) charity for the poor (4) the existence of a warrior's paradise.

9. Which city was the last Moslem stronghold in Spain? (1) Madrid (2) Granada (3) Toledo (4) Barcelona.

10. A country in which Moslem civilization did *not* develop was (1) Syria (2) Persia (3) Egypt (4) Denmark.

11. An Asian people who conquered the Arabs, accepted Islam, and swept into southeastern Europe was the (1) Turks (2) Russians (3) Magyars (4) Bulgarians.

12. Which of these was *not* a contribution of Islamic culture? (1) *The Thousand and One Nights* (2) pyramids (3) medical textbooks (4) architecture featuring minarets.

13. A significant contribution of Islamic culture to western Europe was (1) the introduction of important land reforms into feudal Europe (2) the establishment of the principle of separation of Church and State (3) advancements in mathematics and geography (4) placing of women in a superior position in society.

14. That contact existed between the medieval Moslems and Chinese may be deduced from the fact that the Moslems (1) made Cordovan leather (2) used anesthetics in surgery (3) used the mariner's compass (4) maintained centers of learning.

15. Avicenna, Averroës, and Maimonides—the three outstanding philosophers of the Moslem world—were also (1) military leaders (2) engineers (3) physicians (4) explorers.

## FACT–OPINION QUESTIONS

Some of the statements below are matters of fact and others are expressions of opinion. Write the word *yes* if the statement is based on fact and is true; the word *no* if the statement is contrary to fact and therefore not true; or the letter *O* if the statement is a matter of opinion which may be either true or untrue.

1. Roman law was codified under Byzantine Emperor Justinian.

2. The Byzantine Empire survived long after the fall of Rome because the emperor exercised absolute powers.

3. The head of the Greek Orthodox Church was the Patriarch of Athens.

4. The Greek Orthodox Church sent missionaries into Russia.

5. Even in medieval times, Constantinople contained paved streets that were lighted at night.

6. The famed Byzantine church in Constantinople was the Koran.

7. A famous Moslem literary work is *The Rubaiyat of Omar Khayyam*.

8. Moslem architecture is less beautiful than ancient Greek architecture.

## ESSAY QUESTIONS

1. Describe *three* contributions of the Byzantine Empire to western European civilization.
2. (*a*) Explain *one* way in which the Byzantine *or* Moslem world helped to link medieval Europe with the classical culture of ancient Greece and Rome. (*b*) Explain *one* way in which the Byzantine *or* Moslem world helped to link medieval Europe with the culture of the Far East.
3. Discuss *two* reasons for agreeing or disagreeing with each of the following statements: (*a*) The Moslems helped to advance civilization in Europe. (*b*) Byzantine culture had many similarities with that of the Roman Empire. (*c*) Islam borrowed much from the earlier religions of Judaism and Christianity. (*d*) Justinian deserved to be ranked as a great medieval ruler.
4. Millions of people are believers in Islam. Explain the growth and influence of Islam by discussing (*a*) its origin (*b*) *two* of its important religious concepts (*c*) *two* reasons for its rapid spread in the first century of its existence.
5. During the Early Middle Ages, Moslem civilization was more advanced than European civilization. Discuss (*a*) *three* contributions in learning and in science for which the Moslems are famous (*b*) *two* additional contributions of medieval Moslem civilization to our present-day world.

# Part 4. The Later Middle Ages in Europe

## THE CRUSADES (1095–1291)

**1. Background.** Late in the 11th century, the Byzantine emperor at Constantinople appealed to the Roman Catholic Church for military aid against the Moslem Turks. The Catholic Church sympathized, partly because the Turks threatened Greek Orthodox Christianity, but mainly because the Moslems controlled Palestine, the Holy Land, and molested Christian pilgrims. Consequently *Pope Urban II*, at the Council of Clermont in 1095, summoned western Christiandom to wrest the Holy Land from the Moslems by waging a religious war, or *Crusade*.

The pope's plea aroused enthusiasm among (*a*) religious persons who believed that "God wills it," (*b*) Christians who desired papal forgiveness of their sins, (*c*) nobles who expected to acquire new lands and great riches, (*d*) middle-class merchants who wanted increased trade, (*e*) serfs who sought escape from feudal oppression, and (*f*) adventurers who welcomed travel and excitement.

**2. Leading Events.** Of seven major Crusades over a period of almost 200 years, the most significant were the First and Third crusades.

The *First Crusade,* started in 1096, was a well-organized military expedition.

Its outstanding leader was *Godfrey of Bouillon.* This Crusade drove the Moslems from part of Palestine, established a Christian kingdom in the Holy Land, and gained control of Jerusalem.

Nearly 100 years later, in 1187, Jerusalem was retaken by the Moslems, led by *Saladin.* The loss of the Holy City caused western Europe to undertake the Third Crusade.

The *Third Crusade,* started in 1189, was led by three kings: *Frederick Barbarossa* of Germany, *Philip Augustus* of France, and *Richard the Lion-Hearted* of England. Although this Crusade failed to recapture Jerusalem, Richard persuaded Saladin to grant safe passage to Christian pilgrims.

Subsequent Crusades likewise failed to establish Christian rule in Palestine. By 1291 the Moslem Turks again completely controlled the Holy Land. They retained it until after World War I (1918).

**3. Effects.** Because the Crusades wrought great changes in western European life, they mark the beginning of the end of the Middle Ages.

*a. Broadened the Peoples' Outlook.* The Crusaders were exposed to the advanced Moslem and Byzantine civilizations. They observed powerful governments, great cities, flourishing trade, prosperous industry, and progress in the arts and sciences. The Crusaders also gained increased geographical knowledge. Upon returning home, they introduced new ideas and tastes.

*b. Stimulated Trade and Towns.* The Crusades increased European demand for Eastern products: spices, sugar, silk, rugs, paper, glassware, and precious stones. Throughout western Europe, but especially in Italy, (1) trade increased, (2) money replaced barter, (3) towns grew in number and size, and (4) the bourgeoisie (middle class) acquired wealth and influence. (The Italian cities also grew richer by furnishing supplies to the Crusaders.)

*c. Strengthened the Kings or Central Governments.* The Crusades increased the kings' powers by: (1) *Weakening the nobility.* Some nobles sold their lands to raise money for the Crusades, thereby losing their base of feudal power. Many nobles were killed in the Crusades, thus removing threats to royal power. (2) *Stimulating trade.* Since trade requires a central authority to provide law and order, the rising merchant class opposed the feudal lords and supported the kings.

*d. Weakened Serfdom.* The Crusades enabled many serfs to escape from feudalism. (1) Some serfs gained freedom by joining the Crusades. (2) Other serfs paid for the use of the lord's land in money rather than in products and services. The lords preferred money to buy equipment for the Crusades or to purchase Eastern luxuries; the serfs earned money by selling surplus crops in nearby cities. Slowly the feudal relationship between serf and lord evolved into the modern relationship of tenant and landlord. (3) Still other serfs fled to the growing cities. After a year and a day undetected in a city, a serf became legally free.

*e. Encouraged Learning.* The Crusades stimulated European interest in education by showing that the Byzantines and Moslems had (1) preserved and utilized Greco-Roman knowledge, (2) maintained great universities, and (3) advanced in mathematics, science, literature, and art.

## THE REVIVAL OF TRADE AND TOWNS

Starting in the 10th century, trade gradually revived as the ending of barbarian invasions permitted more settled conditions and safer transportation for persons and goods. Later the Crusades heightened European demand for Eastern luxury products. Increased trade stimulated the growth of favorably located towns.

Towns had not entirely disappeared even during the Early Middle Ages. Now, providing facilities for storage, marketing, transportation, and production of goods, towns were essential to commerce. Medieval towns, first controlled by nearby feudal lords, later secured their freedom (1) by purchasing charters from a lord or monarch or, more rarely, (2) by successful armed uprisings for independence.

## THE RISE OF THE BOURGEOISIE

As trade increased and towns grew, a new economic and social class evolved, the *bourgeoisie*, or townspeople. It consisted of enterprising persons: merchants, shopkeepers, bankers, and professional people. Since it stood between the lowest (serfs) and highest (lords) feudal classes, the bourgeoisie came to be known as the *middle class.*

## LEADING MEDIEVAL TRADE CENTERS

1. **In Italy.** *Venice, Genoa, Pisa,* and *Naples*—cities on the Italian seacoast— soon dominated trade between Europe and the eastern Mediterranean. These cities had the advantages of *(a)* a Mediterranean location and *(b)* a commercial tradition dating back to the Roman Empire. Italian ships carried European wheat, wine, lumber, and wool to such eastern Mediterranean cities as *Alexandria* and *Constantinople.* They returned with valuable Eastern luxuries.

2. **In Belgium.** *Bruges* and *Ghent*—cities in the Belgian province of Flanders— became the leading north European commercial centers. These Flemish (a word derived from Flanders) cities were advantageously situated at the crossroads of the trade routes from northern Europe and Italy. The main trade routes from Italy went *(a)* across the Mediterranean, through the Strait of Gibraltar, and along the the Atlantic coast and *(b)* across the Alps and down the Rhine River. (See map, page 97.)

The Flemish cities imported Eastern products from the Italian cities for sale throughout northern Europe. They also produced and exported their own woolen cloth.

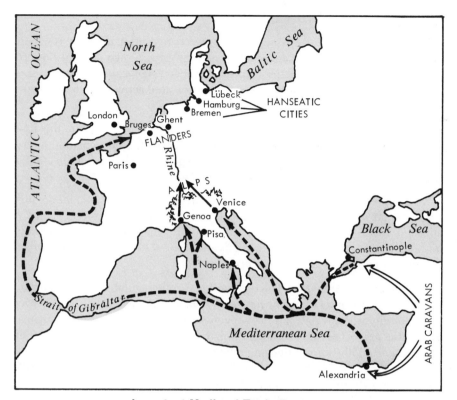

**Important Medieval Trade Routes**

**3. In Northern Germany.** *Bremen, Hamburg, Lübeck,* and other north German cities controlled trade in the Baltic and North seas. In the 13th century these cities organized the *Hanseatic League.* In the 14th century, at the height of its power, the League included the German cities plus other north European cities. To promote the commercial interests of its members, the League *(a)* drove pirates from the northern seas, *(b)* banned non-League cities from trading in the area, and *(c)* maintained regulations for fair trade. The Hanse cities dealt chiefly in timber, grain, iron, leather, and salted fish.

## TRADE FAIRS IN MEDIEVAL TOWNS

To foster trade, the Flemish cities, and later other northern European cities, sponsored fairs. These exhibitions, common by 1200, attracted (1) buyers and sellers of goods, (2) merchants from distant places who exchanged information and introduced new ideas, (3) entertainers who provided fun and frolic, and (4) ordinary people who welcomed the relief from monotony.

## THE GUILDS IN MEDIEVAL TOWNS

**1. Merchant Guilds.** These associations of merchants within the town regulated *trade.* They *(a)* taxed nonmember merchants to discourage competition, *(b)* encouraged fair business practices, such as honest weights and measures, exact quality standards, and uniform prices, *(c)* participated actively in town government, and *(d)* functioned as social clubs.

**2. Craft Guilds.** These associations of skilled craftspeople within the town regulated *industry.* A separate guild existed for each craft, or occupation, such as bakers, candlemakers, weavers, tailors, and carpenters. The craft guilds undertook economic, educational, political, and social activities.

*a. Economic Activities.* The craft guilds answered the basic economic questions of what was to be produced and how it should be produced. They established wages and hours, quality of materials, standards of workmanship, production quotas, and prices. The guilds endeavored to give both producer and consumer a fair price called a *just price.*

*b. Educational Activities.* The craft guilds strictly regulated the training and advancement of workers. (1) The *apprentice*, or beginning worker, bound himself, generally without pay and for a seven-year period, to a master craftsman. The master supported him and taught him the craft, social manners, and morals. After this period, the apprentice might be promoted to the journeyman class. (2) The *journeyman*, or intermediate worker, could be employed in any shop in return for a daily wage. If he passed a test by producing a "masterpiece," he advanced to the master class. (3) The *master craftsman* could open his own shop, where he was both worker and owner.

*c. Political and Social Activities.* The craft guilds (1) were active in town government, (2) supported hospitals and provided special benefits for widows, orphans, and the sick, and (3) arranged holiday entertainment.

In summary, the craft guilds combined features of our modern labor unions, employer associations, political parties, and mutual aid societies.

## LIFE IN MEDIEVAL TOWNS

**1. Disadvantages.** *(a)* Town streets were narrow, unpaved, unlighted, and unguarded. A citizen out alone at night faced danger. *(b)* Most town buildings were dark, dingy, constructed of wood, and close together. Fires spread rapidly from building to building. *(c)* Town walls, although providing protection against pirates, highway robbers, and feudal lords, prevented the town's physical expansion. *(d)* Town sanitation scarcely existed. Inhabitants dumped garbage into streets or nearby rivers, causing pollution. Towns suffered greatly from epidemics and plagues. The *Black Death* (1347–1350), a contagious and deadly bubonic plague, alone killed about one-third of western Europe's population.

**2. Advantages.** In the Later Middle Ages, the towns attracted able and enterprising persons, mainly from the lower class of the rural communities. Towns offered *(a)* freedom from feudal restrictions, *(b)* a fuller, richer, more varied life than at the manor, *(c)* cultural and educational facilities, and *(d)* opportunities for economic advancement.

## CULTURAL ACHIEVEMENTS OF WESTERN EUROPE DURING THE MIDDLE AGES

In the Dark Ages (Early Middle Ages), western European culture retrogressed as a result of barbarian invasions, feudalism, and people's concern for the barest essentials of life. In the Later Middle Ages, western European culture began to progress because (1) the Catholic Church provided leadership and support, (2) the Crusades spread knowledge of the advanced Byzantine and Moslem civilizations, and (3) the towns provided centers of culture and learning.

**1. Architecture.** Medieval people expressed their intensely religious spirit by constructing awe-inspiring cathedrals.

*a. Romanesque Style.* Before the 12th century, architects designed cathedrals in the massive *Romanesque* style, derived from ancient Rome. This style featured thick walls, few windows, rounded arches, and strong columns. A famous example is the Cathedral in Pisa, Italy.

*Italian Government Travel Office*

Romanesque Architecture: The Cathedral and the "Leaning Tower" in Pisa.

*b. Gothic Style.* Starting in the 12th century, architects employed the more graceful *Gothic* style. It utilized thin walls, flying buttresses, pointed arches, tall spires, gargoyles, and many stained-glass windows. Gothic architecture permitted more sunlight to enter the building. Some notable Gothic cathedrals are *Notre Dame* in Paris and *Westminster Abbey* in London.

*French Government Tourist Office*

Gothic Architecture:
The Cathedral of Notre Dame
in Paris.

**2. Higher Education.** In the 11th and 12th centuries, scholars founded many important universities: in France, the University of Paris; in Italy, the universities of Bologna and Salerno; in England, the universities of Oxford and Cambridge. Medieval universities taught geometry, astronomy, music, grammar, and logic—the basis of our modern liberal arts education. Students were prepared for careers in theology (religion), philosophy, law, and medicine. Except in religion, the universities relied chiefly on the writings of the ancient Greek scholar Aristotle.

University students faced difficulties because they (*a*) were taught, not in their own tongue, but in the Church language, *Latin*, and (*b*) lacked books, libraries, laboratories, and comfortable classrooms.

**3. Science and Invention.** Medieval scientists were, in our modern sense, quite unscientific. They rarely experimented or questioned, mainly accepting popular superstitions and the ideas of Aristotle.

*a. Alchemists,* while attempting to transform less valuable metals into gold, gathered information that served as a basis for modern chemistry.

*b. Astrologers,* while seeking to foretell the future, furnished records of the planets and stars helpful to modern astronomy.

*c. Inventors* developed magnifying lenses, mechanical clocks, glass windows, and gunpowder.

*d. Roger Bacon* (1214–1294), alone of the medieval scientists, insisted that science requires experimentation and observation. Bacon's ideas were not accepted for several centuries.

**4. Philosophy and Theology.** Church scholars wrote books on philosophical and theological issues. Their method of using pure reason in the defense of faith is called *scholasticism.*

*a. Peter Abelard* (1079–1142), a famous medieval teacher, wrote *Sic et Non (Yes and No),* which quoted differing views of Church leaders on many religious questions.

*b. St. Thomas Aquinas* (1225–1274), the greatest medieval philosopher, wrote *Summa Theologica.* In this work he summarized Christian doctrine and denied any conflict between reason and religious faith. His philosophy was influenced by the ideas of Aristotle.

**5. Literature.** Although few books were written, many kinds of literature flourished. Epic poems celebrated gallant heroes and stirring adventures. The outstanding medieval epics are *Beowulf,* an Anglo-Saxon (Old English) poem; the *Song of Roland,* a French epic; the *Niebelungenlied,* a German tale; and the *Song of Cid,* a Spanish work.

Beginning in the 11th century, wandering musical entertainers, or minstrels—called *troubadours* in southern France and *minnesingers* in Germany —composed lyrical poems, mostly about love. Later medieval poets wrote stories of love and adventure called *romances.*


## IDENTIFICATION QUESTIONS: WHO AM I?

| | | |
|---|---|---|
| Peter Abelard | Roger Bacon | Richard the Lion-Hearted |
| Thomas Aquinas | Innocent III | Saladin |
| Philip Augustus | Mohammed II | Urban II |

1. I was the Moslem leader who drove the Christian forces from the Holy City.
2. I was the medieval scientist who urged the method of experimentation.
3. As king of England, I played a leading part in the Third Crusade.
4. A philosopher, I summarized Christian doctrine in the book *Summa Theologica.*
5. I was the pope who first issued the call for the Crusades.

## MULTIPLE–CHOICE QUESTIONS

1. The appeal to the pope for military aid against the Moslem Turks in the 11th century came from the (1) sultan of Egypt (2) emperor at Constantinople (3) czar of Russia (4) caliph at Damascus.

2. The ancient city famous for religious shrines and chief goal of the Crusaders was (1) Constantinople (2) Rome (3) Jerusalem (4) Mecca.

3. An important result of the Crusades was that (1) the Turks lost interest in Constantinople (2) serfdom declined in western Europe (3) the Roman and Greek churches were united (4) Italy was united into one nation.

4. The Crusaders hastened the exploratory voyages to America by (1) taking Jerusalem from the Moslems (2) stimulating trade with Asia (3) driving the Turks out of Constantinople (4) increasing the power of the Church.

5. An effect of the Crusades upon western Europe was that the (1) kings lost power (2) Church lost power (3) kings gained power (4) feudal lords gained power.

6. The growth of trade in medieval Europe resulted in (1) invasions by German barbarians (2) the decline of banking (3) an increase in the power of the nobles (4) the rise of a middle class.

7. In *ascending* order, the three major classes in western Europe in the Later Middle Ages were the (1) serfs, nobles, bourgeoisie (2) bourgeoisie, serfs, nobles (3) nobles, bourgeoisie, serfs (4) serfs, bourgeoisie, nobles.

8. In the Later Middle Ages, merchants supported attempts of monarchs to establish strong national states because the merchants (1) had a voice in the government (2) were forced by the Church to support the king (3) had become members of the aristocracy (4) favored a strong central government to preserve law and order.

9. A leading trade center of medieval times in southern Europe was (1) Athens (2) Madrid (3) Rome (4) Venice.

10. In the Middle Ages Europe's main highway of trade was the (1) Atlantic Ocean (2) Mediterranean Sea (3) Indian Ocean (4) North Sea.

11. The Hanseatic League was established to (1) capture the Holy Land from the Turks (2) send trade expeditions to the Far East (3) halt the Moslem invasion of western Europe (4) protect trade and commerce in the North and Baltic seas.

12. Bruges and Ghent, the famous medieval trade centers, are located in (1) Italy (2) Germany (3) England (4) Belgium.

13. Medieval fairs were held chiefly in order to (1) exchange goods (2) buy and sell serfs (3) observe religious holidays (4) exhibit famous works of art.

14. One purpose of the medieval merchant guilds was to (1) drive nonmember merchants from their towns (2) provide relief for the sick in their communities (3) develop trade on a national scale (4) decorate their local cathedrals.

15. Medieval merchant guilds (1) rebelled against the king (2) refused to handle Moslem products (3) developed new industries (4) discouraged competition from nonmember merchants.

16. Medieval craft guilds (1) encouraged competition (2) wanted to restore feudalism (3) established an apprentice system to train craftspeople (4) limited their activities to the production of goods.

17. Buildings in medieval towns in western Europe were generally constructed of (1) brick (2) stone (3) wood (4) dried clay.

18. Which written language was most generally used among scholars in western Europe during the Middle Ages? (1) Italian (2) French (3) Greek (4) Latin.

19. An ancient Greek on whose science and philosophy medieval universities relied heavily was   (1) Plato   (2) Aristotle   (3) Pericles   (4) Herodotus.
20. Which feature identifies a Gothic cathedral?   (1) tall spires   (2) rounded arches   (3) graceful minarets   (4) gilded domes.

## ESSAY QUESTIONS

1. The Crusades failed in their original purpose, but they had far-reaching effects on western Europe. *(a)* State *three* motives that led people to become Crusaders. *(b)* Prove that the Crusades failed in their original purpose. *(c)* Show *three* different ways in which life in western Europe was changed as a result of the Crusades.
2. *(a)* Explain the relationship between the Crusades, the development of trade, and the rise of the middle class. *(b)* Show *one* way in which the development of trade during the Later Middle Ages influenced *each* of the following in Europe: (1) government (2) learning (3) occupations (4) standard of living.
3. Discuss *two* specific reasons for agreeing or disagreeing with each of the following statements: *(a)* Medieval craft guilds benefited the entire community. *(b)* The Hanseatic League furthered unity within Europe. *(c)* The medieval Church encouraged art and architecture. *(d)* The rise of the middle class doomed the feudal system. *(e)* Modern industry should adopt the medieval apprentice system of training workers.
4. Today science plays an important part in our affairs. *(a)* Explain why medieval scientists had less influence on medieval life than modern science has on modern life. *(b)* Describe the work in any *one* scientific area during the Middle Ages.
5. Show *two* differences or *two* similarities between *(a)* medieval craft guilds and modern labor unions *(b)* Gothic and Romanesque architecture *(c)* medieval alchemy and modern chemistry *(d)* medieval and modern universities.

# UNIT V.   THE MIDDLE AGES: IN THE FAR EAST

# Part 1.   India: From Moslem Invasions to British Rule

## INTRODUCTION

Following the destruction of the Gupta Empire in 535 (see page 28), northern India consisted of a large number of independent warring states. India's political disunity and great wealth attracted Moslem invaders.

By the 8th century the Moslem Arabs had extended their power and spread their religion to India's western neighbors, Persia and Afghanistan. For almost 1,000 years thereafter, various Moslem peoples crossed India's northwest mountain passes, invaded the northern plain, and at times expanded into the Deccan plateau. The Moslem conquests greatly influenced India's political and cultural development.

## EARLY MOSLEM INVASIONS OF INDIA (8TH TO 10TH CENTURIES)

The Moslem Arabs conquered territories in the Indus River region of northwest India. These lands were at first part of the Moslem Empire, but they later became independent Moslem states.

## EXPEDITIONS OF MAHMUD (998–1030)

*Mahmud,* a Turkish Moslem who ruled in Afghanistan, led 17 raids into India's northern plain—from the Indus to the Ganges—supposedly to spread the Islamic religion. Mahmud killed and enslaved Hindu natives, destroyed Hindu temples and artistic works, looted rich cities, and carried away much plunder. However, except for annexing the Punjab, a province of northwest India, Mahmud achieved no permanent conquests.

## MOSLEM SULTANATE AT DELHI
## (LATE 12TH TO LATE 14TH CENTURIES)

*Kutb-ud-din Aibak,* a Turk and ex-slave, leading the Moslem forces from Afghanistan, destroyed the Hindu armies and conquered India's entire northern plain. Aibak established his capital at strategically located Delhi and governed as the all-powerful Moslem ruler, or *sultan*, thus founding the Delhi Empire. Later sultans extended Moslem power southward into the Deccan.

Despising Hinduism as idolatry (idol worship), the Delhi sultans tried to convert their conquered subjects to Islam. By persecuting Hindus and by offering tax benefits and social equality to converts, the Moslems gained new adherents, especially from the lowest castes. However, Hinduism survived as the religion of the overwhelming majority in India.

In the 14th century the Delhi sultanate weakened, and portions became independent states, usually under Moslem rulers.

## INVASION OF TAMERLANE (1398–1399)

*Tamerlane*, a Mongol warrior chieftain of central Asia, was one of history's great empire builders. He ruled from Mesopotamia to Afghanistan. In 1398 he overran India's northern plain. Although Moslem, Tamerlane sacked Delhi and, it is estimated, slaughtered 100,000 persons, Moslems as well as Hindus. Inexplicably Tamerlane soon withdrew from northern India, leaving that region physically desolated and politically disunited.

## THE MOGUL EMPIRE (16TH TO 18TH CENTURIES)

Established by Mongol invaders from Afghanistan, the Mogul Empire was the last Moslem Empire in India. The outstanding Mogul emperors were Babar and his grandson Akbar.

1. **Babar** (ruled 1526–1530), a descendant of Tamerlane, conquered much of northern India, including Delhi, thereby founding the Mogul Empire.

2. **Akbar** (ruled 1556–1605), sometimes called "Akbar the Great," invigorated the Mogul Empire by a long, wise, and successful rule. (*a*) He extended the Empire's boundaries throughout the northern plain and southward into the Deccan. (*b*) To provide good government, he established a strongly centralized rule and a competent civil service. (*c*) Akbar supported religious tolerance and treated his realm's Hindu majority fairly. He removed the special tax upon non-Moslems, forbade slave raids upon the Hindus, and himself married a Hindu princess. (*d*) He encouraged learning and furthered art, architecture, and literature. He is rated as one of history's outstanding monarchs.

Under Akbar's successors the Empire continued to flourish (see map, page 106). It eventually declined, so that by the close of the 18th century, the Moguls no longer exercised power over most of India.

## MOSLEM INFLUENCES ON INDIA

1. **Government.** By conquest the Moslem leaders became the ruling aristocracy, chiefly in northern and central India. (Hindu princes retained control

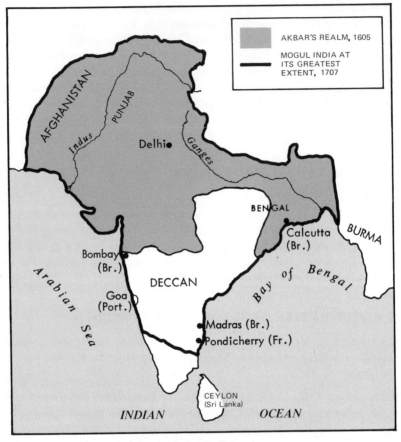

**Mogul India**

mainly in the south.) Moslem rulers exercised absolute power over their own people and over the more numerous conquered Hindus.

**2. Religion.** The Moslem invasions greatly increased religious diversity in India. Some Hindus were converted to Islam, and by the 17th century Moslems in India totaled about 20 percent of the population. They were concentrated in two unconnected territories, the western (Indus) and eastern (Ganges) extremities of India's northern plain. Scattered Moslem communities existed elsewhere in India. The Moslems remained a distinctly separate group from India's overwhelming Hindu majority.

Moslems and Hindus generally regarded each other with hostility. *(a)* Islamic and Hindu beliefs conflicted with each other. For example, the Islamic belief in the close relationship and equality of all Moslems contradicted the caste system; the Moslem paradise in heaven contradicted the Hindu cycle of reincarnations; and the Moslem prohibition against the representation of humans clashed with the Hindu use of religious statues. (b) Most Moslem rulers tolerated Hinduism but considered Hindus to be infidels (nonbelievers in the prevailing religion). Some Moslem rulers inflicted oppressive taxes and forced labor upon the Hindus. The two peoples therefore remained antagonistic.

In 1947, when India became independent, Moslem-Hindu hostility resulted in the partition of the land into two states: Pakistan, chiefly Moslem, and India, chiefly Hindu.

**3. Language.** Arabic and Persian were introduced to India by the Moslem invaders. Persian served as the official language of the Mogul Empire. In time, elements of these two tongues and the native Hindi combined to form a hybrid language, *Urdu*. Today Urdu is a national language of Pakistan.

**4. Architecture.** The Moslems constructed mosques, palaces, gateways, and tombs. In contrast with Hindu ornateness, Moslem structures had greater simplicity and showed the extensive use of the Moslem arch and dome.

The *Taj Mahal*, a marble edifice built in the 17th century by a Mogul emperor as his wife's tomb, is an outstanding example of Moslem architecture. It conveys a sense of beauty, dignity, and grandeur.

*Government of India Tourist Office*

Moslem Architecture: The Taj Mahal near Agra, India.

## COMING OF THE EUROPEANS (LATE 15TH TO 18TH CENTURIES)

In 1498, a few years before the Moguls invaded northern India, a Portuguese merchant ship under *Vasco da Gama* reached southwest India. This contact between western Europe and India was part of Europe's overseas expansion, called the *Commercial Revolution* (see pages 157–164). For many years the Portuguese enjoyed a near-monopoly of the profitable India trade.

In the 17th century England and France—the leading European powers— each chartered East India companies and founded trading posts in India. The two nations quickly became rivals for India's trade and territory. Both trained native armies to add to their own forces and acquired allies among the native princes. By 1763, after a series of wars (see pages 160–162), the British ended French power in India. Thereafter, the British, encountering no effective opposition from the decrepit Mogul Empire or the disunited princes, rapidly expanded their rule throughout the country.

The British conquest was unique, for, unlike previous conquerors of India, the British (1) came by sea, not by land, and (2) ultimately established their control over the entire country, not over only part. From the late 18th century onward, the history of India merges with the history of British imperialism (see pages 407–412).

# Part 2. China:
# Continued Rule by Dynasties

## T'ANG DYNASTY (618–906)

**1. Strong Government and Revival of Confucianism.** T'ang rulers ended the four centuries of disunity and disorder that had followed the downfall of the Han Dynasty (see page 33). The T'ang Dynasty provided a strongly centralized state based on the principles of Confucianism. To recruit government officials, T'ang rulers stressed civil service examinations and provided schools to train scholars. Examinations and schools created a demand for books. Not surprisingly, the T'ang Period witnessed the invention of block printing, the printing of books from carved wooden blocks.

**2. Extent of the Empire.** T'ang warriors expanded the Chinese Empire to its then greatest territorial extent: almost all of China proper; parts of Indo-China, Manchuria, Mongolia, and Tibet; and a vast region in central Asia. The Chinese came in contact with most Asian peoples and even with eastern Europeans. The Chinese developed a flourishing international commerce. They also transmitted their culture, most notably to the Japanese.

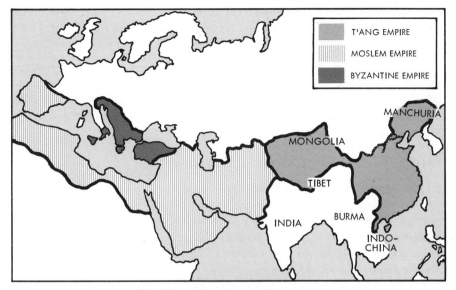

**The T'ang Empire (8th Century)**

**3. Great Cultural Era.** The T'ang emperors encouraged a revival of scholarship and the arts. T'ang writers produced a great literary outpouring, especially of poetry. T'ang artists excelled in portrait and landscape paintings. They often decorated pottery, examples of which are highly prized in Western museums.

In governmental stability, territorial extent, economic prosperity, and cultural progress, the T'ang Era rivaled the Han. Many Chinese consider the T'ang Era their country's most brilliant period.

## SUNG DYNASTY (960–1279)

**1. A Maritime Nation.** Out of the half century of political turmoil that followed the downfall of the T'ang emerged the Sung Dynasty. Sung rulers, surrounded by powerful warlike neighbors, never controlled all of China proper and, in their later period, retreated southward below the Yangtze River.

Since land trade routes were in hostile hands, Sung China became a maritime nation. Its merchant ships sailed southward in the Pacific as far as Java and westward in the Indian Ocean and the Arabian Sea as far as Africa. By the 11th century Chinese sailors were navigating by means of a mariner's compass.

**2. Social and Economic Reforms.** In the 11th century, under Chief Minister *Wang An-shih*, the Sung state imposed a program of reform that (*a*) centralized the control of finances, commerce, and transportation; (*b*) spread the tax burden more equitably among all classes; (*c*) employed hired hands, instead of conscript (forced) labor, on state projects; (*d*) provided government loans at low interest rates to needy farmers; and *(e)* stored food surpluses for distribution during periods of shortage. The reform program encountered upper class opposition and generated great fear of too much government. It was soon abandoned.

**3. Continuation of Chinese Culture.** In many respects the Sung Period continued along T'ang lines. *(a)* Sung rulers centralized government, promoted education, and retained the Confucian civil service examinations but added many practical questions. *(b)* Sung artists and writers maintained high standards in painting and literature.

## CHINA: PART OF THE MONGOL EMPIRE

**1. The Mongol Empire.** *Genghis Khan* (meaning "Universal Ruler"), a cruel and destructive military genius, founded the Mongol Empire. By the early 13th century, he had united his people, the nomadic tribes of Mongolia, into a powerful military force. Then, within a 25-year period, Genghis Khan conquered vast areas: Korea and northern China, central Asia, Persia and the Middle East, and part of European Russia. The great Khan's immediate successors extended Mongol power into central Europe: Hungary, Poland, and Austria. His grandson, *Kublai Khan,* subjugated Sung China. The unified Mongol Empire, the largest known up to that time, was short-lived. By the late 13th century, it had disintegrated into a number of independent states.

**2. The Mongol Dynasty in China (1279–1368)**

  *a. The Wars of Kublai Khan.* Kublai Khan conquered the southern Sung state and reunited the Chinese Empire. However, his efforts to annex Indo-China, Burma, Java, and Japan failed. He sent two naval expeditions against Japan, but they were unsuccessful.

  *b. A Period of Cultural Interchange.* As part of the Mongol Empire, China

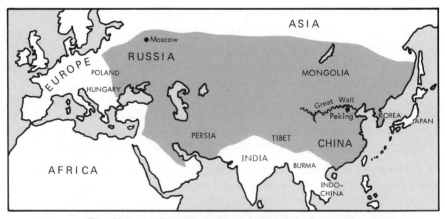

**The Mongol Empire at Its Height (13th Century)**

entered upon a great cultural interchange with the rest of Asia and with Europe. At this time Europeans probably learned of China's gunpowder and printing. The Chinese imported the sorghum (cereal) plant, probably from India, adopted the Arab method of sugar refining, and used Persian techniques in ceramic arts. China's wealth and culture attracted many foreign travelers, including Persians, Arabs, and some Europeans. From western Europe came Catholic missionaries and Italian merchants, most notably *Marco Polo.* His book describing his visit to prosperous Cathay (China) aroused great European interest in the Far East.

*c. Mongol Rule and Decline.* Kublai Khan and his successors improved roads and canals, provided care for the orphaned and sick, and generally allowed religious tolerance. Although the Mongol emperors tried to rule in the Chinese tradition, the Chinese always regarded the Mongols as aliens. In the early 14th century, Mongol power in China declined rapidly. In 1368, after a series of rebellions, the Mongols were forced to withdraw from China.

## MING DYNASTY (1368–1644)

1. **Prosperity and Maritime Activity.** The Ming Era experienced a high level of economic prosperity. Chinese architects erected city walls, temples, and palaces to beautify the southern capital, *Nanking,* and the northern capital, *Peking.* Chinese naval designers constructed great armadas, or fleets of ships. Between 1405 and 1431 seven expeditions carried Chinese people, goods, and culture to the lands of the Pacific and Indian oceans.

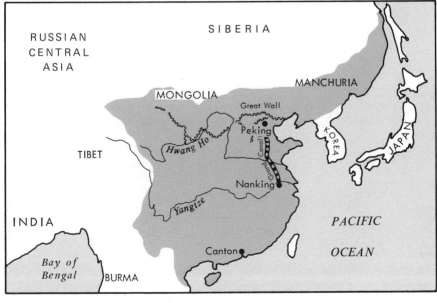

**Ming China**

**2. A Holding Period: Militarily and Culturally.** The Ming did not attain the grandeur or brilliance of the Han or T'ang periods. Ming domains were smaller, and Ming warriors generally were on the defensive against Mongol land attacks and Japanese sea raids. Ming rulers retained the previous governmental organization, law codes, and civil service examinations. They made little effort to adjust to new conditions. Ming painters and writers imitated past works and preserved past thoughts but produced little that was original.

**3. Renewed Contacts with Europe.** Contacts between China and Europe were renewed during the Ming Era and have continued unbroken to this day. Russian adventurers traversed the vast Siberian lands and contacted northern China. From western Europe came Roman Catholic missionaries. West European merchants, under the impetus of the Commercial Revolution (see pages 157–164), sailed halfway around the world to southern China. In 1514 the first Portuguese merchant ship arrived; Spanish, Dutch, and English ships followed. The west Europeans, confined to trade in the Canton area, introduced to China important New World plants: Indian corn, sweet potatoes, peanuts, and tobacco. Nevertheless, the total European impact upon Ming China remained small.

## CHINESE ACHIEVEMENTS DURING THE MIDDLE AGES

**1. Art and Architecture.** Chinese artists during the Middle Ages painted on walls, ceramics, and silk, using brush pens, ink, and watercolors. They depicted religious themes and nature studies, especially of landscapes. A favorite land-

*Courtesy, Museum of Fine Arts, Boston. Ross Collection*

Chinese Painting: 7th century, during the T'ang Dynasty.

scape scene portrayed majestic mountains and seas against which humans appeared insignificant. During the T'ang Period lived the man who is often considered China's outstanding painter, *Wu Tao-hsüan*.

Chinese architects planned cities and constructed impressive temples and vast palaces with beautiful gardens.

**2. Literature.** Chinese writers, encouraged by the invention of printing, produced extensive literary works: poetry, drama, and prose. The prose dealt with such subjects as history, government, geography, architecture, medicine, commerce, and everyday life, as well as fiction. The Chinese prepared many dictionaries and encyclopedias. The T'ang Period claims two outstanding Chinese poets. *(a) Li Po*, a master of words, created an imaginary world of lyric beauty. *(b) Tu Fu*, more of a realist, depicted human suffering.

**3. Inventions.** *(a)* In the 6th century the Chinese invented gunpowder, which they first used for festive fireworks. By the 12th century they were employing gunpowder for military purposes. *(b)* In the 7th century the Chinese printed books from carved wooden blocks. China's earliest known printed books, from the T'ang and Sung eras, are beautiful works of art. In the 11th century the Chinese evolved printing by movable type. *(c)* In the 11th century Chinese navigators determined direction from the magnetic needle enclosed in a mariner's compass. *(d)* Some sources credit the Chinese with developing an inoculation against smallpox.

These advances, however, did not result from the methodical application of scientific principles. Despite their practical-mindedness, the Chinese did not develop theories of science and logical methods of scientific research.

**4. Engineering.** Chinese engineers built roads, bridges, and city walls, dredged river channels, erected sea and river dikes, and expanded irrigation and canal systems. China's waterways, extending over hundreds of miles, were known as the *Grand Canal*.

## MANCHU DYNASTY (1644–1912)

**1. Introduction.** Although coming after the Middle Ages, the Manchu Period is included in this section because the Manchus were China's last dynasty. Manchu China was followed by the Chinese Republic and, more recently, by Communist China. The Manchus received the full impact of European overseas expansion, first felt in China during the Ming Era. Manchu policies toward Westerners help explain modern China's history.

**2. Manchu Power and Government.** With Ming China torn by rebellion, Manchu invaders swept down from Manchuria and seized the country. The invaders required Chinese men to show their loyalty by adopting the Manchu headdress: a shaved head with a *queue* (pigtail).

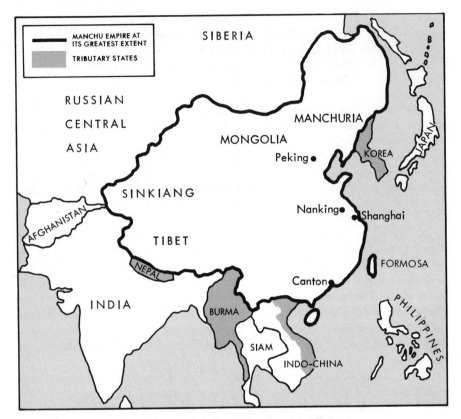

**The Manchu Empire at Its Greatest Extent**

The Manchus ruled the largest Chinese empire ever: China proper, the island of Formosa, and the outlying provinces of Manchuria, Mongolia, Sinkiang, and Tibet. The first Manchu rulers also received tribute from Korea, Burma, Nepal, and part of Indo-China. To prevent uprisings, the Manchus stationed garrisons in strategic cities.

The Manchus ruled as Chinese emperors, using Chinese officials and observing Chinese traditions. Until 1800 the Manchu Dynasty provided strong rule, maintained peace, and furthered prosperity. During these years China's population expanded to an estimated 300,000,000. During the 19th century, however, the Manchu Dynasty lost its vigor and began to decline.

**3. Policies Toward Westerners (Into the 19th Century).** During the Manchu Era, China attracted an ever-increasing number of Westerners—missionaries, diplomats, and merchants. Overland came the Russians; by sea came the west Europeans, especially the French and British; and in 1784 the first American merchant ship arrived in China.

The Manchus pursued the following policies toward the Westerners: *(a)* Manchu rulers viewed the Occidentals as inferior beings and denied diplomatic recognition to Western governments, since that would imply equality. *(b)* Manchu scholars held Chinese civilization to be superior, considering Western culture to be barbarous and refusing to see what they could learn from it. *(c)* Manchu officials restricted Western merchant ships to the port of Canton, imposed import duties unfairly, openly demanded bribes, and subjected the Western merchants to personal indignities. Despite these difficulties, Western merchants continued to come and reap profits from cargoes of Chinese tea, silk, and porcelain.

When the European nations became aware of China's military weakness, however, they used force to impose their will upon China. From the 1840's onward the history of China merges with the history of European imperialism (see pages 397–403).

# Part 3. Japan: From Earliest Days to the Nineteenth Century

## GEOGRAPHIC FACTORS INFLUENCING JAPAN

**1. Location.** Japan consists of four major and many smaller islands in the northern Pacific, with a land area about the size of California. The islands extend in an arc-like shape off the Asian mainland, some 100 miles (160 kilometers) from Korea and 500 miles (800 kilometers) from China. Even before modern transportation Japan was close enough to China to be affected by its history and culture. But Japan was still distant enough from China for the Japanese to remain a homogeneous people able to develop a distinct way of life and retain a sense of isolation. Until World War II Japan had never been occupied by enemy forces, and the Japanese considered their homeland to be divinely protected.

**2. Good Harbors.** Because Japan has numerous good harbors on its long, irregular coastline, many Japanese have turned to the sea for their livelihood. They developed an interest in fishing and overseas trade—two activities that have typified Japan's economic life. Japan remains a major seafaring nation.

**3. Mountains.** The mountains of Japan provide great natural beauty but restrict the farming area to less than 20 percent of the land surface. This lack of farmland limited the number of Japanese who could earn a living from farming. It also

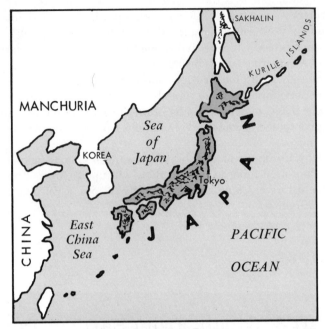

**Japan: Geographic Factors**

compelled those who did farm to expand land areas suitable for crops by building *terraces*. These are a series of flat areas, rising one above the other, created by digging into the mountainside.

Except for a meager supply of coal, Japan is poor in mineral resources. In the 19th century, when Japan turned to industry, the country had to depend heavily on imports for foodstuffs and basic raw materials.

## HISTORY OF JAPAN (TO THE 19TH CENTURY)

**1. Prehistoric Japan (to the 6th Century A.D.).** Little is known about Japan's early history because the Japanese developed writing at a late date. Until the 6th century A.D., the Japanese had no accurate written records.

According to legend, the gods created Japan, and their descendant, *Jimmu,* became the first emperor of Japan in 660 B.C.

According to modern research, the ancestors of the modern Japanese were probably immigrants who came in prehistoric times from northeastern Asia by way of Korea. Also, some early immigrants probably came from southern China and the Malayan Peninsula. These early Japanese formed a number of small states, each headed by a ruling family, or clan. By the 4th century A.D., the *Yamato* clan established a vague leadership over the other clans and became Japan's first imperial family.

**2. Japan Adopts Chinese Culture (6th to 9th Centuries).** For three centuries the primitive Japanese enthusiastically absorbed the advanced Chinese civilization, mainly of China's brilliant T'ang Era (see pages 108–109). Most aspects of Japanese life were affected.

*a. Religion.* Buddhist missionaries, coming from the Asian continent, gained converts, especially among the aristocracy. By the 8th century Buddhism was widespread in Japan. Also brought from China to Japan was the philosophy of Confucius. Japanese society approved the Confucian ideal of strong family ties.

The huge bronze Buddha at Kamakura in Japan.

*b. Art.* Buddhist missionaries introduced Chinese artistic achievements: Buddhist temple architecture, sculptured figures, and religious paintings.

*c. Writing and Literature.* The Japanese adapted the complex Chinese writing system to the Japanese spoken tongue. Also, they shared in China's rich literary heritage and imitated Chinese writings: poetry, history, and the Confucian classics.

*d. Government.* Following the example of T'ang China, the Japanese exalted the position of the emperor, established a centralized government, and adopted a modified civil service examination system.

**3. Feudalism in Japan Under the Shogunates (12th to 19th Centuries).** By the 12th century Japan's imperial central government proved too weak to maintain law and order. The country thereupon entered a 700-year feudal period of rule by the warrior class.

**a. Organization of Feudal Japan.** (1) The *mikado*, or emperor, ruled in theory but in reality was powerless. (2) The *shogun*, or most influential lord, controlled military affairs, as well as justice, lawmaking, and finance. (3) The *daimios*, or local lords, held landed estates and maintained private armies. (4) The *samurai*, or warriors, served in the lords' armies. They observed a warrior's code, *bushido*. This code of chivalry emphasized compliance with daily etiquette, contempt for physical danger, and loyalty to the feudal lord. (5) The *peasants*, who worked the land, were at the bottom of this feudal society. Commoners could not advance to aristocratic status because of rigid class distinctions.

The feudal government and society of Japan in many ways resembled the feudal system of western Europe. (See pages 72–75.)

**b. Major Shogunates.** (1) *Kamakura Shogunate* (1192–1333). The Kamakura shoguns, representing various aristocratic families, ruled from the military capital of *Kamakura*. They shaped Japan's feudal system of land grants in exchange for military services. (2) *Ashikaga Shogunate* (1338–1573). The shoguns of the Ashikaga family exercised only vague control and proved unable to prevent recurring civil wars. (3) *Tokugawa Shogunate* (1603–1867). The shoguns of the Tokugawa family maintained peace and furthered prosperity. *Tokyo*, their political capital, became the nation's leading economic and cultural center. The Tokugawa accustomed the people to centralized military control, but their strong rule delayed Japan's evolution from a feudal structure to modern nationhood.

**c. Important Foreign Developments of Feudal Japan**

(1) *Withstood the Mongols.* In the late 13th century Japanese warriors withstood two separate Mongol invasion attempts. The second invasion fleet was destroyed in 1281 with the help of a typhoon. Hailing this typhoon as "the protector of the sacred homeland," the Japanese named it the "divine wind," or *kamikaze.*

(2) *Failed to Conquer the Mainland.* Hideyoshi, a feudal general, gained control of Japan in the late 16th century and determined to conquer China. As a first step, Hideyoshi invaded Korea, but his death soon ended Japan's first attempt at overseas conquest.

(3) *First Welcomed, Then Excluded Western Influence.* In the last half of the 16th century, Western ships reached Japan. First came Portuguese merchants. Then the Spanish, Dutch, and English followed. In 1549 came a group of Jesuit missionaries led by *St. Francis Xavier.* Japanese converts to Catholicism soon numbered many thousands, and Japanese feudal lords and European merchants developed a mutually profitable trade.

In the first half of the 17th century, Japanese leaders became fearful that European missionary and trade activities would place Japan under foreign domination. Japan, consequently, withdrew into isolation. Japanese rulers expelled the missionaries, wiped out Christianity among the Japanese, and except for a single Dutch station, closed all European trading posts. Until the middle of the 19th century, Japan remained isolated from Western civilization. (For the opening of Japan in 1853–1854 and subsequent developments, see pages 403–407.)

## ASPECTS OF JAPANESE CULTURE

**1. Importance of Foreign Influence.** The Japanese talent for learning and borrowing from foreign civilizations first evidenced itself from the 6th to 9th centuries when primitive Japan accepted the superior culture of China. (This capacity to learn reappeared (*a*) in the 19th century, when feudal Japan transformed itself into a modern, unified, industrialized nation along Western lines, and (*b*) in the 20th century, when Japan shed its militarist dictatorship for the democratic institutions of its World War II conqueror, the United States.)

The medieval Japanese did not merely imitate. By gradually modifying and building upon the borrowed Chinese culture, the Japanese created their own unique civilization.

**2. Language and Literature.** The Japanese used the complex Chinese characters both in their original Chinese meaning and for a simpler, phonetic system of

*Courtesy, Museum of Fine Arts, Boston. Wm. S. and John T. Spaulding Collection.*

"Mt. Fuji in fair weather with gentle wind"
as seen through the eyes of the Japanese artist, Hokusai (1760–1849).

language. From the 8th century onward, the Japanese developed their own literature: poetry, drama, history, and the novel. A favorite romantic theme extolled Japanese military valor. In the 11th century the court lady *Murasaki* wrote a world-famous novel of love and adventure, the *Tale of Genji*.

**3. Arts.** Japanese artists, following the style of the Chinese, created Buddhist religious paintings as well as landscapes, especially scenes of Japan's snow-topped mountain, *Fujiyama*. (See illustration, page 119.) Japanese architects constructed beautiful palaces and temples set in elaborate gardens. Japanese sculptors carved impressive statues of Buddhist divinities. (See illustration, page 117.)

**4. Government Officials.** Although they borrowed the Chinese method of selecting government officials by civil service examinations, the Japanese conformed to their rigid class distinctions by restricting the examinations to the aristocracy.

**5. Religion.** While accepting Buddhist and Confucian doctrines from China, the Japanese retained their native religion, *Shintoism*. This was a form of nature worship inspired by awe in the presence of natural wonders. However, it lacked significant moral content. For many centuries Shintoism was blended with Buddhism and was not a separate religion. Then, in the 18th century, it was revived as a national religion with many temples, shrines, and formal ceremonies. (In the 19th century, after Japan became a modern nation, state Shintoism extolled Japanese nationalism. It was then that great emphasis was given to ancestor worship and to the belief that the emperor descended from the gods.)

**6. Good Manners and Aesthetic Appreciation.** In vivid contrast to their military emphasis, the Japanese displayed a sensitivity in human relations and a love of beauty. They prized good manners and respected personal dignity, a trait that Westerners have often termed "face."

## IDENTIFICATION QUESTIONS: WHO AM I?

| | | |
|---|---|---|
| Akbar | Genghis Khan | Tamerlane |
| Babar | Hideyoshi | Tu Fu |
| da Gama | Kublai Khan | Wang An-shih |
| Francis Xavier | Marco Polo | Wu Tao-hsüan |

1. A great conqueror, I led a single Mongol invasion of northern India, caused much destruction of life and property, and then withdrew.
2. I conquered the southern Sung state and reunited it with the rest of China—all within the Mongol Empire.
3. A Jesuit missionary, I introduced Catholicism to Japan and won many converts.
4. As Mogul emperor in India, I expanded my empire, provided good government, enforced religious tolerance, encouraged culture, and earned the title "the Great."
5. A Japanese feudal lord, my efforts to conquer Korea and China ended with my death.

6. As chief minister during the Sung Era, I introduced a program of social and economic reform that encountered much opposition and was soon abandoned.
7. An Italian merchant, I traveled overland to China and, upon my return home, described my experiences in a book.
8. Uniting the Mongol tribes, I led them in wars of conquest, founding a vast empire.
9. I lived during the T'ang Period, and my works have earned me the title of China's outstanding painter.

## MULTIPLE–CHOICE QUESTIONS

1. In the Middle Ages Moslem peoples were attracted to India because (1) India was the birthplace of Mohammed (2) Hindu princes invited Moslem missionaries (3) the topography of northwest India was similar to that of Arabia (4) northwest India had much wealth.
2. Aibak, founder of the Delhi Empire, was a Moslem and ex-slave. This would indicate that Moslems (1) accepted the caste system (2) rejected the caste system (3) opposed slavery (4) believed in reincarnation.
3. The attitude of the 13th-century Delhi sultans toward Hinduism was one of (1) active support (2) persecution (3) indifference (4) tolerance.
4. By the 17th century the Moslems constituted about (1) 50 (2) 20 (3) 10 (4) 5 percent of the Indian population.
5. Which regions were the centers of Moslem population in India? (1) Indus and Ganges (2) Ganges and Deccan (3) Deccan and Himalayas (4) Himalayas and Indus.
6. Many Moslem rulers accused the Hindus of idolatry because the Hindus (1) accepted caste (2) believed in reincarnation (3) considered the cow sacred (4) carved religious statues.
7. The Taj Mahal was a famous (1) Hindu temple (2) Hindu palace (3) Moslem tomb (4) Moslem victory arch.
8. The European nation that first reached India by sea and monopolized India's trade for many years was (1) Portugal (2) England (3) France (4) Holland.
9. Unlike previous conquerors of India, the British (1) won the Indians' loyalty by prohibiting the Moslem religion (2) sought no profits (3) won control over the entire country (4) declined to introduce foreign ways.
10. A period of Chinese history that compared favorably with the Han Period in military power, economic prosperity, and cultural achievement was the (1) T'ang (2) Sung (3) Ming (4) Manchu.
11. Most similar to the 11th-century Sung economic reforms is today's United States law (1) establishing minimum wages (2) providing social security (3) authorizing the government to purchase agricultural surpluses (4) prohibiting false labeling.
12. At its greatest extent, the Mongol Empire stretched westward from the Pacific Ocean to (1) Persia (2) Sinkiang (3) European Russia (4) central Europe.
13. During the Mongol Era the civilization of China was (1) destroyed by the Mongols (2) opened to new ideas from the rest of Asia (3) tolerated by the Mongols but considered inferior (4) replaced by Indian culture.
14. The medieval Chinese (1) learned block printing from India (2) used gunpowder only for nonmilitary purposes (3) did not develop logical methods of experimentation and research (4) learned of the compass from the Arabs.

15. The Communist Chinese today, to buttress their claims to additional territories in Asia, would use a map of (1) 13th-century Sung China (2) 16th-century Ming China (3) early 19th-century Manchu China (4) 10th-century Sung China.
16. In dealing with the West in the 18th and 19th centuries, China at first (1) enslaved all Westerners who came to China (2) refused to learn from Western culture (3) treated Westerners as equals (4) sent Chinese students to Western universities.
17. The geographic relationship of the Asian continent to Japan is similar to the relationship of Europe to (1) Spain (2) Britain (3) Denmark (4) the United States.
18. The mountains of Japan (1) provide great natural beauty (2) contain much iron ore (3) are a barrier against invasion (4) contain much fertile land.
19. By the 9th century A.D. the Japanese had (1) developed an inbred culture (2) borrowed heavily from China's culture (3) adopted Hinduism from India (4) driven Catholic missionaries from their country.
20. Feudal Europe's closest counterpart to the shogun of feudal Japan was the (1) mayor of the palace (2) pope (3) knight (4) king.
21. Japan's last, or Tokugawa, Shogunate (1) failed to maintain law and order (2) caused economic ruin (3) drove out Buddhist priests (4) delayed Japan's development as a modern nation.
22. Japanese suicide pilots in World War II were called "kamikaze" after a (1) Japanese military leader who invaded Korea (2) Shinto god (3) typhoon that helped destroy a Mongol invasion fleet (4) towering Japanese mountain.
23. Why did Japan isolate itself from Western civilization in the 17th century? (1) Few Japanese had converted to Catholicism. (2) The Japanese resented the poor quality of European goods. (3) The Japanese discovered their own deposits of iron ore. (4) The Japanese feared that European missionary and trade activities would lead to military conquest.
24. Which was *not* an aspect of Japanese culture? (1) a complex system of writing (2) equality of all classes (3) Shinto emphasis on nature worship (4) respect of good manners and personal dignity.
25. Shintoism did *not* (1) originate as nature worship (2) consider the emperor a descendant of the gods (3) emphasize concern for the poor and the unfortunate (4) encourage Japanese nationalism.

## ESSAY QUESTIONS

1. Choose medieval India *or* China *or* Japan and discuss *(a)* *two* developments that were similar to and *(b)* *two* developments that were different from developments in medieval western Europe.
2. Show *three* ways in which the medieval Far East exerted an influence upon the civilization of western Europe.
3. Using *one* fact for each, indicate whether you agree or disagree with each of the following statements: *(a)* Religion played a major role in the history of medieval India. *(b)* In the Middle Ages Chinese culture was superior to west European civilization. *(c)* Chinese civil service examinations provided a good method of selecting government officials. *(d)* Japan benefited greatly from geographic factors. *(e)* The Japanese were fortunate in their ability to learn from foreign civilizations. *(f)* Japanese feudalism was similar to feudalism in western Europe.
4. Describe *one* way in which each of the following persons influenced world history: *(a)* Akbar *(b)* Vasco da Gama *(c)* Genghis Kahn *(d)* Marco Polo *(e)* Hideyoshi *(f)* Francis Xavier.

# Section Three

# Modern History

## UNIT VI. THE TRANSITION: FROM MEDIEVAL TO MODERN EUROPE

## Part 1. The Renaissance: A Rebirth of Learning

### THE RENAISSANCE PERIOD (14TH TO THE 17TH CENTURIES)

The word *Renaissance* means rebirth or revival. The Renaissance, in history, refers to a period of approximately 300 years that in western Europe marked the revival of art, literature, and learning. The Renaissance therefore served as a bridge, or transition, between medieval and modern western Europe.

At one time many historians held that the Renaissance signified a sharp break with the preceding medieval period. More recently some scholars have argued that the Renaissance was an evolutionary change from or an outgrowth of the Later Middle Ages. They point out that the Renaissance had roots in many aspects of the medieval heritage, especially the universities of learning, the forms and subject matter of literature, and the rudiments of science.

### DISTINCTIVE FEATURES OF THE RENAISSANCE

The Renaissance (1) began with the rediscovery of the Greco-Roman civilization, which had been generally neglected during the Middle Ages; (2) emphasized reason, a questioning attitude, experimentation, and free inquiry—in contrast to the medieval concern with faith, authority, and tradition; (3) glorified the individual and approved worldly pleasures, viewing life as worthwhile for its own sake, not chiefly as preparation for the hereafter; (4) focused attention upon worldly matters arising out of a secular society (secularization) rather than the medieval preoccupation with the Roman Catholic Church and religious affairs; and (5) featured great achievements in literature, art, and science.

## THE RENAISSANCE STARTS IN ITALY

The Renaissance arose in the Italian cities because: (1) As the center of Greco-Roman culture, Italy contained sculpture, buildings, roads, and manuscripts that excited curiosity about classical civilization. (2) Located on the Mediterranean, Italy had absorbed stimulating new ideas from the advanced Byzantine and Moslem worlds. (3) Benefiting from the revival of trade that resulted from the Crusades, Italy had wealthy, influential people who became *patrons* (supporters) of literature, art, and science. The leading Renaissance patrons were certain popes in *Rome,* wealthy merchants in *Venice,* the *Sforza* family in *Milan,* and the *Medici* family in *Florence.*

## FLORENCE: THE PREEMINENT ITALIAN RENAISSANCE CITY

Florence is usually considered to be the outstanding city of the Italian Renaissance. In the 15th century the city came under the rule of the Medici— originally a merchant family who amassed a fortune in the wool trade and expanded into banking. The Medici, especially *Lorenzo the Magnificent* (ruled 1469–1492), became the outstanding patrons of Renaissance art.

Florence had many residents who achieved fame as Renaissance painters, sculptors, architects, and writers. Also, by virtue of its artistic leadership and patronage, Florence attracted people of talent from elsewhere in Italy. Thus, the city acquired many priceless works of art. Florence today attracts tourists eager to view its churches, palaces, and libraries with their Renaissance treasures.

## THE RENAISSANCE SPREADS

In the 15th century Renaissance ideas began to spread from Italy to France, the German states, Holland, and England. This cultural diffusion resulted from religious, military, and commercial contacts. Also, many northern scholars traveled to Italy to absorb Italian art and learning.

## HUMANISM ILLUSTRATES THE RENAISSANCE SPIRIT

*Humanism,* a literary movement that began in 14th-century Italy, typified the Renaissance spirit.

Humanists (1) concerned themselves, not with religious matters, but with everyday human problems; (2) drew inspiration from classical civilization— eagerly seeking, studying, and publicizing ancient Greek and Roman manuscripts; and (3) revived interest, chiefly among educated people, in literature and writing.

Early humanist writers were the following:

1. **Petrarch** (1304–1374), Italian, studied the classics and wrote in both Italian and Latin. His beautiful sonnets expressed romantic love and appreciation of nature. In longer works he imitated the style of classical writers.

2. **Pico della Mirandola** (1463–1494), Italian, who lived for a while near Florence, was a scholar of law, philosophy, Greek, Latin, Hebrew, and Arabic. In his writings he expressed unorthodox religious ideas—for some of which he was censured by the Church—and he spoke in praise of the dignity of human beings.

3. **Erasmus** (1466?–1536), Dutch, was a brilliant classical scholar. In his book *Praise of Folly*, he ridiculed superstition, prejudice, upper class privileges, and Church abuses. By satirizing social evils, Erasmus encouraged people to think about reforms.

4. **Sir Thomas More** (1478–1535), English, wrote *Utopia*, a book that portrayed an ideal country, free from war, injustice, poverty, and ignorance. (The word *utopia* now refers to any ideal state.) (See portrait of More, page 128.)

## THE VERNACULAR REPLACES LATIN IN LITERATURE

During the Middle Ages in western Europe, Latin was the language of literature, of the Church, and of educated people. Over the centuries, however, other tongues had been evolving through everyday usage. These included French, Italian, Spanish, German, and English—the *vernacular*, or *national*, languages.

At the end of the Middle Ages, writers began to use vernacular languages in addition to Latin; later writers discarded Latin entirely. Early great writers who used the vernacular were:

1. **Dante** (1265–1321), Italian, born in Florence, served that city in various governmental positions until exiled by a hostile political faction. Known as the "father of modern Italian," Dante was the first to write an important work in the vernacular. His *Divine Comedy*, a long poem, ranks among the greatest literary masterpieces. It describes Dante's imaginary trip through Hell, Purgatory, and Heaven, during which one of his guides is the Roman poet Vergil.

2. **Boccaccio** (1313?–1375), Italian, lived in Florence during his formative years and absorbed the Renaissance spirit. A humanist, poet, and writer, Boccaccio is best known for his Italian prose in his collection of sophisticated short stories, *The Decameron*. Supposedly these stories were related by a group of young men and women who had fled to a villa outside Florence to escape the Black Death plague.

3. **Chaucer** (1340?–1400), English, became familiar with the works of Dante and Boccaccio while traveling in Italy. Chaucer used English in his collection of stories in verse, the *Canterbury Tales*. Supposedly these stories were related by pilgrims journeying to the religious shrine at Canterbury.

## THE INVENTION OF PRINTING ENCOURAGES LITERATURE

About 1450 printing with movable type was invented by a German, *Johann Gutenberg.* As compared to medieval hand copying of books, printing tremendously increased output and accuracy and decreased cost. Inexpensive printed materials afforded all people opportunities for literacy and learning. Moreover, the availability of printing encouraged talented people to write.

## RENAISSANCE LITERARY ACHIEVEMENTS

1. **Machiavelli** (1469–1527), Italian, born in Florence, served the Florentine Republic as secretary and diplomat, gaining firsthand political experience. When the Medici were restored to power in Florence, Machiavelli was dismissed from office and later permitted to retire to his country home where he devoted himself to writing. *The Prince*, Machiavelli's major work on ethics and government, describes how rulers maintain power by methods that ignore right or wrong and accept the philosophy that "the end justifies the means."

Although Machiavelli probably was describing what realistically takes place in government rather than what morally is right, our word *Machiavellian* has come to mean "cunning and unscrupulous."

2. **Rabelais** (1494?–1553), French, wrote the romances *Gargantua* and *Pantagruel.* With tongue-in-cheek humor, he portrayed a comic world of giants whose adventures satirized education, politics, and philosophy.

3. **Montaigne** (1533–1592), French, wrote a series of *Essays.* He expressed skepticism toward accepted beliefs, condemning superstition and intolerance and urging people to live nobly. This collection is sometimes judged the best example of the essay form.

4. **Cervantes** (1547–1616), Spanish, ridiculed feudal society, especially knighthood and chivalry, in relating the adventures of the mad knight of La Mancha, *Don Quixote.*

5. **Shakespeare** (1564–1616), English, is often considered as the greatest poet and playwright of all time. In his sonnets he penned exquisite lines and evoked striking images. In his plays he employed superb dramatic technique to probe historical events and human character. Shakespeare's best-known plays include the histories *Henry IV* and *Henry V*; the comedies *Twelfth Night* and *A Midsummer Night's Dream;* and the tragedies *Romeo and Juliet, Hamlet, Julius Caesar,* and *Macbeth.*

6. **Milton** (1608–1674), English, retold the biblical story of the Creation and the Garden of Eden in his epic poem, *Paradise Lost.* He also strongly advocated freedom of the press in an essay, *Areopagitica.*

7. **Molière** (1622–1673), French, dominated French literature as its leading

comic dramatist. Among his notable plays are *The Misanthrope* and *The Imaginary Invalid*.

## CHARACTERISTICS OF RENAISSANCE ART

1. Renaissance art was considerably influenced by the artistic achievements of classical Greece and Rome. Particularly in sculpture and architecture, Renaissance artists often imitated classical works.
2. Renaissance painting emphasized realism, attention to detail, and desire for perfection.
3. Early Renaissance painters treated religious themes with a lifelike approach. Later Renaissance painters also employed a realistic style and continued to recreate biblical events. In addition they depicted worldly subjects—landscapes, portraits, and scenes of everyday life.
4. Renaissance art continues to evoke admiration. It attracts tourists to western Europe, visitors to art museums, and collectors to art auction sales. In 1967 a da Vinci painting was purchased by Washington's National Gallery of Art for a reputed record price of $5 million to $6 million.

## RENAISSANCE ARTISTIC ACHIEVEMENTS

### Italian

1. **Giotto** (1266?–1337), born near Florence, was a painter and an architect. He realistically portrayed religious themes in his many frescoes (paintings on walls), such as *St. Francis Preaching to the Birds*. For the cathedral of Florence, he designed the famed bell tower, usually called *Giotto's Tower*.

2. **Ghiberti** (1378–1455), born and lived in Florence, was a sculptor. For the bronze doors of the baptistery—a church building—in Florence, he sculpted a series of exquisite biblical scenes. (See illustration, page 129.)

3. **Donatello** (1386?–1466), a Florentine sculptor, carved busts, statuettes, friezes (upper sections of walls) for cathedrals, and an equestrian statue of a Venetian mercenary. Donatello is famed for an early work, the life-size statue of *St. George* in armor.

4. **Leonardo da Vinci** (1452–1519), associated with Florence, Milan, and Rome, was the ideal Renaissance man. He was a versatile genius eager to experiment and skilled as a painter, sculptor, architect, musician, engineer, and scientist. In military engineering he improved the method of loading cannon and devised equipment for scaling walls. With a keen eye for detail, he studied anatomy and from his observations of birds sketched a parachute and a flying machine. He painted such masterpieces as *Self-Portrait*, *The Last Supper*, and the *Mona Lisa*. (See illustration, page 128.)

*French Cultural Services*          *Copyright The Frick Collection, New York.*

Renaissance Painting: (left) *Mona Lisa* by Leonardo da Vinci
(right) *Sir Thomas More* by Holbein.

**5. Michelangelo** (1475–1564), who spent his life in Florence and Rome, was another many-sided Renaissance genius, talented as a painter, sculptor, poet, and architect. He painted biblical scenes and figures on the ceiling of the *Sistine Chapel* in the Vatican; carved the *Pietà*, showing Mary grieving over the dead Jesus; carved massive statues of Old Testament figures, *David* and *Moses;* and designed the dome of *St. Peter's Cathedral* in Rome.

**6. Titian** (1477–1576), a painter associated with Venice, used vivid colors in his portraits of famous people and his scenes from mythology and the Bible, such as the *Assumption of the Virgin.*

**7. Raphael** (1483–1520), a painter who worked in Florence and Rome, captured tranquil beauty in many religious works, such as the *Sistine Madonna.*

**8. Palestrina** (1526?–1594), a composer who spent most of his life in Rome, wrote church music that is still played.

## *Spanish*

**1. El Greco** (1547–1614), a Greek who settled in Spain, painted religious scenes such as the *Assumption,* portraits of church officials, and the famous landscape, *View of Toledo.*

*Italian Government Travel Office*

Renaissance Architecture: St. Peter's Cathedral in Rome.

*The Bettmann Archive, Inc.*

Renaissance Sculpture: The Baptistery Doors in Florence, by Ghiberti.

129

**2. Velasquez** (1599–1660), official painter to the court of King Philip IV of Spain, did many portraits of royalty. He commemorated a Spanish victory against the Dutch in his *Surrender of Breda.*

## Dutch

**1. Hals** (1580?–1666) painted portraits of ordinary people and scenes of everyday life. He is famed for his *Laughing Cavalier.*

**2. Rembrandt** (1606–1669), considered the greatest painter of northern Europe, effectively used contrasts of light and shadow in portraying everyday life and common people. Among his works are *The Night Watch, The Anatomy Lesson,* and *Aristotle Contemplating the Bust of Homer.*

## Flemish

**1. Rubens** (1577–1640), noted for brilliant colors, composed landscapes and portraits, and vigorously depicted action in religious and historical paintings. One of his outstanding works is the *Adoration of the Magi.*

## German

**1. Dürer** (1471–1528) was a painter and a metal and wood engraver. He is famed for his drawing *Praying Hands.*

**2. Holbein** (1497?–1543) in his later life was official painter at the court of Henry VIII in England. Holbein produced lifelike portraits of famous persons, notably Henry VIII, Erasmus, and Sir Thomas More. (See illustration, page 128.)

### CHARACTERISTICS OF RENAISSANCE SCIENCE

Renaissance science (1) built upon the extensive scientific writings of the Greeks and Romans; (2) developed the scientific method of observation and experimentation; (3) challenged medieval superstition and the general acceptance of Aristotle's theories; (4) uncovered much knowledge about the physical world; (5) reduced the importance of humanity in the universal scheme of things by determining that the earth was *not* at the center of the cosmos but rather was one of several planets revolving about its sun in a minor planetary system; (6) encountered considerable opposition at first because its findings were thought to conflict with medieval religious and popular beliefs; (7) increased the ability of people to improve their health and control their environment; and (8) established a firm foundation for modern scientific progress.

Renaissance science is sometimes considered to be the foundation of an ongoing process still evident today—the *Scientific Revolution.*

# RENAISSANCE SCIENTIFIC ACHIEVEMENTS

**1. Copernicus** (1473–1543), a Polish astronomer who had studied in Italy, concluded that *(a)* the sun is the center of our solar system and *(b)* the earth is merely one of several planets revolving about the sun. Copernicus' conclusions, published at the time of his death, disproved the Ptolemaic theory, which claimed that the earth is the center of the universe. (See page 64.)

**2. Vesalius** (1514–1564), a Flemish physician, undertook careful dissections of the human body. He founded the science of anatomy.

**3. Francis Bacon** (1561–1626), an English philosopher, wrote the *Advancement of Learning*. He popularized the new scientific method of observation and experimentation.

**4. Galileo** (1564–1642), who was born in Pisa and for many years lived in Florence, was an Italian astronomer and physicist. He demonstrated the law of falling bodies and greatly improved the telescope. His observations of the heavens confirmed the Copernican theory.

**5. Kepler** (1571–1630), a German astronomer and mathematician, determined that the planets follow an elliptical, not a circular, orbit in revolving about the sun. Kepler's findings help explain the paths followed by human-made satellites today.

**6. Harvey** (1578–1657), an English physician, demonstrated that blood circulates through the body. His research furthered the study of medicine.

**7. Descartes** (1596–1650) was a French scientist, mathematician, and philosopher. He discovered laws of optics and is considered the founder of analytic geometry. His philosophy is summed up in his words "I think, therefore I am."

**8. Boyle** (1627–1691), an English chemist, discovered a law of gases that is fundamental to modern chemistry.

**9. Leeuwenhoek** (1632–1723), a Dutch naturalist, perfected the microscope. With this instrument, Leeuwenhoek studied a heretofore invisible world of bacteria, protozoa, and animal and plant cells.

**10. Newton** (1642–1727) was an English mathematician, astronomer, and physicist. He invented a method of mathematical analysis called calculus, discovered laws of light and color, formulated the laws of motion, and calculated the law of gravitation. Newton's scientific ideas were set forth in his book *Mathematical Principles of Natural Philosophy*.

## IDENTIFICATION QUESTIONS: WHO AM I?

| | | |
|---|---|---|
| Boccaccio | Donatello | Michelangelo |
| Cervantes | Galileo | More |
| Chaucer | Giotto | Newton |
| Copernicus | Gutenberg | Petrarch |
| Dante | Harvey | Rembrandt |

1. A humanist, I portrayed an imaginary ideal country in my book *Utopia*.
2. In my poem *Divine Comedy*, I portrayed an imaginary trip into the hereafter and meetings with famous persons of the past.
3. A physicist and astronomer, I determined the speed at which objects fall and used my telescope to observe the heavens.
4. I am famous for my statues of David and Moses and for my frescoes on the ceiling of the Sistine Chapel in the Vatican.
5. I am considered the greatest painter of northern Europe. Recently my painting *Aristotle Contemplating the Bust of Homer* commanded a price of over $2 million.
6. When I described my hero Don Quixote tilting at a windmill, I was poking fun at feudalism.
7. My mathematical and scientific achievements brought me great fame. I am remembered especially for inventing calculus and discovering the law of gravitation.
8. I advanced the theory, forgotten since the days of the ancient Greeks, that the earth is not the center of the solar system but revolves about the sun.
9. By my invention of movable type for printing, I encouraged the literary Renaissance.

## MULTIPLE–CHOICE QUESTIONS

1. The Renaissance in western Europe was a period marked by (1) unquestioned reliance on the teachings of Aristotle (2) an advance of Moslem culture (3) Christian unity throughout all of Europe (4) a spirit of questioning of formerly accepted authority.
2. An important feature of the Renaissance was an emphasis on (1) alchemy and magic (2) the literature of Greece and Rome (3) chivalry (4) the teachings of St. Thomas Aquinas.
3. Which was an indirect cause of the European Renaissance? (1) the Crusades (2) the discovery of the New World (3) the Mongol invasions of Europe (4) the Black Death.
4. The Renaissance began in Italy because Italy (1) was a united nation with a strong central government (2) had annexed territory in the eastern Mediterranean (3) had a climate that suited artists and writers (4) enjoyed a favorable location for trade with the East.
5. Two early centers of European Renaissance culture were (1) London and Prague (2) Madrid and Berlin (3) Paris and Athens (4) Venice and Florence.
6. The Medicis and Sforzas played a significant part in the Renaissance as (1) painters of everyday scenes (2) rulers of Italian cities and patrons of culture (3) scientists who furthered medical research (4) military leaders whose conquests spread the Renaissance to northern Europe.
7. Francis Bacon and Galileo were alike in that both (1) adopted the ideas of Aristotle (2) limited their discoveries to astronomy (3) believed in the use of the scientific method (4) opposed the Copernican theory.

8. The *Divine Comedy, The Decameron,* and the *Canterbury Tales* were all originally written (1) in the vernacular (2) in Latin (3) by troubadours (4) in the monasteries.

9. Shakespeare's plays (1) were written in Latin (2) protested conditions of the peasants (3) were based upon the plays of Sophocles (4) analyzed problems and motives of the individual.

10. In his book *Praise of Folly,* Erasmus (1) related a series of short stories (2) used satire to attack the evils of society (3) urged people to accept things as they were (4) advised princes how to rule.

11. The term "a da Vinci of today" would best describe a person who seems to be (1) behind the times (2) a genius in many fields (3) a conformist (4) only seeking pleasure.

12. If you referred to a person as "Machiavellian," you would mean that the person is (1) extremely rich (2) a heavy contributor to charitable organizations (3) interested chiefly in material possessions (4) not bound by moral considerations in gaining an objective.

13. The careers of Gutenberg, Copernicus, and Rembrandt best support the conclusion that the Renaissance (1) strengthened religious unity throughout Europe (2) was limited to a specific field of learning but to no one European country (3) occurred in several European countries and in several fields of achievement (4) represents the period of humanity's greatest intellectual progress.

14. During the Renaissance period in western Europe, art and science flourished especially in regions where there was (1) parliamentary government (2) little contact with the outside world (3) little interest in religion (4) a wealthy leisure class.

15. Which present-day concern was most neglected during the Renaissance period? (1) encouragement of creative artistic talent (2) search for new knowledge of the universe (3) emphasis on moral and spiritual values (4) effort to achieve legal recognition of an individual's basic civil rights.

## ESSAY QUESTIONS

1. From its beginning in Italy, the Renaissance spread until almost every country in western Europe felt its influence. *(a)* Discuss *two* reasons why the Renaissance began in Italy. *(b)* Explain *two* ways in which the Renaissance spread to countries outside of Italy. *(c)* Describe *one* Renaissance achievement in *each* of *two* west European countries outside of Italy.

2. Discuss *two* supporting facts for *each* of the following statements: *(a)* The growth of trade and commerce contributed to the development of the Renaissance. *(b)* Leonardo da Vinci symbolizes the spirit of the Renaissance. *(c)* The Renaissance is a "bridge" from classical times to modern times. *(d)* The Renaissance hastened the development of vernacular languages. *(e)* Florence was a leading city in the Italian Renaissance.

3. Explain *one* specific way in which each of the following men contributed to the Renaissance: *(a)* Chaucer *(b)* Copernicus *(c)* Machiavelli *(d)* Erasmus *(e)* Gutenberg *(f)* Michelangelo *(g)* Rembrandt.

4. Discuss briefly *one* specific contribution during the Renaissance in western Europe in each of the following areas: *(a)* architecture *(b)* literature *(c)* painting *(d)* science.

5. Show how people's manner of living and ways of thought have been influenced by the following advances in technology: *(a)* printing from movable type *(b)* the telescope *(c)* the microscope.

6. If you could be transported back in time, in which period would you feel more "at home" in western Europe, the Middle Ages, or the Renaissance era? Support your opinion with *two* specific arguments.

# Part 2. The Reformation: Beginning of Protestant Christianity

## THE PROTESTANT REFORMATION (STARTING IN 1517)

The *Reformation* was a religious revolt against the authority and certain doctrines of the Roman Catholic Church. The Reformation established many *Protestant* sects. (A Protestant is generally considered to be a Christian who is not of the Roman Catholic or Eastern Orthodox faiths.) In western Europe the Reformation shattered Catholic religious unity and led to Christian diversity.

## CAUSES OF THE REFORMATION

**1. Political.** Some rulers resented the Church courts and the Church claim of supremacy over civil authority. Except in Italy, nationalist-minded persons, who were growing in number, considered the pope a foreign ruler.

**2. Economic.** Some rulers envied the Church's wealth and desired to confiscate the vast Church properties. Some business people viewed the Church tithe as a heavy burden and the Church prohibition of interest on loans as a restriction on economic enterprise. Nationalist-minded persons resented the flow of Church taxes from their countries to the papacy in Rome.

**3. Intellectual.** The Renaissance, by its ferment of new ideas, helped contribute to the Reformation. The Renaissance emphasis on individual expression encouraged some persons to seek a direct relationship between the individual and God. The Renaissance questioning attitude led some educated persons to doubt Church religious powers and authority. These persons prepared the way for religious dissent by challenging Church teachings on astronomy, history, and Bible interpretation.

**4. Church Abuses.** Some persons were critical of the following Church practices, which seemed unworthy of religious leaders: *(a) Worldliness*—the luxurious and materialistic life of certain popes and high clergy. *(b) Nepotism*—appointing relatives to Church offices regardless of ability. *(c) Simony*—selling appointments to Church offices. *(d) Sale of indulgences*—accepting money for Church pardons, called *indulgences*, without requiring true repentance. These pardons were granted to reduce punishment in the hereafter for certain sins.

**5. Decline of Church Prestige.** Some persons lost respect for the Church because of *(a)* the *Babylonian Captivity* (1309–1377), a period during which the popes lived at Avignon, France, under the domination of French kings, and (b) the *Great Schism* (1378–1417), a period during which rival popes—at Avignon and at Rome—each claimed to be the true pope and struggled for Church supremacy.

Knowledge of these causes, basic to the Reformation, could be spread widely, quickly, and inexpensively in western Europe after 1450, following the invention of printing with movable type.

## UNSUCCESSFUL EARLY ATTEMPTS AT REFORM (14TH–15TH CENTURIES)

1. **John Wycliffe** (1328?–1384), an English priest, condemned the wealth and worldliness of the Catholic Church. Denying the pope's religious supremacy, Wycliffe argued that the Bible is the highest religious authority. To enable people to guide themselves in religious matters, he translated the Bible into English. Wycliffe was denounced by the pope, and the authorities harshly persecuted Wycliffe's followers, the *Lollards.*

2. **John Huss** (1369–1415), a Bohemian (Czech) religious leader, advocated ideas similar to those of Wycliffe. Arrested and tried as a heretic, Huss was burned at the stake. The *Hussites,* his followers, rebelled against the authorities who opposed religious reform and Bohemian national independence. After a number of years of warfare, the rebels gained a religious compromise but submitted to the rule of the Catholic king of Hungary as Holy Roman Emperor.

3. **Desiderius Erasmus** (1466?–1536), the great Dutch humanist scholar, attacked Church abuses but remained a faithful Catholic. His pleas for internal reform went unheeded.

These early reformers, themselves unsuccessful, helped pave the way for the success of Martin Luther.

## MARTIN LUTHER STARTS THE REFORMATION (1517)

1. **Luther's Background.** *Martin Luther* (1483–1546), born into a poor German family, received an excellent education and entered a Catholic monastic order. At age 25 Luther was appointed professor of Christian theology at the University of Wittenberg.

2. **Luther Attacks the Church.** Luther condemned the sale of indulgences and denounced papal agents selling them in Germany. (The funds obtained were to be used for building St. Peter's Cathedral in Rome.) In 1517 Luther nailed to the door of the church at Wittenberg a statement of his religious beliefs, the *Ninety-five Theses.* The theses aroused tremendous popular support, further encouraging him to attack the Church. Luther denied the pope's supremacy, proclaimed the Bible as the final authority in religious matters, translated the Bible into German, urged each individual to read and understand the Bible, and

criticized a number of Catholic practices. He developed the doctrine of *justification by faith*, that faith alone ensures salvation. Excommunicated by the pope, Luther faced punishment from Charles V, king of Spain, in his capacity as Holy Roman Emperor.

**3. North German Rulers Support Luther.** Powerful northern German rulers welcomed revolt against Rome. In addition to having religious reasons, they desired to seize Church properties, weaken the Holy Roman Emperor, and end their submission to a non-German pope. Consequently they protected Luther against punishment. Throughout northern Germany, these rulers accepted Luther's ideas as the basis of a new religion, *Lutheranism*.

In establishing the new religion, Luther replaced Latin with the vernacular German in church services, wrote catechisms for church members, encouraged congregations to sing hymns, wrote hymns (most notably "A Mighty Fortress Is Our God"), approved marriage by the clergy, rejected the organization of any clerical hierarchy, and recognized the position of the church as subordinate to and an agent of civil authority.

## SCANDINAVIA RAPIDLY ACCEPTS LUTHERANISM

Scandinavian rulers in Norway, Sweden, and Denmark were converted to Lutheranism, established it as the official state religion, and confiscated Catholic Church properties. By the end of the 16th century, Scandinavia had become almost entirely Lutheran.

## OTHER PROTESTANT REFORMERS

Although Luther was intolerant of dissent, even by other Protestant reformers, the success of Lutheranism in northern Germany and Scandinavia encouraged others to challenge Catholic Church authority.

**1. Ulrich Zwingli** (1484–1531), a Swiss priest, taught that the Bible, not the pope, is the supreme religious authority. Zwingli converted certain Swiss cantons (districts) to Protestantism.

**2. John Calvin** (1509–1564), a French religious reformer, fled from Catholic France to safety in Geneva, Switzerland. Author of the *Institutes of the Christian Religion*, Calvin became a leading Protestant spokesman. He taught the doctrine of *predestination*, that only those elected beforehand by God would achieve salvation. He founded a simple form of worship, frowned upon such pastimes as dancing and cardplaying, and extolled a serious, moral, and hardworking life. Those persons predestined for salvation, he held, could be identified by the virtue of their moral lives.

Calvinism spread rapidly. (*a*) In Switzerland Calvinism became the *Swiss Reformed Church*. (*b*) In Holland Calvinism became the prevailing faith, the *Dutch Reformed Church*. (*c*) In Scotland Calvinism became the official state religion, the *Presbyterian Church*. (*d*) In France Calvinism became the faith of a small, influential, middle-class group, the *Huguenots*. *(e)* In England Calvinism became the religion of the *Puritans*. During the 17th century a number of Puritans migrated to the New World colony of Massachusetts, where they introduced Calvinism as the *Congregational Church*.

3. **John Knox** (1505–1572), a Scottish reformer and follower of Calvin, helped establish *Presbyterianism* as the official religion of Scotland.

## ANGLICANISM IN ENGLAND

*Henry VIII*, king of England (1509–1547), at first a loyal Catholic, broke with the Church because (1) the pope refused to grant him a divorce from his Spanish wife, Catherine of Aragon, and (2) Henry desired for the crown the extensive Church properties in England. He induced Parliament to pass the *Act of Supremacy* (1534), which instituted the *Anglican Church of England*, independent of Rome and under the leadership of the English ruler.

Henry's actions won the support of the nationalist-minded English, who considered the pope to be a foreign ruler, and of many people who opposed certain Church practices. After Henry was granted a divorce by the Anglican Church, he married a young English woman, *Anne Boleyn*. Their daughter later became Queen Elizabeth I. During Elizabeth's reign (1558–1603), Anglicanism became firmly entrenched as the English religion.

## THE CATHOLIC REFORMATION, OR COUNTER-REFORMATION

To defend itself against the Protestant movement, the Catholic Church took a number of actions known as the *Catholic Reformation*, or *Counter-Reformation*.

1. **Effective Leadership.** A succession of capable, energetic popes provided strong leadership for Church reform. From all the clergy they demanded devotion to duty and the highest religious standards.

2. **The Council of Trent (1545–1563).** This Church council *(a)* reaffirmed basic Catholic doctrines such as papal supremacy and exclusive Church authority to interpret the Bible; *(b)* prohibited Church abuses—nepotism, simony, and sale of indulgences; *(c)* required the clergy to renounce worldly pleasures; and *(d)* authorized an *Index*, a list of heretical books forbidden to Catholics.

3. **The Holy Inquisition.** These Church courts (see page 82) vigorously combated heretics. In Italy and Spain the Inquisition helped stop the spread of Protestantism.

4. **The Society of Jesus.** This monastic order was founded in 1534 by *Ignatius Loyola*. Known as the *Jesuits*, the members became the leading spiritual soldiers fighting Protestantism. By serving as priests and teachers, they helped preserve Catholicism in Poland, southern Germany, and Belgium. They also won new converts in India, China, Japan, and North America.

## RESULTS OF THE REFORMATION

### 1. Immediate Effects

*a. End of Religious Unity.* The religious unity of western Europe had been destroyed. Henceforth, Europe was divided according to religion, as follows:

(1) Predominantly *Catholic* were Italy, Spain, Portugal, France, Belgium, Ireland, southern Germany, Austria, Poland, and Hungary.

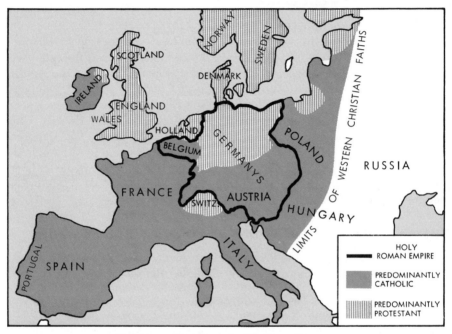

**Religious Divisions in Western Europe**

(2) Predominantly *Protestant* were England, Scotland, Wales, Holland, northern Germany, Switzerland, Denmark, Norway, and Sweden.

The Protestant world at first consisted of the Lutheran, Calvinist, and Anglican denominations. Later there arose other Protestant sects such as Methodists and Baptists.

*b. Religious Wars.* In the 16th and 17th centuries, Europe endured a series of wars, caused partly by religious differences.

(1) *Civil Wars in Germany.* Catholic and Lutheran rulers in Germany fought several civil wars. The *Peace of Augsburg* (1555) provided a compromise permitting German rulers to choose for themselves and their people either Catholicism or Lutheranism.

(2) *Dutch War Against Spain.* The Protestant Dutch revolted against their

Catholic ruler, *Philip II* of Spain, after he ruthlessly tried to suppress Protestantism in Holland. Led by *William of Orange,* the Dutch drove out the Spanish forces and in 1581 declared their political and religious independence. In 1648, after more fighting, Spain recognized Dutch independence.

(3) *Spanish Naval War Against England.* Philip II of Spain desired to *(a)* safeguard Spanish merchant ships and New World colonies against English raids, *(b)* depose Elizabeth I, the Protestant queen of England, and *(c)* restore Catholicism in England. To invade England, he organized a huge war fleet, the *Spanish Armada.* In 1588 the Armada was sighted off the English coast and destroyed by the English navy. Philip's plans were ruined.

(4) *Civil Wars in France.* Protestant and Catholic claimants to the French throne engaged in a series of civil wars. In 1589 *Henry of Navarre,* a Protestant, became King *Henry IV.* Seeking to end religious strife, he *(a)* adopted Catholicism, the predominant French religion, and *(b)* issued the *Edict of Nantes* (1598) granting religious freedom to the Protestant minority, the Huguenots. (Henry IV was the first of the Bourbon family to rule in France.)

(5) *Thirty Years' War (1618–1648).* This war, the bloodiest of the period, originated as a religious struggle in central Europe between Protestant and Catholic rulers. The outstanding Protestant military leader was King *Gustavus Adolphus* of Sweden. The Catholics throughout the war were led by the *Hapsburg* rulers of Austria. In the final stage of the conflict, the Catholic *Bourbon* rulers of France opposed the Catholic Hapsburg rulers of Austria and Spain. The Bourbons, hoping to extend their power and gain land at Hapsburg expense, supported the Protestant cause.

Fought almost entirely in Germany and causing widespread economic ruin, the Thirty Years' War ended in 1648 with the *Treaty of Westphalia: (a)* Catholic France obtained most of Alsace. *(b)* Protestant Sweden acquired territory in northern Germany. *(c)* Calvinist as well as Lutheran and Catholic rulers in Germany gained the right to determine the religion of their people. *(d)* Holland and Switzerland, both Protestant, received recognition of their independence.

(*Hugo Grotius,* a Dutch scholar, was shocked by the behavior of nations in resorting to and callously prosecuting the Thirty Years' War. He wrote *Law of War and Peace,* a book considered the foundation of modern international law.)

*c. Strengthened Civil Authority.* The state gained power at the expense of the Church. In Protestant countries the governments (1) confiscated Catholic Church properties, (2) abolished Catholic Church courts, and (3) assumed control of the new Protestant churches. Even in Catholic countries civil rulers asserted some control over the Church, especially regarding the appointment of Church officials.

## 2. Long-Term Effects

*a. Encouragement of Education.* Protestantism, stressing individual Bible reading in a person's own language, encouraged widespread teaching of reading.

*b. A Step Toward Religious Tolerance.* West European people, torn by contending religious groups during much of the Reformation, experienced great intolerance. Later, as people realized that intolerance threatened their own as well as other faiths, governments permitted some religious diversity. Catholic France granted a degree of toleration to Protestants in the Edict of Nantes (1598); Anglican England extended religious freedom to most other Protestants in the *Toleration Act* (1689). However, these measures were only a first step toward complete religious tolerance.

## RECENT RELIGIOUS TRENDS RELEVANT TO THE REFORMATION ERA

**1. In Western Europe.** The people of western Europe continue to reflect the religious diversity that grew out of the Reformation Era.

In England the people are mainly Anglican, and the Anglican Church of England holds a special position as the official, or established, religion. Because Anglicanism is the state church, the British ruler must be Anglican and the crown—upon advice of the prime minister—appoints the archbishops and other major church officials. The Anglican Church, however, secures funds for its activities from its own members and receives no direct payments from the government.

Other countries in northwestern Europe also maintain state churches, which reflect the religious preference of the greatest number of their peoples. In Scotland the Presbyterian Church is the official church; in the Scandinavian countries—Denmark, Norway, and Sweden—the Lutheran Church is the state church. The relationship of these state churches to their respective governments is similar to that of the Anglican Church and the British government.

In Spain, Portugal, France, and Italy, the people remain predominantly Roman Catholic. Only in Spain and Italy, however, does the Catholic Church hold a special position. In Spain the Catholic Church is the state religion and receives state funds for its support; in Italy the Catholic Church receives state subsidies, and its doctrines are required teaching in state-supported schools. This may change if a 1976 agreement between the Vatican and the Italian government is approved by the Italian parliament.

In the other nations of western Europe, the people continue to reflect the religious diversity that grew out of the Reformation Era. But most of these nations have no established church.

Throughout western Europe, regardless of whether or not a nation has an established church, all peoples are guaranteed full religious freedom.

**2. In the United States.** Because almost 90 percent of the American people trace their origins back to Europe, the United States reflects great religious diversity. Some differences mirror the split between the Eastern Orthodox and Roman Catholic churches and some the split growing out of the Reformation Era. In 1976, when the American population numbered over 215 million, about 133 million Americans had a formal religious affiliation. The largest religious groups represented were: various Protestant sects—73 million; Roman Catholics—49 million; Jews—over 6 million, and Eastern Orthodox—5 million. Of the Protestant sects in the United States, the largest were, in descending order, Baptists, Methodists, Lutherans, and Presbyterians.

By the First Amendment to the Constitution, the United States guarantees all Americans freedom of religion and complete separation of Church and State.

**3. Interfaith Cooperation: Ecumenism.** In the mid-20th century, the three major Western religions—Protestantism, Catholicism, and Judaism—made efforts to achieve understanding and cooperation. These efforts grew out of the need to strengthen the role of religion in the modern world and were spurred by the attacks against religion by Communist nations and by bigotry in the 1930's and 1940's against Jews and devout Christians in Nazi Germany.

The *National Conference of Christians and Jews,* founded in 1928 in the United States, combats religious prejudice and seeks to improve intergroup relations. It sponsors observance of an annual *Brotherhood Week.* The *World Council of Churches,* founded in 1948 in Holland, consists of some 200 Protestant and Eastern Orthodox churches of 80 countries with a total membership of 300 million people. The World Council of Churches furthers cooperation among its member churches, assesses Christian responsibility in international matters, and aids world refugees. The *National Council of Churches,* founded in 1950 in the United States, consists of over 30 Protestant and Eastern Orthodox churches with a membership of over 40 million Americans. The National Council of Churches seeks religious and social cooperation by its affiliated churches.

In 1962 Pope John XXIII convened the *Second Vatican Council.* Its work strongly influenced the Catholic Church toward *ecumenism*—the movement toward Christian unity through dialogue, understanding, and cooperation between Catholics and non-Catholics. The council approved the following significant points: (*a*) the right of all individuals to religious liberty and freedom, (*b*) use of the term "separated brethren," not heretics, in referring to Protestants, (*c*) condemnation of anti-Semitism—an illogical mind-set of prejudice and discrimination against Jews as a group—and reform of Catholic rituals and writings that could give rise to anti-Semitism, (*d*) use of the vernacular language in place of Latin for major portions of the Catholic service, and (*e*) future intergroup discussions to promote Christian cooperation and unity.

**4. The Judeo-Christian Heritage.** While not overlooking doctrinal differences that divide them, religious leaders of the three major Western faiths (Catholic, Protestant, Jewish) have stressed their unifying Judeo-Christian heritage: beliefs that a single God is Father of all human beings who therefore are brothers and sisters; that each individual is a person of worth, entitled to respect and dignity; that relations among persons should be guided by ethical conduct—*negatively,* not to steal and not to lie—*positively,* to honor parents, to give charity, and to provide social justice, especially for the widow, the orphan, and the oppressed; that all persons should observe the *Golden Rule,* "Do unto others as you would have others do unto you"; and finally that a better world can be achieved, and worthy persons will be rewarded in this world or in the afterlife. To implement this Judeo-Christian heritage, many religious leaders have expressed concern and taken action regarding vital social problems—minority civil rights, discrimination, and poverty.

## COMPLETION QUESTIONS

1. The Bohemian (Czech) religious reformer who was tried as a heretic and burned at the stake was _____ .
2. The German religious reformer who started the Reformation by posting his *Ninety-five Theses* on the church door at Wittenberg was _____ .
3. The founder of the Jesuit order and a leading defender of Catholicism was _____ .
4. The English king who broke with Rome and established Anglicanism was _____ .
5. The French religious reformer who fled to Switzerland and wrote the *Institutes of the Christian Religion* was _____ .

## MULTIPLE–CHOICE QUESTIONS

1. The Protestant Reformation was (1) delayed by the questioning attitude engendered by the Renaissance (2) a complete surprise to Catholic leaders (3) supported by many rulers who desired Church properties (4) hastened by the election of an Englishman as pope.
2. The authority of the Catholic Church was strengthened by (1) the Great Schism (2) the Babylonian Captivity (3) simony (4) the Council of Trent.
3. Nepotism meant (1) filling Church positions with relatives (2) filling Church positions by means of competitive examinations (3) failing to live the spiritual and humble life required of Church officials (4) selling Church positions.
4. The *immediate* reason for Luther's protest against the Catholic Church was (1) simony (2) the sale of indulgences (3) the papal refusal to permit Luther to marry (4) German nationalism.
5. Luther and Wycliffe both (1) lived at the same time (2) were German (3) won immediate success as religious reformers (4) translated the Bible into the vernacular.
6. Calvinism was brought to the New World by the (1) English Puritans in Massachusetts (2) French in Canada (3) Swedes in Delaware (4) Spanish in Mexico.
7. Most effective in stopping Protestantism in Italy and Spain was the (1) *Index* (2) Holy Inquisition (3) work of Erasmus (4) work of John Knox.
8. The Protestant Reformation made its greatest gains in which one of the following countries? (1) Germany (2) Spain (3) France (4) Austria.
9. In which country did Protestantism attract the *fewest* followers? (1) England (2) Holland (3) Italy (4) Sweden.
10. The Thirty Years' War was fought almost entirely in (1) Italy (2) England (3) Germany (4) Spain.
11. By the Edict of Nantes, France granted religious toleration to the (1) Huguenots (2) Catholics (3) Moslems (4) Jews.
12. The Treaty of Westphalia in 1648 indicated that in western Europe (1) Catholicism

was victorious    (2) Lutheranism was victorious    (3) religious unity had ended    (4) a Bourbon-Hapsburg alliance had been formed.

13. Which statement about the Protestant Reformation is true?    (1) It sought to reestablish the Holy Roman Empire.    (2) It encouraged the rise of national states. (3) It remained confined to Germany for 200 years.    (4) It brought religious unity to German states.

14. The Reformation    (1) weakened civil authority    (2) prevented the growth of religious tolerance    (3) encouraged the movement for popular education    (4) prevented Catholicism from spreading outside of Europe.

15. The term *ecumenism* refers to a movement to    (1) establish more parochial schools    (2) achieve better understanding between Catholics and non-Catholics    (3) prohibit interfaith cooperation    (4) involve religious leaders in politics.

16. Which *best* describes the major religions in the United States today?    (1) They are supported by government funds.    (2) They have less than half of the population as formally affiliated members.    (3) They have some basic beliefs in common.    (4) They remain apart from national and international politics.

## FACT–OPINION QUESTIONS

Some of the statements below are matters of fact and others are expressions of opinion. Write the word *yes* if the statement is based on fact and is true; the word *no* if the statement is contrary to fact and therefore not true; or the letter *O* if the statement is a matter of opinion which may be either true or untrue.

1. The Renaissance spirit was the chief cause that brought on the Reformation.
2. Wycliffe's followers were known as Lollards.
3. The Reformation resulted in Christian diversity in western Europe.
4. During the Great Schism rival popes resided at Jerusalem and Rome.
5. John Huss was a contemporary of Martin Luther.
6. The *Index* was a list of books that Catholics were permitted to read in Latin only.
7. Philip II of Spain was unwise in attempting to conquer Protestant England.

## ESSAY QUESTIONS

1. (a) Discuss *two* causes of the Reformation. (b) Discuss *two* methods used by the Catholic Church in its Counter-Reformation. (c) Discuss *one* immediate and *one* long-range result of the Reformation.

2. Describe *one* important contribution to the movement for religious reform made by each of the following men: (a) John Wycliffe (b) Johann Gutenberg (c) Charles V (d) John Knox (e) Ignatius Loyola (f) Desiderius Erasmus.

3. Explain *one* way in which each of the following men influenced the Reformation: (a) Luther (b) Calvin (c) Henry VIII (c) Philip II (e) Gustavus Adolphus.

4. Describe *one* effect of the Reformation on each of these countries: (a) France (b) Holland (c) England (d) Germany (e) Spain (f) the United States.

5. The Reformation Era refers to the developments between 1517—the posting of Luther's Ninety-five Theses—and 1648—the end of the Thirty Years' War. Prove that the Reformation Era has influenced today's world by discussing (a) *two* ways in which it has affected your own life (b) *one* reason why it has led to the ecumenical movement and (c) *one* reason why it has led to current emphasis upon our Judeo-Christian heritage.

# Part 3. The Rise of Absolute Monarchs and National States

## RISE OF THE ABSOLUTE MONARCH

**1. From Weak Medieval King to Absolute Monarch.** During the Middle Ages most rulers were men. They were weak kings, exercising little power over feudal lords and usually ruling only the royal domain, the lands belonging to the royal family.

Near the end of the Middle Ages, the king—particularly in England, France, Spain, Russia, Prussia, and Austria—began to extend his rule at the expense of the nobles. By the 17th century the king had become an *autocrat,* or *absolute monarch.* His supremacy was acknowledged by commoners and lords. (In England, however, only the Tudor monarchs approached absolutism. See page 146.)

**2. Factors Strengthening Royal Power.** *(a)* The Crusades and other wars killed many feudal lords. *(b)* The rising middle class supported the monarch to assure protection of property and trade. *(c)* The introduction of gunpowder equipped the monarch with a powerful weapon that could destroy castles of feudal lords. *(d)* The Reformation provided the monarch with some powers formerly held by the Catholic Church. *(e)* The awakening spirit of nationalism made the monarch the symbol of national unity.

**3. "Divine Right of Kings."** This theory attempted to justify unlimited royal power with these arguments: *(a)* The king ruled by God's authority as God's earthly representative. *(b)* Obedience to the king was obedience to God. *(c)* The king could do no wrong.

The divine right concept contrasts with our democratic belief that those who govern derive their authority from the people.

## BEGINNING OF THE NATIONAL STATE

The independent *national state,* or *nation-state,* familiar to us today, arose when a strong ruler expanded control from the limited royal domain to a larger area. Eventually the monarch ruled a nation free from external political or religious control.

In England, France, and Spain, the monarch united people of a common *nationality*—those sharing similar language, history, and customs. Gradually the people transferred their loyalty from local lord and province to monarch and nation. Thus, in these countries, strong monarchs molded unified national states.

In Russia, Prussia, and Austria, however, the monarch ruled diverse nationalities, though one predominated. Even though these monarchs established powerful states, their peoples did not all develop a feeling of national unity.

## DEVELOPMENTS IN ENGLAND: STRONG MONARCHS AND WORLD POWER

**1. Early History.** *(a)* By the 6th century B.C., England was inhabited by the *Celts.* *(b)* From the 1st to the 5th centuries A.D., England was ruled by the *Romans.* *(c)* In the 5th century England was settled by various Germanic peoples, the *Jutes, Angles,* and *Saxons.* *(d)* In the 9th century England was settled by people from the North, the *Danes.* *(e)* In the 11th century England was invaded by the *Normans* who came from Normandy, a northern province in France. Led by William the Conqueror, the Normans were the last people to invade England successfully.

Over the course of years, these many peoples assimilated (blended together) through *(a)* intermarriage, *(b)* the creation of the English language (a mixture of Anglo-Saxon and Norman-French), and *(c)* the development of common laws, traditions, customs, and ideas. Thus, they slowly evolved an English nationality. (A similar blending process occurred in most other European nations.)

## 2. William the Conqueror (Ruled 1066–1087)

*a. Becomes King of England.* William, Duke of Normandy in northern France, claimed the English throne. His claim was opposed by the English Saxon nobles who supported their lord, *Harold.* In 1066 William led his army across the English Channel and defeated the Saxons at the *Battle of Hastings.* Shortly afterward he was crowned king in Westminster Abbey.

*b. Strengthens Royal Power.* (1) *Domesday Book.* William ordered a survey of England's landed property and other wealth. He used this information, recorded in the *Domesday Book,* for levying and collecting taxes. (2) *Salisbury Oath.* William compelled all feudal lords—from highest vassals to lowest knights—to pledge him direct allegiance and military service. Previously English monarchs had received such direct pledges only from their top vassals.

**3. Early Norman Kings.** William's successors likewise strengthened the central government. Gradually they assumed national powers: making and enforcing laws, establishing royal courts, and controlling foreign affairs.

## 4. Hundred Years' War (1337–1453)

*a. Causes.* The Norman kings of England were feudal lords over much French territory, which the French rulers coveted. Futhermore, Edward III of

England claimed the French throne. War began when French forces advanced into English landholdings and King Edward invaded France. The resulting long but intermittent struggle was called the *Hundred Years' War*.

*b. Military Highlights.* English forces invaded France and won notable battles at *Crécy* (1346), *Poitiers* (1356), and *Agincourt* (1415). Late in the war, however, the English lost their military advantage. They met final defeat when the French armies, inspired by Joan of Arc (see page 147), ended the English siege of the city of Orléans and drove the enemy from France. By 1453 the English retained in France only the port of Calais.

*c. Effect on England.* The Hundred Years' War spurred English national patriotism. (1) The English took pride in their notable victories. (2) They were compelled by the loss of their French territory to devote their energies solely to England.

## 5. Wars of the Roses (1455–1485)

*a. Cause.* These civil wars resulted from conflicting claims to the English throne by two families of nobles, the House of *York* (whose badge was a white rose) and the House of *Lancaster* (whose badge was a red rose). After 30 years of bitter strife, *Henry Tudor*, related to the Lancastrians and later, shrewdly, to marry Elizabeth of York, was crowned King *Henry VII*.

*b. Results.* The Wars of the Roses furthered a powerful monarchy in England. (1) Many nobles died in the war, thus removing rivals for royal power. (2) The crown increased its wealth by confiscating properties of deceased nobles who had been hostile. (3) The middle class, having suffered wartime disruption of trade, rallied to Tudor support. (4) The victorious Tudor family provided England with strong, capable rulers.

## 6. Tudor Rule (1485–1603)

*a. Henry VII* (ruled 1485–1509) reestablished the monarch's authority over the nobles, and furthered trade and prosperity.

*b. Henry VIII* (ruled 1509–1547) replaced the Catholic Church with the Anglican Church controlled by the crown (see page 137).

*c. Elizabeth I* (ruled 1558–1603) preserved Protestantism in England and achieved world power for England by humbling Catholic Spain. Elizabeth (1) aided the Dutch revolt against Spain, (2) encouraged such sea captains as *Drake* and *Hawkins* to raid Spanish merchant ships and New World colonies, and (3) organized a navy that defeated the Spanish Armada.

*d. Summary of Tudor Rule.* (1) Tudor rulers expanded central governmental authority and ruled as almost absolute monarchs. Although Parliament held sessions, it was effectively dominated by the Tudors. (2) They furthered economic prosperity and transformed England into a leading world power. (3) They aroused nationalism. (4) They enjoyed immense popularity.

7. **Beginning of Stuart Rule (1603).** James Stuart, king of Scotland and distant cousin to Elizabeth, became King *James I* of England. He and his descendants, the *Stuart* rulers, proved unpopular. Eventually the people rebelled (see pages 169-171).

## DEVELOPMENTS IN FRANCE: ABSOLUTISM AND WORLD POWER

1. **Early History.** *(a)* By the 7th century B.C., France was inhabited by the *Gauls*. *(b)* In 58–50 B.C. France was conquered by the Romans under *Julius Caesar*. *(c)* Until the 5th century A.D., France was ruled by the *Romans*. *(d)* In the 5th century France was settled by Germanic tribes, notably *Burgundians* and *Franks*. *(e)* In the 9th and 10th centuries, northwestern France was invaded and settled by groups of *Norse* searfarers whose territory became known as Normandy. *(f)* From the 8th to 10th centuries, France was ruled by Pepin, Charlemagne, and their descendants, the *Carolingian* family.

2. **Capetian Rule (10th–14th Centuries)**

   *a. Hugh Capet Becomes King.* In 987 Hugh Capet, a French lord, was elected to the throne. Since he controlled only his feudal domain around Paris, his authority elsewhere in France was negated by powerful feudal nobles.

   *b. Capetian Kings Extend Governmental Power.* The Capetian kings struggled to weaken the nobles, expand royal territories, and build a strong central government. The outstanding Capetian kings were (1) *Philip Augustus* (ruled 1180–1223), who seized Normandy and other provinces from their feudal lord, King John of England, and (2) *Philip the Fair* (ruled 1285–1314), who taxed the clergy and forced the Catholic Church into the "Babylonian Captivity" (see pages 134–135).

3. **Hundred Years' War (1337–1453)**

   *a. Joan of Arc Saves France.* In 1429 Joan of Arc, a teenaged peasant from Lorraine, declared that divine voices had directed her to save France from English conquest. From King Charles VII Joan demanded and received command of an army. Her faith and courage inspired the French soldiers. They (1) immediately ended the English siege of the city of Orléans and (2) eventually drove the English from France. Meanwhile, Joan was captured by the English. In 1431 she was condemned as a witch by a clerical court and burned at the stake. (In 1456 another clerical court reversed the decision against Joan, and in the early 20th century, the papacy declared her a saint.)

   *b. Effect on France.* The war (1) *spurred nationalism* by giving the French people a national heroine and a great military triumph and (2) *strengthened royal power* by killing many nobles and enriching the crown with the former English territories. (For a fuller discussion of the Hundred Years' War, see pages 145–146.)

4. **Consolidation of Centralized Power (Late 15th Century).** After the Hundred Years' War, French kings sought to increase their power. *Louis XI* (ruled

1461–1483), the most successful of these monarchs, curbed feudal anarchy, set up efficient central government, and is often considered to be the architect of French absolute monarchy.

**5. Religious Civil Wars (16th Century).** These civil wars were caused by opposing Catholic and Protestant claims to the throne. The conflict ended in 1589 when *Henry of Navarre* became King *Henry IV*. He ended the religious conflict (see page 139), worked to restore central authority, and successfully maintained power.

For 200 years France was ruled by Henry and his descendants, the *Bourbon* family.

**6. Cardinal Richelieu Guides France (1624–1642).** *Richelieu*, a cardinal of the Church and minister to King *Louis XIII*, skillfully directed French affairs to attain supremacy for the king and world power for France.

*a. Supremacy for the King.* Richelieu (1) destroyed the nobles' fortified castles, (2) transferred local governmental functions from the nobles to royal officials, the *intendants*, and (3) levied taxes without consent of the French lawmaking body, the *Estates-General.*

*b. World Power for France.* Richelieu led France into the Thirty Years' War in support of the Protestant cause. France defeated its Catholic Hapsburg rivals, who ruled Austria and Spain (see page 139).

**7. Louis XIV: The Grand Monarch (Ruled 1643–1715)**

*a. The Absolute Monarch.* Louis XIV represented the height of absolutism. Proclaiming that he ruled by divine right, Louis considered himself the *Sun King*. Near Paris he built the magnificent *Palace of Versailles*, where he maintained an extravagant court. At Versailles the nobles fawningly waited upon him and courted his favor. Louis exercised unlimited political powers. Not once during his long reign did he convene the Estates-General. To illustrate his attitude, tradition ascribes to Louis the statement, "L'état, c'est moi," meaning "I am the state."

*b. Economic Affairs.* Louis entrusted economic matters to his able finance minister, *Jean Baptiste Colbert*. To further prosperity, Colbert promoted good farming methods, built roads and canals, protected existing industries with tariffs, aided new industries with subsidies, and helped establish French trading posts in India and colonies in North America.

In 1685, to compel Catholic religious uniformity, Louis revoked the Edict of Nantes. This action damaged the economy because thousands of Protestant Huguenots (mostly skilled workers and enterprising business people) fled France. Many settled in England, Holland, and America.

*c. Foreign Affairs.* Louis pursued an ambitious, aggressive foreign policy. He sought for France its "natural boundaries," especially the Rhine River.

Fighting three major wars, he acquired some territory but failed to achieve the Rhine boundary. In a fourth major war, Louis lost some overseas possessions but placed a Bourbon relative on the Spanish throne.

At Louis XIV's death France was the leading nation on the European continent. But the French people had wearied of wars, taxes, and despotism. Louis XVI, a descendant of the Grand Monarch, was to experience the people's extreme reaction in the 1789 French Revolution (see pages 181–190).

**Territory Gained by Louis XIV**

## DEVELOPMENTS IN SPAIN: ABSOLUTISM AND WORLD POWER, THEN DECLINE

**1. Early History.** (a) Since prehistoric times Spain was inhabited by the *Iberians*. (b) To the 3rd century B.C., Spain was colonized by *Phoenicians, Greeks,* and *Carthaginians.* (c) In 201 B.C. Spain was annexed by Rome. (d) For over 600 years Spain was ruled by the *Romans.* (e) In the 5th century A.D., Spain was settled by Germanic tribes, the *Visigoths.* (f) In the 8th century Spain was invaded by North African Moslems called *Moors.*

After the Moorish invasion, the Iberian Peninsula was divided into a number of Moslem states and Christian kingdoms.

**2. Unification of Spain (11th to 15th Centuries).** The Christian kingdoms warred intermittently against the Moslems and slowly expanded Christian rule in Spain. In 1469 *Ferdinand* of Aragon married *Isabella* of Castile, thus uniting Christian Spain. In 1492 their armies finally conquered Granada, the last Moorish stronghold, thereby ending Moorish rule in Spain.

### 3. Ferdinand and Isabella Rule a United Spain

*a. Absolutism.* Ferdinand and Isabella increased royal power considerably. They weakened (1) the *nobility* by destroying the nobles' fortified castles, (2) the *Catholic Church* by gaining the right to nominate important Church officials, and (3) the *Cortes*, the Spanish legislature, by enacting laws without its approval.

*b. Religious Unity.* Hoping to promote Catholicism, Ferdinand and Isabella persecuted Jews and Moslems, and eventually expelled them from Spain. Spain thus lost energetic merchants and skilled workers.

*c. Foreign Affairs.* Ferdinand and Isabella laid the foundation for Spain's brief period of world power. (1) They financed Columbus' expedition that reached the New World, and they encouraged further exploration. Spain acquired a large New World colonial empire with great wealth in silver and gold. (2) For their three daughters they arranged political marriages to strong allies. The most important marital alliance, Joanna to Philip of Hapsburg, produced an heir who became *Charles V.*

### 4. Reign of Charles V (1519–1556)

*a. Rules an Empire.* Charles of Hapsburg, absolute monarch of Spain and leading ruler of Europe, controlled not only Spain and its colonial empire but also the Netherlands, Sicily, southern Italy, Austria, and other lands in central Europe. In 1520 he became Holy Roman Emperor.

*b. Dominates European Affairs.* To defend his domains, Charles repeatedly fought the French, the Moslem Turks, and the Protestant Germans. A devout Catholic, he most regretted his failure to halt Protestantism in Germany. In 1556 a weary Charles renounced his throne to withdraw into a monastery. His brother Ferdinand became ruler of Austria and Holy Roman Emperor. Charles' son became King *Philip II* of Spain.

### 5. Reign of Philip II (1556–1598): Spanish Power Declines. Philip hastened Spain's military and economic decline. In foreign affairs he expended military power and money but (*a*) was unable to suppress the Protestant Dutch revolt, (*b*) could not halt English raids on Spanish merchant ships and colonies, and (*c*) failed to conquer England with the Spanish Armada (1588).

In Spain Philip's autocratic rule produced inefficient government, a crushing tax burden, and a stagnant economy. His reign began Spain's decline in world prestige and power.

## DEVELOPMENTS IN RUSSIA: ABSOLUTISM AND TERRITORIAL EXPANSION

**1. Early History.** (*a*) By the 8th century A.D., Russia was inhabited by the *Slavs.* (*b*) In the 9th century Russia was settled by the *Norse.* (*c*) In the 10th century Russia was influenced by Byzantine culture and its people converted to *Eastern Orthodox Christianity.* (*d*) In the 13th century Russia was conquered by Asian warriors, the *Mongols,* or *Tartars.* *(e)* For over 200 years Russia was controlled by the Mongols, who introduced Asian ways of living.

**2. Moscow Leads Russia (15th and 16th Centuries).** *Ivan the Great* (ruled 1462–1505), Slavic Grand Duke of Moscow, ended Mongol domination of his dukedom. Thereafter, he struggled to extend his territories, subdue the nobles, and attain absolute power. So too did his grandson, *Ivan the Terrible* (ruled 1533–1584), who often employed great cruelty. Ivan the Terrible was the first ruler to assume the title "Czar and autocrat of all Russia."

After Ivan the Terrible died, Russia endured foreign invasions and civil wars, as the nobles fought for control of the throne. In 1613 an assembly of nobles chose a new czar, *Michael Romanov.* For over 300 years, the Romanov family ruled Russia.

**3. Reign of Peter the Great (1682–1725)**

*a. Furthers Autocracy.* *Peter,* the outstanding Romanov ruler, strengthened absolutism by (1) creating a strong army loyal to him, (2) ruthlessly crushing a revolt of the nobles, (3) appointing royal governors to replace local officials, and (4) extending government control over the Russian Orthodox Church.

*b. Tries to Westernize Russia.* Peter wanted to model Russia after European culture, rather than Byzantine or Asian culture. Having traveled through western Europe, he greatly admired its civilization. He introduced into Russia Western ideas on science, education, military training, and industry. To imitate Western social customs, Peter ordered his male subjects to shave their long beards and discard their Oriental garments. But Peter's westernization efforts made little lasting impression on the Russian masses.

*c. Gains a Seaport.* Peter sought "windows" (seaports) to provide his land-locked country with water routes for trade with western Europe. In a long war against Sweden, he won territories adjoining the Baltic Sea. Here he built his new seaport and capital, *St. Petersburg* (now Leningrad).

**4. Reign of Catherine the Great (1762–1796): Russia Gains More Territory.** *Catherine the Great,* the German wife of a Russian czar, deposed her husband and ruled Russia as an autocrat. She extended Russia's boundaries southward and westward.

*a. Southward.* Warring against the Turks, Catherine gained (1) the northern coast of the Black Sea and (2) the right of Russian ships to sail from the Black Sea into the Mediterranean Sea via the Turkish-controlled Dardanelles.

*b. Westward.* Catherine joined with Austria and Prussia in three partitions that completely eliminated independent *Poland.* (See map, page 153.)

Catherine, building on Peter's accomplishments, ruled an empire consisting of Slavic peoples—Russians, Ukrainians, and Poles, as well as Baltic and Asian peoples. She made 18th-century Russia into a major European power.

## DEVELOPMENTS IN PRUSSIA: ABSOLUTISM AND TERRITORIAL EXPANSION

**1. Early Hohenzollern Rule (15th to 18th Centuries).** The *Hohenzollerns,* a family of German nobles from Brandenburg (the Berlin area), acquired Prussia, a land inhabited by Slavs and Germans. The early Hohenzollern rulers *(a)* established autocratic government, *(b)* created a well-trained army, and *(c)* by war, marriage, and diplomacy, expanded their territory.

For 500 years the Hohenzollern family ruled Prussia; in 1871, when Prussia unified the German states, the Hohenzollern king of Prussia became emperor of Germany.

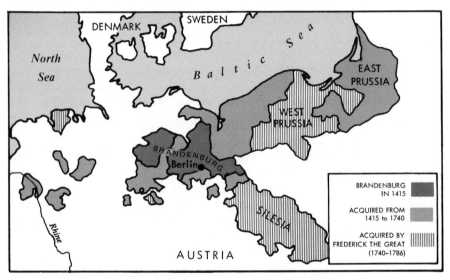

**The Growth of Hohenzollern Domains**

**2. Reign of Frederick the Great (1740–1786): Prussia Gains Territory.** *Frederick the Great,* the most famous Hohenzollern absolute monarch and a military genius, pursued an aggressive foreign policy. In 1740 he seized from Austria the province of Silesia. His action culminated in a major European conflict, the *Seven Years' War* (1756–1763), in which he was pitted against a powerful European coalition of Austria, Russia, and France. Frederick, aided only by England, barely managed to retain Silesia. In 1772 Frederick shared in the first partition of Poland by annexing western Poland.

Frederick thus converted 18th-century Prussia into an important European power.

## DEVELOPMENTS IN AUSTRIA: ABSOLUTISM AND VAST EMPIRE

**1. The Hapsburgs Acquire Austria (13th Century).** The *Hapsburgs* originated as lesser feudal lords with minor territories in Alsace, Switzerland, and southern

Germany. In 1273 *Rudolf I* of Hapsburg became Holy Roman Emperor and, soon afterwards, ruler of Austria. Rudolf laid the foundation for future Hapsburg power. For over 600 years his descendants governed Austria; moreover, with few exceptions, they headed the Holy Roman Empire until its end (1806).

## 2. Highlights of Hapsburg Rule (13th–18th Centuries)

*a. Reverses.* Hapsburg rulers proved unable (1) in the late 15th century to prevent their Swiss subjects from winning virtual independence, (2) in the 16th century to halt the Protestant movement in Germany, and (3) in the 17th century to defeat France in the Thirty Years' War (see page 139).

*b. Achievements.* Despite such setbacks, strong Hapsburg monarchs greatly expanded the family domains. Their methods emphasized political marriages, territorial inheritance, and alliances. In the late 17th century, Hapsburg forces, aided by other Christian troops, ended the Turkish siege of Vienna and drove the Moslems from central Europe.

By the 18th century the Hapsburg rulers exercised absolute power over a vast Austrian Empire of many nationalities: Austrians, Germans, Hungarians, Belgians, Czechs, Poles, Rumanians, Serbs, Slovenes, and Italians.

## 3. Leading Hapsburg Rulers in Austria (18th Century)

*a. Maria Theresa (Ruled 1740–1780).* As prescribed by Charles VI's will, Maria Theresa, his daughter, secured the Austrian throne. Despite the *Pragmatic Sanction,* a document in which most European rulers agreed to guarantee her inheritance, Maria Theresa endured numerous attacks. Eventually she lost Silesia to Prussia but gained part of Poland. A conscientious ruler, Maria Theresa sought to govern efficiently and promote prosperity.

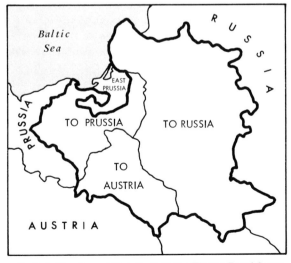

**Polish Territory Distributed by Three Partitions
(1772, 1793, 1795)**

*b. Joseph II (Ruled 1780–1790).* The eldest son of Maria Theresa, Joseph II acted to increase royal authority. He (1) subjected the Catholic Church to state control and seized Church lands, (2) weakened the nobles by taxing them and by canceling many obligations of their serfs, and (3) abolished local self-government. Joseph's policies aroused intense opposition and were later revoked. (For his reforms as an "enlightened despot," see below.)

## ABSOLUTE MONARCHY: A SUMMARY

1. **Achievements.** Absolute monarchs *(a)* weakened the forces tending to disunite a country, *(b)* provided strong central government, and *(c)* generally furthered the growth of national states.

2. **Weaknesses.** Absolute monarchs *(a)* made a nation's welfare depend on the ability of one person, *(b)* often sacrificed the national well-being for the autocrat's personal wishes or dynastic (family) interests, *(c)* led their nations into countless costly wars, and *(d)* disregarded the needs and rights of the common people.

3. **Absolutism Attacked by Intellectuals.** Absolute monarchy was attacked by certain 18th-century philosophers who advocated ideas typical of the *Intellectual Revolution*–also called the *Enlightenment,* or the *Age of Reason.* According to these writers, autocracy *(a)* stemmed from a tradition of brute force that violated all reason, *(b)* perpetuated despotic government, legal and social inequality, serfdom, ignorance, and religious intolerance, and *(c)* prevented progress.

4. **Enlightened or Benevolent Despots.** Influenced by these intellectuals, certain rulers tried to justify their absolutism by claiming to govern in the people's interest. Called *enlightened* or *benevolent despots,* these monarchs introduced various reforms.

*a. Frederick the Great of Prussia* supported literature, music, and science, furthered new agricultural methods, ordered equal legal treatment for all persons, promoted education, and granted religious freedom. Frederick's reforms were largely undone by his successors.

*b. Catherine the Great of Russia* fostered art, literature, and science, permitted greater local self-government, and encouraged legal reforms. Her reforms, however, proved to be of little value to most Russians.

*c. Joseph II of Austria,* the most sincere enlightened despot, improved the conditions of the serfs, expanded educational facilities, attempted to make all persons equal before the law, and advanced religious toleration. Few of his reforms survived his reign.

5. **Failure of Enlightened Despotism.** Enlightened despots did not curb resentment against absolute monarchy. They *(a)* did not remove the basic causes of discontent—autocracy, class distinctions, unfair taxation, and frequent wars—and *(b)* could not assure good government by their successors. In time many European peoples rebelled against royal absolutism.

## IDENTIFICATION QUESTIONS: WHO AM I?

| | | |
|---|---|---|
| Charles V | Joan of Arc | Peter the Great |
| Elizabeth I | Joseph II | Philip II |
| Frederick the Great | Louis XIV | Rudolf I |
| Henry VIII | Maria Theresa | William of Normandy |

1. I introduced Western ideas into Russia and, by war, secured a Baltic "window" for my country.

2. During my reign in England, my sea captains humbled Spanish naval power and established England's mastery of the seas.

3. In accordance with my father's will and the Pragmatic Sanction, I ascended the throne of Austria, but I had to defend my territories against attack.

4. Although a teenaged peasant, I inspired the French armies to victory at the siege of Orléans but later was captured by my enemies, condemned as a witch, and burned at the stake.

5. As ruler of Prussia and military genius, I was fond of war, yet sought to govern as a benevolent despot.

6. Originally a feudal lord in Alsace and southern Germany, I became Holy Roman Emperor. Later I acquired Austria as the base of future Hapsburg power.

7. Known as the Sun King, I built the Palace of Versailles and ruled France at a time of great splendor.

8. I crossed the English Channel from France in 1066 and took the throne of England by defeating the Saxon claimant.

9. Although King of Spain and Holy Roman Emperor, I was unable to halt the spread of Protestantism in Germany.

## MULTIPLE–CHOICE QUESTIONS

1. Which contributed to the rise of national states in western Europe?  (1) the rise of a feudal nobility  (2) the need for protection from barbarian invasions  (3) the acquiring of colonies in the New World  (4) the growth of the middle class.

2. The middle class believed that a strong king would  (1) protect life and property  (2) give the middle class the right to vote  (3) maintain local tariffs  (4) assure religious unity.

3. In 18th-century Europe autocratic rulers based their claim to rule on  (1) the consent of the Church  (2) the support of the nobility  (3) the theory of divine right  (4) the support of the middle class.

4. A result of the Norman conquest of England was the  (1) fusion of French and Anglo-Saxon customs  (2) beginning of the English navy  (3) loss of the English throne to Danish kings  (4) introduction of Christianity to England.

5. Which nations were rivals in the Hundred Years' War?  (1) England and Holland  (2) England and France  (3) France and Portugal  (4) France and Spain.

6. The great aim of Louis XIV was to  (1) preserve the balance of power in Europe  (2) annex the German states  (3) establish colonies throughout America  (4) acquire territories up to France's natural boundaries.

7. The Asian invaders who ruled in Russia from the 13th to the 15th centuries were the  (1) Mongols  (2) Chinese  (3) Turks  (4) Huns.

8. At the end of the 18th century, Poland was partitioned by Prussia, Russia, and  (1) Austria  (2) Belgium  (3) France  (4) Sweden.

9. Which royal family is correctly paired with the country it ruled?  (1) Prussia—Hapsburgs  (2) Spain—Tudors  (3) Russia—Romanovs  (4) England—Bourbons.

10. *Not* a legislative body was    (1) the Cortes    (2) the House of Lancaster    (3) the Estates-General    (4) Parliament.
11. The Wars of the Roses were struggles between    (1) noble families for the English throne    (2) noble families for the French throne    (3) England and Spain for overseas colonies    (4) Prussia and Austria over Silesia.
12. Joseph II of Austria was an outstanding    (1) military leader    (2) enlightened despot    (3) defender of the Catholic Church    (4) author who wrote the Pragmatic Sanction.
13. Writers of the Intellectual Revolution urged people to    (1) rely on faith    (2) obey their rulers without question    (3) retain feudal ways    (4) change society to conform to reason.
14. Enlightened despots during the 18th century    (1) gave their subjects a voice in the government    (2) used their absolute power to make some reforms    (3) united to defeat Louis XIV of France    (4) encouraged the Renaissance.

## ESSAY QUESTIONS

1. Decide whether each of the following statements is true or false. Give *one* fact for each to support your point of view: *(a)* The rule of Louis XIV marked the beginning of a long period of peace for France. *(b)* The French monarchy was less powerful at the end than at the beginning of the Hundred Years' War. *(c)* The use of gunpowder helped cause the decline of feudalism. *(d)* The reign of Queen Elizabeth I was an eventful period in the history of the English people. *(e)* Eighteenth-century Austria was a national state. *(f)* Middle-class support helped the rise of absolute monarchy in western Europe.
2. *(a)* Name *three* invaders who successfully established themselves in Britain. *(b)* Discuss *one* way in which *one* of these invaders influenced the life or the customs of the English people.
3. Discuss *one* influence of *each* of the following on the development of the French nation: *(a)* Philip Augustus *(b)* Henry of Navarre *(c)* Richelieu *(d)* Louis XIV *(e)* Joan of Arc.
4. *(a)* State *two* reasons why Spain under Charles V was the most important country in Europe. *(b)* Describe *two* causes of the later decline of Spain.
5. Before Peter the Great, Russia was more of an Asian than a European nation. *(a)* Give *one* argument to support this statement. *(b)* Discuss *two* ways by which Peter the Great tried to westernize Russia. *(c)* Name *one* territory he gained for Russia. *(d)* Explain *one* reason why Catherine the Great was interested in extending her empire to the Black Sea.
6. Frederick the Great was one of the ablest and one of the most unscrupulous rulers. Describe *one* way in which he was able and *one* way in which he was unscrupulous.
7. *(a)* Mention *three* benevolent despots of the 18th century. *(b)* Describe the work of *one* of these rulers. *(c)* Why were benevolent despots unable to improve conditions significantly for the common people?
8. *(a)* Describe *two* obstacles to world peace *today* that did not exist during the Age of Transition (14th to the 18th centuries). *(b)* Describe *two* obstacles to world peace during the Age of Transition that do not exist today. *(c)* Give *one* argument to show that the maintenance of world peace is more important today than during the Age of Transition.

# Part 4. European Expansion Overseas: The Commercial Revolution

## FACTORS ENCOURAGING OVERSEAS VOYAGES

Europeans during the Middle Ages had a meager knowledge of geography, limited to Europe, northern Africa, and western Asia. Beginning in the 15th century, west European nations—first Portugal and Spain, then England, Holland, and France—undertook expeditions to explore the Americas as well as new regions in Africa and the Far East. The main factors that encouraged these voyages were:

**1. Trade with the East.** Substantial trade between Europe and the East began during the Crusades (see page 95). This profitable business became the monopoly of (a) Asian traders who brought Far Eastern goods by overland caravan to Constantinople, Alexandria, and other east Mediterranean ports and (b) Italian merchants from Italian city-states—such as Venice, Genoa, and Pisa—who shipped the products from the eastern Mediterranean area to western Europe. In the 15th century the lucrative Eastern trade attracted the attention of two newly developed national states on the Atlantic coast, Portugal and Spain. To smash the monopoly of the Asian traders and the Italian city-state merchants, Portugal and Spain financed expeditions seeking an all-water route to the Far East.

**2. European Curiosity About the Far East.** Europeans were interested in the Far East because of (a) the reports of travelers to eastern Asia, particularly *Marco Polo,* a 13th-century Venetian who visited Cathay (China) and then wrote about his adventures and China's great riches, and (b) the Renaissance spirit of inquiry that sought information about the world's size, shape, and people and encouraged travel and exploration.

**3. Wealth and Ambitions of the New National States.** By the 16th century a number of west European nations possessed sufficient wealth to finance expensive voyages of exploration. Their rising middle classes desired increased trade, and their absolute monarchs sought colonial empires. These nations, therefore, were willing to risk capital and prestige in overseas voyages with the hope of reaping great rewards.

**4. Scientific Progress.** Because of scientific progress, European mariners faced fewer hazards in ocean travel. These advances included (a) Renaissance geographical knowledge, especially the realization that the earth is round, *not* flat, (b) improved maps, (c) a better compass for determining direction, and (d) the greater use of the astrolabe, an instrument for determining latitude.

157

## PORTUGAL IS THE FIRST TO REACH THE EAST BY WATER

Prince *Henry the Navigator* inspired Portugal to search for an all-water route around Africa to the East. Portuguese sea captains pushed southward along the Atlantic coast of Africa. In 1488 *Bartholomew Diaz* reached the southern tip of Africa, the Cape of Good Hope. In 1497–1498 *Vasco da Gama* rounded the Cape and sailed on to India. Because he returned with a cargo worth 60 times the cost of the voyage, his trip excited western Europe.

## SPAIN FINANCES TWO SIGNIFICANT EXPEDITIONS

**1. Columbus.** In 1492 *Christopher Columbus,* an Italian navigator, sailed from Spain. Convinced that the earth is round, Columbus planned to reach the East by sailing westward across the Atlantic Ocean. He failed because his ships were blocked by two continents hitherto unknown to Europe. Although Columbus thought he had reached islands off the coast of Asia, he had actually come upon what Europeans later considered to be a *New World.* Because this region was publicized by the Italian explorer *Amerigo Vespucci,* it was later named the *Americas.*

**2. Magellan.** In 1519 *Ferdinand Magellan,* a Portuguese sea captain, led several ships from Spain. He rounded the southern tip of South America and crossed the Pacific but was killed in the Philippine Islands. In 1522 one ship arrived back in Spain, thereby completing the first *circumnavigation* of the world. This daring navigational exploit, covering about 44,000 miles (70,400 kilometers), proved definitely that the world is round.

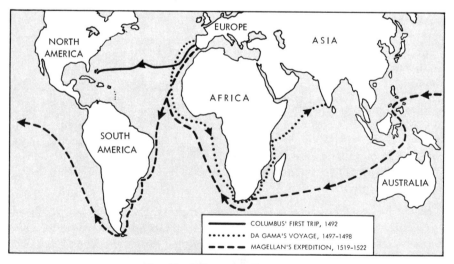

**The First Voyages Overseas**

# EUROPEANS EXPLORE NEW LANDS (15TH TO 18TH CENTURIES)

Spurred by these events, the leading west European nations sent explorers to the New World and the Far East to *(a)* seek a "northwest passage" through or around North America to the Far East, *(b)* secure gold, silver, gems, and other valuable goods, *(c)* convert the natives to Christianity, *(d)* establish claims to the new lands, and *(e)* start trading posts and settlements.

## Important Explorers and Their Accomplishments

| Explorers | Dates | Accomplishments |
|---|---|---|
| **For Spain** | | |
| Balboa | 1513 | First European in America to see the Pacific Ocean. |
| Ponce De Leon | 1513 | Explored Florida. |
| Cortez | 1519–1521 | Conquered the Aztec Indians in Mexico. |
| Pizarro | 1532 | Conquered the Inca Indians in Peru. |
| De Soto | 1541 | First European to see the Mississippi River. |
| **For France** | | |
| Verrazano | 1524 | Explored the Atlantic coast of North America; first European to sail into New York Harbor. |
| Cartier | 1535 | Explored the St. Lawrence River. |
| Champlain | 1603–1608 | Explored eastern Canada and northern New England; founded Quebec. |
| Marquette and Joliet | 1673 | Explored the upper Mississippi River Valley. |
| **For England** | | |
| Cabot | 1497 | Sailed to Labrador and the northeast coast of North America. |
| Drake | 1577–1580 | Led the second expedition to circumnavigate the world. |
| Cook | 1768–1779 | Explored New Zealand, Australia, and the Hawaiian Islands. |
| **For Portugal** | | |
| Cabral | 1500 | Reached Brazil. |
| **For Holland** | | |
| Hudson | 1609 | Entered New York Harbor and sailed up the Hudson River. |

# EUROPEAN NATIONS ESTABLISH COLONIAL EMPIRES (16TH TO 18TH CENTURIES)

## 1. In Asia

*a. Portugal* established an important trading post at *Goa* in India and others in the East Indies.

*b. Spain* annexed the Philippine Islands.

*c. Holland,* by capturing the Portuguese trading posts in the East Indies and establishing its own, won control of the East Indies.

*d. France* established trading posts in India, such as *Pondicherry.*

*e. England* established trading posts in India, such as *Bombay, Madras,* and *Calcutta,* and in a major war against France, gained dominance over India (1763). England also settled Australia.

**2. In the New World**

*a. Portugal* settled Brazil.

*b. Spain* settled the West Indies, Florida, Texas, California, Mexico, Central America, and South America (except for Brazil).

*c. Holland* founded the colony of *New Netherland.* It consisted of Manhattan Island (now part of New York City), eastern Long Island, the Hudson River Valley up to Albany, and part of New Jersey southward to Delaware Bay. Later the Dutch seized the Swedish colony of Delaware.

*d. France* settled Canada along the St. Lawrence River, founding *Quebec* and *Montreal.* France also settled the Great Lakes and Mississippi River regions, founding *Detroit, St. Louis,* and *New Orleans.*

*e. England* settled ten colonies and seized Delaware and New Netherland from the Dutch. New Netherland was divided into New Jersey and New York. These *thirteen English colonies* bordered the Atlantic seaboard from New Hampshire to Georgia. In a major war against France, England acquired Canada (1763).

## COLONIAL RIVALRY CAUSES WARS (16TH TO 18TH CENTURIES)

The west European powers engaged in a number of wars, caused partly by colonial rivalry, in which England achieved victory. (1) England raided Spanish colonies and destroyed the Spanish Armada (1588). (2) England seized the Dutch New World colonies (1664). (3) England fought France, its chief rival in four major wars.

## GREAT BRITAIN DEFEATS FRANCE FOR WORLD EMPIRE

Within almost 100 years Britain and France fought four major wars for European dominance and colonial supremacy. The final and decisive encounter was the *Seven Years' War* (1756–1763). On battlegrounds in Europe, India, and North America, the British triumphed. In India *Robert Clive,* a British empire builder, crushed the French in 1757 at the *Battle of Plassey.* In North

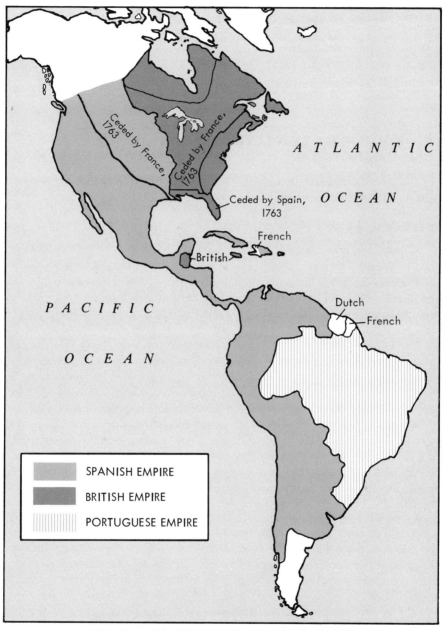

**The Americas After the Treaty of Paris (1763)**

America—where the struggle was called the *French and Indian War* (1754–1763)—the British were also victorious. They invaded French Canada and, under General *James Wolfe,* captured the stronghold of Quebec.

In the *Treaty of Paris* (1763), Great Britain acquired French Canada and all French territory east of the Mississippi (except for the city of New Orleans ceded to Spain). (See map, page 161.) France also agreed not to impede British control of India. By adding these lands to its other possessions, Britain in 1763 became the world's leading colonial power.


## THE COMMERCIAL REVOLUTION: RESULTS OF EUROPEAN EXPANSION

The term *Commercial Revolution* summarizes the effects that overseas expansion had on both western Europe and the rest of the world.

### 1. Effects on Europe

#### a. Increased Imports and World Trade

(1) Western Europe imported many commodities from the New World and the Far East: potatoes, Indian corn (maize), tobacco, chocolate, cane sugar, tea, and quinine. Some of these items were new to western Europe. Others, though previously known, became cheaper and more plentiful. Their availability helped improve west European living standards.

(2) Large quantities of gold and silver received from New World mines substantially affected western Europe's economy. Since these metals served as currency, consumers had more money to spend for goods. Vigorous bidding for these goods raised prices, thus causing inflation. Landlords demanded higher rents; workers required higher wages; governments imposed higher taxes.

(3) To reduce the risk of loss to ships and goods from storm, fire, and piracy, west European merchants originated insurance. Each merchant contributed a specified sum, called a *premium,* to a common fund, from which a businessperson who suffered a loss was compensated. A noted insurance company, founded in the 17th century, was *Lloyd's of London.*

#### b. Shifted Economic Power

(1) Western Europe's major trade routes shifted from the Mediterranean and Baltic to the Atlantic. The Italian city-states and north German cities declined in importance; the European nations, bordering the Atlantic, increased their commerce, wealth, and power. The nation-state became preeminent in world affairs.

(2) Western Europe's population increased, in part due to the availability of additional food supplies. Western Europe's population also began to change residence from rural areas into urban centers. Some lesser nobles and many peasants, both groups having difficulty surviving on the land, moved to the

cities. Cities offered opportunities for business owners (entrepreneurs). In cities workers could find jobs in new industries such as printing and in expanded industries such as shipbuilding and armaments manufacture. Cities also held promises of greater social mobility, richer cultural existences, and a wider variety of life-styles.

(3) Western Europe's middle class—merchants, bankers, capitalists—grew in number and achieved greater economic power. However, the middle class was not content. Considered inferior to the landowning nobles and ruled by absolute monarchs, the middle class lacked social status and political power.

*c. Adopted Mercantilism.* Eager to secure more funds for royal treasuries, west European governments became interested in economic affairs. To further the national prosperity, these governments applied the economic theories of *mercantilism.* The mercantilists argued that a nation must (1) attract the maximum amount of gold and silver, since wealth is measured in these metals; (2) export more than it imports, thereby achieving a favorable balance of trade and receiving payment for the difference in gold and silver; (3) increase exports by stimulating domestic industries with bounties (subsidies); (4) discourage imports of foreign manufactures by levying tariffs; (5) acquire colonies to assure markets for manufactured goods and to guarantee sources of raw materials; (6) restrict colonial manufacturing; and (7) forbid colonies to trade with any country except the mother country. Mercantilists held that colonies exist for the benefit of the mother country. (Mother country is a term commonly applied to a nation that controlled territory in another area. It is historically important from about 1600 to the 1960's.)

### d. Moved Toward the Economic System of Capitalism

(1) Western Europe changed from the relatively static, localized, nonprofit economy typical of the Later Middle Ages to the beginnings of a dynamic, worldwide, profit-oriented system called *capitalism* (see pages 277–278).

Entrepreneurs engaged in business enterprises, taking risks and facing competition, in the hope of making a profit. They operated in a market economy in which the prices of goods and the wages of workers were determined largely by supply and demand. Entrepreneurs sometimes founded joint-stock companies and secured charters from their governments granting monopolies over trade and colonization in specific overseas territories. To raise capital, joint-stock companies sold stock to numerous investors who would share in the profits or losses of the business but who left its management to elected officials. The joint-stock company, as a form of business organization, was the forerunner of the present-day corporation.

(2) Banks arose in western Europe to meet the needs of business enterprises for funds. The growth of banks was aided by *(a)* the increased supply of currency resulting from the importation of New World gold and silver and *(b)* the relaxation of Roman Catholic Church prohibitions against usury—the lending of money for interest. This relaxation came as people realized that capital

played a vital and productive role in business enterprise. In the Age of Transition, two famed banking families—both originating as merchants and evolving into bankers—were the *Medici* in Italy and the *Fuggers* in Germany.

Aware of their role in the developing capitalist economy, bankers devised various new credit facilities: *bills of exchange* for use in international trade enabled a merchant in one country to pay for goods purchased in another country, *checks* for use by business people to pay for goods in local transactions, and *bank notes*, or paper money issued by the banks, for use as a convenient substitute for gold and silver. These credit facilities have survived to the present time.

(3) Limited by guild restrictions, European textile producers proved unable to meet the demand for goods both in Europe and overseas. To increase output, manufacturers employed the *domestic system*—sending out raw materials to be worked on in the home—and later manufacturers adopted the *factory system*—speeding production by using machinery. The Commercial Revolution thus helped pave the way for the Industrial Revolution (see pages 265–267).

## 2. Effects on the Rest of the World

(*a*) Europeans bought slaves in Africa and transported them to the New World to provide labor for the plantations and mines.

(*b*) Many Europeans migrated to overseas colonies, either to escape religious persecution or to improve their personal economic condition.

(*c*) Trade and emigration spread European civilization throughout the world.

## MULTIPLE–CHOICE QUESTIONS

1. The prosperity of Renaissance western Europe was due in part to the (1) sale of works of art and literature throughout Asia (2) sharp rise in commercial activity in western Europe (3) repeal of usury prohibitions by the Church (4) development of power-driven machinery.

2. The Crusaders hastened the voyages to the New World by (1) taking Jerusalem from the Moslems (2) stimulating European demand for goods of the East (3) driving the Turks out of Constantinople (4) increasing the power of the Church.

3. What was the attitude of most merchants and monarchs toward overseas voyages? (1) Both groups supported them. (2) Both groups opposed them. (3) Merchants supported them; monarchs opposed them. (4) Monarchs supported them; merchants opposed them.

4. Which nation was the first to establish trading posts in India? (1) England (2) France (3) Holland (4) Portugal.

5. Which two European countries led in exploration and colonization during the 15th and 16th centuries? (1) England and Germany (2) France and Russia (3) Italy and Holland (4) Portugal and Spain.

6. Two nations that established colonies in North America were (1) France and Portugal (2) Russia and Denmark (3) Spain and England (4) Sweden and Prussia.

7. The eastern part of South America, encompassing Brazil, was once part of the empire of  (1) France  (2) Italy  (3) Portugal  (4) Spain.

8. A bridge spanning part of New York Harbor has logically been named in honor of the explorer  (1) Balboa  (2) Verrazano  (3) Champlain  (4) Cabot.

9. In the 18th century the major colonial rivals were  (1) France and Britain  (2) Britain and Russia  (3) France and Prussia  (4) Britain and Spain.

10. By the 16th century the center of commercial activity had shifted from the Mediterranean to the  (1) Black Sea  (2) Atlantic Ocean  (3) Red Sea  (4) Indian Ocean.

11. By the 17th century the chief export from Africa to the New World was  (1) gold  (2) rubber  (3) slaves  (4) spices.

12. To which of the following pairs of nations did the Commercial Revolution bring the greatest increase in wealth and power?  (1) Spain and Germany  (2) Portugal and Italy  (3) Britain and Holland  (4) France and Russia.

13. The term *mercantilism* is used to describe a policy of  (1) allowing free trade among merchants of different countries  (2) government ownership of domestic industries  (3) regulating trade to benefit the mother country  (4) leaving business alone.

14. Mercantilism held that the wealth of a nation is measured by its  (1) natural resources  (2) skilled workers  (3) precious metals  (4) fertile soil.

15. Which is *not* an aspect of 18th-century mercantilism?  (1) The mother country's exports should be greater in value than its imports.  (2) The mother country should encourage manufacturing in its colonies.  (3) Industry within the mother country should be encouraged by the national government.  (4) Colonies should exist for the benefit of the mother country.

16. Joint-stock companies were important because they enabled business owners to  (1) secure risk capital  (2) move people from rural areas into the cities  (3) compete with the powerful banking families  (4) plot the overthrow of the absolute monarchs.

## TRUE–FALSE QUESTIONS

If the statement is correct write the word *true*. If the statement is incorrect, substitute a word or phrase for the italicized term to make the statement correct.

1. A medieval Italian traveler whose book about his visit to China aroused tremendous interest in Europe was *Leonardo da Vinci*.

2. A scientific advance that reduced the risk of ocean travel was the *astrolabe*.

3. The Portuguese sea captain who first reached India by sailing around Africa was *Prince Henry the Navigator*.

4. The Spanish expedition one ship of which was first to circumnavigate the world was originally led by *Christopher Columbus*.

5. The first European settlement on the present site of New York City was made by the *English*.

6. The military leader who won control of India for Britain was *Robert Clive*.

7. The decisive 18th-century war that established Britain as the world's greatest colonial power was the *Thirty Years' War*.

8. A famous insurance company founded in the 17th century to reduce the risk of merchant ship loss is *Lloyd's of London*.

9. A leading banking family in 16th-century western Europe was the *Medici*.

10. The many results of European expansion overseas are together known as the *Intellectual Revolution*.

## ESSAY QUESTIONS

1. About the year 1500 a change began in west European trade with the Far East. Discuss the change as it affected *(a)* trade routes *(b)* the countries that profited from the trade *(c)* west European relations with the Far East.

2. Discuss fully *(a)* *two* causes and *(b)* *two* results of the voyages of exploration made between 1450 and 1650.

3. The expansion of commerce (1450–1650 A.D.) is called the Commercial Revolution. *(a)* Discuss *two* causes of the Commercial Revolution. *(b)* Discuss *one* effect of the Commercial Revolution on the medieval industrial system. *(c)* Explain *one* way in which the Commercial Revolution affected the native population *(i)* in the New World and *(ii)* in Africa.

4. Decide whether each of the following statements is true or false. In each case explain *two* facts to support your point of view: *(a)* China and India have been important to the economic development of Europe. *(b)* European interest in the New World decreased the importance of the Mediterranean Sea. *(c)* During the 15th and 16th centuries, Portugal became a leading trading power. *(d)* The Seven Years' War had little effect on the colonies of the major powers. *(e)* Astronauts today have the same motives as did explorers during the Age of Exploration.

5. The Commercial Revolution brought about many changes in west European life— changes that are still evident today.

*(a)* Describe *one* change brought about by the Commercial Revolution as it affected each of the following: *(i)* places where people lived *(ii)* how the common people earned their living *(iii)* the extent of business enterprise *(iv)* the importance of capital.

*(b)* For any *one* of the items listed in *(a)*, prove that it is still evident today.

# UNIT VII. THE GROWTH OF DEMOCRACY

## Part 1. Introduction

### MEANING OF POLITICAL DEMOCRACY

Political democracy rests on the principle that government is created by, derives its powers from, and exists to serve the people. In practice today political democracy means a system of government characterized by the following features: (1) Governmental powers are limited by a written constitution or by an unwritten constitution consisting of a group of documents and basic laws that have the prestige of a constitution. (2) The people are protected against possible governmental tyranny by constitutional guarantees of basic civil liberties, especially *(a)* freedom of speech, press, religion, and assembly, and *(b)* the right to bail, impartial trial, and equal treatment under the law. (3) Minority groups, regardless of color, religion, or national origin, have the right to full and free existence. (4) Most governmental officials are chosen by secret ballot in free and frequently held elections. Voters may either reelect the officials or retire them by selecting the opposing candidates. (5) The legislature conducts free and open debate on issues and passes laws by majority vote. (6) More than one political party exists, each free to present its views in seeking to become the majority party.

To summarize, in a democratic government the majority rules, and minority groups are protected in their liberties, especially the right to become the majority or to gain majority support by peaceable means.

### POLITICAL DEMOCRACY THROUGH THE AGES

The democratic form of government (1) *appeared* first in the ancient Greek city-states and in the Roman Republic; (2) *was replaced* by autocracy: the rulers of the Roman Empire, feudal lords of the Middle Ages, and absolute monarchs of the transitional period to modern times; (3) *reappeared* as a result of the 17th-century English Revolution and the 18th-century American and French revolutions; and (4) *developed* into the political systems democratic peoples enjoy today.

In the following chapters we shall trace west European and American history relating to the reappearance and development of democratic government.

167

# Part 2. England (to 1750): Democratic Gains

## FOUNDATIONS FOR DEMOCRATIC GROWTH

During the Later Middle Ages, England established the foundations upon which its people would erect a democracy.

**1. Jury System.** King *Henry II* (ruled 1154–1189) replaced feudal justice with royal courts, grand jury investigations, and, in certain cases, jury trials. Although Henry II's purpose was to strengthen royal authority, not to further democracy, his reforms evolved into our modern system of trial by jury.

**2. Magna Carta (1215).** King *John*, who demanded increased funds from his feudal nobles, was accused by them of being a despot and of violating their feudal rights. At *Runnymede*, outside London, John was compelled by the nobles to sign the *Great Charter*, or *Magna Carta*.

This document limited royal power by stating that the king *(a)* may *not* imprison any free person except by judgment of the person's peers (equals) and in accordance with the laws and *(b)* may *not* levy taxes without consent of the *Great Council*. (This body consisted of the nobility and higher clergy.)

Originally Magna Carta protected the medieval feudal nobility against royal tyranny; in time, the charter's protections were extended to all English people. Magna Carta came to mean that *(a)* the monarch is not an absolute ruler but is subject to the laws, *(b)* all persons are guaranteed trial by jury, and *(c)* the Great Council, which later evolved into Parliament, alone may levy taxes. Magna Carta is therefore usually considered the cornerstone of English democracy.

**3. Model Parliament (1295).** King *Edward I* expanded the Great Council's membership to include middle-class representatives. His purpose was to place taxes upon and still ensure the loyalty of the wealthy middle class, not to further democracy. Because the enlarged Great Council served as a model for England's future legislature, it is called the *Model Parliament*.

By providing representation for aristocrats—nobility and higher clergy—as well as commoners—well-to-do farmers and merchants—Edward hastened the division of Parliament into two houses: the hereditary *House of Lords* and the elected *House of Commons*.

**4. English Common Law.** By the late 13th century, English judges had established the practice of basing their decisions on similar cases decided previously. These legal precedents collectively formed a body of judge-made law called the *common law*. The English common law, both civil and criminal, applied to all the people equally. To protect the individual against possible governmental tyranny, the common law held that life, liberty, and property may not be taken by illegal and arbitrary action. The English common law later greatly influenced the American legal system.

**5. Parliamentary Lawmaking (14th Century).** By threatening to withhold tax laws, Parliament compelled the English monarchs to accept its legislation, not only on taxes but on all matters. Henceforth, all laws required the consent of both houses of Parliament and the approval of the monarch.

## THE POPULAR TUDORS: UNCHECKED BY PARLIAMENT (1485–1603)

The leading Tudor rulers, particularly *Henry VII, Henry VIII,* and *Elizabeth I,* (1) governed capably and intelligently, (2) followed a popular foreign policy by opposing Catholic Spain, (3) aided the middle class by providing law and order, encouraging trade, and furthering overseas expansion, and (4) outwardly appeared to consult Parliament but actually dominated the legislature.

Although forceful monarchs, the Tudors enjoyed tremendous popularity both with the people and with Parliament.

## THE UNPOPULAR STUARTS: CONFLICTS WITH PARLIAMENT (1603–1642)

**1. Reasons for Stuart Unpopularity.** The early Stuart kings, *James I* and *Charles I, (a)* ruled arrogantly and tactlessly, claiming "divine right," *(b)* followed an unpopular foreign policy of friendship for Catholic Spain, *(c)* discriminated against the *Puritans,* a powerful Calvinist sect that considered Anglicanism too close to Catholicism and tried to "purify" Anglican practices, *(d)* harmed the middle class by taxing it heavily while neglecting to further trade, *(e)* violated English law by imprisoning opponents without a fair trial, and *(f)* raised money by means not approved by Parliament.

Popular resentment against Stuart policies encouraged Parliament—with its many middle-class and Puritan members—to reassert its authority.

**2. Parliament Issues the Petition of Right (1628).** In the *Petition of Right* Parliament protested the despotism of Charles I and reaffirmed that the monarch, according to English law, may *not (a)* levy taxes without Parliament's consent, *(b)* imprison persons without a specific charge and without provision for jury trial, and *(c)* quarter (board) soldiers in a private home without the owner's permission. By withholding new tax laws, Parliament finally compelled Charles to sign the Petition of Right.

**3. Charles I Rules Without Parliament (1629–1640).** Charles disregarded the Petition of Right and denied Parliament's authority to curb his "divine right" rule. For 11 years Charles did not convene Parliament. Ruling autocratically, he *(a)* illegally raised money, *(b)* illegally imprisoned his opponents, *(c)* utilized the royal *Star Chamber Courts,* where accused persons were denied a jury and often were tortured to compel them to testify against themselves, and (d) antagonized the Puritans by demanding their conformity to Anglican Church practices, which were similar to Catholicism.

**4. Charles I Calls and Clashes with Parliament (1640–1642).** Desperate for additional funds to suppress a Scottish rebellion in 1640, Charles summoned Parliament into session. He soon realized that the House of Commons was controlled by his enemies, the Puritans. Charles' demand for new taxes was resisted by the Puritans, who insisted that he first abandon his autocratic policies. In 1642 his unsuccessful attempt to arrest the Puritan leaders of Commons led directly to the outbreak of civil war.

## THOMAS HOBBES: PHILOSOPHER DEFENDING STUART ABSOLUTISM

Thomas Hobbes was a 17th-century English philosopher who defended royal absolutism. As England moved toward civil war, he felt personally threatened and in 1640 fled from London to Paris. During his exile he served for a time as tutor to the boy who would become Charles II. More importantly, he completed his major work on government, *The Leviathan*. Hobbes chose this title, after the all-powerful sea monster named in the Bible, to emphasize his belief that government too must be all-powerful and absolute.

Hobbes denied the Stuart claim to rule by "divine right"—a denial that lost him favor in Stuart eyes—but he asserted his support for royal absolutism. Hobbes reasoned that (1) humans in their original state of nature were unhappy and miserable, (2) therefore humans entered into a social compact to surrender their freedom to a ruler and granted the ruler absolute power in order to enable the ruler to maintain law and order, and (3) since the ruler was not a party to the contract, the people have no right to complain about the ruler's policies.

Hobbes' philosophy indicates that some people in the troubled times of 17th-century England were willing to surrender all their liberties in order to gain security. In our own troubled 20th century, we too have seen some people surrender all their liberties in order to gain the supposed advantage of security under dictatorship.

Although a man of integrity and intellect, Hobbes and his ideas never won great popularity because he (1) supported royal absolutism when the popular current of thought in England was flowing strongly toward greater democracy and (2) was overshadowed as a philosopher and exponent of social contract by a contemporary—the democratically minded John Locke (see pages 172–173).

## THE PURITAN REVOLUTION (1642–1660)

**1. Parliament Wins the Civil War (1642–1645).** Parliament rallied the middle class, the small landowners, and the Puritans—groups collectively called the

*Roundheads*. Parliament also had the support of the Scots, who had rebelled against Charles' interference with their Presbyterian religion. Charles had the support of the nobility, the wealthy landowners, the high Anglican clergy, and the Catholics—groups collectively called the *Cavaliers*. The Parliamentary forces were led by an ardent Puritan, *Oliver Cromwell*. He decisively defeated the Cavalier, or Royalist, armies.

**2. Charles I Is Beheaded (1649).** Charles was captured by his enemies. His most bitter foes in Parliament accused him of treason, murder, and tyranny, and placed him on trial. Charles was convicted and executed. Although this extreme measure shocked many people, it reaffirmed that English monarchs rule, not by "divine right," but in accordance with the law.

**3. Oliver Cromwell Rules England (1649–1658).** England was declared a republic, or *Commonwealth*, and Cromwell, the victorious Puritan general, ruled as a military dictator. In 1653 he took the title of *Lord Protector*. A highly capable leader, Cromwell suppressed rebellions in Ireland and Scotland, furthered economic prosperity, and maintained a successful anti-Spanish foreign policy.

Nevertheless, Cromwell's Puritan rule did not gain popular support. Many English people objected to (*a*) Cromwell's dictatorial government and heavy taxes; (*b*) the role of Cromwell and his Puritan followers in the execution of Charles I; (*c*) Puritan intolerance of the Anglican religion—whose members were far more numerous than the Puritan minority; and (*d*) the severe Puritan moral code, which prohibited dancing, athletic games, theatrical performances, and other amusements.

Shortly after Cromwell's death in 1658, Puritan rule ended.

## THE STUARTS RULE AGAIN IN ENGLAND (1660–1688)

**1. Charles II Defers to Parliament (1660–1685).** Upon Parliament's invitation, *Charles II* (the exiled son of Charles I) returned to England and assumed the throne. He pledged to observe Magna Carta and the Petition of Right and to respect the authority of Parliament. Ever mindful of his father's fate, Charles II avoided antagonizing Parliament or the people.

In 1679 Charles yielded to Parliament's wishes and approved the *Habeas Corpus Act*. This act limited the monarch's powers by providing that (*a*) an arrested person may secure from a judge a court order called a *writ of habeas corpus* and (*b*) by this writ the prisoner must be brought before the judge and given a statement of charges. Thereafter, the prisoner may be released on bail, pending a speedy jury trial.

Today, in both England and the United States, habeas corpus protects the individual against arbitrary arrest and imprisonment.

**2. James II Antagonizes Parliament (1685–1688).** Upon Charles II's death his brother assumed the throne as *James II*. A convert to Catholicism, James outraged the people and Parliament by *(a)* his pro-Catholic acts and *(b)* his efforts to dominate Parliament and revive "divine right" rule. Moreover, the birth of his son aroused fear of continuing Catholic rule in England.

## THE GLORIOUS REVOLUTION (1688–1689)

**1. Parliament Overthrows James II.** Parliament secretly offered the English crown to *William*, Protestant ruler of Holland, and his wife *Mary* (Protestant daughter of James II). They accepted. When William arrived in England, James fled the country. Parliament declared the throne vacant and proclaimed William and Mary the new king and queen.

By this bloodless revolution in 1688, Parliament *(a)* finally ended "divine right" in England and *(b)* reaffirmed its supremacy over the monarch.

**2. Parliament Passes Laws Furthering Democracy.** As part of this Glorious Revolution, Parliament passed the following laws:

*a.* The **Bill of Rights** (1689) provided that (1) the monarch may *not* make or suspend laws, levy taxes, or maintain an army without the consent of Parliament; (2) the monarch may *not* interfere with parliamentary elections and debates; (3) Parliament must meet frequently; (4) the monarch must be Anglican in religion; and (5) the people are guaranteed basic civil liberties: the right to petition the government and to an impartial, speedy jury trial and protection against excessive bails and fines and against cruel and unusual punishments.

A hundred years later this great document served as a model for the first ten amendments of our Constitution—the American Bill of Rights.

*b.* The **Toleration Act** (1689) granted freedom of worship to non-Anglican Protestant sects.

## JOHN LOCKE: PHILOSOPHER JUSTIFYING THE GLORIOUS REVOLUTION

John Locke, probably the foremost English philosopher of the 17th century was born into an Anglican family with Puritan leanings. During the English Civil War, his father joined the parliamentary forces but saw little action. Locke was educated at Oxford and later became known for his liberal views and friends. During the reign of Charles II, Locke felt obliged to flee for safety to Holland. In 1689, after James II was overthrown, Locke returned to England. The next year, in a philosophical justification of the Glorious Revolution, Locke published his liberal and democratic statement, *Two Treatises of Government*.

Locke asserted that (1) people in their original state of nature were happy and possessed the natural rights to life, liberty, and property, (2) for the purpose of protecting these natural rights, people entered into a social compact to create a government and grant it limited powers, and (3) if the government—which was a party to the compact—failed to live up to its purpose or exceeded its authority, the people have the right to alter or abolish it—by revolution if necessary. Locke's logic pointed to the conclusion that James II had violated the social contract and therefore deserved to be deposed by the Glorious Revolution.

Locke's ideas greatly influenced later thinkers, especially (1) Thomas Jefferson, who wrote the American Declaration of Independence, (2) the framers of the Constitution of the United States, and (3) Jean Jacques Rousseau, who wrote the *Social Contract*, a book that contributed much to the French *Declaration of the Rights of Man*.

## FURTHER DEMOCRATIC GAINS IN ENGLAND (TO 1750)

**1. Political Parties.** Shortly before the Glorious Revolution, political parties arose. Each party consisted of people of similar interests who banded together to gain control of Parliament. The *Tories*, later known as *Conservatives*, represented mainly the wealthy landowners and favored the royalty. The *Whigs*, later known as *Liberals*, represented mainly the urban middle class and supported Parliament. Political parties tend to further democracy by offering the voters a choice of candidates and ideas.

**2. Cabinet Responsibility to Parliament.** *Cabinet responsibility*, originating during the reign of William and Mary, means that the ruler's chief ministers—together called the *cabinet*—are chosen from and are responsible to the majority party in Parliament. Cabinet responsibility *(a)* insures harmony between the ruler's ministers and the legislature and *(b)* is democratic, since the cabinet holds office only as long as it retains the support of an elected majority in Parliament.

**3. Cabinet Executive Power.** Cabinet executive power developed during the rule of King *George I* (1714–1727), a German prince who inherited the British throne. (His descendants have ruled Britain to this day and are known as the *House of Windsor.*) Since George I spoke no English and was unfamiliar with the workings of the British government, the cabinet, and its leader the *prime minister*, assumed full direction of executive affairs. (Britain's first prime minister was a Whig statesman, *Robert Walpole.*)

Cabinet executive power proved to be a democratic gain, as the British monarch became a mere figurehead.

## SUMMARY: BRITAIN AS A LIMITED MONARCHY (BY 1750)

**1. Democratic Gains.** *(a)* The monarch did not rule by "divine right" but was subject to British law and tradition. *(b)* Parliament controlled the government and was supreme over the monarch. *(c)* The government featured political parties, cabinet responsibility to Parliament, and cabinet executive power. *(d)* The people were guaranteed basic civil liberties.

2. **Undemocratic Features.** *(a)* Property qualifications prevented over 95 percent of the people from voting for members of Parliament. *(b)* Elections were marked by bribery and corruption. *(c)* The hereditary House of Lords was as powerful as the elected House of Commons. *(d)* The government was controlled by the upper classes.

The outbreak of the French Revolution (1789) delayed further British democratic reforms.

# Part 3. The American Revolution (1775–1783): Independence and Democracy

## BRITAIN'S POLICY TOWARD THE THIRTEEN AMERICAN COLONIES

1. **Neglect (Before 1763).** For a long time, Britain neglected its American colonies. They *(a)* enjoyed considerable self-government and *(b)* disregarded British mercantilist laws, the *Navigation Acts*. These acts, in accordance with mercantile doctrine (see page 163), sought to restrict colonial industry and to discourage colonial trade with all countries except Great Britain.

2. **Effect of the French and Indian War (1754–1763).** Although Britain won the French and Indian War (see pages 160–162), the British government considered the aid received from the American colonies inadequate. King *George III* and the Tory party determined to *(a)* reestablish control over the colonies and *(b)* compel the colonies to bear part of the war's cost.

3. **Strict Control (After 1763).** Great Britain then *(a)* vigorously enforced the Navigation Acts; *(b)* combated colonial smugglers *(i)* by authorizing *writs of assistance*—legal documents permitting unlimited search of private buildings—and *(ii)* by denying accused smugglers a jury trial; *(c)* subjected colonists to an import tax, particularly on tea and sugar, and a stamp tax on printed materials; *(d)* prohibited westward migration beyond the Allegheny Mountains; and *(e)* stationed British troops in the colonies, often quartering them in private homes.

## COLONIAL DEFIANCE OF STRICT BRITISH CONTROL

The colonists (1) smuggled goods to evade import taxes, (2) boycotted British goods, (3) demonstrated against British soldiers, (4) organized committees to coordinate anti-British efforts, and (5) spoke and wrote against Britain's colonial policy.

## OUTBREAK OF THE AMERICAN REVOLUTION

In 1773 Massachusetts colonists, protesting the import tax, dumped British tea into Boston Harbor—an event called the *Boston Tea Party*. This action provoked Parliament to punish Massachusetts by restricting that colony's self-government and temporarily closing Boston Harbor—laws that the colonists called "intolerable." The other colonies rallied to support Massachusetts and united in their action against Britain by forming the *First Continental Congress*. Tension increased between colonial patriots and British officials. In 1775, colonial *Minutemen* fired upon British troops marching from Boston to seize colonial military supplies and leaders at *Lexington* and *Concord*. This skirmish marked the start of the American Revolution.

## BASIC CAUSES OF THE AMERICAN REVOLUTION

**1. Economic.** *(a)* Colonial manufacturers and merchants were angered by British mercantilist laws, which hampered their industry and trade. They rejected the doctrine that colonies exist only to enrich the parent country. *(b)* Plantation owners and frontier settlers, eager for new land, disliked the prohibition against westward expansion. *(c)* Professional people opposed the stamp tax on printed matter, such as newspapers, pamphlets, and legal documents. *(d)* Consumers resented import taxes, which raised living costs.

**2. Political.** *(a)* The colonists maintained that they could be taxed only by their colonial legislatures; therefore, they considered taxes voted by Parliament as "taxation without representation." They dismissed the British argument that Parliament legislates for the entire empire. *(b)* The colonists regarded the quartering of British soldiers, the writs of assistance, and the denial of jury trials as violations of their "rights as Englishmen." The colonists claimed that, as the 17th-century English had revolted against the tyranny of the Stuarts, so now they were revolting against the tyranny of George III.

**3. Social.** *(a)* Many colonists of English stock no longer considered themselves to be English; after several generations, the New World environment had transformed them into Americans. *(b)* The non-English colonists—such as the Irish, Dutch, and French—came from countries traditionally hostile to Great Britain.

**4. Misunderstanding.** The colonies were separated from Britain by the Atlantic Ocean, a body of water 3,000 miles (4,800 kilometers) wide and then bridged only by slow-moving ships. This great distance proved a barrier to understanding, negotiation, and compromise.

## REASONS FOR DECLARING AMERICAN INDEPENDENCE

In 1776 the *Second Continental Congress* decided that the colonies were fighting for complete independence from Britain. Colonial patriots (1) complained of brutal British military behavior, (2) considered independence a logical goal, a point of view skillfully argued by *Thomas Paine* in his popular pamphlet *Common Sense*, and (3) hoped that a declaration of independence might secure foreign allies, especially France.

## THE DECLARATION OF INDEPENDENCE (JULY 4, 1776)

The *Declaration of Independence*, written chiefly by *Thomas Jefferson*, was a great democratic document. It reflects Jefferson's thinking, based on the ideas of the English philosopher John Locke (see pages 172–173). In the Declaration, Jefferson outlines the basic principles that underlie democratic governments:

1. "All men are created equal" and "are endowed by their Creator with certain unalienable Rights" (rights that cannot be taken away), including "Life, Liberty and the pursuit of Happiness."
2. To secure these rights, governments are instituted among men, "deriving their just powers from the consent of the governed."
3. "Whenever any Form of Government becomes destructive of these ends, it is the Right of the People to alter or to abolish it, and to institute new Government."
4. However, "governments long established should not be changed for light and transient [temporary] causes."

After stating these democratic principles, the Declaration lists the many and substantial grievances against George III and concludes that the colonies have the right to independence.

## DISAGREEMENT BETWEEN COLONISTS: PATRIOTS VS. TORIES

Not all colonists supported the revolution originally. Of the total population (1) one-third, the well-organized *patriots*, favored independence, (2) one-third were undecided, and (3) one-third, the unorganized *Loyalists*, or *Tories*, remained loyal to Britain. The more prominent Tories consisted of wealthy landowners and government officials. During the war many Tories fled to Canada and Britain, whereupon the patriots broke up the large Tory estates and sold the land in small parcels. Also, the patriots removed royal authority in state governments and took steps to provide more democratic state constitutions.

## REASONS FOR THE AMERICAN VICTORY

The American patriots were (1) fighting on their own soil; (2) experienced wilderness fighters; (3) led by courageous, able men, notably the commander-in-chief, *George Washington;* (4) aided by several capable foreign volunteers, such as the Frenchman *Lafayette;* and (5) joined in the conflict by France in 1778 and later by Spain and Holland. Thus, the American Revolution became part of a larger war in which the colonists, with foreign assistance, achieved victory.

By the *Treaty of Paris* (1783), the thirteen American colonies secured their independence from Britain.

## DEMOCRATIC EFFECTS OF THE AMERICAN REVOLUTION

**1. In the United States.** In 1789 the *Constitution* established the present government of the *United States of America.* Representing many democratic gains, this written Constitution *(a)* created a federal republic headed by an elected *President, (b)* stated the powers of, and limitations upon, the government, *(c)* separated governmental powers among three branches—executive, legislative, and judicial—to prevent any one branch from dominating, and *(d)* in 1791 included a *Bill of Rights* that protected the people from possible governmental tyranny.

The Bill of Rights (1) guaranteed freedom of speech, press, and religion; the right to assemble peaceably, petition the government, and receive a speedy, impartial jury trial and (2) prohibited unreasonable searches, excessive fines, cruel punishments, forcing a person to be a witness against oneself, and the peacetime quartering of troops in homes without the owners' consent.

**2. In Latin America.** The American Revolution inspired most New World colonies of Spain and Portugal to revolt in the early 19th century and achieve independence.

**3. In Britain.** The American Revolution *(a)* discredited George III and his efforts to revive royal executive power and *(b)* led to a gradual change in Britain's colonial policy. To prevent colonial rebellion, Britain eventually granted self-government and independence to most of its possessions, starting in 1867 with Canada.

**4. In France.** The American Revolution, by encouraging the French people to replace their absolute monarchy with a more democratic government, helped inspire the French Revolution of 1789.

## MULTIPLE–CHOICE QUESTIONS

1. Which one of these is the best evidence of democracy? (1) The government is headed by a president. (2) Elections are held. (3) Trials are conducted. (4) Civil liberties are protected.
2. The democratic form of government first appeared in (1) the Roman Empire under Augustus (2) the Middle Ages (3) the ancient Greek city-states (4) England under Henry VIII.
3. An immediate result of Magna Carta was the (1) increase in the power of the monarch (2) increase in the power of the nobles (3) extension of suffrage to the middle class (4) extension of suffrage to the peasants.
4. Magna Carta is considered the cornerstone of English democracy because it (1) limited the power of the Church (2) limited the powers of Parliament (3) was

forced upon the king by the workers in the towns    (4) later became a basis for English political liberties.

5. The English common law evolved out of    (1) acts passed by Parliament    (2) proclamations of the monarch    (3) verdicts handed down by commoners serving on juries    (4) decisions of judges.

6. During the 16th century the main reason for the increase in the power of the English monarch was the    (1) Glorious Revolution    (2) ability of the Tudor rulers    (3) ability of the Stuart rulers    (4) marriage of Queen Mary to Philip II of Spain.

7. The Stuart rulers of England strongly believed in    (1) the supremacy of Parliament    (2) religious freedom    (3) the divine right of kings    (4) rule by the middle class.

8. A reason for the success of the English Parliament in its 17th-century struggle for supremacy was    (1) its control of money appropriations    (2) the Lords' freedom to debate    (3) the attacks by journalists on the English rulers    (4) the empire's loyalty to Parliament rather than to the crown.

9. In 1640 Charles I called Parliament into session because he    (1) became a supporter of democratic principles    (2) wanted to change his religion    (3) needed money to suppress the Scottish rebels    (4) wanted a declaration of war against France.

10. The events of 1640–1660 in English history suggest which idea basic to the concept of democracy?    (1) A written constitution guarantees democracy.    (2) Supreme power should rest in the courts.    (3) Free people often fight for their rights.    (4) A revolution assures greater democracy.

11. Which was an important result of the Puritan Revolution in England?    (1) It ended the union between England and Scotland.    (2) It showed that the execution of a king causes an unfavorable reaction abroad.    (3) It proved that the middle class was not yet ready to assume the ruling power.    (4) It strengthened the belief in parliamentary government.

12. In 1660 Parliament restored the Stuart monarchy mainly because the Commonwealth government had    (1) sought to impose Puritan religious and moral beliefs upon the country    (2) formed an alliance with Spain    (3) caused economic depression    (4) weakened England's naval power.

13. The Habeas Corpus Act made it unlawful for a citizen to be    (1) taxed without the consent of Parliament    (2) held indefinitely in prison without a hearing    (3) persecuted for one's religious beliefs    (4) forced to be a witness against oneself.

14. An immediate effect of the Glorious Revolution in England was    (1) the return of the Tudors as rulers of England    (2) the supremacy of Parliament over the monarch    (3) universal manhood suffrage    (4) the persecution of the Anglican Church.

15. The Bill of Rights of 1689 declared that    (1) no taxes should be levied without the consent of Parliament    (2) the monarch could worship as he or she saw fit    (3) members of Parliament were to be elected by universal suffrage    (4) the Star Chamber Court could be used only in cases of sedition and treason.

16. The Bill of Rights did *not* guarantee all the people the right    (1) to a speedy trial    (2) to petition the government    (3) of protection against cruel punishments    (4) to vote for members of the House of Commons.

17. John Locke justified the Glorious Revolution on the grounds that    (1) monarchs hold power by divine right    (2) government is unnecessary    (3) government is a contract entered into between the ruler and the ruled    (4) rulers are responsible to the House of Lords.

18. Natural rights, according to John Locke, include the right to    (1) obtain a free education    (2) possess private property    (3) receive an old-age pension    (4) work.

19. Which statement is an opinion rather than a fact? (1) Magna Carta marks the beginning of democratic government in England. (2) The English Bill of Rights was passed in 1689. (3) Oliver Cromwell's forces defeated the army of Charles I. (4) England's Parliament is composed of two houses.

20. The British government considered American colonial aid during the French and Indian War (1) inadequate (2) adequate (3) far more than necessary (4) more a hindrance than a help.

21. To show opposition to strict British control, the American colonists did each of the following except (1) smuggle goods (2) defy writs of assistance (3) boycott British goods (4) pass mercantilist laws.

22. The Declaration of Independence (1) guarantees religious freedom to all (2) provides for a system of checks and balances (3) gives all adults the right to vote (4) declares that all men are created equal.

23. The Declaration of Independence (1) guarantees free universal education (2) declares that governments derive their just powers from the consent of the governed (3) declares that every man's house is his castle (4) guarantees equal opportunity.

24. In America the Tories were those colonists who (1) actively supported the Revolution (2) were undecided about the Revolution (3) remained loyal to the king (4) lived west of the Allegheny Mountains.

25. Which nation helped the American colonies in their revolt against Britain? (1) France (2) Italy (3) Sweden (4) Portugal.

26. To keep Stuart Star Chamber Court procedures from the United States, the American Bill of Rights (1) guarantees freedom of the press (2) provides that no person shall be compelled to testify against himself (3) requires judges to be appointed for life (4) orders the keeping of records of court proceedings.

27. Since our chief executive secures office by election rather than hereditary right, the United States is a (1) republic (2) democracy (3) monarchy (4) nation.

28. The American Revolution is important in world history because it (1) delayed the Industrial Revolution in Europe (2) ended British influence in the Western Hemisphere (3) set an example for other colonial peoples (4) adopted reforms from the French Revolution.

## IDENTIFICATION QUESTIONS: WHO AM I?

| | | |
|---|---|---|
| Charles I | James I | Thomas Paine |
| Oliver Cromwell | Thomas Jefferson | Jean Jacques Rousseau |
| George I | King John | Robert Walpole |
| Henry II | Marquis de Lafayette | George Washington |

1. Although a Frenchman, I fought on the side of the American colonists and brought American democratic ideals back to my native land.

2. A German prince who inherited the British throne, I knew little about British government. I permitted executive power to pass into the hands of the prime minister.

3. I was leader of the Puritan army that overthrew tyrannical Stuart rule and established the Commonwealth in England.

4. I drew upon the philosophy of John Locke in writing the American Declaration of Independence.

5. My persecution of Puritans and my clashes with Parliament led to a civil war in which I was captured and beheaded.

6. At Runnymede, in 1215, I was forced by some of my nobles to accept a document, Magna Carta, although its provisions were distasteful to me.

7. To strengthen central authority in England, I expanded royal circuit courts and, in certain cases, authorized trial by jury.

8. In my widely read work *Common Sense*, I urged the American colonists to seek complete independence from Britain.

## ESSAY QUESTIONS

1. Show in *one* way that the growth of democracy in England was influenced by *each* of the following: *(a)* Magna Carta *(b)* the Model Parliament *(c)* the Puritans *(d)* the Glorious Revolution *(e)* the coming of George I from Hanover.

2. The Tudors and the Stuarts were two great ruling families in England. *(a)* Name *one* ruler of the Tudor period and *one* ruler of the Stuart period. *(b)* Discuss *one* effect of Tudor rule on the growth of democracy. *(c)* Explain *two* ways in which democracy gained strength during the time of the Stuarts.

3. Cromwell was a military dictator of England. Explain why *(a)* Cromwell was able to seize control of England *(b)* the English people considered Cromwell to be a powerful ruler *(c)* Cromwell's popularity as a leader declined.

4. Two great philosophers of 17th-century England were Thomas Hobbes and John Locke. Explain *(a)* *one* idea that they held in common and *(b)* *two* ideas upon which they differed greatly. Which of these two philosophers had the greater influence upon world history? Give *one* argument to support your opinion.

5. *(a)* Name *two* English documents of liberty that paved the way for the American Revolution and the United States Constitution. *(b)* Show how *each* document contributed *(i)* to English liberty and *(ii)* to the United States Constitution.

6. For each of the following pairs, show *one* way in which the two items were similar and *one* way in which they were different: *(a)* the Glorious Revolution of 1689 and the American Revolution of 1775 *(b)* the work of John Locke and the work of Thomas Jefferson *(c)* the government of England after 1689 and the government of the United States after 1789.

7. On various occasions in world history, rulers have come into serious conflict with groups of their citizens. Two examples are: Charles I *vs.* Puritans (1640–1649) and George III *vs.* American colonists (1763–1783).
   For *each* of these conflicts, describe *(a)* *two* grievances of the protesting citizens against the ruler and *(b)* *one* important change resulting from the conflict.

# Part 4. The French Revolution of 1789: Democratic Gains

## FUNDAMENTAL CAUSE OF THE FRENCH REVOLUTION: ABUSES OF THE OLD REGIME

The political, social, and economic system of 18th-century continental Europe was called the *Old Regime*. In France, as elsewhere, the Old Regime was characterized by deep-rooted abuses.

**1. Political.** *(a)* The king was an absolute monarch, ruling by divine right. He exercised unlimited powers: made and enforced laws, conducted foreign affairs, dispensed justice, levied taxes, and spent the public funds. *(b)* The king selected his ministers on the basis of noble birth or favoritism, not ability. Frequently royal government was corrupt and inefficient. *(c)* The king censored speech and press to stifle what he considered dangerous ideas. *(d)* By using *lettres de cachet* (letters bearing the royal seal), the king imprisoned his enemies indefinitely, without charge, bail, or trial. *(e)* The king denied the people a voice in the government and a way to make known their grievances.

**2. Social.** The French people were divided into three rigid, distinct classes, called Estates. The *First Estate* consisted of the clergy; the *Second Estate*, the nobility; the *Third Estate*, the rest of the population: the bourgeoisie (merchants, bankers, manufacturers, professionals), city workers, and peasants.

The First and Second Estates, totaling 3 percent of the population, were the *privileged* classes. They *(a)* owned most of the land, *(b)* collected special feudal dues from the peasants, *(c)* received exemption from most taxes, *(d)* held the best government and army positions, and *(e)* enjoyed special treatment before the law. (The First Estate, however, also included poor parish priests, who lived no better than the peasants.)

The Third Estate, or 97 percent of the population, was the *unprivileged* class.

**3. Economic.** The Third Estate bore almost the entire tax burden. The peasants, the most numerous Third Estate group, paid the following taxes: *(a)* to the government: the *taille* (land tax), *corvée* (forced labor on roads and bridges), and *gabelle* (tax on compulsory salt purchases); *(b)* to the Church: the *tithe*; and *(c)* to the lords: *feudal dues*. Such taxes left the peasants with only about half of their meager income.

The bourgeoisie, the most influential group in the Third Estate, was hampered by *(a)* provincial tariffs on trade, *(b)* guild restrictions on manufacturing, and *(c)* government mercantilist regulations on economic life.

## OTHER BASIC CAUSES OF THE FRENCH REVOLUTION

Conditions in France under the Old Regime, although oppressive, were better than elsewhere in continental Europe. Nevertheless, the French led the way in revolt.

**1. The French Bourgeoisie.** Wealthy, well-educated, and ambitious, the bourgeoisie of France was the most powerful group in continental Europe. The bourgeoisie keenly resented the arrogance and political power of the nobility. To remedy Old Regime abuses, the bourgeoisie sought a role in shaping government policies. The bourgeoisie provided many French revolutionary leaders.

The bourgeoisie wanted the government to discard the policy of mercantilism, with its restrictions on industry and trade, and to leave business alone, a policy called *laissez-faire*. These economic ideas had been skillfully presented in the book *Wealth of Nations* (1776) by the Scottish economist *Adam Smith*. Laissez-faire, Smith argued, not only would enable the bourgeoisie to further their own economic interests, but would also increase the national wealth.

**2. The French Philosophers.** In the 18th century the French philosophers led the *Intellectual Revolution*, a movement also called the *Enlightenment* or *Age of Reason*. They believed that humans possessed natural rights and that society could be improved. Insisting that human institutions should conform to logic and reason, they challenged traditional royal and Church authority and called for the end of the Old Regime. Despite censorship, the "enlightened" thinking of the French philosophers reached many people. The leading philosophers were:

*a. Montesquieu* (1689–1755), a baron and landed aristocrat, wrote the book *The Spirit of Laws*. To prevent despotism, he urged that governmental powers be separated among three branches—executive, legislative, and judicial—each checking the other, instead of permitting power to be concentrated in one person, the king.

Montesquieu's proposed separation of powers was adopted in the United States Constitution.

*b. Voltaire* (1694–1778), born into a bourgeois family, won fame as a writer of literature and of political studies. After living in exile in Great Britain for a while, he wrote *Letters on the English*. Voltaire praised Britain's limited monarchy and civil liberties and denounced the French government's censorship, injustice, and despotism. Voltaire urged religious freedom and was especially bitter against the Catholic Church. He believed that its insistence upon authority barred human progress.

Attributed to Voltaire and typical of his outlook is the saying, "I disapprove of what you say, but I will defend to the death your right to say it."

*c. Rousseau* (1712–1778), probably of lower-class origin, was a maladjusted man who lived a disorganized life yet influenced millions by his effective writings. In *Émile* he set forth theories of education new for his time, and in *The*

*Social Contract* he set forth theories of government beginning with the charge: "Man is born free, and everywhere he is in chains."

Rousseau maintained that (1) humans in their original state of nature were happy and possessed natural rights; (2) as inequalities arose, people entered into a social contract among themselves, agreeing to surrender all their rights to the community and to submit to the General Will—the will of the majority; (3) the people created government, as a necessary evil, to carry out the General Will; and (4) if a government fails in this purpose, the people have the right to overthrow and replace it.

Rousseau's ideas were patterned, in part, after those of John Locke (see pages 172–173). But whereas Locke was more concerned with individual rights and limits on the powers of government, Rousseau emphasized the concept that the General Will—the rule of the majority—is supreme. Rousseau further claimed that the government, to enforce the General Will, has unlimited power.

(Rousseau's philosophy has also been used by dictatorships to justify totalitarian rule. They have claimed that the dictator or the single permissible party alone determines, enforces, and speaks for the General Will to which all citizens owe obedience.)

*d. Diderot* (1713–1784), son of a skilled artisan, received a fine education and became editor of the *Encyclopedia.* He included many articles vigorously attacking Old Regime abuses, such as religious intolerance, unjust taxation, and governmental absolutism.

HISTORICAL ANALYSIS: *Importance of the Intellectuals.* Some historians maintain that bad conditions alone do not make a revolution. They point out that the bad conditions of the Old Regime existed in France for hundreds of years before 1789. In addition to bad conditions, these historians believe, the people need a stimulus provided by orators and writers—the intellectuals. In speeches and writings these intellectuals convince the people how bad their conditions are, propose a course of remedial action, and most important, hold out a vision of a better post-revolutionary world. According to this analysis, bad conditions *plus* sufficient intellectual stimulus will cause a revolution.

**3. Influence of the English and American Revolutions.** Of all continental Europeans, the French had been most stimulated by the successful revolts in England and America. France was influenced by the Puritan and Glorious revolutions in England because *(a)* the two countries are geographically close, *(b)* many English—both Royalist and Parliamentary supporters—had taken refuge in France, and *(c)* the French philosophers praised the English parliamentary government.

France was influenced by the American Revolution because *(a)* Lafayette and other French citizens fought for the American cause and spread liberal ideas and *(b)* Benjamin Franklin and Thomas Jefferson, popular American envoys to Paris, inspired French thought.

**4. Incompetent and Unpopular Government.** King *Louis XVI* (ruled 1774–1792) was an incompetent ruler, especially for such difficult times. He was dull of mind, weak in character, and lacking in leadership qualities. Furthermore, his queen, *Marie Antoinette*, was unpopular. She was a foreigner (a Hapsburg from Austria) and a vain, frivolous person.

## IMMEDIATE CAUSE OF THE FRENCH REVOLUTION: FINANCIAL DIFFICULTIES

**1. Louis XVI Brings France to Financial Bankruptcy (by 1788).** As a result of his predecessors' extravagances and wars, Louis XVI inherited an impoverished French treasury. Instead of instituting reforms, he worsened the situation as he *(a)* spent heavily to aid the American colonists against Britain, *(b)* maintained a lavish royal court at Versailles, and *(c)* refused to tax the privileged classes.

Louis ignored the advice of two able finance ministers—first *Turgot* and then *Necker*—to end court extravagances and tax the nobility. Heeding the courtiers (nobles), Louis dismissed these ministers without effecting any financial reforms. By 1788 France was in bankruptcy.

**2. Louis Summons the Estates-General (1789)**

*a. Significance.* To solve the financial crisis, Louis called into session the French legislature, the *Estates-General*. For 175 years (since 1614), French kings had ruled autocratically without convening the Estates-General. By breaking this precedent Louis admitted that the king alone could not solve France's financial difficulties.

*b. Undemocratic Features of the Estates-General*

(1) *Representation.* The Estates-General consisted of the privileged First Estate—300 representatives; the privileged Second Estate—300 representatives; and the unprivileged Third Estate—600 representatives. The two privileged classes, constituting 3 percent of the population, thus had as many representatives as the unprivileged class, totaling 97 percent of the population.

(2) *Voting.* The Estates-General voted by estates, not by individual members. Each estate had one vote. Therefore, the two privileged estates, together having two votes, could outvote the Third Estate.

### Representation in the Estates-General (1789)

| Classes | | Representatives in Estates-General | Votes in Estates-General | Percent of Population |
|---|---|---|---|---|
| Privileged classes | First Estate | 300 | 1 | 3% |
| | Second Estate | 300 | 1 | |
| Unprivileged class | Third Estate | 600 | 1 | 97% |

*c. The Cahiers—Lists of Grievances.* The Third Estate representatives received from many people grievances listed in loose-leaf notebooks called *cahiers.* These documents, while pledging loyalty to the king, demanded far-reaching reforms—an end to Old Regime abuses.

## THE FRENCH REVOLUTION BEGINS (1789)

**1. The Estates-General Becomes the National Assembly (1789).** The Third Estate representatives were led at first by two members of the privileged classes, the *Abbé Sieyès* and *Count Mirabeau.* The Third Estate members demanded that the Estates-General be transformed into a *National Assembly* with each *member,* not each *estate,* having one vote. By this method of voting, the commoners, joined by some liberal clergy and nobility, would gain the Assembly majority and enact a program of basic reform.

When the king rejected the proposed National Assembly, the representatives of the Third Estate took two revolutionary actions: *(a)* They declared themselves to be the National Assembly. *(b)* In the *Tennis Court Oath,* they pledged to provide France with a constitution.

These actions were supported by Paris mobs, who demonstrated against the king. Thereupon, Louis yielded and consented to the formation of the National Assembly.

**2. The Bastille Is Destroyed (July 14, 1789).** Incited by rumors that the king had ordered troops to Paris to disperse the National Assembly, Paris mobs stormed and destroyed a symbol of the Old Regime—the hated prison called the *Bastille.* When this news reached the provinces, the aroused peasants attacked nobles' castles and destroyed the records of feudal dues.

By such violence the commoners *(a)* expressed their support for the National Assembly and *(b)* gave warning to the king and the nobility not to resist reforms.

July 14—the day of the fall of the Bastille—is a French national holiday. Bastille Day is the equivalent of July 4, our Independence Day.

## WORK OF THE NATIONAL ASSEMBLY (1789–1791)

Controlled by its bourgeois, or moderate, members, the National Assembly legislated against Old Regime conditions.

**1. Abolition of Special Privileges.** The National Assembly abolished *(a)* payment of feudal dues by the peasants, *(b)* payment of Church tithes, *(c)* tax exemptions of the privileged classes, *(d)* all class distinctions, and *(e)* guild restrictions on trade and manufacturing.

**2. Declaration of the Rights of Man.** The National Assembly adopted the *Declaration of the Rights of Man.* Its main ideas are: *(a)* Men are born free and equal with rights to liberty, property, security, and resistance to oppression. *(b)* All citizens are entitled to a voice in making the nation's laws. *(c)* All persons are guaranteed equality before the law; freedom from unlawful arrest; and freedom of speech, press, and religion. (This Declaration of the Rights of Man was modeled after the English Bill of Rights and the American Declaration of Independence.)

**3. Financial Measures.** To solve the financial crisis, the National Assembly seized the Church lands, totaling one-fifth of the land area of France. This measure aided the government financially.

*a.* Church lands were used to back a new paper currency, called *assignats.* However, as the government kept printing an ever-increasing amount of assignats, they declined in value and eventually became worthless.

*b.* Church lands (and the domains of some nobles) were broken up and sold at low prices to the peasants. These sales transformed France into a nation of small, independent landowners.

**4. Religious Measures.** To deprive the Catholic Church of the special position it had held under the Old Regime, the National Assembly abolished Church tithes, seized Church lands, guaranteed religious freedom to all groups, and subjected the Church to state control by the *Civil Constitution of the Clergy.*

The Civil Constitution declared that *(a)* the Catholic Church in France is a national church independent of the pope and *(b)* the Catholic clergy in France are paid government officials to be elected by the people.

This document was condemned by the pope and by most of the French clergy. Those of the clergy who refused to swear allegiance to the law were called *nonjuring clergy.*

The Catholic Church—from the highest clerical official to the parish priest and devout Church member—became the revolution's bitter enemy.

**5. Reform of Local Government.** The National Assembly replaced *(a)* the old provinces with 83 *departments* ruled by local assemblies and *(b)* the old provincial tariffs, taxes, and regulations with uniform national taxes and laws. By deemphasizing traditional local loyalties and by making laws nationwide, the National Assembly stimulated loyalty to the nation.

**6. Constitution of 1791.** The National Assembly wrote a constitution providing for a *limited monarchy.* *(a)* The hereditary king retained limited executive powers and received a temporary veto over legislation. *(b)* The elected *Legislative Assembly* passed the nation's laws. *(c)* Members of the Assembly had to be property owners elected by taxpaying citizens.

By these provisions the bourgeoisie, in control of the National Assembly, expected to retain power in the new government.

## THE LIMITED MONARCHY HAS A SHORT LIFE (1791–1792)

**1. Supporters.** Most of the *bourgeoisie* and many *peasants* were well satisfied with their gains under the Revolution. These groups supported the limited monarchy and wanted an end to excitement and change. This proved impossible, however, since too many groups were dissatisfied with the Revolution and opposed the limited monarchy.

## 2. Opponents Favoring a Republic

*a. Girondists,* a *moderate* political party representing some of the bourgeoisie, wanted a middle-class republic (similar to that of the United States).

*b. Jacobins,* a *radical* political party, represented the city workers, who paid no taxes and, therefore, under the constitution of 1791, had no voice in the government. They opposed both the king and the bourgeoisie. The Jacobins desired a republic dominated by the poorer people.

The Jacobins got very close to the people because of (1) their many clubs throughout France, (2) their skillful use of newspapers and street demonstrations to spread their ideas, and (3) their capable leaders: *Marat, Danton, Robespierre.*

## 3. Opponents Favoring the Old Regime

*a. Louis XVI* resented the loss of his absolute power. He conspired with foreign monarchs against the Revolution. In 1791 Louis and his wife, Marie Antoinette, attempted to flee the country but were captured and brought back to Paris.

*b. Devout Catholics,* led by the nonjuring clergy, opposed the Revolution because of its treatment of the Church.

*c. French nobles* were indignant over the loss of their special privileges. The *émigrés,* nobles who had fled the country, urged foreign monarchs to invade France and restore the Old Regime.

*d. Foreign monarchs,* especially the kings of Prussia and Austria, feared that the French Revolution, if successful, would inspire revolt among their own subjects. In 1792 these rulers ordered their armies into France to suppress the Revolution.

**4. End of the Monarchy.** The limited monarchy did not survive the foreign invasion of France. As Austrian and Prussian armies moved toward Paris, French antiroyalist mobs rioted. They accused the king of being in communication with the enemy. The French legislature thereupon deposed the king and called for election of a *National Convention.* It was to govern France and to draw up a new, more democratic constitution.

## THE NATIONAL CONVENTION PROTECTS AND PROMOTES THE REVOLUTION (1792–1795)

**1. The First French Republic.** The National Convention proclaimed France a republic—the *First French Republic.* The Convention then tried Louis XVI on charges of treason and sentenced him to death by *guillotine.* Louis' execution alarmed the other monarchs of Europe. Soon France was invaded by additional foreign armies. Not only Prussia and Austria but also Britain, Holland, and Spain sought to crush the Revolution.

**2. Jacobin Domination: The Committee of Public Safety.** In the face of foreign invasion, the radical, or extremist, Jacobins seized control of the Convention. They were determined to protect the Revolution against its enemies, both foreign and domestic. The Jacobins centralized all governmental powers into the *Committee of Public Safety.* This was a small dictatorial group led first by Danton and later by Robespierre.

**3. Conscript Armies Repel Foreign Invaders.** To protect the Revolution against *foreign* enemies, the Committee of Public Safety appealed to the *nationalism* of the French people. The Committee subjected all Frenchmen to compulsory military service, called the *draft,* or *conscription.* Inspired by French revolutionary ideals, the citizen-soldiers of the conscripted armies decisively drove out the invading mercenary forces.

**4. The Reign of Terror Crushes Domestic Enemies.** To protect the Revolution against *domestic* enemies, the Committee of Public Safety instituted the *Reign of Terror.* The Committee *(a)* arrested all persons suspected of treason, no matter how farfetched the suspicion, and *(b)* sentenced many thousands to death by guillotine, no matter how meager the evidence against them. This Reign of Terror brutally crushed all domestic opposition.

Eventually the horrors of the Reign of Terror turned the French people against the Jacobins and brought an end to the Reign of Terror. In 1794 the rival Jacobin leaders, Danton and Robespierre, were both guillotined. The moderates, or anti-Jacobins, now regained control of the National Convention.

**5. Noteworthy Reforms.** To promote its revolutionary goals, the National Convention *(a)* abolished imprisonment for debt, *(b)* abolished slavery in French colonies, *(c)* adopted the metric system of uniform weights and measures, *(d)* planned a national system of education, and *(e)* prohibited *primogeniture,* a practice that required property to be willed entirely to the eldest son regardless of the existence of other children.

Also, the National Convention drew up a constitution for a republic headed by a five-man *Directory.* Incompetent and corrupt, the Directory lasted only four years before being replaced by the one-man rule of Napoleon Bonaparte. Thus, the French Revolution, which had originated as a movement for democracy, culminated in a military dictatorship.

## SIGNIFICANCE OF THE FRENCH REVOLUTION

**1. Democratic Ideals.** The French Revolution proclaimed the individual's democratic rights in its slogan *liberté, égalité, fraternité.*

*a. Liberty* meant freedom for all persons (1) from despotism, especially absolute rule and unjust imprisonment, (2) from unnecessary and unfair economic restrictions, (3) to influence and change the government, and (4) of speech, press, religion, and other basic civil liberties.

*b. Equality* meant equal treatment for all persons (1) before the law and (2) in business, society, and politics.

*c. Fraternity* meant the brotherhood of all persons working together to make a better world.

**2. Emphasis on Nationalism.** The French Revolution intensified the spirit of nationalism. Loyalty to the nation permeated all classes and influenced every aspect of life. *(a)* War became the concern of the entire nation, as conscript citizen-armies rose to defend—not their province or city, nor their feudal lord or king—but their country. *(b)* The *Marseillaise*, a patriotic song by *Rouget de Lisle*, was adopted as the national anthem. *(c) July 14, Bastille Day*, was proclaimed a national holiday. *(d)* State-controlled education began to serve as a major agency for preserving the nation's ideals.

**3. Worldwide Influence.** The French Revolution, with its ideals of democracy and nationalism, has tremendously influenced peoples throughout the world: first in western Europe, then in Latin America, and later in Asia and Africa. To this very day, peoples everywhere who seek democratic government and national independence reflect the influence of the French Revolution.

HISTORICAL ANALYSIS: *The Pattern of Revolution.* Citing the French Revolution of 1789 as the primary example but also referring to the English Puritan Revolution of 1640 and, to a lesser extent, the American Revolution of 1776, a number of historians have attempted to discern a pattern for revolutions professing democratic goals. These historians acknowledge that each revolution may have individual characteristics considerably different from any other revolution, yet they affirm that democratic revolutions exhibit significant similarities—a logical pattern of events.

Some of these are: (1) On the eve of revolution, the government has failed to meet the needs of the people, has denied political power to new and powerful social or economic groups, and has lost the support of the intellectuals. (2) The revolution begins with a dramatic act that demonstrates the inability of the government to control the course of events. (3) The moderates in the revolutionary movement seize power and attempt a program of moderate reform. (4) The moderate reform program arouses opposition and violence—by counter-revolutionary forces within the country and by fearful foreign countries. (5) To preserve the revolution in this "crisis stage," the extremists of the revolutionary movement seize control and employ force and terror against enemies of the revolution. *Crane Brinton,* in his book *The Anatomy of Revolution,* summarizes these developments as "a tendency for power to go . . . from the conservatives of the old regime to the moderates to the radicals or extremists." (6) With the crisis surmounted and the public sick of the bloodletting, the terror comes to an end.

(7) In the ensuing period of political instability, a powerful leader emerges, seizes power, and rules as a dictator. Crane Brinton states that "dictatorship and revolution are inevitably closely associated because revolutions to a certain extent break down, or at least weaken, laws, customs, habits, beliefs which bind men together in society." (8) The public acceptance of the dictator is based on the belief that he will preserve some of the gains of the revolution while at the same time providing political stability and social cohesion.

The above-described pattern of revolution raises several interesting questions: (1) To what extent is this pattern accurate? (2) In what ways does the American Revolution diverge from this pattern and how would you explain such divergencies? (3) If revolutions for democracy end in dictatorship, are revolutions an advisable technique for seeking democratic reforms?

## MULTIPLE–CHOICE QUESTIONS

1. Which statement best describes the Old Regime in France? (1) No differences existed among social classes. (2) The burden of taxation fell almost entirely on the Third Estate. (3) Citizens enjoyed freedom of speech. (4) The Estates-General controlled the government.

2. The two privileged classes in France under the Old Regime were the (1) nobility and peasants (2) nobility and clergy (3) nobility and bourgeoisie (4) clergy and bourgeoisie.

3. Which aspect of feudalism existed in France until the Revolution in 1789? (1) Feudal dues were paid to the nobility by the peasants. (2) Military protection was provided for the lower classes by the nobility. (3) Most peasants were bound to the land as serfs. (4) Political power was restricted to the knights.

4. The *fundamental* cause of the French Revolution was the (1) Reign of Terror (2) abuses of the Old Regime (3) desire for a republic (4) fact that conditions in France were worse than in most other countries in Europe.

5. Which is most nearly *opposite* in meaning to the *writ of habeas corpus?* (1) *lettre de cachet* (sealed letter) (2) assignat (3) Tennis Court Oath (4) tithe.

6. France was the first country in continental Europe to have a revolution against the Old Regime because (1) Louis XVI was an evil tyrant (2) the middle class was more advanced than in other countries (3) economic conditions were worse than in other countries (4) a French citizen invented the guillotine.

7. In his book *The Social Contract,* Rousseau supported the principle of (1) the totalitarian state (2) the divine right of kings (3) benevolent despotism (4) government by the will of the people.

8. Which was an important contribution of Voltaire and Montesquieu? (1) writing the Declaration of the Rights of Man (2) voting for the execution of Louis XVI (3) publicizing Old Regime injustices (4) acting as advisers to the Girondists.

9. Supporters of Adam Smith's laissez-faire theory advocated (1) high protective tariffs (2) partial regulation of business by government (3) strict regulation of business by government (4) noninterference in business by government.

10. An important characteristic of the 18th-century Intellectual Revolution was (1) criticism of the Old Regime (2) centralization of government (3) dispute resulting in a split in the Catholic Church (4) revival of interest in Latin literature.

11. The *cahiers* of 1789 generally demanded   (1) the death of the king   (2) government reform   (3) the overthrow of the Church   (4) war against Britain.

12. The seizure of the Bastille on July 14, 1789, was important because it   (1) gave the revolutionists a strong fort   (2) released thousands of prisoners who joined the Revolutionary army   (3) placed the royal family in the power of the revolutionists   (4) represented a successful attack on a symbol of the tyranny of the Old Regime.

13. Louis XVI's purpose in summoning the Estates-General in 1789 was to   (1) draft a new constitution   (2) choose a new king   (3) make a treaty of alliance with the United States   (4) consider the question of government debt.

14. The representatives of the Third Estate demanded that the Estates-General be declared a National Assembly in order to   (1) bar representatives of the clergy and nobility   (2) please the king   (3) achieve voting by members rather than by Estates   (4) secure additional representatives from the bourgeoisie.

15. *The Declaration of the Rights of Man,* adopted by the National Assembly, was a   (1) constitution to govern France   (2) document stating the principles of the French Revolution   (3) law confiscating Church lands in France   (4) declaration of war against the monarchs of Austria and Prussia.

16. The Civil Constitution of the Clergy   (1) placed the Church in France under government control   (2) was advocated by the Church   (3) was written by Diderot   (4) was widely accepted by the French clergy.

17. The *assignats* of the French Revolutionary era were   (1) members of a moderate political party   (2) paper currency   (3) nobles who fled from France   (4) plots of land sold to the peasants.

18. During the French Revolution the Jacobins favored the establishment of   (1) a republic   (2) a limited monarchy   (3) an absolute monarchy   (4) a confederation.

19. Foreign intervention during the French Revolution resulted in the   (1) suppression of the Jacobins   (2) establishment of the limited monarchy   (3) establishment of the First French Republic   (4) overthrow of the First French Republic.

20. Which is a statement of opinion rather than a fact about the Reign of Terror?   (1) It employed the guillotine.   (2) It took thousands of lives.   (3) It preserved the gains of the French Revolution.   (4) It was instituted by the Committee of Public Safety.

21. As a result of the French Revolution, the Catholic Church in France   (1) was strengthened   (2) was permanently driven out   (3) became the established church   (4) had its power limited.

22. "Equality" in the slogan "liberty, equality, fraternity" meant equality   (1) of income   (2) of ability   (3) before the law   (4) in land ownership.

23. A permanent result of the Revolution of 1789 for France was the   (1) establishment of a two-party system of government   (2) abolition of the feudal class system   (3) loss of the French overseas empire   (4) destruction of the bourgeoisie.

24. The French Revolution and the American Revolution are similar in that both were   (1) provoked by what was considered to be unfair taxation   (2) discouraged by the failure of the Glorious Revolution in England   (3) supported by advocates of mercantilism   (4) influenced by reformers who urged protection of Catholic interests.

25. The French Revolution had an impact on history in that it   (1) showed how a successful popular revolt should be carried out   (2) brought out the need for an international police organization   (3) portrayed the significance of military might for the first time   (4) influenced people throughout the world with its ideals of democracy and nationalism.

## MULTIPLE–CHOICE QUESTIONS

Select the number of the item that does *not* belong in the corresponding group.

1. *Evidences of nationalism during the French Revolution:* (1) the activities of the émigrés (2) the singing of the *Marseillaise* (3) the celebration of Bastille Day (4) state-controlled education.

2. *Taxes burdening the peasants under the Old Regime:* (1) *gabelle* (2) *taille* (3) *cahier* (4) *corvée*.

3. *Jacobin leaders during the French Revolution:* (1) Robespierre (2) Danton (3) Diderot (4) Marat.

4. *The Declaration of the Rights of Man:* (1) preceded the American Declaration of Independence (2) was greatly influenced by Rousseau (3) appeared during the early stages of the French Revolution (4) drew on Locke's theory of natural rights.

5. *Reforms of the National Assembly:* (1) abolition of special privileges (2) reform of local government (3) a constitution for a limited monarchy (4) adoption of the metric system.

## IDENTIFICATION QUESTIONS: WHO AM I?

| | | |
|---|---|---|
| De Lisle | Montesquieu | Smith |
| Lafayette | Robespierre | Turgot |
| Mirabeau | Rousseau | Voltaire |

1. I fought against intolerance wherever I found it. I am associated with the statement "I disapprove of what you say, but I will defend to the death your right to say it."

2. I composed a patriotic song that became the French national anthem, the *Marseillaise*.

3. I favored the principle of government by the people. The quotations "Back to nature" and "Man is born free, and everywhere he is in chains" are taken from my writings, which included *The Social Contract*.

4. As finance minister to Louis XVI, I urged tax reforms, but my suggestions were not heeded.

5. In *The Spirit of Laws*, I supported the principle of separation of powers. Americans were influenced by my writings when they wrote the United States Constitution.

6. A Scottish economist, I advocated the policy of laissez-faire in my book, *Wealth of Nations*. This idea pleased the rising class of business people.

7. I was called the driving force behind the Reign of Terror in the French Revolution. Some called me "the Incorruptible." Eventually I was a victim of the Reign of Terror.

## ESSAY QUESTIONS

1. The fundamental cause of the French Revolution was the abuses of the Old Regime. (*a*) Explain what is meant by the Old Regime. (*b*) Name *three* abuses of the Old Regime and show how *each* abuse mentioned helped to bring on the Revolution.

2. (*a*) Discuss *three* reforms made by the National Assembly (1789–1791), indicating for *each:* (*i*) conditions that existed before the reform (*ii*) changes introduced by the reform (*iii*) your evaluation of the reform. (*b*) State *one* political reform that was *not* achieved by the National Assembly.

3. For the terms in each of the following pairs (*a*) state the general category to which both belong and (*b*) explain *one* significant difference between them:

| | |
|---|---|
| *a.* writ of habeas corpus—*lettre de cachet* | *d.* storming of the Bastille— Reign of Terror |
| *b.* conscripts—mercenaries | *e.* Jacobins—Girondists |
| *c.* Estates-General—National Assembly | *f.* guild regulations—mercantilist regulations |

4. The French Revolution of 1789 proclaimed the ideals of *liberty, equality, fraternity.* (*a*) Explain fully what is meant by each of these terms. (*b*) Prove that each of these ideals influences world affairs today.

5. Discuss *two* similarities and *two* differences between the French Revolution of 1789 and the American Revolution of 1776.

6. Discuss briefly *two* reasons for agreeing or disagreeing with *each* of the following statements: (*a*) The French philosophers of the 18th century prove the power of the pen. (*b*) Louis XVI had no reason to be surprised by the outbreak of the French Revolution. (*c*) The Reign of Terror outweighed any good effects of the French Revolution. (*d*) The French Revolution marked the beginning of modern nationalism. (*e*) The French Revolution has had little effect outside France. (*f*) Members of the bourgeoisie were the original leaders of the French Revolution, but they lost control of the revolutionary movement. (*g*) The French Revolution, which originated as a movement for democratic reform, had entirely unexpected results.

# Part 5. The Napoleonic Era (1799–1815): Military Dictatorship

## NAPOLEON'S RISE TO POWER: REASONS

*Napoleon Bonaparte,* son of a poor village lawyer, was born on the Mediterranean island of *Corsica.* By 1799, at the age of 30, he had become master of France. His amazing rise was due to:

**1. His Character.** Napoleon possessed a brilliant mind, a keen insight into human nature, tireless energy, and tremendous ambition. In his climb to power, he was ruthless. Napoleon believed himself possessed of a magnetic personality and extraordinary powers—a "man of destiny." He was able to convince others to follow him as a divinely inspired, or *charismatic,* leader.

**2. His Military Ability.** Educated in a French military academy, Napoleon became a renowned general. He devised superior combat tactics, inspired his soldiers, and won astounding victories. Napoleon's troops, who fondly called him the "Little Corporal," supported his political ambitions.

**3. France's Desire for Orderly Government.** By 1799 the French people had become weary of Revolutionary disorder and were displeased with the inefficient, corrupt Directory. They wanted a government that, while safeguarding

Revolutionary gains, would be competent and orderly. For such government the French were willing to accept the popular military hero Napoleon.

## NAPOLEON'S RISE TO POWER: HIGHLIGHTS

1. **First Public Recognition (1793–1795).** Napoleon, as an artillery officer, helped drive British troops from the French seaport of Toulon. Later Napoleon dispersed rioting Paris mobs threatening the National Convention.

2. **Italian Campaign (1796–1797).** Napoleon was now given command of the French army in Italy and won a series of impressive victories in which he routed the larger Austrian forces. He thus became a national hero.

3. **Egyptian Campaign (1798–1799).** To secure a base for attacking Britain's valuable colony of India, Napoleon invaded Egypt. Napoleon's reports of great military victories, although highly exaggerated, enhanced his popularity. Napoleon's career was also aided as the incompetent Directory daily lost public support and French armies in Europe suffered reverses. After the Battle of the Nile, in which the French Mediterranean fleet was destroyed by the British under *Admiral Horatio Nelson,* Napoleon's army in Egypt was cut off from France. In 1799 Napoleon himself eluded the British fleet and returned to France.

4. **Coup d'État (1799).** Napoleon ousted the Directory by a *coup d'état* (a swift overthrow of a government by force). He prepared a new constitution, which the voters approved by a plebiscite (a "yes" or "no" vote). The constitution retained the form of a republic but concentrated governmental power in the *First Consul.* Napoleon ruled France officially as First Consul but in reality as military dictator.

5. **Proclamation of Empire (1804).** Napoleon changed the republic into an empire and crowned himself *Emperor Napoleon I.* Impressed by Napoleon's military and governmental achievements, the people, in a plebiscite, again voted overwhelming approval. The French Revolution had thus led to an undisguised dictatorship.

## NAPOLEON DOMINATES EUROPE

1. **Napoleon's Military Victories (to 1809).** In 1799, when Napoleon seized the government by a coup d'état, France was at war with the Allies, a coalition of Europe's hereditary rulers who were determined to crush the French Revolution. Napoleon took command of the French forces, won significant victories, and in 1802 ended the war favorably for France.

After a brief peace, Napoleon and the Allies resumed the conflict. The Allies wanted to overthrow Napoleon and destroy French power; Napoleon wanted to dominate Europe. From 1803 to 1809 Napoleon achieved great triumphs, defeating Austria and Russia at *Austerlitz*, Prussia at *Jena*, and Russia at *Friedland*. Only Britain, with its powerful navy, remained safe, for Napoleon lacked the sea power to invade the British Isles.

**2. Napoleon at the Height of His Power (1810–1812).** Napoleon now dominated continental Europe from the Atlantic coast to Russia. (See map, below.) Napoleon *(a)* ruled a France enlarged by the annexation of neighboring lands; *(b)* appointed relatives and generals to rule various territories: Spain, northern Italy, Naples, and parts of Germany; *(c)* controlled the newly created dependencies, the Grand Duchy of Warsaw (part of Poland) and the Confederation of the Rhine (an organization of western German states); *(d)* reduced to minor status his defeated enemies, Prussia and Austria; and *(e)* formed an alliance with his former enemy, the only other continental power, Russia. Napoleon's domination of Europe faced serious challenge only from Britain.

## NAPOLEON'S DOWNFALL: REASONS

**1. Personal Weaknesses.** Napoleon's ambition caused him to overreach himself. In conquering most of Europe, he created an empire too complex to be ruled efficiently by one person. His lust for territory and power was limitless. And as he grew older, he became stubborn and unwilling to accept advice.

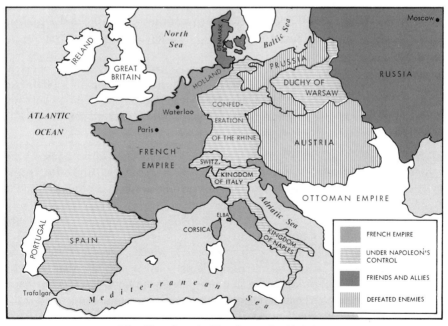

**The Napoleonic Empire at Its Height**

## 2. Britain's Opposition to Napoleon: Reasons

*a.* The British government, a limited monarchy controlled by the upper classes, viewed Napoleon as a symbol of the excesses of the French Revolution: the shattering of tradition, the violence of the Reign of Terror, and the rise of military despotism.

*b.* Napoleon sought to unite Europe under his rule, whereas Britain wanted no one continental nation to be all powerful. In a divided Europe Britain could shift its support from one nation to another and thereby wield the *balance of power.* (For centuries before Napoleon, England's continental policy had been guided by this balance-of-power concept.)

*c.* Napoleon aided French merchants and manufacturers in driving the British from continental markets. Britain, the leading industrial and trading nation, suffered economic hardship and could not tolerate this blow at its economic well-being.

*d.* Napoleon planned to restore French colonial power. In the Seven Years' War (1756–1763), France had lost its major overseas territories, and Britain had become the leading colonial nation. Britain now considered the colonial ambitions of Napoleon as a threat to its possessions.

**3. Britain's Control of the Seas.** Napoleon dominated on land, but Britain ruled the seas. (For this reason their conflict has sometimes been called the struggle between "the tiger and the shark.") Under Admiral Nelson the British navy overwhelmed the French fleets in the battles of the *Nile* (1798) and *Trafalgar* (1805). Naval supremacy saved Britain from invasion and shattered Napoleon's dream of an overseas empire.

(Weakness on the seas forced Napoleon to give up his largest overseas possession, the *Louisiana Territory* in North America. By treaty in 1800 he had acquired this territory from Spain. In 1803, perhaps realizing that he could not defend it against British sea power, Napoleon sold the Louisiana Territory to the United States.)

**4. Napoleon's Continental System.** Unable to invade the British Isles, Napoleon struck at Britain economically by the *Continental System.* In the *Berlin* and *Milan Decrees* (1806–1807), Napoleon ordered the European continent closed to British trade. Russia, his ally, at first agreed to this boycott of British goods. Napoleon despised Britain as a "nation of shopkeepers" and expected the Continental System to effect Britain's ruin.

Britain retaliated by the *Orders in Council,* which barred neutral nations from trading with France and its allies. Thus, Britain not only deprived the Continent of essential products but also interfered with neutral trade. (Britain's seizure of American merchant ships bound for the Continent was one cause of the *War of 1812* between the United States and Britain.)

Throughout Europe people blamed Napoleon for *(a)* a decline in trade, *(b)* an increase in business failures and unemployment, and *(c)* shortages of cloth, machinery, and foodstuffs. In place of hard-to-get imports, Napoleon proposed less popular substitutes: beet sugar (for cane sugar) and chicory (for coffee). Nevertheless, smuggling became widespread.

Although Britain suffered economically from the Continental System, Napoleon was harmed perhaps more by the resentment of the European peoples against his rule.

**5. Russia's Opposition to Napoleon.** As Napoleon achieved domination over Europe, Czar *Alexander I* feared that Napoleon's power threatened Russia. Also, the Russians suffered economic loss under the Continental System, which kept their grain from British markets. When, in 1812, the czar resumed trade with Britain, Napoleon invaded Russia (see below).

**6. Rising Spirit of Nationalism.** Inspired by French example, other European peoples became nationalistic. Spaniards, Prussians, Austrians, and other peoples could no longer tolerate French domination and were ready to fight for liberation. Napoleon now faced the opposition, not of hereditary monarchs and mercenary armies, but of entire nations.

**7. Exhaustion of France.** After many years of warfare, France had depleted its military forces and resources.

## NAPOLEON'S DOWNFALL: HIGHLIGHTS

**1. Peninsular War (1808–1814).** Spain and Portugal occupy the *Iberian Peninsula* in southwest Europe. Their nationalist-minded peoples rebelled against French rule and, by guerrilla warfare, greatly sapped French military strength. To aid the rebellion, Britain sent a force under Sir Arthur Wellesley, who later became the *Duke of Wellington*. This *Peninsular War* resulted in the defeat of the French and their expulsion from Portugal and Spain.

**2. Invasion of Russia (1812).** Leading a huge army, Napoleon invaded Russia to enforce the Continental System. The Russians at first refused battle and retreated, causing Napoleon to overextend his lines. Then, after a costly victory at *Borodino*, Napoleon captured Moscow, but fires, probably set by the Russians, destroyed the city. Lacking shelter, food, and clothing to survive the oncoming winter, Napoleon began a long retreat. Napoleon's retreat became a rout as his forces were harassed by Russian guerrilla attacks and by the bitter cold of "General Winter." Napoleon lost three-fourths of his army and suffered his first great military defeat.

**3. Wars of Liberation (1813–1814).** Heartened by the success of Russia, encouraged by financial subsidies from Britain, and inspired by nationalism, Prussia and Austria again declared war on France. In 1813 the armies of Russia, Prussia, and Austria defeated Napoleon at *Leipzig*, in central Germany, at the *Battle of the Nations*. The following year the Allies invaded France and captured Paris.

Napoleon abdicated his throne and was exiled to the Mediterranean island of *Elba*.

**4. The Hundred Days (1815).** Napoleon escaped from Elba and returned to France—a return that lasted only 100 days. As he regained control of France, the Allies marshalled their forces against him. At the *Battle of Waterloo*, in Belgium, Napoleon met final defeat by Allied armies under the Duke of Wellington. Napoleon was again exiled, this time to the South Atlantic island of *St. Helena*. Until his death, in 1821, Napoleon wrote his memoirs, in which he tried to justify his regime.

## NAPOLEON'S ACCOMPLISHMENTS IN FRANCE

Did Napoleon destroy or preserve the French Revolution?

Napoleon exercised the powers of an absolute monarch. He made the laws, decided on war and peace, censored speech and press, ordered arbitrary arrest and imprisonment, and utilized a secret police. Nevertheless, he claimed to be a "son of the Revolution." He provided efficient government, furthered the Revolutionary principle of equality, and accomplished noteworthy reforms.

**1. Centralization of Local Government.** Napoleon placed local government under national authority. He appointed local governors (prefects), mayors, judges, and police heads, thereby strengthening his control over the country. To this day, France retains a highly centralized, or *unitary*, government.

**2. Furtherance of Public Education.** Napoleon organized a system of state-controlled education under the *University of France*. This was a government agency, not an institution of higher learning. It *(a)* controlled all levels of education from primary grades to college, *(b)* built new schools, *(c)* improved educational standards and made them uniform throughout France, and *(d)* prepared courses of study to extol Napoleon and stimulate French nationalism. As a result, public education progressed in France at the expense of Church schools. (The *University of the State of New York*, directed by its *Board of Regents*, resembles the University of France.)

**3. Settlement of Religious Matters.** Napoleon restored friendly relations between France and the Catholic Church, thus healing a rift that had taken place during the French Revolution (see page 186). The *Concordat of 1801*, a religious agreement, provided that *(a)* the State pay the salaries of the French clergy, *(b)* the Church surrender claims to lands confiscated during the Revolution, and *(c)* bishops be nominated by the State but confirmed by the pope. By this agreement Napoleon protected the peasant owners of former Church lands and pleased the French people, overwhelmingly Catholic. Although Napoleon later annexed the Papal States and was excommunicated by the pope, the Concordat remained in effect. (For later religious developments in France, see pages 229–230.)

Napoleon also gained the support of non-Catholics. He guaranteed religious freedom and gave financial aid to Protestant and Jewish faiths.

**4. Legal Reform.** To establish uniform and just laws throughout France, Napoleon revised the legal system, emphasizing the Revolutionary principle of equality. The *Code Napoleon* (a) provided equal treatment before the law, (b) abolished what remained of serfdom and feudalism, and (c) guaranteed religious toleration and trial by jury. To this day, the Code Napoleon is the basis of law in France, most of western Europe, parts of Asia and Latin America, and the state of Louisiana.

**5. Legion of Honor.** For public recognition of distinguished military and civilian service to France, Napoleon created a society, the *Legion of Honor*. In accordance with the principle of equality, membership in the society was open to all persons regardless of social status. The Legion of Honor still exists.

**6. Improvement of Finances.** By collecting taxes fairly and efficiently, paying the debts of the government promptly, and creating the *Bank of France,* Napoleon restored the government to financial health. The Bank of France, the government's financial agent, maintained sound currency and promoted economic prosperity. Napoleon's financial measures pleased the bourgeoisie and encouraged business enterprise. To this day, the Bank of France heads France's banking system.

**7. Public Works.** Napoleon instituted extensive public works: building roads, bridges, and canals; dredging harbors; and beautifying Paris.

## NAPOLEON'S INFLUENCE UPON EUROPE

**1. Map Changes.** Of Napoleon's many map changes, two survived his downfall: (a) the abolition of the Austrian-dominated Holy Roman Empire and (b) the reduction in the number of German states, which aided German unification.

**2. The Legacy of the Revolution.** Throughout Europe Napoleon and his armies (a) spread French Revolutionary doctrines, especially equality, (b) ended Old Regime abuses of feudalism and serfdom, (c) introduced the Code Napoleon, and (d) encouraged state-controlled education.

**3. The Legacy of War and Empire.** Napoleon, through his armies and puppet governments, (a) promoted the growth of militarism, (b) aroused a spirit of intolerant nationalism among the conquered peoples, (c) caused widespread destruction and a terrible loss of lives, (d) dislocated Europe's economy, (e) placed a heavy tax burden on conquered peoples, and (f) set an example of despotic rule—the first modern dictator.

## MULTIPLE–CHOICE QUESTIONS

1. Which statement describes Napoleon's relation to the French Revolution? He (1) led the attack on the Bastille (2) helped cause the Revolution (3) used Revolutionary ideals to further his own ends (4) was overthrown by the Revolution.

2. In the French Revolution to 1795, Napoleon played (1) no part at all (2) a minor role in support of the Revolution (3) a minor role in support of the monarchy (4) a major role as head of all Revolutionary armies.

3. One reason why the French were willing to accept the leadership of Napoleon in 1799 was his (1) military ability (2) promise to restore the Bourbons (3) intention of building an empire in the Americas (4) royal ancestry.

4. Which list of titles correctly gives the steps by which Napoleon Bonaparte rose to power? (1) general, emperor, first consul (2) emperor, first consul, general (3) first consul, general, emperor (4) general, first consul, emperor.

5. The coup d'état by which Napoleon gained power was a (1) voluntary act of the legislature (2) swift and relatively bloodless revolution (3) gradual change (4) decree issued by the courts.

6. During the Napoleonic Era Britain carried out its policy of balance of power by (1) limiting the power of Parliament (2) maintaining a large standing army (3) using steam power to run machines (4) opposing any nation that threatened to dominate Europe.

7. The main reason the rulers of other countries fought Napoleon was that he was (1) a descendant of Louis XIV (2) irreligious (3) spreading revolutionary ideas (4) of humble birth.

8. A factor contributing to Napoleon's downfall was (1) his defeat in the Egyptian campaign (2) the breakup of his alliance with Russia (3) the failure of the Napoleonic Code (4) the opposition of the pope to the Concordat of 1801.

9. Napoleon's failure to conquer Russia was due chiefly to (1) better-trained and better-equipped Russian troops (2) industrial development of Russia (3) climate and size of Russia (4) aid given Russia by the British navy.

10. Napoleon's Confederation of the Rhine occupied approximately the same area as which country today? (1) Poland (2) East Germany (3) West Germany (4) Belgium.

11. By calling the British a "nation of shopkeepers," Napoleon was (1) complimenting them for their industry (2) admiring their financial strength (3) implying that they lacked military ability (4) complaining about the poor quality of British goods.

12. Napoleon sold the Louisiana Territory to the United States because he (1) was not interested in a colonial empire (2) wanted American military aid against Britain (3) feared that he could not defend the territory against British attack (4) could not continue his war against Britain without the purchase money.

13. Napoleon's Continental System was mainly an effort to (1) increase the exports from the Continent (2) increase the imports to the Continent (3) force the other countries of Europe into war with Britain (4) strike at Britain's trade.

14. Saying that a man has "met his Waterloo" means that he has (1) taken a shower (2) experienced a crushing defeat (3) discovered an opportunity for gaining power (4) found the meaning of life.

15. Napoleon established the University of France as (1) an institution to control all education in France (2) a liberal arts graduate school (3) a military academy (4) a dental and medical college.

16. By the Concordat between Napoleon and the pope, (1) all Church property that had

been confiscated was restored    (2) the Church was given complete control of education    (3) bishops were to be selected by the government and confirmed by the pope    (4) all religions except Catholicism were prohibited.

17. The importance of the Code Napoleon is that it    (1) established democracy in France    (2) is the basis of legal equality in many countries    (3) suppressed the ideas of the French Revolution    (4) was largely responsible for Napoleon's downfall.

18. A feature of present-day French government that may be traced back to Napoleon's reforms is    (1) freedom of the press    (2) dependence upon a large navy    (3) a highly centralized government    (4) a two-party system.

19. An effect of Napoleon's conquests on the nations of Europe was to    (1) discourage the formation of alliances    (2) encourage the growth of intolerant nationalism    (3) spread Catholicism    (4) strengthen feudalism.

## ESSAY QUESTIONS

1. Although the French Revolution of 1789–1795 introduced democratic reforms, it also opened the door to dictatorship. (a) Discuss two reasons why the French Revolution led to the rise to power of Napoleon Bonaparte. (b) Discuss two democratic reforms, begun during the French Revolution, that Napoleon furthered. (c) Discuss two democratic objectives of the French Revolution that Napoleon thwarted.

2. Discuss, under the following headings, Napoleon's place as a dominant leader in Europe: (a) two causes of his rise to power (b) two accomplishments for France (c) two causes of his downfall (d) two influences on Europe.

3. (a) Explain one political and one economic reason for Britain's hostility to Napoleon. (b) Show in two ways how Britain contributed to Napoleon's downfall.

4. Agree or disagree with each of the following statements, providing two facts to support your point of view: (a) Napoleon's relationship to the French Revolution was similar to Cromwell's relationship to the Puritan Revolution in England. (b) Although Napoleon was ambitious, his career was made possible chiefly because he came to maturity in unstable times. (c) Napoleon was justified in claiming to be a "son of the Revolution." (d) Napoleon was the first of the modern dictators.

# Part 6. The Age of Metternich (1815–1848): Failure of Reaction

## THE CONGRESS OF VIENNA (1814–1815)

1. **Purpose and Leading Members.** Following Napoleon's defeat, representatives from the victorious nations and France met at the Congress of Vienna. This was a peace conference to reconstruct war-torn Europe. Its major figures were (a) Britain—the Duke of Wellington; (b) Russia—Czar Alexander I; (c) Prussia—King Frederick William III; (d) France—Prince Talleyrand; and (e) Austria—Prince Metternich.

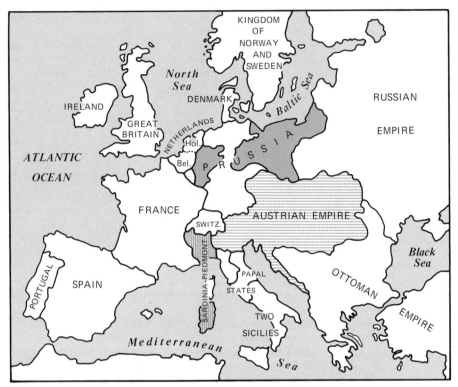

**Europe After the Congress of Vienna**

**2. Domination by Metternich: His Views.** *Metternich,* chief minister of Austria, was a forceful and influential diplomat. An aristocrat, he hated the French Revolutionary ideals of equality, democratic government, and national states; he admired the Old Regime institutions of class distinction, absolute monarchy, and multinational empires. Metternich directed the Congress toward settlements seeking to restore the Old Regime.

**3. Major Settlements**

*a. Principle of Legitimacy.* The rightful, or legitimate, rulers, deposed by the French Revolution or Napoleon, were restored to power. Accordingly a Bourbon king, *Louis XVIII,* brother of the executed Louis XVI, regained the throne of France. Other hereditary rulers returned in Spain, Holland, and in the Italian states of Sardinia-Piedmont, and the Two Sicilies.

*b. Principle of Compensation.* The nations that made important contributions to Napoleon's defeat were compensated (repaid) by territory. *Russia* received Finland and most of Poland. *Prussia* received part of Poland and various German territories, including some bordering the Rhine River; *Britain* received colonial possessions that it had occupied during the war, including Malta, Ceylon (now Sri Lanka), and South Africa.

Also, victorious nations that gave up territory were compensated by other territory. Accordingly *Holland* lost Ceylon and South Africa but acquired Belgium; *Austria* surrendered Belgium but obtained the Italian provinces of Lombardy and Venetia; *Sweden* lost Finland but received Norway.

### 4. Contempt for French Revolutionary Ideals

*a. Denial of Democracy.* The political settlements of the Congress of Vienna denied the people any voice in selecting their rulers and governments. The Congress reinstated the hereditary rulers as absolute monarchs, and most of them used their power to restore the Old Regime. (In France, where Revolutionary ideals were strongest, Louis XVIII granted limited suffrage, legal equality, and freedom of speech and press.)

*b. Denial of Nationalism.* The territorial settlements of the Congress denied many national groups independence and unity. Belgians, Poles, Finns, and Norwegians all were handed over to foreign governments. Germans and Italians each remained disunited and divided among a number of separate states. Many different nationalities were consigned to huge empires, such as Russia and Austria.

## THE METTERNICH SYSTEM

**1. Metternich's Policies.** As chief minister of the autocratic, multinational Austrian Empire, Metternich devoted his full energies to upholding the Vienna settlements and destroying French Revolutionary ideals. Because he sought to "turn the clock back" to Old Regime conditions, the *Age of Metternich* is also called the *Age of Reaction.*

(A *reactionary* wishes to return to previous conditions; a *conservative,* to maintain existing conditions relatively unchanged; a *liberal,* to make moderate changes gradually; and a *radical,* to make basic changes rapidly. These terms became popular during the Metternich Era and survive to this day.)

To enforce his reactionary views, Metternich took stern measures. *(a)* In the Austrian Empire and in the Austrian-dominated regions of Germany and Italy, Metternich employed censorship of speech and press, secret police, spies, and arbitrary arrest. *(b)* Throughout Europe Metternich used military force and diplomacy, especially the *Quadruple Alliance.*

**2. The Quadruple Alliance.** In 1815 Metternich organized the Quadruple Alliance of Austria, Prussia, Russia, and Britain. (In 1818 France became a member.) For several years the Alliance succeeded in its purposes: to enforce the Vienna settlements and to suppress revolutions. This cooperation among the major nations of Europe was called the *Concert of Europe.*

(By 1820 Britain virtually left the Alliance, finding it contrary to British trade interests and liberal traditions.)

## THE HOLY ALLIANCE

In 1815 Russia's Czar Alexander I organized the well-meaning but ineffective *Holy Alliance*. It consisted of most European monarchs, who pledged to rule by Christian principles: charity, peace, and justice. Despite their pledges, the hereditary rulers continued to rule their countries in their repressive ways. (The dormant Holy Alliance is often confused with the active Quadruple Alliance.)

## REVOLTS AGAINST THE METTERNICH SYSTEM (TO 1848)

Despite the expectations of reactionary leaders, people did not forget the French Revolutionary ideals. Reformers steadfastly opposed autocracy and demanded democratic government and independent national existence. Deprived of lawful means to attain their goals, the people resorted to revolutions.

### 1. The Revolutions of 1820–1821

*a. In Spain.* Spanish liberals, supported by Spanish troops, revolted against their reactionary king, Ferdinand VII, and compelled him to approve a limited monarchy under a liberal constitution. The revolt collapsed before an invading French army under Quadruple Alliance orders. The king, restored to absolute power, took cruel vengeance on the Spanish liberals.

*b. In Italy.* Led by the *Carbonari*, a secret liberal society, the Italian people revolted in the Two Sicilies (1820) and in Piedmont (1821). They sought to replace reactionary rule by liberal, constitutional government. Austrian armies, acting for the Quadruple Alliance, invaded Italy, suppressed the revolutions, and restored absolute monarchy.

### 2. The Latin American Revolutions (1810–1823)

*a. Background.* With Spain involved in the Napoleonic Wars, the Spanish colonies of Latin America declared their independence, adopted democratic constitutions, and established republican governments. The Latin Americans thereafter repulsed Spanish efforts to regain control. The outstanding colonial leaders were *Jose de San Martin, Bernardo O'Higgins,* and *Simon Bolivar*—the "George Washington of South America." In 1823 Latin Americans heard rumors of a plan by reactionary European nations to reconquer the Latin American states for Spain.

*b. Britain's Attitude.* Britain sharply opposed this plan of reconquest. British public opinion favored Latin American independence. Furthermore, British merchants had developed a profitable trade with independent Latin America. If Spain regained control, this trade would be destroyed by Spanish mercantilist restrictions.

*c. The United States' Attitude: The Monroe Doctrine.* In the United States popular sympathy and government policy also supported Latin American independence. (1) The American Revolution against Britain in part inspired the Latin American revolutions. (2) The United States preferred having weak independent republics south of its borders instead of having colonies controlled by a more powerful monarchical Spain. (3) American merchants and shippers had built up a profitable Latin American trade that would disappear under Spanish mercantilist control.

In 1823, despite its limited power of enforcement, the United States issued the *Monroe Doctrine*. President Monroe, in a message to Congress, declared that (1) the Western Hemisphere is closed to further European colonization and (2) any European attempt to intervene in the Western Hemisphere will be regarded as "dangerous to our peace and safety."

Since Britain also supported Latin American independence, the fear of its naval power—probably more than the Monroe Doctrine—influenced the reactionary European powers to abandon what plans they had for the reconquest of Latin America.

*d. Significance.* The maintenance of Latin American independence breached the Metternich System for the first time and heartened other peoples seeking democracy and independence.

**3. The Greek Revolution (1821–1829).** In their rebellion against Turkey, the Greek nationalists received military aid from Britain and, surprisingly, from France and Russia also. France and Russia temporarily ignored their distaste for revolution in order to weaken the Moslem Turks. In 1829 Greece achieved independence.

**4. The Revolutions of 1830–1832**

*a. In France.* In 1824 *Charles X* succeeded his brother, Louis XVIII, as king. Whereas Louis had followed a middle-of-the-road policy, Charles rejected compromise and attempted to restore Old Regime conditions. In 1830 the French revolted under liberal middle-class leadership. They (1) drove out Charles X, (2) enthroned *Louis Philippe*, Duke of Orleans, as a limited monarch, (3) enacted a liberal constitution, and (4) reduced property qualifications for voting in order to enfranchise more members of the middle class.

French success in 1830 ignited other European revolutions.

*b. In Belgium.* Rebelling against Holland, Belgian nationalists received support from France under Louis Philippe and from Britain. In 1839 Belgium secured international recognition of its independence and neutrality.

*c. In Italy.* In a series of uprisings, Italian democrats again revolted against their absolute monarchs. The rebels were ruthlessly suppressed by Austrian troops under Metternich's orders.

*d. In Poland.* Polish nationalists rebelled against Russian rule, but their uprising was cruelly suppressed by the Czarist army.

The successful revolutions of 1830–1832 in France and Belgium proved that, even in western Europe, the Metternich System could not hold back the forces of democracy and nationalism.

## 5. The Revolutions of 1848

*a. In France.* Louis Philippe's rule eventually aroused opposition. (1) *Republicans* opposed monarchy. (2) *Liberals* deplored the government's conservative policies, press censorship, corruption, and voting restrictions. (3) *City workers* suffered poor economic conditions and had no vote. In 1848 rioting Paris mobs compelled Louis Philippe to flee from France.

The revolutionists proclaimed the *Second French Republic* and guaranteed universal male suffrage. *Louis Napoleon*, nephew of the former emperor, Napoleon Bonaparte, was overwhelmingly elected president.

*b. In the Austrian Empire.* Inspired by French success and incited by poor economic conditions, the peoples within the Austrian Empire revolted. The Austrians demanded democracy; the Czechs and Italians claimed national independence, as did the Hungarians under *Louis Kossuth.* The avalanche of revolutions forced Metternich to flee the country. However, the revolutionary groups, belonging to different nationalities, started quarreling among themselves. Thus divided, they were conquered one at a time by the reactionary forces. The Hungarians, the last to succumb, fell when Austrian troops received help from a Russian army. Restored to full power, Austria's Hapsburg emperor abolished serfdom but rejected demands for national independence and annulled the previously proclaimed liberal constitution.

*c. In Italy and Germany.* Revolutions for democracy and national unity in northern Italy and in Germany were crushed. However, Sardinia-Piedmont in northern Italy retained its new liberal constitution. Prussia, the leading German state, also adopted a constitution, but it was undemocratic.

SIGNIFICANCE. Although mainly unsuccessful, the revolutions of 1848 were noteworthy. They (1) brought about the downfall of Metternich and the collapse of the Metternich System, (2) resulted in a republic and universal male suffrage in France, a liberal constitution in Piedmont, and abolition of serfdom in the Austrian Empire, (3) marked the last effort in Europe to overthrow reactionary government by revolution *alone.*

Subsequently European peoples groped toward democracy with uneven and varied results: In some countries there was no movement; in others, some measure of democracy developed by peaceful political and economic pressure; and in still others, some democratic gains were made through war and revolution. Also, suppressed and disunited European national groups moved toward national independence and unity through diplomacy and war.

# MULTIPLE–CHOICE QUESTIONS

1. The chief purpose of the Congress of Vienna was to   (1) stimulate nationalism   (2) protect western Europe from autocratic Russia   (3) restore the Old Regime as far as possible   (4) preserve the basic reforms of the French Revolution.

2. The principle of legitimacy at the Congress of Vienna meant the   (1) restoration of monarchs previously dethroned by Napoleon   (2) extension of democracy   (3) establishment of equality before the law   (4) self-determination of peoples.

3. In regard to France the Congress of Vienna succeeded in   (1) restoring the Old Regime   (2) abolishing the Napoleonic Code   (3) making France give up its recent territorial gains   (4) preventing the Bourbon family from regaining the throne.

4. At the Congress of Vienna, Belgium was   (1) granted its independence   (2) given to Holland   (3) neutralized   (4) given to France.

5. Which pair contains the nation that lost and the nation that gained South Africa at the Congress of Vienna?   (1) Holland—Britain   (2) Belgium—Portugal   (3) Austria—Prussia   (4) Belgium—Britain.

6. The Metternich System supported   (1) independence for Belgium   (2) the Greek revolution against Turkey   (3) restoration of the Bourbon monarchy in France   (4) a written constitution for Austria.

7. Because Metternich attempted to "turn the clock back" to before 1789, he has been classified as a   (1) reactionary   (2) conservative   (3) liberal   (4) radical.

8. Which position would a liberal be most likely to take?   (1) a return to the policies of the past   (2) opposition to all change   (3) moderate social and economic change   (4) immediate political and economic change brought about by force.

9. In the years immediately following the Congress of Vienna, the Great Powers of Europe generally   (1) granted democratic reforms to prevent revolutions   (2) suppressed democratic movements   (3) cooperated to bring about the downfall of Metternich   (4) checked Russian expansion in central Europe.

10. The author of the Holy Alliance, pledging rulers to govern according to Christian principles, was   (1) Metternich   (2) Talleyrand   (3) Alexander I   (4) Wellington.

11. Nationalism was largely responsible for the   (1) French Revolution—1830   (2) Belgian Revolution—1830   (3) Spanish Revolution—1820–1821   (4) Glorious Revolution—1689.

12. In 1820 and 1831 Austrian troops suppressed revolutions in   (1) Poland   (2) France   (3) Italy   (4) Spain.

13. The Monroe Doctrine declared that   (1) the Western Hemisphere was no longer open to European colonization   (2) no European country could own territory in Latin America   (3) Latin America could not trade with Britain   (4) Spain had to give up its possessions in the Western Hemisphere.

14. The Quadruple Alliance did *not* seriously challenge the Monroe Doctrine because   (1) the United States was a great world power   (2) Spain was willing to give up its colonies   (3) Great Britain was opposed to intervention in Latin America   (4) Russia was opposed to intervention in American affairs.

15. The Metternich System was most seriously challenged by the   (1) Revolutions of 1848   (2) Concert of Europe   (3) Revolutions of 1820–1821   (4) Carbonari.

16. A democratic gain of the Revolutions of 1848 was   (1) a liberal constitution in Prussia   (2) independence for Poland   (3) a liberal constitution for Sardinia-Piedmont   (4) overthrow of Hapsburg rule in Austria.

17. The history of Europe during the period 1815–1848 supports the generalization that (1) the Congress of Vienna destroyed the spirit of nationalism (2) the revolutionary spirit in France influenced other countries (3) the Austrian Empire had ceased to be a power in European affairs (4) Britain was the leader of the reactionary powers.

## MATCHING QUESTIONS

| *Column A* | *Column B* |
|---|---|
| 1. Louis Philippe | *a.* French delegate at the Congress of Vienna |
| 2. Duke of Wellington | *b.* Latin American revolutionary leader |
| 3. Simon Bolivar | *c.* Bourbon king restored to the French throne |
| 4. Louis Napoleon | *d.* Austrian leader at the Congress of Vienna |
| 5. Metternich | *e.* Bourbon king overthrown by revolution |
| 6. James Monroe | *f.* Orleanist king in France |
| 7. Louis Kossuth | *g.* Russian leader at the Congress of Vienna |
| 8. Talleyrand | *h.* Hungarian revolutionary leader |
| 9. Alexander I | *i.* President of the Second French Republic |
| 10. Louis XVIII | *j.* Belgian revolutionary leader |
| | *k.* American president opposed to European intervention in Latin America |
| | *l.* British delegate at the Congress of Vienna |

## ESSAY QUESTIONS

1. "The Congress of Vienna applied the principle of legitimacy but ignored the principle of nationalism." In relation to the Congress of Vienna, explain *(a)* one of its purposes *(b)* the principle of legitimacy, giving *one* example of its application *(c) two* instances in which the Congress ignored the principle of nationalism.

2. The Congress of Vienna was controlled by reactionaries. *(a)* Explain what is meant by a reactionary. *(b)* Describe *one* circumstance that enabled the reactionaries to control the Congress of Vienna. *(c)* Show how *two* decisions of the Congress illustrate the power of the reactionaries.

3. Select any *one* person in the news recently and state whether you would consider this person to be: reactionary *or* conservative *or* liberal *or* radical. Present *two* facts to support your opinion.

4. *(a)* Mention *three* territorial changes made by the Congress of Vienna. *(b)* Select *one* of the territories mentioned and describe its present status.

5. In regard to the Monroe Doctrine, explain *(a) one* provision of the doctrine *(b) two* reasons why the United States issued this doctrine *(c)* Britain's attitude toward the Monroe Doctrine *(d) two* effects of the doctrine on the Metternich System.

6. From 1815 to 1848 European peoples took part in many revolutions. Select any *two* revolutions of this period and explain for *each (a) one* condition that the people sought to remedy by revolution *(b) one* reason why the people resorted to revolution rather than peaceful methods of change *(c) one* result of the revolution.

# Part 7. Britain: Democracy Through Evolution

## UNDEMOCRATIC FEATURES OF THE BRITISH GOVERNMENT (1750)

Although the British people had taken important steps toward democracy (see pages 168–174), Britain in 1750 retained many undemocratic features in its government.

**1. Voting Restrictions.** By property qualifications voting for members of the House of Commons was limited chiefly to wealthy landowners. More than 95 percent of the adult male population could not vote. Women had no political rights.

**2. Open Ballot.** Voting took place by an open show of hands, not by secret ballot. The open ballot deterred many persons from voting their true beliefs and encouraged intimidation and bribery.

**3. Unfair Representation.** In apportioning representation to the House of Commons, the law ignored population shifts, caused by the Industrial Revolution, from rural districts to urban centers. Whereas the newly populated factory cities, such as Manchester and Leeds, remained unrepresented in Parliament, areas with greatly reduced populations retained their original representation. These depopulated districts were called *rotten boroughs*. A district in which a powerful landowner personally selected the representative to the House of Commons was called a *pocket borough*.

**4. Officeholding Restrictions.** A man could *not* hold public office unless he *(a)* owned considerable property, *(b)* could afford to serve without salary, and *(c)* was a member of the Church of England or of some other Protestant sect. These restrictions closed government service to Catholics, Jews, women, and poor people.

**5. Power of the Hereditary House of Lords.** Since laws required the consent of both branches of Parliament, legislation desired by the elected House of Commons could be defeated by the hereditary House of Lords.

## DEMOCRATIC REFORM IN BRITAIN TEMPORARILY HALTED BY EVENTS IN FRANCE (1789–1815)

The movement for democratic reform in Britain was delayed during the French Revolutionary and Napoleonic eras. At first the British people associated

209

reform with the violence and bloodshed of the French Reign of Terror. Later they were too preoccupied with defeating Napoleon to devote efforts to domestic reform. However, after Napoleon's exile in 1815, British liberals revived the movement for democratic reform.

## DEMOCRATIC REFORM IN BRITAIN: PROGRESS THROUGH EVOLUTION

In the struggle to bring political democracy to Britain, the opposing sides each gave way a little to avoid violence. They thus practiced the method of *compromise*. Reformers sought to accomplish their purpose by a gradual approach. Opponents of reform yielded under the pressure of overwhelming public sentiment. For these reasons we say that Britain achieved democracy through *evolution*.

This British approach contrasts with France's search for democracy through *revolution*. Some historians maintain that democratic reforms achieved through evolution come more slowly but prove more permanent than reforms achieved through revolution. Evolutionary changes are rooted in widespread public acceptance; whereas revolutionary changes are introduced only over vehement opposition, sharpen divisions within society, and may be rolled back by counter-revolutionary forces.

## EXTENDING THE RIGHT TO VOTE

**1. The Reform Bill of 1832.** Representing a moderate step forward and enjoying widespread public approval, this bill constituted the first important test of the evolutionary method. In the House of Commons the bill was strongly opposed by the Tories but passed by votes of the Whig members. In the House of Lords, dominated by the Tories, the bill was approved only after the king threatened to appoint enough new liberal Lords to ensure its passage. (Whereas the English aristocracy yielded peacefully and enfranchised the middle class, the French ruling classes, at about the same time, employed repression, which led to the Revolution of 1830.)

This "Great Reform Bill" (a) reduced property qualifications for voting so as to enfranchise the middle class, thereby increasing the number of voters from 500,000 to over 800,000 (still only about 5 percent of the British adult male population); (b) took representation away from many rotten and pocket boroughs; and (c) granted representation to many populous industrial cities. By these provisions the bill shifted control of the House of Commons from the landed aristocracy to the commercial and industrial middle class. The well-to-do middle class groups—factory owners, bankers, and merchants—associated with the Industrial Revolution were eager for a voice in shaping government policies.

**2. The Chartist Movement.** City workers, not enfranchised by the Reform Bill of 1832, organized the *Chartist Movement*. In the "People's Charter" they petitioned the government for *(a)* universal manhood suffrage, *(b)* equal election districts, *(c)* the secret ballot, *(d)* annual elections of Parliament, *(e)* removal of property qualifications for members of Parliament, and *(f)* salaries for members of Parliament. To rally support, the Chartists used mass meetings and parades.

The Chartist Movement died out following its failure to secure reforms from Parliament in 1848—a year of revolutions on the Continent. Subsequently, however, almost all Chartist demands were enacted into law.

**3. The Reform Bill of 1867.** This bill further reduced property qualifications for voting so as to enfranchise city workers. It was guided through Parliament by *Benjamin Disraeli,* who dominated the Conservative (formerly Tory) party. Disraeli hoped that the newly enfranchised city workers would join with the landed aristocracy in the Conservative party and together outvote the merchants and factory owners in the Liberal (formerly Whig) party. In this hope Disraeli was largely disappointed. The city workers usually supported the Liberals to obtain further democratic reforms. Later they formed their own Labor party.

**4. The Reform Bill of 1884.** This bill extended the right to vote to agricultural workers. It was passed by the Liberal party under its prime minister, *William Gladstone.*

**5. The Reform Bill of 1918.** All men over 21 years of age received the right to vote, thus achieving *universal manhood suffrage.* Also, the bill granted the vote to most women over 30.

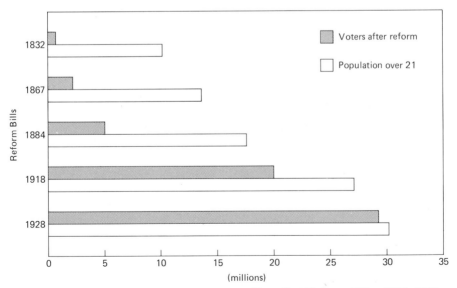

**Increase in Number of British Voters as the Result of Reform Bills, 1832–1928**

This latter reform was in appreciation of the contributions made by women during World War I. It represented a triumph for the women suffrage advocates, called *suffragettes*. They were part of the *women's rights* movement for educational, professional, legal, and occupational equality with men. The outstanding leader of the British suffragettes at the turn of the century was *Emmeline Pankhurst*.

**6. The Reform Bill of 1928.** In 1928 Parliament granted the right to vote to all women over 21 years of age. By this bill Britain finally achieved the goal of *universal suffrage*.

## LIMITING THE POWER OF THE HOUSE OF LORDS

**1. Undemocratic Aspects of the House of Lords.** Regardless of the extension of the suffrage, Parliament could not be a truly democratic body while the House of Lords had equal powers with the House of Commons. Whereas the House of Commons is elected, the House of Lords is chiefly hereditary. As long as both houses had to approve laws, the Lords could block any measure voted by the people's elected representatives in the Commons. Furthermore, one party, the Conservative, was assured permanent control of the House of Lords, since the Lords were mostly wealthy landowners, conservative in outlook.

**2. The Issue of the 1909 Budget.** The House of Commons and the House of Lords came into major conflict over new taxes in the *Budget of 1909*. *David Lloyd George*, Chancellor of the Exchequer (Treasury) in the Liberal party government, proposed placing heavy taxes on large incomes and estates. The budget was passed in the Commons but was rejected by the landowners controlling the House of Lords. The Commons was dissolved and new elections held in January, 1910, with the budget as the issue. By returning the Liberals to power, the voters indicated their approval of the Lloyd George proposals. The budget was reintroduced and, in view of the election results, accepted by the Lords.

**3. The Parliament Act of 1911.** Believing that public opinion was now sufficiently aroused against the House of Lords, the Liberals introduced a bill to weaken the Lords' legislative powers. After passage in the Commons, the bill was defeated in the House of Lords. The Commons was again dissolved and new elections held in December, 1910, on the issue of curbing the Lords' powers. By again giving the Liberals a majority, the voters indicated their support of the bill. When the Lords still refused to accept the bill, the king threatened to appoint enough new liberal Lords to ensure the bill's passage. Finally in 1911 the bill was passed.

The *Parliament Act of 1911* provided that, even if the House of Lords withholds its consent, (*a*) money bills approved by the Commons once become law after 30 days and (*b*) other bills approved by the Commons three consecutive times over at least two years become law. Thus, the act reduced the Lords' power over legislation to a temporary, or *suspensive, veto.* The act established the supremacy of the elected House of Commons over the hereditary House of Lords.

**4. The Parliament Act of 1949.** The Labor government, expecting Conservative opposition to its program of nationalizing basic industries, proposed in 1947 to reduce the Lords' suspensive veto over general legislation to only one year. The government bill, twice rejected by the Lords, was three times passed by the Commons and in 1949 became law. Thus, in the British government today, the House of Lords plays only a minor role.

## OTHER DEMOCRATIC REFORMS

1829—*Catholic Emancipation Act* granted Catholics the right to serve in Parliament. (The act also required Catholics to take an oath denying any intention to upset the established Anglican Church and denying the authority of the pope to interfere in Britain's domestic affairs.)

1833—slavery abolished in all British possessions.

1858—Jews received the right to serve in Parliament.

1858—property qualifications for members of Parliament removed.

1872—open voting replaced by the secret, or *Australian,* ballot. (The secret ballot had originated in Australia.)

1885—*Redistribution Bill* established election districts approximately equal in population.

1911—House of Commons elections required at least once every five years.

1911—members of the Commons received salaries.

1918—women received the right to serve in Parliament.

## THE BRITISH GOVERNMENT TODAY:
## REPRESENTATIVE AND RESPONSIBLE

The government of Great Britain (1) illustrates peaceful evolution from aristocracy to democracy and (2) has served as a model for other democratic nations, including Canada, Australia, and New Zealand in the British Commonwealth, and Sweden, Norway, Denmark, Holland, and Belgium in Western Europe. The major features of the British *parliamentary system* are:

**1. No Formal Constitution.** Britain, unlike other democracies, has no formal, written constitution. Instead, the British consider their constitution to be made up of *(a) written documents and laws of significance,* such as Magna Carta (1215), the Bill of Rights (1689), and the suffrage reform bills (1832–1928), and *(b) unwritten precedents* (customs and traditions), such as cabinet responsibility to the Commons.

**2. The Monarch.** Great Britain is a monarchy, officially headed by a king or queen. At one time an absolute ruler, the British sovereign today is a *figurehead,* said to "reign but not rule." The sovereign performs certain political duties but is restricted by precedent. *(a)* The monarch selects the prime minister but by precedent must choose for this position the leader of the majority party in the Commons. *(b)* The monarch considers the bills passed by Parliament but by precedent must approve them. (The last royal veto of a bill occurred in 1707.) *(c)* The monarch reads the "Speech from the Throne" at the opening of Parliament but by precedent must advocate the program of the cabinet.

The monarch's chief duties are social and ceremonial, such as welcoming foreign diplomats and dedicating public improvements. Most important, the monarch serves as a symbol of unity for the people of Britain and the British Commonwealth of Nations.

**3. Parliament.** The English legislature consists of two houses.

*a.* The *House of Lords,* the lesser body, may only delay legislation temporarily. Lords consists of about 1,000 members, mostly hereditary, of whom on the average some 100 attend sessions.

*b.* The *House of Commons,* the supreme legislative body, has unlimited power to pass laws. The Commons consists of 630 members, called MPs, meaning members of Parliament. They are directly elected by the people voting by districts. (The House of Commons is often referred to as Parliament.)

**4. Cabinet Membership.** The cabinet consists of *(a)* the prime minister, who is the leader of the majority party in the Commons, and *(b)* about 20 members of Parliament selected by the prime minister from the majority party. To promote national unity during crises, the prime minister may include in the cabinet some members of Parliament from the opposition party, thereby forming a *coalition government.* This was done during both world wars.

**5. Cabinet Powers.** The cabinet exercises both executive and legislative functions.

*a. Executive.* (1) The prime minister is the head of the government and directs and coordinates its activities. (2) Each cabinet member heads a department, such as Foreign Affairs, Exchequer (Treasury), Commonwealth Relations, or Defense. (3) The cabinet enforces laws passed by Parliament.

*b. Legislative.* (1) Cabinet members are also members of the Commons. (Occasionally a cabinet member is chosen from the House of Lords.) (2) The cabinet draws up the legislative program of the majority party, prepares the necessary bills, introduces them into the Commons, defends them in debate, and guides them to passage.

**6. Cabinet Responsibility.** The prime minister and the cabinet remain in office as long as they command the support of a majority in the Commons. If the

Commons votes "no confidence" in the cabinet or rejects a major cabinet-sponsored bill, the cabinet no longer controls the Commons. Then the cabinet must either *(a)* resign, whereupon the opposition majority in the Commons forms a new cabinet, or, as is done more frequently, *(b)* *"go to the country"*—dissolve the Commons and call for new elections with the cabinet's policies or a specific bill as the issue. In the newly elected House of Commons, if the majority supports the cabinet, it remains in office, its policies considered approved by the voters; and the Commons enacts the disputed cabinet-sponsored bill. If the majority is hostile, the cabinet resigns; its bill remains dead, and a new government is formed by the opposition leader.

At all times the cabinet is directly responsible to the majority in the Commons and thereby indirectly responsible to the people. The practice of "going to the country" on major issues allows the British electorate to affect directly the policies of the prime minister—much more so than the American electorate can influence the policies of a president in office for a fixed four-year term.

**7. Influences on the Government.** The minority party in the Commons is called "Her (or His) Majesty's Loyal Opposition." Its leader receives an extra salary for services rendered as head of the opposition. In the Commons the opposition criticizes government policies, delays somewhat the passage of government bills, and proposes alternatives that it would adopt if in power. Parliamentary debates are brought to the attention of the people by newspapers, magazines, radio, and television. MPs belonging to the opposition report to their constituents by mail and at local meetings. The loyal opposition reflects the British view that, in a democracy, opposition does not constitute treason but furthers public understanding by free and open discussion of issues.

The public may express opposition to (or support for) government policies by various means: letters to MPs and to the press, petitions, attendance at local meetings and mass rallies, and of course by voting in elections.

Special-interest groups—such as farmers, doctors, teachers, veterans, and ethnic minorities—may use their own members or employ paid lobbyists to present their points of view, influence public opinion, and pressure MPs regarding their votes on specific bills.

## POLITICAL PARTIES IN BRITAIN

### 1. Introduction

*a. Two-Party System.* The two-party system—typical of democracies in the United States and Britain—has provided the British people with a choice of policies and candidates, with a loyal opposition, and with relatively stable government.

In contrast, the one-party system—typical of the Communist nations and of many newly independent Asian and African nations—denotes dictatorship. The one-party system denies the people a choice of policies and candidates, considers

## Two Democracies: Differences in Government

| Great Britain | The United States |
| --- | --- |
| 1. *Not* a single, formal, written constitution, the fundamental principles of government are contained in historic precedents, documents, and laws. These are subject to easy change. | 1. A formal, written constitution, drawn up at Philadelphia in 1787, established the fundamental structure and principles of government. The constitution may be amended only by a complex process. |
| 2. Great Britain is a monarchy, headed by a hereditary ruler. The king or queen is a *figurehead,* having no power but serving as a symbol of unity. | 2. The United States is a republic, headed by an elected president. This person is the chief executive and exercises great power. |
| 3. Parliament is the legislature, consisting of *(a)* the hereditary House of Lords with minor powers and *(b)* the elected House of Commons with unlimited legislative powers. | 3. Congress is the legislature, consisting of two elected houses—the House of Representatives and the Senate—both exercising practically equal powers. |
| 4. The House of Commons is elected for a maximum term of five years but may be dissolved earlier if the prime minister calls for new elections. | 4. Congressional terms of office are definite. Representatives serve for two years, Senators for six. |
| 5. The prime minister secures office as the leader of the majority party in Parliament. | 5. The president is chosen by a nationwide vote as expressed through the electoral college. (The only exception was Gerald Ford, who became president in 1974 through other constitutional means.) |
| 6. *(a)* The cabinet is selected by the prime minister from members of the majority party in Parliament. <br><br> *(b)* The cabinet exercises executive and legislative functions, thereby ignoring the principle of separation of powers. <br><br> *(c)* The prime minister and the cabinet remain in office as long as they command a majority in the Commons. Their term of office may be less or more than the life of one House of Commons. <br><br> *(d)* Cabinet responsibility to Parliament assures that the same party controls the executive and legislative branches. Thus, the two branches always work in harmony. | 6. *(a)* The cabinet is selected by the president from persons outside of or resigning from Congress. They take office with the consent of the Senate. <br><br> *(b)* The cabinet exercises executive functions chiefly, thereby observing the principle of separation of powers. <br><br> *(c)* The president serves a four-year term and is limited to no more than two terms. The cabinet remains in office at the will of the president. <br><br> *(d)* The president (and the cabinet) may belong to one political party, while Congress (or either house) may be under control of another party. Thus, conflicts may arise between the executive and legislative branches. |

opposition to government policies to be treason, and may or may not provide stable government.

In still another contrast, the multiparty system—typical of the West European parliamentary democracies such as France, Italy, and Belgium—offers the people a wide choice of policies and candidates. Because no one party controls a legislative majority, a coalition of several parties is required to form a government. Since the withdrawal of one party from the coalition may cause the government to lose its parliamentary majority and resign, the multiparty parliamentary democracy frequently experiences unstable government.

*b. Party Discipline.* The two major British parties exercise considerable discipline upon their own members elected to the Commons. Each member is expected to adhere to the party ideology or doctrines, to attend sessions when votes are taken on important bills, and to uphold the party stand on issues. Although some dissent is possible, an MP who consistently defies party discipline may be expelled from the party. Expulsion means the loss of the party label and party support in the next election and almost certain political defeat. Strong party discipline is considered essential to the British parliamentary system.

In contrast, the two major American parties exercise little discipline upon their members in Congress. The American parties are not tied to a consistent ideology but include a broad spectrum of views so that each party contains liberal, moderate, and conservative members. Party members frequently vote against the wishes of their party leaders, and expulsion from a party is practically unknown.

**2. Liberal Party.** The *Liberals* (formerly called Whigs) played a leading role in British history in the 19th and early 20th centuries. As the Labor party developed, however, the Liberals lost their upper-class supporters to the Conservatives and their lower-class supporters to the Laborites. Today the once-powerful Liberal party exists only as a minor party.

**3. Conservative Party.** The *Conservatives* (called Tories before the 1832 suffrage bill) remain one of Britain's two major parties. They draw strong support from the aristocracy and upper middle class: large landowners, prosperous farmers and shopkeepers, industrialists, merchants, bankers, and professionals. However, their success in recent elections shows that their leaders and programs appeal also to less prosperous citizens. The Conservatives *(a)* praise the values of the existing society and seek to preserve its beneficial features, *(b)* advocate free enterprise under capitalism, with government regulation limited to preventing abuses, *(c)* favor the continuation of existing social services, and *(d)* seek close cooperation with the United States on international affairs.

**4. Labor Party.** In 1901 the Labor party was created by labor union leaders and Socialist reformers. These Socialists included a group of intellectuals—members of the *Fabian Society*—whose thinking greatly influenced the Labor party ideology. Not revolutionaries, they opposed the Marxist doctrine of class warfare and favored gradualism as the way to achieve the goal of democratic socialism (see pages 296–297). Union leaders and Socialists both held that the existing parties were not representing the wishes of the working classes.

Since the 1920's Labor has been one of Britain's major parties. This party draws its support mainly from the lower middle class: city and farm workers, small farmers and shopkeepers, reform-minded intellectuals, and union members. The Laborites *(a)* deplore defects of the existing society and seek to build a different one, *(b)* believe in a Socialist economy with government ownership of basic industries and government economic planning, *(c)* urge expanding national welfare programs, and *(d)* favor cooperation (but to a lesser degree than the Conservatives) with the United States.

Labor's defeat in the 1979 election led to a serious split in the party. The left-wing faction seized control, elected as new party leader and potential prime minister *Michael Foot,* and proclaimed their party policies: within Britain— more radical socialist measures; in foreign affairs—withdrawal from the Common Market, opposition to NATO, and unilateral nuclear disarmament. This shift in Labor party control and policy dismayed its right-wing factions. Some MPs and former Labor cabinet members, notably *Roy Jenkins,* withdrew declaring that the party they had loved and worked for "no longer exists." The right-wingers, buoyed by expressions of public support, formed what they hoped would be a broad-based centrist *Social Democratic* party. They declared their support: within Britain—for a mixed economy of public and private enterprise that recognized the ability of market forces to create wealth but urged the government to assure equitable distribution of economic rewards; in foreign affairs—for a firm commitment to the Common Market and NATO.

In a 1981 by-election, *Shirley Williams*—a former Labor cabinet member— ran as the Social Democratic candidate with Liberal party support and won a strong and surprising victory. Mrs. Williams claimed that "the mold of British politics has been totally shattered" and predicted that the Social Democratic- Liberal alliance would win the next general election.

## OUTSTANDING GOVERNMENT LEADERS (19TH AND 20TH CENTURIES)

### 1. Liberals

*a. Charles Grey,* a Whig (the former name of the Liberal party), secured passage of the Reform Bill of 1832.

*b. William Gladstone* promoted land distribution to Irish peasants and won passage for the Reform Bill of 1884.

*c. Herbert Asquith* won passage of the Parliament Act of 1911 and guided Britain at the beginning of World War I (1914–1916).

*d. David Lloyd George* fought for the Budget of 1909 and led Britain to victory in World War I (1916–1918).

*Bruce Shanks in The Buffalo Evening News, June 28, 1971*

**"Longest Channel Swim Yet"**

It took Britain 12 years (1961 to 1973) to secure membership in the Common Market. Why did it take so long? How does this fact explain the title, "Longest Channel Swim Yet"? Did Britain act wisely in joining the Common Market?

## 2. Conservatives

*a. Robert Peel* ended the tariff on grain imports by securing the repeal of the Corn Laws (1846). This move lowered food costs for British workers but meant increased competition for British farmers.

*b. Benjamin Disraeli* sponsored the Reform Bill of 1867 and expanded British colonial power by acquiring the Suez Canal (1875).

*c. Winston Churchill* exemplified British courage and determination as he guided the nation to victory in World War II (1945).

*d. Harold Macmillan,* prime minister from 1957 to 1963, faced troublesome economic problems but maintained a high level of general prosperity.

*e. Edward Heath* secured agreement for Britain to join the Common Market (1973). Heath's success in this matter was due in major part to the fact that Charles de Gaulle—who had vetoed two previous British applications for membership—no longer governed France. (Check the Index for Common Market.)

## 3. Laborites

*a. Ramsay MacDonald* headed Labor's first government (1924). He, however, had to depend on Liberal votes for his parliamentary majority.

*b. Clement Attlee,* prime minister from 1945 to 1951, nationalized the electric, coal, and steel industries. His government also began a government program of medical, dental, and hospital service.

*c. Harold Wilson,* who headed two Labor governments (from 1964 to 1970 and again from 1974 to 1976), lowered the voting age in Britain from 21 to 18 years (1969) and authorized a referendum in which the British people, by a wide margin, voted to remain in the Common Market (1975).

## PROBLEMS FACING GREAT BRITAIN SINCE WORLD WAR II

**1. Loss of Overseas Possessions.** Labor and Conservative governments both have granted, to almost all of Britain's overseas possessions, independence and membership in the Commonwealth of Nations. (Check the Index.) British leaders had hoped that, as Commonwealth members, the newly independent nations would maintain their ties with Britain and would respect British leadership.

The Commonwealth has grown from six to about 41 members—the overwhelming majority being newly independent African, Asian, and West Indian nations. Because of its increased and diverse membership, the Commonwealth has been weakened by conflicts among its members and by the withdrawal of two major nations—in 1961 the Republic of South Africa and in 1972 Pakistan. (For details, check these nations in the Index.)

Great Britain today no longer controls a vast and wealthy empire, and its influence has waned in the Commonwealth—as the newly independent nations have asserted their own national ideologies and interests. In assessing Britain's position, an American statesman declared that Britain had lost an empire and not yet found a new world role.

**2. Breakaway Regime in Rhodesia (Zimbabwe).** The former British colony of Rhodesia—now the independent nation of Zimbabwe—in southern Africa con-

*Tom Little in the Nashville Tennessean*

**"—Farewell
to all my greatness!"**

tains a population that is 95 percent black and 5 percent white. The whites are mainly of British stock. The blacks had been disenfranchised by the whites, who ruled the country.

The Labor and Conservative parties in Britain agreed on the need for more representative government in Rhodesia. In 1964 the Labor government proposed that Rhodesia move rapidly from white-minority to black-majority rule. The British proposal was rejected by the white-minority regime, and in 1965 Rhodesian Prime Minister Ian Smith declared his country independent. The British Labor government labeled the breakaway regime "illegal" and secured a UN resolution asking all members to apply sanctions against Rhodesia. Britain, however, rejected the demand of African nations to crush the white-minority regime by force. For 14 years, Labor and Conservative governments were unable to resolve this problem.

In late 1979, as Zimbabwe Rhodesia faced continued guerrilla warfare and the possibility of Russian and Cuban intervention, Britain's Conservative government convened a London conference of all Rhodesian parties to seek a peaceful settlement. The conference reached agreement for a democratic government, guarantee of personal liberties, protection of white-minority rights, and free elections, which in 1980 were supervised by Great Britain. This election gave Patriotic Front leader *Robert Mugabe* a legislative majority and he became prime minister. In mid-1980 Great Britain formally granted independence to Zimbabwe. (For details, check the Index for Rhodesia and for Zimbabwe.)

**3. Racial Problems in Britain.** By the early 1960's Great Britain had admitted about one million immigrants from Commonwealth members and territories, mainly India, Pakistan, the West Indies, and Africa. Of various ethnic and racial backgrounds, they are called "colored" immigrants. These people settled in the large industrial cities, forming ethnic ghettos and presenting problems of social services, housing, education, and employment. These newcomers aroused considerable resentment among many British people. In 1962 the Conservative government passed the Commonwealth Immigration Act limiting the inflow of "colored" immigrants, and in 1965 the Labor government announced further restrictions. The Labor government also passed laws to prohibit racial discrimination in public places, housing, and employment and to forbid incitement to race hatred. Labor and Conservative leaders supported spending for social services and education to integrate the "colored" immigrants into British life.

In 1969 the Labor government took a further step against the admission of "colored" immigrants into Britain. Labor decided to exclude from Britain the Asians being expelled from the former British colony of Kenya under its "Africanization" policy. At the time of Kenya's independence, these Asians—many of whom were successful merchants and professionals—had chosen to retain their British citizenship rather than become citizens of Kenya. Although Labor's action was approved by many British, a considerable number expressed their moral dismay. In 1972 the Conservative government under Prime Minister Heath faced a similar situation that arose in another former British African colony, Uganda. Idi Amin, black nationalist president of Uganda, announced that 45,000 Asians—who had not become Ugandan citizens but who had retained British citizenship—would be expelled within three months. The Conservative government declared that Britain was morally obligated to accept those Ugandan Asians seeking admission, and the government's position was supported by Labor party leaders. By airlift Britain received 27,000 Ugandan Asians, and the government tried to integrate them into British life. (Recently the British government estimated that 300,000 people in former British colonies have no local citizenship and, if expelled, could claim refuge in Britain.)

In 1981 black and Asian youths in a number of cities rioted on a scale previously unknown in Britain. The rioters, who destroyed much property, were believed to be expressing resentment against racism—especially against police brutality toward nonwhites. In some cities, the "colored" rioters were later joined by white youths. Both groups were believed to be expressing frustration at the lack of opportunity resulting from massive unemployment.

**4. Violence in Ulster (Northern Ireland).** In 1921 Ulster, or Northern Ireland, voted to remain part of Great Britain rather than unite with the Irish Republic to the south. Ulster contains a Protestant majority and a Catholic minority while the Irish Republic is mainly Catholic.

In 1969 violence erupted in Ulster between the Catholic and Protestant communities. The Catholic minority, protesting against the local Ulster Protestant-dominated government, cited discrimination in voting, jobs, and public housing. Some Catholics further wanted to unite with their Catholic coreligionists in the Irish Republic. The Labor government of Prime Minister Wilson sent troops to stop the street fighting and secured pledges from the local authorities to remedy justifiable Catholic complaints. Violence continued, nevertheless, and in 1972 the Conservative government of Prime Minister Heath suspended the local Ulster regime, imposed direct British rule, and sought to persuade the opposing groups to negotiate a peaceful settlement—to no avail. Violence has continued, deaths have risen above 2,000 persons, and the British government—whether under Laborites or Conservatives—has been unable to resolve the Ulster problem. (For details, check the Index for Ulster.)

**5. Economic Problems.** Since the mid-1960's Britain has been beset by major economic problems: stagnant or declining industrial production; unemployment that in 1975 affected 1.2 million workers, or over 5 percent of the labor force; inflation that in 1975 rose to an annual rate of 25 percent; and an unfavorable balance of payments—meaning that the funds spent abroad, chiefly for foreign goods and services, exceeded funds earned from abroad, chiefly for British goods and services. At times these problems seemed to ease and then to worsen.

The domestic reasons for these economic problems include: depletion of Britain's natural resources, especially the more accessible coal and iron-ore deposits; the failure to replace outmoded and inefficient equipment with new plants and new machinery; high wage settlements in excess of cost-of-living needs secured by powerful unions; government budget deficits that pumped additional money into the economy and increased the demand for goods and services; and the high cost of British goods and services in world markets.

Since the mid-1960's both Laborites and Conservatives have controlled the British government, but neither party has been able to deal with Britain's economic problems effectively.

(a) To spur industrial production and modernization, Labor urged increased nationalization of industry and more government economic planning. The Conservatives, on the other hand, stressed free enterprise to spur individual initiative and lower corporate taxes to enable industry to accumulate investment funds. Both Labor and Conservative governments have provided loans to "sick" companies to keep them in business and thereby save jobs. Both parties look forward to increased tax revenues, from newly developed North Sea oil resources, to provide funds for Britain's industrial resurgence.

(b) To contain inflation, both Labor and Conservative governments imposed temporary wage-price controls—but to no avail. In 1973 Conservative Prime Minister Heath attempted, unsuccessfully, to limit a wage increase for coal miners. Two years later the Labor government failed to stop unions from securing excessive wage settlements.

(c) To reverse Britain's unfavorable balance of payments, the Labor government in 1967 lowered the value of the pound, the British monetary unit, from $2.80 to $2.40. With the pound devalued in terms of foreign currency, British consumers would find imports more costly and foreigners would find British goods less costly. The government hoped that imports would therefore decrease and exports increase. In 1972 the Conservative government abandoned efforts to keep the British pound at a fixed ratio to the American dollar. Instead, the government permitted the pound to "float"—meaning to allow the international supply and demand for currency to set the value of the pound in relation to the dollar. By 1976 the pound had fallen below $1.80. Britain's recent balance of payments, nevertheless, remained unfavorable.

Some economists insist that, for Britain to solve its economic problems, the British people, political parties, labor unions, and government must be prepared to accept drastic and unpopular measures—including the curtailment of government services and the lowering of living standards.

## 6. Recent Political Developments

*a. Conservative Control (1970–1974).* In response to the demand in 1973 by the coal miners union for a 30 percent to 40 percent wage increase, the Conservative government of Prime Minister Heath offered only a 16 percent increase. This offer was turned down by the union, and the miners voted to strike. Heath thereupon called for a new parliamentary election, hoping that the public would support his policy of wage restraint as necessary to curtail inflation. Heath narrowly lost the election, held in early 1974, and resigned.

*b. Labor Control (1974–1979).* Harold Wilson became prime minister, governing with a scant majority in the Commons. Labor allowed the coal miners a 35 percent wage increase, and the strike ended. The Wilson government continued to face the same problems that had plagued Britain for years: unemployment,

Ashley in The Blade, Toledo, Ohio

**"There'll always be an
England . . . I 'opes!"**

inflation, unfavorable balance of payments, the breakaway regime in Rhodesia, and violence in Ulster.

With these problems still unsolved, Prime Minister Wilson in 1976 announced his resignation for personal reasons.

*James Callaghan,* the former foreign minister, was selected by the Labor party to be prime minister. Labor continued to govern Britain, but the nation's problems remained worrisome. In 1979 Callaghan was defeated, by one vote, on a parliamentary motion of "no confidence." He resigned and arranged for a new parliamentary election.

*c. Conservative Control (1979–    ). Margaret Thatcher* led the Conservative party to victory—a 43-seat majority in the Commons. Mrs. Thatcher became prime minister, the first woman in British history to hold that position and the first woman to be prime minister of a major European nation. The Conservative victory was interpreted as a voter protest against Labor's socialist and trade union programs.

To revive the economy, the Thatcher government moved to curtail spending programs so as to reduce the budget deficit, to limit the money supply so as to lower the inflation rate, to return certain nationalized industries to private ownership, to encourage competition, individual initiative, and free enterprise, and to sharply reduce the government's role in the economy. Nevertheless, by 1981, economic conditions remained unfavorable, with unemployment rising to above 8 percent of the work force, inflation continuing above 15 percent, and high interest rates impeding industrial growth. Whereas even some Conservatives suggested other economic approaches, Mrs. Thatcher—nicknamed the "Iron Lady"—remained determined to maintain her economic program. Pointing out that Britain's economic problems were deep-rooted, Mrs. Thatcher insisted that her program eventually would revive the economy.

## IDENTIFICATION QUESTIONS: WHO AM I?

| | | |
|---|---|---|
| Herbert Asquith | Benjamin Disraeli | Ramsay MacDonald |
| Clement Attlee | David Lloyd George | Harold Macmillan |
| James Callaghan | William Gladstone | Margaret Thatcher |
| Winston Churchill | Edward Heath | Harold Wilson |

1. Famed as an orator and writer, I was the Conservative prime minister who led Britain to victory in World War II.

2. I took office as Labor prime minister immediately after World War II and nationalized several major industries.

3. I was the Conservative prime minister who led Britain into the Common Market.

4. As Conservative leader, I secured passage of the Reform Bill of 1867, hoping that the city workers would join with the landed aristocracy against the industrialists.

5. I was the Liberal prime minister who secured the vote for farm workers by the Reform Bill of 1884.

6. I was the Liberal chancellor of the exchequer who fought for passage of the 1909 Budget and as prime minister led Britain to victory in World War I.

7. After a close Labor victory in the 1974 elections, I became prime minister.

## MULTIPLE–CHOICE QUESTIONS

1. In 1800 the British government was undemocratic in that (1) Parliament lacked the power to pass laws (2) no cabinet existed (3) the king controlled Parliament (4) the House of Lords was as powerful as the House of Commons.

2. Another undemocratic feature of the British government in 1800 was that (1) the king appointed the prime minister (2) the king vetoed many laws (3) most citizens did not have the right to vote (4) Parliament was a hereditary body.

3. The term "rotten borough" refers to (1) an area that had lost population and was overrepresented in Parliament (2) a city slum area with inadequate sanitation facilities (3) lands used for hunting (4) a large city unrepresented in Parliament.

4. In 1815 Manchester and Leeds were unrepresented in Parliament because these cities (1) contained no persons of wealth (2) were under naval rule (3) were almost completely depopulated (4) had not secured a reapportionment of parliamentary seats in accord with their increase in population.

5. The chief cause of the shift in population in Britain resulting in unequal representation in Parliament before 1832 was the (1) Napoleonic Wars (2) Industrial Revolution (3) repeal of the Corn Laws (4) decline of British naval power.

6. Democracy in Britain developed chiefly through a process of (1) violent upheaval (2) gradual evolution (3) rapid changes (4) royal decrees.

7. Which group gained suffrage as a result of the Reform Bill of 1832? (1) the middle class (2) peasants (3) factory workers (4) landed aristocracy.

8. The Reform Bill of 1832 (1) abolished many rotten boroughs (2) deprived the House of Lords of veto power (3) provided funds for slum clearance in factory towns (4) outlawed the open ballot.

9. Why did the House of Lords approve the Reform Bill of 1832? (1) The bill strengthened the power of landlords. (2) The king threatened to appoint new liberal lords. (3) The king threatened to abolish the House of Lords. (4) The bill did not affect the pocket boroughs.

10. The Chartist Movement (1) led the successful Revolution of 1848 in Britain (2) won immediate acceptance of its demands (3) was outlawed by Parliament (4) collapsed, but its demands eventually became law.

11. One Chartist demand was (1) the right of workers to collective bargaining (2) government ownership of industry (3) unemployment insurance for workers (4) the abolition of property qualifications for members of Parliament.

12. The history of Great Britain in the 19th century best supports the generalization that political reforms often occur as a result of (1) a series of violent revolutions (2) the democratic progress made by neighboring countries (3) important changes in the economic structure of a society (4) isolation from involvement in world affairs.

13. Great Britain gave women equal voting rights with men (1) shortly after the French Revolution (2) just before World War I (3) shortly after World War I (4) during World War II.

14. The Parliament Act of 1911 weakened the House of Lords by (1) discontinuing its judicial functions (2) making its membership elective rather than hereditary (3) limiting its lawmaking function to a suspensive veto (4) providing that no cabinet member may come from this body.

15. The Catholic Emancipation Act of 1829 (1) gave Catholics freedom to worship (2) gave Catholics the right to hold public office (3) disestablished the Anglican Church in Ireland (4) freed Catholics from paying certain taxes.

16. The prime minister of Britain is (1) leader of the majority party in the House of Commons (2) directly elected to that office by the people (3) the independent choice of the monarch (4) by law a member of the House of Lords.

17. The British cabinet has (1) both executive and legislative powers (2) only legislative powers (3) only executive powers (4) only those powers assigned to it by the monarch.

18. Members of the British cabinet (1) are elected directly to the cabinet by the people (2) are chosen by the prime minister (3) hold office by hereditary right (4) are elected by a joint meeting of both Houses of Parliament.

19. The prime minister and the cabinet usually resign if a major government bill is (1) vetoed by the monarch (2) opposed by public opinion (3) defeated in the House of Lords (4) defeated in the House of Commons.

20. When the British cabinet "goes to the country," it (1) takes a vacation (2) establishes a new foreign policy (3) calls for elections of a new House of Commons (4) protests the actions of the monarch.

## COMPARISON OF GOVERNMENTS

Consider the following statements in relationship to government in Britain and the United States. For each statement 1-10, write the letter of the appropriate phrase below. (A letter may be used more than once.)

(A) if the statement is true of the British government only.

(B) if the statement is true of the American government only.

(C) if the statement is true of both the British and American governments.

(D) if the statement is not true of either government.

1. The government is a limited monarchy.
2. The chief executive may serve for no more than five years.
3. Requirements for voting meet with the approval of the suffragettes.
4. The fundamental principles of government may be changed by a new law passed by the legislature only.
5. The chief executive is elected by the members of both houses of the legislature.

6. The chief executive remains in office even though a major law requested of the legislature is defeated.
7. Cabinet members are members of the legislature.
8. The government is a democracy.
9. The two houses of the legislature are approximately equal in power.
10. The right to hold public office is not legally restricted by religious qualifications.

## ESSAY QUESTIONS

1. Discuss fully *one* important step in the progress toward democracy made by Great Britain during *each* of the following periods: *(a)* 1815–1849 *(b)* 1850–1899 *(c)* 1900–1925 *(d)* 1926–present.
2. "Britain has progressed toward democracy by evolution rather than by revolution." Prove this statement by reference to the *(a)* Reform Bill of 1832 *(b)* Chartist Movement *(c)* Parliament Act of 1911.
3. *(a)* Explain why the Liberal party in Great Britain in the first decade of the 20th century wished to limit the power of the House of Lords. *(b)* State *two* provisions of the Parliament Act of 1911 that limited the power of the House of Lords.
4. Discuss the cabinet system of the British government, bringing out the following points: *(a)* how the cabinet obtains office *(b)* how the cabinet may be removed from office *(c)* the powers and duties of the cabinet.
5. Show how the American and British systems of government *differ* from each other with respect to each of the following: *(a)* constitution *(b)* relationship between the cabinet and the legislature *(c)* the *official* head of government *(d)* selection of the chief executive.
6. For the years since the end of World War II *(a)* state *one* problem faced by Britain and prove that it is similar to a problem faced by the United States *(b)* state *one* problem unique to Britain and prove that it has no parallel in the United States. *(c)* For *each* of these problems, evaluate the efforts of the British government to resolve it.

# Part 8. France: Democracy Through War and Revolution

## SECOND FRENCH REPUBLIC (1848–1852)

By the Revolution of 1848 (see page 206), the French people established the Second French Republic and elected Louis Napoleon as president. From this nephew of Napoleon Bonaparte, the French envisioned stable government, economic prosperity, and foreign glory.

Louis Napoleon used his elected position to further his personal power and popularity. He posed as the defender of democratic government, but in 1852 Louis Napoleon ended the republic and proclaimed the *Second French Empire* with himself as Emperor *Napoleon III*. In a plebiscite the people approved these changes.

## SECOND FRENCH EMPIRE (1852–1870)

**1. Government.** Napoleon III retained outward democratic forms: a constitution, a legislature, and universal male suffrage. In reality his government was a dictatorship typified by secret police, censorship of the press, and state-controlled elections.

**2. Early Popularity.** Napoleon III gained support among *(a) city workers*—by legalizing unions and granting them a limited right to strike, and by providing employment on public works, *(b)* the *middle class*—by improving banking and credit facilities, by promoting railroad and canal building, and by encouraging the growth of industry, and *(c) nationalists*—by expanding French colonial control in Algeria, by seizing part of Indo-China, and by joining with Britain to defeat Russia in the Crimean War.

**3. Later Discontent.** Napoleon earned the hostility of *(a) advocates of democracy*—who realized that the Second Empire was a veiled dictatorship (Victor Hugo, the French writer and outspoken democrat who had to flee France, ridiculed the emperor as "Napoleon the Little."); *(b) Catholics*—who feared that Napoleon's aid to Italian unification was a threat to Church control of the Papal States; and *(c) nationalists*—who felt a loss of pride over Napoleon's humiliating failure in Mexico—the *Maximilian Affair*.

In 1863, with the United States engaged in the Civil War, the French sent troops into Mexico and enthroned their puppet, the Hapsburg Archduke *Maximilian*. By attempting to control Mexico, Napoleon violated the Monroe Doctrine (see pages 204–205). In 1865, when the Civil War ended, the United States placed an army at the Mexican border and ordered the French to withdraw. Napoleon removed his troops. Maximilian remained, was captured by Mexican forces, and died before a firing squad.

**4. Downfall.** To revive his popularity and to check Prussian power, Napoleon opposed German unification. Bismarck, the chief minister of Prussia, wanted a war and goaded Napoleon into beginning hostilities. In the Franco-Prussian War (1870–1871), the French army was overwhelmed, and Napoleon III was taken prisoner. French republicans, led by *Leon Gambetta*, declared the end of the Second French Empire.

## ESTABLISHMENT OF THE THIRD FRENCH REPUBLIC (1871–1879)

The National Assembly, elected in 1871, contained a majority of royalists, or monarchists. They had won the election on the pledge to bring about an immediate peace; the republican minority, on the other hand, had favored continuing the war against Prussia. The royalists promptly accepted Prussia's harsh peace terms in the Treaty of Frankfurt (see page 247).

Regarding government, the National Assembly agreed to reestablish a monarchy but was unable to decide between a Bourbon or an Orleanist king. In moves meant to be temporary, the royalists in 1871 set up a republic, and in 1875 outlined a governmental framework by four *Organic Laws*. These laws became the constitution of the *Third French Republic*. In elections between 1875 and 1879, the royalists lost control of the government to the republicans. These elections doomed royalist plans to restore monarchy.

## EARLY CRISES IN THE THIRD REPUBLIC

The royalists, chiefly nobles and army officers, bitterly assailed the Republic and plotted its destruction. The royalists were supported by the clericals, who included devout lay Catholics and high clergy. The clericals, remembering the Revolution of 1789, feared that a republic would weaken the Catholic Church in France.

Two major attempts by the royalist forces to overthrow the republican government were:

1. **Boulanger Affair.** In the late 1880's General *Georges Boulanger*, hero of the antirepublican groups, apparently planned to seize the government. To forestall a coup d'état, the Republic in 1889 charged him with treason and ordered his arrest. Boulanger fled the country and soon afterwards committed suicide. By successfully handling the Boulanger threat, the Republic increased its prestige.

2. **Dreyfus Affair.** In 1894 *Alfred Dreyfus*—a French army captain, republican, and Jew—was court-martialed by royalist officers and declared guilty of selling military documents to Germany. Monarchists, clericals, and anti-Semites (persons prejudiced against Jews) all cited the Dreyfus case to discredit the Republic. To Dreyfus' defense rallied the republicans. *Emile Zola,* a leading French literary figure, penned an open letter, "J'Accuse." He charged the army high command with "framing" Dreyfus and seeking to destroy the Republic. In 1906, following several dramatic trials, Dreyfus was finally declared innocent, restored to military service, promoted, and awarded the Legion of Honor. (According to the evidence, the man guilty of selling the military documents to the Germans was a heavily-in-debt gambler and royalist army officer, Count Esterhazy.)

The Dreyfus Affair *(a)* swung French public opinion strongly toward the Third Republic, *(b)* discredited anti-Semitism in France, *(c)* spurred the government to replace monarchist army officers with loyal republicans, and *(d)* brought about laws to weaken clerical influence.

## ANTICLERICAL LAWS (1901, 1905)

1. The **Associations Law** of 1901 had the effect of closing schools conducted by religious orders. The law aimed to compel pupils to attend public schools, where they would be exposed to republican books and teachers.

2. The **Separation Law** of 1905 abrogated (ended) the Concordat of 1801 (see

page 198). No longer would the government nominate bishops and pay salaries to the clergy. The law meant full separation of Church and State.

## GOVERNMENT OF THE THIRD FRENCH REPUBLIC (1875–1940)

**1. Constitutional Framework.** The Third Republic's constitution (the Organic Laws of 1875) established a democratic government as follows: *(a)* All men received the right to vote. *(b)* The elected legislature—the Chamber of Deputies and the Senate—passed the laws. *(c)* The president, chosen by the legislature, served as a figurehead. *(d)* The cabinet, headed by the premier, governed the country, exercising both executive and legislative powers. The cabinet was responsible to the Chamber of Deputies and remained in power as long as it commanded a majority of the deputies.

**2. Political Parties.** Many political parties arose and elected members to the Chamber of Deputies. They were seated by party: *(a)* radicals at the *left*, *(b)* moderates at the *center*, and *(c)* reactionaries at the *right*. (This seating arrangement illustrates the political meaning of the terms *Leftist*, *Centrist*, and *Rightist*.)

**3. Bloc Government.** Since many parties were represented in the Chamber of Deputies, no one party alone could command a majority. Consequently a cabinet was formed by a coalition of several parties, called a *bloc*. If one party in a bloc disagreed with the others on a major issue, it left the cabinet. As a result, the cabinet lost its majority in the Chamber. Then a new bloc, representing a new majority, formed a new cabinet. During the 65 years of the Third Republic, such cabinet changes occurred more than 100 times. Although democratic, the bloc system did not provide stable, efficient government.

**4. Accomplishments.** In *domestic matters* the Third Republic *(a)* survived royalist plots aimed at its destruction, *(b)* separated Church and State, *(c)* provided free, compulsory public elementary education, *(d)* established a social security system of sickness and old age insurance, and *(e)* encouraged business growth and prosperity.

In *foreign affairs* the Third Republic *(a)* expanded the French colonial empire in northern Africa and Indo-China, *(b)* joined with the other Allied powers to defeat Germany in World War I, and *(c)* in the late 1930's prepared, though inadequately, to meet the threat of an aggressive Nazi Germany.

**5. Downfall.** The Third Republic ended when German armies overran France at the beginning of World War II (see page 493). The Nazis directly ruled over northern and western France, called the *occupied zone*. The Nazis permitted a puppet French government, with its capital at the city of Vichy, to rule unoccupied France. Under Marshal *Henri Pétain*, the Vichy regime was a French version of an authoritarian state.

Meanwhile, in England, General *Charles de Gaulle* established a *Free French* government-in-exile to continue the war against Nazi Germany.

## GOVERNMENT OF THE FOURTH FRENCH REPUBLIC (1946–1958)

**1. Constitutional Framework.** After liberation from German occupation, France established the *Fourth Republic*. Its constitution, modeled on that of the Third Republic, provided a similar democratic but unstable government.

*a. Universal Suffrage.* All men and, for the first time, women received the right to vote.

*b. Weak President.* Elected for a seven-year term by the legislature, the president was a figurehead.

*c. Powerful Legislature.* The elected legislature consisted of the *Council of the Republic*, which could hold up legislation temporarily, and the *National Assembly*, which *alone* could pass laws. Also, it could overthrow the cabinet.

*d. Responsible Cabinet.* Headed by the premier, the cabinet governed France, exercising both executive and legislative powers. The cabinet remained in office as long as it controlled a majority in the Assembly.

**2. Leading Political Parties**

*a. Extreme Left.* The *Communist party* opposed France's pro-Western foreign policy and favored a French Communist regime.

*b. Center.* Four main parties existed in the "center": the left center *Socialists*, the center *Radicals* and *Popular Republicans* (Christian Democrats), and the right center *Independent Republicans*. These parties differed regarding business controls, labor policies, tax measures, Catholic interests, and the Algerian rebellion. However, they united in allegiance to the Republic.

*c. Right.* The *Rally of the French People*, founded by Charles de Gaulle, favored revising the constitution so as to strengthen the office of president and assure stable government. By 1953 de Gaulle, despairing of achieving his aims through his party, dissolved it and withdrew from political life.

**3. Unstable Bloc Government.** Since no one party commanded a majority in the Assembly, government was by bloc—a coalition of the center parties. However, differences on issues frequently led one center party or another to withdraw from the bloc and overthrow the government. During its 12-year life, the Fourth Republic had 25 different center-bloc cabinets.

**4. Accomplishments.** The Fourth Republic *(a)* fostered France's economic recovery after World War II, *(b)* cooperated in West European moves toward economic unity, *(c)* joined pro-Western alliances against communism, and *(d)* granted independence, although reluctantly, to the French colonies of Indo-China, Tunisia, and Morocco.

**5. Downfall.** The downfall of the Fourth Republic resulted from, *(a) fundamentally*, the inability of the multiparty center-bloc system to provide stable and effective government and, *(b) immediately*, the failure to settle the Algerian crisis.

*a. Rebellion in Algeria.* Algeria was inhabited by 9 million Moslems and 1 million European (chiefly French) settlers called *colons.* In 1954 the Moslem *National Liberation Front* began guerrilla warfare to win independence from France. This Algerian rebellion tied down a large French army, drained the French treasury, and caused many cabinet crises. When a new cabinet took office in May, 1958, rumors arose that the government was ready to make substantial concessions to the Algerian rebels. French army officers and settlers in Algeria rebelled, denied the authority of the government in Paris, and demanded that all governmental power be given to General de Gaulle. In Paris the center-bloc government resigned, an admission that it could not control the defiant army officers.

*b. De Gaulle as Premier: End of the Fourth Republic.* Fearing civil war as the alternative to de Gaulle, the National Assembly confirmed de Gaulle as premier, granted him unlimited power for six months, and agreed to submit his constitutional reforms directly to the people. Premier de Gaulle reestablished the authority of the Paris government over the French army and settlers in Algeria and prepared far-reaching constitutional reforms.

## GOVERNMENT OF THE FIFTH FRENCH REPUBLIC (1958 TO THE PRESENT)

The Gaullist constitution for the *Fifth Republic* received overwhelming popular approval. The vote was a personal triumph for de Gaulle and an endorsement of his plans for a strong presidential system. The Gaullist constitution, with later amendments, provided a government that differs markedly from that of the Fourth Republic.

1. **Popularly Elected President.** Instead of being elected by the legislature, the president is directly elected to a seven-year term by a majority vote of the people. (In case no one candidate secures a majority of the popular vote, the two top candidates engage in a runoff election.)

2. **Powerful President.** No longer a figurehead, the president dominates the government as a strong executive with substantial powers. The president *(a)* appoints personal choices to the premiership and to other government positions; *(b)* serves as commander-in-chief of the armed forces; *(c)* negotiates treaties; *(d)* issues executive decrees on matters not subject to legislation; *(e)* after the first year of any legislature, may dissolve the National Assembly and call for new elections; and *(f)* in a national emergency, may temporarily assume dictatorial powers.

3. **Weakened Cabinet.** The cabinet, headed by the premier, has less authority than before, since the president now exercises many of its former powers. The cabinet directs everyday governmental operations and enforces the laws. Members of the cabinet no longer sit in the National Assembly. Although appointed

by the president, the cabinet is responsible to the National Assembly. However, constitutional provisions make it very difficult for the National Assembly to overthrow a cabinet.

**4. Weakened Legislature.** The legislature consists of the indirectly elected *Senate* and the directly elected *National Assembly.* The legislature no longer dominates the government, and its powers are severely limited. The legislature *(a)* meets only twice a year for no more than three months each time and *(b)* may pass laws only on matters specifically listed in the constitution; all other matters are handled by executive decree. Furthermore, the National Assembly *(a)* is restricted in its ability to defeat a government bill or to overthrow a cabinet by a vote of censure and *(b)* after its first year may be dissolved and new elections ordered by the president.

**5. Single District Election of Assembly Members.** Under the Fourth Republic's method of *proportional* representation, each party received seats in the National Assembly in proportion to its total popular vote. This method enabled the Communists, who polled up to 30 percent of the popular vote, to receive up to 30 percent of the Assembly seats. Under the Gaullist constitution, each district elects a single member to the Assembly. If no candidate receives a majority, the two top candidates engage in a runoff election. This method permits the other parties to join in support of one anti-Communist candidate.

**6. Constitutional Council.** This judicial body determines the constitutionality of new laws.

## OBSERVATIONS ON THE DE GAULLE CONSTITUTION

**1. Democratic Aspects.** Like the constitution of the Fourth Republic, the Gaullist constitution guarantees civil liberties, especially legal equality, religious freedom, and universal suffrage; provides for direct election of the National Assembly; and makes the cabinet responsible to the Assembly.

**2. Strong President.** Two new features of the Fifth Republic borrowed from the United States are the strong president and the separation of executive from legislative powers. The president is not responsible to the legislature and, unlike the president of the Fourth Republic, has real powers.

Some observers wonder whether the constitution has sufficient safeguards to prevent an unscrupulous president from becoming a dictator.

## FIFTH REPUBLIC: THE DE GAULLE ERA (1958–1969)

**1. Elections**

*a. Presidential.* In 1958 Charles de Gaulle was overwhelmingly elected as the Fifth Republic's first president. In 1965 de Gaulle was reelected but with diminishing support. Failing to secure an absolute majority, de Gaulle was forced into a runoff election that he won with 55 percent of the vote.

*b. National Assembly.* In 1958 the *Union of the New Republic,* the new Gaullist group, emerged as the largest party in the National Assembly. Together with other conservatives, the Gaullists held a comfortable legislative majority. The other major parties—center *Radicals* and *Popular Republicans,* left-center *Socialists,* and the extreme-left *Communists*—all registered sharp declines. The Gaullists retained control of the Assembly—in 1962 with a strong majority, in 1967 with a bare majority, and in 1968 with an overwhelming majority.

The 1968 elections were called by de Gaulle as France faced a possible revolutionary situation: massive sit-ins, demonstrations and strikes by students and workers, and demands by anti-Gaullist parties for de Gaulle's resignation. The 1968 Gaullist victory indicated that the French, when faced by the possibility of revolution, preferred de Gaulle and his promise of orderly reform.

**2. Accomplishments.** De Gaulle *(a)* settled the Algerian crisis by granting Algeria independence, *(b)* made France a nuclear power, *(c)* sustained general prosperity, and *(d)* maintained a stable, democratic government.

**3. Downfall of De Gaulle.** In 1969 de Gaulle demanded a "yes" vote on a government-reorganization referendum, warning that, if the voters defeated the referendum, he would step down. When 52.4 percent of the electorate voted "no," de Gaulle resigned. (The next year, at age 80, de Gaulle died.)

De Gaulle's defeat has been explained by the following factors:

*a. Economic and Social.* Workers protested low wages, high prices, inadequate welfare benefits, and poor housing; small merchants complained of tax discrimination; students at government-run universities resented the overcrowded classrooms, outmoded courses of study, and lack of any student voice in educational matters. These groups resented de Gaulle's neglect of domestic reforms and his preoccupation with foreign affairs.

*b. Foreign Policy.* Voters were disquieted as de Gaulle's foreign policies alienated France's traditional friends. De Gaulle embargoed arms to Israel, vetoed British membership in the Common Market, withdrew French forces from NATO, and opposed American influence in European affairs.

*c. Political.* Voters were disturbed by de Gaulle's authoritarian style as seen in his use of "personal power" and his insistence that only he could lead France to greatness. Many believed that it was "time for a change," especially since several capable men were available to succeed to the presidency.

**FIFTH REPUBLIC: AFTER DE GAULLE**

**1. Pompidou Government (1969–1974)**

*a. Presidential Election of 1969.* Georges Pompidou, for six years premier under de Gaulle, was the Gaullist candidate. He vowed to maintain stable government, to foster domestic reforms, and to reconsider de Gaulle's foreign policies. Pompidou won the runoff election and became president.

*b. Domestic Matters.* Pompidou inherited the long-term problems facing France. Students agitated for educational reforms; workers complained of unemployment, low wages, and inflationary prices. The government (1) introduced some educational reforms but also adopted severe antiriot regulations to curb student protests and (2) sought to moderate union wage demands and to battle inflation. Pompidou's policies appealed to the middle and upper classes, who feared violence and wanted law and order.

c. *Foreign Affairs.* Pompidou maintained, with one exception, the policies of de Gaulle. French military forces remained apart from NATO, France continued atmospheric testing of nuclear weapons, and Pompidou reaffirmed France's independent but pro-Western foreign stance. Pompidou maintained the embargo on arms to Israel but agreed to sell Libya 100 *Mirage* fighter-bombers. Pompidou, however, approved British membership in the Common Market.

d. *National Assembly Elections of 1973.* The Gaullists faced a leftist "united front" formed by the Socialists under *François Mitterrand* and the Communists under *Georges Marchais.* These two leftist parties agreed to support each other's candidates in the runoff elections. Although the Gaullists and their allies lost some seats, they retained a comfortable majority in the new Assembly.

## 2. Giscard d'Estaing Government (1974–1981)

a. *Presidential Election of 1974.* With Pompidou's death in 1974, France held a new presidential election. François Mitterrand, candidate of the leftist Socialist-Communist coalition, polled 43 percent of the vote. *Valéry Giscard d'Estaing*—the aristocratic former finance minister, head of the Independent Republicans allied with the Gaullists, and candidate of the center and right—polled 33 percent. In the runoff election, Giscard edged out Mitterrand by polling 51 percent of the vote and became president.

b. *Foreign and Domestic Affairs.* In foreign affairs Giscard acted to strengthen French ties with the Arab states by encouraging personal visits, furthering business arrangements, and agreeing to sell 44 *Mirage* fighter-bombers to Egypt. In Africa Giscard expanded French military activity: supporting Mauritania against Polisario Front rebels (check the Index), supporting Chad in a border dispute with Libya, assisting Zaire to repel an invasion by Katanga rebels (check the Index), and overthrowing a brutal dictator so as to return the nation of Central Africa to republican government. In domestic matters Giscard struggled with France's long-term problems: spurring industrial production, reducing unemployment, curbing inflation, expanding social services, providing low-cost housing, and moderating student unrest. The Giscard government raised the minimum wage, lowered the voting age to 18, and granted tax and credit incentives to private enterprise.

c. *National Assembly Elections of 1978.* The center-rightist coalition defeated a leftist alliance of Socialists and Communists. The progovernment parties secured 291 seats—a secure majority of the National Assembly—as compared with 200 seats for the leftist opposition. (Of the leftist seats, 86 were held by the Communists, 103 by the Socialists, and the rest by other leftists.)

Observers claimed that the election results indicated that the voters wanted to (1) keep the Communists out of power despite the French Communist party's avowal of Eurocommunism (see page 531), and (2) rebuff the Socialists for their strategy of alliance with the Communists.

### 3. Mitterrand Government (1981–    )

*a. Presidential Election of 1981.* François Mitterrand, the Socialist candidate, thwarted Giscard's bid for reelection. In the runoff election, Mitterrand polled 52 percent of the vote and became president. Observers held that the voters blamed Giscard for not improving the economy and for remaining aloof from the people's worries and problems; they were willing to risk new leadership for France; Mitterrand's victory marked a major political shift for the Fifth Republic as control of the presidency passed from the right and center-right to the left and center-left.

*b. National Assembly Elections of 1981.* To solidify his political power, President Mitterrand dissolved the National Assembly and called for new legislative elections. Mitterrand won strong support from the voters, who gave the

*Tim Menees in the Pittsburgh Post-Gazette*

**"Life's full of difficult questions, ma chère: Am I really awake at 5:30 a.m.? Is this the new dawn for France? Why did I ever go into banking??!"**

Socialists 285 seats—a secure majority of the 491-seat National Assembly. The right and center-right parties fell to 156 seats; the Communists fell to 44 seats.

*c. Socialist Domestic and Foreign Policies.* Mitterrand pledged to pursue a moderate course and to govern in the interests of the "entire national community." The Mitterrand government immediately raised the minimum wage by 10 percent (to the equivalent of $503 per month), increased social security benefits, and provided funds to build low-cost housing. After the Socialist victory in the Assembly elections, the government officially presented its economic program: nationalization of most private banks and some military aircraft, armaments, and steel companies; creation of 210,000 public sector jobs; reduction of the workweek from 40 to 35 hours within four years; increase of taxes by 25 percent on the wealthy. The Socialists insisted that their program would benefit those at the bottom of the economic ladder and would stimulate economic growth; it was not designed to collectivize the entire economy.

In foreign affairs, Mitterrand expressed support for the NATO alliance (but did not plan to return French forces to a unified command); for continued development of French nuclear weapons; and for Israel and the Camp David accords while recognizing Palestinian demands for a homeland. Toward the Soviet Union, Mitterrand adopted a hard line. He called upon the Soviet Union to withdraw its troops from Afghanistan, to refrain from interfering in Poland, and to remove from Eastern Europe Soviet missiles aimed at West European targets.

*d. Communists in the French Cabinet.* Mitterrand appointed four Communists to his 44-member cabinet. He explained that Communist voters had helped the Socialists attain power, that the four Communists filled technical posts—not politically or militarily sensitive, and that the French Communist party had agreed to support Socialist domestic and foreign policies—notably Socialist anti-Soviet stands. Nevertheless, Mitterrand's appointment of the four Communist cabinet members raised fears—especially in the United States—that the appointments would endanger military secrets, undermine the Western alliance, and set an undesirable precedent for other West European countries where Communists had voting strength.

## MULTIPLE–CHOICE QUESTIONS

1. Following in Napoleon Bonaparte's footsteps, Louis Napoleon (1) was a great military leader (2) completely revised the French legal code (3) donated lands in Italy to the papacy (4) established a dictatorial government in France.
2. Napoleon III established French imperialist control over (1) Indo-China (2) China (3) India (4) Indonesia.
3. As a result of the Maximilian Affair, Louis Napoleon (1) gained popularity in France (2) lost popularity in France (3) earned the hatred of Bismarck (4) joined in a military alliance with Britain.
4. Defeated in the Franco-Prussian War, France (1) adopted the Declaration of the Rights of Man (2) restored the Bourbon monarchy (3) established a republic (4) lost its colonies in Africa.

5. The National Assembly elected in 1871 contained a majority of royalists because (1) the royalists pledged an immediate peace with Germany (2) voting was restricted to the upper classes (3) the German military commanders appointed the members of the Assembly (4) the republicans refused to stand for office.

6. The Dreyfus Affair was (1) a business scandal (2) an effort to weaken the Catholic Church in France (3) a plot to discredit the Republic (4) an attempt by a military hero to lead a coup d'état.

7. Which group was charged with treason to the government by Emile Zola in his letter "J'Accuse"? (1) Jews (2) royalist army officers (3) republican politicians (4) middle-class business people.

8. The Dreyfus Affair in France led to (1) Napoleon's downfall (2) a scandal in regard to the Panama Canal (3) the passage of the Civil Constitution of the Clergy (4) laws separating Church and State.

9. Under the Fourth French Republic, a group of parties that acted together to form a cabinet was called (1) the center (2) an alliance (3) a bloc (4) a ministry.

10. Bloc governments under the Fourth Republic proved unstable because they (1) did not include Communists (2) failed to stop antigovernment strikes by unions (3) lost their Assembly majority when one party withdrew from the bloc (4) were limited constitutionally to six months in office.

11. The constitution for the Fifth Republic (1) allowed the president to rule by decree in emergencies (2) granted all legislative power to the Constitutional Council (3) gave independence to Algeria (4) adopted the two-party system.

12. The Fifth French Republic borrowed from American practice when it (1) made the cabinet responsible to the legislature (2) gave the president power to dissolve the legislature (3) prohibited cabinet members from serving in the legislature (4) limited legislative sessions to two three-month periods a year.

13. The name of the Gaullist party in the Fifth Republic was (1) Union of the New Republic (2) Radicals (3) Socialists (4) Popular Republicans.

14. Under the Fifth Republic the president is elected (1) directly by the voters (2) indirectly by the voters through an "electoral college" (3) by the National Assembly (4) jointly by the National Assembly and the Senate.

15. Under the Fifth Republic if a district fails to give any Assembly candidate a majority in an election, (1) the seat is left vacant (2) the candidate with more votes than any other candidate is the winner (3) a runoff election is held (4) the president fills the position by appointment.

## COMPLETION QUESTIONS

1. Louis Napoleon lost French Catholic support when he aided the unification of _____.

2. Louis Napoleon failed in his attempt to gain imperialist control over _____ in the Western Hemisphere.

3. The leader of the Free French government during World War II was _____.

4. Under the Fourth French Republic, the position most similar to that of the king of England was that of the _____.

5. The immediate cause that led to the overthrow of the Fourth French Republic was the army-created crisis in _____.

6. In order to provide stability in government, the Fifth French Republic strengthened the powers of the _____.

7. Elected as first president under the Fifth French Republic was _____.

## ESSAY QUESTIONS

1. Show how each of the following influenced the life of Louis Napoleon: *(a)* the career of his uncle, Napoleon Bonaparte *(b)* the failure of the Maximilian Affair *(c)* defeat in the Franco-Prussian War.

2. Discuss how the Third French Republic *(a)* came into existence *(b)* overcame a plot to destroy it *(c)* was overthrown.

3. Discuss *(a)* *one* factor that led to the creation of the Fourth French Republic *(b)* *two* reasons for its downfall.

4. *(a)* Compare the French and British governments today by showing *(i)* *two* ways in which they are similar *(ii)* *two* ways in which they are different. *(b)* Evaluate *one* of the differences, indicating whether you think the French or the British practice is better.

5. *(a)* Compare the French and American governments today showing *(i)* *two* ways in which they are similar *(ii)* *two* ways in which they are different. *(b)* Evaluate *one* difference, indicating whether you think the French or the American practice is better.

6. Agree or disagree with each of the following statements, providing *two* arguments to support your opinion: *(a)* The French Revolution of 1789 may be considered to have ended in 1958 with the establishment of the Fifth French Republic. *(b)* Americans can learn much from the British and French experiences in developing their democracies. *(c)* To determine if a nation is a democracy, you must look beyond the formal structure of its government. *(d)* The Gaullist constitution for the Fifth Republic opens the way for dictatorship. *(e)* Cabinet responsibility to the legislature promotes stability in a country. *(f)* Democracy is an ideal that has grown in meaning from century to century.

# Part 9. Some Concluding Observations on Democracy

## DEMOCRATIC NATIONS IN THE WORLD TODAY

Of over 150 nations in the world today, those that may be considered democratic total about 20. The 20 democracies reflect (1) the British democratic heritage—in such nations as the United States, Great Britain, Ireland, Canada, Australia, and New Zealand; (2) in part the British example and, perhaps more, the French Revolution of 1789—in a group of West European nations including France, Italy, Belgium, the Netherlands, and the Scandinavian countries; (3) the encouragement of democratic government by the Western powers following World War II—in two nations, West Germany and Japan; and (4) the commitment of Jewish Zionist leaders, mostly Westerners, to democratic ideals—in establishing the state of Israel.

The other 130 nations reflect, in varying degrees, dictatorial government, military rule, a one-party system, and denial of civil liberties. The undemocratic states include (1) the Communist nations, especially the Soviet Union and China; (2) nations whose societies remain primarily feudal with sharp class distinctions—land ownership by the aristocracy, widespread illiteracy and low living standards—most Latin American, Asian, and Arab countries; and (3) nations whose peoples are just emerging from tribalism—most black African regimes.

Of the 80-plus nations in Asia, Latin America, and Africa that have gained independence since World War II, almost all have undemocratic regimes. Even those few nations that started out as democracies—such as Pakistan, Kenya, and Nigeria—have adopted the techniques of dictatorship. In a 1976 report Freedom House, which describes itself as a nonpartisan organization of Americans dedicated to freedom, reported the continuing decline of freedom around the world. The question for us is why?

## CONDITIONS NECESSARY FOR DEMOCRATIC SOCIETY

Democracy rests upon the belief that the people are able to govern themselves. For people to do so, history would seem to indicate that they must possess the following qualifications:

*(1) Decent Living Standards.* With sufficient food, clothing, and shelter, people have the time and energy to be concerned about their form of government and their rights as individuals. People who live at a starvation level are so occupied with securing the bare necessities of life that they have no time and no energy for political matters.

*(2) Democratic Traditions.* People cherish their national traditions. Democratic actions or events, such as successful resistance against royal power, may become part of the national heritage. These actions or events are praised by philosophers, extolled by political leaders, and transmitted from generation to generation. The democratic heritage becomes an integral part of the people's way of life. To people without such a tradition, democracy seems to have no strong claim on their loyalty.

*(3) Literacy.* For democratic government to succeed, the people must be able to read and understand the issues facing the voters, to consider conflicting points of view, to contribute to the discussion of the issues, and to vote intelligently. Thus, a literate people are necessary for democracy. However, literacy itself does not ensure democracy. The German people in the 1930's were highly literate, but they accepted the cruel Nazi dictatorship. The Russian people today are literate, by they may read only those materials permitted by their Communist dictatorship.

*(4) Political Maturity.* To ensure a successful democratic government, the people must possess a high degree of political maturity. They must realize that opposition to government policies does not constitute treason but represents alternative proposals designed to further the same goal—the national welfare. They must be willing to compromise on issues—to give a little and get a little—in order to preserve the nation's social cohesion. They must accept the members of minority groups as human beings with individual weaknesses and strengths and must grant minorities the right to full and free existence.

# DEMOCRACY VERSUS DICTATORSHIP

In the struggle between democracy and dictatorship, democratic peoples have confidently developed a belief in the eventual triumph of democracy. This is a superficial point of view and not necessarily supported by history. In ancient Greece the Spartan military state defeated democratic Athens. In ancient Rome the Roman Republic was overthrown and replaced by the Roman Empire— essentially a military dictatorship. In our own day almost all of the newly independent nations have turned, not to democracy, but to one-party states and military dictatorships.

Democratic peoples must remember that a successful democracy requires their concern and cooperation. Each generation must heed anew the warning contained in the statement: "Eternal vigilance is the price of liberty."

# DEMOCRATIC HOPES AND RECENT GAINS

Democratic peoples hope that additional nations, not now democratic, eventually will evolve toward political freedoms and human rights. This hope rests on the following bases: (1) Human beings—it is believed—naturally dislike dictatorial rule and desire a government responsive to their wishes. (2) Most nations seek to raise their people's living standards. As progress is made toward this goal, people will devote more attention to improving their form of government. (3) Most nations seek to improve their people's literacy—that is an essential ingredient for democratic rule. (4) With literacy and the influence of the mass media, people will develop the political maturity and social cohesion necessary for a democratic society.

In recent years democratic peoples have been cheered by several developments: (1) In Spain, following the death of dictator Franco, the government under King Juan Carlos I moved definitely toward democracy. In 1981 the King, rallying the army to his side, protected Spain's democratic regime by suppressing an attempted right-wing coup. (2) In Portugal an army coup ended over 40 years of dictatorial rule and led to free elections and a representative government committed to seek democracy. (3) In Greece the military dictatorship collapsed following the failure of its attempt to annex Cyprus, and Greece returned to civilian and democratic rule. (4) In India Prime Minister Indira Gandhi moved toward dictatorial rule by declaring a "state of emergency," instituting press censorship, and arresting political opponents. With economic conditions improving in India, Mrs. Gandhi in 1977 risked free elections. She and her Congress party were decisively defeated. The victorious opposition formed a government that ended press censorship and restored personal liberties. (In 1980, however, Mrs. Gandhi and her party won a remarkable election victory. Mrs. Gandhi again became prime minister as she pledged to respect India's constitution.) (5) In three African countries—Uganda, Equatorial Guinea, and Central Africa—brutal dictators were overthrown in 1979, and these nations moved toward more responsive and humane regimes.

# UNIT VIII. THE INFLUENCE OF NATIONALISM

## Part 1. Introduction

### TERMS: MEANING AND APPLICATION

**Nationality (or nation)**—people united by a belief that they share social and cultural bonds: language, history, traditions, ideals, and goals.

In some few countries people considered to be of the same nationality but residing in different regions speak different native tongues. For example: Canada is bilingual (French and English); Switzerland is trilingual (German, Italian, and French). Such diversity of language within a country tends to weaken the people's feeling of being a single nationality.

**Nationalism**—the feeling of patriotism and supreme loyalty that a nationality has toward its own country. If a nationality lacks its own independent country, nationalism provides the driving force to create one.

**National state (or nation-state)**—an independent country containing a single nationality.

**Subject nationality**—a nationality that has not achieved its own independent state but is subject to the rule of a different people.

An illustration of the above terms: For over 100 years after 1795 there existed no Polish national state. The Polish people, constituting a single nationality, survived as a subject nationality under Russian, German, and Austrian rule. Inspired by nationalism, the Polish people dreamed and worked to resurrect a Polish state. After World War I, their nationalist aspirations were realized with the formation of an independent Poland.

**Chauvinism**—extreme nationalism that exaggerates the nation's accomplishments. Whereas nationalism makes people say, "We are just as good as anyone else," chauvinism makes people say, "We are far better than anyone else."

### DEVELOPMENT OF NATIONALISM

**1. During the Middle Ages.** Until the 15th century, nationalism and national states did not exist. People gave their greatest loyalty to their church, feudal lord, city-state, or province.

242

**2. With the Rise of Absolute Monarchs and National States.** From the 15th century into the 18th century, *moderate nationalism* emerged as people became aware and proud of their own distinct nationality. They gave their loyalty to the monarch, the symbol of national unity. Moderate nationalism only mildly affected people's lives.

AN EXAMPLE: The English people were motivated, in part, to support their Tudor rulers—Henry VIII in his confrontation with the Catholic Church and Elizabeth I in her struggle against Spain—by moderate nationalism. When it was centered upon the members of a ruling family or dynasty, moderate nationalism assumed the aspects of a *dynastic nationalism.*

**3. With the French Revolution.** *Intense nationalism* originated during the French Revolution of 1789 and spread throughout Europe and the rest of the world. People transferred their loyalty from monarch to country and placed the national interest above all other considerations. Intense nationalism greatly influenced the actions of the people.

AN EXAMPLE: During the French Revolution the First French Republic began military conscription—the first time in modern history. French citizens responded approvingly, willing to risk life and limb for the defense of their homeland against invading foreign mercenary armies.

**4. To the Present Day.** In the 19th and 20th centuries, intense nationalism has been fostered by a number of developments. *(a) State control of education.* Public schools teach pride in the customs, ideals, and glories of a nation. *(b) Culture.* Artists, writers, and musical composers—in considerable numbers— produce works expressing nationalist themes. *(c) Mass communication.* Newspapers, magazines, books, radio, and television standardize and thus unify a nation's culture and outlook on life. *(d) Rapid transportation.* Railroads, automobiles, and airlines unite a national state physically.

## NATIONALISM: A FORCE FOR BOTH GOOD AND EVIL

Imbued with intense nationalism, people have supported movements and actions to further what they consider to be the well-being of their nationality.

**Democracy.** *(a)* During the French Revolution French patriots set up democratic institutions and defended them against invading foreign armies. *(b)* During the Metternich Era Italian revolutionists sought unsuccessfully to gain national unity and democratic government.

**Dictatorship.** *(a)* Italian patriots in the 1920's supported Mussolini in ending a democratic regime and establishing a dictatorship when he appealed to their Italian nationalism. *(b)* German nationalists in the 1930's rallied to Hitler's side and helped him overthrow the democratic German government and establish a Nazi dictatorship.

**Imperialism.** Powerful industrial nations—Britain, France, Germany, Italy,

Japan—were each inspired by nationalism to acquire colonial empires. Imperialist advocates claimed that colonies meant prestige, economic resources, and military bases for the mother country.

**Anti-Imperialism.** In the 20th century colonial peoples developed their own nationalism and struggled to end foreign domination. After World War II Indian nationalists ended British rule, and Algerian nationalists ended French rule. However, Hungarian and Czech efforts to throw off Russian domination of their countries proved unsuccessful.

**Militarism and War.** Modern peoples have made great sacrifices when convinced that their national existence was in peril. In the 20th century Germans and French endured peacetime conscription, tolerated heavy taxation for military expenditures, and suffered the hardships of two world wars.

**National Unification.** *(a)* In 1815 the German people inhabited 38 independent states. By 1871 German nationalists, led by Bismarck, had unified their country. *(b)* In the 19th century Italy also achieved unification.

**Empire Disruption** *(a)* The subject nationalities in the Austro-Hungarian Empire desired independence. Their leaders plotted revolution and war. Finally, when Austria-Hungary was defeated in World War I, the various subject nationalities achieved their goals. *(b)* The multinational Turkish Empire, too, came to an end following its defeat in World War I.

# Part 2.   German Unification by "Blood and Iron"

## THE GERMAN STATES (1789–1848)

### 1. Factors Promoting Unity

*a. Common Nationality.* Beginning in the late 18th century, some German people began to think of themselves as a distinct nationality and agitated for a unified "fatherland," as they called their country. This nationalist awakening reflected the efforts of German educators, poets, writers, historians, and philosophers.

FOR EXAMPLE: (1) *Johann Fichte* (1762–1814) was a philosopher whose feelings of nationalism became aroused as Napoleon conquered the German states. Fichte proclaimed the existence of a "German spirit" more noble than that of other peoples and declared that it was the mission of a unified Germany to lead the civilized world. (2) *Georg Hegel* (1770–1831) was a philosopher who predicted the unification of Germany and asserted that the state was not bound to respect any individual rights. (3) The brothers *Jakob* (1785–1863) and *Wilhelm* (1786–1859) *Grimm*, were linguists who traveled about the German states studying various dialects and collecting folktales published as *Grimm's Fairy Tales*. The brothers claimed that German was preeminent over other languages and that the folktales expressed the unique "German spirit."

*b. Napoleon's Influence.* Napoleon aided German unification, although unintentionally. He aroused German nationalism against him, weakened Austrian authority in the German states by abolishing the Holy Roman Empire, and reduced the more than 300 German states to fewer than 100.

*c. Congress of Vienna.* This peace conference in 1815 helped German unity, although unwittingly. It reduced the number of German states to 38 and organized them into an Austrian-dominated league of rulers, the *German Confederation*. The confederation proved weak and ineffective, incapable of providing Germany with a unified government. Its failure stirred German nationalists to seek unity by other means.

*d. Zollverein.* In 1819 Prussia formed a German customs, or tariff, union, known as the *Zollverein*. By the 1840's it included most German states except Austria. The Zollverein encouraged free trade between member states but maintained high tariffs against nonmembers. The removal of internal tariff barriers benefited German workers, merchants, and maufacturers and promoted the country's economic unity.

## 2. Factors Hindering Unity

*a. Differences Among the German People.* In Prussia and other north German states, the people were, in the main, Protestant, were interested in commerce, and were turning toward manufacturing. In Bavaria and other south German states, the people were predominantly Roman Catholic and were interested chiefly in agriculture. Outnumbered by the northerners, the south Germans realized that, in a united country, they would be a minority.

*b. Opposition of Austria.* Austria emerged from the Congress of Vienna as an influential central European empire containing many different peoples. Austria's rulers feared that the growth of nationalism, particularly in nearby Germany, might inspire their subject nationalities to seek independence. Austria's rulers also realized that, in the event of German unification, they would lose their influence over German affairs.

In 1819 Metternich, chief minister of Austria, induced the German Confederation to issue the *Carlsbad Decrees*. Aimed at suppressing liberal and nationalist ideas in Germany, these laws provided for (1) strict supervision of universities, teachers, and student organizations and (2) censorship of newspapers, pamphlets, and books.

*c. Opposition of the Lesser German States.* The rulers and officials of the smaller German states feared that a unified Germany might centralize governmental power, thereby ending their authority.

*d. Opposition of France.* French leaders feared that a unified Germany would be sufficiently powerful to challenge France's leadership in Europe. France also felt militarily more secure with weak, disunited neighbors.

## FAILURE OF THE 1848 REVOLUTION

German liberals led a series of revolts in 1848 aimed at ending autocracy and unifying Germany. Encouraged by early successes, they convened a parliament, the *Frankfurt Assembly.* The liberals prepared a democratic constitution, proclaimed a united Germany, and after months of debate offered the position of emperor to the king of Prussia. He rejected the Assembly's offer as "a crown out of the gutter" and also because he feared that acceptance might lead to war with Austria. Since the liberals lacked the military power to enforce unification, the king's refusal spelled the failure of the Frankfurt Assembly.

The conservatives regained control throughout the German states, and the liberals experienced severe persecution. Many fled the country. A considerable number came to the United States, where they contributed to our growing democracy.

In Germany the way was now open for the successful attempt at unity under autocratic and anti-democratic leadership.

## LEADERS OF GERMAN UNIFICATION

**1. Bismarck,** appointed chief minister of Prussia in 1862, belonged to the dominant, landowning aristocracy, the *Junkers.* A reactionary who despised democracy, Bismarck planned to unite Germany—not by speeches and votes as at the Frankfurt Assembly, but by "blood and iron," meaning military power.

**2. William I,** *Hohenzollern* king of Prussia (1861–1888), who became emperor of Germany in 1871, fully supported Bismarck's policies.

**3. Moltke,** Prussian general and chief of staff, assured Bismarck's success by building a strong army and achieving impressive military victories.

## STEPS IN GERMAN UNIFICATION (1862–1871)

**1. Creation of Prussian Military Power.** In 1862 the government's request for increased military funds was defeated in the Prussian legislature; its liberal majority opposed militarism and distrusted Bismarck. Thereupon, Bismarck ignored the lawmakers, violated the Prussian Constitution, and from 1862 to 1867 governed virtually as a dictator. He and Moltke created a powerful Prussian military machine.

## 2. Elimination of Austrian Influence

*a. The Danish War (1864).* Bismarck brought about a war with Denmark over the provinces of *Schleswig* and *Holstein*. Prussia, joined by Austria, easily defeated Denmark and compelled it to cede Schleswig-Holstein. Prussia and Austria became the joint owners of the two provinces.

*b. The Austro–Prussian War (1866).* Bismarck deliberately quarreled with Austria regarding the administration of the conquered provinces and provoked a war. Bismarck's purpose was to end Austrian power in Germany. Most German states supported Austria since they were fearful of Prussian domination. Prussia was allied with Italy, which wanted the Italian-inhabited territory held by Austria. General von Moltke's armies overwhelmed Austria so quickly that the war is also called the *Seven Weeks' War.*

By the treaty of peace, Austria (1) agreed to Prussia's annexation of Schleswig-Holstein, (2) ceded Venetia to Italy, and (3) agreed to dissolve the Austrian-dominated German Confederation, thus withdrawing from German affairs. By treating Austria generously, Bismarck expected to gain its friendship for the emerging German state.

**3. Establishment of the North German Confederation (1867).** Following the Austro–Prussian War, Bismarck annexed several north German states and compelled the remaining ones to join in a Prussian-dominated *North German Confederation.* Only the four south German states remained outside the confederation, but they were tied to Prussia by the Zollverein and by a defensive military alliance.

**4. The Franco–Prussian War (1870–1871).** Bismarck now desired a war with France so that the south Germans, by fighting a common enemy and experiencing wartime nationalism, would voluntarily merge into a Prussian-controlled, unified Germany. When Napoleon III of France opposed a Prussian Hohenzollern candidate for the throne of Spain, Bismarck rewrote the *Ems Dispatch*—a vital telegram dealing with the issue—so as to intensify Franco-German enmity. Thus provoked, Napoleon III declared war upon Prussia, which was joined by the four south German states. General von Moltke's armies invaded France, destroyed the French forces at the battle of *Sedan,* and quickly overran the country.

By the *Treaty of Frankfurt,* France *(a)* ceded to Germany the provinces of *Alsace* and *Lorraine* (rich in coal and iron and inhabited mainly by French people), *(b)* agreed to pay Germany a huge war indemnity, and *(c)* consented to German military occupation until the indemnity was paid. By treating France harshly, Bismarck planted the seeds of World War I.

**5. Establishment of the German Empire (1871).** During the Franco-Prussian War, the four south German states consented to unification with Prussia. In 1871, at the Palace of Versailles outside Paris, Bismarck proclaimed William I as Emperor *(Kaiser)* of the German Empire.

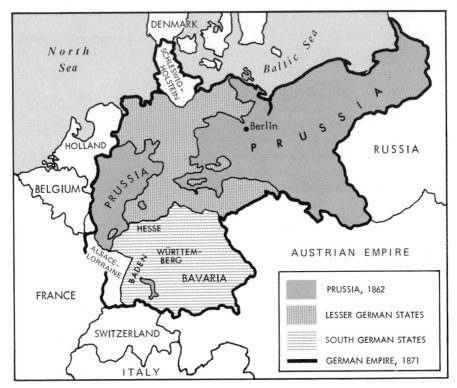

**The Unification of Germany Under Prussian Leadership**

Bismarck's success—by military might and autocratic rule—established a tradition that, according to many historians, greatly impeded the development of democracy in Germany and paved the way for the Nazi dictatorship.

## THE GERMAN EMPIRE: UNDEMOCRATIC GOVERNMENT

**1. Autocracy.** *(a)* Unlike the British king, the German ruler was no figurehead. The kaiser commanded the armed forces, conducted foreign affairs, and appointed his choices to major government positions. *(b)* The *Chancellor* (prime minister) and other cabinet members were responsible to the kaiser, not to the legislature. *(c)* In the two-house legislature, the *Bundesrat*—whose members were appointed by the heads of the various states—exercised important lawmaking powers; the popularly elected *Reichstag* had few powers.

**2. Prussian Domination.** Prussia contained almost two-thirds of the area and the population of the Empire. The king of Prussia automatically became emperor of Germany. The chief minister of Prussia usually served as chancellor of Germany. Prussia controlled enough votes in the Bundesrat to block any military law, tax measure, or constitutional amendment.

## THE GERMAN EMPIRE UNDER BISMARCK'S DIRECTION (1871–1890)

As the *Iron Chancellor* of Germany, Bismarck pursued conservative and nationalist policies.

**1. Centralization of Power.** To promote uniformity within Germany, the national government took away from the states their control over railways, telegraph lines, postal service, banking, and coinage. Also, national codes of law replaced the varying state legal systems.

**2. Continuation of Militarism.** The Empire adopted the Prussian system of compulsory, peacetime military service. Militarism was extolled by government officials, patriotic societies, and nationalist writers. In conducting foreign affairs, Bismarck emphasized military alliances.

**3. Encouragement of Industrialization.** Unification encouraged industrial growth. Germany rapidly changed from an agricultural to a predominantly industrial nation and experienced great prosperity. The German government, eager to attain economic self-sufficiency, assisted the industrialists by *(a) high tariffs* to protect home industry against foreign competitors and *(b) imperialism* to secure colonies for raw materials and markets.

**4. Persecution of Subject Nationalities.** Bismarck tried to compel the Empire's minorities—Poles, Danes, and French—to forsake their own cultures and adopt German ways. Despite persecution, these minority groups resisted *Germanization*.

**5. Measures Against Catholics: The Kulturkampf.** The German Catholics, who inhabited chiefly the four southern states, opposed Bismarck and feared domination by Protestant Prussia. To protect their interests, Catholics organized the *Center party*, which advocated stronger states' rights. Bismarck opposed the Catholics because of their support of states' rights and because of their ties to the pope in Rome. This loyalty to an international church, Bismarck believed, evidenced a lack of German nationalism.

To weaken the Catholic Church, Bismarck in 1872 started a struggle called, by his supporters, the battle for civilization, or *Kulturkampf*. He secured laws placing the Catholic clergy under state control, ending Church influence in education, and requiring civil marriage ceremonies. These measures, denounced by the pope and defied by clergy and devout Church members, intensified Catholic resistance and helped the Center party increase its Reichstag representation. Eventually Bismarck permitted the repeal of most anti-Catholic laws as he realized their failure and desired Catholic support against another of his enemies, the Socialists.

**6. Measures Against the Socialists.** As German industry grew, city workers became more numerous and sought higher wages and better working conditions. The workers voted for the Reichstag candidates of the *Social Democratic (Socialist) party*. The Socialists pleaded the workers' cause and denounced

Bismarck's policies of autocracy and militarism. Bismarck detested the Socialists because of their democratic, antimilitarist stand and their ties to the international Socialist movement. He felt that supporters of any worldwide organization could not be true German patriots.

To combat the German Socialists, Bismarck employed: *(a) Repression.* In 1878 he secured laws that forbade Socialist meetings, banned their publications, and subjected their leaders to arrest. *(b) Social Security.* Bismarck believed that the workers would reject the Socialist party if they received government help toward economic security. Between 1883 and 1889, therefore, he secured laws to assist workers financially in case of sickness, accident, and old age. (Bismarck's social insurance program set an example later followed by most industrial nations. See pages 292–293.)

Neither repressive laws nor social legislation weakened socialism in Germany. Even operating under severe handicaps, the Socialist party spread its ideas and increased its Reichstag membership.

**7. Propaganda Against Jews.** In Bismarck's Germany anti-Semitism exerted considerable influence. Bigots published pamphlets and gave lectures claiming that Jews had too much influence over German industry and commerce. In the royal court the kaiser's chief chaplain, Adolf Stocker, often preached that Jews sought to destroy Germany's social order. Bismarck himself used the Jews as a scapegoat, blaming Jewish leaders for his failure in the Kulturkampf and his failure to eradicate liberal democratic ideas in Germany.

**8. Foreign Policies.** See page 431.

## THE GERMAN EMPIRE UNDER WILLIAM II

In 1888 *William II,* grandson of the Prussian ruler who first appointed Bismarck as chancellor, inherited the German throne. A strong-willed believer in the "divine right" of kings, William II was determined to direct German affairs personally. In 1890, following a policy disagreement, the new kaiser dismissed Bismarck from office.

Kaiser William II reversed two of Bismarck's policies: friendship for Russia and repression of Socialists. Otherwise he maintained Bismarckian conservatism and nationalism. William II ruled autocratically. He favored Junker landlords, industrialists, and military officers; strengthened the army and built an imposing navy; and furthered imperialism.

The kaiser's policies of militarism and imperialism helped bring about World War I. Still later, Adolf Hitler followed a similar course of militarism and imperialism and brought on World War II.

## MULTIPLE–CHOICE QUESTIONS

1. Nationalism may best be defined as   (1) a feeling of unity within a country   (2) the desire to rule over other peoples   (3) a respect for law and order   (4) opposition to autocracy.

2. Within a national state the group likely to be least nationalistic is   (1) workers   (2) employers   (3) women   (4) recent immigrants.

3. A subject nationality is a people   (1) of low living standards   (2) of primitive culture   (3) lacking its own independent country   (4) lacking a national religion.

4. Chauvinists would be most likely to say that their people   (1) are as good as any other people   (2) have a backward culture   (3) constitute the master race   (4) have a tradition of democracy.

5. Nationalism became an important factor in European affairs during   (1) the Middle Ages   (2) the French Revolution   (3) World War I   (4) the Renaissance.

6. Which did *not* strengthen nationalism?   (1) state control of education   (2) the social classes of the Old Regime   (3) modern communication methods   (4) improved transportation facilities.

7. At different times and in different countries, nationalism has supported conflicting ideals such as democracy and dictatorship. This proves that   (1) nationalists are illogical   (2) democracy and dictatorship are not too different   (3) nationalists will support that form of government they identify with their country's history and interests   (4) nationalists prefer war and dictatorship.

8. Nationalists would be most aroused if their country's   (1) unemployment rate went up   (2) flag flying before the embassy in a foreign nation was torn down   (3) printing of history books increased   (4) exports of goods decreased.

9. Napoleon I affected German history by   (1) bringing about immediate German unification   (2) consolidating many small states into fewer larger ones   (3) making his brother emperor of Germany   (4) enlarging Prussian territory.

10. An obstacle to German unification in the period from 1815 to 1860 was the   (1) lack of common language   (2) rivalry between Prussia and Austria   (3) power of the Holy Roman Emperor   (4) territorial changes made by Napoleon I.

11. In the mid-19th century, the German people were   (1) almost all Protestant   (2) almost all Catholic   (3) Protestant in the north; Catholic in the south   (4) Catholic in the north; Protestant in the south.

12. The Carlsbad Decrees sought to   (1) bring about war with France   (2) suppress nationalist agitation at German universities   (3) democratize the government of Prussia   (4) remove Austria from German affairs.

13. The liberals failed to unify Germany because they   (1) were not nationalistic   (2) lacked knowledge of parliamentary procedure   (3) lacked military power   (4) were pro-Austrian.

14. The Zollverein was   (1) a German tariff union   (2) a German legislative body   (3) the Prussian land-owning aristocracy   (4) the cavalry unit of the Prussian army.

15. Bismarck's plan to unify Germany included   (1) beginning a tariff union   (2) securing the cooperation of Austria   (3) compelling the other north German states to join Prussia in a confederation on Prussia's terms   (4) holding a plebiscite on unification in all German states.

16. Bismarck expelled Austria from German affairs by means of   (1) a diplomatic agreement   (2) paying Austria a monetary indemnity   (3) allowing Austria to annex Schleswig-Holstein   (4) the Seven Weeks' War.

17. Bismarck completed the formation of the German Empire by means of the (1) Austro-Prussian War (2) Franco-Prussian War (3) Napoleonic Wars (4) Danish War.

18. After unifying Germany, Bismarck undertook the *Kulturkampf* to (1) encourage music and literature (2) weaken the power of the Catholic Church (3) destroy the Socialist party (4) Germanize subject nationalities.

19. Bismarck advocated social insurance in Germany because he (1) wished to compete with Britain in industry (2) wished to satisfy workers and to discourage socialism (3) represented the working class (4) was the leader of the Social Democratic party.

20. Between 1871 and 1914 Germany became a(an) (1) democratic republic (2) highly industrialized nation (3) Fascist dictatorship (4) advocate of disarmament.

## COMPLETION QUESTIONS

1. During the Revolution of 1848, German liberal groups proclaimed their country's unity at the _____ Assembly.

2. Bismarck's method of uniting Germany was expressed in the slogan _____.

3. As a result of the Franco-Prussian War, Germany annexed the provinces of _____ and _____.

4. The prime minister of the German Empire, appointed by the emperor, was called the _____.

5. Under the German Empire, the cabinet was responsible to the _____.

## ESSAY QUESTIONS

1. Using specific examples, show how *each* of the following influenced the development of nationalism: *(a)* French Revolution *(b)* building of railroads *(c)* spread of free public education *(d)* the work of an artist or a writer or a musical composer.

2. "Nationalism has been an important factor in the development of Europe, but its influence has not always been desirable." Explain and illustrate with examples *(a) one* way in which nationalism has been desirable *(b) one* way in which it has been undesirable.

3. Explain the relationship of *each* of the following to the unification of Germany: *(a)* Zollverein *(b)* Carlsbad Decrees *(c)* Schleswig-Holstein *(d)* the Ems Dispatch *(e)* Germanization *(f)* the Kulturkampf.

4. Using *one* specific reference for *each*, describe Bismarck's attitude toward or influence upon the following: *(a)* autocracy *(b)* militarism *(c)* nationalism *(d)* civil liberties *(e)* minorities under German rule *(f)* problems facing workers *(g)* powers of the central government.

5. "Germany was unified *not* under democratic but under autocratic leadership." *(a)* Show *one* way that democratic forces tried but failed to unify Germany. *(b)* Explain *two* factors that enabled autocratic forces to unify Germany *(c)* Discuss *one* significance of German unification under autocratic leadership.

6. Contrast the government of the German Empire with the government of Britain as to *(a)* powers of the monarch *(b)* cabinet responsibility *(c)* powers of the Reichstag and the House of Commons.

# Part 3. Unification of Italy

## ITALY IN 1815: A "GEOGRAPHIC EXPRESSION"

### 1. Factors Hindering Unity

*a. Political Divisions.* At the Congress of Vienna, Metternich insisted that Italy not be a united nation but a "geographic expression." The Congress divided the country as follows: (1) The kingdom of *Sardinia-Piedmont* (also called Sardinia or Piedmont)—under Italian control. (2) The provinces of *Lombardy* and *Venetia*—annexed to Austria. (3) The duchies of *Parma, Modena,* and *Tuscany,* as well as the *Kingdom of the Two Sicilies* (also called Naples)—under local rulers dominated by Austria. (4) The *Papal States*—under Church control.

*b. Opposition of Austria.* The rulers of Austria fought Italian unification to (1) discourage nationalist uprisings within their empire, (2) retain Lombardy and Venetia, and (3) maintain Austrian influence in the duchies and the Two Sicilies—whose reactionary rulers also feared unification.

*c. Opposition of the Papacy.* Church leaders believed that a united Italy would end the pope's temporal, or civil, rule over the Papal States.

*d. Discord Among Nationalists.* The leading Italian nationalists were in conflict on a type of government for a united Italy. *Mazzini* and *Garibaldi* sought a democratic Italian republic; *Gioberti* urged an Italian federation under the leadership of the pope; *Cavour,* an admirer of the British government, worked for a liberal Italian monarchy.

### 2. Factors Promoting Unity

*a. Nationalist Feeling.* Beginning with the Napoleonic Era, the Italians became increasingly conscious of their nationality. They recalled the past glory of Italy during the Roman Empire and the Renaissance, resented their present subjugation to Austria, and desired unity and greatness.

*b. Patriotic Societies*

(1) The *Carbonari,* a secret society of limited membership, conspired to establish a united Italian republic. It fomented uprisings in 1820, 1821, and 1831—all suppressed by Austria. Thereafter, Carbonari secrecy and intrigue lost favor among Italian nationalists.

(2) *Young Italy,* founded in 1831 by Mazzini, was a nonsecret society. It openly and successfully propagandized democratic and nationalist ideas among the people.

253

*c. Leadership of Sardinia-Piedmont.* The *House of Savoy*, a patriotic Italian family, ruled Sardinia and aspired to unify Italy. In 1848 the king of Sardinia granted his people a liberal constitution and led his armies in support of an Italian uprising against Austria. The Sardinians were defeated, and Austria reestablished its control within Italy. Although unsuccessful in 1848, Sardinia-Piedmont won the loyalty of Italian nationalists.

## LEADERS OF ITALIAN UNIFICATION.

**1. Mazzini,** writer, orator, and founder of Young Italy, dedicated his life to securing democracy and unity for his country. Preaching through newspapers, pamphlets, and speeches, Mazzini transmitted his patriotic ardor to the masses. In the Revolution of 1848, his followers seized the Papal States, and Mazzini proclaimed the Roman Republic. When French troops crushed this uprising, he fled the country and continued his propaganda efforts from abroad. Mazzini has been called the *soul* of unification.

**2. Garibaldi,** a friend of Mazzini, was a military leader. He defended Mazzini's Roman Republic against the French, several times fought for Sardinia against Austria, and in 1860 conquered the Two Sicilies. Garibaldi was known as the *sword* of unification.

**3. Cavour,** liberal statesman appointed prime minister of Sardinia-Piedmont in 1852, strengthened the country by promoting industry, building railroads, improving agriculture, fostering education, and enlarging the army. Until his death in 1861, he executed a series of diplomatic moves to achieve Italian unity. Cavour has been called the *brain* of unification.

**4. Victor Emmanuel II,** who became king of Sardinia-Piedmont in 1849, retained his nation's liberal constitution and fully supported Cavour's policies. In 1861 he became king of Italy.

## SARDINIA-PIEDMONT UNIFIES ITALY BY TERRITORIAL ANNEXATIONS (1859–1870)

**1. Lombardy (1859).** Cavour shrewdly secured from Napoleon III of France a pledge of military assistance if Austria attacked Sardinia. Thereupon, Cavour maneuvered Austria into declaring war. In a short conflict French and Sardinian troops defeated the Austrians. As a result of this Austro-Sardinian War, *(a)* Austria ceded Lombardy to Sardinia and *(b)* following a plebiscite, Sardinia ceded Savoy and Nice to France.

Sardinia's success aroused nationalist revolts elsewhere in Italy.

**2. The Duchies (1860).** In Parma, Modena, and Tuscany, the people drove out their pro-Austrian rulers and, by plebiscites, voted for annexation to Sardinia-Piedmont.

**The Unification of Italy (1859–1919)**

**3. The Two Sicilies (1860).** In 1860 Garibaldi came to the aid of the Sicilian and Neapolitan revolutionaries. He sailed from Piedmont to Sicily with a volunteer army of 1,000 men, called *Red Shirts*. Garibaldi, joined by rebels in southern Italy, soon gained complete control of the Two Sicilies. In the national interest Garibaldi put aside his republican sentiments and proposed that the Two Sicilies unite with Sardinia under Victor Emmanuel II. By a plebiscite the southern Italians so voted.

**4. The Papal States (1860).** While Garibaldi conquered the Two Sicilies, Cavour ordered Sardinian troops into the Papal States. The Sardinians, welcomed by nationalist groups, overran central Italy. Cavour then announced the annexation of the Papal States (except for Rome, protected by French troops), thereby joining northern and southern Italy. In 1861 the Kingdom of Italy was proclaimed.

**5. Venetia (1866).** Italy allied itself with Prussia in the Seven Weeks' War against Austria. The Italians invaded Venetia but were defeated. However, the Prussian armies quickly overwhelmed the Austrians. By the peace treaty Austria ceded Venetia to Italy.

**6. Rome (1870).** Because of the Franco-Prussian War, France withdrew its troops protecting the pope in Rome. Thereupon, Italian forces occupied the city. Following a plebiscite, Rome was annexed and designated the capital of Italy.

## PROBLEMS FACING ITALY AFTER UNIFICATION

**1. Government Weaknesses.** Italy's limited monarchy featured a king with few powers, an elected Chamber of Deputies, and a cabinet responsible to the Chamber of Deputies. Although modeled after Britain's parliamentary system, the Italian government operated far less successfully. (*a*) The Italian masses, illiterate and impoverished, lacked a democratic tradition and demonstrated little public responsibility. (*b*) Until 1904, when the pope relaxed the ban forbidding Catholics to take part in the Italian government, devout Catholics shunned government positions and did not vote. (*c*) Until 1912, when universal manhood suffrage was adopted, only the wealthier classes could vote. (*d*) The existence of many political parties caused a number of cabinet crises. (*e*) Bribery and corruption pervaded public life.

**2. Church Hostility.** The Italian government sought peace with the papacy. By the *Law of Papal Guarantees* of 1871, Italy (*a*) acknowledged papal rule of an independent Vatican state within Rome and (*b*) offered the papacy an annual indemnity. Pope Pius IX rejected these terms, denying Italy's right to seize the Papal States. Until this dispute was settled in 1929 (see page 472), the popes considered themselves "prisoners" in the Vatican.

**3. Poor Economic Conditions.** Italy lacked the coal, iron, and oil necessary for extensive industrialization; it also lacked sufficient fertile land to support an increasing population. Despite government efforts to improve economic conditions, living standards remained low. Many Italians migrated to South America and to the United States.

**4. Ambitious Nationalism.** Italy also became weakened by trying to play the part of a great world power. (*a*) *Militarism.* Italy adopted compulsory military service and maintained a large army and navy. (*b*) *Imperialism.* Italy acquired the African colonies of Eritrea, Italian Somaliland, and Libya. Italy's attempt to conquer Ethiopia in 1896 met with defeat. (*c*) *World War I.* By joining the Allies and fighting Austria, Italy gained most of its demands for further European territory, called *Italia Irredenta* (unredeemed Italy): *Trentino, Istria,* and *Trieste* (see map, page 255).

Italy's nationalist policies created heavy personal and financial burdens. Nevertheless, nationalist feeling remained strong and after World War I helped pave the way for Fascist rule under Mussolini (see pages 471–473).

## MULTIPLE–CHOICE QUESTIONS

1. During the last half of the 19th century, which problem was common to both Italy and Germany? (1) absorbing the Papal States into the nation (2) checking the influence of communism (3) consolidating separate states into a unified nation (4) ending the rule of fascist dictators.

2. The principal obstacle to Italian unification during the 19th century was (1) domination by Sardinia-Piedmont (2) interference by foreign powers (3) lack of common traditions (4) lack of a common language.

3. The founder of the Young Italy Society to arouse Italian nationalist feeling was (1) Gioberti (2) Cavour (3) Victor Emmanuel II (4) Mazzini.

4. Cavour believed that Sardinia-Piedmont could unify Italy because Sardinia-Piedmont was (1) a liberal monarchy whose ruling house was Italian (2) friendly to Austria (3) under control of the pope (4) an enemy of France.

5. In unifying their respective countries, both Bismarck and Cavour followed the policy of (1) winning the friendship of France (2) extending democratic reforms (3) maintaining neutrality in the Crimean War (4) provoking Austria into declaring war.

6. Who performed the military exploits responsible for bringing Sicily into the Kingdom of Italy? (1) Mazzini (2) Garibaldi (3) Cavour (4) Victor Emmanuel II.

7. Italy was able to annex Rome because of the (1) Seven Weeks' War (2) Franco-Prussian War (3) Austro-Sardinian War (4) Revolution of 1848.

8. The ruling family of the Kingdom of Italy was the House of (1) Savoy (2) Bourbon (3) Hapsburg (4) Parma.

9. Both Mazzini and Garibaldi wanted the government of a united Italy to be a (an) (1) limited monarchy (2) dictatorship (3) republic (4) absolute monarchy.

10. For many years the Catholic Church was hostile toward the Italian government over the issue of (1) militarism (2) lack of religious education in public schools (3) seizure of the Papal States (4) interference by the state in papal elections.

11. After unification in 1871 the Kingdom of Italy (1) became a prosperous country (2) adopted policies of militarism and imperialism (3) discovered rich iron ore and coal resources (4) became a leading industrial nation.

12. After Italy was unified in 1871, many Italians migrated to the United States because they (1) lacked Italian nationalism (2) resented the undemocratic features in the Italian government (3) supported the Catholic Church in its dispute with the Italian government (4) found it difficult to earn a living in Italy.

## ESSAY QUESTIONS

1. In the mid-19th century, Italy and Germany both achieved unification. Compare these two countries to show that, in the process of unification, they exhibited the following *similarities:* ( *a* ) *two* factors encouraging unification ( *b* ) *two* factors opposing unification ( *c* ) *two* methods used to achieve unification.

2. In regard to Italian unification, Mazzini has been called the *soul*, Garibaldi the *sword*, and Cavour the *brain*. For each of these men, present *one* argument to prove the appropriateness of the description.

3. *(a)* Explain briefly *two* similarities between the government of the Kingdom of Italy and that of Great Britain. *(b)* Give *two* reasons why the Italian government was less democratic in operation than the British government.

4. *(a)* Discuss *three* ways in which the Kingdom of Italy followed a policy of ambitious nationalism after 1871. *(b)* Was this policy a wise one for Italy? Explain *one* reason to support your opinion.

# Part 4. Disruption of Multinational Empires

## A. The Austrian Empire

### AUSTRIA IN 1815: AN EMPIRE OF MANY NATIONALITIES

**1. Dominant Nationality.** The German-speaking Austrians, constituting one-fifth of the population of the Empire, were the dominant nationality. They held the leading positions in government, Church, education, and army. The Empire's ruling family, the Hapsburgs, was also Austrian.

**2. Subject Nationalities.** These included Hungarians (or Magyars), Italians, Rumanians, and Slavic-speaking peoples: Czechs, Slovaks, Poles, Serbs, Croats, and Slovenes. (These latter three are also known as southern Slavs, or Yugoslavs.) As these subject peoples absorbed nationalist ideals—spread from France after 1789—they aspired to independence.

### AUSTRIA COMBATS NATIONALISM

Until 1848 Prince Metternich directed Austrian efforts to suppress nationalist movements. He employed press censorship, spies, secret police, arbitrary prison terms, and armed forces. Nevertheless, in 1848, revolutions erupted throughout the Empire, Metternich fled the country, and several subject nationalities seemed on the verge of partial or complete independence.

By 1849, however, the Empire had regained complete control because (1) the army remained loyal to the Hapsburgs and (2) the government succeeded in its *divide-and-rule* policy: setting one nationality against another—Austrians to suppress Czechs and Italians; Slavs to subdue Hungarians.

Austria's exertions to repress its subject nationalities sapped its military strength. In two wars—in 1859 against France and Sardinia and in 1866 against Prussia—the Austrian armies were easily defeated.

## THE EMPIRE BECOMES THE DUAL MONARCHY (1867)

To buttress their hold over the Empire, the Austrians granted an equal partnership to the Hungarians. This *Ausgleich,* or *Compromise,* of 1867 transformed the Austrian Empire into the *Dual Monarchy* of Austria-Hungary. The Hapsburg ruler now was entitled "Emperor of Austria and King of Hungary." Austria and Hungary each had its own government, independent in local matters but joined together on common problems: foreign affairs, military defense, tariffs, and finances.

## DISCONTENT WITH THE DUAL MONARCHY (1867–1914)

The Slavic peoples, as well as Rumanian and Italian minorities, remained restless and agitated for freedom because, (1) unlike the Hungarians, they gained nothing from the Ausgleich and (2) in Hungarian domains they were oppressed even more than they had been before the Ausgleich. Following 1878, when an independent Serbia was created out of Turkish territory, the Serbs in Austria-Hungary became especially rebellious.

## AUSTRIA-HUNGARY AND WORLD WAR I (1914–1918)

Serbian nationalists ignited World War I by assassinating Archduke Francis Ferdinand, the heir to the Austro-Hungarian throne. Austria-Hungary declared war upon Serbia, hoping to crush the Serbian threat to the Dual Monarchy. This initial conflict evolved into World War I (see pages 433–434).

Austria-Hungary was weakened in the war by the disloyalty of its subject nationalities. The Slavic subjects engaged in sabotage, mutiny, and in 1918 outright revolt. Even the favored Hungarians revolted. These revolutions, coming when Austria-Hungary's military position was desperate, hastened the end of Hapsburg rule and Austria-Hungary's surrender to the Allies.

## BREAKUP OF THE AUSTRO-HUNGARIAN EMPIRE (1919–1920)

By the peace treaties, the territories of Austria-Hungary were divided so that its many nationalities each achieved an independent existence. (1) Trentino, Istria, and Trieste, all having large Italian populations, were transferred to Italy. (2) Rumanian-inhabited territory was ceded to Rumania. (3) Polish-inhabited territory was combined with territories previously held by Germany and Russia to recreate a sovereign Poland. (4) Territory inhabited by southern Slavs was combined with Serbia and Montenegro to form Yugoslavia. (5) Czechoslovakia was formed out of territory inhabited mainly by Czechs and Slovaks. (6) Austria and Hungary were separated into small independent republics. (See map, page 260.)

**The Breakup of the Austro-Hungarian Empire (1919–1920)**

The heavy black line shows the size of the
Austro-Hungarian Empire prior to World War I.

## PROBLEMS RESULTING FROM AUSTRIA-HUNGARY'S DISSOLUTION

**1. New Nationalist Discontent.** It proved impossible to draw boundaries that would include all the people of one nationality in one state. Consequently a minority of Austrians and Hungarians was assigned to Czechoslovakia; some Hungarians were included in Rumania; the territory given to Italy contained some Austrians and Yugoslavs. These newly created subject nationalities agitated for further territorial revision. (When Hitler claimed the Czechoslovakian Sudetenland because of the German-speaking population that had been transferred from Austria, the fate of the Sudetenland became a matter of international concern. (See page 491.)

**2. Economic Distress.** The Empire, in which industrial and agricultural regions supplemented each other's needs, had constituted a prosperous free trade area. The nations replacing the Empire adopted high tariffs, which hampered their trade relations and caused widespread economic distress.

## B. The Turkish Empire

### OTTOMAN TURKEY: ANOTHER MULTINATIONAL EMPIRE

**1. Dominant Nationality.** In the early 19th century, the Ottoman Turks, by religion Moslem, governed an empire that included parts of Asia, Africa, and

Europe. The Turks themselves inhabited Asia Minor and a small European area that included the city of Constantinople.

**2. Subject Nationalities.** These included *(a)* Arabs in the Middle East and North Africa, *(b)* Egyptians (also considered Arabs) in North Africa, and *(c)* southern Slavs, Albanians, Rumanians, Bulgarians, and Greeks in the Balkans. Whereas the Arabs and Egyptians are Moslem, the Balkan peoples are mainly Eastern Orthodox Christian.

## REASONS FOR BALKAN DISCONTENT

The Balkan peoples, inspired by nationalism, desired independence. They also detested Turkish rule. (1) *Autocracy.* Absolute power was in the hands of the sultan. (2) *Corruption.* Money raised by heavy taxation was diverted from public use to private hands. (3) *Inefficiency.* Disorder existed in many parts of the Turkish Empire. (4) *Discrimination.* Christians were singled out for economic and religious persecution. (5) *Cruelty.* Unusual cruelty was used to suppress rebellious subjects.

## TURKEY LOSES THE BALKANS

Over a 100-year period, from 1815 to 1914, the Balkan peoples gained freedom from an enfeebled Turkey, *"the sick man of Europe."* The highlights of this struggle, often marked by atrocity and barbarism, were as follows:

**1. Greek Revolution (1821–1829).** Revolting against Turkey, the Greeks received aid from *(a)* Russia, which sought influence in the Balkans, and *(b)* Britain and France, which cherished the ancient Greek heritage and wanted to restrain Russian efforts in the Balkans. By 1829 the Greeks had gained Turkish recognition of their independence.

**2. Crimean War (1853–1856).** From Turkey, Russia wanted Constantinople and the Straits (the Dardanelles and the Bosporus) so as to control the water route connecting the Black and Mediterranean seas. Britain opposed these Russian ambitions as threatening British interests in the eastern Mediterranean.

In 1853 Russia demanded the right to protect Orthodox Christians within the Turkish Empire. When Turkey refused, Russia began hostilities. Britain and France aided Turkey, and together their armies defeated Russia. For the time being, the Turkish Empire remained intact.

**3. Russo-Turkish War (1877–1878).** Supposedly enraged by Turkish atrocities against Slavic peoples, Russia declared war and defeated the sultan's forces. Russia forced upon Turkey a peace treaty that gave Russia great influence in the Balkans. Britain and Austria-Hungary denounced this treaty and demanded a Balkan settlement by international conference. Under threat of a new war, Russia agreed to a conference in Berlin.

**The Breakup of the Turkish Empire in Europe (by 1914)**

**4. Congress of Berlin (1878).** By this conference Turkey granted (a) Austria-Hungary the southern Slavic provinces of Bosnia and Herzegovina; (b) Britain the Mediterranean island of Cyprus; (c) Serbia, Montenegro, and Rumania independence; (d) Bulgaria self-government within the Turkish Empire; and (e) Russia certain Balkan territory. (In 1882, shortly after this conference, Turkey recognized British domination over Egypt.)

**5. Balkan Wars (1912–1913):** (a) *The First Balkan War.* Greece, Bulgaria, Montenegro, and Serbia attacked and defeated Turkey. In disposing of the ceded Turkish lands, the victors agreed, under Austrian pressure, to form an independent Albania (for Austria's reasons, see Balkan Crises of 1912–1913, page 433). However, the victors quarreled bitterly over the remaining territory. (b) *The Second Balkan War.* Bulgaria battled its former allies and Turkey. By the final peace treaty, Turkey retained in Europe only a small area including Constantinople. The Balkans now consisted primarily of independent national states.

# TURKEY BECOMES A NATIONAL STATE (By 1823)

**1. The "Young Turks."** In 1908 this nationalist group of Turks seized control of the government. The Young Turks hoped to modernize Turkey, establish constitutional government, revitalize Turkish military power, and preserve what was left of the Empire. Some reforms were made, but the Young Turks failed to stop the breakup of the Empire: In 1908 they could not prevent Bulgarian independence; in 1911–1912 Turkey was defeated by Italy and was forced to cede Tripoli (Libya); in 1912–1913 Turkish forces were defeated by the Balkan states; in 1914–1918 Turkey joined Germany against the Allies and again met defeat.

**2. Mustafa Kemal and the Nationalists.** After World War I Turkish nationalists, led by army officer *Mustafa Kemal*, rejected the severe Allied peace treaty of 1920 and continued to fight until they secured more favorable terms. In 1923, by the *Treaty of Lausanne*, Turkey surrendered only its remaining non-Turkish territories (chiefly Arab) but retained its Turkish areas: Constantinople and Asia Minor. To prevent nationalist friction, Turks living in Greece and Greeks living in Turkey were compelled to migrate to their respective homelands. Turkey, no longer an empire, was now reduced to a national state.

## TURKEY UNDER MUSTAFA KEMAL (1923–1938)

The nationalists declared Turkey a republic, transferred the capital from Constantinople (renamed Istanbul) to Ankara, and elected Mustafa Kemal as president. Ruling as virtual dictator, he (1) modernized the country by prohibiting polygamy, outlawing Oriental dress, introducing Western law codes, and encouraging industry and (2) appealed to Turkish nationalism through press, radio, and the public school system.

## TRUE–FALSE QUESTIONS

If the statement is correct, write the word *true*. If the statement is incorrect, substitute a word or phrase for the italicized term to make the statement correct.

1. The German-speaking people in the Austro-Hungarian Empire were the *Croats*.
2. Another name for the people of *Rumania* is Magyars.
3. The plan to change the Austrian Empire into the Dual Monarchy was called the *Ausgleich*.
4. The subject nationalities who gained nothing from the Dual Monarchy arrangement included the *Slavs*.
5. The heir to the Austrian throne, Archduke Francis Ferdinand, was assassinated by a *Polish* nationalist.
6. The Austro-Hungarian Empire came to an end after *the Austro-Sardinian War*.
7. In 1920 Serbs, Croats, and Slovenes were united to form the independent state of *Yugoslavia*.

8. In drawing the boundaries of Czechoslovakia, the World War I treaty makers gave it a minority of Hungarians and *Italians*.
9. Another name for the Turkish Empire was the *Egyptian* Empire.
10. For the most part, the Christian peoples in the Balkans are members of *Eastern Orthodox* churches.
11. The first Balkan people to achieve independence in the 19th century were the *Serbs*.
12. Russia's interest in the Turkish Empire was to secure control over the *Dardanelles*.
13. In the Turkish Empire the subject peoples of the same religion as the Turks included the *Arabs*.
14. In the Crimean War France and Britain fought against *Turkey*.
15. In 1912 Turkey ceded its African territory of Tripoli (Libya) to *Britain*.
16. During World War I Turkey fought on the side of *the Allies*.
17. Following World War I Turkey was ruled by a nationalist leader, *Mustafa Kemal*.
18. Following World War I *Greeks* living in Turkey were compelled to return to their native land.

## ESSAY QUESTIONS

1. Explain clearly *one* relationship of nationalism to *each* of the following: (*a*) establishment of the Dual Monarchy (*b*) assassination of the Austrian Archduke Francis Ferdinand (*c*) the Greek Revolution (*d*) the Young Turk movement.
2. "The breakup of the Austro-Hungarian Monarchy after World War I may have had political justification, but it had bad economic effects." (*a*) Name *five* states that were created from the former Austro-Hungarian Monarchy or that received territory from it. (*b*) Explain *one* political justification for breaking up Austria-Hungary. (*c*) Explain *one* bad economic effect that resulted from this action.
3. The Balkans have frequently figured in the wars between the great European powers. (*a*) Discuss *two* reasons why the Balkans have been a bone of contention among the great powers. (*b*) Show how the Balkans figured in *one* war involving the European powers prior to 1920.
4. (*a*) Name *five* countries of Europe that were created from the Ottoman Empire or that received territory from it. (*b*) Describe and evaluate *two* measures taken by Mustafa Kemal to strengthen modern Turkey.
5. For the years 1815 to 1920, describe fully *two* ways in which nationalism affected (*a*) the Austrian Empire (*b*) the Ottoman Empire.

# UNIT IX. THE IMPACT OF THE INDUSTRIAL REVOLUTION

## Part 1. The Revolution in Production

### INDUSTRIAL REVOLUTION: MEANING

*In a narrow sense.* The *Industrial Revolution* refers to the changes, beginning in the 18th century, in manufacturing methods. These changes were (1) from slower, more expensive production by hand to quicker, less costly production by machine and consequently (2) from work in the home to work in the factory.

*In a broad sense.* The Industrial Revolution refers to the effect of machinery upon humanity. Our entire way of living, as citizens, workers, and consumers, reflects the influence of the Industrial Revolution.

### INDUSTRIAL REVOLUTION: CHRONOLOGY

1. **Old, or First, Industrial Revolution (1750–1870).** The first phase of the Industrial Revolution consisted of *(a)* the invention of the first complex machines and the building of the first factories, *(b)* the development of steam as a source of power and its application to manufacturing and transportation, *(c)* the expansion of the output of basic materials—coal, iron, and steel—and *(d)* the introduction of new methods of transportation and communication. These developments changed living patterns considerably.

2. **New, or Second, Industrial Revolution (1870–Still Continuing).** The second phase of the Industrial Revolution witnessed inventions in greater number and brought even more sweeping changes to industry and society. This phase, still continuing, consists of *(a)* the use of new sources of power—electricity, petroleum, natural gas, atomic energy, and solar energy—which in turn makes possible new industries; *(b)* the deliberate application of science to industry and the development of artificial, or synthetic, products such as nylon and plastics; *(c)* the invention of newer and faster means of transportation and communication such as the airplane, radio, and television; *(d)* the construction of machines equipped with electronic brains capable of running other machines, a process called *automation;* and *(e)* the placing of space vehicles in orbit around the earth and on flights into and beyond our solar system.

265

## ROOTS OF THE INDUSTRIAL REVOLUTION

**1. Renaissance Spirit.** By emphasizing life in this world, the Renaissance encouraged west European peoples to seek material comforts. By furthering a scientific approach to problems, the Renaissance helped pave the way for inventions.

**2. Commercial Revolution.** West European expansion overseas uncovered new markets and created a vast demand for goods, at first especially textiles. Western Europe moved from a static, localized, agrarian economy toward the beginnings of a dynamic, worldwide economy of trade, banking, and manufacturing. Entrepreneurs acquired large sums of money, and many invested their capital in new and faster manufacturing methods.

**3. The Domestic System.** In the Later Middle Ages the guilds, by restricting the number of workers, hours of work, and type of tools, had limited the output of goods. In the 16th century capitalists and workers, chiefly in the English textile industry, defied the guilds and devised a new way of producing goods, the "putting out," or *domestic, system.* Capitalists provided the raw cotton and wool and paid the workers on a piecework basis for the finished product. The workers, ususally entire families, labored at home for unlimited hours and with hand-operated tools. (Many workers supplemented their incomes by small-scale farming.) Not bound by guild restrictions, the domestic system increased the supply of textiles, but the demand for such goods increased even more rapidly. Beginning in the 18th century, the domestic system gave way to a still newer method of production, the *factory system.*

## INDUSTRIAL REVOLUTION STARTS IN BRITAIN: FAVORABLE CONDITIONS

**1. Markets.** A prosperous nation and major colonial power, Britain experienced a heavy demand for goods from domestic and overseas markets.

**2. Population.** The British population included (a) skilled workers who designed the needed machines, (b) wealthy entrepreneurs who invested capital in such equipment, and (c) many individuals who sought employment.

**3. Agricultural Changes.** Powerful landowners benefited from numerous *Enclosure Acts* in the 18th century that legalized their land-grabbing practices: "fencing in" for their exlusive use open field strips and village commons and evicting tenant farmers from leased lands. Many peasants, thus deprived of lands previously available to them, abandoned farming and migrated to the cities to seek work in factories. The powerful landowners, now able to pursue large-scale production, increased Britain's output of meat, wool, and grain.

These agricultural changes—creating a pool of unemployed workers and increasing the supply of farm produce—prepared Britain for what Professor W. W. Rostow, in his study *The Stages of Economic Growth,* has termed the "industrial takeoff."

**4. Natural Resources.** Britain had coal to provide steam power, iron ore to make machines, and good harbors to facilitate trade. Also, the British colonies sent valuable raw materials, including lumber and cotton.

**5. Government.** The British entrepreneur had the advantage of a stable government that *(a)* levied relatively fair and light taxes, *(b)* had established a sound money system and a well-organized banking system (the *Bank of England* was chartered in 1694), and *(c)* maintained a competent administration in a unified country.

**6. Other Factors:** *(a)* An island apart from the European continent, Britain had *not* been invaded and devastated by the many 18th-century wars. *(b)* In their trading and colonizing ventures, the British acquired experience with joint-stock companies—the forerunner of the modern corporation and a basic institution of a capitalist economy. *(c)* The British government encouraged science—its study, spread, and application to industry—by chartering and utilizing many scientific groups, especially (1) the *Royal Society of London* (1660), the world's oldest scientific society, (2) the *Royal Society for the Encouragement of Arts, Manufactures and Commerce* (1754), and (3) the *Royal Institution* (1800), to spur scientific research and further public understanding of scientific matters.

## TEXTILES: THE FIRST MECHANIZED INDUSTRY

The making of cloth was the first industry to feel the full effects of the Industrial Revolution. Cloth is made by (1) spinning raw fiber (wool or cotton) into thread and then (2) weaving thread into cloth. To meet the need for cotton goods, spinning and weaving had to be greatly sped up and the supply of raw fiber greatly increased. In devising new machines to achieve these goals, inventors illustrated two now-familiar sayings: "necessity is the mother of invention" and "one invention leads to the next."

| Inventors | Inventions |
|---|---|
| John Kay (British) | *Flying shuttle* (1733), hand-operated, sped up weaving by loom and created a demand for more thread. |
| James Hargreaves (British) | *Spinning jenny* (1764), hand-operated, sped up spinning by forming eight threads at one time. |
| Richard Arkwright (British) | *Water frame* (1769), water-powered, increased the rapidity of spinning. |
| Samuel Crompton (British) | *Spinning mule* (1779) combined the best features of the spinning jenny and the water frame. |
| Edmund Cartwright (British) | *Power loom* (1785), water-powered, provided rapid and automatic weaving. |
| Eli Whitney (American) | *Cotton gin* (1793), hand-operated at first, sped up removal of seeds from the raw cotton fiber. |

## STEAM: A SOURCE OF POWER

From prehistoric times to the 18th century, people secured *power*—the force or energy to do work—from limited and unreliable sources: their own exertions, animals, wind, and water. People dreamed of a new kind of power to achieve freedom from fickle nature and physical drudgery. The Industrial Revolution provided the answer—*steam*. Formed by boiling water, steam exerts pressure that can be harnessed to drive engines and operate machines.

In 1705 *Thomas Newcomen* (English) devised a crude *steam engine*. It served chiefly to operate pumps draining water from coal mines.

In 1769 *James Watt* (Scottish) greatly improved upon Newcomen's work and constructed an efficient steam engine, thus opening up the *age of steam*. Watt's success illustrates the observation that "an important invention often results from the work of several persons."

Watt's engine was soon adapted for textile-mill use and then for other factories and for transportation.

## STEAM ENGINE IN TRANSPORTATION

The horse-drawn wagon and wind-driven sailing vessel for centuries had transported goods. When factories began producing large quantities of finished products for worldwide markets, these vehicles proved too slow and uncertain. They were replaced by steam-driven means of transportation.

**1. Steamboat.** In 1807 *Robert Fulton* (American) successfully launched the *Clermont*, a steam-driven side-paddle ship. Steamboats soon appeared on rivers and along coasts and then crossed the oceans. In 1838 the *Great Western* crossed the Atlantic in 15 days, using only steam power. Luxury passenger liners in the 1950's completed the same trip within five days. Today tankers and freighters carry raw materials, consumer goods, and machinery to all parts of the world.

**2. Locomotive.** In 1814 *George Stephenson* (British) built the first successful steam locomotive. In 1830 his *Rocket* traveled at the then astounding speed of 29 miles per hour while pulling a train of cars. This achievement spurred a tremendous increase in rail-track mileage, and railroads soon became the leading means of land transportation. Today's trains are safer, speedier, and more versatile. They can carry passengers in Pullman sleeping cars and freight in refrigerated cars and on piggyback flatcars.

## COAL, IRON, AND STEEL

**1. Coal.** This fossil fuel became essential to industry, providing the heat necessary to (*a*) change water into steam and (*b*) remove iron from its ore. To reduce coal gas explosions ignited by miners' open lamps in mines, Sir *Humphrey Davy* (British) in 1815 invented the closed *safety lamp*.

**2. Iron and Steel.** These metals were used in the manufacture of many products, especially machines. At first iron predominated because steel, although stronger and less brittle, was costly to produce. In 1856 *Henry Bessemer* (British) devised the inexpensive Bessemer process of refining iron into steel. Subsequent improvements in steelmaking included the open-hearth, electric-furnace, and crucible processes. Alloys were developed for special types of steels, such as stainless steel. Steel—used to make products from tiny watch springs to immense skyscraper structures—is the basic metal of our industrial society.

## NEW SOURCES OF POWER

**1. Electricity.** For years scientists conducted experiments to learn more about electricity. In 1831 *Michael Faraday* (British) moved a magnet inside a wire coil and generated an electric current. This discovery led to the invention of the *dynamo*, an electric generator that transforms mechanical energy into electricity. Today dynamos are driven by falling water (hydroelectric power) and by steam produced by means of coal, oil, natural gas, or atomic energy. Inventors have employed electricity to run motors; provide heat, cooling, and light; and transmit signals, sounds, and pictures.

| Inventors | Inventions |
|---|---|
| Samuel F. B. Morse (American) | *telegraph*, 1844 |
| Alexander Graham Bell (American) | *telephone*, 1876 |
| Thomas A. Edison (American) | *electric light bulb*, 1879 |
| Guglielmo Marconi (Italian) | *wireless telegraphy*, 1896 |
| Lee DeForest (American) | *radio vacuum tube*, 1907 |
| Vladimir Zworykin (American) | *television*, 1934 |
| William Shockley, Walter Brattain, John Bardeen (Americans) | *transistor*, 1948 |

**2. Petroleum.** In 1859 *Edwin Drake* in the United States drilled the first successful oil well. Oil, a fossil fuel, was at first used for lubrication and lighting but soon was put to use as a source of power.

*a. The Automobile.* In the 1880's *Gottlieb Daimler* (German) developed a practical *internal combustion engine*. It was powered by a petroleum product, *gasoline*. Daimler used his engine to propel a four-wheel vehicle, thereby opening up a new use for petroleum as a source of power. In 1908 *Henry Ford* (American) brought automobile ownership out of the luxury class and within reach of most Americans by low-cost, mass-production, assembly-line methods. Today almost every American family owns at least one car, and automobile production is a key industry. Its growth has (*a*) stimulated related industries: oil, rubber, glass, steel, and aluminum; *(b)* created new enterprises: gasoline stations, garages, parking lots, motels; and *(c)* necessitated the building of new and improved highways.

**b. The Diesel Engine.** In 1892 *Rudolf Diesel* (German) utilized diesel oil, a fuel less expensive than gasoline, in his *diesel internal combustion engine.* Today diesel engines power heavy machinery, buses, trucks, autos, locomotives, and oceangoing ships.

**c. The Airplane.** In 1903 *Wilbur* and *Orville Wright* (American) flew, for less than a minute at Kitty Hawk, North Carolina, the first heavier-than-air flying machine. It was powered by a gasoline engine. Subsequently aeronautical engineers designed larger and speedier aircraft. Many modern jet planes are longer than a city block and can fly at over 600 miles (960 kilometers) per hour. Today commercial airlines, flying national and international routes, represent a major means of transportation.

By its very speed the airplane has "shrunk the size of the earth" and changed our concept of distance. We tend to measure distance no longer in miles but in the time necessary to traverse that distance. For example: We view the distance from New York to London not as some 3,000 miles (4,800 kilometers) but rather as some seven hours flying time. Our lives have been affected by the airplane in such areas as recreational opportunities, freight transporation, business contacts, and military defenses.

**3. Natural Gas.** Often found together with petroleum, natural gas is also a fossil fuel. At first it was burned at the well site as a waste product. Subsequently the value of natural gas was recognized; it was collected and transported to homes for lighting, heating, and cooking and to electric power plants for making steam to run dynamos. (Both natural gas and petroleum are sources of organic chemicals used by industries producing synthetic rubber, plastics, and drugs.)

**4. Solar Energy.** Solar energy derives from the sun's radiation of heat and light. Although only a minute portion reaches the earth—one part in two billion—the sun's radiation suffices to warm the earth, affect our weather, and make possible plant growth.

In the 1970's the industrialized powers—west European nations, Japan, and the United States—began to realize that they were using too much oil and natural gas, which are irreplaceable fossil fuels, and that they were depending too heavily on unreliable, politically motivated Arab countries for such supplies. (For details, check the Index for Organization of Petroleum Exporting Countries.)

During these years the industrialized nations became seriously interested in developing solar energy, at least for heating purposes. In the United States the government has made grants to corporations to further solar energy research and to develop the necessary hardware such as radiation collectors. These corporations have predicted that solar energy will be competitive in cost with fossil fuels by 1985 to 1990, beginning in the sun-drenched American Southwest, and that by the next century solar energy will become a major source of power.

**5. Atomic Energy.** See pages 308–309.

## AGRICULTURAL REVOLUTION: AN ASPECT OF THE INDUSTRIAL REVOLUTION

**1. Primitive Agricultural Methods.** At the beginning of the 18th century, farm methods had not progressed since feudal manor days. Farmers still relied upon a few simple tools: the wooden plow, the hoe, and the scythe. Many continued the three-field system, idling one-third of the land each year to restore fertility. Of fertilizers, crop rotation, and animal breeding, they knew very little. Although farmers labored hard and long, they produced scanty crops.

**2. Industrial Growth Spurs Agriculture.** The revolution in industry influenced farming by *(a)* demonstrating that laborsaving machinery and science increase output, *(b)* requiring greater quantities of agricultural raw materials, such as cotton, wool, and leather, and *(c)* demanding increased food supplies for city populations.

**3. Meaning of Agricultural Revolution.** *Agricultural Revolution* refers to the change from primitive to modern farm-production methods—the use of farm machinery and scientific agriculture. The Agricultural Revolution began in England, spread to other countries in Europe, penetrated thoroughly into American farming, and to this day continues its advance in the underdeveloped areas of the world.

**4. Farm Machinery.** The following table lists some of the basic inventions that led to the "mechanization" of agriculture:

| Inventors | Inventions |
|---|---|
| Jethro Tull (English) | *Seed drill* (1701) planted seeds in rows. It improved upon "broadcast," or hand, sowing by providing space for cultivation and growth. |
| Charles Newbold (American) | *Cast-iron plow* (1797) turned soil deeper and more easily than the wooden plow. |
| Cyrus McCormick (American) | *Reaper* (1834) cut grain many times faster than a scythe. |
| John Deere (American) | *Self-cleaning steel plow* (1837) improved upon the cast-iron plow. |

Other agricultural machines include the thresher (to separate grain from the stalk), the harvester (to cut and bind the grain), the combine (to cut, thresh, and sack the grain), the tractor (to pull equipment through the field), the corn planter, the potato digger, the electric milker, and the cotton picker.

### 5. Scientific Agriculture

*a. Charles Townshend* (British) in the early 18th century preserved soil fertility by *rotation of crops.* He alternated grains with soil enriching plants such as turnips and clover.

*b. Robert Bakewell* (British) in the late 18th century improved the weight of cattle by *scientific breeding.* His experiments led to better plant and animal selection.

*c. Justus von Liebig* (German) in the mid-19th century discovered how to improve soil fertility by using chemicals as *artificial fertilizers.* His discovery enabled farmers to harvest a greater quantity of crops from the same amount of land.

*d. George Washington Carver* (American black) in the late 19th century discovered many uses for a major Southern crop, the peanut. His work encouraged researchers to discover new uses for other farm products.

*e.* Other applications of science to agriculture include contour plowing to prevent soil erosion, draining swamps to augment the land supply, irrigating dry lands, combating insect pests and plant diseases by chemicals, and improving the processes for canning, refrigerating, and freezing foods.

### 6. Effects of the Agricultural Revolution

*a.* Agricultural production increased greatly, both in output per worker and in total amount. The cost of foodstuffs dropped.

*b.* Large farms, best able to employ machines and scientific methods, began to dominate agriculture. The number of small farms declined.

*c.* The number of farmers, in proportion to total population, decreased sharply. Many moved to the cities.

*d.* Farmers found their work less laborious because machines performed the backbreaking tasks.

*e.* Farming changed from a self-sufficient way of life to big business. Farmers today specialize in a few crops, sell them on national and international markets, and purchase foodstuffs for their own use.

## INDUSTRIAL REVOLUTION: A SURVEY BY COUNTRY

**1. Britain.** By 1850, after a century of the Industrial Revolution, more British workers were employed in factories than on farms. British manufacturers produced vast quantities of cotton and woolen textiles, shoes, cutlery, and tools for sale in domestic and foreign markets. Nineteenth-century Britain experienced great economic prosperity as the "workshop of the world."

Today Britain faces some difficult industrial problems. *(a)* British coal resources are being depleted and mining costs are rising. *(b)* British factories need capital to replace outmoded machinery. *(c)* British products are meeting stiff competition in world markets.

**2. The United States.** In 1790 *Samuel Slater*, a British immigrant, built America's first textile factory. Slater had left Britain in disguise and designed the factory equipment from memory. Until 1825 Britain sought to prevent industrial development elsewhere by prohibiting the emigration of textile workers and the export of textile machines.

American textile manufacturing prospered, especially after the War of 1812 halted the importation of British goods. After the Civil War (1861–1865), the United States had an era of great industrial expansion spurred by the *(a)* wealth of natural resources, *(b)* availability of capital, *(c)* existence of domestic markets easily accessible by water and rail transportation, *(d)* pro-business policies of the government, *(e)* supply of capable workers, and *(f)* abilities of a group of inventive and enterprising individuals. Two such business leaders were oil refiner *John D. Rockefeller* and steel magnate *Andrew Carnegie*. By 1914 the United States equaled Britain in manufacturing; today the United States is the world's leading industrial power.

**3. France.** After 1815, the end of the Napoleonic Era, the Industrial Revolution penetrated more deeply into France. The French built railroads, mined coal and iron, and constructed factories. However, French industry retained much handicraft labor and concentrated on such luxury items as laces, silks, wines, perfumes, and jewelry.

In the 19th century France did not industrialize thoroughly because the country lacked *(a)* political stability, with new governments arising in 1815, 1830, 1848, 1852, and 1871; *(b)* sufficient coal resources, especially after the 1871 loss of Alsace-Lorraine; and *(c)* an adequate labor supply because France's small independent landowners preferred farming to factory life. In recent years, however, France has pushed forward in the mass production of steel, automobiles, and airplanes.

**4. Germany.** After unification in 1871 Germany industrialized rapidly, aided by *(a)* extensive coal and iron resources, *(b)* skilled workers, *(c)* talented scientists who created such new industries as dyes and chemicals, *(d)* efficient water and rail transportation, *(e)* favorable government policies, and *(f)* industrial leaders, such as the *Krupps*, who founded business empires. By 1914 German iron, steel, textile, and chemical products were world famous. Today West Germany is a leading industrial power.

**5. Russia.** Before 1914 Russia was overwhelmingly agricultural. Russian industry was limited chiefly to several iron and steel mills and some railroad construction. The reactionary Czarist regime, the emphasis upon maintaining past traditions, and the rigid social classes all served to deter the development of industry. After the Revolution of 1917, Soviet rulers drove Russia toward industrialization. Today the Soviet Union is a major manufacturing power, second only to the United States.

**6. Japan.** Late in the 19th century, Japan abandoned feudalism, modernized its government, and started to industrialize. Japan was the first Asian nation to turn to industry. Although Japan lacked most mineral resources and sufficient farmland, Japanese manufacturers had the advantages of cheap labor, government assistance, and nearness to populous Far Eastern markets. Today the Japanese export large quantities of electronic equipment, machinery, textiles, cameras, and toys.

**7. Underdeveloped, or Developing, Countries.** In Latin America, Africa, and Asia, many countries still have primitive agricultural economies. But they are eager to industrialize, believing that is the way to raise living standards. Their progress toward industrialization has been hindered by their lack of governmental stability, capital, skilled labor, and technical "know-how." Today many underdeveloped (developing) countries receive financial and technical aid from the United States, the Soviet Union, Japan, France, West Germany, and agencies associated with the United Nations.

## MULTIPLE–CHOICE QUESTIONS

1. As used in the term "Industrial Revolution," the word "Revolution" means (1) popular uprising (2) sweeping change (3) rebirth (4) turning of a wheel.
2. The principal cause of the Industrial Revolution was the (1) effort to eliminate child labor (2) increase in population (3) need of more manufactured goods for foreign trade (4) desire for colonies.
3. What was the relationship between the Renaissance and the Industrial Revolution? (1) None existed. (2) The earliest inventions came during the height of the Renaissance. (3) Renaissance painters created a heavy demand for paints and canvas. (4) The scientific spirit of the Renaissance encouraged inventions.
4. The chief objection to the guilds in the 18th century was (1) the poor quality of goods (2) unsatisfactory training of workers (3) substandard working conditions (4) limited output of goods.
5. In the "putting-out," or domestic, system in Britain, (1) overseas trade was discouraged (2) piecework was done in the home (3) agriculture was the only means of making a living (4) no capital was needed.
6. One reason why the Industrial Revolution began in Britain was that (1) Parliament had ended the mercantile system (2) the monarch granted subsidies to inventors (3) considerable money was available for investment (4) nationwide technical schools produced skilled workers.
7. The 18th-century Enclosure Acts in Britain resulted in (1) an increase in the

number of small farms    (2) an increase in the number of landless farmers    (3) a decrease in Britain's food supply    (4) a deemphasis of scientific farming.

8. The first machines were invented mainly by    (1) trained scientists    (2) skilled workers    (3) capitalists    (4) guild apprentices.

9. Stephenson's work on the locomotive was most directly related to the earlier work of    (1) Kay    (2) Bessemer    (3) Watt    (4) Faraday.

10. The first series of inventions affecting the domestic system of production occurred in    (1) agriculture    (2) mining    (3) transportation    (4) textiles.

11. Steam is a source of power because it    (1) can be used as a substitute for coal    (2) condenses back to water    (3) contains no living germs    (4) exerts pressure.

12. That one invention leads to the next is shown by the relationship of    (1) the steam engine to the automobile    (2) the diesel engine to television    (3) the power loom to the cotton gin    (4) plastics to the seed drill.

13. An example of automation in the modern home is a (an)    (1) electric can opener    (2) vacuum cleaner    (3) television set    (4) oil burner thermostat.

14. The invention of machinery for spinning and weaving benefited farmers by increasing the    (1) difficulty of farm work    (2) market for farm produce    (3) government's aid to farmers    (4) number of farm workers.

15. The term "Agricultural Revolution" refers to the    (1) distribution of small farms to the peasants    (2) end of taxation of farmland    (3) flight of city workers to the farms    (4) introduction of machinery into farming.

16. During the 19th century which was an important result of the Agricultural Revolution in Britain?    (1) Serfdom became unprofitable.    (2) It became unprofitable to own large estates.    (3) Commercial farming became less widespread.    (4) The proportion of the population engaged in farming declined.

17. Of the following inventors, whose work was basic to the work of the other three?    (1) Faraday    (2) Edison    (3) Morse    (4) Marconi.

18. Which person's invention sped the cutting of grain?    (1) McCormick    (2) Newcomen    (3) Newbold    (4) Tull.

19. Liebig discovered the    (1) advantages of scientific breeding    (2) use of artificial fertilizer    (3) use of natural fertilizer    (4) rotation of crops.

20. George Washington Carver is connected with what major crop in the southern United States?    (1) peaches    (2) cotton    (3) peanuts    (4) tobacco.

21. In which one of these countries did the Industrial Revolution occur last?    (1) Russia    (2) France    (3) the United States    (4) Germany.

22. In which one of these Asian countries did the Industrial Revolution develop first?    (1) India    (2) China    (3) Japan    (4) Burma.

23. Which country would be most likely to consider Samuel Slater an industrial hero?    (1) Britain    (2) the United States    (3) Russia    (4) Germany.

24. The Industrial Revolution    (1) ended with the discovery of atomic power    (2) continues today at a slow pace    (3) continues today at a rapid pace    (4) ended about 1870.

## ESSAY QUESTIONS

1. (a) What is meant by the term "Industrial Revolution"? (b) Explain *three* reasons why the Industrial Revolution started in Britain. (c) Discuss *two* ways by which the Industrial Revolution brought about an Agricultural Revolution.

2. (a) List *two* sources of power in use before the Industrial Revolution. For *each* source of power listed, state *one* use. (b) Using *two* examples, prove that the steam engine revolutionized 19th-century life. (c) Show how *two* other sources of power are revolutionizing life today.

3. For *each* of the following pairs, state which item you consider more important, and explain *one* reason for your choice. (a) the Industrial Revolution or the Agricultural Revolution (b) the steam engine or the steamboat (c) iron or steel (d) the dynamo or the diesel engine (e) rotation of crops or artificial fertilizer.

4. In the 20th century great developments have taken place in aviation. (a) Describe *two* important improvements in aviation. (b) Discuss *two* peacetime uses of the airplane. (c) Explain how the airplane has affected our concepts of time and distance.

5. Decide whether *each* of the following statements is true or false. Provide *two* facts to support your point of view. (a) An invention is often the result of the work of many people. (b) The steam and internal combustion engines have freed people from hard physical labor. (c) One invention leads to the next. (d) The industrial development of Britain and Germany can be attributed to the same factors. (e) Industrial development would have been stifled without the expansion of transportation facilities. (f) The Industrial Revolution is still going on. (g) Underdeveloped nations today find it difficult to industrialize.

# Part 2. Results of the Industrial Revolution

## INTRODUCTION

Now in its third century, the Industrial Revolution has decidedly changed our world. At first it caused economic dislocation and many hardships. In the long run, however, the Industrial Revolution has brought widespread benefits to the people of industrialized nations. Hardly a phase of life remains unaffected by it. Whatever we are, whatever we think, whatever we do are directly or indirectly touched by the effects of industrialization.

### A. *Economic Results*

#### FACTORY SYSTEM

Because machines are heavy, bulky, and power-operated, only specially designed factory buildings can provide for their proper installation. Consequently the factory replaced the home as the center of production.

#### MASS PRODUCTION METHODS IN FACTORIES

**1. Division of Labor.** The worker does not make the entire product but performs only one operation. The worker can be trained for the job quickly but never achieves varied skills and often finds the work boring.

**2. Standardization.** Some workers turn out quantities of the same parts, which are standardized, or *interchangeable*. Other workers assemble the components into the finished product.

**3. Assembly Line.** Workers take positions alongside a moving belt that brings them the product being processed. As one worker performs one task, the belt moves the product to the next worker for the next operation. The belt moves along from worker to worker until the product is completed.

EVALUATION: (1) *Advantages.* Mass production makes possible the efficient use of workers and machines, the economical use of raw materials, and the speedy output of more goods at lower cost. (2) *Disadvantages.* Mass production requires workers to perform monotonous and repetitive tasks that stifle creativity and offers consumers identical or very similar products that push society into uniformity.

## HIGHER STANDARD OF LIVING

Today our economic system produces a greater volume and variety of goods—at lower cost—than ever before. The average American enjoys material comforts undreamed of by past monarchs.

## MODERN CAPITALISM

**1. Emergence.** With the coming of the Commercial Revolution (see pages 162–164), western Europe began to move toward a dynamic, worldwide, profit-oriented economic system called capitalism. Entrepreneurs devised the domestic system for production and engaged in trade—taking risks, facing competition, and operating in a market economy where prices were set largely by supply and demand. Entrepreneurs secured money sometimes by forming joint-stock companies and other times by borrowing from newly formed banks.

With the coming of the Industrial Revolution, the new production methods required large amounts of capital—economic wealth usually thought of as money. Capital was necessary to build factories, purchase machines, secure raw materials, and pay workers—all before any goods were sold. Consequently the capitalist, who risked money by investing in a business, controlled the entire process of production. This economic system, based on private capital, is known as *capitalism*.

**2. Laissez-faire.** In the late 18th century, capitalists urged the government to abandon mercantilism (see page 163) and cease its regulation of the economy. Opposed to restrictions on production and trade, capitalists wanted to manufacture and sell their goods free from government interference. They favored *laissez-faire* (leave business alone), a principle advocated by the economist Adam Smith (see page 182). In the 19th century such thinking greatly influenced

Britain and other industrialized nations, but it has been sharply modified or rejected by industrial nations today.

**3. Basic Principles of Capitalism.** *(a) Private ownership.* Individuals (persons and corporations) own the means of production and distribution of goods. *(b) Free enterprise.* Individuals are free to enter any business and run it as they wish. *(c) Profit motive.* Business leaders direct their affairs to avoid loss and make profit. *(d) Competition.* To excel all rivals, each producer strives to improve the quality and lower the cost of goods. *(e) Market economy.* Supply and demand, operating under conditions of free competition in the marketplace, determine the price of goods.

**4. Philosophy of Interdependence.** Today capitalist nations acknowledge the interdependence of capital, labor, and government. Capital provides the means of production and the managerial skills; labor provides the work; government provides law and order and protects the people against economic abuses.

## RISE OF THE CORPORATION

In the late 19th century, the corporation became the dominant form of business organization. A corporation, operating under state charter, enables a group of individuals to engage in business as a single "person," or legal entity. The advantages of a corporation are: (1) *Ability to raise capital.* Whereas an individual entrepreneur or a partnership has limited capital resources, the corporation can raise large sums of money by selling securities (stocks and bonds) to the public. The corporation belongs to its stockholders, each a part owner. (2) *Limited liability.* If the corporation proves unsuccessful, each stockholder is liable only for the money invested in the business, not other personal assets. (3) *Perpetual life.* The existence of the corporation is unaffected by the death of any stockholder, for the corporation has perpetual life.

Today the individual entrepreneur and the partnership exist chiefly in farming, the professions, small retail shops, and services. The corporation dominates the major economic areas: public utilities, transportation, communication, and manufacturing.

## AGE OF BIG BUSINESS

Corporations grew to "giant" size in assets, volume of sales, and number of employees. Big business has the advantages of utilizing mass-production methods, maintaining research laboratories, promoting large-scale advertising, and securing capital easily. Sometimes big business has been criticized for certain abuses: paying low wages, selling inferior goods, competing unfairly against the small entrepreneur, and creating monopolies to restrict competition and keep up prices.

## GOVERNMENT REGULATION OF INDUSTRY

Aroused by abuses resulting from the Industrial Revolution, the people protested against laissez-faire and demanded government action. In the second half of the 19th century, governments began to pass laws designed to protect workers, consumers, and small business people.

## ECONOMIC INTERDEPENDENCE OF NATIONS: WORLD TRADE

The Industrial Revolution helped unify the world economically and expand international trade. Industrial nations exported manufactured goods and imported foodstuffs, fuels, and raw materials. Agricultural nations imported manufactured goods and exported foodstuffs. Nations rich in natural resources provided fuels and raw materials. Also, as different countries specialized in different manufactured goods, trade developed among industrial nations. Mutually profitable trade among nations, some political leaders believed, aided the cause of world peace.

## ECONOMIC COMPETITION AMONG NATIONS

As more nations became industrialized, they engaged in bitter rivalry for world markets and for regions containing raw materials. Their disputes helped cause World War I (see page 434).

Also, industrial nations hindered world trade by adopting *protective tariffs*—duties on imports that raise the price of foreign goods. This policy, each nation contended, saved domestic manufacturers and workers from foreign competition and furthered the nation's economic self-sufficiency.

From about 1850 to 1932, Britain, alone of the industrial nations, promoted world commerce by levying no tariffs. That is, it followed a policy of *free trade*. The British operated without tariffs because their industries could compete successfully against foreign imports. In 1932, as foreign competition became more intense, even Britain adopted protective tariffs.

## LABOR PROBLEMS

For a discussion of labor problems, see pages 288–291.

# B. Political Results

## GROWTH OF DEMOCRACY

**1. Rise of the Middle Class and Working Class.** Before the Industrial Revolution the landed aristocracy ruled throughout western Europe. With industrialization, the middle class (which included the capitalists) grew in number and economic wealth; the working class also became more numerous. Both classes desired political influence to make the government responsive to their interests. Therefore, both capitalists and workers battled for democracy, which would give them representation in government. Their efforts in most west European countries led to the extension of the suffrage, the rise of new political parties, and changes in old political parties to reflect the interests of business leaders and workers.

By the mid-19th century, the landed aristocracy in Britain and France had lost its political power to the middle class. In Britain especially the interests of landed aristocrats and wealthy capitalists tended to merge by marriage of their children and by the entrance of capitalists into landowning and of aristocrats into business ventures. Thereafter, the upper middle class constituted a "new elite" of economic and political power whose needs greatly influenced government policy. As workers called attention to their problems, organized unions, and engaged in political action, the needs of the working class also strongly affected government policy.

Industrialization by itself does not guarantee the development of democracy. This lesson may be learned from the histories of Imperial Germany before World War I, Nazi Germany and Imperial Japan before World War II, and Communist Russia today.

2. **Informed Citizenry.** Radio, television, newspapers, and magazines—the "mass media" of communication—have enabled citizens, as never before, to keep informed on civic matters. Modern democracy operates best with an informed citizenry.

## AID TO NATIONALISM

The Industrial Revolution helped strengthen the feeling of nationalism. A whole nation could read the same newspapers and magazines and get the same programs on radio and television. Improved transportation encouraged nationwide travel. Thus, local points of view and customs gave way to a national culture.

## IMPETUS TO IMPERIALISM

Modern industry needs large quantities of raw materials as well as mass markets. Consequently the leading industrial nations promoted imperialistic undertakings in Africa, Latin America, and Asia.

## LEADERSHIP OF INDUSTRIAL NATIONS

Because industry creates military power and financial strength, industrial nations have come to dominate world affairs. In the late 19th century, the major powers were Britain, Germany, and the United States; in the early 20th century, Japan assumed leadership in Asia; today the world's major powers are Russia and the United States.

# C. Social Results

## DYNAMIC SOCIETY

For centuries before the Industrial Revolution, people had lived in a feudal agrarian society in which their life-style had remained static (relatively the same). They expected the present and future to be a repetition of the past. With industrialization people entered upon a new, dynamic world of speed, variety, change, and opportunity. They engaged in new occupations and professions; they expanded their intellectual and scientific horizons. No longer satisfied to maintain existing ways, people welcomed innovation and believed in the inevitability of progress.

## INCREASE IN WORLD POPULATION

As a result of the Industrial Revolution, (1) new production methods increased the supply of manufactured goods and foodstuffs, and (2) medical science combated disease and lengthened the human life span. These developments have led to a great increase in world population.

To the mid-20th century, the greatest population growth occurred in the industrialized regions: Britain, western Europe, and the United States. Since World War II, with medical care expanding throughout the world, the greatest population growth has taken place in the underdeveloped areas: Asia, Africa, and Latin America.

In 1950 the world population totaled 2.5 billion; 20 years later, in 1970, it was 3.7 billion. If the current unprecedented 2 percent annual growth rate con-

"Strain"

*Fischetti, Reprinted by permission of NEA.*

tinues, by the year 2000 the world population will total 6.5 billion. Demographers (population experts) named this astounding growth since the end of World War II the *population explosion.*

Some observers now question whether the world's resources will prove sufficient to provide so many people with a decent living standard.

## GROWTH OF CITIES

People have flocked to cities to secure jobs in industry. Also, many have been attracted to cities by social and cultural opportunities: theaters, concert halls, schools, libraries, and sports arenas. Cities traditionally have been centers of culture.

By means of improved transportation facilities, especially railroads and trucks, city dwellers were able to receive foodstuffs and other necessities of life and to distribute the products they made in city factories. Today, in countries such as the United States and Britain, the urban, or city, population far exceeds the rural population.

Cities face many problems: clearing slums, constructing decent housing, preventing crime, halting air and water pollution, providing mass transportation, improving education, and assuring efficient local government.

In the United States since World War II, many middle- and upper-class families, especially whites, have fled the central cities for the suburbs. They reasoned that they would be close enough to the central cities to work there and use the cultural facilities. But their belief that they could escape the many city problems proved wrong, for these problems soon emerged in the suburbs.

The flight to the suburbs has had the following effects: decreasing the city tax base and increasing the proportion of minority groups—primarily blacks and Spanish-speaking people—in the total city population.

## IMPROVED STATUS OF WOMEN

Before the Industrial Revolution women occupied a status inferior to men. Women took care of the home and family, while depending upon the men to be the breadwinners. With industrialization, women secured factory and office jobs and became economically independent.

To better their status in society, women in the 19th century organized the *feminist movement.* In Britain the leading feminists were *Mary Wollstonecraft* and *Emmeline Pankhurst.* In the United States the leading feminist was *Susan B. Anthony.* Gradually, in various parts of the world, women secured equal rights to vote, hold political office, pursue an education, engage in the professions, own property, and obtain justice before the law.

## NEW FAMILY PATTERNS

Before the Industrial Revolution, most west European families lived in an agrarian society and performed two basic functions: (1) educational—instructing the children in religion, good citizenship, and occupational skills—and (2) economic—organizing the family members to work together in agriculture and under the domestic system. In such a society children were an economic asset. As a result, large families were typical. These families were *patriarchal*—ruled by the father, who made the important decisions and exercised full family authority. Usually the family consisted of husband, wife, and children—called the *nuclear family*. When joined by grandparents and other close relatives, the enlarged family became known as the *nuclear extended form*.

Today in our industrial society, the family has lost many of its educational functions to schools, other societal agencies, and labor unions; also, the family is no longer an economic unit. The father works in an office or in a factory; the mother works at home or secures outside employment; and the children are at school. Modern families are small, and the cost of educating children is high. The patriarchal family has given way to the *equalitarian family,* in which mother and father share in making family decisions and children possess a great deal of freedom.

Most families today are nuclear. They live in relatively small houses or apartments, usually at some distance from relatives. Grandparents or other elderly close relatives generally live by themselves or in senior-citizen homes.

## MORE COMFORTABLE HOMES

Industrialization has produced countless conveniences for the modern home. Our dwellings are warmed by central heating, cooled by air conditioning, cleaned by vacuum machine, and illuminated by electric light. Our foods are preserved in refrigerators and cooked on gas or electric stoves. Our entertainment comes from radio and television.

## LEISURE TIME

As machine production increased, the individual's average working day decreased from about 15 hours in the late 18th century to 7 or 8 hours today. Workers today also receive more holidays and vacations, and many workers receive pensions that enable them to retire with an assured income.

To occupy their leisure time, individuals pursue their own interests, giving free reign to "individual expression" in such areas as education, culture, and recreation. Many people also use leisure time to search for their "individual identity"—to know themselves and understand their relationships to family and society.

## IMPETUS TO EDUCATION

With the Industrial Revolution, education became increasingly important to all people. (1) In industry workers need the basic skills—reading to understand written instructions, writing to prepare reports, and arithmetic to perform simple computations. Many positions require workers with special skills, such as shorthand, typing, drafting, and computer programming. Industrialization also increased the need for the training of such professionals as accountants, engineers, and librarians. (2) As individuals and, through their unions, workers have supported free public schools so as to educate their children and to remove children from the labor market. (3) With industrialization, the world became an interdependent unit and government grew in function and importance. All people require education to understand complex world affairs and to perform the duties of good citizenship. (4) Industrialization has affected the educational process. For teaching purposes today, educators have available various products of our industrial economy: paper and pens, textbooks and other printed materials, films and recordings, and radio and television programs.

## HUMANITARIANISM

*Humanitarianism* is a feeling of deep concern for the welfare of unfortunate peoples, usually coupled with a desire to improve conditions. With industrialization, humanitarians could draw upon the newly created wealth to combat many social injustices.

**1. Abolition of Slavery.** In 1833 British humanitarians secured the abolition of slavery throughout the British Empire. Somewhat later France and Holland abolished slavery. The United States granted freedom to blacks as a result of the Civil War (1861–1865).

**2. Expanded Missionary Services.** Starting in the 19th century, Christian missionaries, sent to underdeveloped areas of the world, expanded their activities to include educational and medical services. Famous medical missionaries in Africa were, in the 19th century, *David Livingstone* (British) and, in the 20th century, *Albert Schweitzer* (French). Also famed as a philosopher and musician, Schweitzer devoted hs life to providing hospital care for the natives.

**3. Care for Sick and Wounded Soldiers.** *Florence Nightingale* (British), during the Crimean War (1853–1856), provided the first wartime nursing service. She became known as "the lady with the lamp." In 1864 *Jean Henri Dunant* (Swiss) founded the *International Red Cross.* In 1881 *Clara Barton* (American) organized and headed the *American Red Cross.* Today the Red Cross serves not only war casualties but also peacetime disaster victims.

**4. Improved Treatment of the Insane and Criminals.** *Elizabeth Fry* (British) sought better treatment of imprisoned criminals, and *Dorothea Dix* (American) fought for better treatment of the insane. Today the insane are treated as being mentally sick, not as being possessed of the devil. Imprisoned criminals are taught a trade in order to help them earn a living when they are released. Reform, not punishment, is the modern approach.

**5. Free Public Education.** Humanitarians enlisted support to help schoolchildren enjoy their youth, remain out of the labor market, and become the educated citizenry essential to a successful democracy.

In 1867 Britain granted suffrage to city workers, and three years later, in 1870, Parliament passed the *Forster Act*. It supplemented private schools by a system of state-supported elementary schools. In 1918 the *Fischer Act* made school attendance compulsory until age 14.

In the United States *Horace Mann* and *Henry Barnard* fought for free public education, which by 1860 became the rule on the elementary level.

**6. Philanthropy.** *Philanthropists* are persons of great fortune who devote their wealth to promote the welfare of society.

*a. Alfred Nobel* (Swedish), the inventor of dynamite, founded the annual *Nobel Prizes.* These awards honor individuals who make outstanding contributions to science, literature, economics, and world peace.

*b. Andrew Carnegie* (American), the steel magnate, established free public libraries, the *Carnegie Endowment for International Peace*, and other agencies to promote education and aid worthy causes. He also built *The Hague* (Holland) *Peace Palace.*

*c. Cecil Rhodes* (British), the South African diamond and gold millionaire, created the *Rhodes Scholarships.* These enable outstanding students from the United States and from the British Commonwealth (except for Britain itself) to study at Oxford University in England.

*d. John D. Rockefeller* (American), the oil magnate, through the *Rockefeller Foundation*, provided grants to colleges and universities, and encouraged research in the social sciences and humanities. He also founded the *Rockefeller Institute* (now *Rockefeller University*) for medical research.

*e. Henry Ford* (American), the automobile manufacturer, established the *Ford Foundation.* It grants funds to universities, medical schools, and hospitals, and finances studies of such human problems as civil liberties, democracy, and international peace.

## MULTIPLE–CHOICE QUESTIONS

1. Which was an immediate result of the Industrial Revolution? (1) a decrease in population (2) an increase in the number of guilds (3) the growth of the factory system (4) less need for capital.

2. With the invention of machinery, the textile mills employed more workers because (1) the first machines were less efficient than hand labor (2) women and children could work the machines (3) goods were cheaper and in greater demand (4) division of labor required more workers to produce the same amount of goods.

3. Which is *not* a result of division of labor? (1) quick training of workers (2) increased production (3) interesting work (4) repetitive work.

4. The development of capitalism in western Europe was accompanied by a great increase in the (1) power of the aristocracy (2) influence of the bourgeoisie (3) taxes on the clergy (4) power of absolute monarchs.

5. Capitalists are best defined as persons who (1) own or control business enterprises (2) give large sums of money to charity (3) favor government ownership of industry (4) invent machines.

6. As a result of the Industrial Revolution, the power of the capitalist class was (1) transferred to the landed aristocracy (2) increased tremendously (3) weakened slightly (4) transferred to the working class.

7. *Not* a principle of capitalist economy is (1) the profit motive (2) competition (3) free enterprise (4) government ownership of major industries.

8. Adam Smith pointed out the advantages of (1) rule by divine right of kings (2) separation of governmental powers (3) price regulation by the laws of supply and demand (4) mercantilist regulations of trade.

9. Laissez-faire is the economic theory that government should (1) regulate all business strictly (2) not interfere in business (3) own the railroads (4) give the public lands free to the people.

10. A major reason for forming corporations was to (1) avoid government control (2) raise large sums of capital (3) regulate labor unions (4) promote better advertising.

11. The consumer may be harmed if big business achieves (1) low prices (2) monopoly (3) greater variety of goods (4) research for new products.

12. Britain adopted free trade about 1850 because Britain then (1) did not fear foreign competition (2) grew grain more cheaply than other countries (3) opposed industrialization in the United States (4) was not interested in increasing exports.

13. Which was an important political result of the Industrial Revolution in 19th-century Britain? (1) establishment of the Bank of England (2) end of free public education (3) assembly-line production (4) suffrage for the middle class.

14. The Industrial Revolution has affected American family life by (1) strengthening patriarchal control (2) encouraging large families (3) weakening the nuclear family group (4) furthering greater equality among family members.

15. As a result of the Industrial Revolution, women have (1) become more dependent upon men (2) decreased in number (3) become heads of many large corporations (4) gained equal rights with men.

16. The "population explosion" since World War II has created serious food problems in (1) India (2) Sweden (3) France (4) Ireland.

17. Between 1870 and 1914 industrialization was *not* accompanied by democracy in (1) Britain (2) the United States (3) Germany (4) France.

18. In the term "dynamic society," the word "dynamic" means (1) modern (2) electrical (3) changing (4) warlike.

19. *Not* a humanitarian movement is (1) abolishing slavery (2) lowering the cost of goods (3) sending medical missionaries to Africa (4) providing free public education.

## IDENTIFICATION QUESTIONS: WHO AM I?

| | | |
|---|---|---|
| Susan B. Anthony | Henry Ford | Emmeline Pankhurst |
| Clara Barton | Horace Mann | Cecil Rhodes |
| Andrew Carnegie | Florence Nightingale | John D. Rockefeller |
| Jean Henri Dunant | Alfred Nobel | Albert Schweitzer |

1. I led the fight in Britain to win the suffrage for women.
2. I established prizes for contributions to science, literature, economics, and world peace.
3. A musician and author, I spent my life as a medical missionary in central Africa.
4. An Englishwoman, "the lady with the lamp," I began nursing services for soldiers.
5. An American suffragette, I fought to give women the right to vote.
6. A Swiss humanitarian, I founded the International Red Cross.
7. An Englishman, I made my fortune in South Africa's gold and diamond mines. I provided scholarships for outstanding students to study at Oxford University.
8. An American steel magnate, I sought to further international peace and provided the funds to build The Hague Peace Palace.
9. I organized the American Red Cross and served as its first president.

## ESSAY QUESTIONS

1. Explain *one* way in which the Industrial Revolution is related to *each* of the following: (*a*) standard of living (*b*) strengthening of nationalism (*c*) development of democracy (*d*) growth of imperialism (*e*) organization of business (*f*) development of capitalism (*g*) present-day family patterns.
2. (*a*) Explain what is meant by the "economic interdependence of nations." (*b*) Describe *one* way in which the Industrial Revolution has helped bring about economic interdependence. (*c*) Discuss *one* argument to support your opinion of the statement: Economic interdependence promotes world peace.
3. Describe *one* way in which the industrial development of Western Europe and the United States has affected *each* of the following: (*a*) cities (*b*) women in industry (*c*) population growth (*d*) education (*e*) transportation (*f*) amusements and recreation.
4. Explain how the great increase in population during the Industrial Revolution brought about new problems in relation to the following: (*a*) city living (*b*) agriculture (*c*) science (*d*) government responsibility.
5. The 19th century saw great advances in the field of social reform. Give evidence to show gains in *each* of the following areas: (*a*) slavery (*b*) care of the wounded in war (*c*) treatment of the insane (*d*) status of women (*e*) public education.
6. Indicate whether *each* of the following statements is true or false, and explain fully *two* reasons for your answer: (*a*) The Industrial Revolution has lowered the standard of living of the average family. (*b*) Modern imperialism may be considered a result of the Industrial Revolution. (*c*) Because of the Industrial Revolution, the nations of the world depend more upon one another than they did before. (*d*) The Industrial Revolution has promoted the unequal distribution of wealth. (*e*) The modern advances in communication and transportation have benefited humanity. (*f*) A nation's economic and cultural progress may be measured by the size and growth of its cities. (*g*) More leisure time, by reducing the 5-day, 40-hour workweek, may not necessarily be a benefit to the average person.

# Part 3. Problems of Labor
# and Industrialization

## EARLY LABOR DISCONTENT

As workers left farming and the domestic system for factory employment, they became completely dependent upon the employer for their livelihood. In the early years of industrialization, workers faced many hardships. (1) Wages were low, just above the starvation level. (2) Hours were long, up to 16 per day. (3) Children from age 5 and women held jobs in factories and mines. Since they were less demanding and accepted lower wages, they often replaced men. (4) Factories were unlighted and unsanitary; machines lacked proper safeguards against accidents. (5) As invention followed invention, workers lost jobs to machines, thus causing *technological unemployment*.

Reacting to these distressing conditions, some few British workers attempted to undo the Industrial Revolution. Known as *Luddites* after a supposed destructive guild apprentice Ned Ludd, these workers tried to halt factory production by deliberately destroying textile machines. The Luddite movement disappeared in the early 19th century as the authorities executed a number of machine-breakers and as most Britishers realized the impossibility of reversing industrial development.

Concerned and involved people considered other approaches to remedying the conditions of the worker.

## A. *Labor Unions*

## WORKERS SEEK STRENGTH IN UNIONS

In small business enterprises employers often worked alongside the employees, and the two groups frequently maintained personal relationships.

As business enterprises grew in size, employers and employees became separated from each other and their relationship became impersonal. Workers soon found that they could not improve conditions by *individual bargaining*. A single worker appealing to the employer could be refused and discharged without disrupting production.

By *collective bargaining*, that is, acting together as a group, the workers were in a stronger position to secure their demands. If refused, they could all strike, and the employer would be hurt by a complete halt in production. To represent them collectively in bargaining with the employer, workers formed labor unions.

## BRIEF HISTORY OF BRITISH UNIONS

**1. Legal Restrictions.** Workers' efforts to unionize were hindered by *(a)* court decisions holding unions illegal and *(b)* Combination Laws (1799–1800) declaring workers who joined together to improve conditions liable to imprisonment. Workers defied these restrictions until Parliament, in 1824–1825, granted them the right to form unions but not to strike.

**2. Workers' Suffrage.** Unions agitated for the Reform Bill of 1867, which gave the vote to city workers. Shortly thereafter, unions secured legislation removing the restriction upon strikes.

**3. Labor Party.** In 1901 the *Taff Vale Decision* held unions financially responsible for strike damages. Unions believed that this judicial ruling imperiled their existence. They decided to protect themselves by establishing the British Labor party. In 1906, with 29 Labor members elected to the Commons, Parliament set aside the Taff Vale Decision.

**4. Present Influence.** The Labor party, the unions' political arm, developed into a major party and several times headed the government. Membership in British unions has grown from 1.5 million in 1892 to 11 million today. Unions now represent about 50 percent of Britain's total working population. In present-day Britain the trade unions are a powerful force in politics and industry.

## UNIONS IN OTHER COUNTRIES

Unions overcame legal restrictions and emerged to defend worker interests. Today they are a vital force in the economic and political life of most democratic nations. In the United States some 16 million workers are members of 120 different unions affiliated with the *American Federation of Labor and Congress of Industrial Organizations (AFL-CIO)*. About 5 million more workers are unionized outside the AFL-CIO. Total union membership constitutes less than 25 percent of the American labor force. Instead of forming its own political party, American labor primarily works to achieve legislative goals through existing political parties.

## OBJECTIVES OF LABOR UNIONS

Labor unions seek (1) recognition of the union as the sole bargaining agent, (2) higher wages, (3) fewer working hours, (4) security against unemployment, (5) safe and sanitary factory conditions, (6) vacations with pay, and (7) *fringe benefits*, such as medical care, hospitalization, old-age pensions, and general welfare.

## PEACEFUL SETTLEMENT OF LABOR DISPUTES

The great majority of labor disputes are settled, with little or no publicity, by the following peaceful methods:

1. **Collective Bargaining.** The union and employer meet to discuss and agree upon the terms of a labor contract.

2. **Mediation.** A third party, respected by both the union and the employer, secures concessions from both sides, making an agreement possible.

3. **Arbitration.** A third party, accepted by both sides as neutral, hears the dispute and hands down a decision, or *award*. Union and employer often pledge beforehand to accept the award. This method is used only rarely.

## INDUSTRIAL WARFARE

A small minority of labor disputes erupt into industrial battles, frequently accompanied by much publicity. The union and the employer each seeks to pressure the other to secure better terms.

## WEAPONS OF THE UNION

1. **Strike.** Employees refuse to work until union demands are satisfied.

2. **Picket.** Workers parade outside the strikebound premises. They seek to enlist public support for their cause and to deter strikebreakers from entering the premises and taking the jobs.

3. **Boycott.** Workers request the consumer not to patronize the strikebound company.

4. **Publicity.** Unions appeal for public support through mass demonstrations, newspapers, radio, and television.

## WEAPONS OF THE EMPLOYER

1. **Lockout.** The employer keeps the workers from entering the premises and pursuing their jobs until management's terms are satisfied.

2. **Strikebreakers.** The employer hires new workers to take the jobs of the strikers.

3. **Injunction.** Under certain conditions the employer (or the government) may obtain a court order forbidding workers to strike, picket, or boycott. Violators of the injunction are liable to punishment for "contempt of court." (In the United States the power of Federal courts to grant injunctions in labor disputes has been limited by the 1932 Norris-LaGuardia Act.)

4. **Publicity.** The employer presents management's case to the public through the mass communication media.

"Nonprofit Enterprise"

## COSTS OF INDUSTRIAL WARFARE

Industrial warfare causes much hardship. (1) *Employers* suffer halted production, decreased profits, and unfavorable publicity. (2) *Workers* face unemployment and loss of income. (3) The *community* endures loss of services, shortage of products, and decreased income tax revenues.

# B. Labor and Social Legislation

## GOVERNMENTS ABANDON LAISSEZ-FAIRE IN LABOR MATTERS

Many groups urged governments to interfere in industry to improve labor conditions. (1) Workers demanded laws to consolidate and supplement gains achieved by unions. (2) Humanitarians deplored factory abuses and viewed oppressed workers as unfortunates. (3) Political leaders argued that a healthy and contented working class strengthens the nation.

Despite strong opposition by employers, governments began in the early 19th century to enact protective labor legislation.

## BRITISH FACTORY AND MINE LAWS

1. The **Factory Act of 1819,** applying to cotton factories only, prohibited employers from *(a)* hiring children under age 9 and *(b)* working older children more than a 12-hour day. However, this law was inadequately enforced.

2. The **Factory Act of 1833,** applying to all textile factories, prohibited employers from *(a)* hiring children under age 9 and *(b)* working 9- to 13-year-old children more than a 9-hour day and 13- to 18-year-olds more than a 12-hour day. The law also called for strict inspection and enforcement.

3. The **Mines Act of 1842** prohibited mine employment for children under age 10 and for women.

4. The **Ten-Hour Law of 1847,** for all textile factories, limited child and woman labor to a maximum 10-hour day.

5. Subsequent laws, too numerous to list, *(a)* raised the factory employment age for children, *(b)* prohibited children and women from working in mines, *(c)* required safety devices on dangerous machinery, and *(d)* established standards of factory sanitation.

Achieved through the democratic process, Britain's factory and mine laws set an example followed by most industrialized nations.

## SOCIAL SECURITY LAWS

With industrialization workers were beset by economic insecurity. They feared unemployment resulting from technological improvement and business depression; they feared their own inability to work due to accident, sickness, and old age. Generally they did not earn enough money to save for a "rainy day." Workers gained some protection as governments enacted social security laws.

1. **Germany.** Between 1883 and 1889 Germany under Bismarck led the way in social security, passing sickness, accident and old-age insurance laws.

2. **Britain.** Between 1906 and 1911 Britain began accident, old-age, sickness, and unemployment insurance. In 1946, under a Labor government, Britain adopted a comprehensive program of social security from "cradle to grave." The *National Insurance Act* includes unemployment, sickness, accident, and maternity benefits, old-age and survivors' pensions, and death grants. The *National Health Service Act* provides for dental, hospital, and medical service. Under both acts membership is compulsory, and costs are borne by workers, employers, and government. Because these social security acts indicate the government's concern for its citizens' welfare, Britain is often called a *welfare state.*

Britain's comprehensive program survives despite opposition. Employers claim that it costs too much and discourages labor's incentive to work. Some doctors resent government control and protest "socialized medicine." In recent years Britain has faced a multitude of economic problems, causing the government to cut back somewhat on social service expenditures.

**3. The United States.** In 1935 Congress passed our first *Social Security Act,* providing old-age and unemployment insurance. This act has been revised many times to increase old-age benefits, to extend coverage to additional workers, and to provide protection to totally disabled persons, orphans, and widows. In 1965 Congress enacted for persons over 65 a health insurance program called *Medicare.* It provides for social security taxes to finance compulsory hospital insurance and for payments by the enrollee and the government to finance medical insurance.

## C. Movements to Displace Capitalism

### MEANING OF SOCIALISM

Some reformers who blamed factory abuses, unemployment, and depression upon capitalism urged that it be replaced by a new political and economic system, *socialism.*

| Socialism | Capitalism |
|---|---|
| 1. *The government as representative of the people* owns and operates the major means of production (farms, mines, and factories) and distribution (transportation and retail stores). | 1. *Private individuals and corporations* own and operate business enterprises. The government maintains law and order, encourages private industry, and prevents abuses. |
| 2. The government determines the needs of the people and provides goods and services for the people's *use.* | 2. Private owners provide the people with goods and services they want in order to make a *profit.* |
| 3. The government plans the economy, determining which new industries to start, and which existing ones to contract or expand. According to its master plan, the government allocates capital, directs the flow of raw materials, and supplies the workers. These economic functions, performed by the government under socialism, are summed up by the term *state planning.* | 3. Individual owners and corporate managers make the basic decisions about starting new industries and contracting or expanding existing ones. They plan how to secure capital, to arrange the flow of raw materials, and to provide workers. These economic functions, performed by private owners who are oriented to the consumer and the marketplace, are summed up by the terms *individual planning* and *corporate planning.* |

### UTOPIAN SOCIALISM (EARLY 19TH CENTURY)

Utopian Socialists believed that capitalists, once convinced of the merits of socialism, would voluntarily discard private ownership and the profit motive. To many people, the possibility that this would happen seemed unlikely. Therefore, these reformers were considered dreamers, or *Utopians*.

1. **Robert Owen,** a wealthy British cotton manufacturer, created a model industrial community in Scotland at *New Lanark*. Contrary to general practice, he paid high wages, reduced working hours, provided sanitary factory conditions, built decent homes for workers, established schools for their children, and permitted the workers to share in management and profits. Owen's New Lanark community prospered, but he was disappointed that other manufacturers ignored his enlightened example.

In 1825 in the United States, Owen established a model agricultural-industrial community in Indiana at *New Harmony*. This venture failed.

2. **Claude Saint-Simon,** a French reformer, envisioned an ideal social order. He taught that the wealthy and educated classes should devote their energies to activities that would benefit the lower classes.

3. **Charles Fourier,** a French philosopher, advocated the establishment of ideal communities. In such Utopias, he believed, members working together for the common good would demonstrate the superiority of socialism. His followers established several experimental communities, which proved unsuccessful. In the 1840's American idealists, inspired by Fourier, maintained the famed but short-lived community in Massachusetts of *Brook Farm*.

## LOUIS BLANC AND NATIONAL WORKSHOPS

*Louis Blanc*, a French Socialist, believed that (1) every person has a right to a job and (2) the state should provide work for the unemployed in government-financed factories, or *national workshops*.

Blanc organized a workers' party and played a major role in the French Revolution of 1848. For a while the provisional government provided the unemployed with work: digging ditches and improving parks. However, as the middle class regained control, the government ended the work program and suppressed the subsequent workers' revolt. (During the depression of the 1930's, Blanc's ideas were applied in the United States when the government sponsored an extensive public works program.)

Blanc is considered more practical than the Utopians since he looked for reform, not to capitalists, but to workers and the government.

## "SCIENTIFIC" SOCIALISM

*Karl Marx* (1818–1883), German writer and economist, founded modern socialism. Exiled from Prussia after the failure of the 1848 Revolution, Marx settled in England. A learned man, Marx was familiar with the writings of west European philosophers and economists and with the manuscripts kept in the British Museum. Although he lived in poverty, Marx persevered to complete his studies and publicize his ideas.

Marx wrote the following important works: (1) The *Communist Manifesto* (co-authored by *Friedrich Engels*), 1848, was a pamphlet outlining his socialist ideas in a simple, propagandistic style. (Marx used the term "communist" to distinguish his views from those of the Utopian Socialists, whom he scorned as dreamers.) (2) *Das Kapital* was a detailed study containing Marx's critical analysis of the mid-19th-century capitalist system and expounding his theories of socialism. These works present the basic ideas of *Marxian socialism*, or *Marxism*.

**1. Economic Interpretation of History.** Marx argued that economic conditions determine the course of history. The class that possesses economic power— whether through ownership of land, merchant ships, banks, or factories— controls the government and social institutions. In an industrial society based on private ownership, the capitalist class rules.

**2. Class Struggle.** Marx also viewed history as a "class struggle" between economic groups: the "have-nots" against the "haves." In ancient Rome plebeians battled patricians; in feudal society serfs opposed lords; under the guilds apprentices and journeymen resisted master craftsmen; under private enterprise workers, or the *proletariat*, clash with capitalists, or the *bourgeoisie*. The "class struggle," Marx believed, was international since workers in each nation faced the same problems and battled the same capitalist oppressors. Marx concluded that "the proletarians have nothing to lose but their chains," and he coined the slogan "workingmen of all countries, unite."

**3. Surplus Value.** Capitalists exploit, or take advantage of, workers by paying them just enough wages to keep them alive, that is, just above the subsistence level. The difference between their wages and the price of the goods the workers produce, Marx called *surplus value*. Although the capitalists contribute nothing to production, according to Marx, they take the surplus value as profit. Consequently workers lack sufficient income to purchase all the goods produced, and this in turn, Marx claimed, leads to depression.

**4. Inevitability of Socialism.** Marx predicted that capitalism would destroy itself as depressions became more and more severe. In time, he said, wealth would concentrate in fewer and fewer hands, while workers' conditions would steadily deteriorate. Eventually the workers would be driven to overthrow the capitalists and establish a socialist state. Marx did not make clear whether the overthrow of capitalism would come by peaceful means or by violence. However, he was certain that socialism would first come not to agricultural but to industrial nations.

**5. Ultimate Communist Society.** With the triumph of socialism, Marx predicted that eventually the proletariat would establish an equalitarian, or "classless," society and that the state would tend to wither away. Also, eventually under socialism the production of goods and the availability of services would be so great, Marx believed, that society would apply the principle "from each according to his ability, to each according to his needs."

Since Marx believed that socialism would be achieved, not by appeals to the capitalist class, but by the working class as an inevitable result of "scientific" economic laws, Marxism is known as "scientific" socialism.

## CRITICISMS OF "SCIENTIFIC" SOCIALISM

Defenders of capitalism attack Marxian economics and warn against a socialist economy as follows:

1. **Marxian Errors.** Opponents of Marxism point out: *(a)* The economic interpretation of history neglects the vital role of noneconomic factors—for example, religion and nationalism. *(b)* The interests of capitalists and workers often coincide—for example, increased production makes possible both higher wages and greater profits. *(c)* Capitalists are entitled to profits, since they risk money and manage industry. *(d)* Major Marxian predictions have proven erroneous: for example, the conditions of workers have improved steadily, not worsened; socialist revolutions came first to semi-feudal agricultural nations—Russia and China—not to industrial nations; and in socialist countries the state has become all powerful rather than tending to wither away. *(e)* Basing his analysis upon mid-19th-century capitalism, Marx did not foresee that capitalism, operating within the democratic process, would change and evolve to remedy abuses and institute reforms.

2. **Defects of Socialism.** Opponents predict that under socialism *(a)* individuals will lose their incentive to work and progress; *(b)* the government, to spur industrial output, will have to maintain a state of continuous national crisis and to adopt capitalist concepts: stimulating individual initiative to increase production by offering factory managers and workers special pay incentives; *(c)* the government, exercising economic as well as political power, will become a dictatorship controlling every phase of a citizen's life; *(d)* the government will place the needs of the state ahead of the needs of the people; and *(e)* the government will have great difficulty in managing a complex economic system and will commit serious errors in planning.

Defenders of capitalism assert that we can retain the full advantages of the free-enterprise system while remedying its defects.

## BRIEF HISTORY OF SOCIALIST PARTIES

Marx's followers founded *Socialist*, or *Social Democratic*, parties to achieve, (1) as the *immediate objective*, greater democracy and improved labor conditions and, (2) as the *ultimate objective*, a socialist state. During the 19th century they employed peaceful methods, such as publicity and the ballot, in seeking to gain control of governments.

In 1889, to coordinate world Socialist activities, the various Socialist parties formed the *Second International*. (The *First International*, founded by Marx in

1864, had been short-lived.) The Second International proclaimed the unity of all workers, regardless of nationality. Nevertheless, in World War I, most Socialist parties ignored their international ties and supported the war efforts of their respective countries. After World War I Socialists kept their parties from being absorbed by the more radical Communists.

Since World War II Socialist parties have exercised considerable influence in West European countries: Sweden, Norway, Denmark, the Netherlands, Italy, West Germany, France, and Britain. While controlling the government in some of these countries, the Socialists have (1) maintained democratic institutions— including freedom of speech and press and the right to criticize the government; (2) conducted free elections—surrendering control when defeated at the polls; and (3) instituted a wide and varying range of socialist reforms. (For the British Labor party, check the Index.)

## SWEDEN: A CASE STUDY OF SOCIALISM IN WESTERN EUROPE

**1. Brief Description of Sweden.** Located in northern Europe, Sweden contains over 8 million people and possesses valuable resources of timber, iron ore, and water power. Sweden's mountainous terrain limits farming, but its irregular coastline encourages fishing and shipping. Sweden has a democratic government: a monarch who serves as a figurehead, an elected one-house parliament called the *Riksdag*, and a prime minister and cabinet who remain in office as long as they control a Riksdag majority. The government protects individual rights, permits speech and press freedom, and conducts honest elections.

**2. Social Democratic Control (1932–1976)**

*a. Political Developments.* During the Great Depression of the 1930's, Sweden, like other Western nations, faced rising unemployment, falling farm prices, and diminishing foreign trade. As a result of the 1932 elections, the Social Democrats, a moderate Socialist party, gained control of the government. For the next 44 years, with free elections held regularly, the Social Democrats alone or with minority party support maintained a Riksdag majority and controlled the government.

*b. Social Democratic Record*

(1) *Little Nationalization.* When the Social Democrats took office in 1932, they found that the state already owned various economic enterprises: much of the country's natural resources (timber, iron ore, and water power) and almost all rail transportation. The Swedish Socialists, despite their theoretical belief in nationalization, permitted most industry to remain under private ownership. Their approach was not to nationalize but rather to compel private enterprise to undertake major social goals: guaranteeing employment, spurring economic growth, and providing superior products. To pressure private industry toward these ends, the Social Democratic government used its control of natural resources, rail transport, credit facilities, and tax policies.

(2) *Welfare State.* The Social Democrats concentrated on making Sweden a preeminent welfare state. Over the years the Socialist government provided unemployment insurance, aid to low-income families and benefits for children, free education from elementary school through university, health insurance, sickness benefits, old-age pensions and survivors' benefits, housing subsidies, and rent controls. The Socialist government also assumed responsibility for encouraging full employment and decent living standards. The Swedes enjoy the highest per capita income of any European people and are second in this respect only to the Americans. The Swedish people, however, pay for their social services by taxes on personal incomes, corporate incomes, sales, and luxury items. Together these taxes are the highest of all industrial nations and far more burdensome than those paid by American taxpayers.

Some observers have questioned whether Sweden represents a socialist economy or a capitalist welfare state.

**3. Social Democratic Defeat in the 1976 Elections.** The Social Democrats and their minority-party allies lost control of the Riksdag by a narrow margin. Their defeat was attributed to the following causes: resentment against exorbitant taxes and the regulation of people's lives by insensitive bureaucrats; fears that the labor unions were becoming too powerful; doubts about the wisdom of Socialist plans to end Sweden's reliance on imported oil for power by constructing 13 additional nuclear power plants; and the feeling that it was "time for a change."

Socialist leader *Olof Palme* resigned as prime minister and the position was filled by the three-party center coalition leader, *Thorbjorn Fälldin.* The new non-Socialist government indicated that it would scrap plans for additional nuclear power plants, lower taxes, limit the power of labor unions, and reduce the government's role in the economy. But it would maintain Sweden's social welfare programs. Once in office, the non-Socialist government made little change in Sweden's welfare benefits, high taxes, and other economic policies.

**4. The 1979 Elections.** By tacit agreement, the political parties avoided the nuclear power issue since it was to be the subject of a 1980 national referendum. On other issues, the political parties were not sharply divided, but the elections attracted a voter turnout of 90 percent. The non-Socialist coalition retained control of the Riksdag by a margin of one seat and therefore remained in office.

**5. The 1980 Referendum on Nuclear Power.** With 75 percent of the electorate going to the polls, Swedish voters faced three complex and involved choices. They strongly approved choices for doubling the country's nuclear facilities, by the mid-1980's, up to 12 plants. They split, however, on choices for eventually phasing out nuclear power—some voting for a vague timetable, others endorsing the early 21st century.

## BRIEF HISTORY OF COMMUNIST PARTIES

In Russia before World War I, the left-wing Socialists broke with the moderate Social Democrats and formed their own organization, the Bolsheviks, later called the *Communist party.* In 1917 the Bolsheviks seized control of Russia by revolution (see pages 447–448). This accomplishment encouraged left-wing Socialists in other countries to establish their own Communist parties.

In 1919, to further world revolution, Russia linked the various Communist parties by the *Third International*, or *Comintern*. During World War II, to foster unity with its capitalist British and American allies, Russia ended the Comintern.

Today Communist parties control Russia, many East European nations, China, Mongolia, North Korea, Vietnam, Cambodia, Laos, and Cuba. Also, Communist candidates poll substantial votes in France and Italy.

## THE SOVIET UNION: A CASE STUDY OF COMMUNISM IN EASTERN EUROPE   (Check the Index.)

## COMMUNISTS VS. SOCIALISTS

Although both Communists and Socialists claim to follow Marxian ideas, they have disagreed on the following major points:

| Communists | Socialists |
| --- | --- |
| 1. Communism can be achieved only by *revolution*—a violent overthrow of the capitalist government and economy. | 1. Socialism can be achieved by *evolution*—a peaceful and legal gaining of control by publicity and the ballot. |
| 2. To protect the revolution, a Communist government must at first be a "dictatorship of the proletariat." It must suppress, by all available means, any movement considered procapitalist or counterrevolutionary. | 2. A Socialist government, assuming power by consent of the people, must always be a democracy. It must retain the people's support by providing political liberty and economic justice. |
| 3. Communism requires government ownership and operation of all the means of production and distribution—without significant exception. | 3. Socialism requires nationalization only of the major industries. Small farms, small factories, and retail stores may remain under private ownership but subject to government regulation. |

## CHRISTIAN SOCIAL MOVEMENTS

Many devout Christians took a strong interest in social reform but opposed "scientific" socialism, holding its economic interpretation and doctrine of class struggle to be irreligious. Instead they urged reform based upon religious principles, especially the Golden Rule. This movement was encouraged by religious leaders. (1) *Pope Leo XIII* in 1891 advised employers to treat workers in a Christian manner and appealed to workers to form Catholic labor unions. (2) *Pope Pius XI* in 1931 proposed that workers share in the management and profits of industry. (3) *Pope John XXIII* in 1961 deplored low wages that condemned workers to "subhuman conditions of life." He urged that labor receive a greater share of the fruits of its industry and preached the responsibility of society for the well-being of all its members. (4) *Pope Paul VI* in 1967 deplored the abuses of unrestrained capitalism. On behalf of poor individuals and underdeveloped nations, the pope urged a major effort to overcome misery, hunger, disease, and ignorance. (5) *Protestant religious leaders* have called for economic and social justice.

Today the *Christian Democratic party* in Italy, the *People's party* in Austria, and the *Christian Social party* in Belgium each commands a considerable following for its program of protecting Catholic interests and advancing social reform.

## MULTIPLE–CHOICE QUESTIONS

1. The beginning of the factory system caused (1) acute labor problems (2) a greater personal bond between employees and employers (3) equality of economic status (4) workers to turn to agriculture.
2. In 1825 British industrialists paid low wages to their employees because of (1) German competition (2) minimum wage laws (3) the absence of tariffs on food imports (4) an oversupply of labor.
3. The Industrial Revolution caused the modern labor movement because (1) workers immediately had more security (2) the standard of living improved (3) more people worked for a living (4) workers were more dependent on the capitalist.
4. Collective bargaining means that the (1) workers go out on strike (2) workers act as a group in making demands on the employer (3) employer may not discharge a worker (4) employer must agree to raise wages.
5. The first British labor unions were (1) welcomed by the employers (2) started by foreigners (3) declared illegal by the courts (4) encouraged by the Combination Laws.
6. A neutral third party hands down a decision in a labor dispute under (1) collective bargaining (2) arbitration (3) mediation (4) an injunction.
7. Labor unions generally advocate (1) strikes to overthrow capitalism (2) formation of worldwide trusts (3) social legislation for workers (4) individual bargaining.
8. In labor disputes unions do *not* advocate (1) picketing (2) boycotting (3) lockouts (4) publicity.
9. British legislation to end factory and mine abuses was (1) in harmony with the laissez-faire doctrine (2) guaranteed in the British Bill of Rights (3) provided by the 1832 Reform Bill (4) important to the health and welfare of the working class.
10. The purpose of social security is to (1) provide cheap life insurance (2) curtail employers' profits (3) help relieve workers of the fear of destitution (4) provide more business for the big insurance companies.
11. *Not* included in the British system of social security is protection in case of (1) old age (2) sickness (3) unemployment (4) automobile accidents.
12. Britain has been termed a "welfare state" because of its (1) Labor party (2) factory laws (3) social security legislation (4) universal suffrage laws.
13. Socialism means (1) abolition of factory managers (2) abolition of all government (3) ownership of land by the peasants (4) ownership of the major means of production by the government.
14. The early Socialists, such as Robert Owen and Charles Fourier, who wished to reform society by establishing model communities, were called (1) "scientific" Socialists (2) Christian Democrats (3) Utopians (4) Communists.

15. The Utopians believed that socialism would come mainly through the efforts of the (1) workers (2) capitalists (3) government (4) consumers.

16. The basic concepts of world communism may be traced to the (1) writings of Marx and Engels (2) republican uprisings in France (3) activity of Russian Bolsheviks (4) writings of Voltaire and Diderot.

17. Marx believed in (1) private ownership of land (2) the right to inherit property (3) the economic interpretation of history (4) cooperation with the capitalists.

18. Which is *not* one of the beliefs of Karl Marx? (1) Capitalist countries will experience more and more serious depressions. (2) Workers' conditions will slowly improve under capitalism. (3) Labor is the most important factor in production. (4) Wealth in capitalistic countries will be concentrated in fewer and fewer hands.

19. The word "proletariat" refers to (1) capitalists (2) workers (3) Russians (4) soldiers.

20. According to "scientific" socialism (1) the interests of workers and capitalists often coincide (2) workers throughout the world basically have the same interests and problems (3) there will always be a class struggle (4) capitalism does not provide enough surplus value for the economy.

21. Marx would *not* have expected the 1917 Communist Revolution to take place in Russia because Russia (1) was largely agricultural (2) had too many moderate leaders (3) retained many Oriental ideas (4) had a large population.

22. The meaning of "a government nationalizes an industry" is that (1) offices are established throughout the country (2) the workers gain control (3) the government becomes the owner of the industry (4) all foreigners lose their jobs.

23. In Sweden the Social Democrats emphasized (1) nationalizing all industry (2) establishing a one-party state (3) providing social welfare programs (4) fomenting revolution in the other Scandinavian countries.

24. The Socialists disagreed with the Communists on all of the following *except* (1) the need of revolution to overthrow capitalism (2) "dictatorship of the proletariat" (3) nationalization of small retail stores (4) the inevitability of socialism.

25. Christian social movements (1) oppose the formation of labor unions (2) preach that the "meek" will be rewarded in the hereafter (3) urge that society accept responsibility for all persons in economic matters (4) favor the overthrow of capitalism.

26. Today a strong Christian (Catholic) Democratic party exists in (1) Norway (2) Britain (3) Poland (4) Italy.

## ESSAY QUESTIONS

1. (*a*) Describe *two* conditions in Great Britain after 1750 that caused the government to turn its attention to the problems of labor. (*b*) Explain to what extent labor legislation in Great Britain has remedied each condition.

2. Discuss: (*a*) *two* causes for the rise of labor unions (*b*) *two* methods used by unions to secure their demands (*c*) *two* weapons used by employers to fight unions (*d*) *one* argument for and *one* argument against unionism.

3. Explain *one* way in which *each* of the following has influenced the labor movement: (*a*) Louis Blanc (*b*) Robert Owen (*c*) Otto von Bismarck (*d*) Karl Marx (*e*) Adam Smith (*f*) Pope Leo XIII (*g*) Pope John XXIII.

4. Many people face the problem of economic insecurity. (*a*) Describe, in *one* way, how industrial development has contributed to insecurity. (*b*) Give *two* provisions of a law adopted in an industrial country to provide greater economic security.

5. Discuss the development of the British labor movement and include the following points: (a) the status of labor in the early days of the Industrial Revolution (b) two gains made by labor in the 19th century (c) two accomplishments of the British Labor party.

6. Explain (a) two basic ideas of Marxian socialism (b) two criticisms of Marxian ideas (c) one reason why Marxian ideas achieved greater public support in Europe than in America (d) two reasons for the development of Christian social movements.

7. From 1932 to 1976 Sweden was governed by the Social Democratic party. Explain (a) one factor that enabled the Social Democrats in 1932 to gain control of the government (b) one way by which the Social Democratic government influenced the policies of Swedish private industry (c) two evidences that the Social Democrats transformed Sweden into a welfare state (d) one reason why the Social Democrats lost the 1976 elections. Decide whether you think Sweden under Social Democratic control illustrates a socialist economy or welfare capitalism. Give one argument to defend your opinion.

8. (a) Contrast capitalism and socialism as to (1) the role of the government in economic affairs (2) role of the marketplace in economic affairs (3) incentives to work and progress. (b) Contrast socialism and communism as to (1) methods of displacing capitalism (2) views on democracy (3) ownership of the means of production and distribution.

# UNIT X. DEVELOPMENTS IN SCIENCE AND CULTURE

## Part 1. Achievements in Science

### DEFINITION OF TERMS

**Science** is an intellectual study—an experimental method of gathering and interpreting data—regarding the world of nature: humanity, matter, and the universe. Science also is an organized body of knowledge regarding the world of nature. To arrange such knowledge logically, science is divided into branches, such as chemistry, physics, geology, biology, medicine, and astronomy.

**Pure,** or **basic, science** is concerned primarily with gathering knowledge for its own sake, better to understand ourselves and the universe. Pure scientists are not concerned with knowledge for any immediate practical value.

**Practical,** or **applied, science** is concerned with utilizing the discoveries of pure science for specific purposes. Applied scientists seek cures for disease, inventions of new machines, and discoveries of new products.

**Technology** is the study of the industrial arts for their practical value. Technologists work in industry seeking to achieve the most efficient methods of production and the highest quality of product. Technologists may depend upon the work of applied scientists or may themselves be applied scientists. In the general sense technology and applied science are used interchangeably.

### SCIENTIFIC METHOD

To investigate and solve a problem, scientists (1) state the problem clearly, (2) gather data by precise observation and experimentation that include rigid controls, (3) analyze the data to arrive at a well-reasoned conclusion—a scientific theory or law—and (4) test and retest the conclusion because a scientific law must always hold true.

The scientific method has been applied to the study of the problems of society—for example, human behavior, economic security, race relations, and world peace. In so doing the *social scientist* in economics, sociology, and history and the *behavioral scientist* in psychology and psychiatry try to eliminate variables and prejudices and strive for truth through a factual, logical, and open-minded attitude.

## BRIEF HISTORY OF SCIENCE

**1. Prehistoric Times Through the Middle Ages.** Until the Renaissance Era humanity slowly accumulated knowledge about the physical environment. The method was trial and error; the emphasis was upon practical discoveries. Peoples of many races, religions, and nationalities contributed. Prehistoric peoples devised the lever and wheel; other advances originated with the ancient Egyptians, Greeks, Indians, and Chinese, and with the medieval Moslems. (For details, check the Index under Science.)

**2. Renaissance Era.** In the 16th century west Europeans began modern science by inaugurating a *scientific revolution.* Renaissance scientists, extolling free inquiry and employing the scientific method, made important contributions to pure science. Their work in the fields of mathematics, medicine, chemistry, and astronomy (see pages 130–131) was basic to later research.

**3. Enlightenment and Early Industrial Revolution.** In the 18th century scientists were stimulated by both philosophical developments and practical industrial motives. Scientists were encouraged by the Enlightenment—a west European philosophical movement typified by a skepticism toward tradition, a drive for knowledge, and an emphasis upon natural law and reason. This climate of enlightenment spurred research utilizing the scientific method. Scientists also were encouraged by the early Industrial Revolution to speed production by inventing new machines and improving farming methods. During this era scientists engaged in pure research and, perhaps to a greater degree, in applied research or technology.

**4. Modern Science.** In the 20th century science has continued to grow in importance and has assumed characteristics that, in many ways, distinguish it from previous scientific ages. *(a)* Research scientists require equipment that may be very expensive. For example, the big telescope to scan the heavens and the atom smasher to delve into the atom cost many millions of dollars each. *(b)* Scientific research is financed increasingly by large corporations and governments. Corporations, some maintaining their own research laboratories, recognize the interdependence of science and industry. They seek scientific progress to provide them with salable products. Governments fund scientific research, usually conducted at university and industrial laboratories, for consumer safety, environmental protection, and military strength. *(c)* Research often involves several scientific areas and has become complex. The individual scientist, no matter how talented, has given way to teamwork under centralized supervision—the creative scientific team. *(d)* Scientists engage in pure as well as applied research. They have become increasingly aware that discoveries in basic research are essential for progress in technology. *(e)* Scientific developments have resulted in the opening up of new, previously unknown areas of investigation. These disciplines are primarily in the social and behavioral fields such as anthropology, sociology, and psychology. *(f)* The achievements of science and technology affect our lives—at work and play and in war and peace. We live in an *age of science.*

## MEDICAL SCIENCE

### 1. Scientists and Their Contributions

*a. Edward Jenner* (1749–1823), British, discovered a method of preventing *smallpox* by vaccination. Jenner's approach, preventing disease by building body resistance, illustrates an important aspect of *preventive medicine.*

*b. Louis Pasteur* (1822–1895), French, formulated the *germ theory of disease.* He proved that certain diseases result from the invasion of the body by microscopic organisms called *germs.* Pasteur developed a vaccine that enables the body to resist the germ that causes *rabies.* He also discovered that heating such fluids as milk destroys many disease-producing bacteria. This discovery is used in the process called *pasteurization.*

*c. Joseph Lister* (1827–1912), British, prevented infection during surgery by the use of special germ-killing substances called *antiseptics.*

*d. Robert Koch* (1843–1910), German, isolated the specific bacteria causing *anthrax* (a cattle disease) and *tuberculosis.*

*e. Elie Metchnikoff* (1845–1916), Russian, explained the disease-fighting role of *white blood corpuscles.*

*f. Wilhelm Roentgen* (1845–1923), German, discovered *X rays.* By making shadow pictures of bones and internal organs, X rays help in diagnosing illness and performing surgery.

*g. Walter Reed* (1851–1902), American, proved that a mosquito transmits *yellow fever.* By draining swamps where mosquitoes breed and by using insecticides, sanitary engineers have largely eradicated yellow fever.

*h. Sigmund Freud* (1856–1936), Austrian, pioneered the study of human behavior by looking inward into the human mind. To treat certain types of mental illness, he developed the technique of psychoanalysis. His theories regarding the workings of the subconscious mind influenced surrealist art and stream-of-consciousness writing. Freud's pioneer work inspired the growth of psychology and psychiatry.

*i. Alexander Fleming* (1882–1955), British, found that some harmful bacteria are destroyed by the antibiotic *penicillin.*

*j. Selman Waksman* (1888–    ), naturalized American, developed the antibiotic *streptomycin.*

*k. Jonas Salk* (1914–    ), American, created a vaccine effective against *infantile paralysis,* or *polio.*

*l. Christiaan Barnard* (1923–     ), South African, led a surgical team in performing the first human heart transplant.

**2. Results of Medical Advances.** *(a)* In 1900 the average American life span was about 50 years. Today, with infant and child deaths sharply reduced, American life expectancy has increased to over 70 years. *(b)* Since World War II, in underdeveloped countries, medical scientists have significantly reduced death-causing diseases and thus created a "population explosion" (see pages 281–282). *(c)* Surgery gained in importance as a tool for the treatment of certain injuries and diseases. *(d)* Scientists developed a better understanding of human behavior and some success in the treatment of certain mental illnesses. *(e)* In the United States and other medically advanced countries, doctors emphasize preventive medicine. They use inoculations against smallpox, diphtheria, tetanus, whooping cough, measles, and polio. Nations seek to prevent other diseases by modern sanitation, a balanced diet, and adequate exercise. People have faith that research will conquer today's major diseases: heart ailments and cancer.

## GEOLOGY AND BIOLOGY

### 1. Scientists and Their Contributions

*a. Carolus Linnaeus* (1707–1778), Swedish, devised a system, still used today, for classifying plants and animals on the basis of similarities in structure. He is known as the "father of modern botany."

*b. Charles Lyell* (1795–1875), British, the "father of modern geology," believed that natural forces—water, wind, volcanoes—have continually shaped the surface of the earth. Lyell estimated the age of the earth at many millions of years.

*c. Matthias Schleiden* (1804–1881) and *Theodor Schwann* (1810–1882), Germans, demonstrated that all living things, plant and animal, are composed of microscopic units, called *cells.*

*d. Charles Darwin* (1809–1882), British, in his book *The Origin of Species* stated the *theory of evolution.* Darwin was influenced by Lyell's work in geology and by his own observations in South America and the South Pacific while serving as a naturalist for five years on the naval vessel *Beagle.* Darwin held that, during vast time eras, human beings and other complex life forms evolved from simpler types by the process of *natural selection,* or *survival of the fittest.*

*e. Gregor Mendel* (1822–1884), Austrian, experimenting with the cross-breeding of pea plants, developed the *laws of heredity.* "Mendelianism" gave impetus to scientific breeding of plants and animals.

**2. Effects of These Contributions.** *(a)* People acquired a better perspective of themselves and their civilization in relation to the vast age of the earth. They began to realize that the 6,000 years of known human history spanned but a tiny fragment of the earth's vast existence. *(b) Social Darwinists* applied Darwin's theory of evolution to explain the development of human institutions. They cited "natural selection" to support the economic policy of laissez faire. (According to this idea, if business were left to develop without regulations, only the strongest and best managed would survive.) They also cited "survival of the fittest" to justify doctrines of racial superiority and wars of conquest. *(c)* Farmers raised improved agricultural products and greatly increased the food supply.

## CHEMISTRY AND PHYSICS (EXCLUDING ATOMIC ENERGY)

**1. Scientists and Their Contributions**

*a. Joseph Priestley* (1733–1804), British, discovered the gas *oxygen*.

*b. Henry Cavendish* (1731–1810), British, demonstrated that water consists of two gases, hydrogen and oxygen.

*c. Antoine Lavoisier* (1743–1794), French, pioneered quantitative research methods and is known as the "father of modern chemistry." He proved that, in burning, a substance unites with oxygen.

*d. Alessandro Volta* (1745–1827), Italian, invented the *electric cell*. It made possible discoveries in electricity and magnetism.

*e. André Ampère* (1775–1836), French, made discoveries concerning the relationship between magnetism and electricity.

*f. Michael Faraday* (1791–1867), British, discovered the principle of *electromagnetic induction*, producing electricity by moving a magnet through a wire coil. This principle led to the generating of electricity by use of the *dynamo*.

*g. Dmitri Mendeleev* (1834–1907), Russian, classified chemical elements according to their atomic weights, thereby developing the *Periodic Table*. By its use he was able to predict the existence of elements not then known.

**2. Recent Developments.** These scientists provided the foundation for two of today's giant industries, chemicals and electronics. *(a)* Chemists, usually working in research laboratories, have furnished an array of useful products, such as explosives, building materials, synthetic dyes, flavoring extracts, drugs, synthetic fibers (rayon, nylon, Orlon, Dacron), synthetic rubber and leather, and a wide range of plastics. *(b)* Electronics engineers have produced automatic control devices: thermostats to regulate heating systems, electronic eyes to adjust camera lenses and operate doors, instruments to guide space vehicles, and control panels to direct factories through automation. Scientists have also devised giant *computers*, or electronic brains, which outspeed humans in performing clerical tasks and mathematical calculations.

## ATOMIC ENERGY

### 1. Scientists and Their Contributions

*a. John Dalton* (1766–1844), British, explained the structure of matter by his *atomic theory.* He held that matter is composed of tiny, invisible particles, called *atoms.*

*b. Marie Curie* (1867–1934), Polish-born, together with her husband, *Pierre Curie* (1859–1906), French, discovered the chemical element *radium.* Physicists have used radium to help determine the structure of the atom.

*c. Ernest Rutherford* (1871–1937), British, discovered that the atom consists largely of empty space, with almost all of its mass concentrated in its center, or *nucleus.*

*d. Lise Meitner* (1878–1968), Austrian, predicted that using neutrons to bombard an unstable element, such as uranium, could split its atomic nucleus. Fleeing Nazi Germany in 1938, she later communicated her findings to atomic scientists in America.

*e. Albert Einstein* (1879–1955), a Jew born in Germany, fled his native land because of Nazi religious persecution and became a naturalized American. Einstein, hailed as the outstanding modern theoretical physicist, expressed the complex relationship of matter, space, motion, and time in his *theory of relativity.* Einstein predicted that a small amount of matter could be converted into a tremendous quantity of energy according to the formula $E = mc^2$ (energy equals mass multiplied by the speed of light—186,000 miles [300,000 kilometers] per second—squared). In 1939 Einstein informed President Franklin D. Roosevelt that an atomic bomb could be built and that Nazi scientists were working to that end. Einstein's advice, heeded by the president, was to initiate an American atomic-bomb project.

*f. Niels Bohr* (1885–1962), Danish, described the atom as a miniature solar system. A refugee from Nazi-occupied Europe during World War II, Bohr worked on the American atomic-bomb project.

*g. Enrico Fermi* (1901–1954), born in Italy, fled in 1938 from Fascist Italy and became a naturalized American. He employed slow-speed neutrons to split the nucleus of the uranium atom. Fermi served with the United States atomic-bomb research team and in 1942 achieved the first human-made nuclear chain reaction.

*h. J. Robert Oppenheimer* (1904–1967), American, directed the Los Alamos (New Mexico) laboratory of the *Manhattan Project.* This was the World War II scientific effort that designed and built the first atomic bomb (A-bomb).

*i. Edward Teller* (1908– ), born in Hungary, studied in German universities until 1933, when he fled Nazi rule. He moved to the United States and became a naturalized American. After working on various aspects of atomic energy, Teller headed the American project that in 1952 produced the first hydrogen bomb (H-bomb).

**2. Atomic Energy and War.** America's World War II leaders, determined to secure an atomic bomb before the Germans, inaugurated the Manhattan Project. They mobilized the top scientists—American, British, Canadian, and refugees from Nazi-occupied Europe—and produced an A-bomb containing about two pounds (.9 kilogram) of uranium, which had the explosive power of 20,000 tons (18,000 metric tons) of TNT. In 1945 American airmen dropped the first nuclear bomb in the history of warfare on *Hiroshima,* Japan, killing or injuring 130,000 people and destroying 60 percent of the city. Subsequently scientists developed the hydrogen bomb. With its explosive power several thousand times that of the first A-bomb, a single H-bomb can wipe out all life within a 60- to 100-mile (96- to 160-kilometer) radius.

The destructiveness of nuclear weapons results from their explosive blast, tremendous heat, and radioactivity, which can contaminate large areas. Widespread fear exists that a nuclear war could mean the end of civilization. (For efforts at international control of nuclear weapons, check the Index.)

**3. Atomic Energy and Peacetime Uses.** Scientists devised methods to control nuclear reactions and utilize the tremendous heat to change water into steam. In turn, steam can be used to propel boats and to generate electricity. The United States possesses a fleet of atomic-powered surface ships and submarines and about 70 atomic-powered plants for the production of electricity.

Atomic scientists have also produced radioactive chemical substances called *isotopes.* These have significant uses *(a) in medicine* to diagnose body ills, *(b) in agriculture* to study plant growth and to preserve foods, *(c) in industry* to measure the flow of oil in pipelines and to uncover flaws in metal, and *(d) in science* to explore the structure of matter.

**4. Opposition to Nuclear Power Plants.** With America's growing dependence upon foreign natural gas and oil imports and the depletion of America's domestic petroleum reserves, the United States would be expected increasingly to generate electricity by nuclear power. In recent years, however, many Americans have opposed and delayed the building of nuclear power plants. Community leaders fear the danger of an accidental nuclear explosion and accidental discharge of radioactive wastes; environmental groups fear the effect of the plants' discharge of heated water upon the ecology of nearby rivers and lakes. These groups have maintained their opposition despite the reassuring statements of knowledgeable scientists and despite the government's requirements for plant licensing set by the *Nuclear Regulatory Commission.*

In 1976, voters in seven states defeated proposals to limit the growth of nuclear power plants. These people evidently believed that the need for more energy was greater than the risks posed by nuclear power.

In 1979 nuclear power received a severe setback because of an accident at the Three Mile Island (Pennsylvania) nuclear power plant. Although causing considerable damage to the plant, the accident seemingly caused negligible harm to people and the environment. Nevertheless, the accident aroused public concern and spurred mass antinuclear demonstrations. Opponents charge that nuclear power is not safe, endangers the environment, and lacks facilities for the proper disposal of nuclear waste materials. Nuclear advocates deny these charges, insisting that nuclear power poses less danger to people and the environment than coal or hydroelectric power, and that scientists have solved the problem of nuclear waste disposal. President Carter asserted that, for the foreseeable future, the United States cannot "abandon the nuclear supply of energy." This view was upheld by the President's commission investigating the Three Mile Island accident. After recommending a new regulatory setup and improvements in licensing procedures and safety standards, the commission concluded that, by keeping nuclear risks "within tolerable limits," the country could if it wished continue to develop nuclear power.

## SPACE AGE

**1. The Rocket Engine.** The *rocket*, a cylindrically shaped engine propelled by burning high-energy fuel, provides the powerful thrust necessary to lift vehicles into outer space. Following World War II both Russia and the United States began to develop rockets. In rocket-thrust power the Russians were ahead at first; however, by the mid-1960's, the Russians were overtaken and surpassed by the United States with its mighty *Saturn* rockets.

**2. Beginning of the Space Age.** In 1957 Russian scientists placed into orbit around the earth the first human-made satellite, *Sputnik I*. It weighed 184 pounds (82.8 kilograms) and carried scientific equipment to transmit data regarding outer space. In 1958 the Americans orbited their first earth satellite, the 18-pound (8-kilogram) *Explorer I*. Subsequently both nations placed weather, communications, and other satellites into earth orbit. Also, they launched spaceships to the moon, to Mars, and to Venus. In 1961 the Russians placed into orbit the world's first cosmonaut, Major *Yuri Gagarin*. In 1962 the Americans launched their first orbiting astronaut, Colonel *John H. Glenn*.

In 1969 the United States achieved a historic first as the flight of *Apollo 11* enabled astronaut *Neil Armstrong* to be the first human being to set foot on the moon. In 1972 the United States launched the 570-pound (256.5-kilogram) spaceship *Pioneer 10*, which completed a 21-month journey past the planet Jupiter and was programmed to leave our solar system, traveling toward other star systems in the universe. Pioneer 10 carries a metal plate etched with pictures of a man and a woman and with symbols indicating that it was launched from earth—the third planet of our solar system. Many scientists believe that intelligent beings, capable of interpreting the metal plate, exist elsewhere in the universe. In other words, these scientists hold the opinion that earthlings are not the universe's only intelligent beings. (For further details of the space program, check the Index.)

## IMPACT OF SCIENCE UPON HUMANITY TODAY

1. **Expansion of Scientific Knowledge.** In the four centuries since the "scientific revolution" began during the Renaissance, humanity has witnessed a tremendous expansion of scientific knowledge. The effects of this scientific information explosion include the following: (a) Scientists usually receive intensive training in one restricted area of specialization. They frequently receive little training in related scientific areas and even less in the humanities and social sciences. The scientifically trained person reflects, for better or worse, a "narrow education." (b) To solve major scientific problems, scientists must work together in a spirit of cooperative teamwork. (c) Scientists depend upon computers to store the vast amounts of knowledge and to retrieve such data as they may need for solving problems. (d) Average individuals have little understanding of the scientific principles underlying our industrial society—even of such widely used items as the automobile, refrigerator, air conditioner, and television set. They are concerned mainly with "Does it work?" not with "How does it work?" Society witnesses an ever-widening gulf between the few technically trained persons and the many who are dependent upon them.

2. **Moral and Philosophical Issues Raised by Scientific Progress.** Scientists increasingly realize that their discoveries and inventions raise moral and philosophical issues such as: how to limit the use of nuclear power to peaceful purposes; how to gain the benefits and avoid the ill effects of automation; how to protect the environment against pollution resulting from our mechanized society; and how to determine whether to use complex medical equipment to prolong somewhat the lives of terminally ill people. Especially since World War II, scientists have begun to speak out on such public issues and have sought to exert leadership. Scientists, however, do not speak with a single voice. Depending upon their upbringing, education, and outlook on life, they frequently differ among themselves. Concerned citizens who are not scientists also speak out on public issues raised by scientific progress. These issues, however, are complex and do not permit any easy answers.

One additional philosophical issue raised by scientific progress concerns humanity's view of itself in relationship to the universe. Before the "scientific revolution" humanity viewed itself as standing alone at the apex of creation and the earth as being at the center of the solar system. Scientists now think that other intelligent beings probably exist throughout the universe. Through observation they know that the earth is but one of nine planets revolving about the sun and that our solar system is an ordinary one located toward the edge of the immense Milky Way galaxy. These ideas cause some thinkers to question the importance of humanity in the scheme of life and the meaning of our existence.

3. **Evaluation of Science: Good or Evil?** It is impossible to state whether science is a force for good or evil. Science is a body of knowledge and a method of acquiring such knowledge. Consequently science is merely the servant of hu-

manity. More properly the question that should be asked is whether humanity is a force for good or evil.

Humanity has used science for good purposes: to build laborsaving devices, to provide more leisure, to further human comfort and well-being, to extend the average life span, to wipe out disease, and to employ natural resources more efficiently. But humanity has also used science for evil purposes: to wage war, to torture innocent people, to kill; to bomb and destroy cities, and to seek world domination. What does the future hold? Will humanity use science to further its mastery over nature or to destroy its civilization? That answer lies not with science but within humanity itself.

## MULTIPLE–CHOICE QUESTIONS

1. The pure scientist would be most concerned with   (1) purifying gasoline so as to achieve more miles per gallon   (2) producing complex computers   (3) writing manuals for operating atomic-powered ships   (4) studying the basic truths of our universe.

2. The practical scientist   (1) seeks knowledge for its own sake   (2) usually disregards the findings of pure science   (3) searches for new consumer products   (4) has contributed little to the American standard of living.

3. The scientific method does *not* include   (1) reliance upon written authority   (2) observation   (3) experimentation   (4) retesting the conclusion.

4. The beginnings of modern science may be traced to the   (1) ancient Greek city-states   (2) Roman Empire   (3) Renaissance Era   (4) Industrial Revolution.

5. A theory becomes a scientific law when it is   (1) propounded by a famous scientist   (2) clearly understood by the average citizen   (3) proven true by repeated tests utilizing observation and experimentation   (4) used in constructing machines.

6. Medical science has made the *least* progress in   (1) reducing the strains of urban and industrialized living   (2) increasing the average life span   (3) reducing the death rate in underdeveloped countries   (4) developing preventive medicine.

7. The factor that most sped atomic energy research in the 1940's was the   (1) depletion of coal reserves essential for producing electricity   (2) need of an improved tool for cancer research   (3) desire for more devastating weapons   (4) curiosity of scientists about the structure of the atom.

8. An automated factory would have to   (1) produce only synthetic products   (2) increase its number of workers   (3) decrease its number of machines   (4) employ machines that would control other machines.

9. Which can *best* be described as a reaction against the impersonal nature of a modern technological society?   (1) the assembly line   (2) a union strike for higher wages   (3) the organization of a scientific research team   (4) the movement of some families back to farm life and a more self-sufficient way of living.

10. Which is the *most* accurate statement concerning scientific development?   (1) The future of science is completely predictable.   (2) Humanity must find a balance between the risks and the opportunities being created by scientific progress.   (3) The interaction of science and society is less important today than in earlier ages.   (4) Today's social structure is keeping pace with the invention of new machinery.

## MATCHING QUESTIONS: BIOLOGY AND MEDICINE

| Column A | Column B |
|---|---|
| 1. Freud | *a.* use of antiseptics |
| 2. Jenner | *b.* penicillin |
| 3. Roentgen | *c.* study of white blood corpuscles |
| 4. Metchnikoff | *d.* transmission of yellow fever |
| 5. Mendel | *e.* theory of evolution |
| 6. Salk | *f.* smallpox vaccine |
| 7. Darwin | *g.* use of X rays |
| 8. Pasteur | *h.* germ theory of disease |
| 9. Lister | *i.* streptomycin |
| 10. Waksman | *j.* study of mental disease |
| | *k.* infantile paralysis vaccine |
| | *l.* laws of heredity |

## MATCHING QUESTIONS: GEOLOGY, CHEMISTRY, AND PHYSICS

| Column A | Column B |
|---|---|
| 1. Faraday | *a.* theory of relativity |
| 2. Fermi | *b.* head of the Manhattan Project |
| 3. Teller | *c.* originator of atomic theory |
| 4. Curie | *d.* discovery of radium |
| 5. Einstein | *e.* head of the H-bomb project |
| 6. Dalton | *f.* electromagnetic induction |
| 7. Lyell | *g.* father of modern chemistry |
| | *h.* slow-speed neutrons to split atom |
| | *i.* father of modern geology |

## ESSAY QUESTIONS

1. Explain *one* way in which science has contributed to *each* of the following: *(a)* increased population *(b)* increased material comfort *(c)* more accurate ideas about earth and the universe *(d)* greater utilization of natural resources *(e)* more destructive warfare.

2. Scientific progress is not confined to any one nation or race. *(a)* Prove the truth of this statement by naming *four* great scientists, each of a different nationality. *(b)* Show how the discoveries of *two* of these scientists have affected modern life.

3. For *each* of the following scientists, explain *(a)* his contribution to scientific knowledge and *(b)* the impact of his contribution upon humanity's beliefs or problems.

|  |  |  |
|---|---|---|
| (1) Darwin | (2) Einstein | (3) Freud |
| (4) Jenner | (5) Mendel | (6) Pasteur |

4. More important than the scientific discoveries of the past 400 years is the development of the scientific method or attitude of mind. *(a)* Explain what is meant by the scientific method or attitude of mind. *(b)* Show why the scientific attitude of mind may be considered more important than any scientific discoveries. *(c)* In your opinion may the scientific method be applied successfully to the study of a social or economic question? Give *one* argument to support your point of view.

5. Developments in science in the 19th and 20th centuries have given humanity the power either to advance human welfare or to bring about the complete destruction of civilization. Discuss this statement, giving *one* specific fact to support each of the opposing alternatives facing humanity.

6. Agree or disagree with *each* of the following statements, presenting *two* specific facts to support your opinion: (*a*) The applied scientist depends greatly upon the work of the pure scientist. (*b*) Scientific developments in the 20th century differ considerably from those of the three preceding centuries. (*c*) Because democracy encourages the spirit of free inquiry, democratic nations lead in scientific progress. (*d*) Scientific progress has raised basic moral and philosophical issues for humanity. (*e*) The atomic age has introduced an era of great progress for humanity. (*f*) If modern science enables us to see new worlds, it is because we are standing on the shoulders of giants.

# Part 2. Achievements in Literature and the Arts

## CULTURAL MOVEMENTS

In any time period writers and artists are affected by conditions in society. As a result their works contain certain common characteristics, usually classified as cultural movements.

**Classicism,** which dominated most of the 18th century, was inspired by the classical Greek and Roman civilizations. The style and subject matter aimed to please the aristocracy, who, under the Old Regime, were the main patrons (supporters) of art. Classical works adhered to established rules and emphasized emotional restraint, formality, and dignity.

Typical classicists: in literature—Alexander Pope; in painting—Joshua Reynolds and Thomas Gainsborough; in music—Joseph Haydn.

**Romanticism,** which dominated the early 19th century, expressed the spirit of revolt encouraged by the French Revolution of 1789. Romanticists rebelled against classical tradition. They extolled the worth of the ordinary person; and they asserted the individual's right to live in freedom, to exercise imagination, and to express emotion. Romantic writers and painters described the beauties of nature and the glories of past eras; romantic musicians often expressed nationalist themes.

Typical romanticists: in literature—Walter Scott, John Keats, Alexandre Dumas, Heinrich Heine; in painting—Joseph Turner; in music—Georges Bizet, Giuseppe Verdi, Ludwig van Beethoven, Peter Tchaikowsky, Frederic Chopin, Edvard Grieg.

**Realism,** which arose by the mid-19th century, described the world as it existed, even in its less attractive aspects. Realistic writers dealt with ordinary people and everyday affairs, especially problems emerging from the Industrial Revolution. Realistic painters pictured people and things in a true-to-life style.

Typical realists: in literature—Charles Dickens, Emile Zola, Henrik Ibsen; in painting—Honoré Daumier, Francisco Goya.

**Victorian Age** refers to the years from 1837 to 1901, when Britain was under the reign of Queen Victoria. During this period Britain witnessed the growth of industry, the extension of suffrage to city and farm workers, and the worldwide expansion of British imperial power (influence in and control of other countries). Victorian Age, as a cultural term, is applied chiefly to British literature. Some Victorian writers were romanticists and others realists, but generally they reflected Victorian society: middle-class domination, high moral standards, growth of democracy, and interest in social reform.

Typical Victorian writers: in history—Thomas Carlyle; in poetry—Alfred Tennyson, Robert Browning; in the novel—George Eliot, Thomas Hardy, Robert Louis Stevenson.

**Impressionism,** popular toward the late 19th century, was a revolt against realism. Although some impressionists won fame in music, they were prominent chiefly in painting. They expressed not "photographic" accuracy but the artist's personal reactions.

Typical impressionists: in music—Claude Debussy; in painting—Edouard Manet, Paul Gauguin, Pierre Renoir.

**Modern Tendencies.** Twentieth-century writers and artists have utilized the older movements and also experimented with newer methods of expression: abstract painting, such as *cubism;* nonmelodic and nonharmonic music called *dissonance;* disconnected thoughts of characters in novels, a form of writing called *stream of consciousness;* and *surrealism*—a movement in writing and painting that is influenced by psychology in its attempt to give expression to the subconscious mind.

Modern literature and art have become, within limits, increasingly internationalized. With science providing quick, inexpensive means of worldwide communication and transportation, cultural ideas and works are able to spread rapidly. Many modernists search for originality and individuality, protest against war and brutality, and emphasize the complexity of our society.

Typical modernists: in literature—Marcel Proust, André Breton, Albert Camus, Erich Maria Remarque, James Joyce, Alexander Solzhenitsyn; in music—Arnold Schönberg, Igor Stravinsky; in painting—Henri Matisse, Pablo Picasso, Salvador Dali.

## IMPACT OF SCIENTIFIC PROGRESS UPON CULTURE

**1. Providing New Techniques and Materials:** *(a) Literature.* Modern methods of printing and paper production have substantially lowered the cost of manufacturing literary works, thus making them available to more people. *(b) Music.* Electronics has provided amplification systems that increase musical volume and has devised electronic musical instruments such as the Moog synthesizer. *(c) Performing Arts.* Lighting and staging effects have improved the production of plays, ballets, and operas. *(d) Sculpture.* Stainless steel, aluminum, plywood, wire, metal tubing, and plastics are some of the materials being utilized by modern sculptors.

**2. Introducing New Ideas:** *(a) Psychology.* Writers employ psychology in their works to probe motives and analyze the characters of their subjects. The psychological novel has soared into literary prominence. Novelists have drawn upon psychology for new writing techniques—stream of consciousness and surrealist ramblings. Artists too have looked to psychology to provide inspiration for their works, especially surrealist paintings. *(b) View of Life and the Universe.* New scientific ideas regarding the age of the earth, the process of evolution, the diversity of the universe, and the possibility of intelligent beings elsewhere—all have spurred the imagination of modern writers. Some modernists have developed a new literary field—science fiction. In this field the stories deal with such themes as space travel and life on other planets. Science fiction has gained in popularity with the emergence of the space age.

**3. Inventing New Media of Cultural Expression.** Scientific progress has provided humanity with new art forms, including photography, the motion picture, high-fidelity (hi-fi) sound reproduction, and television.

## BRITISH CONTRIBUTORS

### 1. Writers

*Jonathan Swift* (1667–1745), essayist and writer of fiction, berated humanity for stupidity and intolerance. His *Gulliver's Travels*, intended as a biting satire of society, has become a children's classic.

*Alexander Pope* (1688–1744), classical poet, stated "whatever is, is right" in his often-quoted poem, *Essay on Man.*

*William Wordsworth* (1770–1850), romantic poet, acclaimed the beauty of nature and analyzed human character in *Tintern Abbey, The World Is Too Much with Us*, and *Ode: Intimations of Immortality.*

*Walter Scott* (1771–1832), romantic novelist, wrote adventure stories glorifying the Middle Ages in *Kenilworth* and *Ivanhoe.*

*Jane Austen* (1775–1817), Britian's first important woman novelist, wrote of the daily lives of ordinary people and satirized provincial society. Her best known work, orginally published anonymously, is *Pride and Prejudice.*

*Lord Byron* (1788–1824), romantic poet, died while assisting the Greeks in their revolt against Turkey for independence. With humor and satire, he protested the evils of society in his narrative poem *Don Juan*.

*Percy Shelley* (1792–1822), romantic poet, pleaded for freedom and justice in *Prometheus Unbound*. He proclaimed the wonders of nature in *Ode to the West Wind*.

*John Keats* (1795–1821), romantic poet, praised beauty for is own sake in *Ode to a Grecian Urn*, *The Eve of St. Agnes*, and *To a Nightingale*.

*Thomas Carlyle* (1795–1881), historian of the Victorian Age, held that great men, not impersonal social and economic forces, determine history. Carlyle wrote a famed study *The French Revolution*.

*Alfred Tennyson* (1809–1892) was appointed poet laureate (court poet) of Britain by Queen Victoria. He exalted world peace in *Locksley Hall*, extolled the heroism of British soldiers during the Crimean War in *The Charge of the Light Brigade*, and glorified King Arthur's court in the *Idylls of the King*.

*Charles Dickens* (1812–1870), Victorian novelist, was a realist and social reformer. He portrayed lower-class poverty and attacked the abuses of the Industrial Revolution in *David Copperfield* and *Oliver Twist*. Dickens also wrote the humorous *Pickwick Papers* and a novel of the French Revolution, *A Tale of Two Cities*.

*Robert Browning* (1812–1889), Victorian poet, analyzed individuals in his dramatic poems *Rabbi Ben Ezra*, *My Last Duchess*, and *Andrea del Sarto*.

*Charlotte Brontë* (1816–1855) and her sisters *Emily Brontë* (1818–1848) and *Anne Brontë* (1820–1849) published their works under pseudonyms (pen names) to hide their identities as women. The Brontë sisters possessed vivid imaginations and great writing talent. They are best known for their novels: Charlotte for *Jane Eyre*, Emily for *Wuthering Heights*, and Anne for *Agnes Grey*.

*George Eliot* (1819–1880) was the pen name of Mary Ann Evans, a Victorian novelist. She portrayed common people realistically in *The Mill on the Floss* and described the effect of machinery on a weaver in *Silas Marner*.

*Thomas Hardy* (1840–1928) probed character in realistic novels such as *The Mayor of Casterbridge* and *The Return of the Native*.

*Robert Louis Stevenson* (1850–1894), Victorian romanticist, wrote the adventure novels *Treasure Island* and *Kidnapped* and the poetry collection *A Child's Garden of Verses*.

*George Bernard Shaw* (1856–1950), Socialist and member of the Fabian Society, was an outstanding drama critic and playwright. Shaw satirized prevailing customs and crusaded against war, poverty, and ignorance. He is witty, entertaining, and provocative in such plays as *Caesar and Cleopatra*, *Major*

*Barbara, Man and Superman, Saint Joan,* and *Pygmalion.* (In 1956 *Pygmalion* was transformed into a popular musical comedy, *My Fair Lady.*)

**Rudyard Kipling** (1865–1936), the romantic "poet of imperialism," glorified the British Empire and preached the "white man's burden"—the duty to look after the world's "backward" peoples. He wrote poems, such as *The Ballad of East and West* and *Gunga Din,* and prose works, such as *Soldiers Three* and *Kim.*

**H. G. Wells** (1866–1946), Socialist and Fabian Society member, envisioned the future in imaginative science fiction novels, such as *The Time Machine, The War of the Worlds,* and *A Modern Utopia.* Wells deplored the waste of human resources in realistic novels such as *Tono-Bungay* and *The History of Mr. Polly.* Wells also wrote a very popular one-volume Outline of History.

**John Galsworthy** (1867–1933) traced the life of an English family in his series of realistic novels, *The Forsyte Saga.* Also, he dissected social and economic conflict in the plays *Strife* and *Loyalties.*

**John Masefield** (1878–1967), poet laureate of Britain, wrote realistically of the sea in such poems as *Dauber* and the collection *Salt-Water Ballads.*

**T. S. Eliot** (1888–1965), poet and playwright, although born in the United States, adopted a British outlook and citizenship. He expressed humanity's search for spiritual values in his poem *The Waste Land* and in his poetic drama *Murder in the Cathedral.*

## 2. Painters

**Joshua Reynolds** (1723–1792), classical painter, specialized in portraits of the British aristocracy.

**Thomas Gainsborough** (1727–1788), classical portrait painter, won fame for *Blue Boy.*

**Joseph Turner** (1775–1851), romantic painter of landscapes and water scenes, depicted the old warship *Fighting Temeraire* and *The Battle of Trafalgar.*

## FRENCH CONTRIBUTORS

### 1. Writers

**Victor Hugo** (1802–1885), romantic novelist, sympathized with the downtrodden in his *Hunchback of Notre Dame* and *Les Misérables.* Hugo opposed Napoleon III's dictatorship, disparaged him as "Napoleon, the Little," and was forced to flee France.

**Alexandre Dumas** (1803–1870), romantic novelist, wrote adventure stories, including *The Count of Monte Cristo* and *The Three Musketeers.*

**George Sand** (1804–1876) was the pen name of Amandine Dupin, a novelist who shocked society by her unconventional life-style. She advocated social reforms and urged women's rights as evidenced in her early novels, especially *Indiana*.

*Emile Zola* (1840–1902), realist, wrote a series of novels of 19th-century France depicting life in its sordid aspects. For example, *Nana* exposed Parisian social climbers and *Germinal* portrayed the misery of French coal miners. Zola was a courageous man who championed Manet's paintings when impressionism was unpopular and challenged royalist groups by defending Alfred Dreyfus and the Third French Republic. (See page 229.)

**Guy de Maupassant** (1850–1893) was a realistic writer of novels and especially of dramatic short stories. He portrayed ordinary people and exposed their failings with satire and irony.

**Marcel Proust** (1871–1922), psychological novelist, provided insight into the actions of individuals and society as well as the workings of memory in his cycle of novels, *Remembrance of Things Past*.

**André Breton** (1896–1966), poet and essayist, who had studied Freudian ideas, founded the surrealist school of writing. He also greatly influenced surrealist painting. Dismayed by the human slaughter of World War I, Breton sought to lift humanity to a higher moral level by utilizing the powers of the subconscious mind.

**Albert Camus** (1913–1960), philosopher and novelist, illuminated individual suffering caused by hatred, illness, and war. He is noted for his novels *The Stranger* and *The Plague*.

## 2. Composers

*Hector Berlioz* (1803–1869), romantic composer, was noted for combining music with story and for melodic style. He wrote symphonies, such as *Harold in Italy*, and operas, such as *The Trojans*.

*Charles Gounod* (1818–1893) wrote romantic operas, including *Faust* and *Romeo and Juliet*.

**Georges Bizet** (1838–1875) composed the romantic opera *Carmen*.

**Claude Debussy** (1862–1918) appealed to imagination and mood in such impressionistic works as *Clair de Lune* and *The Afternoon of a Faun*.

**Maurice Ravel** (1875–1937) achieved unusual musical effects in *Rhapsodie Espagnole*, *Bolero*, and *Mother Goose Suite*.

## 3. Painters

*Jacques David* (1748–1825), who painted in both classical and realistic styles, actively supported the 1789 French Revolution and later became court painter for Emperor Napoleon. In addition to many portraits, David created notable historical canvases: *Tennis Court Oath, Coronation Ceremony,* and *Distribution of the Eagles.*

*Eugene Delacroix* (1789–1863), romantic painter, used bold colors and expressed intense emotions. He chose subjects from romantic literature and from history, such as *The Crusaders Entering Constantinople* and *Liberty at the Barricades: 28 July 1830.*

*Honoré Daumier* (1808–1879) became famous chiefly by use of a special printing process called lithography. He produced thousands of *caricatures,* many biting and satirical, of social values and of public figures.

*Edouard Manet* (1832–1883), "father of impressionism," achieved striking landscapes. He is also famous for *Lunch on the Grass.*

*Paul Cézanne* (1839–1906), impressionist, painted landscapes and still lifes. He also depicted the *Card Players.*

*Pierre Renoir* (1841–1919), impressionist, painted the popular *Canoeists' Luncheon.*

*Paul Gauguin* (1848–1903), impressionist, employed startling colors and distortions of shape. Gauguin spent his last years painting the scenery and people of the South Pacific islands.

*Henri Matisse* (1869–1954), modernist, achieved striking effects with his primitive style in such works as *The Piano Lesson.*

### 4. Sculptor

*Auguste Rodin* (1840–1917) conveyed a feeling of power and intensity in his many statues, such as *The Thinker.*

## ITALIAN CONTRIBUTORS

### 1. Composers

*Gioacchino Rossini* (1792–1868), operatic composer, is best known for *The Barber of Seville* and *William Tell.*

*Giuseppe Verdi* (1813–1901), operatic composer, expressed romantic and nationalist themes in *Rigoletto, La Traviata,* and *Aïda.*

*Giacomo Puccini* (1858–1924) was a romantic composer of operas, including *La Boheme, La Tosca,* and *Madame Butterfly.*

### 2. Conductor

*Arturo Toscanini* (1867–1957), orchestra conductor, eventually fled from Fascist Italy and became a naturalized American. Toscanini won acclaim as leader of the *New York Philharmonic Orchestra* and the *NBC Symphony Orchestra.* During the 1930's he refused to perform in Fascist countries.

# GERMAN CONTRIBUTORS

## 1. Philosophers

*Georg Hegel* (1770–1831), strong nationalist, extolled Prussia's monarchical government, equated war with progress, and placed the well-being of the state above that of its citizens. Hegel's ideas encouraged antidemocratic forces.

*Friedrich Nietzsche* (1844–1900) condemned Christianity as a slave religion and democracy as the rule of mediocrity. He believed that a small group of "supermen" would eventually dominate the world. Nietzsche, probably unwittingly, provided the philosophical background for Germany's Nazi movement.

## 2. Writers

*Johann von Goethe* (1749–1832) portrayed the conflict between good and evil and held out hope for the salvation of humans in his dramatic poem *Faust*.

*Friedrich von Schiller* (1759–1805), romantic poet and playwright, won fame for his drama *William Tell*.

*Heinrich Heine* (1797–1856), romantic poet and essayist, attacked despotism and reaction. His most famous poem is *Die Lorelei*.

*Thomas Mann* (1875–1955), realistic novelist, fled Nazi Germany and spent many years in the United States. He probed individual character and the problems of modern Western civilization in *Buddenbrooks, Death in Venice,* and *The Magic Mountain.*

*Erich Maria Remarque* (1898–1970), a refugee from Nazi Germany, became an American citizen. A novelist, he attacked the stupidity and destruction of war in *All Quiet on the Western Front* and portrayed a German refugee doctor in *Arch of Triumph.*

## 3. Composers

*Johann Sebastian Bach* (1685–1750), church organist, experimented with new musical techniques in his many sonatas, concertos, suites, and cantatas.

*Ludwig van Beethoven* (1770–1827), possibly the greatest of all composers, wrote romantic music: sonatas, concertos, an opera, and nine symphonies. His works marked the transition of music from the court and aristocracy to the concert hall and general public. About the *Third (Eroica) Symphony,* it is said that Beethoven tore up a dedication to Napoleon upon hearing that Napoleon had taken the title of emperor. The *Fifth Symphony,* perhaps best known of all symphonies, opens with four notes that Beethoven likened to fate knocking at the door. Beethoven combined orchestra and chorus, which sings Schiller's *Ode to Joy,* in the final movement of the *Ninth (Choral) Symphony.*

*Felix Mendelssohn* (1809–1847), romanticist, created much delightful music. His incidental music for the play *A Midsummer Night's Dream* provided the ever-popular *Overture* and *Wedding March.* He is also known for his *"Italian"* and *"Scotch"* symphonies.

**Richard Wagner** (1813–1883), romantic composer and German nationalist, employed Germanic themes in his operas *Lohengrin, Die Walküre, Die Meistersinger,* and *Tristan and Isolde.*

**Johannes Brahms** (1833–1897), in a romantic style, wrote symphonies, concertos, and a series of *Hungarian Dances.*

## AUSTRIAN CONTRIBUTORS

### 1. Composers

**Joseph Haydn** (1732–1809), classical composer, wrote over 100 symphonies, including the *Clock Symphony* and the *Toy Symphony.*

**Wolfgang Mozart** (1756–1791) helped bridge classicism and romanticism by his symphonies, concertos, chamber music such as *Eine Kleine Nachtmusik,* and such operas as *The Marriage of Figaro* and *Don Giovanni.*

**Franz Schubert** (1797–1828) wrote romantic songs and the ever-popular *Unfinished Symphony.*

**Johann Strauss** (1825–1899), the "Waltz King," composed several operattas and many waltzes, such as *By the Beautiful Blue Danube* and *Tales from the Vienna Woods.*

**Arnold Schönberg** (1874–1951), Austrian-born, taught music in Berlin until 1933 when he fled Nazi rule. Schönberg came to the United States and became an American citizen. He composed symphonies and string quartets. A modernist, Schönberg experimented with musical dissonance and with a 12-tone musical scale.

## RUSSIAN CONTRIBUTORS

### 1. Writers

**Ivan Turgenev** (1818–1883), realistic novelist, described the revolutionary movement in Czarist Russia in his *Fathers and Sons.*

**Feodor Dostoevski** (1821–1881) probed human suffering in his psychological novels *The Brothers Karamazov* and *Crime and Punishment.*

**Leo Tolstoi** (1828–1910), social reformer and novelist, explored life among the aristocracy in *Anna Karenina.* He related Napoleon's invasion of Russia and condemned warfare and hero worship in *War and Peace.*

**Anton Chekhov** (1860–1904) reflected realism and pessimism in the plays *The Sea Gull* and *The Cherry Orchard.*

**Boris Pasternak** (1890–1960), poet and novelist, criticized Communist ethics and rule in his novel *Doctor Zhivago*, only published outside Russia. Awarded the 1958 Nobel Prize for literature, Pasternak rejected the award because of pressures brought by his country's Communist rulers.

*Alexander Solzhenitsyn* (1918–    ), novelist, related his experiences in a Stalinist labor camp in *One Day in the Life of Ivan Denisovich*. His later works, *The First Circle, The Cancer Ward,* and *The Gulag Archipelago,* all highly critical of Soviet society, were denied publication in Russia. Awarded the 1970 Nobel Prize for literature, he accepted and was berated by Soviet government officials. A brave man who defied the Communist regime by upholding the right to dissent, Solzhenitsyn in 1974 was exiled from Russia and eventually settled in the United States.

### 2. Composers

*Peter Tchaikovsky* (1840–1893), romantic and nationalist composer, commemorated Russia's victory over Napoleon with the *1812 Overture*. Tchaikovsky utilized Russian folk themes in his symphonies and concertos, in his opera *Eugene Onegin*, and in his ballet music such as *Swan Lake* and *The Nutcracker*.

*Nikolai Rimski-Korsakov* (1844–1908) wrote romantic and nationalist music based on-folk themes. His works included the opera *The Snow Maiden* and the tone poem *Scheherazade*.

*Igor Stravinsky* (1882–1971) left Russia before World War I and later settled in the United States. A modernist, Stravinsky achieved striking effects in his ballet music *The Rite of Spring, Petrouchka,* and *The Firebird*.

*Aram Khatchaturian* (1904–1978)  used folk themes in his ballet music *Masquerade* and *Gayne*.

*Dmitri Shostakovich* (1906–1975), noted Soviet composer, wrote many nationalist works. He honored the defense of Leningrad during World War II by his *Seventh Symphony*.

## OTHER EUROPEAN CONTRIBUTORS

### 1. Writers

*Henrik Ibsen* (1828–1906), Norwegian playwright, exposed pretense and hypocrisy in realistic plays such as *A Doll's House, An Enemy of the People,* and *Hedda Gabler*.

*James Joyce* (1882–1941), Irish novelist, experimented with stream-of-consciousness writing and innovations in his use of language. He wrote *A Portrait of the Artist as a Young Man, Finnegans Wake* and *Ulysses*.

*Arthur Koestler* (1905–    ), Hungarian-born political essayist and novelist, by 1938 had become disillusioned with communism. He attacked Stalinism in *The Yogi and the Commissar* and *Darkness at Noon*.

## 2. Composers

*Frederic Chopin* (1810–1849), Polish romanticist and nationalist, wrote delightful piano pieces, such as the *Polonaise* and the *Minute Waltz*.

*Franz Liszt* (1811–1886), Hungarian pianist, composed the melodic *Hungarian Rhapsodies*.

*Anton Dvořak* (1841–1904), Czech composer, created romantic and nationalist music, including the *New World Symphony* and the *Humoresque*.

*Edvard Grieg* (1843–1907), Norwegian nationalist, employed native folk themes in his stirring piano concerto and in his *Peer Gynt Suite*.

*Jean Sibelius* (1865–1957), Finnish composer, expressed nationalist feeling in his symphonies and in his tone poem *Finlandia*.

## 4. Painters

*Francisco Goya* (1746–1828), Spanish, excelled in portraits of nobility as well as in realistic, everyday scenes. He also depicted the Spanish uprising against Napoleon and the French reprisals in his works *The Second of May* and *The Executions of the Third of May*.

*Vincent van Gogh* (1853–1890), Dutch modernist, used brilliant colors in still lifes and landscapes such as *Starry Night*.

*Pablo Picasso* (1881–1973), Spanish modernist, who lived chiefly in France, was the "father of cubism." He also painted in other styles and did sculpture, etchings, and illustrations. He achieved unusual effects in his *Three Musicians*.

*Salvador Dali* (1904– ), born and educated in Spain, moved in 1940 to the United States. After a brief early interest in abstract art, Dali became a surrealist painter. Influenced by Freudian psychology, he placed on his canvases dreamlike images, hallucinations, and fantasies. Dali has produced surrealist religious paintings, two surrealist movies, his autobiography, and various books on art.

## MULTIPLE–CHOICE QUESTIONS

1. Classicism in music and painting   (1) originated in the 20th century   (2) sought to please the average citizen   (3) was formal, dignified, and restrained   (4) drew inspiration from primitive cultures of Asia and Africa.
2. The beginnings of the romantic movement in literature and art are sometimes associated with the   (1) Protestant Reformation   (2) Glorious Revolution of 1689   (3) French Revolution of 1789   (4) Russian Revolution of 1917.
3. A realistic writer would probably choose which subject?   (1) difficulties of earning a living in a factory town   (2) beauties of nature   (3) battles of knights against barbarians   (4) happy story of a poor boy's rise to fame and wealth.
4. *Not* an aspect of the Victorian Age in Britain was   (1) growth of democracy   (2) high moral standards   (3) despair about the future   (4) faith in the British Empire.

5. An impressionist landscape painting would (1) show every blade of grass (2) convey the artist's feelings about the scene (3) be best viewed standing close to the canvas (4) show nature to be ugly.

## IDENTIFICATION QUESTIONS: LITERATURE

| | | | |
|---|---|---|---|
| Breton | Hugo | Nietzsche | Solzhenitsyn |
| Byron | Ibsen | Remarque | Swift |
| Dickens | Joyce | Scott | Tolstoi |
| Goethe | Kipling | Shaw | Zola |

1. A nobleman and social reformer, I described Napoleon's invasion of Russia in my novel *War and Peace*.
2. A Victorian novelist, I portrayed the unfortunate effects of the Industrial Revolution in such books as *David Copperfield* and *Oliver Twist*.
3. A Norwegian dramatist, I exposed pretense and hypocrisy in such plays as *An Enemy of the People* and *A Doll's House*.
4. My work *Gulliver's Travels*, intended to satirize humanity's stupidity and intolerance, has become a children's adventure classic.
5. A German philosopher, I criticized Christianity and democracy and predicted world domination by a group of "supermen." Years after my death, my ideas were utilized to justify Nazism.
6. Hoping to point the way to a better world for humanity, I founded the surrealist school of writing.
7. A great German literary figure, I depicted the struggle between good and evil and expressed hope for humanity in my dramatic poem *Faust*.
8. A romantic poet, I protested against corruption and convention in my verse tale *Don Juan*. I died while assisting the Greeks in their revolt against Turkey.
9. A Russian writer, I insisted upon exposing the slave labor camps in the Soviet Union. Although I won the Nobel Prize for literature, I was forced into exile in 1974 by the Communist rulers of my homeland.
10. As the "poet of imperialism," I proclaimed the "white man's burden" and extolled the British Empire.
11. I was a Socialist and writer of satirical plays. My play *Pygmalion* provided the story for the musical show and movie *My Fair Lady*.
12. I was a French romantic novelist and author of *The Hunchback of Notre Dame* and *Les Misérables*. Because I opposed Napoleon III, I was forced to flee from France.

## IDENTIFICATION QUESTIONS: PAINTING AND MUSIC

| | | | |
|---|---|---|---|
| Beethoven | Debussy | Mozart | Tchaikovsky |
| Chopin | Gauguin | Picasso | Van Gogh |
| Dali | Goya | Sibelius | Verdi |
| Daumier | Mendelssohn | Strauss | Wagner |

1. A Russian composer, I utilized native folk themes in many works, such as the ballet music for *The Nutcracker* and *Swan Lake*.
2. Born in Spain, I became a leading exponent of surrealist painting.
3. An operatic composer and German nationalist, I employed Germanic themes in such operas as *Die Meistersinger* and *Lohengrin*.
4. A Spanish painter known for realistic, everyday scenes, I portrayed the resistance of my people against Napoleon.

5. Although known as the "father of cubism," I experimented with many painting styles. A famous work of mine is *Three Musicians*.

6. A romantic composer whose works remain immensely popular, I wrote nine symphonies, including the *Third*, or *Eroica*, and the *Ninth*, or *Choral*, symphonies.

7. An operatic composer and Italian nationalist, I am known for my music for the operas *La Traviata* and *Aïda*.

8. A French lithographer, I won fame for my satirical caricatures.

9. Despite my short life, I helped bridge classicism and romanticism in music. I composed the operas *Don Giovanni* and *The Marriage of Figaro*.

10. A French composer, I applied impressionism to music in such works as *The Afternoon of a Faun*.

11. Born in France, I left my native land for the South Pacific islands, where I utilized impressionist techniques in painting native scenes and peoples.

12. A pianist and Polish patriot, I wrote charming piano compositions such as the *Minute Waltz*.

## ESSAY QUESTIONS

1. The people of certain countries are especially remembered for their contributions in the fields of *(a)* art, *(b)* literature, and *(c)* music. For *each* of these fields, select *one* country and discuss the contributions of *two* famous nationals of that country.

2. *(a)* Name *five* persons who contributed to art or music during the 19th or the 20th century. *(b)* Give *one* specific contribution made by each person mentioned. *(c)* Discuss *one* reason why it is important to learn about a nation's culture.

3. Name *one* European writer of the last 200 years in each of the following fields: *(a)* fiction *(b)* drama *(c)* poetry *(d)* philosophy. For each of *two* of these writers, discuss *one* important idea that was expressed.

4. Many of our great works of literature deal with historical conditions and social problems. Discuss *one* literary work of each of the following, showing how the author used historical facts or social problems: *(a)* Charles Dickens *(b)* George Eliot *(c)* Rudyard Kipling *(d)* Leo Tolstoi *(e)* Victor Hugo *(f)* H. G. Wells *(g)* Erich Maria Remarque *(h)* Alexander Solzhenitsyn.

5. *(a)* Over the past 250 years, literature and art have reflected three major cultural movements: (1) classicism (2) romanticism (3) realism. For each movement explain *two* of its characteristics and name *one* of its leading exponents. *(b)* Name *two* tendencies seen in modern culture. For each tendency named explain whether you think it to be a passing fad or to have permanent value.

6. We have lived in a complex world in which many factors are interrelated. Explain *one* specific way that the items in each of the following groups have been interrelated: *(a)* science and music *(b)* psychology and painting *(c)* war and literature *(d)* nationalism and music *(e)* totalitarianism and culture.

7. Agree or disagree with each of the following statements, discussing *two* specific facts to support your position: *(a)* Victorian novels generally ignored the social and economic problems of the time. *(b)* The advance of the machine age has greatly extended the appreciation of literature. *(c)* The smaller countries of continental Europe have made important cultural and scientific contributions to Western civilization. *(d)* In recent times literature and art have tended to become increasingly internationalized. *(e)* Technological advances have created new and diverse forms of artistic expression.

# UNIT XI. IMPERIALISM AND COLONIAL NATIONALISM

## Part 1. Introduction to Imperialism

### DEFINITION OF IMPERIALISM

*Imperialism* means *control by a powerful nation over an underdeveloped or weaker area.* The powerful nation is usually characterized by an advanced economy, strong government, and considerable military strength. The underdeveloped area is characterized by untapped natural resources, a primitive economy, weak government, and limited military power. Since World War II imperialism has also been called *colonialism.*

### OLD IMPERIALISM (16TH TO EARLY 19TH CENTURY)

**1. Aspect of Commercial Revolution.** During the Renaissance west European nations, desiring trade with the Far East, pioneered direct water routes; explored the New World; founded settlements and trading posts in the Americas, Africa, and Asia; conquered native peoples; and established European rule over them. European nations fought many wars over colonial trade and territory. By 1763 France retained little overseas territory; considerable empires belonged to Holland, Portugal, and Spain; and the leading colonial power was Britain.

**2. Reasons for Decline.** By the early 19th century, west European nations had lost interest in empire building. They were *(a)* exhausted by the Napoleonic Wars, *(b)* occupied with democratic and nationalist movements, *(c)* engaged in industrial development, and *(d)* convinced that the cost of colonies outweighed the benefits to the mother country.

### MODERN IMPERIALISM (SINCE MID-19TH CENTURY)

**1. Fundamental Cause: Industrial Revolution.** Industrialized nations desired colonies to provide *(a)* a cheap and certain supply of *raw materials, (b) markets* reserved for the mother country's manufactured goods, and *(c)* large profits with minimum risk on investment of *surplus capital.*

**2. Other Causes: Related to Nationalism.** The advocates of imperialism used nationalist arguments to gain public support for empire building. They claimed that the parent country would *(a)* gain glory and achieve "a place in the sun," *(b)* secure essential military bases and war materials, *(c)* provide an outlet for surplus population, *(d)* safeguard missionaries spreading Christianity and other humanitarians promoting public health and education, and *(e)* bring to the underdeveloped areas the blessings of the superior culture of the West—a duty labeled by the British writer Rudyard Kipling as the "white man's burden."

## TYPES OF IMPERIALIST CONTROL

**1. Concession.** An underdeveloped country granted to foreign business interests specific economic privileges, or *concessions,* such as to build railroads, open mines, or drill for oil. The underdeveloped country eventually came under the economic and political influence of the imperialistic nation. Example: Before World War I Turkey granted German interests permission to construct the Berlin-to-Bagdad railroad through Turkish territory. Turkey thereafter came under considerable German influence.

**2. Sphere of Influence.** A powerful nation secured *exclusive* economic privileges in an underdeveloped region, thereby establishing a *sphere of influence.* Usually such an economic monopoly was respected by other imperialist nations. Example: Before World War I France, Britain, Germany, and Russia each had exclusive control over tariffs, trade, and economic development in separate parts of China.

**3. Protectorate.** The native ruler remained in power outwardly, but the imperialist nation controlled affairs behind the scenes. Examples: French officials advised the Bey of Tunisia and the Sultan of Morocco. British authorities advised the Sheik of Kuwait.

After World War II a new form of protectorate appeared in eastern and central Europe. Several countries there came under Communist control and became subject to Russian authority. These nations, which may be considered protectorates, are known as *satellites.* (For details, check the Index.)

**4. Colony.** A powerful nation formally took over and governed an underdeveloped area, which became its colony. Examples: Britain annexed Gibraltar and Hong Kong. France took over Indo-China.

**5. Mandate and Trusteeship: Under International Supervision.** Following World War I an attempt was made to introduce reforms in the field of imperialism. Colonies of defeated Germany and Turkey were assigned to victorious nations to be governed under League of Nations supervision as *mandates.* Following World War II the colonies of defeated Italy and Japan, together with the remaining mandates, were placed under United Nations supervision as *trust territories.* Countries administering trusteeships pledged to prepare the native peoples for self-government and to accept the supervision of the *UN Trusteeship Council.* (For details, check the Index.)

EXAMPLES: As mandates, *(a)* Britain received Palestine and Iraq and *(b)* France received Lebanon and Syria. As trusteeships, *(a)* Italy retained Italian Somaliland, *(b)* Australia retained New Guinea, and *(c)* the United States received the former Japanese-mandated islands in the Pacific.

# Part 2. British Empire to Commonwealth of Nations

## IMPORTANCE OF THE BRITISH EMPIRE

**1. Size.** Over three centuries the British assembled history's largest empire. By 1920 the British Empire had reached its greatest extent. It contained one-fourth of the world's land area and population. Its territories, found on every continent, led proud Britons to boast, "The sun never sets on the British Empire."

### The British Empire (1920)

| Location | Members |
|---|---|
| **Europe** | Great Britain, Gibraltar, Ireland, Malta |
| **Africa** | Egypt, Gambia, Gold Coast, Kenya, Nigeria, Nyasaland, Rhodesia, Sierra Leone, Sudan, Tanganyika, Uganda, Union of South Africa, Zanzibar |
| **Indian Ocean** | Mauritius, Seychelles |
| **Asia**<br>1. Middle East<br>2. Far East | <br>Aden, Cyprus, Iraq, Kuwait, Palestine<br>Burma, Ceylon, Hong Kong, India, Malaya, North Borneo, Singapore |
| **Australasia** | Australia, Fiji, New Zealand, Tonga |
| **Americas**<br>1. North America<br>2. South America<br>3. West Indies | <br>Bermuda, British Honduras (Belize), Canada<br>British Guiana<br>Bahamas, Barbados, Grenada, Jamaica, Tobago, Trinidad |

**2. Resources.** The British Empire was a tremendous military force: peoples, raw materials, industries, and strategic bases.

**3. Government Variety.** The British Empire illustrated *(a)* the use of many forms of imperialist control and *(b)* evolution of an empire into a free association of self-governing nations.

**4. Independence and Commonwealth.** The British pioneered in *(a)* granting colonies the status of self-governing, independent *dominions* and *(b)* relating them to Britain in a voluntary association, or *commonwealth.* Insofar as the Commonwealth nations remain loyal to Britain and its democratic traditions, these policies strengthen the free world.

The British Empire has been transformed into the *Commonwealth of Nations,* and the dominions are called *Commonwealth members.*

## INDEPENDENT COMMONWEALTH MEMBERS

**1. Brief History.** Prior to the 19th century, Britain permitted little or no colonial self-government. Usually London appointed colonial officials, and the British Parliament enacted colonial laws. Following the successful revolt of the thirteen American colonies (1775–1783) and an unsuccessful Canadian uprising (1837), Britain questioned the wisdom of strict colonial rule. Thereafter Britain granted Canada limited self-government; from this beginning evolved independent Commonwealth membership.

**2. Self-Government of Commonwealth Members.** Each member exercises full control over its own domestic and foreign affairs, such as coining money, levying tariffs, negotiating treaties, and declaring war.

**3. Independence of Commonwealth Members.** The 1931 *Statute of Westminster,* enacted by the British Parliament, declared that the Commonwealth nations and Great Britain are *(a)* equal in status as independent nations, *(b)* united by common allegiance to the British Crown, and *(c)* voluntarily associated as members of the Commonwealth of Nations.

## STRUCTURE AND MEMBERSHIP OF THE COMMONWEALTH

**1. Structure.** The Commonwealth possesses no rigid organization. It is not based upon formal treaty obligations; it exercises no central control of economic or foreign policy; it cannot prevent member nations from changing their form of government or from seceding from the Commonwealth.

In essence the Commonwealth provides its members with a means of discussing and cooperating upon issues of mutual interest.

**2. Members**

*a. The United Kingdom.* This is the official name for the union of Great Britain (England, Scotland, and Wales) and Northern Ireland.

*b. Old Dominions.* Canada, Australia, and New Zealand, inhabited chiefly by peoples of British origin, received dominion status prior to World War I. Although independent, these members recognize the British Crown both as head of their own governments and as head of the Commonwealth. The crown is

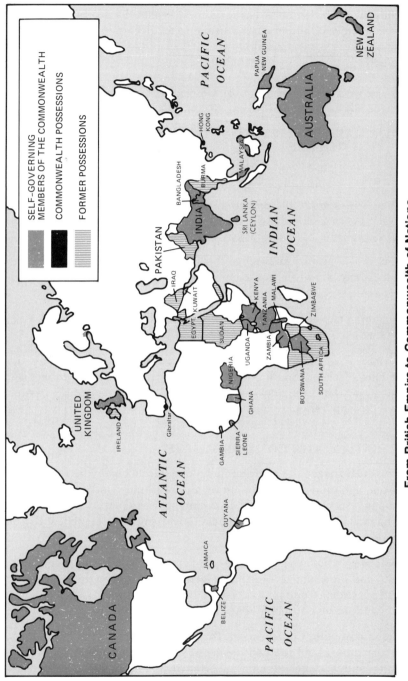

**From British Empire to Commonwealth of Nations**

represented in each of these members by a governor general, who serves as a figurehead. Each dominion has a cabinet, headed by a prime minister, who controls a majority in and is responsible to an elected legislature.

    *c. New Commonwealth Nations.* Many countries, peopled chiefly by native stock, received independence after World War II.

    (1) *In Africa:* Botswana, Gambia, Ghana, Kenya, Lesotho, Malawi, Nigeria, Sierra Leone, Swaziland, Tanzania, Uganda, Zambia, Zimbabwe

    (2) *In Asia:* Bangladesh, India, Malaysia, Singapore, Sri Lanka

    (3) *In the Pacific:* Fiji, Papua New Guinea, Tonga, Western Samoa

    (4) *In the Indian Ocean:* Mauritius, Seychelles

    (5) *In the Mediterranean:* Cyprus, Malta

    (6) *In the Atlantic:* Bahamas; *the West Indies islands of* Barbados, Grenada, Jamaica, Trinidad-Tobago

    (7) *In Central and South America:* Belize, Guyana

These nations all acknowledge the British Crown as head of the Commonwealth. Many, however, are republics, and a few have native rulers—both governmental types that permit no governor general.

**3. Dependencies of Commonwealth Nations.** Some Commonwealth members have possessed colonies, protectorates, and trusteeships.

**4. Former Possessions Rejecting the Commonwealth.** *(a)* Three former dominions—Ireland, South Africa, and Pakistan—became republics and seceded from the Commonwealth. *(b)* Two former colonies—Burma and Sudan—became republics outside of the Commonwealth.

## TIES BINDING THE COMMONWEALTH

**1. British Heritage.** The mother country and the old dominions share a common language, a sentimental attachment to the royal family, and similar customs and traditions, especially a belief in democratic government.

    The new Commonwealth members, in varying degrees, reflect British culture and political ideals.

**2. Defense.** In both world wars the old dominions voluntarily fought alongside Britain, and the Commonwealth received protection from the powerful British navy. Today some Commonwealth members maintain defense agreements with Britain and permit British military bases.

**3. Commonwealth Conferences.** To discuss Commonwealth problems, the member nations hold frequent conferences. These include finance ministers' meetings and top-level but informal prime ministers' meetings. At times, some or all members have agreed upon common action.

**4. Economic Affairs.** Most Commonwealth members depend to a great extent upon Britain to purchase their raw materials, supply manufactured goods, and provide investment capital and technical assistance.

At the 1932 Ottawa Conference, the members encouraged inter-Commonwealth trade by agreeing mutually to reduce tariff rates, a system called *preferential tariffs*. At the 1950 Colombo Conference, the more prosperous Commonwealth members agreed to give economic aid to less developed south and southeast Asian countries. This agreement was called the *Colombo Plan*. In 1960 the Commonwealth decided to encourage financial and technical aid to its African members. This decision became known as the *Special Commonwealth African Assistance Plan*.

## THE COMMONWEALTH TODAY: AN EVALUATION

Some observers question the value of the Commonwealth today, pointing out that:

(1) With some 41 member nations, the Commonwealth includes diverse peoples and cultures, which are also widely separated geographically. The Commonwealth lacks any significant unifying theme or purpose.

(2) The member nations often have conflicting viewpoints and interests. For example: economically, the underdeveloped members compete for aid to spur industrial and agricultural output; socially, Asian nations resent the persecution practiced by several African members against Asian minorities—some of whom have lived in Africa for over 300 years; politically, Britain and the old dominions are democracies and side with the West in the cold war, whereas many newly independent members are one-party states and claim neutrality in the cold war.

"Strained, mate, strained."

(3) Commonwealth Conferences, by tradition, may not discuss internal affairs of members or disputes between members without the consent of the parties involved. Furthermore, the Commonwealth takes no formal decisions on international affairs and has no enforcement powers.

(4) When displeased with the Commonwealth, for any reason whatsoever, member nations may promptly and easily leave the association.

(5) Britain—having declined as a world power, having experienced serious economic problems, and having moved closer to Europe in 1973 by joining the Common Market (check the Index)—lacks the ability to provide the Commonwealth with cohesiveness and leadership.

Defenders of the Commonwealth, while not minimizing its weaknesses, emphasize its value in providing scientific and educational exchanges, financial assistance, people-to-people contacts, and an international forum.

# A. Canada: Commonwealth Member

## ECONOMY AND PEOPLE

Canada possesses rich natural resources: minerals (iron ore, copper, uranium), oil, natural gas, forests, waterpower, and fertile soil. Predominantly agricultural, Canada is a leading producer of foodstuffs, especially wheat. Its industries—food processing, forest products, iron, and steel—are dominated by American corporations. The country exports newsprint, wheat, lumber, and minerals and imports manufactured goods. Canada trades chiefly with the United States.

Canada's population of 23 million encompasses a large minority of French descent and a near majority of British origin. The people generally support compulsory education and enjoy a high standard of living.

## BRIEF HISTORY

Originally French, Canada became a British possession by the Treaty of Paris (1763) that ended the French and Indian War. During the American Revolution (1775–1783), the Canadians remained loyal to Britain, but in 1837 they revolted unsuccessfully. In 1839 self-government for Canada was recommended by a British statesman, Lord Durham, in the famous *Durham Report*. By the *British North America Act* in 1867, Canada became the first dominion.

## CURRENT PROBLEMS

1. **French-English Friction.** Since they constitute an overwhelming majority in the province of Quebec, the French Canadians oppose increased power for the British-dominated central government. Also, they are less enthusiastic than the British about maintaining Commonwealth ties and more concerned with preserving their French heritage. To quiet French-Canadian demands, the central

government enacted laws guaranteeing the use of both French and English in carrying out federal services and in labeling products sold in Canada. The Quebec provincial government contrarily declared the province's official language to be only French. (In 1979, after a Canadian Supreme Court decision, Quebec was compelled to restore the official status of the English language.)

In 1970 *René Levesque*, an ardent advocate of Quebec independence from Canada, founded the *Quebec party—Parti Québécois*. In the 1976 provincial elections, the Parti Québécois defeated the Liberal party, which favored Canadian unity and had controlled the provincial government. The Liberals labored under several handicaps: charges of corruption and economic problems of labor strife, high unemployment, and inflation. The Parti Québécois, meanwhile, played down its demand for independence and emphasized honest government and economic improvement. The Parti Québécois won 41 percent of the popular vote and 69 assembly seats—a clear legislative majority—giving it control of the provincial government. The Liberals fell to 34 percent of the popular vote and only 28 assembly seats.

As Quebec's prime minister, Levesque promised no unilateral move toward independence but pledged to hold a referendum on that issue. Meanwhile, Canada's prime minister, *Pierre Elliott Trudeau*—himself a French Canadian—warned Levesque that he had "been granted a mandate to form a government in the province, not to separate that province from the rest of Canada."

In 1980 Levesque organized a referendum asking the Quebec voters to approve a carefully worded and somewhat ambiguous question—to grant the provincial government a mandate to negotiate with Canada for Quebec to achieve "sovereignty-association"—a term meaning political independence with economic ties. As 60 percent of the electorate voted disapproval, Levesque met a decisive defeat. He pledged to respect the voters' decision.

In the 1981 provincial elections, Levesque and the Parti Québécois promised no new moves toward independence but emphasized their social and economic record. The Parti Québécois won the election, gaining 50 percent of the popular vote and 80 of the 122 seats in the provincial legislature. The Liberals had 46 percent of the popular vote but only 42 legislative seats. Seemingly, the majority

Does this cartoon favor or oppose Quebec independence?

of Quebec's voters opposed Levesque's dream of Quebec independence but supported Levesque's efforts to govern in the interest of the province.

**2. Small Population.** Relative to its size and resources, Canada is sparsely populated. Canada restricts immigrants except from France, the United States, the old dominions, and the British Isles. Since these peoples are little inclined to migrate, Canada's population growth is slow.

**3. Defense.** A free world nation and NATO member, Canada coordinates its defense efforts with the United States. They cooperate in a *Permanent Joint Board of Defense* and a *North American Air Defense Command (NORAD)*. Since planes and missiles may attack via the North Pole region, Canada and the United States maintain, across the top of the continent, defense systems such as the radar *DEW (Distant Early Warning) Line*.

**4. Latent Anti-United States Sentiment.** As democratic nations, Canada and the United States have a history of close and friendly cooperation. Canadians, nevertheless, have protested that the United States exerts too much influence on Canada's culture, economy, and defense. In the 1970's, with its oil reserves declining, Canada sharply curtailed oil exports to the energy-hungry United States. Canada also enacted a tax measure to discourage the circulation in Canada of American magazines and television programs—so as to reduce the American impact upon Canadian culture.

# B. Australia: Commonwealth Member

## ECONOMY AND PEOPLE

Australia possesses mineral resources (gold, coal, uranium, and iron ore), fertile soil, and grazing land. At first mainly agricultural, Australia has been developing industry, including iron and steel, machinery, chemicals, textiles, electrical equipment, cars, aircraft, and ships. It exports wool, meat, wheat, minerals, and some industrial products. Its major trading partners are Japan, the United States, and the Common Market members, especially Britain.

Australia's 14 million people, primarily of British stock, have free compulsory education and a good living standard.

## BRIEF HISTORY

Explored by Captain *James Cook* in 1770, Australia became a British possession. Until 1840 the country served as a penal colony for British criminals and debtors. After the discovery of gold in 1851, Australia attracted many British settlers. In 1900 the country received dominion status.

Famed as an economic and political *experimental laboratory,* Australia pioneered in adopting government railroad and telephone ownership, universal suffrage, and the secret, or Australian, ballot.

## CURRENT PROBLEMS

1. **Population.** Relative to its size, Australia is sparsely populated. In 1901 the government adopted a *white Australia* immigration policy, welcoming British settlers, accepting some other white immigrants, but completely barring Asians. After 1945 racial restrictions were somewhat modified, and in 1973 Australia discarded skin color as a factor in admitting immigrants. Australia's new emphasis was upon the individual's qualifications and the nation's need for skilled workers. Nevertheless, population growth remains very slow.

2. **Defense.** Australia supports Britain, Commonwealth unity, and the free world. Australia is a member of the free world defensive alliance, ANZUS (check the Index).

# C. New Zealand: Commonwealth Member

## ECONOMY AND PEOPLE

New Zealand consists of two large islands 1,200 miles (1,920 kilometers) southeast of Australia. The country exports wool, meat, and dairy products and imports oil, industrial raw materials, and machinery. It trades mainly with Australia, the United States, Japan, and Common Market members, especially Britain.

New Zealand's 3 million people, chiefly of British stock, enjoy high literacy and a comfortable living standard.

## BRIEF HISTORY

Explored by Captain Cook and later annexed by Britain, New Zealand in 1907 received dominion status. The country experimented with new ideas: universal suffrage, income tax, social security, government ownership of basic industries, and compulsory arbitration of labor disputes.

## CURRENT PROBLEMS

New Zealand (1) favors British settlers, (2) supports Britain and the Commonwealth, and (3) belongs to ANZUS.

(Other Commonwealth members, discussed elsewhere in this unit, include India, Bangladesh—formerly East Pakistan, and the African members. For pages, check the Index.)

## D. Ireland: Former Commonwealth Member

### ECONOMY AND PEOPLE

Ireland, the *Emerald Isle,* engages in agriculture—raising grains, potatoes, and sugar beets—and in industry—processing foods and manufacturing metal products, chemicals, and textiles. Ireland trades mainly with France, West Germany, United States, and Britain.

The country contains a population of 3 million, almost entirely Roman Catholic.

### BRIEF HISTORY

England conquered Ireland during the Middle Ages and, for several hundred years, ruled the country harshly. In the 19th and early 20th centuries, the British gradually enacted reforms to eliminate major Irish grievances.

**1. Religious Issue.** Protestant England discriminated against Catholic Ireland by *(a)* forbidding Catholics to hold political office and *(b)* taxing Catholics to support the Anglican Church in Ireland.

SOLUTION. In 1829 the *Catholic Emancipation Act* declared Catholics eligible for public office. In 1869 the *Disestablishment Act* ended taxation of Irish Catholics for the support of a church to which they did not belong.

**Ireland and Great Britain**

**2. Land Issue.** Through conquest and rule, English landlords gained ownership of most Irish farmlands. Chiefly *absentee landlords,* the English extorted high rents from the Irish peasants who remained as tenant farmers. (The Irish raised potatoes as their principal crop and main food. During Ireland's potato famine of the 1840's, many Irish migrated to the United States.)

SOLUTION. From 1870 to 1903 Parliament passed several *Land Acts* providing long-term, low-interest government loans to enable Irish tenant farmers to purchase their landholdings. The leading advocate of such legislation was Britain's prime minister, *William Gladstone.*

**3. Independence Issue.** Britain denied Irish demands for self-government and independence. Twice in the late 19th century, Parliament defeated Gladstone's proposals for Irish *home rule.*

In 1905 Irish nationalists formed the *Sinn Fein party.* Its outstanding leader was *Eamon de Valera.* In 1916, while Britain was fighting World War I, the Irish revolted in the unsuccessful *Easter Rebellion.* Thereafter, the Sinn Fein began guerrilla warfare to evict the British.

SOLUTION. In 1921 Ireland (without Ulster province) received dominion status. Gradually the Irish government severed its political ties to Britain. During World War II Ireland remained officially neutral. In 1949 the *Republic of Ireland* withdrew from the Commonwealth.

## ULSTER: A REMAINING AND COMPLEX ISSUE

**1. Economy and People.** Ulster, or Northern Ireland, constitutes one-fifth of the area of the entire Irish island. Although its farms grow agricultural surpluses, Ulster is mainly industrial—producing textile machines, building ships, and manufacturing Irish linens. The major cities are *Londonderry* and the capital, *Belfast.*

Ulster contains 1.5 million people divided into two groups hostile toward each other: (1) Protestants, descendants of 17th-century English and Scottish settlers (the Scotch-Irish), totaling two-thirds of the population and (2) Irish Catholics. In 1921 Ulster voted to remain part of the United Kingdom. The vote was condemned by Ireland, which demanded the return of Ulster. Ulster, however, remained part of Great Britain, electing members to Parliament in London but being ruled locally by its own government. Because of their majority, the Protestants through their *Unionist party* controlled the local legislature and executive and dominated the Ulster government.

**2. Violence in Ulster.** In 1969, as tensions between Protestants and Catholics mounted, Ulster erupted into violence. The Protestant-dominated government pledged to remedy justifiable Catholic grievances of police brutality and of discrimination in voting, jobs, and public housing. Despite this pledge, Catholic militants in the outlawed *Irish Republican Army (IRA)* continued bombings and shootings and demanded that Ulster be reunited with the rest of Ireland.

Protestant militants organized their own paramilitary force, the *Ulster Defense Association*. As violence continued, Britain sent troops to Ulster, suspended the local government, and imposed direct British rule. (Thereafter, the IRA also engaged in terrorist bombings in England.)

**3. Actions of the Irish Republic.** Believing that the reunification of Ireland must come through consent, not coercion, the Irish Republic began a crackdown on the IRA. The Irish Republic's government argued that IRA terrorism hindered reunification by embittering relations between Ulster Catholics and Protestants. Also, Irish voters in 1972 strongly approved a referendum deleting from the Irish Constitution the clause granting the Roman Catholic Church a "special position." Although this referendum did not remove Irish laws reflecting Catholic views on birth control, mixed marriages, and divorce, it was hailed by Irish leaders as a move for "peace and reconciliation." In 1976, after IRA bombings in the Irish Republic, Prime Minister *Liam Cosgrave* requested drastic legislation to crush the terrorists. Cosgrave termed the IRA a "conspiracy of hate and evil" and charged that IRA crimes "have brought discredit to the name of Irishmen throughout the world and death and damage to our own people."

**4. Recent Developments.** In 1974, operating under a new constitution that required a sharing of power in the executive branch between Protestant and Catholic leaders, a new Ulster government took office. *Brian Faulkner*, a Protestant moderate, was executive head and *Gerry Fitt*, a Catholic moderate, served as deputy. This compromise arrangement was opposed by the IRA and also by Protestant militants led by the Reverend *Ian Paisley*. The new Ulster government soon collapsed under pressure of a general strike called by Protestant militants. Britain reimposed direct British rule, violence continued, with the number of deaths rising to about 2,000 persons; and the Ulster problem was no nearer to solution.

In 1979 prominent voices were raised against terrorism in Ireland. American political leaders of Irish ancestry condemned violence by all parties in Ulster and urged Americans to cease contributions of guns and money to the IRA. Prime Minister *Jack Lynch* of the Irish Republic told Americans that money given to the IRA "goes to make widows and orphans." *Pope John Paul II,* on a visit to Ireland, condemned terrorism, appealed for an end to "hatred and violence," and warned that "violence destroys the work of justice."

In 1980–1981, a number of IRA members jailed in Ulster demanded special political status and undertook hunger strikes. As the British government rejected their demand, some fasted to death. Their funerals occasioned further outbreaks of violence.

# E. South Africa: Former Commonwealth Member

## ECONOMY AND PEOPLE

South Africa is a prosperous country. Its farm and grazing lands raise corn, wheat, fruit, and wool. Its cities contain food processing, chemical, textile, armament, and iron and steel industries. Its mines—in addition to providing coal, uranium, iron ore, copper, and platinum—lead the world in the production of gold and diamonds. (By dominating the diamond industry, one South African company—it is claimed—keeps world diamond prices high.) South Africa exports minerals and agricultural produce and imports oil and manufactured goods. Its major trading partners are West Germany, Japan, United States, and Britain.

South Africa has a population of 22 million. *(a)* Eighteen percent are *European,* or *white,* of Dutch and British origin. The Dutch, or *Afrikaners* (formerly called the *Boers*), by a ratio of 3 to 2, outnumber the British. The whites speak Afrikaans or English, both official languages of the republic. *(b)* Sixty-nine percent are *black,* mainly various Bantu tribes. The blacks speak several Bantu dialects. *(c)* Nine percent are *colored,* of mixed black and European ancestry. *(d)* Four percent are *Asian,* of Indian origin.

## BRIEF HISTORY

**1. Boers Resent the British.** In 1815 Holland ceded the Cape Colony to Britain. The Dutch settlers detested British rule, British abolition of Negro slavery, and British immigrants. In the 1830's the Boers left British territory in a northward mass migration called the *Great Trek.* Eventually they founded two republics: the *Orange Free State* and *Transvaal.* The discovery of Transvaal gold in the 1880's attracted British fortune seekers. The Boers resented their coming and restricted their political rights.

**2. Rhodes Incites the Boer War.** In 1890 *Cecil Rhodes*—the Kimberley (South Africa) diamond-mine millionaire—became head of Britain's Cape Colony. Rhodes envisioned a British African empire extending the full length of Africa, from Capetown to Cairo. As a necessary step, Rhodes set out to annex the two

Boer republics. In the Boer War (1899–1902) that followed, Britain, with considerable difficulty, defeated the resolute Dutch settlers and annexed their territories.

**3. South Africa Becomes a Dominion and Supports Britain.** In 1910 Britain combined its South Africa colonies into a self-governing dominion, the *Union of South Africa*. The dominion constitution limited voting and officeholding essentially to the white population. The Boers, who outnumbered the British settlers, assumed political control.

*Louis Botha* and *Jan Smuts*, former Boer generals, each of whom served as prime minister, urged their people to uphold the dominion arrangement. During World War I Botha suppressed a Boer anti-British revolt and aligned his country with Britain. During World War II Smuts barely secured legislative approval for South Africa to join Britain against Nazi Germany. In the 1948 elections Smuts met defeat; the *United party*—supported by most British and some Dutch voters—lost control of the government.

**4. South Africa Becomes a Republic and Leaves the Commonwealth.** Since 1948 the Afrikaner *Nationalist party* has governed South Africa. The Nationalists secured a slim majority in 1960, authorizing South Africa to change from a dominion to a republic. At a Commonwealth conference in 1961, South Africa, agreeing to a discussion of its black segregation policy, came under bitter attack from Asian, African, and Canadian members. Prime Minister *Hendrik Verwoerd* thereupon announced that South Africa would not remain in the Commonwealth. Later Verwoerd indicated that South Africa wished to maintain its historic friendship and economic ties with Britain.

In 1966 Verwoerd was succeeded as prime minister by *Balthazar Johannes (John) Vorster*. In 1978, after serving for 12 years, Vorster resigned because of poor health and was succeeded by *Pieter Botha*.

## CURRENT PROBLEMS

**1. Racial Strife: Apartheid.** South Africa has long followed a policy of discrimination against and segregation of nonwhites. Since 1948 the Nationalists have intensified segregation by adopting an apartness program, called *apartheid*. City blacks, who provide the major source of labor for South Africa's industries, are restricted to the lowest-paying jobs. Also, they must carry identification passes and must reside in designated sections called *black townships*. Rural blacks must occupy special tribal reserves. Blacks have no vote and no say in the national government. Blacks and some whites—mainly of British descent—have protested apartheid by riots, strikes, and violations of segregation laws. In a major confrontation at Sharpsville in 1960, rioters were suppressed by South African forces only after the killing of 70 blacks.

In addition to severe anti-riot actions, the government passed repressive laws—notably the *Suppression of Communism Act* and the *Suppression of*

*Terrorism Act.* It also imprisoned protest leaders, often holding them in jail for considerable periods without trial or subjecting them to "house arrest." The best known person restricted to "house arrest" was the black civil rights leader of the *African National Congress* and 1960 Nobel Peace Prize winner Chief *Albert Luthuli.* The government also adopted other "internal security" measures, such as banning public protest gatherings and prohibiting "subversive" organizations.

**The Soweto Riots.** In 1976 black and colored youths rioted intermittently for several months. The riots began in the urban black township of *Soweto,* spilled over into nearby white-inhabited *Johannesburg,* and spread throughout the country. The riots at first protested the government's decision that black school children above the 4th grade be instructed in only the Afrikaans tongue. The riots later expanded into a major protest, including a strike by some black workers, against South Africa's racial policies. The blacks, however, were not united, and several skirmishes took place between Bantu tribes hostile to each other. Altogether, the riots resulted in some 300 dead, many more injured, and almost 2,000 arrested before the government was able to end the unrest.

The government made minor concessions: withdrawing the order for the compulsory use of Afrikaans in teaching black students and permitting blacks to buy houses with secure land titles—instead of leaseholds—in black townships. The government, however, viewed the riots as a "Communist plot" and indicated that it remained fully committed to the policy of apartheid.

**2. Bantustans: Transkei.** By the 1959 *Promotion of Bantu Self-Government Act,* the South African regime legislated the policy of "separate development" of racial groups by calling for the establishment of black homelands, or *Bantustans.* (*a*) There are now nine black homelands. One—Transkei—is a compact area; the others consist of scattered land parcels in the process of being consolidated. Of South Africa's total area, the nine black homelands comprise 13 percent. They do not contain any great wealth-producing resources but are mainly the less desirable rural land areas. (*b*) All blacks are considered citizens, not of South Africa, but of their homelands—whether or not they live there. They have the right to vote for and hold office in their homeland governments. (*c*) Urban blacks, who live in the white-designated areas and work in mines and factories, are considered to be "guest workers." (*d*) All Bantustans are to be trained in self-government and are eventually to receive full independence.

The Afrikaners justify the "separate development" policy as follows: (*a*) They are the "white tribe" of Africa—mostly the descendants of 17th-century Dutch settlers who were the first ones in the area. The whites found and developed South Africa's resources. (*b*) Subsequently the blacks came to South Africa— brought in as slaves or attracted by the country's prosperity. The blacks today are the descendants of these later arrivals. (*c*) "Separate development" will limit friction between and allow for the independent progress of different peoples— whites as against blacks and black tribes hostile toward one another.

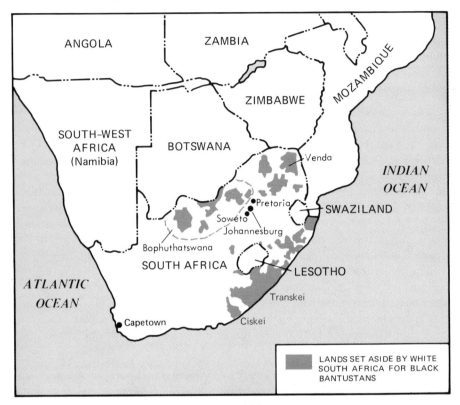

**Southern Africa**

Black South African leaders, supported by most world speakers, condemn the Bantustan policy, for many reasons: (a) Although they total 69 percent of South Africa's population, the blacks are to receive only 13 percent of the land area and, at that, the least desirable lands. (b) Urban blacks, who total over half the black population and whose labor is essential for South Africa's economy, are permanent dwellers in the white areas. Nevertheless, they are denied civil rights and subjected to discrimination by the fiction that they are "guest workers." (c) Bantustans perpetuate white supremacy and will lead inevitably to racial conflict. The solution for South Africa's racial problems, say black leaders, is full equality for all its peoples in a multiracial state.

**Transkei.** In 1976 Transkei became the first Bantustan to receive independence. Located in southeastern South Africa with a coastline on the Indian Ocean, Transkei is inhabited by 1.7 million people of a Bantu tribe known as the Xhosa. (An additional 1.3 million Xhosa live and work elsewhere in South Africa.) In size and population Transkei is larger than one-third of the UN member nations. Chief *Kaiser Matanzima*, in accepting independence for his country, admitted that Transkei was economically dependent upon South Africa but pointed out that so were most nations in South Africa. He warned South Africa that failure to treat blacks fairly "will lead to an increase in black militancy."

At the UN the General Assembly, by a 134–0 vote, adopted a resolution declaring Transkei independence to be a sham. It called upon its members to refrain from "all contacts" with Transkei or any future Bantustans.

South Africa has granted independence to additional Bantustans—in 1977 to *Bophuthatswana*, in 1979 to *Venda*, and in 1981 to *Ciskei*.

**3. South-West Africa (Namibia).** A large territory bordering on the Atlantic Ocean, South-West Africa contains farms, ranches, copper mines, and diamond fields. Its population, now about 900,000, is *(a)* one-ninth white—of German, Afrikaner, and British descent and *(b)* eight-ninths black—of various tribes with a history of tribal warfare.

Captured by South African troops during World War I, South-West Africa was taken from Germany and assigned to South Africa as a League of Nations mandate. After World War II South Africa was refused UN permission to annex the territory, and in turn South Africa refused to place the territory under the UN Trusteeship Council (check the Index). In 1966 the UN General Assembly passed a resolution declaring the South-West Africa mandate ended and ordering UN control of the territory—later given the name *Namibia*. In 1971 the International Court of Justice advised that South Africa was occupying the territory illegally. In 1973 the General Assembly declared the *South-West Africa People's Organization (SWAPO)* to be the "authentic representative of the Namibian people." SWAPO, with arms from Communist nations, has conducted sporadic guerrilla warfare against South African control.

In defiance of these UN initiatives, South Africa continued to rule the territory and warned that it would resist any UN interference. In 1975, however, after the Portuguese colonies of Mozambique and Angola in southern Africa gained independence, Prime Minister Vorster stated that South Africa would grant independence to South-West Africa. The Afrikaner government refused to recognize SWAPO—a refusal supported by rival black groups in Namibia. In 1978 South Africa held elections, boycotted by SWAPO, for a South-West African National Assembly and later granted it some local legislative powers. The elections gave an overwhelming majority to a moderate, multiracial South African-backed party, the *Democratic Turnhalle Alliance (DTA)*. Also, South Africa agreed to an independence plan—proposed by five Western nations—that called for UN-supervised elections with SWAPO participation. In early 1981 negotiations to implement this plan ended in failure amidst charges of South African intransigence against and UN bias for SWAPO.

In mid-1981 South African forces crossed the border into Angola and attacked SWAPO guerrilla bases. South Africa reported knocking out radar and antiaircraft installations and wounding and killing several hundred Angolan and guerrilla troops as well as a number of Soviet advisers. At the UN, a Security Council resolution condemning South Africa for the raid was vetoed by the United States. The American delegate explained that the United States deplored the South African raid but that the Security Council resolution was unbalanced—not mentioning SWAPO raids into South-West Africa nor Cuban and Russian support for SWAPO-incited violence.

Copyright © 1976. The Chicago Sun-Times. Reproduced by courtesy of Wil-Jo Associates, Inc. and Bill Mauldin.

"I'm sure we have
a little more time . . ."

**4. International Censure.** Because of its racial policies, South Africa faces the world almost alone. The other African nations, mostly black-led, have demanded full rights for South Africa's blacks. The Asian nations, especially India (concerned over the Indian population in South Africa), have protested South Africa's discriminatory practices. The Communist nations have denounced South Africa in their propaganda against the West. The free-world nations have condemned apartheid as morally wrong.

The African nations have secured UN resolutions (a) censuring South Africa for racial discrimination, (b) threatening to expel South Africa from the UN, and (c) urging UN members to act against South Africa by severing diplomatic relations, imposing economic boycotts, and banning military shipments.

The South African government has (a) insisted that apartheid is a domestic issue over which the UN has no authority and (b) argued that, in a multiracial country, the outnumbered whites would lose control to the black majority. South Africa stands almost alone but defiant.

**5. Recent Developments:** (a) Prime Minister John Vorster acted to eliminate apartheid practices that "cause offense and serve no purpose." Accordingly the government removed "white only" signs from park benches; desegregated some luxury hotels, restaurants, libraries, and opera houses; allowed some racially mixed sports events; and sent a multiracial delegation to the UN General Assembly. (b) Prime Minister Vorster fostered efforts to improve relations with some black African states by expanding trade, extending financial aid, and promoting discussions and visits between South African and black African leaders. (c) Prime Minister Botha granted most black workers the right to join black trade unions that have the power to negotiate with management regarding labor conditions. He also announced plans to ease restrictions on blacks under the identification pass system. (*d*) Prime Minister Botha urged the voluntary recruitment of nonwhites—coloreds, Asians, and blacks—into South Africa's defense forces. (*e*) The Botha government in 1980 replaced the all-white upper house of Parliament by a multiracial advisory President's Council. Its members, appointed by the prime minister, include whites, coloreds, and Asians but no blacks. (*f*) The Botha government announced that beginning in 1981 it would gradually institute compulsory schooling for black children.

Botha's moves to ease certain disabilities against South Africa's nonwhite population aroused strong criticism among apartheid supporters in the Africaner communities and the ruling Nationalist party.


# F. Commonwealth Colonies

The Commonwealth also includes a number of British colonies. Each is headed by a governor appointed by the British government. Some colonies control their internal affairs through locally elected legislatures.

The remaining British colonies, chiefly small military bases, include (1) in the Mediterranean—Gibraltar, (2) in the Pacific—Hong Kong, and (3) in the Atlantic—Bermuda.

Former British colonies include (1) the independent republic of Burma and (2) the Commonwealth members of Cyprus, Ghana, Guyana, Jamaica, Lesotho, Malta, Nigeria, Trinidad-Tobago, Sierra Leone, Sri Lanka, and Zimbabwe.


# G. Commonwealth Protectorates

The Commonwealth no longer has protectorates. Former British protectorates are (1) the independent nations of Egypt, Kuwait, and Southern Yemen and (2) the Commonwealth members of Botswana, Malaya (part of Malaysia), Malawi, Swaziland, Uganda, Zambia.


# H. Commonwealth Trusteeships

The Commonwealth's last major trust territory (part of a South Pacific island), which had been administered by Australia, received independence and Commonwealth membership in 1975 as Papua New Guinea.

Former British mandates and trust territories are (1) Tanganyika, the major portion of the Commonwealth member Tanzania, and (2) the independent Middle East nations of Iraq, Israel, and Jordan.

# Part 3. Other Empires

## A. *The French Empire*

### EXTENT PRIOR TO WORLD WAR II

As a colonial power, France before World War II ranked second only to Britain. In 1939 the French Empire included: (1) In Africa—Algeria, French Cameroon, French Equatorial Africa, French Morocco, French Somaliland, French Togoland, French West Africa, Madagascar, and Tunisia. (These African territories constituted the major portion of France's empire.) (2) In the Middle East—Lebanon and Syria. (3) In the Far East—the Indo-Chinese states of Cambodia, Laos, and Vietnam. (4) In the Americas—French Guiana and several small Caribbean and Atlantic islands. (5) In the Pacific—several small islands.

The French Empire contained 20 times the area and twice the population of France.

### TERRITORIAL LOSSES SINCE WORLD WAR II

Weakened by World War II and challenged by colonial nationalism, France granted independence to almost all its African, Middle Eastern, and Far Eastern possessions. Today France retains only French Guiana and some small islands of relatively minor importance.

### FRENCH COMMUNITY: NOW DEFUNCT

Under the 1958 Gaullist constitution, the Fifth Republic established the *French Community.* This organization, modeled after the British Commonwealth, was to associate France with certain possessions scheduled for independence. Community members were to (1) exercise complete self-government, (2) follow common economic and defense policies and consult regarding foreign affairs, and (3) retain the right to withdraw from the Community.

Twelve African nations, formed from the French territories of West Africa, Equatorial Africa, and Madagascar, in 1960 received independence within the French Community. As a number of these former French possessions withdrew, the French Community became a nonfunctioning organization.

France, however, maintains strong ties with most French-speaking African nations by granting economic aid, staffing military bases, providing technical military assistance, and holding regular consultations on common problems.

## B. *Other West European Empires: Now Vanished*

Several other West European nations that had acquired colonies subsequently gave up control over major territories. These nations are Belgium, Germany, Italy, Spain, and Portugal, which gave up colonies in Africa; and the Netherlands, which gave up the East Indies—now called Indonesia.

# C. The United States Empire

## IMPETUS TOWARD IMPERIALISM

The United States embarked upon overseas imperialism following (1) the rapid expansion of American industry after the Civil War (1861–1865) and (2) the disappearance of cheap land with the close of the frontier (after 1890). Americans looked abroad for new markets, sources of raw materials, and opportunities for capital investment. Some Americans also held that the United States needed foreign possessions (1) to be considered a first-class power and (2) for strategic military reasons.

With victory in the Spanish-American War (1898), the United States emerged as an imperialist power.

## AMERICAN COLONIAL POSSESSIONS: FROM ACQUISITION TO PRESENT STATUS

The United States, recalling its own colonial history, has followed an enlightened policy toward its possessions. The United States has improved economic conditions, provided health and educational facilities, and generally trained dependent peoples for self-government.

### American Territorial Acquisitions and Present Status

| Possessions | How Acquired | Present Status |
| --- | --- | --- |
| Alaska | Purchased from Russia (1867). | State since 1959. |
| Hawaii | Annexed at request of American settlers (1898). | State since 1959. |
| Philippines | Ceded by Spain (1898). | Independent since 1946. Remains an American ally. |
| Puerto Rico | Ceded by Spain (1898). | Commonwealth since 1952. Remains freely associated with the United States and exercises complete local self-government. |
| Guam | Ceded by Spain (1898). | Colony. Serves as a military base in central Pacific. |
| Some Samoan Islands | Annexed (1899). | Colonies. Serve as military bases in the Pacific. |
| Panama Canal Zone | Leased in perpetuity by treaty with Panama (1904). | In 1978 the United States agreed to turn over the canal to Panama by the year 2000. |
| Virgin Islands | Purchased from Denmark (1917). | Colonies. Serve as military bases in the Caribbean to protect Panama Canal. |
| Many West Pacific Islands | Transferred from Japanese control by UN Security Council (1947). | Trusteeship. The United States has defense posts but grants local self-rule to some islands. |

## D. *The Soviet Russian Empire: Communist Imperialism*

Since World War II Soviet Russia—powerful and industrialized—has extended control over additional non-Russian peoples by (1) annexing territories on its borders, in particular the small Baltic nations of Estonia, Latvia, and Lithuania, and (2) dominating a group of East and Central European Communist nations—Bulgaria, Czechoslovakia, East Germany, Hungary, Poland, and Rumania—as protectorates, or *satellites* (check the Index). By trade agreements, military occupation, intervention, and alliance, and by Communist party interrelationships—the Soviets compel the supposedly independent satellite governments to accept Russian leadership in domestic and foreign affairs. The Russians permit some deviations but stand ready to crush forcibly any satellite government that "goes too far astray"—as in Hungary (1956) and Czechoslovakia (1968). (For these countries, check the Index.)

Also, the Russians seek to extend their influence into the newly independent Afro-Asian nations by supporting colonial nationalists against the West and by offering military, technical, and economic aid. To thwart Russian expansion into the underdeveloped nations, the free world, led by the United States, (1) offers economic and military assistance and (2) attempts to convince these nations not to exchange their newly won independence for Russian imperialist control.

### MULTIPLE–CHOICE QUESTIONS

1. The *least* significant factor in bringing about colonial expansion in the 19th century was (1) religious persecution (2) the growth of manufacturing (3) improved transportation and communication (4) accumulation of surplus capital.

2. What did imperialist nations most look for in a colony? (1) stable government (2) natural beauty (3) undeveloped natural resources (4) a cultural heritage.

3. Another word for imperialism is (1) communism (2) colonialism (3) capitalism (4) racism.

4. The Old Imperialism arose as a result of the (1) Crusades (2) Commercial Revolution (3) Reformation (4) French Revolution.

5. *Not* an aspect of the Old Imperialism was the (1) desire for trade with the Far East (2) establishment of colonies in the New World (3) establishment of trading posts in Asia (4) need for oil.

6. Which sequence best shows the historical development of a 19th-century colonial power? (1) nationalism, imperialism, industrialization (2) imperialism, nationalism, industrialization (3) nationalism, industrialization, imperialism (4) industrialization, imperialism, nationalism.

7. An important factor in establishing western Europe's dominant position in world affairs (1763–1914) was its (1) abundance of natural resources (2) outstanding achievements in literature (3) political revolutions (4) technological developments.

8. When Morocco was outwardly ruled by its sultan but really controlled by the French, it was considered to be a (1) dominion (2) mandate (3) protectorate (4) concession.

9. When an oil company was granted permission to drill for oil, as in a certain part of

Saudi Arabia, the arrangement was generally known as a   (1) concession   (2) mandate   (3) protectorate   (4) trusteeship.

10. A phrase used by Kipling to describe British imperialism is   (1) "spread culture"   (2) "long live the Queen"   (3) "white man's burden"   (4) "a place in the sun."

11. In the British Empire self-government was first extended to   (1) crown colonies   (2) dominions   (3) mandated territories   (4) naval bases.

12. Which legally established the Commonwealth of Nations?   (1) Reform Bill of 1832   (2) Glorious Revolution   (3) Statute of Westminster   (4) Durham Report.

13. The Statute of Westminster (1931) provided for   (1) abolition of slavery in colonial areas   (2) land reform in Ireland   (3) religious freedom in Canada   (4) political equality for the dominions with the mother country.

14. Which phrase best describes the Commonwealth of Nations today?   (1) an English-speaking union   (2) a voluntary union of independent states   (3) a confederation with equal representation in the British Parliament   (4) a military alliance.

15. The Durham Report recommended that Canada   (1) lift its immigration restrictions   (2) be subject to strict British control   (3) set up a joint board of defense with the United States   (4) be given self-government in internal affairs.

16. Which marked a step in the growth of self-government within the British Empire?   (1) the policy of apartheid in South Africa   (2) the Colombo Plan   (3) the British North America Act of 1867   (4) the Parliament Act of 1911.

17. One limiting factor in the economic development of Canada is insufficient   (1) mineral resources   (2) exportable products   (3) available foreign capital   (4) population.

18. In 1976 Quebec elections the Parti Québécois   (1) gained a majority of the popular vote   (2) won a majority of seats in the Quebec assembly   (3) came in second to the Liberal party   (4) dropped its demand of independence for Quebec.

19. Because it originated in that country, the secret ballot is also known as the   (1) Australian   (2) British   (3) Irish   (4) South African ballot.

20. During the 1840's many Irish migrated to the United States because   (1) America lifted its immigration restrictions   (2) Britain suppressed the Irish Easter rebellion   (3) Ireland gained home rule   (4) Irish farms had several crop failures.

21. During the 19th century absentee landlordism was a major cause of discontent in   (1) Canada   (2) India   (3) Ireland   (4) South Africa.

22. Sinn Fein was the name of   (1) an Irish nationalist party   (2) a British imperialist   (3) a South African nationalist party   (4) a Bantu tribe.

23. The Irish Republican Army is the   (1) Irish volunteer brigade that helped Britain in World War II   (2) military arm of the Irish Republic   (3) terrorist group seeking to unite Ulster with the rest of Ireland   (4) terrorist group seeking to make Britain a republic.

24. Of South Africa's total population, the whites consist of about   (1) 20%   (2) 40%   (3) 60%   (4) 70%.

25. What American event is comparable to the Great Trek in South African history?   (1) War of 1812   (2) westward migration   (3) emancipation of the slaves   (4) establishment of Indian reservations.

26. The policy of apartheid in the Union of South Africa was   (1) imposed by the British after the Boer War   (2) advocated by the Afrikaner Nationalist party   (3) proposed by the Bantus   (4) introduced by the Communists.

27. The apartheid program in South Africa calls for separation of   (1) blacks from whites   (2) British from Afrikaner   (3) farming from grazing   (4) powers between the central and provincial governments.

28. In 1976 South Africa granted independence to a Bantustan known as (1) Namibia (2) Soweto (3) Rhodesia (4) Transkei.

29. The major portion of France's empire before World War II was in (1) Africa (2) Asia (3) North America (4) South America.

30. The United States emerged as an imperialist power following (1) the Civil War (2) the Spanish-American War (3) World War I (4) World War II.

31. A former American colony that has become an independent nation is (1) Puerto Rico (2) Alaska (3) Panama (4) the Philippines.

32. An aspect of Communist Russian imperialism is (1) acquiring colonies in Africa (2) sending Soviet artists to perform in the United States (3) suppressing free speech in Soviet Russia (4) acquiring satellites in Eastern and Central Europe.

## MATCHING QUESTIONS

| *Column A* | *Column B* |
|---|---|
| 1. Leader of Irish independence party | *a.* Cecil Rhodes |
| 2. Author of a report on Canada | *b.* Ian Paisley |
| 3. English explorer in South Pacific | *c.* Lord Durham |
| 4. Afrikaner leader who took South Africa out of the Commonwealth | *d.* John Vorster |
| | *e.* James Cook |
| 5. Leader of Quebec separatists | *f.* René Levesque |
| 6. British advocate of Irish home rule | *g.* William Gladstone |
| 7. British imperialist who advocated a Cape-to-Cairo railroad | *h.* Jan Smuts |
| | *i.* Kaiser Matanzima |
| 8. Black South African civil rights leader who won 1960 Nobel Peace Prize | *j.* Albert Luthuli |
| | *k.* Eamon de Valera |
| 9. Boer general who later supported Britain | *l.* Hendrik Verwoerd |
| 10. Prime minister of South Africa who sought to improve relations with some black African nations | |

## ESSAY QUESTIONS

1. (*a*) Discuss *two* economic causes for the growth of imperialism in the second half of the 19th century. (*b*) Describe *two* ways in which a nation exercised imperialistic control without annexation of territory.

2. (*a*) Give *two* specific facts to prove that the Commonwealth dominions are independent countries. (*b*) Discuss *two* bonds between Britain and its old dominions. (*c*) Explain whether or not each of these bonds exists between Britain and the newer members of the Commonwealth.

3. Illustrate *one* way in which each of the following strengthened or weakened the British Empire: (*a*) Durham Report (*b*) Statute of Westminster (*c*) Boer War (*d*) Catholic Emancipation Act (*e*) Colombo Plan (*f*) Sinn Fein.

4. The Republic of South Africa is a land of great wealth and great racial strife. (*a*) Show in *two* ways that the Republic of South Africa is a land of great wealth. (*b*) Explain *two* reasons for racial strife in South Africa. (*c*) Explain *one* reason why the democratic world is concerned over the racial issue in South Africa.

5. The British Empire enjoyed a predominant position in the world for over 200 years. (*a*) Discuss *two* reasons for Great Britain's rise to world power during the period 1750–1940. (*b*) Describe *two* conditions that helped to bring about the decline of the British

Empire. *(c)* Select *one* of the former British colonial areas herein listed and show that it continues to have major problems even though it has achieved independence: (1) Canada (2) Ireland (3) South Africa.

6. Discuss whether *each* of the following is true or false, giving *two* reasons to support your point of view: *(a)* The policy of imperialism was not motivated entirely by economic factors. *(b)* The "white Australia" immigration policy served the best interests of that country. *(c)* Canada has benefited greatly, both economically and militarily, from its relations with the United States. *(d)* For Quebec to separate from Canada would be a tragic mistake. *(e)* The solution to the Ulster problem requires, not violence, but goodwill and understanding on all sides. *(f)* The UN General Assembly was justified in calling the independence of Transkei a sham. *(g)* The United States has followed a policy of strict rule over its colonies. *(h)* Although the Communists denounce imperialism, the Soviet Union is itself an imperialist nation.

7. "When [the imperialist] wants a new market for his adulterated . . . goods, he sends a missionary to teach the natives the gospel of peace. The natives kill the missionary; [the imperialist] flies to arms in defense of [religion]; fights for it, conquers for it; and takes the market as a reward from heaven."

—George Bernard Shaw

*(a)* Which aspect of imperialism is Shaw most clearly criticizing? Explain your answer. *(b)* Has Shaw provided a balanced statement or a biased statement on imperialism? Present *two* arguments to support your point of view. *(c)* In reply to Shaw, how would missionaries justify their activities in underdeveloped countries?

# Part 4. Africa

## AFRICA: LAND AND PEOPLE

**1. Geography.** Africa is a huge continent, three times as large as Europe. Africa extends from west to east at its widest part about 4,500 miles (7,200 kilometers) and from north to south about 5,000 miles (8,000 kilometers). It is geographically divided into several areas: *(a)* The northern coast, in the north temperate zone, borders the Mediterranean Sea. *(b)* To the south lies a vast region of sand, the Sahara Desert. It extends over 3,000 miles (4,800 kilometers) west to east across the width of Africa and ranges north to south from 800 to 1,400 miles (1,280 to 2,240 kilometers), reaching into the tropical zone. The Sahara Desert has been a major land barrier to the movement of African peoples. *(c)* Still farther southward in the tropics lies sub-Saharan Africa. An immense area, it contains tropical grasslands, rain forests, or jungles and in its eastern part mountains and highland plateaus. *(d)* The southernmost portion of the continent extends into the south temperate zone.

Africa's Mediterranean and Atlantic coasts have for centuries been accessible to European ships. However, until the late 19th century, its inhospitable interior—desert, mountain, plateau, and jungle—discouraged exploration and remained unknown to the outside world. Hence, Africa was called the *Dark Continent*.

**2. Resources.** Africa possesses great wealth in the form of: *(a)* Minerals—gold in South Africa, diamonds in South Africa and Zaire, copper in Zaire and Zambia, bauxite in Ghana, phosphates in Morocco, and uranium in South Africa and Zaire. *(b)* Oil—in Algeria, Libya, and Nigeria. *(c)* Agricultural produce. Although large portions of Africa's lands—desert, semi-arid grassland and rain forest areas—are not suited for farming, the continent contains sufficient fertile soil to produce substantial crops—rubber in Liberia; cacao in Ghana; coffee in Ethiopia, Kenya, and Tanzania; and cotton in Uganda, Sudan, and Egypt. The African continent also produces much palm oil, sisal fiber, and tropical woods.

**3. Population.** Africa contains the following peoples: *(a)* Fewer than 5 million whites of European descent reside in Africa's cooler regions. Some remain on the Mediterranean coast and the interior plateaus, but most are found at the southern tip of the continent in South Africa. *(b)* Some 80 million Moslems, primarily Arabs along with some Berbers, reside on Africa's northern coast. They constitute the five North African nations: Morocco, Algeria, Tunisia, Libya, and Egypt. These five nations are separated from the rest of Africa geographically by the Sahara Desert and ethnically by their inhabitants being not blacks but Arabs. *(c)* Over 300 million blacks reside in Africa from the Sahara Desert southward.

# OLD IMPERIALISM IN AFRICA

From the 16th through the 18th centuries, Europeans looked to Africa (1) for bases to supply their ships sailing to the Far East and (2) for slaves to sell to the New World. In the early 19th century, however, Europeans lost interest in imperialism generally and in Africa specifically. (1) The advent of the steamship lessened the need for African supply bases. (2) Humanitarian and other considerations led to the outlawing of the slave trade.

# MODERN IMPERIALISM: INTEREST IN AFRICA (SINCE MID-19TH CENTURY)

**1. Work of Explorers.** *David Livingstone*, Scottish missionary and doctor, spent many years (1840–1873) serving the peoples and exploring the lands of central Africa. *Henry M. Stanley*, American newspaper reporter, headed an expedition in 1871 that "found" the presumably "lost" Livingstone. Later Stanley undertook additional explorations. In well-publicized reports these two men, as well as other explorers, described the geography, resources, and peoples of Africa.

**2. Other Groups Interested in Africa.** The glowing reports of explorers reawakened Europe's interest in Africa. Business leaders saw economic opportunities. Missionaries wanted to convert the blacks to Christianity. Nationalists dreamed of empire building unopposed by the primitive Africans.

# EUROPEAN NATIONS PARTITION AFRICA

## 1. Britain

*a. To Protect Trade Routes to the East.* In 1815 Britain acquired from Holland the *Cape Colony*. It included Capetown, a port at southernmost Africa that served as a supply base for British ships enroute to India. In 1875 Prime Minister *Disraeli* purchased from the bankrupt ruler of Egypt sufficient stock to give Britain control of the *Suez Canal*. By sailing through the canal, British ships eliminated the long voyage around Africa. In 1882 Britain established a protectorate over Egypt. Britain's trade route to India—via Gibraltar, the Mediterranean Sea, the Suez Canal, and the Red Sea—became known as the *lifeline of the British Empire*. (See map, page 356.)

(The non-African territories on this lifeline Britain acquired as follows: (1) Gibraltar, guarding the western entrance to the Mediterranean Sea, was seized in the early 18th century during a war with Spain. (2) Malta, an island in the central Mediterranean, was occupied by British forces who evicted the French during the Napoleonic Wars. (3) Cyprus, an island in the eastern Mediterranean, was transferred to British control in the late 19th century by Turkey. (4) Aden, on the south Arabian peninsula coast at the entrance to the Red Sea, was seized by Britain in the mid-19th century to suppress Indian Ocean pirates and to serve as a coaling station.)

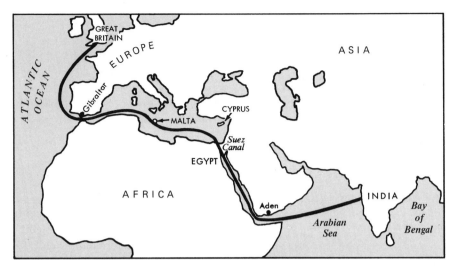

**The British "Lifeline" to India**

*b. To Gain a Rich Empire.* Cecil Rhodes, foremost empire builder in Africa, dreamed of an unbroken north-south line of British territory to be linked by a *Cape-to-Cairo* railroad. Rhodes' ambition became British policy. By 1914 the British dominated South Africa, Rhodesia, Northern Rhodesia (now Zambia), Kenya, Uganda, and the Sudan, as well as Egypt. After World War I, Britain acquired the final link for the railroad, the former German East Africa, or Tanganyika (now Tanzania).

Also, by the beginning of the 20th century, British control was firmly established in Sierra Leone, Gambia, the Gold Coast (now Ghana), and Nigeria—all on the west coast of Africa.

**2. France.**

*a. Colonial Acquisitions.* For economic gain and nationalist glory, the French gained a considerable African domain. By 1847 the French had subdued the Moslem tribes and gained control of Algeria. Between 1881 and 1912 France acquired Tunisia, Morocco, West Africa (now Benin, Guinea, Ivory Coast, Mali, Mauritania, Niger, Senegal, and Upper Volta), Equatorial Africa (now Chad, Central Africa, Congo, and Gabon), and Madagascar.

*b. Imperialist Conflicts.* French expansion clashed with the aims of other imperialist nations. *(a)* Italy resented French seizure of Tunisia (1881) and allied itself with Germany. (See Triple Alliance, page 431.) *(b)* Britain took over the Sudan (1898), and France surrendered its claims in order to win Britain's friendship. (See Fashoda Affair, page 431.) *(c)* Germany challenged France over Morocco (1905, 1911), but France retained control. (See Crises Preceding World War I, pages 432–433.)

**3. Germany.** Late unification delayed Germany's imperialist ventures. Nevertheless, by 1914 Germany possessed several African colonies. But after Germany's defeat in World War I, these colonies were distributed as mandates: Tanganyika to Britain; Togoland and most of the Cameroons to France; South-West Africa to South Africa.

**4. Italy.** Another late starter was Italy. By 1914 it controlled Eritrea, Italian Somaliland, and Libya. In 1936 Italy conquered and annexed Ethiopia. Defeated in World War II, Italy surrendered its African possessions.

**5. Portugal.** As a 16th-century maritime power, Portugal early established supply bases and trading posts on the east and west coasts of Africa. (In the mid-1970's Portugal granted independence to its African territories: Portuguese Guinea [now Guinea-Bissau], Mozambique, and Angola.)

**6. Spain.** By the early 20th century, Spain controlled Spanish Morocco (opposite Gibraltar) and Spanish Sahara on the Atlantic coast of Africa. (In 1956 Spain ceded Spanish Morocco to newly independent Morocco. In 1976 Spain surrendered Spanish Sahara [now Western Sahara] to Mauritania and Morocco.)

**7. Belgium.** In 1876 King *Leopold* II and a group of Belgian capitalists founded a private company to manage the Congo region (now Zaire). The company reaped huge profits from rubber and ivory but shockingly mistreated the natives. In 1908 the Belgian government took control of the Congo.

## AFRICANS OPPOSE IMPERIALISM: REASONS

The native Africans felt that any benefits of imperialism—such as industries, jobs, public works, schools, and health facilities—were outweighed by its evils.

**1. Economic.** (*a*) The Europeans seized the fertile lands and the rich mineral resources. Often they tricked the natives. (*b*) The Africans worked long hours for low wages and lived in unbelievable poverty. (*c*) The continent's wealth benefited the foreign investors, not the native peoples.

**2. Social.** The Africans were considered inferior, subjected to humiliating discrimination, limited as to educational opportunities, and belittled culturally.

**3. Political.** The Africans received little training for self-government, their countries remained under European rule, and their nationalist demands for self-government went unheeded.

## AWAKENING AFRICAN NATIONALISM

Emerging after World War I, colonial nationalism swept Africa and, especially after World War II, became a powerful anti-imperialist force. By agitating for political independence, social equality, and economic betterment, African nationalists reflected the impact of world forces.

1. **Western Influences.** Africans became aware of Western ideals as expressed in the American Declaration of Independence, which proclaimed that "all men are created equal" and endowed "with certain unalienable rights," and in the French Revolution, which inspired democracy and nationalism. They also learned of the improved living conditions that resulted from industrialization, labor unions, and government regulation. This knowledge came to Africa through colonial and missionary schools, printed materials, radio programs, movies, and the few African leaders educated in West European and American schools.

2. **Communist Propaganda.** Communists told Africans that they could achieve a brighter future if they drove out the imperialists. Then the Africans could utilize their natural wealth for their own betterment. Such propaganda stimulated African nationalists, most of whom were not Communists.

3. **Effects of World War II.** World War II sapped the military and economic strength of the major African colonial powers: Belgium, France, and Britain. They became more inclined to yield to African nationalist demands.

4. **Newly Independent Asian Nations.** Following World War II Africans became hopeful that they too would achieve independence when they saw one Asian nation after another free itself from European control.

5. **United Nations.** Africans were cheered as the UN proclaimed the right of all peoples to self-determination, declared independence the objective of trusteeships, and provided an international forum to discuss grievances.

6. **Changing World Attitude.** Especially after 1945, the world came to realize the evils of imperialism and the justice of many African demands.

## Africa Today

### INDEPENDENT AFRICAN NATIONS IN 1945

**Liberia,** a black republic, was founded in 1822 by the United States as a haven for freed slaves. In 1980, as Liberia faced unemployment, inflation, and political corruption, a military coup ousted the government that, since the country's founding, had been dominated by the descendants of freed American blacks. President William Tolbert, Jr. was killed, and political control passed to a descendant of native Liberians, Master Sergeant *Samuel K. Doe.* He announced plans to improve the economy but no change in Liberia's friendship for the United States.

**South Africa,** granted self-government by Britain in 1910, later became an independent white-ruled republic that discriminates against its large black majority. (For a discussion of South Africa, check the Index.)

**Egypt** in 1922 ended the British protectorate and gained independence. (For a discussion of Egypt, check the Index.)

Ethiopia fell in 1936 to an invading Italian army. With Italy's defeat in World War II, Ethiopia regained independence and thereafter acquired as a federated province the former Italian colony of Eritrea. In 1974 a military coup deposed Emperor *Haile Selassie* and instituted military rule.

*Recent Developments Affecting Ethiopia.* The military government changed Ethiopia's foreign policy from pro-Western to pro-Soviet. It ordered the closing of American military, communications, information, and health centers in Ethiopia; it proclaimed policies of socialism; and it received considerable quantities of Soviet arms and numbers of Russian military advisers.

The Ethiopian military regime faced conflict in two areas. In the northeast, Arab-supported Eritrean rebels battled for independence for Eritrea. In the southeast region of Ogaden, Somali guerrillas supported by Somali regular troops sought to transfer the Ogaden region from Ethiopia to Somalia.

Since both Ethiopia and Somalia were Soviet "client" states and received Soviet arms, their conflict endangered Soviet plans to dominate the strategic East African region known as the *Horn of Africa.* Unable to persuade Moscow to cease its aid to Ethiopia, the Somali government in late 1977 ended its "client" relationship with the Soviet Union. Somalia (1) renounced its 1974 treaty of friendship and cooperation with the Soviet Union; (2) ordered all Soviet advisers—military and civilian, numbering several thousands—out of Somalia; and (3) ended Soviet use of all land and sea bases in Somalia. Also, Somalia broke relations with Communist Cuba as 12,000 troops of Cuba's African contingent, originally employed in Angola (check the Index), came to the aid of Ethiopia.

Thus strengthened, the Ethiopian forces gained the upper hand in the Ogaden region. Thereupon, in 1978 Somalia withdrew its troops from Ethiopian territory. The fighting, however, has continued on a limited scale. Somali

## African Nations Gaining Independence Since 1945

| Former Colonial Power | African Nations |
| --- | --- |
| **Great Britain** | 1. *Outside the British Commonwealth:* Sudan<br>2. *Within the British Commonwealth:* Botswana, Gambia, Ghana, Kenya, Lesotho, Malawi, Nigeria, Sierra Leone, Swaziland, Tanzania, Uganda, Zambia, Zimbabwe |
| **France** | 1. *In North Africa:* Algeria, Morocco, Tunisia<br>2. *In West and Equatorial Africa:* Benin, Cameroon, Central Africa, Chad, Congo, Gabon, Guinea, Ivory Coast, Mali, Mauritania, Niger, Senegal, Togo, Upper Volta<br>3. *In East Africa:* Djibouti<br>4. *Off the southeast coast of Africa:* Malagasy |
| **Italy** | Libya, Somalia (a union of Italian and British Somaliland) |
| **Belgium** | Burundi, Rwanda, Zaire |
| **Portugal** | Angola, Guinea-Bissau, Mozambique |

guerrillas have ambushed Ethiopian and Cuban forces; Ethiopian fighter planes, believed to be piloted by Cubans and East Germans, have bombed Ogaden villages. An estimated 1 million Ogaden refugees have fled into Somalia.

Somalia received American economic, military, and refugee aid. In 1980 Somalia granted the United States use of the naval and air base at Berbera just south of the Red Sea.

In Eritrea, meanwhile, Ethiopian and rebel forces battled inconclusively.

## LAST AREAS OF EUROPEAN CONTROL IN AFRICA

**French Somaliland (Territory of the Afars and Issas).** Located on the east African coast at the southern entrance to the Red Sea, this small but strategic area is at the center of the Horn of Africa. The area is inhabited by the Afars—a people of Ethiopian ancestry—and the Issas—a Somali-speaking people. The Afars and Issas are hostile toward each other, as are the territory's two bordering nations, Ethiopia and Somalia.

Ethiopia is concerned over the territory economically because 80 percent of Ethiopia's imports and exports are carried, via railroad, through the territory's seaport of Djibouti. Ethiopia charges that Somalia plans to annex the territory and interfere with Ethiopia's trade, which charges Somalia denies.

In 1977, in a referendum conducted by France, the territory's inhabitants voted overwhelmingly for independence. The nation took the name *Republic of Djibouti.*

**Western (Spanish) Sahara.** Located on the northwest coast of Africa, Western Sahara recently discovered rich phosphate deposits, used for making fertilizer. The territory was claimed by three bordering nations: Mauritania, Algeria, and Morocco. In 1976 Spain withdrew from Western Sahara, the southern one-third going to Mauritania and the northern two-thirds to Morocco. In 1979 Mauritania withdrew from the southern region, which Morocco then annexed.

Since 1976 Morocco has fought a difficult guerrilla war against forces of the local independence group, the *Polisario Front.* The Polisario rebels are equipped with the latest Soviet-bloc arms supplied by Algeria and Libya. The war has drained Morocco's economy, weakened the morale of its soldiers, and, according to some observers, endangered the regime of King *Hassan II*—a friend of the United States. To combat the rebels, the United States sold Morocco considerable military equipment. At the UN, however, the General Assembly declared the Polisario Front the valid representative of the Western Saharan people.

**Portuguese Colonies in Africa.** Portugal for many years managed to suppress various African rebellions against its rule. In 1974 Portugal experienced a revolution that overthrew the rightist dictatorship and established a leftist government. The new Portuguese regime granted independence to its colonies in Africa:

**Portuguese Guinea.** Located on the west coast of Africa just below Senegal, tiny Portuguese Guinea received independence in 1974 as *Guinea-Bissau.*

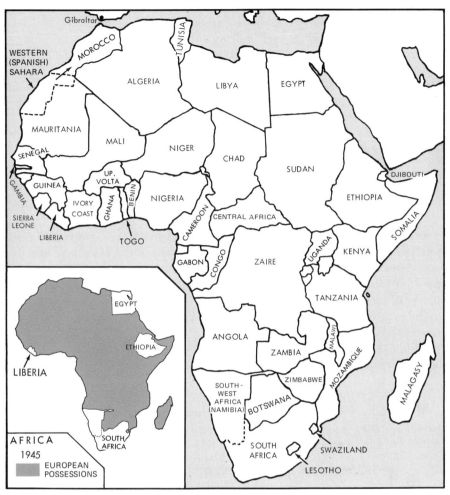

**Africa Today**

*Mozambique.* Located on the southeast coast of Africa, Mozambique in mid-1975 became independent. The *Mozambique Liberation Front (FRE-LIMO)*, which for years had waged guerrilla warfare against Portuguese rule, took control. Mozambique became a one-party, pro-Marxist state. Its first president was the FRELIMO leader, *Samora Machel.* Although a black nationalist committed to ending white-minority rule in Africa, Machel was aware of Mozambique's economic dependence upon South Africa. Some 100,000 Mozambicans were migrant workers in South African mines, and many others held jobs created by South African exports through Mozambique ports.

Following independence, Mozambique's economy declined so that President Machel in 1980 announced measures to improve conditions. While reaffirming his belief in socialist nationalization and central planning, Machel pledged to return small businesses to private ownership and invited foreign corporations to invest in his country. Machel appealed to the 200,000 Portuguese settlers who had fled after 1975 to return to Mozambique with their skills as farmers, business managers, and professionals.

Mozambique's economy benefited from the 1980 independence of Zimbabwe. Previously, Mozambique had closed its borders to pressure the white-minority regime in Rhodesia, and Mozambique had suffered over $500 million in lost port, trade, and transport revenues. With Zimbabwe now independent, Mozambique and Zimbabwe resumed normal economic relations.

The Machel regime faces sporadic attacks by guerrilla groups, possibly supported by South Africa.

*Angola.* Located on the southwest coast of Africa, Angola is twice the size of Texas and contains some 6 million blacks—mainly of various Bantu tribes. The country is predominantly agricultural but also mines diamonds, iron ore, and copper and produces petroleum from offshore oil wells.

In late 1975 Portugal withdrew from Angola, leaving the country independent but without any official government. Battling for control were three groups, each reflecting in part tribal divisions. Two groups were pro-Western and one—the *Popular Movement for the Liberation of Angola (MPLA)*—was pro-Soviet. The pro-Western groups were supported by black-ruled Zaire and Zambia and by white-ruled South Africa. The pro-Western groups also received some covert (secret) military aid from the United States, but this aid was soon prohibited as Congress overwhelmingly passed the *Clark Amendment*. (Although President Ford considered such aid vital for American foreign policy, the congressional vote reflected fears of American involvement in another Vietnam-type situation.)

Meanwhile, the Soviet Union strengthened the MPLA by sending massive amounts of military equipment and military advisers. Communist Cuba also sent 15,000 troops to Angola. Thus reinforced, the MPLA by 1976 established mili-

"It never fails to give me a quiet chuckle when I read all
that chat about black or white majority rule . . ."

*Mac, London Daily Mail ROTHCO*

tary control. (The MPLA, however, still faces guerrilla attacks by rival groups, especially the pro-Western *National Union for the Total Independence of Angola (UNITA)*, led by *Jonas Savimbi.*)

The MPLA victory had various repercussions. White-ruled Rhodesia and South Africa feared that leftist black Africans, supported by the Cuban force, would subject their regimes to military pressure. The United States warned Cuba that "we cannot tolerate again a Cuban military adventure anywhere" and told the Soviet Union that its behavior in Angola harmed efforts to improve Soviet-American relations. Finally the United States became increasingly involved, trying peacefully to solve the problem of Rhodesia.

## AMERICAN INTERESTS IN SOUTHERN AFRICA

1. **Social.** Of the total American population, over 10 percent are blacks. They view Africa as their ancestral homeland and are concerned over the status of black Africans.

2. **Economic.** The United States depends upon southern Africa for imports of diamonds, copper, manganese, chromium, and oil; for markets for American manufactured goods; and for profitable investment opportunities. In South Africa alone, American corporations have invested 1.5 billion dollars.

3. **Foreign Policy.** The United States wishes to prevent any further expansion of Communist, especially Soviet, influence in southern Africa. If the Soviet Union were to dominate southern Africa, the Communists would be able to control the sea lanes around Africa and to enhance their prestige in the developing nations comprising the "Third World."

4. **Humanitarian.** The United States wishes to prevent a race war in southern Africa. Such a war would be costly in terms of people killed or maimed and of material goods destroyed. It would heighten racial tensions, thus poisoning international relations, and, further, might involve the major powers, which, in turn, would raise the threat of a nuclear holocaust.

Aware that Rhodesia was a major danger spot, Secretary of State Henry Kissinger undertook personal diplomacy to achieve a peaceful solution.

## RHODESIA BECOMES INDEPENDENT AS ZIMBABWE

1. **Geography.** Located in south central Africa, Zimbabwe is a landlocked country. It is bordered by three black African nations—Botswana, Zambia, and Mozambique—and by white-ruled South Africa.

2. **Economy and People.** Mostly a high, level plateau, Zimbabwe contains good grasslands and fertile soil. Its farmers raise tobacco, sugar, cotton, maize (corn), and meat. The country possesses rich mineral resources, especially asbestos, copper, gold, and chromium. It manufactures mainly chemicals and clothing.

The population is about 6 million. The blacks, constituting 95 percent, are mostly members of various Bantu tribes. The whites, numbering 300,000, or the remaining 5 percent, are of European descent, chiefly British.

**3. The Breakaway Regime.** Until 1965 Rhodesia, as a British colony, exercised local self-government under a white-minority regime. Its black African population had no vote. The Rhodesian government rejected Britain's proposal to move rapidly toward majority, meaning black, rule. In 1965 Rhodesian Prime Minister *Ian Smith* unilaterally declared his country independent.

The British government labeled the breakaway regime "illegal" and applied economic sanctions: suspending preferential tariffs, banning purchases of Rhodesia's sugar and tobacco, and embargoing oil shipments. Britain, however, rejected the demands of African nations to crush the rebellion by force.

In 1966 Britain secured a UN resolution requesting all member nations to apply economic sanctions against Rhodesia. The breakaway regime was not moved to change its policies by economic sanctions. They proved ineffective—evaded by Rhodesia and disregarded in whole or part by other nations. For example: South Africa ignored the call for sanctions; black-ruled Zambia, facing a food shortage in 1971, purchased large quantities of Rhodesian maize; and the United States, by vote of Congress in 1971, lifted the ban against importing Rhodesian chromium—so as to reduce American dependence upon Russia for this vital defense metal. (In 1977 the United States Congress, at the insistence of President Carter, reinstated the American ban on Rhodesian chrome.)

In 1976, after Mozambique gained independence, it closed its border with Rhodesia, throttling Rhodesia's traditional trade routes to the outside world. Thereafter, Rhodesia faced stepped-up black guerrilla attacks.

**4. The American Initiative.** In 1976, after the Angolan civil war ended with the pro-Soviet group in control, Secretary of State Henry Kissinger acted to achieve a peaceful transition to black-majority rule in Rhodesia and thereby forestall any Soviet or Cuban intervention. Kissinger undertook many months of personal diplomacy. Finally he secured acceptance by Prime Minister Smith of Rhodesia of proposals for a temporary biracial government in Rhodesia, pending a peaceful transition to black-majority rule.

Britain convened a Geneva conference to work out the details. In attendance were Smith and several black leaders, each claiming to speak for the Zimbabwe blacks. The conference became deadlocked and adjourned in failure. Smith, however, stated that he was still committed to a transfer of power, now by discussions with moderate black leaders in Rhodesia.

**5. The Internal Rhodesian Agreement.** In 1978 Prime Minister Smith and three moderate black leaders in Rhodesia reached an internal agreement that provided for (a) black-majority rule on the basis of free elections open to all citizens; (b) safeguards of white-minority rights; (c) a transitional government to seek a cease-fire with the guerrillas and hold elections.

The agreement was denounced by most black African states, who distrusted Smith, by the Communist nations, and by the leftist Rhodesian *Patriotic Front,* whose different factions were led by *Joshua Nkomo* and *Robert Mugabe.* The Patriotic Front included guerrilla fighters based in Zambia and Mozambique and equipped with Soviet and Chinese arms. Patriotic Front orators rejected the agreement as a "sellout" perpetuating white-minority rule and pledged to continue the fighting.

**6. The Zimbabwe Rhodesia Elections (1979).** The elections attracted a voter turnout of 65 percent, despite Patriotic Front efforts at sabotage. The elections gave Zimbabwe Rhodesia a new government headed by a black prime minister, Bishop *Abel Muzorewa*. The Muzorewa government was labeled by Patriotic Front leaders as a "puppet regime," and it was condemned as illegal by the UN Security Council.

**7. The London Conference (1979).** In late 1979, as Zimbabwe Rhodesia faced continued guerrilla warfare and the possibility of Russian and Cuban intervention, Britain convened a London conference at Lancaster House to seek a peaceful settlement. In attendance were all the interested parties. Britain urged the various factions to accept reasonable compromises. Behind the scenes Zambia and Mozambique—two African states that harbored guerrilla bases and suffered economic and military hardships—pressured the Patriotic Front leaders to be flexible. After hard negotiations, the conference agreed to the following: *(a)* a democratic government with a prime minister responsible to a parliament, *(b)* a parliament of 100 members chosen in free elections open to all citizens and all political parties, *(c)* a guarantee of personal and individual rights, *(d)* safeguards for the white minority by reserving, for at least seven years, 20 seats for whites in the 100-seat parliament and by requiring the government to compensate whites for any seizure of their lands (the funds to be provided by Britain, the United States, West European nations, and international agencies), *(e)* a cease-fire, and *(f)* appointment of a British governor, with a 1,200-troop Commonwealth force, to assume temporary control of Rhodesia, enforce the cease-fire, and organize early 1980 elections. Thereafter, Britain will grant legal independence to Rhodesia. Following the London conference, economic sanctions against Rhodesia were lifted by Britain, the United States, the United Nations Security Council, and most black African nations.

**8. The 1980 Elections.** The campaign among blacks for the country's parliament was strongly contested and reflected tribal divisions. Robert Mugabe, leading the *Zimbabwe African National Union* (ZANU)-Patriotic Front, secured a clear majority of 57 seats. Joshua Nkomo gained 20 seats and Bishop Muzorewa took 3 seats. (Ian Smith at the head of the *Rhodesian Front* party received the 20 seats reserved for whites.) Despite some intimidation of voters, the results—according to the British election commissioner—broadly reflected the wishes of the people.

Robert Mugabe, during the years of guerrilla warfare, had received support from Communist China and was known as a radical Marxist-Leninist. Now, following his election victory, Mugabe adopted a moderate and conciliatory position. He urged blacks and whites to "remain calm," "work for unity," and "forget our grim past." He pledged to form a broadly based government and offered four cabinet posts to members of the Nkomo party and two cabinet posts to whites. Mugabe reassured the whites that his government would not seize their farmlands and other properties. Acknowledging that the country's economic structure was based on capitalism, he pledged to build on that foundation to further prosperity. Although committed to improving conditions for blacks, Mugabe warned them that "change cannot occur overnight." Mugabe's conciliatory stance gave hope that his government would create a free, democratic, and prosperous Zimbabwe.

White inhabitants in Zimbabwe remained fearful and in large numbers continued to flee the country.

## Case Studies of Selected African Nations

### GHANA (FORMER BRITISH COLONY OF GOLD COAST)

1. **People.** The people are blacks, divided into many tribes and speaking some 50 different tribal languages. Ghana's official language is English. The people have a per capita income of about $500 a year, and some 70 percent are illiterate.

2. **Road to Independence.** After riots, Ghana won independence in 1957 and became the first black nation in the Commonwealth. In 1960 Ghana became a republic but remained within the Commonwealth.

3. **Government.** *Kwame Nkrumah,* Ghana's independence leader, headed the new government. He established a personal dictatorship, suppressed opposition, mismanaged the economy , and followed a pro-Communist foreign policy. Nkrumah was overthrown in 1966 by army leaders, who thereafter improved the economy and followed a foreign policy of neutrality. In 1969 the military returned the country to civilian rule, but in 1972 they charged the civilian regime with "mismanagement" and again imposed military rule. In 1979 the military yielded power to an elected parliament and an elected president, *Hilla Limann.*

4. **Economy.** The people are engaged mainly in agriculture and also in forestry and mining. Ghana is the world's leading producer of cacao; it also exports hardwoods, gold, and industrial diamonds. It imports chiefly manufactured goods and oil. The chief trade partners are Britain and the United States. Ghana attracted Western capital to build a hydroelectric power plant on the Volta River and an aluminum industry.

Ghana's economy now faces serious problems: soaring inflation, food shortages, heavy foreign debts, a declining cacao crop, and high oil prices.

### ZAIRE (FORMER BELGIAN COLONY OF THE CONGO)

1. **People.** The Zairians (Congolese) are blacks divided among some 200 tribes, mainly Bantu. Few whites remain in the country. Most Zairians speak their tribal tongues, but the country's official language is French. The people have a per capita income of about $125 a year, and some 70 percent are illiterate.

2. **Road to Independence.** After anti-Belgian riots by the Congolese people, the Congo in 1960 received independence from Belgium.

**3. Government.** The new republic faced serious problems: rivalry between pro-Communist Premier *Patrice Lumumba* and pro-Western President *Joseph Kasavubu*, army mutinies, tribal conflicts, secession by mineral-rich Katanga province (now Shaba), the continued presence of Belgian troops, and involvement in the cold war. (For the UN and the Congo, see page 509.)

Slowly, painfully, the Congo resolved these problems and established an anti-Communist central government. In 1965 General *Joseph Mobutu*, a Congo nationalist and anti-Communist, seized control and established a stable military regime. In 1971 he renamed the country Zaire and ordered the replacement of European designations with African names for cities, geographic features, and families. Joseph Mobutu became *Mobutu Sese Seko*.

In 1977 leftist Katanga rebels living in Angola invaded Shaba province. When the Zairian army proved unable to repel the invaders, Morocco sent some 1,500 troops, transported in French planes, to the fighting front. Thus strengthened, the Zairian forces reestablished control. Zaire thereafter broke diplomatic relations with Cuba and East Germany, accusing these Communist nations of having supported the rebels. In 1978 leftist Katanga rebels from Angola again invaded Shaba. They were driven out by Zairian forces aided by French and Belgian units transported in American planes. Thereafter, Mobutu met with Angolan leaders and they agreed to stop supporting each other's guerrilla opposition.

Although Mobutu's regime gave the Zairian people a measure of peace and unity, by 1981 it had become corrupt, repressive, and increasingly unpopular. Mobutu, however, retained army support and was firmly in control.

**4. Economy.** Zaire's economy consists of *(a)* agriculture, which employs most of the people, many as subsistence farmers, *(b)* mining, and *(c)* light industry. Rich in mineral resources, Zaire exports chiefly copper, tin, industrial diamonds, cobalt, and uranium, and some coffee and palm oil. It imports foodstuffs, oil, and manufactured goods. Its chief trading partners are free world nations: Belgium, Britain, other Common Market members, and the United States.

Zaire nationalized the properties of Belgian companies and later moved to "Africanize," in whole or part, all other foreign-owned companies. Nevertheless, the country attracted loans and investment capital from many Western nations.

Zaire's economy now is seriously burdened by declining agricultural production, heavy foreign debt, soaring inflation, high oil prices, and lower mineral output as mine workers fled from twice-invaded Shaba province.

## NIGERIA (FORMER BRITISH COLONY AND PROTECTORATE)

**1. People.** The most populous African state, Nigeria contains many small tribes and three major ones: the Hausa, the Yoruba, and the Ibo. English is the official language, but the people speak some 250 tribal dialects. The Nigerians observe two major religions: in the north they are mainly Moslems, and in the south they are mainly Christians. The people have a per capita income of about $700 a year, and some 75 percent are illiterate.

**2. Road to Independence.** In a peaceful transition, Nigeria in 1960 gained independence and Commonwealth membership.

**3. Government.** Nigeria originally adopted a British-type parliamentary democracy. The government, however, was torn by tribal rivalries for control. In 1966 two army coups led to a military regime under a Hausa tribesman, *Yakubu Gowon*. Fearful of this military regime, the Ibo tribe, in Nigeria's eastern region, in 1967 seceded to form the republic of *Biafra*. The central government moved to suppress this secession, and Nigeria experienced almost three years of civil war. In 1970, after casualties estimated at over 1 million, the central government won. In 1975, as Nigeria experienced poverty, inflation, and political unrest, Gowon was overthrown by a bloodless military coup. In 1979 Nigeria adopted a constitution—modeled after that of the United States—providing for an elected president, an independent judiciary, a two-house legislature, and a federal-state division of powers. After elections, the military yielded control to a civilian president, a Moslem from the north, *Shehu Shagari*. He pledged to seek national unity, to improve the economy, and to "fight racism" in Africa.

**4. Economy.** The people are engaged in forestry, fishing, and mainly agriculture. The country contains valuable oil resources, developed by British and American companies, that provide the major portion of government revenues. Nigeria belongs to the Organization of Petroleum Exporting Countries (OPEC) and is a major oil supplier of the United States. Nigeria exports crude oil, cacao, and peanuts; it imports manufactured goods, chiefly from Britain, West Germany, and the United States; it also imports foodstuffs. In 1972 the government moved to "Nigerianize" the oil industry, retail trade, and banks, but such government-dominated businesses are plagued by corruption and inefficiency.

In 1981 the Shagari regime began a five-year program—called the "green revolution"—to achieve self-sufficiency in food crops. The program faces problems: shortages of seed, fertilizer, machinery, and farm managers, as well as the dangers of bureaucratic interference.

## ALGERIA (FORMER FRENCH POSSESSION)

**1. People.** The people are 25 percent Berber and 75 percent Arab. Of the 1 million French settlers in Algeria before independence, fewer than 10 percent remain. Algeria's official language is Arabic. The Algerians have a per capita income of about $800 a year, and 65 percent are illiterate.

**2. Road to Independence.** After nine years of guerrilla warfare, Algeria in 1962 received independence from France under de Gaulle (check the Index). Algeria was to receive French technical, cultural, and financial aid and to permit joint French-Algerian development of the Saharan oil fields.

**3. Government.** Algeria immediately became a one-party state under military rule and moved toward socialism by nationalizing factories, mines, and large farms, many being French-owned. Algeria equipped its army with French and Soviet weapons and followed a pro-Communist foreign policy. In 1965 an army coup placed Algeria under the rule of a leftist, Colonel *Houari Boumediene*. In 1978, Boumediene died. His successor, chosen by Algeria's only political party, the National Liberation Front, was Colonel *Benjedid Chadli*.

Although Algeria voices strong support for Arab unity and Arab nationalism, the country has engaged in a bitter dispute with the bordering Arab state of Morocco. This dispute, since 1975, has been over the phosphate-rich territory known as Western (Spanish) Sahara (check the Index).

**4. Economy.** Most Algerians are engaged in agriculture; some work in fishing, mining, and extracting oil. Algeria exports crude oil, natural gas, wine, and citrus fruit; it imports foodstuffs and consumer goods. Its trade is mainly with the United States, West Germany, and France, but it is being oriented toward the Soviet Union by government trade pacts. In 1971 Algeria nationalized French-owned oil companies. In response the French government limited imports of Algerian wine and reduced the number of Algerian workers in France.

The Algerian government had emphasized the construction of heavy industry such as iron and steel works, oil refineries, and gas liquefication plants. To finance such projects, Algeria borrowed heavily from the Soviet Union and from several Western nations. In 1980 Algeria moved to deemphasize heavy industry to meet the needs of its people for housing and light industry producing consumer goods. Algeria is a member of OPEC and has been a strong advocate of high oil prices.

Algeria faces problems of explosive population growth, insufficient agricultural output, and mass unemployment.

## KENYA (FORMER BRITISH COLONY AND PROTECTORATE)

**1. People.** Blacks of some 40 different tribes constitute 95 percent of the people; the rest are Arabs, Indians from Asia, and British. The official languages are English and the major native tongue, Swahili. The people have a per capita income of about $300 a year, and 65 percent are illiterate.

**2. Road to Independence.** In the 1950's Kenya experienced terrorism against white farmers by a secret native group, the *Mau Mau Society*. Britain restored order, began training the blacks in self-government, and in 1963 granted Kenya independence and Commonwealth membership.

**3. Government.** Beginning with a democratic government, Kenya chose as its first president the former Mau Mau leader, *Jomo Kenyatta*. He belonged to Kenya's largest tribe, the Kikuyu. Aware of Kenya's many races and tribes, Kenyatta advocated "Harambee," a Swahili word meaning "Let us all work together." Although torn by tribal rivalries for control, the government remained stable. In 1969 the government outlawed the major opposition party, allegedly for "subversive activities," leaving Kenya with one party, the Kikuyu-dominated Kenya African National Union (KANU).

In 1978 President Kenyatta died and was succeeded in a peaceful and constitutional transition by *Daniel Arap Moi*—a member of a tiny Kenyan tribe.

In 1980 Kenya granted the United States use of air and naval facilities at the Kenyan city of Mombasa on the Indian Ocean. In return Kenya received food supplies, agricultural aid, and military equipment.

**4. Economy.** Although most Kenyans work in agriculture, the country also has food processing and consumer goods industries, mainly privately owned. Kenya attracts tourists to enjoy its mountains, parks, and wild-game preserves. The country exports coffee and tea and imports manufactured goods. Its chief trading partners, which also provide it with investment capital, are Great Britain, West Germany, and the United States. In 1968 Kenya began to "Africanize" the retail trade, thereby evicting many Kenya-born Indian merchants who had retained their British passports when Kenya received independence.

With inflation and unemployment besetting the nation in the mid-1970's, Kenya experienced a series of strikes. President Kenyatta then issued an order prohibiting all strikes. Kenya's economy also has been seriously burdened by OPEC's explosive increase in the price of oil. Funds earmarked for agricultural development projects have been diverted instead to pay for oil imports.

## UGANDA (FORMER BRITISH PROTECTORATE)

**1. People.** Ugandans are almost entirely blacks, divided into four major and many minor tribes. The people speak their tribal tongues, but the country's official language is English. Ugandans have a per capita income of about $200 a year, and 75 percent are illiterate.

**2. Road to Independence.** In a peaceful transition Uganda in 1962 gained independence and Commonwealth membership.

**3. Government.** Uganda adopted a constitution providing local autonomy and establishing a central government. Uganda's first head was Prime Minister *Milton Obote.* After several years of political turmoil, Obote secured approval of a new constitution strengthening the central government. Obote took the title of president and ruled in a dictatorial manner. In 1971 he was ousted by a military coup led by General *Idi Amin.*

Idi Amin became president and governed as a military dictator. Employing terror, his regime was responsible for the torture of prisoners, the killing of opponents, and the massacre of tribes whose loyalty Amin doubted. The Amin regime was estimated to have murdered as many as 300,000 Ugandans. In foreign affairs Amin denounced the United States and Britain, strained relations with the bordering black-ruled countries of Tanzania and Kenya, and cultivated the friendship of the oil-rich Arab states by speeches attacking Western imperialism and Israel. In 1976 Amin assisted Palestinian terrorists who had hijacked a passenger plane from Athens to Entebbe airport in Uganda. After an Israeli air raid on Entebbe had rescued most hostages, Amin spoke bitterly against Kenya for permitting the homebound Israeli plane to land and refuel.

In 1978 Amin's troops, armed with Soviet weapons, entered northwest Tanzania—supposedly to wipe out Ugandan exile guerrilla bases—and then withdrew. Thereafter, President *Julius Nyerere* of Tanzania ordered his forces to invade Uganda. Tanzanian forces and Ugandan exile units routed Amin's native and Libyan troops. The invaders were hailed by the Ugandan populace as liberators. Amin fled to safety, and was last known to be in Saudi Arabia.

After much political instability, Milton Obote won a disputed 1980 election marked by tribal rivalries, and again became president. Obote benefited from the support of Tanzania, whose troops remained in Uganda. To combat a Ugandan guerrilla movement seeking his ouster, Obote resorted to mass executions and repressive tactics—as had been employed by Idi Amin.

**4. Economy.** Uganda is mainly an agricultural country but also has some mining. It exports coffee, copper, and cotton; and it imports machinery, transportation equipment, and clothing. Uganda's foreign trade passes through ports in Kenya. Uganda's major trading partners are Britain, Kenya, and West Germany.

In 1972, to achieve "Africanization" of the economy, Amin expelled 55,000 Uganda-born Asians—chiefly merchants and professionals—who had retained their British passports when Uganda received independence. For these people Uganda had been their ancestral home for many generations.

In 1978, to express its opposition to Amin, the United States imposed a trade embargo, mainly halting American purchases of Ugandan coffee.

In 1979, after Amin's downfall, Uganda faced massive economic problems: securing food and medical care, overcoming a severe drought, restoring agricultural output, rebuilding foreign trade links, and improving living standards.

## Outlook for the Future

### PROBLEMS BESETTING THE INDEPENDENT AFRICAN NATIONS

**1. Developing National Unity.** African nationalism has been largely negative—based more on hostility toward imperialists than on a sense of nationhood. The boundaries of most African colonies were determined by imperialist considerations rather than by related population groups. Since the new nations are based on the old colonies, most African states consist of many distinct tribes. Some tribes have long histories of tribal conflict and speak different dialects and languages, often totally unrelated. Although education, intermarriage, urban living, and mine and factory employment have discouraged tribalism, it remains a deeply engrained tradition. African peoples face a difficult transition from tribal loyalties to 20th-century nationalism.

**2. Securing Professional Personnel.** Before the black African states achieved independence, Europeans had provided them with most professional skills. Few native Africans had training as educators, doctors, scientists, engineers, and civil servants. When independence came, many skilled Europeans, fearing for their future, left Africa, especially the Congo, Algeria, Mozambique, and Angola.

Some black Africans sent to Western countries for professional education have preferred to remain in the West—attracted by the higher living standards and the climate of freedom. This flow of bright people out of the developing nations and into the industrialized countries has been termed the *brain drain.*

Africa's shortage of professional people handicaps efforts to wipe out illiteracy, raise health standards, improve agriculture, further industry, and provide efficient government.

**3. Maintaining Popular Government.** The African people lack democratic traditions and experience in running a government. Most African peoples received no political training before independence. Living close to the subsistence level, they are concerned mainly with securing the necessities of life and have little time or energy for political matters. Many African leaders are sincere and hardworking but inexpert.

In North Africa's Arab states of Egypt, Libya, and Algeria and in many African black nations, the people have acquiesced in army rule and one-party governments, essentially dictatorships.

In 1979 Africans witnessed a trend toward more responsive and humane regimes. In Central Africa, Equatorial Guinea, and Uganda, brutal dictators were ousted; in Ghana and Nigeria, military rule was replaced by elected civilians.

**4. Improving Living Standards.** Most Africans live in poverty. Farmers produce scanty crops; many city workers are unemployed. African nations seek to improve agricultural methods and diversify their crops. Also, they seek to develop their mineral resources and establish industries.

Lacking capital for development, African nations need foreign aid. They have received some aid from foreign governments, mainly from the Soviet Union and the United States. However, private investors are deterred by threats of political instability, unfair taxation, and nationalization.

Many African nations, adversely affected since 1973 by OPEC's high oil prices, have been compelled to pay for oil imports by diverting funds from needed development projects.

Independent Africa has made some economic progress, but living standards remain low. The desire of peoples in developing countries to achieve higher living standards has been called the *revolution of rising expectations.*

In the 1980's, some 150 million Africans faced famine. The reasons were the continent's explosive population growth, high oil prices, declining food production due to poor farming methods and the emphasis on exportable cash crops such as coffee and tea, and the property destruction and refugee problems caused by local wars.

**5. Determining a Foreign Policy.** African nations oppose colonialism, applaud the end of the European holdings in Africa, and resent white-dominated South Africa. Toward the cold war, most African nations proclaim a policy of neutrality. In the UN they often vote with the new Asian states and constitute an influential Afro-Asian "Third World" bloc.

Despite official neutrality, the African states have at times revealed their sympathies in the cold war. Some have consistently been pro-Communist; others have strongly adhered to pro-Western policies. The greater number have taken a stand based on specific issues but have shown a leftward tendency.

**"Man, that big jump is really rough."**

©1966 HERBLOCK
THE WASHINGTON POST

From The Herblock Gallery (Simon & Schuster, 1968)

**6. Seeking African Unity.** In 1963 the independent African states (with the chief exception of white-dominated South Africa) met at Addis Ababa, Ethiopia, to further African unity. President Nkrumah of Ghana urged a strong union similar to that of the United States. He argued that, since no single African state is powerful enough to stand by itself economically and militarily, Africa must unite or perish. Emperor Haile Selassie of Ethiopia pointed to the vast differences—linguistic, racial, economic, and political—among the African nations and recommended a loose organization. Haile Selassie's views prevailed.

The independent African states formed the *Organization of African Unity (OAU)*. They adopted a charter that called for: *(a)* A loose confederation. Its major agencies are (1) a top-level conference of heads of state to meet annually, (2) a Council of Ministers to meet every six months, and (3) a Commission on Mediation and Conciliation to settle inter-African disputes peacefully. *(b)* African cooperation in foreign policy, economics, education, and defense. *(c)* The liberation of all African territories still under foreign rule and the extension of full rights to blacks in white-dominated lands.

Now totaling 50 member nations, the OAU has served to focus African opposition to white-minority rule—by 1982 remaining only in Namibia and South Africa. The OAU, however, has been unable to resolve many intra-African disputes: most recently between Ethiopia and Somalia over the Ogaden region; between Morocco and the Polisario Front over Western Sahara; and between Egypt and Libya over Libyan intervention in the civil war in Chad. The OAU remains a viable organization available for use by its member nations.

## MULTIPLE–CHOICE QUESTIONS

1. In comparison with the size of Europe, the size of Africa is  (1) smaller  (2) about the same  (3) slightly greater  (4) much greater.

2. In addition to spreading Christianity, missionaries in Africa  (1) headed white armies of conquest  (2) provided capital for business ventures  (3) maintained health clinics and schools  (4) established the Organization of African Unity.

3. French expansion in Africa between 1875 and 1914 did *not* conflict with the ambitions of  (1) Italy  (2) Portugal  (3) Germany  (4) Britain.

4. The country that secured the largest part of Africa during its partition was  (1) Britain  (2) Italy  (3) Germany  (4) Spain.

5. The lifeline of the British Empire after 1875 did *not* include  (1) Gibraltar  (2) Capetown  (3) the Red Sea  (4) the Suez Canal.

6. Before 1914 Britain's efforts to acquire an unbroken north-south line of territory in Africa were thwarted by  (1) France  (2) Italy  (3) Germany  (4) Portugal.

7. Two late starters in the race for African territories were  (1) Spain and Portugal  (2) the United States and Russia  (3) Italy and Germany  (4) Belgium and France.

8. Since World War II European control in Africa has been opposed by the growth of colonial  (1) nationalism  (2) imperialism  (3) laissez-faire  (4) industrialization.

9. Colonial nationalism in Africa was  (1) in part influenced by the American Declaration of Independence  (2) a plot for Communist seizure of the continent  (3) very different from nationalism in Ireland  (4) in favor of agriculture over industry.

10. Which two African countries were independent before World War II?  (1) Egypt and Liberia  (2) Algeria and Morocco  (3) Libya and Sudan  (4) Kenya and Guinea.

11. Which nation was conquered by Italy in 1936 and regained its independence after World War II?  (1) Egypt  (2) Ethiopia  (3) Libya  (4) Liberia.

12. Which former British colony, granted independence in 1960, has the largest native population in Africa?  (1) Ghana  (2) Uganda  (3) Somalia  (4) Nigeria.

13. Which African country gained its independence from France in 1962 following a drawn-out rebellion?  (1) Tunisia  (2) Algeria  (3) Malagasy  (4) Morocco.

14. Which problem is common to emerging nations in Africa?  (1) exhaustion of natural resources  (2) United Nations interference in internal affairs  (3) continuing oppression by European powers  (4) insufficient technically trained people.

15. The Organization of African Unity (OAU) is a  (1) tariff union similar to the Common Market  (2) loose confederation of most independent African states  (3) military alliance of Africa's black nations  (4) political union of Africa's Arab states.

16. In its charter the OAU did *not* propose  (1) settling inter-African disputes peacefully  (2) liberating the remaining colonies in Africa  (3) eliminating Communist influence from Africa  (4) securing African cooperation in economic matters.

17. The African nations gaining independence since 1945 have had disputes on all of the following *except*  (1) control of seaports  (2) territorial acquisitions  (3) OAU membership  (4) Israeli raid to free hostages at Entebbe.

18. The Asian people expelled from Kenya and Uganda were  (1) newly arrived immigrants  (2) wealthy vacationers  (3) conspirators plotting to seize the government  (4) middle-class business and professional people whose families had lived in Africa for generations.

19. The United States Congress cut off aid to pro-Western groups in the Angolan civil war because Congress  (1) believed we were too busy with Vietnam  (2) feared that we might get involved in another Vietnam-type situation  (3) insisted we had no interests in Angola  (4) did not want to oppose the president.

20. Which is a major problem facing the new African nations? (1) joining in mutual defense pacts with the major world powers (2) fulfilling requirements for admission to the United Nations (3) establishing stable political systems (4) guaranteeing the safety of Europeans remaining after independence.

21. The actions of emerging nations in Africa are most often determined by (1) sentiments in the United Nations (2) advice given by their scientists (3) orders of the Russian Communist party (4) consideration of their national goals and needs.

## TRUE–FALSE QUESTIONS

If the statement is correct, write the word *true.* If the statement is incorrect, substitute a word or phrase for the italicized term to make the statement correct.

1. The famous Scottish missionary who explored central Africa was *Henry M. Stanley.*

2. To protect the Suez Canal, Britain established a protectorate over *Egypt.*

3. The Mau Mau Society employed terrorism against white settlers in *Rhodesia.*

4. In north Africa, from Egypt to Morocco, live large numbers of *Moslems.*

5. A former Italian colony in north Africa, now an independent nation, is *Libya.*

6. Zaire, rich in uranium and copper, was formerly under the control of *Portugal.*

7. Liberia, a republic in Africa, was founded by *Russia* as a haven for former slaves.

## MAP QUESTIONS

For each area described below, write *both* its name and the letter indicating its location on the map.

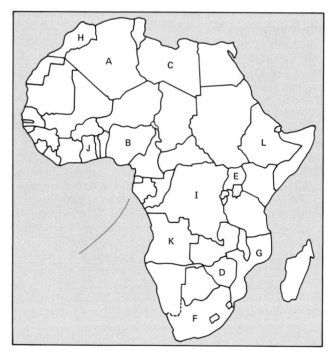

1. This country, granted independence by Belgium in 1960, was torn by civil war and violence.
2. Acquired by France during the 19th century, this nation gained independence following nine years of guerrilla warfare.
3. This country, conquered by Italy in 1936, is now an independent nation. In 1974 an army coup deposed its emperor, Haile Selassie.
4. This former British colony, with the largest native population in Africa, became independent in 1960 after a period of preparation for self-government.
5. This country was ruled by a white-minority regime. In 1980 following a London conference at Lancaster House, it became independent under black-majority rule.
6. This Portuguese colony, located on the Atlantic side of Africa, was set free in 1975. It came under leftist control with the aid of Cuban troops.
7. This former British colony, once known as the Gold Coast, is now a member of the Commonwealth of Nations.
8. A daring Israeli air raid rescued hostages held by Arab terrorists in this country.
9. Formerly an Italian colony, this independent Moslem country has prospered because of its newly discovered oil resources.
10. This monarchy, which borders on both the Atlantic Ocean and the Mediterranean Sea, ended the French protectorate in 1956 and gained its independence.

## ESSAY QUESTIONS

1. Discuss, in *one* way for each, how geography has influenced the history of *two* specific countries or areas in Africa.
2. (*a*) Give *one* reason why either Italy *or* Germany was late in acquiring a colonial empire. (*b*) Name *one* African colony acquired by Italy or Germany before 1914 and trace its history up to the present day.
3. Show *one* difference in the way each of the following African nations achieved independence: (*a*) Nigeria (*b*) Algeria (*c*) Congo (*d*) Angola.
4. (*a*) Define "colonial nationalism." (*b*) Show in *two* ways that colonial nationalism in Africa was an outgrowth of world conditions. (*c*) Describe *two* grievances of African nationalists against the European empire builders.
5. For Africa "independence is only the beginning." (*a*) Discuss *two* problems facing the independent African states. (*b*) Giving *one* argument to support your opinion, indicate whether the OAU will be effective in overcoming these problems. (*c*) Evaluate *two* other efforts by the African nations to overcome these problems.
6. For each of the following, discuss *one* effect upon any newly independent African nation. You must name a specific nation and use a different one for each item: (*a*) tribalism (*b*) Sahara Desert (*c*) subsistence agriculture (*d*) lack of capital (*e*) high price of oil since 1973 (*f*) exodus of white settlers.

# Part 5. The Middle East

## MIDDLE EAST: LOCATION AND IMPORTANCE

The Middle East consists of northeastern Africa and southwestern Asia. The region's importance lies in its (1) *vital waterways*—the Suez Canal and the Dardanelles; (2) *valuable oil resources*—in Saudi Arabia, Kuwait, Iraq, and Iran; and (3) *strategic location*—at the crossroads of Europe, Asia, and Africa, and on the southern flank of Russia (see map, page 378).

## IMPERIALISM IN THE MIDDLE EAST

### 1. Britain

*a. To Secure Its "Lifeline" to the Far East.* In the late 19th century, Britain purchased controlling interest in the Suez Canal, established a protectorate over Egypt, and acquired the militarily valuable island of Cyprus.

*b. To Restrain Other Powers.* By the Crimean War (1853–1856) and the Congress of Berlin (1878), Britain kept Russia out of the eastern Mediterranean and prevented Russia from seizing the Turkish-controlled Dardanelles. By World War I Britain removed German influence from the Middle East.

*c. To Acquire Oil Resources.* By 1914 British companies had obtained oil concessions in Iraq (then part of the Turkish Empire), Kuwait, and Persia (now Iran). During World War I Britain encouraged revolt by the subject Arab peoples under Turkish rule. After the war Britain received mandates over the former Turkish territories of oil-rich Iraq and strategically located Palestine.

**2. Russia.** Under both Czarist and Communist rule, Russia has sought to extend its influence into the Middle East. Before World War I Czarist Russia helped dismember the Turkish Empire and gain independence for several Balkan states close to the Middle East. Since World War II the Soviet Union has dominated its Balkan satellites of Rumania and Bulgaria. Also, the Soviet Union exerts considerable influence in several Arab countries.

**3. Germany.** For investments, trade, and nationalist glory, German imperialists were attracted to the Turkish Empire. In 1899 German bankers secured Turkey's consent to complete the *Berlin-to-Bagdad* railroad. Because this railroad would enable German manufacturers to compete in Asian markets, it aroused British opposition. Germany's defeat in World War I temporarily ended its Middle East ambitions.

**4. France.** France in 1920 secured mandates over the former Turkish territories of Lebanon and Syria.

## MIDDLE EAST OPPOSES IMPERIALISM

### 1. Decline of British Power

a. **Egypt** demonstrated against Britain and in 1922 gained independence. The Suez Canal, however, remained under British control. In 1954 Egypt became a military dictatorship under *Gamal Abdel Nasser*. In 1956 he defied Britain (and France) by nationalizing the Suez Canal. An Arab nationalist, Nasser sought to end British and French influence in the Arab world.

b. **Iraq** in 1932 ended the British mandate. As an independent state, Iraq experienced several revolutions. In 1968 the leftist Baath party seized control. This regime has been anti-Western, especially anti-American. In 1972 it nationalized the major Western-owned oil company in Iraq. It has been friendly to the Communist bloc, accepting Communist loans, granting Russia oil exploration rights, and in 1972 signing a treaty of military aid with the Soviet Union. In 1980 Iraq unilaterally canceled its border treaty with Iran and invaded that country. (For details, check the Index.)

c. **Jordan** in 1946 became an independent Arab state. With the creation of Israel in 1948, Jordan annexed the Arab Palestinian territory west of the Jordan River, including the Old City of Jerusalem, and acquired a large Palestinian

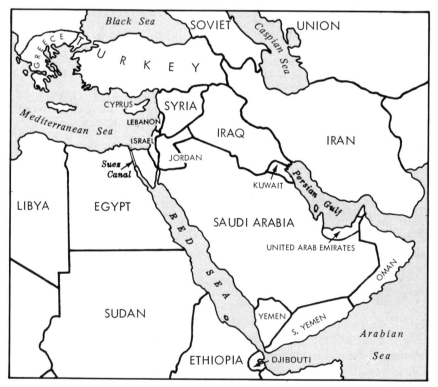

**The Middle East Today**

population. In the 1967 Arab-Israeli War, Jordan lost this territory to Israel. King *Hussein* of Jordan, maintaining a pro-Western but anti-Israeli stand, was opposed by the Palestinian guerrillas as not sufficiently devoted to their cause. In 1970–1971 Hussein's army drove out the Palestinian guerrillas.

**d. Israel** in 1948 became an independent Jewish state (check the Index).

**e. Iran** by religion is a Moslem state whose people are mainly Persians. Iran has a major oil industry—originally developed by the British and later nationalized—and is a member of OPEC.

Iran was a monarchy ruled by a Shah. The last Shah, who ruled from 1941 to 1979, was *Mohammed Riza Pahlevi*. He ruled autocratically, employed secret police, and permitted no political opposition. The Shah, however, spurred economic and social modernization, including land reform, literacy, and women's rights. He followed a pro-Western foreign policy and maintained a "special relationship" with the United States. (For recent events, check the Index.)

**f. Cyprus** in 1960, after four years of violence, became an independent republic within the British Commonwealth and permitted Britain to retain its military bases. Archbishop *Makarios* was elected the first president.

The *Cypriotes* (inhabitants of Cyprus) are 80 percent Greek and 20 percent Turkish. Their constitution (1) guaranteed many rights to the Turkish minority and (2) provided for a Turkish Cypriote vice president and a Greek Cypriote president, each with veto power over laws. (For recent events, check the Index.)

**g. Kuwait** in 1961 ended the British protectorate and became an independent Arab sheikhdom. The new nation received Britain's pledge of military protection. Kuwait, although small in size, is one of the world's largest producers of oil. In 1975 Kuwait nationalized its oil properties.

**2. Decline of French Power.** By 1944 Syria and Lebanon, after riots and strikes, ended the French mandates and became independent Arab republics.

In 1975–1976 Lebanon was torn by civil war between its Christian and Moslem Arabs. (Check the Index for Lebanon.)

With Britain and France no longer dominant in the Middle East and with the Soviet Union exerting pressure, the United States has become increasingly involved in the area. (Check the Index for the Middle East in the cold war.)

## SURVEY OF ARAB NATIONALISM (ESPECIALLY SINCE 1945)

**1. Roots.** Arab peoples have become aware of their common cultural background: Arabic language, Moslem religion, and the great Arab civilization of the Middle Ages. They wish to govern themselves free of foreign domination.

**2. Meanings.** Arab nationalism has many advocates, and they may differ as to its meaning. *(a)* Some Arab nationalists, as did Egypt's President Nasser, dream of creating one united Arab nation, from the Atlantic Ocean to the Persian Gulf, as had existed during the Middle Ages. *(b)* Other Arab nationalists, probably more realistic, believe in maintaining separate Arab states, each with its own government but working together to protect Arab interests.

### 3. Evidences of Arab Unity

*a. Arab League.* Founded in 1945, the Arab League seeks to unify Arab policy on world issues, especially Arab efforts against Israel. The Arab League enforces an economic boycott against Israel, against private companies doing business with Israel, or having Jewish ownership or management.

*b. Organization of Petroleum Exporting Countries (OPEC).* Founded in 1960, OPEC consists of six non-Arab and seven Arab states—the major oil-producer being Saudi Arabia. Dominated by its Arab members, OPEC's economic purpose is to increase its members' oil revenues. (For OPEC and Arab unity during the 1973 Arab-Israeli war, check the Index.)

*c. Palestine Liberation Organization (PLO).* Because the PLO has been both a unifying and a divisive force, it is discussed at greater length.

## PALESTINE LIBERATION ORGANIZATION (PLO)

**1. Background.** The Palestine Arab refugee problem arose out of the 1948–1949 war when the Arab nations tried to destroy the newborn state of Israel. Mainly fearing for their safety, some 540,000 Arabs, out of 700,000 living in Israeli territory, fled to neighboring Arab nations. After the war the Arab nations demanded that Israel readmit the Arab refugees. Israel insisted that the refugee problem be part of an overall settlement involving boundaries and diplomatic recognition, which the Arab nations refused.

The Arab nations also refused to assimilate the refugees into their societies. Many refugees were compelled to live apart in squalid camps dependent upon international charity for food and other necessities and without any visible prospects for a decent future. This environment gave rise to various guerrilla groups committed to destroy Israel. By the mid-1960's these guerrilla groups formed an umbrella organization, the *Palestine Liberation Organization (PLO)*. Eventually *Yasir Arafat*—leader of the largest guerrilla group, *Al Fatah*, and its *Black September* terrorist faction—became head of the PLO. He claims to speak for all Palestinians. These people, according to rough estimates, include Palestinians under Jordanian rule—1 million; Palestinian refugees in Lebanon, Syria, and other Arab states—1 million; Palestinians in Israel—500,000; and Palestinians in the Israeli-occupied West Bank and Gaza Strip—over 1 million—a total of about 3.5 million.

**2. Arab Summit Conference at Rabat, Morocco (1974).** The Arab nations unanimously declared the PLO the "sole legitimate representative of the Palestinian people" and called for the creation of a Palestinian state "on any Palestinian land that is liberated" from Israeli control.

**3. UN General Assembly (1974).** The Arab nations, with the support of the Communist and Third World blocs, secured a General Assembly invitation for the PLO, as "representative of the Palestinian people," to take part in the debate on the "Palestine question." After hearing Yasir Arafat demand establishment of a Palestinian state, the General Assembly voted overwhelmingly to approve the right of the Palestinian people to national independence and sovereignty. The General Assembly also voted to restrict Israel's right to rebuttal. (For Israel's answer, check the Index for United Nations and Arab-Israeli conflicts.)

**4. PLO as a Divisive Force in the Arab World.** In 1970–1971 Palestinian guerrillas threatened the rule of King Hussein of Jordan, but his army defeated them and drove them from Jordan. In the Lebanese civil war (1975–1976) leftist Palestinian guerrillas joined with leftist Lebanese Moslems to battle against rightist Lebanese Christian Arabs. Fearful of a hostile leftist regime in Lebanon, Syria sent its army into Lebanon, suppressed the leftist Palestinians and Lebanese Moslems, and enforced a cease-fire. (Check the Index for Lebanon.)

## SURVEY OF ARAB DISUNITY

**1. Differences Among the Arab Nations.** The Arab nations, in many ways, reveal great diversity. *(a)* Libya, Algeria, and Iraq are leftist, radical, and pro-Soviet, whereas Saudi Arabia, Jordan, and Tunisia are rightist, conservative, and generally pro-Western. *(b)* Saudi Arabia, Jordan, Morocco, and Kuwait are monarchies headed by hereditary rulers; most others are republics—in reality military dictatorships and one-party states. *(c)* Saudi Arabia, Kuwait, Libya, and Algeria have extensive oil resources and are relatively well-to-do, whereas Yemen and Sudan have no oil resources and are relatively poor.

**2. Disputes in the Arab World**

    *a. Yemen Civil War (1962–1970).* In 1962 a republican revolt erupted against Yemen's hereditary ruler. Egypt, then a leftist nation under President Nasser, provided troops for the republican forces. Saudi Arabia gave arms and money to the royalists. In 1970 this civil war ended as royalist supporters accepted posts in the republican regime.

    *b. Jordan vs. Palestinian Guerrillas (1970–1971).* King Hussein thwarted the efforts of the Palestinian guerrillas to overthrow his regime and Hussein's army drove the guerrillas out of Jordan. They fled into Syria and Lebanon.

    *c. Algeria vs. Morocco (Since 1975).* These nations have bitterly disputed control of the phosphate-rich Western (Spanish) Sahara. (Check the Index.)

    *d. Lebanon Civil War (1975–1976).* A small Arab republic, Lebanon lies west of Syria and north of Israel. Lebanon had a flourishing economy based upon banking, trade, and Arab tourism. Lebanon's population of 3 million is roughly equally divided between Arab Moslems and Arab Christians, with the Arab Christians being the more prosperous. They controlled the government, generally pursued a pro-Western foreign policy, and stayed out of the Arab-Israeli wars. After the Palestinian guerrillas were expelled from Jordan in 1971, their number in Lebanon increased considerably. The Lebanese government, with its small army, was unable to control the Palestinians, who mounted guerrilla attacks against Israel and incurred Israeli reprisal raids.

In 1975 Lebanon erupted into civil war between rightist Arab Christian militia and leftist Arab Moslem forces supported by leftist Palestinian guerrillas. Syria—on unfriendly terms with leftist Iraq to its east—now feared the rise of a hostile leftist regime in Lebanon. Syrian President *Hafez al-Assad* therefore sent his troops into Lebanon, giving battle to the leftist forces. Arab leaders approved a peacekeeping force for Lebanon—to consist mainly of Syrians. Some 30,000 Syrian troops occupied most of Lebanon, enforced a cease-fire, and upheld a Lebanese government under a pro-Syrian Christian Arab, President *Elias Sarkis*. The Lebanese civil war resulted in killing some 30,000 people, wounding many more, destroying the Lebanese economy, and weakening the PLO.

To expand their control, the Syrian occupation forces later launched sporadic attacks on their former allies, the Christian Arabs, some centered in southern Lebanon. These Syrian attacks perturbed Israel, whose government had aided the Christian Arab communities and fighting units.

*e. Iran-Iraq War (Beginning in 1980).* Check the Index. Libya and Syria expressed support for non-Arab Iran as a revolutionary Moslem state. Iraq thereupon broke diplomatic relations with Libya and Syria. However, Jordan backed Iraq as defending Arab interests.

*f. Syria vs. Jordan (1980).* Supporting opposing sides in the Iran-Iraq war, Syria and Jordan became bitter enemies. Syria accused Jordan of aiding a terrorist organization, the Moslem Brotherhood, which Syria claimed was seeking to overthrow the regime of Syrian President al-Assad. For Jordan, King Hussein denied these charges. As Syria and Jordan massed troops along their common border, a Saudi Arabian envoy helped defuse the situation.

*g. Egypt vs. Libya (Since 1977).* These countries became bitter enemies as Egypt under President Sadat adopted a pro-American stance, while Libya under Colonel *Muammar al-Qaddafi* moved into the Soviet orbit. In 1977 the two nations clashed in air and land border battles. In 1980 Libya sent troops southward across the border into Chad. This Libyan invasion, Egypt feared, endangered its security and the security of Egypt's ally, the Sudan. Sadat and Qaddafi called for the overthrow of each other's governments and Sadat considered Qaddafi a fanatic and terrorist supporter. In 1981, when Sadat's assassination become known, Libya was officially jubilant. Meanwhile, Sudan's president, General *Gaafar al-Nimeiry*, voiced fear that Libya, which had been attacking Sudanese border areas, was planning to use Chad for an invasion of his country. Libya, however, announced that it was withdrawing its troops from Chad.

## Israel

### JEWISH CLAIMS TO PALESTINE

*Theodor Herzl*, a journalist and Jewish intellectual, in 1897 founded modern *Zionism*, the movement for a Jewish homeland in Palestine. Zionists point out that the Jewish people (1) lived in Palestine during ancient times, (2) possess the attributes of a nationality entitled to its own state, and (3) need a refuge in case of anti-Semitic persecution. In 1917 the British government gave support to the Zionist movement through the *Balfour Declaration,* which viewed "with favor the establishment in Palestine of a national home for the Jewish people." To fulfill the Balfour Declaration, Britain in 1922 received the League of Nations mandate over Palestine.

By 1938 over 500,000 Jews had migrated to Palestine. They built modern cities, founded agricultural settlements, started industries, restored desert lands to fertility, reduced death from disease, and established schools.

## ARAB OPPOSITION AND A NEW BRITISH POLICY

Opposition to Jewish immigration came from (1) Arab nationalists, who desired an Arab Palestine; (2) Arab ruling classes, who feared incoming Western ideas of democracy; and (3) Arab peasants and nomads, who feared the loss of their traditional ways of living. In 1939, just before the outbreak of World War II, Britain severely limited Jewish immigration to Palestine. By so appeasing the Arabs, Zionists claimed, Britain was violating the Balfour Declaration.

During World War II, 6 million European Jews—men, women, and children—were savagely murdered by the Nazis. Of those who survived, most sought admission to Palestine. Britain, however, still kept the gates closed. Britain's policy was (1) defied by Palestinian Jews, who smuggled immigrants into the Holy Land, and (2) condemned by the United States. Britain rejected the repeated requests of President Truman to ease immigration restrictions.

## PALESTINE AND THE UN

In 1947 Britain gave the Palestine problem to the UN General Assembly. It voted to (1) end the British mandate, (2) place Jerusalem under international control, and (3) partition Palestine into separate Arab and Jewish states.

Thereupon, in 1948 Israel proclaimed its independence under President *Chaim Weizmann* and Prime Minister *David Ben-Gurion.* The Israeli republic is the Middle East's only modern democratic state.

## ISRAEL MAINTAINS ITS EXISTENCE

1. **Israeli War for Independence (1948–1949).** The Arab nations defied the UN decision for a Jewish state and attacked Israel. Despite their greater numbers, the Arabs were driven back and lost territory. In 1949 the Arab states accepted, as temporary, armistices arranged by UN mediator *Ralph Bunche.*

(The Arab nations also defied the UN decision for a Palestinian Arab state. The areas proposed for such a state were seized—the Gaza Strip by Egypt and the land on the West Bank of the Jordan River by Jordan.)

2. **Continued Arab Hostility (1949–1956).** (*a*) The Arab League enforced an economic boycott against Israel. (*b*) Egypt barred Israeli ships from the Suez Canal. (*c*) Egyptian artillery on the Sinai Peninsula blockaded ships bound for

Israel's port of *Elath* on the *Gulf of Aqaba* (see map, below). (*d*) Egypt allowed *fedayeen* (guerrilla) raids from its territory against Israeli settlements.

**3. Sinai Campaign (1956).** Israel feared Egypt's military buildup, which resulted chiefly from an arms deal in 1955 between Egypt and the Communist bloc. In 1956 Israel invaded the Sinai Peninsula to wipe out fedayeen bases and end the Aqaba blockade. Israeli forces quickly scattered Nasser's armies. (Britain and France also invaded Egypt to regain control of the Suez Canal. Check the Index.) The UN condemned the attacks, secured withdrawal of the invading forces, and stationed a *United Nations Emergency Force (UNEF)* in Egypt on the border with Israel and at the tip of the Sinai Peninsula. For ten years Israel was free from Egyptian fedayeen raids and free to use the Gulf of Aqaba.

**4. Arab-Israel War (1967)**

*a. Background.* Egypt entered into military alliances with Syria and Jordan; and the Arab states moved their armies toward their borders with Israel. Nasser secured removal of the UNEF and closed the Gulf of Aqaba to Israeli shipping. Israel called up its military reserves. Eventually war started.

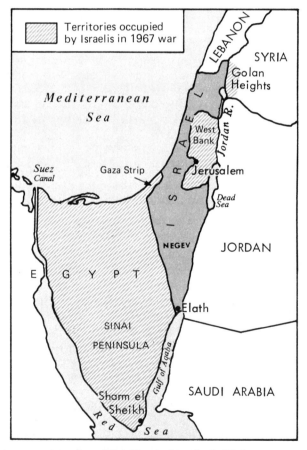

**Israel and the Bordering Arab States**

*b. The War.* In a six-day war, the Israelis routed the Arab forces. The Israelis seized (1) *from Egypt*—the Gaza Strip and the entire Sinai Peninsula westward to the Suez Canal and southward to Sharm el Sheikh, opening the Gulf of Aqaba to Israeli shipping; (2) *from Jordan*—the West Bank of the Jordan River, including the Old City of Jerusalem; and (3) *from Syria*—the Golan Heights.

UN Security Council resolutions helped end the fighting. Israel urged peace talks, but Egypt and Syria spoke of another round of fighting.

## 5. Postwar Developments (1967–1973)

*a. No War but No Peace.* Arab guerrilla groups gave Israel no peace. They increased terrorist raids against Israeli settlements and gunned Israeli commercial airplanes at airports in Greece and Switzerland. In 1972 Arab extremists employed Japanese leftists to massacre innocent civilians at the Tel Aviv airport; also the *Black September* terrorists murdered 11 Israeli Olympic athletes at Munich. In response Israel raided guerrilla bases in Syria and Lebanon.

The main threat to Israel, however, was Egypt, whose leaders called for "fire and blood." Israel bested Egypt in artillery and airplane duels along the Suez Canal. Egypt became dependent upon Russia for military equipment and for 20,000 military personnel, who manned missile sites and trained Egypt's forces.

*b. Egypt Under Sadat.* In 1970 Nasser died, and his position was assumed by *Anwar al-Sadat.* This Egyptian president directed his nation's foreign policy away from dependence on the Soviet Union. Although in 1971 Sadat signed a Soviet-Egyptian treaty of friendship, a year later he ordered Soviet military personnel to leave Egypt. They left, but Soviet military equipment remained, and the Soviets continued to supply Egypt with spare parts.

Sadat, however, was determined to regain Egyptian territory lost to Israel in the 1967 war—if necessary by a new war.

## 6. Arab-Israeli War (1973)

*a. Military Front.* By attacking on Yom Kippur, the most holy day of the Jewish religion and a day devoted to prayer, the Syrians and Egyptians gained an initial surprise advantage. Israeli forces, hastily mobilized, slowly reversed the tide of battle. The Israelis achieved air supremacy, advanced against the Syrians on the Golan Heights, and crossed the Suez Canal westward into Egypt proper, trapping a 20,000-man Egyptian force in the Sinai desert. Against this military background, the three warring nations accepted the UN cease-fire calls.

*b. Arab Unity Moves* (1) *Military Matters.* To the aid of Syria and Egypt rushed the other Arab states, sending troops and planes. (2) *Oil Embargo.* The oil-rich Arab states, joined together in OPEC, have supplied significant amounts of the oil needs of industrialized nations: the United States, West European nations, and Japan. With the outbreak of the 1973 Arab-Israeli War, the Arab states raised oil prices fourfold, and, using oil as a political weapon, reduced shipments to most West European nations and Japan, and totally embargoed oil shipments to the United States. As the diplomatic price for easing their oil cutoff, the Arab states demanded that the oil-consuming nations voice support for the

Arab position in the Mideast. Japan and most West European nations did so. After the UN cease-fire, American Secretary of State *Henry Kissinger* negotiated an Israeli-Egyptian troop-separation agreement that restored Egyptian control of both sides of the Suez Canal. Thereafter, most Arab oil-producing states ended the embargo against the United States.

*c. Superpower Involvement.* After the outbreak of the 1973 war, the United States acted unsuccessfully to halt the hostilities. The Soviet Union, in contrast, acted to spur hostilities, voicing support for Egypt and Syria and urging the other Arab states to join in the struggle. As the war took a heavy toll of military equipment, the Soviets began airlifting additional supplies to Egypt and Syria. The United States thereupon acted to resupply Israel.

After the Israelis gained the military advantage, the Soviet Union and the United States jointly sponsored a balanced UN resolution that achieved a Mideast cease-fire. A rumored Soviet plan to send Russian troops into the Mideast to bolster Egyptian forces led President Nixon to place the American military on a "precautionary alert." The danger of this possible confrontation was eased with the creation of the UNEF peacekeeping force—to serve as a buffer between the Israeli and Egyptian armies.

*d. Observations.* (1) Israel "won" the war militarily but in other ways "lost." With its small population, Israel suffered heavy casualties, although they were only one-tenth those inflicted on the Arabs. With its limited resources, Israel incurred heavy war costs. Israel finally was more isolated diplomatically than ever before. (2) Egypt experienced a tremendous upsurge of confidence as its armies demonstrated ability to master modern military equipment. Egypt also regained full control of the Suez Canal. (3) The United States increased its *leverage*, that is, its ability to influence Mideast affairs. While reaffirming its support for Israel's right to exist, the United States avoided an extreme partisan stand and gained increased respect among moderate Arab states, especially Egypt. (4) The Soviet Union demonstrated its ability to influence Mideast affairs.

## RECENT DEVELOPMENTS

**1. Egyptian-Soviet Discord.** In 1976 Sadat, bitter that the Soviet Union had refused to replenish Egypt's weapons and to ease Egypt's debt repayment, moved to end the 1971 Soviet-Egyptian friendship treaty.

**2. The Entebbe Air Rescue Mission.** In 1976 Palestinian guerrillas in Greece hijacked an Air France plane coming in from Israel. After compelling the pilot to fly the plane to Entebbe airport in Uganda, the hijackers threatened death to over 100 Israeli hostages unless Israel released jailed Palestinian terrorists. To save the hostages, Israel launched a daring long-distance air rescue mission. Israeli commandos landed at Entebbe airport, wiped out the Palestinian hijackers and some 20 Ugandan soldiers assisting the hijackers, and flew back all but four hostages and one commando safely to Israel.

**3. PLO Terrorism and the Israeli Invasion of Southern Lebanon.** In early 1978 PLO terrorists came from southern Lebanon by boat into Israel. They killed more than 30 civilians and injured over 70 others before being suppressed by Israeli forces. In response, Israel sent a force into southern Lebanon to deprive the PLO of this area for attacks upon Israel. As the Palestinian guerrillas and refugees fled northward, the Israelis strengthened the Christian Arab militia, who were hostile to the PLO. At the UN the Security Council approved a resolution for Israel to withdraw its force from southern Lebanon and for a UNEF to replace the Israelis. Israel agreed, despite skepticism that the UNEF could prevent the return of PLO guerrillas to southern Lebanon.

**4. The Sadat Visit to Israel.** In late 1977 President Sadat informed the Egyptian parliament that, to further Mideast peace, he was ready to journey to Israel. Sadat thereupon received an official invitation from Israeli Prime Minister *Menachem Begin.* Sadat became the first Arab leader ever to visit Israel. He received a warm welcome from the Israeli people, worshipped in a mosque in Jerusalem, paid his respects at Yad Vashem—the Israeli memorial to the 6 million Holocaust victims of Nazi Germany, and addressed the Knesset.

In his speech Sadat acknowledged that Israel's existence is a fact and stated that we Arabs "welcome you to live among us in peace and security." However, he reiterated Arab demands for the return of all lands occupied by Israel in the 1967 war and for the recognition of Palestinian rights to a homeland, but he significantly did *not* mention the PLO. In response Prime Minister Begin praised Sadat for his courage and vision but reiterated Israeli demands for secure borders so as to protect the nation against the danger of destruction. In final statements the two leaders pledged "no more war."

Sadat's visit sharply divided the Arab world. His initiative was hailed overwhelmingly by the Egyptian people and was approved by the governments of Sudan, Tunisia, and Morocco. Sadat was denounced as a traitor to the Arab cause by the PLO and by the radical Arab states of Libya, Algeria, and Iraq. These states were known as "rejectionists" because they rejected any compromise that provided for the existence of Israel. Syria, while not fully joining the rejectionists, also condemned the Sadat visit.

**5. The Camp David (Maryland) Summit Conference (1978).** Following the Sadat visit to Israel, the Egyptian-Israeli peace talks faltered. President Carter, thereupon, invited President Sadat and Prime Minister Begin to meet with him at Camp David. For 13 days the leaders conferred and reached two agreements:

*a.* "Framework for Peace in the Middle East" dealt with the West Bank of the Jordan River and the Gaza Strip. It provided: (1) Palestinians living in these areas will receive self-rule through an elected council. Thereafter the Israeli military government will end and Israeli troops will be partially withdrawn. These arrangements will prevail during a five-year transition period. (2) Within three years, Israel, Egypt, Jordan, and the elected Palestinian representatives will begin discussions on the "final status" of the areas. (3) This document was designed to provide a basis for peace between Israel and the three bordering Arab states of Jordan, Syria, and Lebanon.

*b.* "Framework for a Peace Treaty Between Egypt and Israel" dealt with the Sinai Peninsula. It provided: (1) Israel agreed to return the Sinai Peninsula to

Egypt and, within three years, to withdraw all Israeli troops from the area. (2) Egypt agreed to demilitarize much of Sinai and to permit peacekeeping forces to be stationed in the strategic Sinai areas. (3) Israeli ships were guaranteed free passage through the Suez Canal and the Gulf of Aqaba. (4) Egypt and Israel will negotiate a peace treaty and thereafter establish normal relations.

The agreements evoked widely different responses. President Carter was jubilant. The Egyptian and Israeli peoples were pleased that the agreements had resolved many issues. The PLO was bitter that its existence had been ignored. Syria, the "rejectionist" Arab states, and Russia denounced the agreements.

**6. The Israeli-Egyptian Peace Treaty** (1979): *(a)* reaffirmed the Camp David provisions regarding Israeli withdrawal from the Sinai, the stationing of a peacekeeping force, free passage through the Suez Canal and the Gulf of Aqaba for Israeli ships, and the establishment of normal relations between Israel and Egypt and *(b)* contained provisions for Israel to buy oil from the Sinai fields being returned to Egypt and for Israel and Egypt to hold negotiations regarding Palestinian self-rule in the West Bank and the Gaza Strip.

As part of the peace process, the United States agreed to *(a)* extend extensive economic and military aid and loans to both Israel and Egypt, *(b)* assist Israel in case of Egyptian violations of the peace treaty, *(c)* help meet Israel's oil needs for up to 15 years, and *(d)* take part in negotiations on Palestinian self-rule.

Although the peace treaty was welcomed by the Egyptian people, it received a hostile reception elsewhere in the Arab world. Most Arab nations—moderates as well as hard-liners—broke diplomatic relations with Egypt. Saudi Arabia ended economic aid to Egypt, and the Arab League moved its headquarters out of Cairo. Despite Egypt's isolation in the Arab world, President Sadat remained confident that his policies would bring genuine Middle East peace.

**7. Negotiations on Palestinian Autonomy.** Beginning in 1979, these negotiations were attended by Egypt, Israel, and the United States but were boycotted by Palestinians of the West Bank and Gaza and by Jordan. The negotiations soon revealed sharp disagreement. Egypt insisted that the Palestinians be granted full local autonomy with the right, after five years, to establish an independent Palestinian state. Israel declared a "united Jerusalem" to be its "eternal capital" and asserted the right to establish additional Jewish settlements in "Judea and Samaria"—the biblical names for the West Bank region. Israel rejected any Palestinian state as a threat to its security and as a potential Soviet satellite nation in the Middle East. Israel insisted upon maintaining its military forces in the West Bank but offered the Palestinians local autonomy with the right after five years to choose between Israeli and Jordanian citizenship. The United States urged flexibility, asked the Palestinians to join the negotiations, expressed concern for Palestinian rights and for the security of Israel, but condemned new Jewish settlements in the West Bank as "harmful to the peace process."

**8. The Syrian-Soviet Treaty** (1980). Increasingly isolated in the Arab world and concerned over the loss of Egyptian support in a future war against Israel, President al-Assad of Syria signed a 20-year treaty of friendship with the Soviet

Union. The treaty called for the two nations to consult in case of a security threat and to cooperate in military, economic, scientific, and cultural areas.

**9. Israeli Raid on the Iraqi Nuclear Facility (1981).** Israeli warplanes bombed and destroyed the Iraqi nuclear facility—named *Osirak*—that was purchased from and being built by France. Israel explained that the surprise raid was conducted on Sunday—so that the fewest foreign technicians would be at the plant—and conducted before the facility became operational—so that its destruction would not release radiation upon the people of nearby Baghdad.

Israel justified the raid as an "act of national self-defense" and claimed that the Iraqi facility was meant to produce nuclear weapons. Israel supported this claim by citing technical data such as the design of the reactor to require weapons-grade uranium. The Israelis further pointed out that Iraq had never signed an armistice and considered itself in a "state of war" with Israel; that Iraq had often stated its goal of destroying the "Zionist entity"; and that Iraqi President *Saddam Hussein* was an "evil" and "crazy" person who would not hesitate to use nuclear bombs against Israeli cities. To provide historical perspective for the raid, Israeli Prime Minister Begin vowed, "There won't be another Holocaust in history. Never again."

Iraq insisted that its nuclear facility was designed for peaceful purposes. (Expert opinion was divided as to whether the destroyed Iraqi facility could have produced nuclear bombs.) Iraq further claimed that Israel was seeking to deter Arab technological progress, and that Iraq would rebuild the nuclear facility. Iraqi President Hussein also called upon "all peace-loving nations" to help the Arabs acquire nuclear weapons to offset what he claimed was Israel's nuclear power. France warned that before it would help rebuild the destroyed reactor, Iraq must accept strict safeguards against possible military use.

The UN Security Council voted unanimously to "strongly condemn" Israel for the raid, but the resolution was considered moderate since it did not call for sanctions against Israel. Before voting for the resolution, American delegate *Jeane Kirkpatrick* delivered a brief speech reaffirming America's commitment to Israel as a friend and an ally.

**10. Assassination of Egypt's President Sadat (1981).** While observing a military parade, Anwar al-Sadat was assassinated by four men who were later identified as Egyptian *Moslem fundamentalists* holding similar beliefs to the religious party in control of Iran. In the month preceding his assassination, Sadat had begun a crackdown against such extremist groups in Egypt, and had jailed over 1,000 Moslem fanatics. (Whether this crackdown led to the assassination plot is not known.) Sadat's death was mourned in Egypt, the Sudan, Israel, the United States, and most pro-Western nations, where he was viewed as a man of courage and peace. His death was greeted with joy by the PLO, Libya, and other "rejectionist" Arab states, where he was viewed as a "traitor" to the Arab cause.

*Hosni Mubarak*—a former air force commander trained in the Soviet Union—had been handpicked by Sadat as his vice-president and successor. Mubarak now became Egypt's new president. He pledged to continue the peace process.

Despite Mubarak's pledge, political observers held that Sadat's death introduced greater uncertainty into Middle Eastern affairs. Will Mubarak be able to consolidate his power inside Egypt? If yes, will Mubarak continue the peace process with Israel after the final Israeli withdrawal, in April 1982, from the Sinai Peninsula? Or will he return Egypt to the Arab fold by denouncing the Camp David agreements? Will he maintain Sadat's pro-American and anti-Soviet foreign policy? One conclusion seems certain—the Middle East will remain an area of instability, tension, and major-power rivalry.

**11. United States Sale of AWACS to Saudi Arabia (1981).** The Reagan administration proposed to sell to Saudi Arabia $8.5 billion of military equipment including five Airborne Warning and Control System (AWACS) planes. These are complex high-technology radar planes capable of detecting approaching aircraft at a distance of several hundred miles. The administration defended the proposed sale as (a) enhancing the military security of the Persian Gulf area against any Soviet threat, (b) providing vital early-defense information, (c) encouraging the Saudis to be more supportive of American Middle East peace efforts, (d) representing no threat to the security of Israel, and (e) removing any need for the Saudis to purchase similar equipment from Britain.

Opponents argued that the sale does not serve the "best interests of the United States" because Saudi Arabia (a) is an unstable country, creating the danger that the AWACS might fall into unfriendly hands, (b) has rejected proposals for joint AWACS control with the United States and for American military bases on its territory, (c) has been a "negative" influence on the Middle East peace process by financing the PLO, opposing the Camp David accords, and condemning Egypt, (d) in possession of the AWACS, threatens the security of America's ally, Israel. In condemning the sale, Israeli leaders accused Saudi Arabia of "a fanatic hatred of Jews and Israel" and expressed fears that Saudi Arabia could use the AWACS to undermine Israeli military security.

With a majority vote in each House of Congress required to halt the sale, the House of Representatives, by a three-to-one margin voted against the President. Reagan then engaged in an intensive lobbying effort with Senators—emphasizing the need to support Presidential foreign policy leadership. The Senate, by a 52-to-48 vote, narrowly upheld the President. The AWACS are scheduled for delivery in late 1985—four years hence.

## PROBLEMS FACING ISRAEL

**1. Assimilating Immigrants.** Since independence, the population of Israel has quadrupled, chiefly through Jewish immigration from Europe, North Africa, and the Middle East. Israel seeks to unite these diverse peoples culturally and to provide for them economically.

**2. Expanding the Economy.** Israel needs capital to develop its limited natural resources, to build industries, and to bring water to desert lands, especially the southern, or Negev, region. Its plans to tap the Jordan River waters have been opposed by the Arab states.

**There are several alternatives.**

*Reprinted with permission from the Minneapolis Tribune.*

**3. Negotiating a Peace Agreement.** Israel wants a permanent peace settlement with the Arabs. Three major obstacles are the future of the Palestinian Arab refugees, the boundaries of Israel, and the refusal of most Arab states to recognize the existence of Israel.

**4. Raising Funds.** With Arab hostility undiminished, Israel spends considerable sums on military preparedness. Its people bear an extremely heavy tax burden. Israel sells economic development bonds, mainly to people in the Western democracies. In addition to interest on the bonds, these people gain the satisfaction of knowing that they have helped Israel's economic progress. Israel also benefits from charitable contributions collected worldwide in most Jewish communities and used in Israel for health, education, and immigrant assistance.

**5. Coping with Russia.** Israel, democratic and Western in outlook, must contend with the pro-Arab policy of Soviet Russia.

## *Iran*

**BACKGROUND.** See page 379.

**UPHEAVAL AND UNREST**

**1. Khomeini Seizes Control.** By 1979 the Shah faced uncontrollable opposition by workers protesting low wages and inflation, by democratic and radical groups protesting autocratic rule, and by conservative religious groups protesting efforts to modernize the country. As the Shah fled Iran, the country came under the control of *Ayatollah* (holy man) *Ruhollah Khomeini*. This Moslem religious leader, who exercised dictatorial rule, planned to make Iran an Islamic republic based on the principles of the 7th-century Moslem bible, the Koran.

**2. Problems Facing Iran.** Iran faces many problems: resentment of Marxist groups for being excluded from the government; resentment of moderate democratic groups against strict observance of the Koran and against Khomeini's dictatorial rule, which included a ban on broadcasts of music, a call for women to dress modestly in accordance with Islamic tradition, and a shutdown of opposition newspapers; revolts by ethnic minorities—Arabs to the south and Kurds and Turks (Iran's largest minority) in the north; assassinations; unemployment; inflation; and a sharp cut in oil production. Nevertheless Iranian voters approved an Islamic constitution that granted Ayatollah Khomeini dictatorial powers for life.

**3. Ouster of Bani-Sadr.** In 1980 Iranian voters elected a civilian president—a moderate, French-educated economist, *Abolhassan Bani-Sadr*. For 17 months Bani-Sadr struggled against the clergy-dominated *Islamic Republican* party that controlled the Iranian Majlis (Parliament) and the Cabinet members—but he was unsuccessful. Removed from office by Khomeini, Bani-Sadr fled for his life, eventually surfacing in France. With Bani-Sadr's removal, still more violence erupted in Iran. The authorities mounted a crackdown against "counterrevolutionaries" and some 2,000 persons were executed, many before firing squads. Guerrilla groups opposed to the regime fought street battles against revolutionary guards and planted bombs that took the lives of major figures in the Islamic Republican party and government. The authorities blamed various opposition groups, especially a leftist Islamic organization, the *People's Mujahedeen*. The Mujahedeen, who had fought against the Shah and had supported Bani-Sadr, wanted, not a clergy-dominated Iran, but a modern nation.

## PROBLEMS FOR THE UNITED STATES

**1. Khomeini's Anti-American Attitude.** Khomeini spurred anti-American feeling and blamed the United States for Iran's problems. Iran canceled contracts for the purchase of American arms and other goods, curtailed the shipment of oil to the United States, and closed the American intelligence posts in northern Iran that had monitored Soviet missile tests.

**2. Americans Taken Hostage in Iran.** In late 1979 President Carter allowed the Shah to enter the United States for surgery and postoperative treatment for cancer. Thereupon, in *Teheran*, capital of Iran, militants—supposedly students—occupied the American embassy and seized some 50 Americans as hostages. For release of the hostages, the "students" demanded that the United States deliver the Shah to Iran to be punished for his "crimes." The militants, urged on by Khomeini, charged the Shah with massacring antigovernment demonstrators, torturing political prisoners, plundering the nation's wealth, eroding Iran's traditional Islamic values, and placing Iran under the control of Washington. As the United States refused to hand over the Shah, the Iranians then charged that the American embassy had been a "spy center" and threatened to place some hostages on trial for spying.

The United States condemned the seizure of the American embassy and its staff as violations of international law and "blackmail." The United States demanded that the hostages be released unconditionally—a position supported by a unanimous vote of the UN Security Council and by a unanimous decision of the World Court. As Iran still refused, President Carter prohibited American purchases of Iranian oil, froze Iranian assets in the United States, and ordered the deportation of Iranian students illegally in the United States. President Carter also warned that he might take other actions.

In early 1980, although the Shah had left the United States, the American hostages were still in captivity. The United States then broke diplomatic relations with and embargoed American exports to Iran. Later, President Carter ordered a military mission to rescue the hostages, but three helicopters malfunctioned and the President called off the mission.

**3. Release of the American Hostages.** In late 1980, the Iranian Parliament proposed to free the 52 hostages upon American acceptance of certain conditions. With Algeria serving as intermediary, the United States and Iran negotiated, but excessive Iranian demands slowed progress. After President-elect Reagan denounced the Iranians as "criminals and kidnappers," Iran concluded negotiations with the outgoing Carter Administration as follows: (a) The United States would not interfere in Iran's internal affairs and would end its embargo against Iran. (b) The United States would return, through Algeria, some $7–$8 billion of frozen Iranian assets—of which up to $5 billion would be used to repay American banks for previously made loans to Iran. (c) The United States would later transfer additional frozen Iranian assets of up to $2 billion—part to be turned over to Iran and part to be held to satisfy private American claims against Iran. (d) The two nations would establish an arbitration commission to decide claims of American individuals and corporations against Iran (the hostages were excluded from claiming damages from Iran). (e) Iran could sue in American courts for any of the late Shah's assets found in the United States.

On January 20, 1981, as President Reagan was being inaugurated, the hostages, after 444 days of captivity, departed from Iran in an Algerian plane. Several days later they returned to the United States where they received heroes' welcomes. As the hostages told of the physical and mental brutality practiced by their Iranian captors, President Reagan expressed America's outrage, but he pledged to honor the agreement. The President also cautioned Americans against attempting business with Iran.

## THE IRAN-IRAQ WAR (BEGINNING IN 1980)

Under the Shah, Iran had been considered a military power and had secured Iraq's signature to a 1975 treaty establishing the boundary between the two nations so as to share control of the *Shatt al-Arab* waterway—at the northern tip of the Persian Gulf. (In return, Iran ended its aid to the rebellious Iraqi Kurds.)

Under Khomeini, Iran by 1980 was considered militarily weak—its military leaders purged, military supplies from the United States frozen, and Iranian society chaotic. Thereupon President Saddam Hussein of Iraq abrogated the "humiliating" 1975 treaty and attacked Iran. Hussein's motives were to gain full control of the Shatt al-Arab waterway, to seize three small islands near the center of the Persian Gulf at the Strait of Hormuz, to overthrow Khomeini, who had called upon Iraqis to rebel against Hussein, and to emerge as the Arab "strongman." Iraqi forces penetrated some 30 miles into Iran's oil-rich province of Khuzistan but thereafter were contained by fanatic Iranian resistance.

Although stalemated, the Iran-Iraq war has had serious effects. It *(a)* curtailed oil shipments to the West from both Iran and Iraq, *(b)* sharply divided the Arab world as Libya and Syria voiced support for Iran whereas Jordan pledged aid to Iraq, *(c)* raised the possibility that the war might involve other Persian Gulf nations, and *(d)* heightened fears that the Soviets, who have supplied Iraq with military equipment, might expand their influence in the Persian Gulf area.

## MULTIPLE–CHOICE QUESTIONS

1. Of Great Britain's Middle East policies, which one led to the other three?   (1) purchase of the Suez Canal   (2) protection of the Empire's "lifeline"   (3) annexation of Cyprus   (4) control of Egypt as a protectorate.

2. The Suez Canal shortened the water route between   (1) New York and Istanbul   (2) London and Singapore   (3) Tokyo and San Francisco   (4) Cairo and Venice.

3. During the 19th century, Russian efforts to seek control of the straits uniting the Black and Mediterranean seas were most strongly opposed by   (1) Austria-Hungary   (2) France   (3) Great Britain   (4) Italy.

4. Archbishop Makarios was noted as   (1) the leader of the Greek Cypriotes   (2) the prime minister of Greece   (3) the Patriarch of Eastern Christianity   (4) a Roman Catholic missionary in the Middle East.

5. Which *two* countries were most concerned with the conflicts on Cyprus?   (1) Israel and Egypt   (2) Turkey and Greece   (3) Bulgaria and Rumania   (4) Italy and France.

6. Two nations intervening on opposing sides in the Yemen civil war were   (1) Egypt and Israel   (2) Egypt and Saudi Arabia   (3) Syria and Jordan   (4) Sudan and Libya.

7. Which country controlled Palestine prior to World War I?   (1) Britain   (2) Egypt   (3) Turkey   (4) Saudi Arabia.

8. When did Jews first live in Palestine?   (1) after World War I   (2) during the Crusades   (3) with the founding of the state of Israel   (4) in ancient times.

9. Which event in modern times caused large-scale Jewish immigration to Palestine?   (1) Nazi persecution of Jews   (2) Russian discrimination against Jews   (3) discovery of oil in Palestine   (4) British violation of the Balfour Declaration.

10. By the Balfour Declaration Britain supported   (1) the Berlin-to-Bagdad railroad   (2) Arab nationalism   (3) Cyprus independence   (4) a Jewish homeland in Palestine.

11. The first prime minister of the state of Israel was   (1) Herzl   (2) Weizmann   (3) Ben-Gurion   (4) Bunche.

12. One factor encouraging unity among Arab countries is   (1) a common hostility toward Israel   (2) similar types of government   (3) common ownership of valuable oil reserves   (4) the acceptance of Egypt's leadership by most Arab rulers.

13. One purpose of the Arab League has been to (1) resettle Arab refugees from Palestine (2) establish an Arab free trade area (3) settle the Cyprus dispute (4) destroy the state of Israel.

14. By the 1956 Sinai Campaign, Israel (1) won the friendship of the Soviet Union (2) gained complete control of the Jordan River (3) ended the blockade of the Gulf of Aqaba (4) secured a military alliance with the United States.

15. OPEC is an organization of (1) only Arab states (2) all Arab states (3) only non-Arab states (4) oil-producing Arab and non-Arab states.

16. Al Fatah is the name of the (1) president of Syria (2) large guerrilla group in the PLO (3) Moslem Bible (4) major port city in Lebanon.

17. Syria entered the Lebanese civil war (1975–1976) because Syria (1) feared an Israeli takeover (2) wanted to help the PLO (3) feared a hostile leftist government in Lebanon (4) wanted control of Lebanon's oil resources.

18. President Sadat of Egypt (1) followed all the policies of his predecessor (2) followed none of the policies of his predecessor (3) lessened Egypt's dependence on Russia (4) opposed the 1973 Arab attack on Israel.

19. Israel's "victory at Entebbe" refers to (1) a 1973 Sinai battle (2) the capture of Yasir Arafat (3) the rescue of hostages held by Palestinian guerrillas in Uganda (4) the PLO defeat in the Lebanese civil war.

20. Which represents the *major* goal of Israeli foreign policy? (1) ending Communist influence in the Middle East (2) destroying the Organization of Petroleum Exporting Countries (OPEC) (3) gaining control of both sides of the Suez Canal (4) assuring the physical and economic security of Israel.

21. American foreign policy in the Middle East has sought (1) a confrontation with the Soviet Union (2) a compromise settlement of Arab-Israeli issues so as to end the recurrent crises (3) peace in the area enforced by American marines (4) an end to American investments in Arab countries.

## TRUE–FALSE QUESTIONS

If the statement is correct, write the word *true*. If the statement is incorrect, substitute a word or phrase for the italicized term to make the statement correct.

1. The leading natural resource of the Middle East is *uranium*.

2. *Lebanon* was formerly a French mandate in the Middle East.

3. The Arab nationalist who wanted but failed to unite the Arab countries under his leadership was *Syria's Assad*.

4. The Arab states vehemently oppose Israel's plan to irrigate its desert lands by utilizing the waters of the *Mediterranean Sea*.

5. The port city of Elath, at the southern tip of Israel, is on the *Persian Gulf*.

6. Morocco's control of the Western (Spanish) Sahara was challenged by *Tunisia*.

7. The Arab state whose population is divided between Arab Christians and Arab Moslems is *Iraq*.

8. *President Carter* assisted Egypt and Israel to reach agreement at Camp David.

9. *Elias Sarkis* was the American secretary of state who, after the 1973 Arab-Israeli War, negotiated a Sinai accord that restored full Egyptian control of the Suez Canal.

## MAP QUESTIONS

For each country described below, write *both* its name and the letter indicating its location on the map.

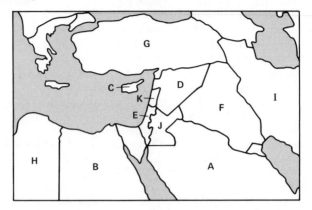

1. This nation, which controls the Dardanelles, was the center of the Ottoman Empire.
2. In this country, formerly a British colony, the Greek and Turkish peoples have been unable to live in harmony.
3. This oil-rich Arab country borders on both the Red Sea and the Persian Gulf.
4. Formerly a British mandate, this nation is surrounded by hostile Arab states.
5. This country, which contains the Suez Canal, was once a British protectorate.
6. In 1970–1971 this Arab country ruled by King Hussein drove out the Palestinian guerrillas.
7. In this oil-rich Middle East nation, a 1979 revolution overthrew the Shah and shifted control to a religious leader.
8. This oil-rich nation in North Africa is one of the radical Arab states.

## ESSAY QUESTIONS

1. *(a)* Discuss *two* reasons for Britain's interest in the Middle East. *(b)* Name *three* Middle East territories that Britain previously controlled, and for *each* describe the form of British control and the present status of the territory.
2. In regard to Arab nationalism, discuss *(a)* *two* factors that led to its growth *(b)* *two* evidences of Arab unity *(c)* *two* causes of Arab disunity.
3. Strong convictions and support of specific ideas cause people to join together to work for a common goal. Discuss *one* goal of each of the following groups: *(a)* Zionists *(b)* Arab League *(c)* Turkish Cypriotes *(d)* OPEC.
4. In regard to the state of Israel, discuss *(a)* *two* arguments for a Jewish homeland in Palestine *(b)* *one* military action by which Israel defended its existence *(c)* *three* problems that currently face the state of Israel.
5. State whether you agree or disagree with each of the following statements, giving *two* arguments to support your position: *(a)* Arab nationalism has been responsible for unrest in the Middle East. *(b)* The Suez Canal is less important, economically and militarily, today than it was before World War I. *(c)* Israel was justified in its 1956 invasion of Egypt. *(d)* The Cyprus issue can be solved only by partition of the island. *(e)* The PLO has caused more disunity than unity among the Arab nations. *(f)* Regardless of the cause, terrorism against innocent civilians is never justified. *(g)* The Arab-Israeli conflict could be solved if each side showed a little flexibility.

# Part 6. The Far East

## A. China

### APPEAL TO MODERN IMPERIALISTS (STARTING IN MID-19TH CENTURY)

China attracted imperialist nations for several reasons. (1) China's huge population offered a tremendous market for manufactured goods and a supply of cheap labor to work in foreign-owned enterprises. (2) China's untapped mineral resources—coal, tin, and tungsten—interested investors. (3) China's tea and raw silk could be readily sold in European markets. (4) The inefficient Manchu government lacked military power and could be easily intimidated (see pages 113–115).

### VICTIM OF MODERN IMPERIALISM

1. **Britain,** by the *Opium War* (1839–1842), (*a*) compelled China to allow imports of opium, a habit-forming narcotic, (*b*) annexed Hong Kong, and (*c*) acquired the privilege of *extraterritoriality*. This entitled a Briton accused of a crime in China to be tried in a British court. (Extraterritoriality, soon conceded to other foreign nations, affronted Chinese justice and pride.) Britain later established a sphere of influence over the Yangtze River Valley.

2. **France** annexed Indo-China and gained a sphere of influence in southeastern China.

3. **Germany** acquired a sphere of influence in northeastern China over the Shantung Peninsula.

4. **Russia** annexed the Amur River district, the Pacific seaport of Vladivostok, and the central Asian territory bordering Sinkiang Province; secured a lease to ice-free Port Arthur; and established a sphere of influence over Manchuria.

5. **Japan,** by the *Sino-Japanese War* (1894–1895) annexed Taiwan (also called Formosa) and secured a sphere of influence over Korea. (In 1910 Japan annexed Korea.) By victory in the *Russo-Japanese War* (1904–1905), Japan took over Russia's lease to Port Arthur and Russia's sphere of influence in southern Manchuria.

The imperialist nations seemed poised to annex their respective spheres of influence, thereby threatening to dismember China.

## OPEN DOOR POLICY (1899)

The United States was interested in China, not for territory, but for commerce. Our trade, however, was threatened by the spheres of influence and the prospect of China's dismemberment. *John Hay*, American secretary of state, therefore suggested the *Open Door Policy*. It proposed equal trade rights in China for all nations. Later it also came to mean the preservation of China's independence and territory.

The "open door" was accepted by the imperialist nations in principle but not in practice. However, it earned us China's goodwill and for many years served as the cornerstone of American policy toward the Far East.

## BOXER REBELLION (1900)

The *Boxers*, a Chinese society encouraged by Manchu government officials, staged an uprising to drive out all foreigners and restore China to isolation. After an international military force suppressed the rebellion, the foreign nations demanded damages from China.

The United States successfully urged that China pay, not by loss of territory, but by a monetary indemnity. The other nations agreed but imposed excessive indemnities. The United States disapproved and returned half of its indemnity money to advance education in China and to enable Chinese students to attend American colleges.

## THE NATIONALISTS ESTABLISH THE CHINESE REPUBLIC (1911–1912)

The *Kuomintang*, or *Nationalist party*, was founded by Dr. *Sun Yat-sen*, who was educated in British Hong Kong and American Hawaii, and well traveled in the Western world. Dr. Sun advocated for China a program of "three principles": (1) *nationalism*—to replace the weak Manchu Dynasty by a strong central government capable of freeing China from imperialist control, (2) *democracy*—to elect government officials responsible to the people, and (3) *people's livelihood*—to adopt Western industrial and agricultural ways in order to improve economic conditions.

As the Chinese became nationalistic and the Manchus failed to halt the imperialists, the Kuomintang attracted supporters. In 1911–1912 the Nationalists overthrew the Manchu emperor and proclaimed a republic.

## NATIONALISTS STRUGGLE AGAINST WARLORDS (TO 1928)

The Kuomintang failed to gain control of the entire country, ruling only a small region in the south. Most of China was controlled by local warlords. For several years Kuomintang armies made little progress in subduing the warlords. Dr. Sun asked for foreign military assistance, but only Russia, then recently turned Communist, offered help. With Soviet armaments and military advisers, Kuomintang armies became an effective fighting force.

After Dr. Sun Yat-sen died (1925), the Kuomintang came under the direction of a conservative military leader, *Chiang Kai-shek*. By 1928 Chiang had destroyed the power of the warlords and achieved control over most of China.

## NATIONALISTS STRUGGLE AGAINST COMMUNISTS (TO 1937)

1. **Communists Gain Supporters.** The Chinese Communist party, organized in 1921, at first operated within the Kuomintang. The party steadily increased its membership and influence by winning over *(a)* some Kuomintang members who were grateful for Soviet military assistance, *(b)* landless peasants who were attracted by Communist promises to break up the estates of the rich landlords, *(c)* low-paid city workers who applauded Communist demands to seize foreign-owned businesses, and *(d)* nationalists who acclaimed Communist propaganda attacks against Western imperialists.

2. **Nationalists Battle Communists.** Chiang Kai-shek opposed the spread of Communism within China. His stand received strong support from *(a)* landlords and the emerging middle class, who feared Communist economic doctrines, *(b)* democratic groups who feared Communist totalitarian rule and hoped that the Kuomintang would move toward democracy, and *(c)* nationalists who feared that the Communists would place China under the domination of the Soviet Union.

In 1927 Chiang ousted the Russian advisers, drove the Chinese Communists from the Kuomintang, and sought to destroy the Communist movement. The Communists fought back, and for ten years China experienced inconclusive civil war. In 1934–1935 the Communists, now led by *Mao Tse-tung*, undertook a perilous *long march* of several thousand miles northward and established their stronghold around the city of *Yenan* in north central China somewhat south of the Russian border. In 1937 Nationalists and Communists agreed to a truce to meet the challenge of Japanese imperialism.

## CHINESE STRUGGLE FOR INDEPENDENCE AGAINST JAPAN (TO 1945)

1. **Japanese Imperialism in China.** Modern, industrialized Japan represented the major imperialist threat to China's independence. Japan had taken Taiwan (Formosa) (1895), Port Arthur (1905), Korea (1910), and Manchuria (1931)—all without effective Chinese opposition. In 1937 Japan invaded China proper. This time Japan met with considerable resistance from both Chinese Nationalists and Communists. The Japanese seized the coastal areas with their large seaport cities and occupied about one-quarter of the country but were unable to destroy the Chinese armies. The Chinese retreated into the interior and waged guerrilla warfare. The Chinese Nationalists received armaments and loans from Britain and the United States.

**2. China and World War II.** In 1941 China's struggle for independence merged into World War II when Japan attacked Britain and the United States. To strengthen China's determination to fight, the Allies *(a)* gave up their extraterritorial and other special privileges, *(b)* pledged to restore Taiwan and Manchuria to China, and *(c)* elevated China to United Nations "Big Five" status.

Although China fought on, its military contribution was not significant. American armed might, with some Allied help, crushed Japan by 1945 and thus saved China from Japanese conquest. As World War II ended, the Nationalists and Communists resumed their civil war.

## NATIONALISTS LOSE CHINA TO THE COMMUNISTS (1949)

**1. Nationalist Weaknesses.** The Chiang Kai-shek regime lost public support in China because it *(a)* was a thinly veiled dictatorship marked by corruption and inefficiency, *(b)* wasted a considerable portion of the $2 billion in American loans and military supplies, *(c)* failed to earn the soldiers' loyalty and prevent army desertions, and *(d)* ignored the peasants' desire for land and the workers' demand for better living conditions. Chiang did not heed American advice to improve political and economic conditions.

**2. Communists Gain China.** Following World War II Chinese Communist armies, strengthened by considerable equipment captured from the Japanese and supplied by the Soviet Union, achieved military supremacy over the Nationalists. By the end of 1949, Communist armies had driven Chiang Kai-shek to his only remaining stronghold—the island of Taiwan (Formosa).

Since then the Communists have controlled mainland China with its current population of over 1,000 million (one billion) people.

## CHINA AS A COMMUNIST STATE (SINCE 1949)

At Peking (Beijing) the Communists proclaimed the *People's Republic of China* under the leadership of Premier *Chou En-lai* (Zhou Enlai) and Communist party head *Mao Tse-tung* (Mao Zedong). (The spellings in parentheses conform to the Pinyin phonetic transcription system recently adopted officially by China.)

**1. Government.** The government is a one-party dictatorship under the Communist party. By army and secret police, the government enforces its authority and deals ruthlessly with domestic opposition. In purges the Communists executed several million Chinese as counterrevolutionists. Others were imprisoned for "reeducation," a process labeled by non-Communists as *brainwashing.*

**2. Economy**

*a. Industry.* The government nationalized industry and inaugurated Five-Year Plans for economic development. The plans emphasize heavy industry—iron and steel, chemicals, electric power, machinery—but neglect consumer goods. Although workers' living standards may have improved slightly, wages

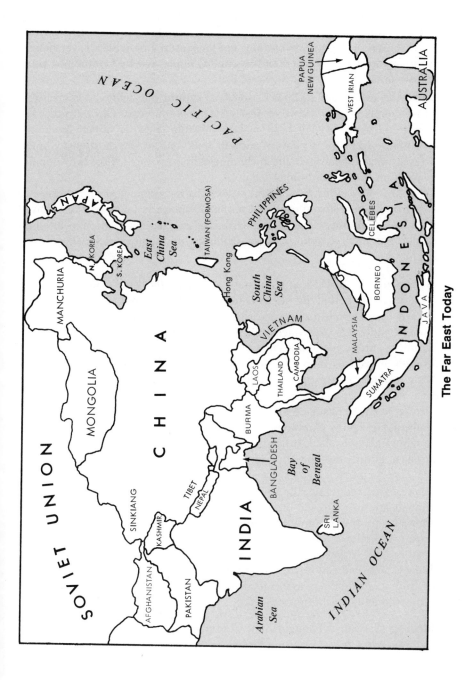

The Far East Today

remain low, working hours are long, factory conditions are poor, and in practice strikes are forbidden. Under Mao Tse-tung's economic theories, workers are to labor for the success of the revolution, not for material benefits. Nevertheless, some labor unrest has surfaced and has been suppressed by Communist party and army units.

Since the early 1960's China's industrial output has achieved remarkable growth—averaging an increase of nearly 10 percent a year. This output, however, started from a very low base, making possible large percentage increases. Some Chinese industry is modern and efficient, but for the most part China's factories are poorly managed and technologically backward. Also, they depend excessively on the use of human labor.

To improve its industry, Communist China in recent years has turned to imports from industrialized capitalist nations, especially Japan and the United States. The Communist Chinese emphasize the purchase of modern technological equipment, such as steel mills, oil drilling equipment, and advanced computers.

*b. Agriculture.* In 1958, announcing a *great leap forward,* Communist chief Mao Tse-tung compelled the peasants to transfer land to and join in *communes.* These are huge agricultural establishments in which the state owns all the equipment and land, pays wages to the workers, takes care of the children in community centers, maintains communal dining halls, and compels farm work by women as well as men. By thus freeing individuals from family responsibilities, Communists expected to increase the number of people available to work on farms.

Strong peasant resistance exists against the commune system, and agricultural output lags badly. Commune mismanagement and natural calamities, such as droughts and floods, have caused severe food shortages. China has been forced to purchase grain from abroad, especially Canada, Australia, and the United States.

To increase production, the commune system has been somewhat modified. Individuals are now allowed incentives such as private peasant plots and wage differentials. For the commune system to increase output significantly, Western farm experts believe, the Communists must expand available farmlands by reclamation and irrigation projects, mechanize production by providing farm machinery, improve soil fertility by applying large quantities of chemical fertilizer, and persuade the peasants to abandon traditional methods of farming for modern production techniques.

**3. Ideology (System of Thought).** The Communist government drove out Western influence in China by closing foreign schools, expelling Christian missionaries, and banning "dangerous" books. Through mass communications media and schools, the Communists tried to *(a)* promote their ideology based upon the Chinese Communist interpretations of the doctrines of Marx and Lenin and upon the teachings of Mao Tse-tung and *(b)* wean the people away from the ethical precepts of Confucianism. In particular the Communists stress that the primary loyalty of the individual is to the state, not as Confucius taught, to the family.

(For China's split with the Soviet Union, other foreign relations, and recent developments, check the Index.)

# B. Japan

## OPENING OF JAPAN (1853–1854)

In the mid-17th century, feudal Japan withdrew into isolation and for 200 years remained unaffected by Western civilization (see pages 118–119).

In 1853–1854 Commodore *Matthew C. Perry*, heading an American naval squadron, convinced Japan to open its ports to American trade. Soon afterward the leading European powers demanded and received similar trade rights. In 1864 European and American warships bombarded a Japanese seaport in retaliation against antiforeign outbreaks.

## WESTERNIZATION OF JAPAN (STARTING 1867)

Impressed by Western military might, the Japanese were fearful of foreign domination. Therefore, they rapidly transformed their country from a medieval feudal state into a modern nation.

**1. Government.** The nobles removed the shogun (the highest lord) from power and transferred full governmental control to Emperor *Mutsuhito*. He assumed the reign name *Meiji,* meaning enlightened peace. Mutsuhito's reign (1867–1912) and the accompanying transformation of Japan became known as the *Meiji restoration.*

In 1889 Mutsuhito granted Japan a constitution that provided an autocratic government (modeled upon that of Bismarck's Germany). The cabinet was dominated by military leaders and responsible only to the emperor. (The emperor's authority was further strengthened by Shintoism, the state religion, which began to preach his divine origin.)

**2. Military.** The government created a powerful British-type navy and Prussian-type army.

**3. Education.** The state began a compulsory public education system, and the Japanese became a highly literate people.

**4. Agriculture.** The nobles voluntarily surrendered their feudal privileges. The peasant farmers were no longer bound to the soil, and many became landowners.

**5. Industry.** The government encouraged a sweeping program of industrialization. Japan soon produced textiles, steel, machinery, and ships, and became a major trading and manufacturing nation.

## JAPAN TURNS TO IMPERIALISM

**1. Reasons.** *(a)* With Japan deficient in natural resources, Japanese industrialists needed supplies of raw materials—especially cotton, iron ore, and oil; they also wanted secure markets for their manufactured goods. *(b)* Japanese nationalists sought honor for the emperor and glory for the military forces. They thought that colonies would raise Japan to the rank of a "major power." *(c)* Densely populated and lacking arable land, Japan wanted colonial outlets for its surplus population. *(d)* Japan's location placed the country within easy reach of eastern Asia's underdeveloped nations.

**2. Early Events**

*a. Sino-Japanese War (1894–1895).* Japan overwhelmed China and acquired Taiwan and a sphere of influence in Korea. (In 1910 Japan annexed Korea.)

*b. Russo-Japanese War (1904–1905).* Japan, to the world's surprise, defeated Russia. By the *Treaty of Portsmouth* (New Hampshire), Japan acquired the southern half of Sakhalin Island, Port Arthur, and Russia's sphere of influence in southern Manchuria. (For promoting the peace treaty, American President Theodore Roosevelt received the 1906 Nobel Peace Prize.)

*c. World War I (1914–1918).* Although contributing little to the Allied victory, Japan acquired Germany's concessions on China's Shantung Peninsula and mandates over the former German islands in the Pacific.

## JAPAN AND THE UNITED STATES COME INTO CONFLICT

Made bold by easily won successes, Japanese militarists determined to create and dominate a *New Order,* or *Co-Prosperity Sphere,* for eastern Asia. Japan's ambitions, however, clashed with the Open Door Policy of the United States. Japanese aggressions kept the two nations in conflict and led both into World War II.

**1. Washington Conference (1921–1922).** During World War I, while the Western powers were preoccupied in Europe, Japan tried to turn China into a protectorate by making the *Twenty-one Demands.* The Western powers were alarmed, and after the war the United States arranged the Washington Conference on naval and Far Eastern problems. Under Western persuasion, Japan joined in the *Nine-Power Treaty,* pledging to respect the Open Door principles: *(a)* equal trade rights in China and *(b)* China's territorial integrity and independence. Also, Japan agreed to restore Chinese control over Shantung.

**2. Japanese Invasion of Manchuria (1931).** In violation of the Nine-Power Treaty, Japan invaded China's northern province of Manchuria, which is rich in coal, iron, and fertile soil. The *Lytton Commission,* investigating for the League of Nations, condemned Japan and ordered it to withdraw its troops. Instead, Japan withdrew from the League.

*Henry L. Stimson*, the United States secretary of state, informed Japan that America disapproved of the aggression im Manchuria. His statement, that the United States would recognize no territory taken by force, became known as the *Stimson Doctrine*. Neither the League nor the United States took further action.

By 1932 Japan exercised full control over Manchuria, which was now the puppet state of *Manchukuo*. In violation of the Open Door Policy, the Japanese expelled foreign business interests and monopolized the region's economic development. They built railroads, developed hydroelectric power, and created a sizable iron and steel industry, thereby increasing Japan's economic and military power.

**3. Japanese Invasion of China (1937).** Japan invaded China proper, seeking control of the entire country. Initially Japanese armies met with success and occupied most of coastal China. By 1939, however, their advance into the interior was slowed, often to a standstill, by Chinese guerrilla resistance. Meanwhile, the United States, in support of China, *(a)* extended government loans for the purchase of war materials, *(b)* permitted American volunteer pilots to fight for China as the *Flying Tigers,* and *(c)* in 1940 embargoed the sale to Japan of scrap iron and aviation gasoline. Also, many American importers and consumers unofficially boycotted Japanese goods.

**4. Japanese Attack on Pearl Harbor (December, 1941).** To dominate the Far East, Japanese leaders held that they must drive out Great Britain and the United States. In 1937 Japan joined the Axis alliance of Fascist Italy and Nazi Germany. When World War II began in 1939, Japanese leaders believed that their opportunity was at hand. Britain was at war against Germany; the United States was busy supplying military equipment to the Allied nations in Europe. Consequently, in December, 1941, Japan staged a surprise air attack against the American naval base at *Pearl Harbor,* Hawaii. At the same time Japanese armies invaded British-owned Malaya and the American-owned Philippines. (For Japan's defeat in World War II, check the Index under "Japan.")

## JAPAN SINCE WORLD WAR II

**1. Territorial Losses.** Following its surrender in 1945, Japan was stripped of the territories it had seized during many years of aggression. Japan lost Taiwan and Manchuria to China, southern Sakhalin Island and the Kurile Islands to Russia, and the Japanese-mandated islands in the Pacific to the United States as a trusteeship. The Ryukyu Islands, which include Okinawa, were temporarily occupied by the United States. Korea was divided into Russian and American zones supposedly pending independence. (For developments in Korea, check the Index.)

**2. American Occupation (1945–1952).** American military forces occupied Japan until the 1952 peace treaty. General *Douglas MacArthur*, as Supreme Allied Commander in Japan, introduced sweeping reforms.

3. **New Constitution (1947).** Under MacArthur's direction, the Japanese people adopted a democratic constitution that *(a)* renounced the waging of war and the maintaining of offensive armed forces; *(b)* denied the emperor's divine origin but retained him as a symbol of national unity; *(c)* contained a Bill of Rights guaranteeing civil liberties—including freedom of speech and press, separation of church and state (ending government support for Shintoism), equality under the law (including equal rights for women), and the right to a standard of "wholesome" living; and *(d)* provided for a cabinet responsible to an elected legislature, called the *Diet*.

4. **Economic and Social Reforms.** MacArthur took steps by which Japan *(a)* dissolved the huge business monopolies, such as the *Mitsui* and *Mitsubishi*, which had controlled much of Japan's economic life, *(b)* encouraged free labor unions empowered with the right to strike, *(c)* provided farms for landless peasants, and *(d)* reformed education by removing ultranationalist teachers and textbooks and encouraging democratic learning.

5. **War Trials.** Japanese war leaders received trials before Allied courts on war crime charges: aggressive warfare and atrocities against prisoners. Of those found guilty, some were sentenced to long imprisonment; others were executed.

6. **Treaty of Peace with Japan (1952).** Drawn up by the United States, the Japanese peace treaty was accepted by the major Allied nations, except the Soviet Union. Russia refused to sign the treaty, chiefly because it confirmed Japan's position as an ally of the United States. (In 1956 Russia signed a separate declaration of peace with Japan.)

Considered lenient, the 1952 treaty included the following provisions:

*a. Territory.* Japan lost all its conquests since 1895 but retained its four large home islands. Japan consented to American administration of the Ryukyu Islands, including Okinawa, but reserved the right to claim their return. (For their return to Japan, check the Index under Okinawa.)

*b. Reparations.* Japan was not required to pay reparations in money for war damages. Japan, however, agreed to contribute goods and services to countries damaged by Japanese aggression in World War II.

*c. Defense.* Japan was recognized as an independent sovereign nation possessing the right of military self-defense. (In a separate pact the United States and Japan agreed that American troops would remain stationed in Japan.)

7. **Limited Rearmament.** The Japanese government interpreted the constitutional prohibition against armed forces to apply to offensive—but not defensive—military units. It therefore built up air, sea, and land units, constituting a "self-defense" force of 235,000 troops. These troops are insufficient to defend the nation. However, Japanese public opinion, strongly pacifist, remains unwilling to amend the constitution to permit more extensive rearmament.

Meanwhile, the people are free of heavy military expenditures and depend on the United States to protect their homeland.

**8. Stable, Democratic Government.** Under the Japanese constitution, the people choose the two-house Diet, the more powerful branch being the House of Representatives. The major Liberal-Democratic party—actually a broad coalition of conservative groups—is pro-capitalist, pro-American, and anti-Communist. It has controlled postwar Japan since 1955 and provided stable, democratic rule.

In the 1976 elections the Liberal-Democrats suffered a setback, securing only 258 seats—a razor-thin majority of the 511-seat House of Representatives. The Liberal-Democratic setback was due to two factors: *(a)* a number of Liberal-Democrats were involved in a bribery scandal regarding orders from an American airplane manufacturing company, and *(b)* since 1973 Japan, as did most free world industrial nations, experienced an economic recession. The Socialists increased their representation slightly to 123 seats; the Communists fell sharply to 17 seats.

In the 1980 elections the Liberal-Democrats, despite intraparty disputes, secured 284 seats—a comfortable majority; the Socialists, the major opposition party, held 107 seats; the Communists held 29 seats. The Liberal Democrats, remaining in control of the government, pledged close ties with the United States and increased defense spending. (For Japan and the cold war era, check the Index.)

# C. India

## FACTORS ENABLING BRITAIN TO DOMINATE INDIA

By 1763 Britain had driven its chief European rival, France, from India. Thereafter, relatively few British military and civilian personnel gradually expanded British control throughout vast, heavily populated India. The British conquest was facilitated by India's backwardness and disunity.

**1. Military Inferiority.** The Indians could not cope with the superior British military knowledge, training, and equipment.

**2. Many Languages.** The people of India were divided linguistically among more than a dozen main languages and over 200 dialects. Their many tongues reflected geographic and cultural separation.

**3. Religious Divisions.** Of India's total population, the Moslems constituted about 20 percent and the Hindus the overwhelming majority. Because of their divergent religious traditions and past conflicts, the Moslems and Hindus were bitterly antagonistic to each other (see pages 105–107).

**4. Caste System.** Within Hinduism, the caste system rigidly divided the people and kept them from cooperating effectively (see pages 28–29).

**5. Political Disunity.** India was divided among more than 600 independent states, each headed by its own native prince, or *rajah*.

Britain's method of extending its authority throughout India illustrates the principle of *divide and conquer*.

## INDIA AS A BRITISH POSSESSION

**1. Political Control.** To the mid-19th century, Britain controlled India through a private business enterprise, the *British East India Company*. Its rule resulted in an Indian revolt in 1857, led by the British army's native soldiers, called *sepoys*. After suppressing the *Sepoy Mutiny*, the British government assumed control of the country, ruling British India directly as a colony and ruling the native states indirectly as protectorates through British "advisers" to the Indian princes. In 1876, after Prime Minister Disraeli had secured the Suez Canal, which shortened the water route to India, Parliament proclaimed Queen Victoria as Empress of India.

The British freed India of local wars, guarded its borders against invasion, and generally provided efficient rule. In response to Indian demands, Britain in 1919 permitted the Indian people limited self-government.

**2. Economic Control.** Britain profited greatly from India, called the "brightest jewel of the British Empire." British manufacturers and workers depended upon India to purchase their textiles and machines. British merchants sought India's exports of raw jute and tea. British investors developed India's mineral resources, built railways, and established factories. By the mid-20th century, India was an important Asian producer of textiles, iron and steel, and cement.

By industrializing India, the British provided employment for many Indian workers. Also, the British government improved the country by public works: schools, roads, hospitals, and irrigation and sanitation projects.

The Indian masses, however, continued to live close to the starvation level. The population almost doubled between 1850 and 1900, and job opportunities could not keep up with the increase in population. Handicraft workers could not compete with factories, and factory workers received extremely low wages. Farmers, the overwhelming majority in the population, were beset by uncertain rainfall, crude cultivation methods, high rents, and heavy taxes.

**3. Social Control.** The British had little respect for the native Indian culture, particularly the barbaric practices of slavery, *suttee* (the Hindu custom of burning the widow on the funeral pyre of her deceased husband), and *female infanticide* (killing unwanted baby girls). The British halted these practices. Also, they instituted modern health methods, thus lowering the death rate, began English-oriented educational programs, and introduced the English language and English concepts of law, justice, democracy, and nationalism. However, the funds that the British made available for health and education were hardly adequate for India's massive needs.

## INDIAN INDEPENDENCE MOVEMENT

By the early 20th century, the Indian nationalist movement for self-government and independence centered in the *Indian National Congress party*.

### 1. Leaders

*a. Mohandas K. Gandhi.* A high-caste Hindu educated in Britain, Gandhi absorbed Western ideals of democracy and nationalism. He became the political and spiritual leader of the Indian masses—revered as a prophet and called "saintly one," or *Mahatma*. Gandhi sought to end British rule, not with violence, but with *passive resistance*, also called *noncooperation* or *civil disobedience*. His followers boycotted British goods, shunned government service, refused to pay taxes, and disregarded British laws. Gandhi believed that passive resistance would compel Britain to withdraw from India.

To provide work for India's masses and to avoid the need for foreign capital, Gandhi urged India to produce goods by ancient hand methods. Gandhi also struggled to improve the status of India's untouchables.

*b. Jawaharlal Nehru.* Also a high-caste Hindu educated in Britain, Nehru was a practical political leader with socialist leanings. He accepted Gandhi's ideas of passive resistance and aiding untouchables, but he rejected Gandhi's proposal for hand production. Instead, Nehru urged industrialization to develop India's economy and raise living standards.

*c. Mohammed Ali Jinnah.* A Moslem, Jinnah in the 1930's led his coreligionists out of the Congress party and into the *Moslem League*. Because he feared Hindu domination, Jinnah demanded that the Moslem sections of India become a separate independent state, *Pakistan*.

### 2. India Gains Independence (1947).
Following World War I, Indian nationalists intensified their campaign against British rule. Undeterred by repeated jail sentences, they practiced civil disobedience. Even Gandhi and Nehru were several times imprisoned.

During World War II the Congress party rejected Britain's offer of postwar independence, continued its policy of civil disobedience, and demanded immediate freedom. The Indians, however, could not convince the British to act more rapidly. After the war, in 1947, India (chiefly Hindu) and Pakistan (predominantly Moslem) both received dominion status.

### 3. Moslem–Hindu Violence Accompanies Independence.
With British control removed, Moslems and Hindus engaged in bloody religious riots and sought safety by mass migrations. Because Gandhi preached against such violence, he was assassinated in 1948 by a Hindu fanatic.

## INDEPENDENT INDIA: DEVELOPMENTS IN GOVERNMENT

**1. Introduction.** At first a dominion, India in 1950 became an independent republic but remained within the Commonwealth of Nations.

India had a democratic government with a cabinet responsible to an elected legislature. Until his death in 1964, Nehru was prime minister. From 1966 until 1977 the prime minister was Nehru's daughter, Mrs. *Indira Gandhi*. By 1975 her popularity had fallen because of inflation and political corruption.

**2. Mrs. Gandhi and a "State of Emergency."** In 1975 India entered upon a governmental crisis. A high court found Mrs. Gandhi guilty of violating election laws and barred her for six years from public office. In reaction Mrs. Gandhi charged a "conspiracy," declared a "state of emergency," arrested thousands of her political opponents, and instituted press censorship. Her Congress party, in control of Parliament, retroactively legalized her disputed election practices and acted to restrict the courts from interfering with the prime minister. In response to charges that she had "killed democracy," Mrs. Gandhi replied that India remained "more democratic" than any other developing country.

In 1976 Mrs. Gandhi insisted that India still faced a "state of emergency." Her government therefore postponed parliamentary elections, enacted a code of permanent press censorship, and secured constitutional amendments to strengthen Parliament and the prime minister. These measures, the government contended, would enable it to achieve a "revolution which would end poverty and ignorance and disease and inequality of opportunity."

Those opposition leaders still free to speak declared that India faced no emergency and demanded the release of opposition members of Parliament in prison. The opposition charged that the government was seeking to "throttle democracy and impose authoritarian rule."

**3. The 1977 Elections.** In early 1977, with India improving economically, Mrs. Gandhi called for parliamentary elections. The elections centered on the theme of "dictatorship versus democracy." Mrs. Gandhi lost her parliamentary seat, and the Congress party—which had ruled India for the 30 years since independence—was humiliatingly defeated. Mrs. Gandhi resigned as prime minister, saying the "judgment of the people must be respected."

*Morarji Desai*, the 81-year-old leader of the *Janata* party, became prime minister. Imprisoned for 18 months under Mrs. Gandhi's state of emergency," Desai had been released and permitted to take part in the election campaign. His Janata party, together with its political allies, overwhelmingly controlled Parliament. The Desai government pledged to fully restore personal liberties, to end press censorship, and to pursue democratic ways. Also, the Desai government promised to better the economy, to pursue family planning programs but to avoid compulsory birth control methods employed by Gandhi officials, to shun the development of nuclear weapons even though the Gandhi regime in 1974 had set off a nuclear explosion, and to seek "genuine nonalignment" in foreign affairs, implying that Mrs. Gandhi had followed a pro-Soviet policy.

In 1979, because of feuds within the Janata party, Desai lost his parliamentary majority and resigned. India experienced political instability that led to the dissolving of Parliament and the scheduling of new elections.

**4. The 1980 Elections.** Indira Gandhi conducted an energetic and effective campaign. She pledged to curb crime by enforcing law and order, to battle inflation by rolling back prices, and to ease shortages of essential commodities such as sugar and kerosene. She emphasized her family's role in India's history and her leadership qualities. She avoided reference to her previous emergency dictatorial rule, and the voters either chose not to remember or believed that she had learned a lesson and would not again resort to antidemocratic practices.

Mrs. Gandhi achieved a remarkable triumph. She won election to Parliament—and her faction of the Congress party captured over two-thirds of the legislative seats. Mrs. Gandhi's victory left her political opponents demoralized. Mrs. Gandhi commented that the voters now realized that in 1977 they had made a "big mistake." Upon being sworn in as prime minister, she solemnly affirmed her allegiance to India's constitution.

**5. The Gandhi Regime (Since 1980).** Using a provision of the Indian Constitution that permits the executive to enact ordinances when Parliament is not in session, the Gandhi regime announced measures enabling it to *(a)* jail individuals for up to a year without trial—justified as necessary to prevent ethnic, regional, and economic unrest, and *(b)* prohibit strikes for up to a year in industries providing essential services—justified as necessary to curb inflation and prevent labor unrest. Mrs. Gandhi's opponents protested these measures and claimed that she was reviving her previous dictatorial rule.

## PROBLEMS FACING THE REPUBLIC OF INDIA

**1. Unifying India's People.** To combat the country's divisive cultural heritage, the Indian government guaranteed religious freedom, outlawed certain caste restrictions, abolished the class of untouchables and improved their economic conditions, and encouraged the use of a single official language, *Hindi.* Slowly the people are developing a feeling of national unity.

**2. Raising Living Standards by Increasing Production.** India permits private and public enterprise in a mixed economy. To supplement the efforts of private businesses, the Indian government has undertaken *Five-Year Plans:* constructing irrigation projects, electric power plants, railroads, and steel mills; distributing land to the peasants; and fostering modern farming methods. India's efforts to better economic conditions and raise living standards have benefited from some Russian and considerable American and British funds.

In improving economic conditions, India faces a challenge from certain Hindu beliefs: *(a)* that cows are sacred and not to be slaughtered for food, *(b)* that farm pests may contain reincarnated human souls and are not to be destroyed, and *(c)* that higher castes may not work alongside untouchables.

**3. Wiping Out Illiteracy.** Only 29 percent of the people are able to read and

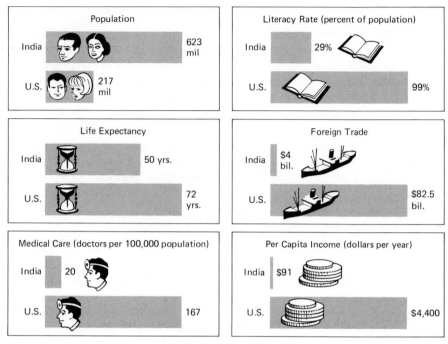

**Problems Facing India**

How can India help itself? Should the U.S. help? How?

write. India's constitution calls for free compulsory education through the age of 14. The government is seeking to realize this goal but must overcome a staggering shortage of schools and teachers.

**4. Settling the Kashmir Dispute.** India and Pakistan both claimed *Kashmir,* a native state where a Hindu prince ruled a chiefly Moslem people. Both nations agreed in principle to a UN plebiscite, but in practice India prevented any vote. In 1957, despite protests by the UN and Pakistan, Nehru annexed the Indian-occupied portion of Kashmir. (Check the Index.)

**5. Determining a Foreign Policy.** Nehru hoped to devote India's energies to solving domestic problems. Consequently in the cold war between Communism and the West, he set a policy of *nonalignment,* or *neutrality.*

At first Nehru expressed great fear of Western colonialism. Later, as Red Chinese troops invaded northern India in a series of border disputes, Nehru awakened to the Communist Chinese menace. After Nehru's death, Indian leaders reaffirmed their determination to protect India's borders and to maintain India's neutrality. (For India and the cold war, check the Index.)

# D. Pakistan and Bangladesh

## PAKISTAN SPLITS INTO TWO NATIONS

From independence (1947) until defeated in war (1971), Pakistan was one nation. It consisted of two nonadjacent regions separated by 1,000 miles (1,600 kilometers) of Indian territory. West Pakistan was larger in area but had fewer people than East Pakistan. Aside from their Moslem religion, the people of the two regions had little in common. The West Pakistanis were mostly Punjabis, who spoke Urdu and looked westward to the Moslem Arabs; the East Pakistanis were Bengalis, who spoke Bengali and felt close to the Hindu Bengalis living in India.

Despite their smaller population, the West Pakistanis controlled the central government, but in 1970 elections the Bengali *Awami League* gained a legislative majority. President *Yahya Khan* and Bengali leader Sheik *Mujibur Rahman* negotiated regarding East Pakistan's demand for autonomy but failed to agree. Thereupon the West Pakistani army seized control of the East, killing many civilians and occupying the major cities. The Bengalis declared their region's independence and retained control mostly of rural areas.

India meanwhile voiced support for East Pakistan, received over 9 million Bengali refugees—creating a tremendous relief burden—and trained Bengali guerrilla fighters. India also gained international support by signing a 20-year treaty of friendship with the Soviet Union. In late 1971 Indian military forces crossed into East Pakistan and in a two-week war defeated the West Pakistani army, making independence a reality for the new Bengali nation, *Bangladesh*. (For UN developments, check the Index.)

In 1972, after Britain formally recognized the new Bengali nation, Pakistan withdrew from the Commonwealth while Bangladesh joined it. In 1975 Pakistan officially recognized the independence of and established diplomatic relations with Bangladesh.

## PAKISTAN: FEDERAL ISLAMIC REPUBLIC

1. **Developments in Government.** As a result of Pakistan's disastrous defeat in the 1971 war, *Zulfikar Ali Bhutto* replaced Yahya Khan as president. Bhutto acted to remove incompetent officials, assert the authority of the central government, restore civilian rule, and draw up a new constitution. Concluded in 1973, the new constitution provided for a two-house legislature and a powerful prime minister.

Bhutto assumed the position of prime minister. Although he announced the restoration of some civil rights, Bhutto had his government censor the news media, imprison opposition leaders, and suppress dissent.

In early 1977, Pakistan held national elections. Bhutto's Pakistan's People's party won an overwhelming victory, but opposition leaders of the Pakistan National Alliance charged that the elections had been rigged and demanded new, honest elections. Pakistan experienced political violence during which 300 persons lost their lives and thousands were arrested. General *Mohammed Zia ul-Haq* then led the Pakistani army in a coup and seized control of the government. (Bhutto was arrested; he later was tried for the murder of a political opponent, found guilty, and hanged.) General Zia ul-Haq stated that the army had acted to end the political violence and pledged new, honest elections and a return to civilian rule eventually.

## 2. Problems Facing Pakistan

*a.* Because of religious antagonisms, the Kashmir issue, disputes over water resources, and the 1971 war, Pakistan's relations with India remained strained. When India in 1974 exploded a nuclear device, Pakistani leaders declared it "a nuclear bomb directed at us." As India continued a military build-up with Soviet equipment, Pakistan in 1975 convinced the United States to lift its ten-year-old embargo on the sale of arms to Pakistan.

*b.* The Pakistani people themselves are divided into a number of distinct linguistic and cultural groups. With the example set by the Bengalis, the Pathans of Pakistan's North-West Frontier Province have agitated for independence. This independence movement, generating considerable unrest in the province, has been supported by the bordering nation of Afghanistan.

*c.* The Pakistanis are mainly farmers, especially in the Indus River Valley. They use primitive agricultural methods, suffer adverse floods and droughts, and have a low standard of living. Many are tenants on large estates and do not have their own lands. The government began a moderate land reform program.

*d.* The country is beset by inflation and rising prices, the loss of its markets for cotton textiles and cement in the former East Pakistan, and heavy defense expenditures to rebuild its military strength. Hurt by OPEC's increases in oil prices since 1973, Pakistan has secured loans and grants from oil-rich Iran and Saudi Arabia as well as from the United States and Communist China.

*e.* Although the United States had "leaned" toward Pakistan in the 1971 war with India, Pakistan resigned from SEATO, diluted its pro-Western foreign policy, and turned for friendship to Communist China.

*f.* In 1976 Pakistan arranged to purchase from France a nuclear reprocessing plant. Such a plant, using the waste materials from a nuclear electric power facility, could derive the element plutonium—the basic component of an atomic bomb. The United States was concerned that Pakistan would use the plutonium to explode an atomic device and set off an Indian-Pakistani nuclear race. Heeding American concern, France in 1978 canceled the sale. Thereafter, the United States learned from a Central Intelligence Agency report that Pakistan secretly was building its own plant to produce nuclear weapons. In 1979 the United States ended its economic and military assistance to Pakistan. Pakistan denied the CIA report but was unwilling to place its atomic facilities under international safeguards. (For recent events, check the Index.)

# BANGLADESH

**1. Developments in Government.** The first head of the new Bengali nation was Sheik Mujibur Rahman. He acted to establish a one-party state, wipe out corruption, create a national army, and restore law and order. Sheik Mujibur proved unable to solve the nation's many problems; his popularity waned and his regime was accused of "corruption, injustice, and autocracy." In 1975 Mujibur Rahman was overthrown and killed by a military coup. After some political instability, the army gained control and established a military government headed by Major General *Ziaur Rahman* (no relative of Sheik Mujibur Rahman).

In 1981 General Rahman, then president, was killed by a coup that failed. Thereafter, Bangladesh voters elected as president a 75-year-old judge, *Abdus Sattar*.

**2. Problems Facing Bangladesh**

*a.* Bangladesh must recover from the wounds of war. The war resulted in considerable loss of life, hatred for the Pakistanis, razing of cities and villages, disruption of transportation, and serious food shortages.

*b.* Aside from the fertile land in the Ganges River Valley, Bangladesh has few natural resources. Most of its large population are farmers who use primitive methods to raise chiefly jute and tea. They also face hostile weather conditions: monsoon rains that cause the rivers to flood and violent cyclonic storms. The Bengalis have an extremely low living standard and poor health conditions.

To alleviate population pressures, the Bangladesh government has encouraged the use of birth control methods.

*c.* Bangladesh has depended upon India—itself impoverished—for food and other economic aid. Bangladesh has received some foreign economic aid but it is insufficient for the country's massive needs.

Since 1976 Bangladesh's relations with India have deteriorated. The major issue has been India's diversion of Ganges River waters needed, so India claimed, to flush silt from Calcutta harbor. Bangladesh condemned the diversion of Ganges waters for drying up its irrigation ditches, hurting industries requiring water, and reducing the availability of drinking water.

# *E. Indonesia*

## LAND AND PEOPLE

Formerly the Netherlands East Indies, Indonesia consists of several thousand Pacific islands, notably Sumatra, Java, Celebes, most of Borneo, and West New Guinea (West Irian). The islands, extending about 4,000 miles (6,400 kilometers) from east to west, possess great wealth in (1) mineral resources—oil, coal, and tin—and (2) agricultural produce—rubber, quinine, sugar, pepper, and copra. Nevertheless, the people, chiefly farmers, have a low standard of living. The Indonesians, numbering 130 million, are predominantly Moslem.

## FROM DUTCH COLONY TO INDEPENDENT NATION

For over 300 years Holland ruled the islands and developed their resources. During World War II Dutch colonial forces fell before Japanese invaders. After the war, Indonesian nationalists set up a republic. When the Dutch tried to win back Indonesia by force, the UN Security Council secured a cease-fire. In 1949 Holland granted independence to Indonesia.

## INDONESIA SINCE INDEPENDENCE

The Republic of Indonesia was first headed by President *Achmed Sukarno*. He faced problems of providing stable government, improving economic conditions, and replacing skilled Dutch personnel who fled the country. In the early 1960's Sukarno dismissed the elected legislature, appointed his own group of legislators, and later had himself named president-for-life.

In 1964–1965 Sukarno displayed friendship for Communist Russia and China and enmity toward the West. He antagonized Britain by claiming the Borneo territories of Malaysia. After Malaysia was elected to the UN Security Council, Sukarno withdrew Indonesia from the United Nations.

In late 1965 the Indonesian Communist party attempted a military coup. The Communist rebels were defeated by the Indonesian army, which emerged as the major power. With General *Suharto* replacing Sukarno as president, the military government ended the "confrontation" with Malaysia, returned to the United Nations, and welcomed Western and Japanese investors.

In 1978 Suharto was elected by the People's Consultative Assembly for his third five-year term as president.

## RECENT PROBLEMS

1. Although oil rich and a member of OPEC, Indonesia has experienced financial problems because of corruption and mismanagement, especially at the state-owned oil and general development company *Pertamina*. In 1975 Pertamina defaulted on its huge foreign debts. The Indonesian government assumed responsibility for Pertamina's debts, changed the management of the company, and straightened out the company's finances.

2. Indonesia faces problems of a high birthrate, considerable unemployment, and insufficient production of foodstuffs to feed its population, with an estimated 60 percent being undernourished. To deal with these problems, Indonesia: encouraged family planning to lower the birthrate; secured foreign loans to speed industrialization and provide jobs; imported foodstuffs and sought to increase agricultural output.

3. A South Moluccan independence movement seeks to free the Moluccan Islands from Indonesia and to establish them as an independent nation. In 1950 a

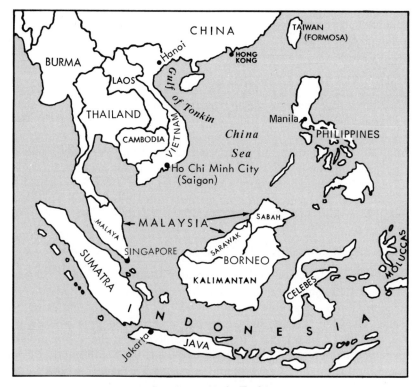

**Southeast Asia Today**

South Moluccan rebellion was suppressed, and many thousands of South Moluccans migrated to the Netherlands—the former colonial power over Indonesia. In the mid-1970's South Moluccan bands operating in the Netherlands committed several acts of terrorism, seizing numerous Dutch hostages. The terrorists sought to call world attention to their demands for Moluccan independence and to compel the Dutch government to support their cause. The terrorist acts were suppressed by the Netherlands government.

## F. The Nations of Indo-China

### INDO-CHINA UNDER FRENCH RULE

In the 19th century France annexed Indo-China. This was an agricultural country in Southeast Asia with a predominantly Buddhist population. During World War II, while France was overrun by the Nazis, Indo-China was occupied by the Japanese. Indo-Chinese nationalists, opposed to both Japan and France, joined an independence movement called the *Vietminh*. Although this movement contained some non-Communist nationalists, it was controlled by Communists and led by Moscow-trained *Ho Chi Minh*.

## COMMUNISTS SEEK CONTROL (1946–1954)

After the war, France promised partial independence to the three states of Indo-China: Laos, Cambodia, and Vietnam. The Vietminh rejected the French offer and gained popular support by appealing to (1) *nationalism*, with promises to drive out the French completely, and (2) *land hunger*, with promises to distribute land to the peasants. For eight years civil war raged in Indo-China. The Vietminh received aid from Communist China. The French and their Indo-Chinese allies received equipment from the United States. In 1954 the Vietminh won the crucial *Battle of Dien Bien Phu*.

## GENEVA CONFERENCE: TRUCE FOR INDO-CHINA (1954)

Britain, the Soviet Union, the United States, Communist China, France, and the states of Indo-China sent representatives to Geneva to negotiate a settlement. The Geneva Agreements, not signed by the United States or South Vietnam, called for: (1) *Laos* and *Cambodia* to be independent and to observe neutrality in the cold war. (2) *Vietnam* to be divided at the 17th parallel: the North under a Communist government in *Hanoi*, the South under a French-sponsored anti-Communist government in *Saigon*. The people in both the North and the South were to vote by mid-1956 for a single all-Vietnam government.

## DEVELOPMENTS IN INDO-CHINA (1955–1974)

**1. Communist North Vietnam.** Ho Chi Minh established a Communist dictatorship, increased the army's strength, eliminated most private enterprise, and received considerable Russian and Chinese aid. The Communists were determined to gain control of South Vietnam.

**2. Anti-Communist South Vietnam.** The Saigon government became fully independent of France, was strongly anti-Communist, and rejected plans for all-Vietnam elections. It argued that honest elections were impossible in the Communist north. To undermine the Saigon government, the Communist Vietcong waged guerrilla warfare throughout the south—terrorizing villagers and killing government supporters—and established Vietcong control over large rural areas. Saigon requested American aid. This was first granted by President Eisenhower and later expanded by President Kennedy. American leaders feared that a Communist takeover in South Vietnam might cause the bordering nations in Southeast Asia to fall to the Communists like a row of "falling dominoes."

**3. Escalation of the War.** In 1964 a limited number of American troops and military advisers were in South Vietnam, and American naval units patrolled the international waters of the Gulf of Tonkin. When North Vietnamese torpedo boats attacked American destroyers in the gulf, President Johnson ordered an air strike against North Vietnam's naval bases. The president's action received almost unanimous support from Congress in its vote for the *Gulf of Tonkin Resolution*. (In 1970 Congress repealed this resolution.)

In 1965, after American bases in South Vietnam had been attacked by Communist forces, President Johnson ordered continuous air strikes against North Vietnamese military targets. The United States increased its forces in South Vietnam, eventually to over 500,000 individuals. Also, four SEATO members—Australia, New Zealand, the Philippines, and Thailand—augmented the South Vietnamese and American forces.

The Communist nations increased their support for the Vietcong and Hanoi. Moscow provided additional military equipment. Peking assigned service troops to maintain transportation in the North.

### 4. Sharp Debate in America Regarding Vietnam

*a.* The "hawks" argued for increased military action to halt aggression and contain Communist expansion in Asia. Many hawks demanded that we drastically step up military pressures on Hanoi.

*b.* The "doves" urged the United States to seek peace by reducing its military activities in Vietnam. They argued that America was (1) lacking vital interests in Vietnam, (2) risking war with Communist China, and (3) supporting a Saigon government that commanded no loyalty among the people. (This government was dominated, from 1967 to 1975, by the military leader who was elected as president, *Nguyen Van Thieu*.)

### 5. The Move to Peace Talks (1965–1968).
President Johnson made several efforts to move the Vietnam conflict from the battlefield to the conference table—all unsuccessful. In 1968 President Johnson again halted the bombing, this time of most of North Vietnam, and Hanoi agreed to peace negotiations. The two nations began talks in Paris. Later the peace talks were expanded to include the Saigon government and the Vietcong.

### 6. Nixon Administration and Vietnam (1969–1974)

*a. Diplomatic Stalemate Continues.* President Nixon sought a Vietnam settlement that would free American prisoners of war and enable the South Vietnamese people to decide their own future by honest, internationally supervised elections. Communist leaders demanded complete withdrawal of American forces and replacement of the "puppet" Thieu government by a pro-Communist regime. The Paris talks remained deadlocked.

*b. Vietnamization.* Nixon spurred *Vietnamization*, that is, shifting the burden of fighting the war to South Vietnamese forces. By late 1972 he had withdrawn over 500,000 men from Vietnam, leaving there only 27,000 American troops. American casualty lists grew much shorter.

### c. The War Spills Over Into the Other Indo-Chinese States

(1) *Cambodia.* In 1970 a new, rightist-leaning regime took control. It reaffirmed Cambodia's neutrality and demanded the withdrawal of North Vietnamese and Vietcong forces from bases in Cambodia. Instead, the Communist forces attacked Cambodian towns. Thereupon, President Nixon ordered American forces to join with South Vietnamese troops in a limited "incursion" into Cambodia to destroy the Communist bases.

(2) *Laos.* In 1970 North Vietnamese and local Communist Pathet Lao forces overran much of southern Laos. In 1971 South Vietnamese forces with American air support began a limited "incursion" into southern Laos to disrupt enemy supply routes.

Both incursions aroused much controversy in the United States between the "hawks" and the "doves."

### d. Secret Peace Talks.
Since 1969 Washington and Hanoi had held, around Paris, a series of secret peace talks. The American negotiator was President Nixon's national security adviser, *Henry Kissinger;* the Hanoi negotiator was *Le Duc Tho.* In 1973 they reached an agreement.

## 7. The Paris Peace Agreement for Vietnam (1973)

### a. Major Provisions

(1) *Military. (a)* The United States, North Vietnam, South Vietnam, and the Vietcong all agree to a cease-fire. *(b)* The United States shall withdraw its remaining forces and dismantle its remaining military bases in South Vietnam. *(c)* Hanoi and the Vietcong shall return all American prisoners of war and provide the fullest possible accounting for persons "missing in action" (MIA). *(d)* All foreign troops shall be withdrawn from Laos and Cambodia. *(e)* No additional troops and military supplies shall be introduced into South Vietnam.

(2) *Reunification. (a)* The reunification of Vietnam shall be achieved only by peaceful means. *(b)* Pending reunification, both North Vietnam and South Vietnam shall respect the provisional demarcation line at the 17th parallel.

(3) *Political Arrangements for South Vietnam. (a)* Saigon and the Vietcong shall each retain the areas under its control at the time of the cease-fire. *(b)* The South Vietnamese shall decide their political future through honest elections.

### b. Observations.
(1) The agreement was a compromise, with neither side gaining all its objectives. The United States did *not* secure *(a)* the withdrawal of an estimated 145,000 Hanoi troops out of the South and back to the North or *(b)* a cease-fire for Laos and Cambodia. Hanoi did *not* secure *(a)* the overthrow of the Thieu regime in Saigon or *(b)* the establishment of a Communist-dominated coalition government in the South. (2) The Vietnam War cost the United States over an 11-year period $140 billion, more than 300,000 wounded, and 46,000 killed. It was one of the costliest and most divisive wars in American history.

# COMMUNIST FORCES TRIUMPH IN INDO-CHINA (SINCE 1975)

**1. Cambodia (Kampuchea).** The rightist-leaning government faced increasing military pressure from Communist forces—some North Vietnamese units and the local *Khmer Rouge*. The government forces, despite a Congress-imposed cutoff of American air support, withstood the Communist insurgents for more than a year. In 1975 the government forces collapsed. Communist troops occupied the capital, Phnom Penh, and took control of the entire country.

The Khmer Rouge executed Cambodian leaders who had opposed them; forced urban residents to move out of the major cities into the rural areas, which caused many deaths; and on charges of spying seized an American merchant vessel, the *Mayaguez*. When diplomatic efforts failed, President Ford ordered American forces to rescue the crew and vessel, which was done at a cost of almost 70 American casualties.

**2. Laos.** The anti-Communist and Communist Pathet Lao forces reached a cease-fire agreement and established a coalition government. In 1975, following the Communist victories in Cambodia and South Vietnam, the Pathet Lao took full control of the country.

In 1976 reports out of Laos indicated that the Pathet Lao held 50,000 rightists and neutralists in harsh prison camps for punishment and "reeducation." Many inmates died from lack of food and medical attention.

**3. Vietnam.** (*a*) The United States withdrew its remaining military forces but continued to give limited economic and military aid to the Thieu regime. (*b*) North Vietnam, in violation of the Paris agreement, increased its strength in the South to an estimated 400,000 troops. In 1975 the North Vietnamese and Vietcong mounted a major military offensive and gained full control of the South.

During this final phase of the Vietnam War, the United States proceeded as follows: (1) President Ford pledged that American forces would not return to Vietnam. (2) The United States helped evacuate thousands of South Vietnamese, many of whom had worked with the Americans and feared for their lives under Communist rule. Congress voted funds to assist some 120,000 Vietnamese refugees to come to the United States. (3) President Ford reassured our allies who, viewing the downfall of the pro-American governments in Cambodia and South Vietnam, were concerned regarding the direction of American foreign policy and the credibility of American defense treaties. The president warned any potential enemies that "we will stand up to them" and affirmed that "no allies or time-tested friends of the United States should worry or fear that our commitments to them will not be honored."

In 1976 reports out of South Vietnam indicated that the Communists held between 100,000 and 300,000 persons in labor camps where brutal conditions caused many deaths. Also in 1976 the Communists proclaimed the official reunification of the country as the *Socialist Republic of Vietnam.*

(For the effect of the Vietnam War on American foreign policy, check the Index.)

Wright in The San Diego Union
Copley Newspapers

"It makes a nice shield."

How did North Vietnam violate the Paris truce agreement?
How did these violations further the Communist victory in South Vietnam?
Should we generalize, on the basis of North Vietnam's violations,
that international agreements with Communist nations have little value?

## REFUGEES FROM INDO-CHINA (SINCE 1975)

Following the Communist takeovers, more than 1 million people fled from
the three Indo-Chinese states and became refugees. They were driven by varied
motives: (1) the earliest refugees were those Indo-Chinese closely identified with
the overthrown anti-Communist regimes, who feared for their lives under
Communist rule. (2) The ethnic Chinese, many of families who had lived in
Vietnam for generations, were pressured to leave by the Hanoi regime. The
Chinese had been merchants and moneylenders—capitalist enterprises; they
were considered of doubtful loyalty by Hanoi; and they were disliked by the
Vietnamese. Many Chinese were compelled to pay large sums to the Hanoi
regime before being permitted to depart. (3) Cambodians fled political instability
and renewed warfare as Vietnamese troops invaded Cambodia to oust a pro-
Chinese regime and install a government subservient to Hanoi. (4) Other refugees fled harsh Communist rule, forced evacuation from cities into the rural
areas, and the lack of food, clothing, and other essentials.

Some refugees fled overland to Thailand and China; others fled by sea and
became known as the *boat people*. Fewer than half the boat people were
estimated to have survived their unsafe vessels, the hazards of the sea, and pirate
attacks and to have reached land in the Philippines, Malaysia, Indonesia, and
southern Thailand. The refugees were not welcomed—and in many cases were

forcibly driven out—by the southeast Asian nations. These nations insisted that they lacked the facilities and resources to care for the refugees and were unwilling to absorb the refugees into their societies.

Refugees in large numbers were accepted by the United States and in lesser numbers by other Western nations—notably Canada, Australia, and France. Some 250,000 ethnic Chinese found temporary safety in Hong Kong and southern China.

The plight of the refugees led to a 1979 UN conference at which (1) Hanoi promised to stem the flow of refugees, (2) the UN promised—with funds mainly from Western nations and Japan—to care for the refugees in temporary transit camps, and (3) Western nations promised to accept additional refugees.

Vietnam meanwhile was viewed with grave mistrust by many Western powers, the Southeast Asian nations, and China.

## VIETNAM VS. CHINA: HOSTILITY BETWEEN COMMUNIST NATIONS (BY 1979)

**1. Reasons.** By 1979 Vietnam had aroused the anger and hostility of Communist China. (*a*) Vietnam indicated its preference for the Soviet Union, which country China viewed as its major enemy. In 1978 Vietnam signed a 25-year friendship treaty with Russia, receiving pledges of economic aid and of "effective measures" in case of attack by a third party. Hanoi was cooperating with Moscow, so Peking believed, in encircling China with hostile states. (*b*) Vietnam moved to control all Indo-China. Whereas Laos yielded to Vietnamese dominance, Cambodia did not. Under *Pol Pot*, this Cambodian regime ruled with great brutality. It was pro-Chinese and received extensive Chinese military and economic aid. After a series of border skirmishes, Vietnam in late 1978 launched a full-scale invasion of Cambodia, overthrew the Pol Pot regime, and installed a puppet government, under *Heng Samrin*, subservient to Hanoi. China resented the ousting of its ally and held that Moscow was using the Vietnamese in Asia as it had used the Cubans in Africa. (*c*) Vietnam harassed, exacted funds from, and expelled over 250,000 of its ethnic Chinese residents.

**2. The Limited War (1979).** After several border incidents, China announced that it would no longer tolerate "being pushed around" and would act to "teach Vietnam a lesson." Embarking upon a limited invasion, Chinese armies crossed the border into northern Vietnam and met strong resistance. Russia warned China to withdraw "before it is too late" and speeded military equipment to Vietnam but itself undertook no military moves. At the UN, Russia vetoed a Security Council resolution calling upon Vietnam to withdraw from Cambodia and upon China to withdraw from Vietnam. After four weeks of fighting, with heavy casualties on both sides, the Chinese withdrew their forces. Thereafter, China and Vietnam engaged in peace talks but arrived at no meaningful understandings.

# Part 7. Imperialism and Colonial Nationalism: Evaluation and Summary

## EFFECTS OF IMPERIALISM UPON COLONIAL POWERS

1. **Good Effects.** Imperialism *(a)* provided manufacturers with cheap raw materials and with protected markets, investors with profitable business opportunities, exporters and importers with increased trade, and factory workers with steadier employment; *(b)* raised the parent country's living standards; *(c)* opened up colonial careers for government officials and military men; and *(d)* gave the imperialist nation more military bases, human resources, and world prestige.

2. **Bad Effects.** Imperialism *(a)* burdened taxpayers to finance colonial improvements and defense, *(b)* caused colonial rivalries that threatened war, *(c)* perpetuated the antidemocratic belief that colonial peoples are inferior, and *(d)* aroused colonial ill will toward the ruling peoples.

## EFFECTS OF IMPERIALISM UPON COLONIES

1. **Good Effects.** Imperialist nations *(a)* developed their colonies' natural resources, improved transportation and communication, furthered agriculture, and established industries; *(b)* trained workers in new skills and provided the colonial peoples with employment; *(c)* constructed educational and health facilities, such as schools, hospitals, and sanitation projects; *(d)* halted native warfare and prohibited barbarous practices; *(e)* introduced Western culture: Christian ethics, democracy, science, and the belief in progress; and *(f)* trained the colonial peoples in self-government.

2. **Bad Effects.** Imperialist nations *(a)* drained wealth from the colonies, *(b)* maintained unbalanced economies in many colonies by emphasizing mineral and agricultural production and discouraging colonial manufacturing, *(c)* exploited the native workers by requiring long hours for little pay, *(d)* assumed an attitude of racial and cultural superiority, discriminated against the colonial peoples, and degraded their native cultures, *(e)* introduced previously unknown vices and diseases, and *(f)* aroused in the colonies feelings of antagonism toward the imperialists, who were considered to be oppressors.

## COLONIAL NATIONALISM AND THE DECLINE OF WESTERN IMPERIALISM

1. **Factors Encouraging Colonial Nationalism.** Emerging in the 20th century, especially after World War II, colonial nationalism resulted from *(a)* Western ideals of democracy and nationalism, *(b)* Communist propaganda against

"capitalist exploitation," (c) exhaustion of the West European colonial powers following World War II, (d) United Nations support of self-determination, and (e) revived native pride in their own cultures.

Colonial nationalists—many of whom were educated in Europe and the United States—led the struggle against imperialist rule.

**2. Extent of Imperialist Decline.** Greatly weakened by World War II, the West European powers have yielded to colonial nationalism. They have relinquished control, willingly or unwillingly, over almost all their empires. Since 1945 more than 50 nations in Africa and Asia have achieved independence.

## PROBLEMS FACING NEWLY INDEPENDENT NATIONS

**1. Economic Problems:** (a) Raise living standards from the poverty level. (b) Secure foreign capital to develop natural resources, further industry, and purchase the latest technology. (c) Decrease economic dependence on the former parent country. (d) End reliance on a single agricultural or mineral product. (e) Provide employment for factory workers and land for peasants.

The desire of peoples in developing countries to achieve higher living standards has been called the *revolution of rising expectations*.

**2. Social Problems:** (a) Instill in the people a sense of national pride and unity. (b) Eliminate illiteracy. (c) Improve health conditions. (d) Train personnel for professional, industrial, and governmental service. (e) Become aware of the "population explosion" and its implications.

**3. Political Problems:** (a) Maintain stable, efficient, and possibly democratic government. (b) Develop civic responsibility among their peoples. (c) Break down tribal organizations and regional loyalties. (d) Suppress military revolts and secessionist movements. (e) Combat Communist attempts to gain control.

**4. Foreign Problems:** (a) Aid peoples still subject to imperialist rule. (b) Maintain adequate military defenses against hostile neighbors. (c) Determine a policy toward the cold war. (d) Obtain foreign aid from the Communist bloc or the free world or both.

## PROBLEMS FACING FORMER IMPERIALIST POWERS

The former colonial powers face the need to: (1) Assuage national pride wounded by military defeats and territorial losses and direct it into constructive domestic channels. (2) Absorb the European settlers who fled the newly independent countries and returned to their homelands. (3) Establish mutually satisfactory relations with their former colonies so as to maintain cultural and economic ties. (4) Secure new foreign outlets for manufactured goods and capital investment. (5) Help former colonies escape Communist domination and provide them with technical and economic aid.

## MULTIPLE–CHOICE QUESTIONS

1. The Western powers were interested in 19th-century China because it (1) had a large supply of oil (2) was a good market for farm machinery (3) was an outlet for Europe's surplus population (4) offered opportunities for profitable trade.

2. As a result of the Opium War (1) the United States issued the Open Door Policy (2) Britain acquired Hong Kong (3) Russia annexed the Amur River area (4) Japan seized Formosa.

3. By granting extraterritorial rights to the foreign powers, China permitted them to (1) build railroads (2) establish tariff rates (3) lease seaports (4) try in their own courts their citizens accused of crimes in China.

4. The Open Door Policy meant that (1) all nations were equally free to trade in China (2) Britain gave up its lease holdings in China (3) Russia had a "free hand" in China (4) American missionaries were free to establish churches in China.

5. An important aim of the Open Door Policy was to (1) prevent the imperialist powers from dividing up China (2) encourage the Chinese to emigrate (3) speed China's industrial development (4) introduce democratic government into China.

6. The Boxers of China favored the (1) creation of a democratic government (2) overthrow of the Manchu Dynasty (3) expulsion of foreigners (4) opening of all Chinese ports to foreign trade.

7. As a result of the Boxer Rebellion, (1) Japan paid an indemnity to China (2) the United States withdrew its Open Door Policy (3) China ceded territory to the imperialist powers (4) the United States returned part of the indemnity to advance Chinese education.

8. An aim of the Kuomintang in China was to (1) eliminate foreign domination (2) declare war against Japan (3) prevent industrialization (4) expel missionaries.

9. What important iron-producing area was seized by Japan in 1931 and is now a part of Communist China? (1) Tibet (2) Sinkiang (3) Mongolia (4) Manchuria.

10. As a result of its invasion of China proper in 1937, Japan (1) gained control of all China (2) failed to capture any key Chinese cities (3) captured many key cities but failed to gain full control of China (4) introduced communism in China.

11. One factor enabling the Communists to seize control of China after World War II was that (1) Japan had wiped out the Kuomintang armies (2) the United States refused to aid the Nationalists (3) Russia had never been imperialist toward China (4) the Chinese Communists promised to drive out the imperialist powers.

12. Which group in China before 1949 supported the Chinese Communists *least?* (1) peasants (2) city workers (3) landlords (4) anti-imperialists.

13. The "great leap forward" refers to Communist China's effort to increase (1) its total population (2) the amount of territory under its control (3) the number of men in its armies (4) the output of agricultural and other goods.

14. The communes in Communist China are (1) the basic membership units of the Communist party (2) huge housing projects in the major cities (3) newly constructed industrial communities (4) huge farms on which peasants labor for wages.

15. Where does the government of Nationalist China maintain its headquarters? (1) Cambodia (2) Taiwan (3) Hong Kong (4) Korea.

16. Japanese ports were opened to world trade as a result of (1) Commodore Perry's expedition (2) World War I (3) the Opium War (4) the Washington Conference.

17. As a result of the Russo-Japanese War, Japan (1) became recognized as a world power (2) annexed Taiwan (3) began to Westernize (4) ceded Korea to Russia.

18. Japan withdrew from the League of Nations because (1) the United States refused to recognize Manchukuo (2) the Lytton Report condemned Japan's actions in

Manchuria    (3) Germany urged its withdrawal    (4) it feared the power of Russia.

19. An important reform in Japan after World War II was the    (1) return to the emperor of his powers lost during the war    (2) recognition of Shinto as the state religion    (3) nationalization of industry    (4) adoption of a democratic constitution.

20. The Japanese Constitution of 1947 contained all of the following *except* a    (1) guarantee of civil liberties    (2) denial of the emperor's divine origin    (3) surrender of the right to wage war    (4) state subsidy for Shintoism.

21. According to the 1952 peace treaty, Japan    (1) must pay cash reparations    (2) retains ownership of Taiwan    (3) has the right of military self-defense    (4) may not trade with Communist China.

22. Since World War II Japan's government has    (1) been dominated by the Socialists    (2) advocated pro-American policies    (3) been unstable because of many small parties in the Diet    (4) been controlled by the military.

23. India was valuable to Great Britain especially as a    (1) place for surplus population    (2) means of lowering taxes in Britain    (3) field for missionary work    (4) place for investment of British capital.

24. The British government assumed control of India after    (1) the Sepoy troops mutinied    (2) Gandhi started a movement to free India    (3) the East India Company's charter expired    (4) the French threatened to take control.

25. Under British rule in the 19th century, India's population    (1) declined slightly    (2) remained about the same    (3) increased slightly    (4) increased considerably.

26. Which of the following is an example of civil disobedience as it was practiced in India?    (1) dynamiting factories    (2) attacking British army outposts    (3) voting against British officials in elections    (4) refusing to pay taxes.

27. India seeks to raise living standards by    (1) abolishing Hinduism    (2) adopting a mixed economy of public and private enterprise    (3) turning to communism    (4) encouraging handicraft labor.

28. Pakistan is referred to as an underdeveloped nation today because it    (1) lacks sufficient population    (2) is predominantly Moslem    (3) has a poorly equipped army    (4) has an agricultural economy and a low standard of living.

29. Before gaining independence in 1949, Indonesia belonged to    (1) Belgium    (2) China    (3) France    (4) the Netherlands.

30. The Indo-Chinese people mainly observed which religion?    (1) Christianity    (2) Hinduism    (3) Buddhism    (4) Islam.

31. Which European country was directly involved in the 1946–1954 civil war in Indo-China?    (1) Great Britain    (2) France    (3) Italy    (4) the Netherlands.

32. Which American president began the United States policy of aid to South Vietnam?    (1) Truman    (2) Eisenhower    (3) Kennedy    (4) Johnson.

33. Following the Communist triumph in Indo-China in 1975, Vietnam    (1) extended its control over Laos and Cambodia    (2) showed greater friendship for China than for Russia    (3) urged its ethnic Chinese residents to remain and help rebuild the country    (4) granted a blanket pardon to all South Vietnamese who had worked with the Americans.

34. "The nation began to make itself over according to Western standards" refers to    (1) India after the Sepoy Rebellion    (2) Russia following the Treaty of Portsmouth    (3) China following the Opium War    (4) Japan under the Meiji Restoration.

35. Which explains why Europeans, although heavily outnumbered, were able to conquer territory in southern and southeastern Asia during the 18th and 19th centuries?    (1) European soldiers were more courageous than Asian soldiers.    (2) Europeans were able to capitalize on Asian disunity.    (3) Asians did not believe in fighting.    (4) Asians were more interested in making money than in retaining land.

36. Which conclusion can be drawn from a study of Western imperialism (1870–1914)? (1) The Western Hemisphere was the chief target of European imperialism. (2) Human beings are naturally restless and must keep moving. (3) European imperialists were responsible for the great civilizations of Asia. (4) Historical movements are explained by political, economic, and psychological motives.

37. In general which is the most immediately pressing need of developing nations? (1) a Westernized, democratic form of government (2) a culture of their own (3) adequate military and naval defenses (4) technical know-how and funds for economic growth.

38. In the late 19th century, a beneficial result of the expansion of European interest and holdings in Asia was (1) a rise in standards of living in industralized Europe (2) a slowing down of industrialization in the West (3) a decline in rivalry among the industrialized nations (4) mass emigration of Europeans to the colonial areas.

39. Which has been a major cause of recent change in world cultural patterns? (1) widespread religious conflict (2) growth of two opposing political and military powers (3) scientific and technological advances (4) climatic changes.

40. "Despite the apparent decline of European imperialism, Europe has still triumphed." The author of this statement is referring to the fact that (1) Europe still has political control of most former colonies (2) Christianity has had a tremendous impact on China and India (3) European culture and ideas have had a great impact on the world (4) European peoples are found in many lands.

## MULTIPLE–CHOICE QUESTIONS

Select the number of the item that does *not* belong in the corresponding group.

1. *Nations that had spheres of influence in China in the 19th century:* (1) France (2) the Netherlands (3) Russia (4) Germany.
2. *Chinese territories seized by Czarist Russia:* (1) the Amur River district (2) part of central Asia (3) the Yangtze River Valley (4) Vladivostok.
3. *Policies of Communist China:* (1) develop heavy industry (2) encourage workers to strike (3) purge counterrevolutionists (4) weaken family ties.
4. *Territories acquired by Japan between 1890 and 1945:* (1) Korea (2) Port Arthur (3) Formosa (4) Sinkiang.
5. *Problems facing India:* (1) strengthening national unity (2) countering the hostility of Great Britain (3) developing industry (4) reducing illiteracy.
6. *Chief products of Indonesia:* (1) radios (2) quinine (3) rubber (4) oil.

## IDENTIFICATION QUESTIONS: WHO AM I?

Chiang Kai-shek    Mohammed Ali Jinnah    Jawaharlal Nehru
Chou En-lai    Henry Kissinger    Richard Nixon
Mohandas Gandhi    Douglas MacArthur    Mujibur Rahman
John Hay    Mao Tse-tung    Henry L. Stimson
Ho Chi Minh    Mutsuhito    Sun Yat-sen

1. Opposed to Japan's conquest of Manchuria, I stated that the United States would recognize no territory taken by force.
2. As leader of the Chinese Nationalists, I fought the warlords, the Japanese, and the Chinese Communists. By 1950 I had lost the mainland to the Communists and ruled only a small island off the China coast.
3. As leader of the Congress party and first prime minister of India, I sought to set my country on the road to economic development and political democracy.

4. Educated in Western schools, I founded the Kuomintang and led the revolution that overthrew the Manchu Dynasty.
5. Fearful of Hindu domination after independence, I secured the creation of the Moslem state of Pakistan.
6. After leading my people to independence from Pakistan, I was overthrown by a military coup and killed.
7. Known as the "saintly one," I combated British rule by passive resistance and secured independence for my country.
8. A Communist trained in Moscow, I successfully combated French rule and became head of North Vietnam.
9. I was head of the Communist party when it gained control of China. In 1958 I proclaimed a "great leap forward" to develop China economically.
10. As Supreme Allied Commander in the Pacific, I accepted the surrender of Japan in World War II. I occupied that country and introduced democratic reforms.

## MAP QUESTIONS

For each area described below, write *both* its name and the letter indicating its location on the map.

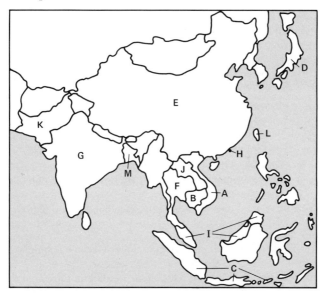

1. This heavily populated country is mainly Hindu in religion. In 1977 its people voted to oust the Congress party from control of the government.
2. This country, once divided by imperialist powers into a number of spheres of influence, is today unified under a Communist regime.
3. This country was defeated in World War II and occupied by American forces. In 1947 it adopted a democratic constitution.
4. This country consists of former British possessions in southeast Asia: the Malay states and two Borneo territories.
5. This country, mainly Moslem in religion, lost its eastern province following defeat in a 1971 war.

6. This country was reunited by Communist forces after the 1973 Paris Agreement secured the withdrawal of all American troops.

7. This area, formerly a possession of Japan, is now held by the Chinese Nationalists.

8. This colony, acquired by Great Britain during the Opium War, is one of its last footholds in Asia.

9. This country, granted independence by the Netherlands, is rich in oil, tin, and rubber.

## ESSAY QUESTIONS

1. (a) Discuss briefly *two* reasons why European powers in the 19th century became interested in the continent of Asia. (b) Explain fully how *each* of the following nations freed itself from imperialistic control by Western European powers during the 20th century: (1) China (2) India (3) Indonesia.

2. (a) State *two* reasons why Manchu China became an easy victim of imperialism. (b) Describe *two* factors that enabled the Communists to seize power in China. (c) Discuss *two* changes within China resulting from the rise to power of the Chinese Communists.

3. (a) Give *two* reasons why Japan Westernized more rapidly than did China. (b) Describe *two* ways in which Japan was undemocratic before World War II. (c) Discuss *two* changes within Japan since the end of World War II.

4. India was once called the "brightest jewel of the British Empire." (a) Explain *two* factors that enabled Britain to gain control of India. (b) Discuss *two* ways in which India was valuable to Britain economically. (c) Relate *two* episodes in India's struggle to gain independence. (d) Show *one* importance of India in the cold war.

5. State an issue on which the men in each of the following groups differed and describe the point of view of each person on the issue.

   a. Otto von Bismarck—          c. Jawaharlal Nehru—
      Mohandas Gandhi                Mohammed Ali Jinnah
   b. Chiang Kai-shek—            d. Ho Chi Minh—
      Mao Tse-tung                  Lyndon B. Johnson

6. From the point of view of the parent country, explain (a) *three* arguments in favor of imperialism (b) *three* arguments against imperialism (c) *one* problem resulting from the loss of overseas colonies.

7. (a) Describe *three* good effects on an underdeveloped region that resulted from its control by a more advanced country. (b) Discuss *three* reasons why, in spite of these advantages, the people of an underdeveloped country usually resented imperialist control. (c) Explain *one* problem facing an underdeveloped country after it gained independence.

8. In various countries of Africa and Asia, there are different levels in the standard of living. (a) Name an African or Asian country that has a high standard of living and discuss *two* reasons for the high standard of living. (b) Name an African or Asian country that has a low standard of living and give *two* reasons for the low standard of living. (c) Describe *two* efforts being made to improve the low standard of living in the above country.

9. In the 20th century there frequently have been conflicts between traditional institutions in a society and developments in that society. For the traditional institutions listed, discuss a conflict that has arisen between the traditional institution and the recent developments in a specific society: (a) tribalism in an African nation, (b) the family in China, (c) the caste system in India.

# UNIT XII. WORLD WARS AND DICTATORSHIPS IN A TROUBLED WORLD

## Part 1. World War I

### FORMATION OF EUROPEAN ALLIANCES

**1. Triple Alliance (Germany, Austria-Hungary, and Italy).** Germany, under Bismarck's leadership, had triumphed in the Franco-Prussian War and had imposed a humiliating peace treaty on France (see page 247). To deter the French from a "war of revenge," Bismarck pursued policies to isolate France and gain allies for Germany. Bismarck sought an alliance with Austria-Hungary, whose expansion into the Balkans conflicted with Russian ambitions. In 1879 Germany and Austria-Hungary—Europe's *Central Powers*—joined in a defensive military alliance.

Italy was enraged at France, whose seizure of Tunisia in 1881 thwarted Italian plans. In 1882 Italy agreed to a defensive military alliance with Germany and Austria-Hungary, thereby completing the *Triple Alliance*.

The *weaknesses* of the Triple Alliance were Italy's historic enmity for Austria-Hungary and Italy's desire for the remaining Italian-inhabited Austrian territories.

**2. Triple Entente (France, Russia, and Britain).** France aspired to regain European leadership and win back its "stolen provinces" of Alsace and Lorraine from Germany. France therefore sought allies, particularly Russia. However, France could not overcome Bismarck's skillful diplomacy, which kept Russia friendly to Germany. Soon after Bismarck was dismissed as chancellor in 1890, Germany refused to renew its treaty of friendship with Russia. France thereafter extended military and industrial loans to Russia and gained its confidence; in 1894 the two nations entered into the *Dual Alliance*.

Britain considered its industrial leadership and colonial empire threatened most by Germany. Nevertheless, in 1898 Britain clashed with France over control of the Sudan in the *Fashoda Affair*. Because both nations feared Germany more than each other, they agreed to a peaceful settlement. Eventually Britain gave France a free hand in Morocco, and France confirmed British dominance in the Sudan. By this settlement in 1904, Britain and France began a close diplomatic understanding, the *Entente Cordiale*.

In 1907 Britain and Russia settled differences over spheres of influence in Persia and China. This agreement completed the *Triple Entente*.

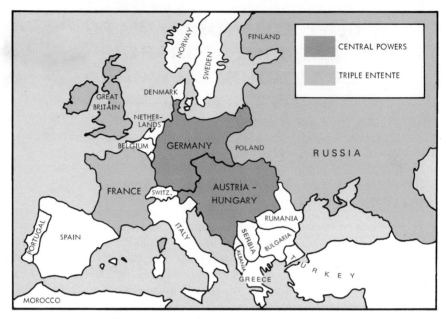

**Europe on the Eve of World War I (1914)**

## ALLIANCES AND THE BALANCE OF POWER: EFFECTIVENESS AS A GUARANTEE OF PEACE?

The alliances preceding World War I divided Europe into two opposing armed camps, representing a roughly equal *balance of power*. Such equilibrium, its advocates argued, was an effective method of guaranteeing the peace. Since neither alliance could be sure of military victory, the individual nation-states would proceed cautiously in foreign affairs and avoid the risk of war.

Critics of the balance-of-power theory held that the existence of the two alliances eventually would lead to war. Since each alliance represented tremendous military power, the individual nation-states would miscalculate, abandon caution, and adopt an aggressive attitude in international affairs. Unfortunately for world peace, this latter analysis proved correct.

## CRISES PRECEDING WORLD WAR I

The rival alliances confronted each other in a series of diplomatic clashes.

1. **Moroccan Crisis of 1905.** Germany challenged France's sphere of influence in Morocco. The German kaiser visited Morocco and pledged his support for that country's independence. Not ready for war, France agreed to submit the question of Morocco to an international conference. The *Algeciras Conference (a)* reaffirmed the independence of Morocco but *(b)* recognized France's special interests in that country.

**2. Moroccan Crisis of 1911.** Germany challenged France's attempt to convert Morocco into a protectorate. War was averted when both nations agreed to a compromise. Germany withdrew its objections to a French protectorate over Morocco in exchange for a small area of the French Congo.

The Moroccan crises of 1905 and 1911 *(a)* constituted diplomatic setbacks for Germany, *(b)* drew France and Britain into closer alliance as Britain supported French claims, and *(c)* intensified hostility between the Entente and the Central Powers.

**3. Balkan Crises of 1912–1913.** Russia supported the expansion plans of its Balkan ally and kindred Slavic state, Serbia. With Russian approval, four Balkan nations—Serbia, Montenegro, Bulgaria, and Greece—warred against, defeated, and seized territory from Turkey.

Austria thereupon intervened to force the creation of Albania out of former Turkish lands and thus deny Serbia an outlet to the Adriatic Sea. Austria's attitude reflected its *(a)* opposition to Russian influence in the Balkans and *(b)* fear that a powerful Serbia would cause unrest among Serbians and other Slavic peoples in the Austro-Hungarian Empire.

In the Second Balkan War (1913), Serbia gained some territory from defeated Bulgaria but *not* an outlet to the sea.

The Balkan crises of 1912–1913 *(a)* brought Russia and Serbia closer together and *(b)* intensified the hatred of Russia and Serbia for Austria-Hungary.

## IMMEDIATE CAUSE OF WORLD WAR I: ASSASSINATION OF THE AUSTRIAN ARCHDUKE

Serbian nationalists, both in Serbia and in Austria, plotted the breakup of the Austro-Hungarian Empire and wanted to establish a strong Serbian state. In June, 1914, a Serbian nationalist assassinated Archduke *Francis Ferdinand,* heir to the throne of Austria-Hungary. The assassination took place in the Serbian-populated region of the Austrian Empire, at *Sarajevo.* Although several Serbian government officials had been aware of the plot, no one had warned the Austrian government.

The assassination sparked a chain reaction that led Europe into World War I.

1. Austria decided to deal harshly with Serbia and obtained from Germany a promise of unconditional support—a diplomatic *blank check.* Thus fortified, Austria presented an ultimatum demanding that Serbia *(a)* stop anti-Austrian propaganda, *(b)* dismiss anti-Austrian officials, and *(c)* permit Austria to investigate, within Serbia, the assassination plot. Austria denounced Serbia's reply as unsatisfactory and declared war on Serbia.

2. Germany was alarmed when Russia mobilized its forces in preparation for helping Serbia and in anticipation of a major war. Germany therefore seized the initiative and declared war against Russia and France.

3. Germany's armies moved toward France, not by crossing the mountains on the fortified Franco-German border, but by going through the Belgian level plain. By invading Belgium, Germany violated its pledge to respect that country's neutrality.

4. Britain feared German control of Belgium—opposite the British Isles—as a threat to its security. When Germany rejected a British ultimatum to withdraw from Belgium, Britain declared war on Germany.

## FUNDAMENTAL CAUSES OF WORLD WAR I

All the European powers were to blame for World War I, although not in equal measure. The major causes were the following:

1. **Nationalism.** (a) France was determined to recover the French-inhabited provinces of Alsace and Lorraine. (b) Serbia wanted Austro-Hungarian territory inhabited by Yugoslav peoples. (c) Subject nationalities—Yugoslavs, Czechs, Slovaks, and Poles—sought independence, even at the price of war. (d) Intense patriotism assured popular support for warlike measures.

2. **Imperialism.** (a) France and Germany clashed over Morocco. (b) Russia and Austria-Hungary were rivals in the Balkans. (c) Britain and Germany, both highly industrialized, competed for imperialist control in Africa and the Middle East and for world markets.

3. **Militarism.** (a) By conscripting (drafting) soldiers, lengthening their training period, and providing them with modern equipment, the continental European nations each sought military superiority. (b) Germany had a military tradition and extolled armed might. (c) Armament manufacturers—Krupp in Germany and Schneider in France—encouraged increased production of military equipment. (d) Britain, which relied heavily upon its navy for protection of its island homeland, considered Germany's huge naval building program a threat to British security.

4. **International Anarchy.** (a) No strong international organization existed with facilities to enable nations to settle disputes peacefully. (b) The *Hague Court of Arbitration* (also called the Hague Tribunal), established in 1899, was ineffective. It could not compel nations to submit their quarrels to its judgment or to accept its decisions.

## OTHER NATIONS ENTER THE WAR

1. **The Central Powers** (Germany and Austria-Hungary) were joined by two nations: (a) Turkey in 1914—to combat its traditional enemy, Russia—and (b) Bulgaria in 1915—to secure revenge against Serbia (see Balkan Crises, page 433).

**2. The Allied Powers** (Britain, France, Russia, Serbia, and Belgium) were joined by more than 25 nations. Most notable were *(a)* Japan in 1914—to acquire German territories in the Pacific; *(b)* Italy in 1915—won over by secret Allied promises of territory at the expense of Turkey and Austria-Hungary (previously Italy claimed that the Central Powers were the aggressors and therefore refused to honor its defensive alliance with Germany); and *(c)* the United States in 1917.

## AMERICAN ENTRANCE INTO WORLD WAR I: REASONS

When war started in 1914, President *Woodrow Wilson* urged the American people to be "neutral in fact as well as in name" and issued a *Proclamation of Neutrality*. However, confronted by world events, neither Wilson nor the American people could remain neutral. In April, 1917, Wilson asked Congress to declare war on Germany. The main reasons, historians believe, were the following:

**1. German Unrestricted Submarine Warfare.** To blockade Britain and to counteract British superiority in surface warships, German resorted to *unrestricted submarine warfare*. German submarines, called *U-boats*, attacked without warning and without attempting to save crews and passengers. They torpedoed ships of neutral nations as well as of belligerents. In 1915 over 100 American lives were lost when a German U-boat sank the British passenger vessel *Lusitania*. The American people were outraged as German U-boats took an increasing toll of American ships and lives.

(In spite of our protests, British warships searched and seized our vessels to prevent vital supplies from reaching the Central Powers. Americans, however, were less angered since such interference did not endanger American lives.)

**2. Allied Propaganda.** Americans were receptive toward Allied propaganda because *(a)* we felt a kinship for Britain, based upon common language and culture, and *(b)* our friendship for France went back to France's support of the colonial cause in the American Revolution.

**3. Hostility Toward Germany.** The American people became increasingly hostile toward Germany because the Germans *(a)* invaded neutral Belgium, *(b)* waged unrestricted submarine warfare, *(c)* attempted sabotage of American industries, and *(d)* plotted to draw Mexico into war against the United States—a plot revealed in the 1917 *Zimmermann Note*.

**4. American Economic Interests.** Because Britain effectively blockaded the Central Powers, Americans sold foodstuffs and manufactured goods almost entirely to the Allies. When the Allies exhausted their funds, American investors extended them substantial loans. Americans feared that, if Germany won the war, American loans to the Allies might never be repaid.

**5. American Idealism.** Americans felt that a better world would emerge if the Allied nations triumphed over the autocratic Central Powers. President Wilson called World War I "a war to end all wars" and proclaimed that "the world must be made safe for democracy."

**6. American Security.** Germany, if victorious, would replace democratic Britain as the dominant European power on the Atlantic. From this location, aggressive Germany might threaten the security of the United States.

## AMERICAN ENTRANCE INTO WORLD WAR I: SIGNIFICANCE

American entrance into the war (1) turned the tide of battle in favor of the Allies, (2) broke sharply with America's traditional avoidance of foreign entanglements—that is, a *policy of isolation*—and (3) marked America's emergence as a world power and eventually as a world leader.

## MILITARY ASPECTS OF THE WAR

**1. Worldwide Involvement.** For the first time in history, all major nations throughout the world were involved in the same war. Peoples from every continent provided combat forces.

**2. New Weapons.** The following military devices were used for the first time in warfare: dirigibles, submarines, giant artillery guns, tanks, and poison gas. Also used for the first time in warfare was the airplane. It was employed at first mainly for observation purposes but later for small-scale bombings and for attacks on ground forces.

**3. Naval Warfare.** On the high seas the British navy, aided by the French and later the American navies, kept control of the Atlantic shipping lanes, dealt successfully with the German submarine menace, and effectively blockaded the Central Powers. In 1916 Germany attempted to break the blockade but was halted by Britain in the North Sea naval battle of *Jutland*.

**4. Europe: Major Theater of Warfare**

*a. Eastern Front.* From 1914 to 1917 Russian forces suffered crushing defeats, inflicted chiefly by German armies. Russia experienced two 1917 revolutions (see pages 447–448) and, under a Communist regime, withdrew from the war in early 1918 by accepting the harsh *Treaty of Brest-Litovsk*.

*b. Southern Front.* By 1917 the Central Powers had overrun most of the Balkans but had won no decisive battle in Italy. In 1918 an Allied force won back much of the Balkans, and an Italian offensive compelled the surrender of Austria-Hungary.

*c. Western Front.* In 1914 German armies overran Belgium and northern France until halted by desperate French and British resistance at the battle of the *Marne*. The opposing armies then dug into the ground for *trench warfare;* the western front became deadlocked. In 1916 the Germans attempted to smash the Allied defenses but were thrown back at *Verdun* and the *Somme*. In 1918 Allied forces were reinforced by fresh American troops and unified under the command of the French Marshal *Foch*.

**5. American Military Contribution.** The *American Expeditionary Force (AEF)* of 2 million men was led by General *John J. Pershing*. In 1918 American soldiers helped halt a German offensive at *Château-Thierry* and *Belleau Wood*. Later they led the Allied end-the-war counteroffensive at *St. Mihiel* and the *Argonne Forest*.

**6. German Surrender.** By late 1918 the German High Command under Generals *von Hindenburg* and *Ludendorff* realized that the German armies, although still fighting on foreign soil, had lost the war. Germany sued for peace and on November 11, 1918, ended hostilities by accepting an *armistice*.

## PRESIDENT WILSON'S FOURTEEN POINTS

In 1918, before the end of the war, President Wilson addressed Congress on American war aims. His program for a lasting peace consisted of the *Fourteen Points:* (1) open covenants (treaties) of peace openly arrived at, (2) freedom of the seas, (3) removal of international trade barriers (such as tariffs), (4) reduction of armaments, (5) impartial adjustment of colonial claims with due regard for the interests of the native peoples, (6–13) adjustment of European boundaries in accordance with the principle of *nationality,* that is, the right of any national group to self-determination regarding its own government and independent state, and (14) establishment of a League of Nations.

Allied leaders approved Wilson's Fourteen Points only with significant reservations. In particular each leader upheld his nation's claims to territorial gains and to protection of vital national interests.

## THE TREATY OF VERSAILLES WITH GERMANY (1919)

**1. Different Allied Objectives.** The "Big Four," the allied leaders who dominated the peace conference, each sought different objectives. *(a) David Lloyd George,* prime minister of Britain, sought to expand Britain's colonial empire, preserve its naval and industrial supremacy, and "make Germany pay for the war." *(b) Georges Clemenceau,* premier of France, sought to ensure France's security against future German invasion and to weaken Germany by imposing military limitations, financial payments, and territorial losses. *(c) Vittorio Orlando,* premier of Italy, sought to enlarge Italy's territory in Europe and expand its empire overseas. *(d) Woodrow Wilson,* president of the United States, sought to provide a just peace and create a better world by implementing the Fourteen Points.

Out of these different and often conflicting objectives and after months of argument and compromise emerged the Treaty of Versailles.

**Europe Following World War I**

## 2. Major Treaty Provisions

*a. Territorial.* Germany surrendered (1) Alsace-Lorraine to France; (2) the Saar Valley to League of Nations authority and Saar coal mines to French control with the provision that, after 15 years, the Saar inhabitants decide their political future by a plebiscite (in 1934 they voted for union with Germany); (3) minor border regions to Denmark and Belgium; (4) parts of Posen and West Prussia, including a corridor to the Baltic Sea, to the new Polish Republic (this "Polish Corridor" cut off East Prussia from the rest of Germany); (5) Danzig, a Baltic seaport bordering on Poland, placed under League of Nations authority as a *free city* for Polish use.

The Saar and Danzig, predominantly German-inhabited, were transferred for economic considerations. Saar coal mines compensated France for property destruction caused by the German invasion. Danzig provided Poland with its only seaport.

The other territorial changes were in accord with the principle of nationality. The territory granted Poland, however, contained a considerable German minority.

*b. Colonial.* Germany ceded all its colonies to the Allies to be held as League of Nations mandates.

*c. Disarmament.* The German army was limited to 100,000 volunteers. Conscription was forbidden. The Rhineland, in western Germany, was demilitarized. The German navy was reduced to a few small ships. Submarines, military aircraft, and war industries were prohibited.

These military restrictions were intended to prevent Germany from again waging war.

*d. War Guilt and Reparations.* Germany accepted sole responsibility for causing the war and agreed to pay reparations for all damages. (Germany made a few payments until 1931 and afterwards repudiated the debt.)

*e. League of Nations.* The first article of the treaty provided for the establishment of the League of Nations (see pages 486–488).

3. Differing Views of the Treaty

*a. Arguments Against: A Harsh Treaty That Planted the Seeds of World War II.* The treaty transferred German-inhabited territory, seized all colonies of Germany, and compelled Germany to accept sole war guilt. It forced Germany to be unarmed while other nations remained armed, and it wounded German pride. By attacking the treaty the Nazi party gained the support of the German people, achieved power, and brought on World War II.

*b. Arguments For: A Fair Treaty That Was Not Enforced.* The treaty transferred German territory chiefly on the basis of nationality, assigned German colonies as League of Nations mandates with the objective of eventual independence, disarmed Germany as a start toward world disarmament, and provided a League of Nations. The treaty alone cannot be blamed for the German people's support of Nazism. Furthermore, if the military provisions of the treaty had been enforced, Nazi Germany would not have been able to wage war.

## TREATIES WITH THE OTHER DEFEATED NATIONS

1. The **Treaty of St. Germain** (1919) with Austria and the **Treaty of Trianon** (1920) with Hungary ended the Hapsburg Empire. *(a)* Austria and Hungary became independent national states. *(b)* Czechoslovakia, a new republic, was created out of Austro-Hungarian territories. *(c)* Italy, Rumania, the recreated Poland, and Yugoslavia (the enlarged former Serbia) each secured areas inhabited by its own nationals.

Both Austria and Hungary were required to limit their armies and pay reparations. Also, Austria was forbidden *Anschluss*, union with Germany.

2. The **Treaty of Neuilly** (1919) with Bulgaria provided that it cede minor territories, limit its army, and pay reparations.

3. The **Treaty of Lausanne** (1923) with Turkey contained slightly better terms than the **Treaty of Sèvres** (1920), which Turkey had rejected. In the Lausanne settlement Turkey lost its non-Turkish territories but retained Asia

Minor, Constantinople, and the Dardanelles. Turkey was exempted from arms limitations and payment of reparations.

## RESULTS OF WORLD WAR I

**1. Social.** *(a)* Almost 10 million soldiers were killed and over 20 million wounded. *(b)* Millions of civilians died as a result of the hostilities, famine, and disease. *(c)* The world was left aflame with hatred, intolerance, and extreme nationalism.

**2. Economic.** *(a)* The total cost of the war was over $350 billion. Paying for the war brought heavy taxation and lower living standards to European peoples. *(b)* International trade suffered because nations raised tariffs and sought economic self-sufficiency. *(c)* In Russia the Communists seized power and introduced a new economic system. *(d)* Economic dislocations caused by the war helped bring on the 1929 depression.

**3. Political.** *(a)* The United States emerged as a leading world power though reluctant to assume international responsibilities. *(b)* Three major European dynasties were dethroned: the Hohenzollerns of Germany, the Hapsburgs of Austria-Hungary, and the Romanovs of Russia. *(c)* New national states arose in central Europe. Several contained subject nationalities, especially the German-speaking populations of Poland and Czechoslovakia. *(d)* The League of Nations was established to solve international problems and advance world peace. *(e)* Many European nations, beset by economic and political discontent, turned to dictatorship—notably Russia, Italy, and Germany.

## COMPLETION QUESTIONS

1. The members of the Triple Alliance were Italy, Austria-Hungary, and _____.
2. The members of the Triple Entente were France, Britain, and _____.
3. Before World War I Germany twice challenged French claims to the North African territory of _____.
4. The new Balkan state created, at Austria-Hungary's insistence, to block Serbia's access to the sea was _____.
5. In 1914 Archduke Francis Ferdinand, heir to the Austro-Hungarian throne, was assassinated by a _____ nationalist.
6. President Wilson's statement in 1918 intended to serve as a basis for peace was the _____.
7. The British prime minister who attended the World War I Peace Conference was _____.
8. Two provinces taken by Germany from France in 1871 but restored after World War I were _____ and _____.
9. By the Treaty of Versailles, the German army was limited to no more than _____ volunteers.
10. The nation that had control of the Dardanelles according to its peace treaty after World War I was _____.

## MULTIPLE–CHOICE QUESTIONS

1. During the period 1900–1914, the political leaders in Europe believed that the "balance of power" could best be maintained by (1) a policy of isolation (2) an effective international organization (3) a system of alliances (4) a program of free trade.

2. The division of the major European powers into two rival alliances in the years preceding 1914 resulted in a (1) reduction of world tensions (2) decline of imperialism (3) decrease in military expenditures (4) series of international crises.

3. Italy entered the Triple Alliance because it was (1) grateful for German aid in the Austro-Sardinian War (2) angered by France's seizure of Tunisia (3) promised territory (4) afraid of the Triple Entente.

4. Britain joined the Triple Entente because (1) it feared rebellion in India (2) the member nations were Britain's traditional allies (3) the ruling families of the member nations were related (4) it feared Germany's trade and naval policies.

5. The basic weakness of the Triple Alliance was that (1) its members lacked common borders (2) Germany lacked a conscript army (3) Italy desired Austrian territories (4) Serbia desired Austrian territories.

6. In the decade before World War I, the two chief rivals for control of the Balkans were (1) Russia and Italy (2) Italy and France (3) Austria-Hungary and Great Britain (4) Russia and Austria-Hungary.

7. During World War I both Italy and Japan (1) joined forces with Germany (2) participated in the war to gain territory (3) were forced into the war by direct attack on their land (4) declared their position in the last year of the war.

8. Which nation withdrew from the Triple Alliance and entered World War I to fight on the other side? (1) Germany (2) Austria (3) Italy (4) Russia.

9. In 1914 German armies invaded Belgium because Belgium (1) had declared war on Germany (2) contained important munitions works (3) consisted of level land leading to the French border (4) refused to surrender the assassin of Archduke Francis Ferdinand.

10. One reason for America's entrance into World War I was (1) a treaty with Britain (2) the desire to stop the spread of communism (3) France's refusal to repay American loans (4) our fear that Germany would emerge as an Atlantic power.

11. President Wilson's ideals were best expressed in the provision of the Treaty of Versailles concerning (1) reparation payments by Germany (2) division of Germany's colonies among the Allies (3) war guilt (4) the League of Nations.

12. Which was true of both the Congress of Vienna (1815) and the Versailles Conferences (1919)? (1) Many of the boundaries of Europe were changed. (2) France attended both conferences as a victorious nation. (3) Small nations had as much influence as the large powers. (4) The principle of self-determination was an important basis for deciding issues.

13. Two nations created following World War I were (1) Belgium and Denmark (2) Czechoslovakia and Poland (3) Siberia and Yugoslavia (4) Sweden and Bulgaria.

14. The treaties ending World War I created a new minority problem of (1) French in Alsace-Lorraine (2) Magyars in Hungary (3) Germans in Poland (4) Serbs in Yugoslavia.

15. The treaty of peace with Austria after World War I forbade Anschluss, which meant (1) establishment of war industries (2) maintenance of a submarine fleet (3) government by dictatorship (4) union with Germany.

16. One result of World War I was that (1) the United States became a world power (2) Italy annexed Tunisia (3) France and Germany became allies (4) Britain lost its colonial empire.

17. An important result of World War I was that in many European nations (1) living standards rose (2) foreign trade increased (3) nationalism became less intense (4) dictators seized control.

### ESSAY QUESTIONS

1. (a) Discuss *two* circumstances that led to the formation of the Triple Alliance. (b) Discuss *two* circumstances that led to the formation of the Triple Entente. (c) Present *one* reason for agreeing or disagreeing with the statement that alliances preserve peace.

2. (a) Show *one* way in which each of the following helped cause World War I: (1) alliances (2) imperialism (3) militarism (4) nationalism (5) international anarchy. (b) Select *one* of these factors and show that it is still a cause of world tension.

3. With reference to World War I, illustrate the following terms: (a) ultimatum (b) principle of nationality (c) reparations (d) idealism (e) unrestricted submarine warfare.

4. (a) List *four* important provisions of the Treaty of Versailles. (b) Explain *two* reasons why Germany criticized this treaty. (c) Would you agree or disagree with *each* of the German criticisms? Defend your answer. (d) Did the Treaty of Versailles plant the seeds of World War II? Support your opinion with *one* reason.

5. Describe *two* important results of World War I for each of the following headings: (a) social (b) economic (c) political.

6. The settlements made at the Congress of Vienna (1815) and at the Paris Peace Conference (1919) provided for organizations to keep the peace. Yet each settlement contained provisions that sowed the seeds of future wars. (a) Name *one* organization established by the Congress of Vienna and *one* organization established by the Paris Peace Conference, and state *one* reason for the need for *each* organization mentioned. (b) Show how *one* action taken at the Congress of Vienna and *one* action taken at the Paris Peace Conference led to conflict or war.

# Part 2. Russia: From Czarist Absolutism to Communist Dictatorship

## RUSSIA: GEOGRAPHIC SETTING AND POPULATION

1. **Tremendous Size.** Russia, which since 1924 has also been known as the Soviet Union, is the world's largest country. It contains two and one-half times the area of the United States, or one-sixth of the world's land surface. Russia extends 7,000 miles (11,200 kilometers) from central Europe eastward across Asia to the Pacific Ocean. At easternmost Siberia, bordering on the Bering Strait, Russia approaches within a few miles (kilometers) of the United States at Alaska.

Since most of European Russia consists of a low, level plain, the country has been open on its western borders to easy military invasion. Russia's tremendous size, however, has enabled Russian forces to retreat considerable distances, thereby compelling invaders to lengthen their supply lines. Then the Russians have turned on and destroyed the invaders, as was done in the 19th century to Napoleon and in the 20th century to the Nazi German armies.

**2. Rich Natural Resources.** Russia possesses extensive natural wealth: fertile soil, forests, oil, and minerals—coal, iron ore, manganese, aluminum, nickel, chrome, and copper. By utilizing these resources, Russia today is a leading nation in agriculture and industry.

Russian agriculture, however, is affected by several adverse geographic factors. Much of the land lies in northern regions that have long, severe winters and short, cool summers. This short growing season makes the northern lands unsuitable for farming so that less than 25 percent of the country's land area can be successfully cultivated. In the southern regions that have warmer climates, farming is often hampered by uncertain and inadequate rainfall.

**3. Limited Transportation Facilities.** *(a) Inland.* Russia's 83,000 miles (132,800 kilometers) of railroad, some single track, is equal to about two-fifths of the railroad mileage in the United States. Russia's 267,000 miles (427,200 kilometers) of surfaced roads constitute less than 10 percent of American surfaced road mileage. Russia also utilizes about 82,000 miles (131,200 kilometers) of natural and human-made inland waterways. *(b) Seaports.* The ports of Leningrad on the Baltic Sea and Vladivostok on the Pacific Ocean are icebound part of the year. Odessa on the Black Sea is a warm-water port serviceable the whole year. However, ships from the Black Sea must sail through the Turkish-controlled Dardanelles to reach the Mediterranean.

**4. Many Peoples.** Russia's population of 250 million, chiefly Slavic-speaking, consists of *(a)* Great Russian, over 50 percent; *(b)* Ukrainian, or Little Russian, about 20 percent; *(c)* Byelorussian, or White Russian, almost 5 percent; and *(d)* about 100 other nationalities totaling about 25 percent. This portion includes a variety of Asian peoples and several peoples of Eastern Europe, whose lands were annexed during the World War II era.

European Russia, which lies west of the Ural Mountains, is heavily populated, whereas central Asia and Siberia are lightly populated.

## RUSSIA: HISTORICAL BACKGROUND— AN INTERPRETIVE ANALYSIS

Geographically Russia is part of Europe—and therefore may be considered as part of the West—but actually Russia lies at the continent's periphery, or eastern edge, far distant from Western Europe. As a result the Russian people for the most part have been historically isolated from Western Europe. The Russians developed their own civilization shaped by uniquely Russian experiences and largely unaffected by the major historical movements that molded Western civilization.

**1. The Byzantine Influence.** The Russian inheritance, from ancient times through most of the medieval era, came largely from the Byzantine Empire. The Russians traded with Constantinople and were converted to Greek Orthodox Christianity by Byzantine missionaries. The Byzantine Empire set an example of autocratic government, preoccupation with military defense, a church subservient to political control, and a static, relatively unchanging society. Because the Greek Orthodox Church did not require its liturgy (services) to be in Greek, the Russian clergy were not compelled to learn Greek and so lost contact with the writings of the ancient Greek world.

During the same time period, the west European peoples derived their inheritance from the classical Greco-Roman civilization. This civilization illustrated, in addition to autocracy, the development of democratic city-states, the rise of a powerful church independent of civil control, the use of a Latin liturgy compelling the clergy to learn Latin and to be able to read the works of the ancient world's writers, and the example of certain dynamic, changing societies.

**2. The Mongol (Tartar) Rule (13th Century into the 15th Century).** The Mongols, or Tartars, a warrior people from central Asia, conquered and for over 200 years ruled most of Russia. The Tartars set an example of autocratic rule, disdain for human life, and ruthlessness in the collection of tribute. While contributing little to Russian culture, the Tartar invaders isolated Russia from the West and fostered an era of cultural and social stagnation. Even as the Tartars were being driven out, the Russian peasants fell more deeply into serfdom.

During the same time period, the west European peoples experienced (a) the Renaissance with its interest in the ancient Greco-Roman writers, its emphasis upon individualism, and its encouragement of literature, art, and science; (b) the Reformation, a successful revolt against religious authority; and (c) the Commercial Revolution that gave rise to a wealthy middle class of merchants and bankers, witnessed the beginnings of capitalist institutions, and created a demand for manufactured goods that would lead to the Industrial Revolution. These west European historical movements had little or no impact on Russia.

**3. Russian Contacts with Western Europe (Late 17th Century into Early 19th Century):** (a) Czar Peter the Great of Russia (1689–1725), attempted to Westernize his country. His purposes, however, were to strengthen his army and support his autocratic rule. Peter's reforms were superficial, affected only a thin top layer of Russian society, and lacked permanence. (b) Czar Alexander I (1801–1825) and the Russian armies played a major role in the downfall of the French Emperor Napoleon. The Russian people, however, remained largely unaware of the French Revolutionary ideals—liberty, equality, fraternity—that so affected civilization in western Europe.

# CONDITIONS IN CZARIST RUSSIA

Up to World War I, Russia in many respects resembled France under the Old Regime. Unlike most west European nations, Czarist Russia had made little progress away from absolutism, inequality, and poverty.

## 1. Political Conditions

*a. Absolutism of the Czar.* The czar ruled as an unlimited monarch and exercised all powers. Through the secret police he vigorously suppressed demands for reforms and punished reformers by imprisonment, execution, or exile to penal colonies in Siberia.

*b. Terrorism by Reformers.* Denied lawful means of expressing discontent, many Russian reformers, especially intellectuals, identified with a radical movement called *nihilism*—a word derived from the Latin meaning *nothing.* Nihilists believed that nothing was worthwhile in Czarist Russia and that all must be destroyed in order to apply reason and science to the building of a better society. The nihilists therefore turned to underground activity and terrorism. They spread anti-Czarist propaganda among the peasants, and turning to violence, they assassinated a number of government leaders including, in 1881, reformist Czar Alexander II.

Thereafter the nihilist movement was destroyed by the new czar—indicating that individual acts of terrorism could not undermine the Czarist government.

## 2. Social Conditions

*a. Rigid Class Distinctions.* (1) *Privileged classes.* The clergy of the state-controlled Russian Orthodox Church preached obedience to the czar. The nobility owned much land and held important army and government positions. (2) *Unprivileged classes.* The peasants, constituting the masses, lived impoverished lives and worked hard without prospect of advancement. The city workers, few in number, faced conditions that were hardly better. The unprivileged classes remained mostly illiterate, for the czar's government feared that education would teach the common people "dangerous" ideas.

*b. Russification.* Subject peoples, such as Poles, Finns, Estonians, Latvians, Lithuanians, and Armenians, were pressured to adopt the Russian language, culture, and religion. They bitterly resisted the government's attempts to destroy their national heritages.

*c. Persecution of Jews.* Jews were forbidden to own land, were almost completely barred from educational institutions, and were required to live in restricted districts, called the *Pale of Settlement.* They were victimized recurrently by government-inspired outbursts of violence, called *pogroms.* Anti-Jewish riots served the Czarist government by diverting the attention of the people away from their own deplorable conditions. After a series of brutal pogroms in 1881, following the assassination of Czar Alexander II, many Jews began to flee Russia, migrating chiefly to the United States.

## 3. Economic Conditions

*a. An Agricultural Country.* Russia raised great quantities of sugar beets and grains. Its peasants, using primitive methods and lacking sufficient land, eked out a wretched living.

*b. Beginnings of Industrialization (Late 19th Century).* With landless peasants providing cheap labor and French investors supplying capital, Russia began its industrial revolution. The Russians constructed iron and steel mills, textile factories, and railroads. An ambitious project, spanning the width of Russia from St. Petersburg (now Leningrad) to Vladivostok, was the *Trans-Siberian Railroad.*

Russia's industrial beginnings created two new economic classes: workers and capitalists. The workers resented their low wages and slum conditions. The business owners resented the privileged position of the nobility. Both groups desired a voice in the government and opposed Czarist absolutism.

## REFORMS IN CZARIST RUSSIA

Fearing unrest that accompanied military defeats, two czars made concessions to the people. Czarist reforms, in the long run, brought little change. Czarist Russia's failure to solve its problems made revolution almost inevitable.

## 1. Emancipation of the Serfs (1861)

*a. Background.* Although serfdom had long ago disappeared in western Europe, the peasants in Russia remained serfs. They were bound to the soil, required to pay feudal dues and services, and subjected to the will of the nobles. Peasant discontent led to occasional but easily suppressed uprisings. However, after Russia's defeat in the Crimean War (1853–1856), the peasants intensified their complaints and gained the support of many intellectuals. The movement for reform began to frighten the government.

*b. Reform Measures.* In 1861 reformist Czar *Alexander II*, by edict, freed the serfs, purchased land from the nobles, and sold this land to peasant village communities called *mirs*. The mirs were instructed to assign plots to their members, who would pay for the land over a period of 49 years.

*c. Weaknesses.* The peasants remained dissatisfied because (1) the nobles retained more than half the land, which left the peasants with inadequate acreage; (2) the amount of land assigned to each peasant decreased as the population of the mirs increased; (3) the mirs, not the peasants, held title to the land; and (4) the peasants were compelled to make land payments they could not afford.

In 1906, following Russia's defeat by Japan, Czar *Nicholas II* canceled all debts on land, permitted peasants to abolish the mirs, and transferred land titles to the peasants. These measures failed to calm the peasants. They needed more land and hungered for the fertile fields in the nobles' estates.

## 2. Establishment of a Legislature (1905)

*a. Background.* In the Russo-Japanese War (1904–1905), Russia met defeat amidst evidence of government inefficiency and corruption. The people demanded reforms in a series of strikes, demonstrations, riots, and scattered uprisings. A group of workers, trying to deliver a petition to the czar, were fired upon by troops, an event called "Bloody Sunday." These developments, reflecting widespread discontent, became known as the *Revolution of 1905.*

*b. Reform Measures.* Czar Nicholas II (1) promised to guarantee certain personal liberties, (2) established a lawmaking body, the *Duma,* and (3) permitted Duma elections by universal male suffrage.

*c. Absolutism Restored.* As the revolutionists quarreled among themselves, the czar used the soldiers returning from the war to spread terror and reestablish his control. Thereafter, he restricted suffrage to the upper classes and limited the power of the Duma, making it into a "debating society."

## FOREIGN AFFAIRS OF CZARIST RUSSIA

**1. Imperialism and Pan-Slavism.** Czarist Russia pursued imperialist policies toward China and Persia (Iran) and in the Balkans. Because many Balkan peoples—Bulgars, Serbs, Croats, and Slovenes—spoke Slavic languages related to Russian, the czars justified Russian expansion into the Balkans by claiming Slavic unity, *Pan-Slavism.* Up to 1914 Russia helped many Balkan peoples gain independence from Turkey (see pages 261–262).

**2. Triple Entente and World War I.** Russia came in conflict with Austria-Hungary over the Balkans and Pan-Slavism. To counter the alliance between Austria-Hungary and Germany, Russia reached agreements with France and Britain, thereby forming the Triple Entente. In 1914 Russia supported Serbia in the chain of events that led to World War I. (See pages 433–434.)

## RUSSIAN REVOLUTIONS OF 1917

Some historians contend that Russia, in 1917 and afterward, experienced three major stages of revolution, similar in certain respects to those of the 1789 French Revolution. As we discuss developments in Russia, we shall identify these three stages and call attention to seeming similarities.

**1. First, or "Moderate," Stage: March Revolution—The Czar Is Overthrown**

*a. Underlying Causes: Conditions in Czarist Russia.* (1) *Political.* The people wanted an end to Czarist absolutism and repression. Especially the middle class and workers desired a voice in the government. (2) *Economic.* Peasants wanted the nobles' fertile lands. City workers wanted better economic conditions. (3) *Social.* Subject nationalities wanted an end to discrimination and Russification.

**b. Immediate Causes: Czarist Wartime Incompetence.** (1) *On the battlefront.* Soldiers received inadequate food, clothing, and battle equipment; officers, chiefly nobles, often lacked ability; Russian armies met with defeat after defeat; casualties ran high. (2) *On the home front.* Factories proved unable to satisfy military and civilian needs; railroad transportation broke down; cities faced food shortages; prices soared.

With soldiers war weary and deserting, peasants rioting, workers striking, and Duma members demanding reform, Russia was ripe for revolution. In March, 1917, soldiers defied government orders to fire on striking city workers in Petrograd (St. Petersburg); railroad workers delayed the czar's return from the fighting front to Petrograd; and the Duma spurned Czarist commands to dissolve. Czar Nicholas II, realizing that his authority was gone, abdicated the throne.

**c. The Provisional Government Fails (March–November, 1917).** This temporary government was headed first by the liberal Democrat Prince *George Lvov* and later by the moderate Socialist *Alexander Kerensky.* Dominated by middle-class liberals, this temporary government guaranteed civil liberties, freed political prisoners, and sought to establish a west European type of democratic regime.

The provisional government, however, (1) insisted upon continuing the war, (2) proved unable to provide the cities with food, and (3) refused to approve land seizures by the peasants. It therefore lost support among the public and especially among the newly organized *soviets* (councils) of workers and soldiers.

**2. Second, or "Radical," Stage: November Revolution—The Communists Seize Control.**

**a. Communist Party and Leaders.** The Communist party, a small but well-organized and highly disciplined group, originated with left-wing Russian Socialists, the *Bolsheviks.* They had fanatically defied Czarist rule. Hunted by Czarist police, many Bolshevik leaders had been sent to Siberian prison camps; others had fled to exile. In 1917 the Bolsheviks gained skilled leadership by the return from exile of *Leon Trotsky* and *Nikolai Lenin.* The realistic, shrewd, iron-willed Lenin headed the party and was assisted by Trotsky, a brilliant orator and organizer.

**b. Communist Tactics.** By demanding *"Peace, Bread, and Land"* for soldiers, city workers, and peasants, respectively, the Bolsheviks appealed to the masses. The Bolsheviks attracted considerable support because the Russian people— then overwhelmingly not Communist and not aware of fundamental Communist aims—were displeased with the Kerensky regime.

The Bolsheviks quickly gained influence in the soviets, extended the authority of the soviets, and undermined the Kerensky government. Finally, in November, 1917, Red troops toppled the provisional government. The Bolsheviks established a regime led by Premier Lenin and War Minister Trotsky.

## RUSSIA UNDER LENIN: CONSOLIDATION OF COMMUNIST POWER (1917–1924)

**1. Sought Popular Support.** Lenin took Russia out of World War I by accepting Germany's severe terms in the *Treaty of Brest-Litovsk*. Russia lost much territory, especially Finland, Estonia, Latvia, Lithuania, Russian Poland, and the Ukraine. In domestic affairs Lenin *(a)* organized the workers to take over the factories and then nationalized industry and *(b)* directed the peasants to seize the nobles' estates and then nationalized all land. Thus, the Communists carried out their program of "Peace, Bread, and Land."

**2. Crushed Opposition.** The Communists under Lenin encountered strong enmity from several groups. *(a)* **Within Russia** were the anti-Bolsheviks, or "Whites," who were led by former Czarist officers. *(b)* **Outside Russia** were the newly created state of Poland (which desired additional Russian territory) and the Allies (who resented Communist Russia's withdrawal from the war and its policy of world revolution).

From 1917 to 1920 the Communist regime faced attack by Polish troops, Allied intervention forces, and Russian "Whites" armies. To protect their revolution, the Communists acted ruthlessly. In 1918 they put to death Czar Nicholas II and his family. Communist secret police, often influenced by hearsay evidence and prejudice against the upper classes, executed thousands as counter-revolutionaries. (This "Red Terror" in Russia was remindful of the Reign of Terror during the 1789 French Revolution.)

The Communist "Red" army smashed all military threats. Its success resulted from *(a)* Trotsky's ability as military organizer and inspirational leader, *(b)* the peasant soldiers' determination to prevent the nobles' return, *(c)* Russian nationalism, which made Russians resent foreign intervention, and *(d)* disunity and war-weariness among the "Whites" and the various foreign armies.

**3. Gained Diplomatic Recognition.** By 1921 the Communists had conceded the independence of Finland, Estonia, Latvia, Lithuania, and Poland but had recovered the Ukraine. They ruled Russia unchallenged. Thereafter, Lenin's government received diplomatic recognition from most foreign nations. The United States waited until 1933 before recognizing the Soviet Union. (Recognition meant official acknowledgment that the Communists had effective control over Russia; it did *not* imply approval of the Communist regime.)

**4. Lenin's Death.** In 1922 Lenin suffered the first of a series of strokes. His illness touched off a struggle among top Communists for the eventual leadership of Russia. Lenin's death in 1924 brought this struggle into the open.

## RUSSIA UNDER STALIN (1924–1953)

**1. Overview.** *Joseph Stalin,* General Secretary of the Communist party, battled War Minister Leon Trotsky for supreme power. Stalin emerged victorious. In

1929 Trotsky was sent into exile; in 1940, in Mexico, he was slain by an assassin, supposedly an agent of Stalin.

Stalin's control over the party made him dictator of Russia, although he waited until 1941 to become premier. Stalin destroyed internal opposition by brutality and terror: secret arrests, fake trials, inhuman forced-labor camps, and mass executions. On the constructive side Stalin transformed Russia from a backward agricultural nation into a modern industrial state and guided it to victory in World War II.

**2. Third, or "Return to Stability," Stage of Revolution: Stalinist Russia.** Historians, who perceive similarities in the "anatomy of revolution," contend that the third stage of the Russian Revolution—similar to the Napoleonic Era in France—was Stalinist Russia.

While restoring Russia to stability, Stalin preserved certain revolutionary goals: no restoration of hereditary Czarist rule, no restoration of the privileged noble class possessing land and dominating government and army positions, and improvement of Russian living standards somewhat above Czarist levels.

Stalin, however, departed from Communist ideology: (1) He utilized the capitalist practice of paying interest on savings and bonds. (2) Instead of "to each according to need," Stalin permitted wide wage discrepancies between unskilled and skilled workers. (3) Instead of acting to weaken the family as a "bourgeois institution," Stalin's government encouraged strong family ties and large families.

Stalin also perpetuated certain practices typical of Czarist Russia: (1) Stalin himself was the new czar, ruling with absolute power, utilizing secret police, and suppressing opposition. (2) His regime encouraged the rise of a new upper class composed of professionals, artists and writers, factory managers, and Communist party and government officials. (3) Stalin's collective farm program was reminiscent of the Czarist mir system. (4) Stalin's government revived militarism, played power politics, and sought territorial expansion. (5) Stalin employed the mass media to extol Russian nationalism and to praise selected heroes of Czarist times.

## RUSSIA UNDER KHRUSHCHEV (1953–1964)

When Stalin died in 1953, *Nikita Khrushchev*, then little known to the Western world, became First Secretary of the Communist party. By shrewdness, intrigue, and party manipulation, Khrushchev eliminated his chief rivals. Internal Affairs Minister *Lavrenti Beria* was denounced as a foreign agent, arrested, and executed; Premier *Georgi Malenkov* was compelled to confess blunders and resign; other important officials, including another premier, a foreign minister, and a defense minister, were removed from office. By 1958 Khrushchev felt secure enough to assume the premiership and openly rule the Soviet Union. Although Khrushchev halted the worst aspects of Stalinist terror, he maintained a tightly controlled dictatorship.

Khrushchev directed Russian efforts toward space flights, with considerable success. However, in economic matters Khrushchev failed to halt the decline in the rate of Russian industrial growth and failed to spur Russian agricultural output. Toward the European satellite nations, Khrushchev somewhat relaxed Russian control. In the cold war Khrushchev acted cautiously. He agreed to the Limited Nuclear Test Ban Treaty and advocated a policy of "peaceful coexistence" with the West. His cautious policy toward the West was one factor in the split between the Soviet Union and Communist China.

## RUSSIA UNDER BREZHNEV (1964–    )

In a surprising development in 1964, Khrushchev was removed from his positions as first secretary of the Communist party and as premier. In *Pravda*, the Communist party newspaper, Khrushchev was denounced (by implication but not by name) for "harebrained scheming, immature conclusions, and hasty decisions." Khrushchev's removal, according to Western observers, was caused by his undignified personal conduct, his worsening of the dispute with Communist China, and his failure to spur industrial and agricultural output. From Khrushchev himself the peoples of the Soviet Union and the world heard nothing. He became a "nonperson" in Russia—his writings removed from bookstores, his picture removed from public buildings, his name not mentioned in newspapers or on radio.

Khrushchev was succeeded by two men long associated with him. *Leonid Brezhnev*, who had been Khrushchev's deputy in the Communist party Secretariat, became first secretary. *Aleksei Kosygin* became premier. This leadership (1) continued the policy of peaceful coexistence toward the West, (2) sought—so far unsuccessfully—to lessen the breach with Communist China, and (3) worked to improve the Soviet economy.

In time Brezhnev emerged as the most powerful leader in the Soviet Union.

## GOVERNMENT OF COMMUNIST RUSSIA

The Soviet government uses the outward forms of democracy to conceal the actuality of Communist dictatorship. What the Soviet government claims to be *in theory* is very different from what it is *in fact.*

1. **Federal Organization.** The *Union of Soviet Socialist Republics* (U.S.S.R. or Soviet Union) is a federation of 15 republics. Thus, the Soviet Union has *(a)* one central government—housed in Moscow's famous fortress, the *Kremlin*—which exercises extensive nationwide powers, and *(b)* 15 republics, which are smaller governmental units. Each republic represents a major national group.

The *Russian Soviet Federated Socialist Republic*, with four-fifths of the country's area and over half of its population, is by far the largest of these republics. Consequently the Soviet Union is still commonly called Russia.

*In theory,* each republic is independent and may secede from the U.S.S.R.

*In fact,* each republic is dominated by the highly centralized Communist party, views secessionist activity as treasonable, and dares not deviate from the policies set by the central government at Moscow.

## 2. The Central Government

*a. Legislature.* The *Supreme Soviet,* the chief legislative body, serves a four-year term. It consists of two houses: the *Soviet of the Union,* elected on the basis of population, and the *Soviet of Nationalities,* elected from the major national homelands. The two houses jointly select a small permanent committee—called the Supreme Soviet's *Presidium.* Between sessions of the Supreme Soviet, its powers are exercised by the Presidium. (The chairman of the Supreme Soviet's Presidium is the titular head of state—the *President* of the Soviet Union.)

*In theory,* the Supreme Soviet enacts Russia's laws. *In fact,* the Supreme Soviet—meeting no more than twice a year for about a week at a time—automatically approves laws previously issued by its Presidium and by the executive branch.

In 1977 the Supreme Soviet, under the leadership of Leonid Brezhnev, unanimously approved a new Soviet constitution. As with the three previous Soviet constitutions, it did not provide any means for a citizen to legally challenge the constitutionality of a law.

*b. Executive.* The *Council of Ministers,* or cabinet, the chief executive body, consists of the heads of the major ministries—such as Foreign Affairs, Defense, Trade, Agriculture, Conservation of Resources, and Culture. The chairman of the Council of Ministers is the Soviet Union's *Premier.*

*In theory,* the Supreme Soviet appoints these top officials. *In fact,* it unanimously approves the individuals previously designated by the Communist party.

*In theory,* the Council of Ministers enforces the laws and directs the government. *In fact,* in addition to its other powers, the Council of Ministers also makes laws by issuing decrees.

*c. Judiciary.* The *Supreme Court,* the chief judicial body, consists of about 80 judges appointed for five-year terms by the Supreme Soviet.

*In theory,* the Supreme Court, in accordance with the constitution, renders independent judgments. *In fact,* the Supreme Court may not declare laws unconstitutional, may not void ministerial decisions, and has never deviated from Communist party policy.

*d. Civil Rights. In theory,* Soviet citizens are guaranteed freedom of speech, press, and assembly. The 1977 Constitution, however, declared that such freedoms may be exercised only to "strengthen and develop the Socialist system" and to "safeguard the interests of the Soviet state."

*In fact,* persons who speak, print, or assemble in opposition to the government are regarded as mental defectives or criminals. In searching out opposition the secret police ignore the constitutional guarantees of civil rights. Political prisoners are denied the right to counsel until after the police have completed their investigations. The secret police may extort confessions from such prisoners before bringing them to trial. Also, accused persons are denied the presumption of innocence until legally proven guilty.

*e. Elections. In theory,* the Soviet government is controlled by the voters. All Soviet citizens over 18 years of age may vote—chiefly for legislature members. *In fact,* since only one slate of candidates, picked by the Communist party, is permitted, the people have no choice. Citizens who fail to vote risk being considered hostile to the regime and being treated accordingly.

## 3. The Communist Party

*a. Membership.* With nearly 15 million members, the Communist party contains about 6 percent of the total Soviet population. Most party members are recruited from Communist youth groups. Party members are carefully selected and accept iron discipline. They devote their leisure time almost entirely to party work, which may involve difficult assignments. As compensation, party membership offers special privileges and is essential for personal advancement in almost any field of work.

Party members are carefully watched. Those who do not measure up to standards or who are suspected of opposing the existing leadership are expelled by *purges.*

*b. Pyramidal Organization.* At its base the Communist party consists of local units (formerly called "cells") organized within factories, farms, offices, and schools. These primary units elect representatives to higher party groups, each of which elects representatives to the next highest body up to the *All-Union Party Congress.* Since this Congress meets infrequently—supposedly every four years—it delegates its powers to its *Central Committee,* which in turn chooses the members of the two all-powerful party organs, the Presidium and the Secretariat.

(1) The *Presidium,* or *Politburo,* consists of a small group that determines party policy.

(2) The *Secretariat* directs party work and membership. In practice the First, or General, Secretary—the position held by Stalin, later by Khrushchev, and now by Brezhnev—dominates the party and thereby the country.

*c. Power Over Russia.* The Communist party dominates the Russian people and government. (1) The Communist party is Russia's only party. No opposition party is permitted to exist. (2) The Communist party selects all candidates for government office. Candidates for key positions usually are leading party members; candidates for less important posts may be nonmembers approved by the party. (3) The Communist party keeps a watchful eye on the government. If the party is dissatisfied with the attitude or accomplishment of any official, it will take steps to remove that person from office. (4) The Communist party controls the

The Kremlin, a fortress enclosed by walls built in the 1400's, contains government buildings, churches, museums, and residences.

army, the regular police, and the secret police—all instruments for destroying opposition and enforcing the party's will. (5) The Communist party controls education, the radio, the theater, and the press. These sources of information and means of propaganda are used to extol the party leaders, to glorify the party's role in Russian history, and to justify the Communist stand on issues—known as the *party line.*

In 1977 Leonid Brezhnev, General Secretary of the Soviet Communist party, also assumed the title of President of the Soviet Union. Brezhnev was the first Soviet leader simultaneously to hold the powerful position as chief of party and the largely ceremonial position as chief of state. He did so, Brezhnev explained, to emphasize the dominant role of the party over the state.

The 1977 Constitution defined, for the first time, the status of the Communist party as the "leading and guiding force of Soviet society and the nucleus of its political system."

**4. Transferring Power in a Dictatorship.** *In theory,* when the Russian head of government dies, that person's successor is selected by the Supreme Soviet. *In fact,* after the deaths of Lenin and Stalin (check the Index), a bitter struggle, marked by violence, took place within the Communist party. Both times the successor was the person with the most power over the Communist party, its first secretary. (In contrast with the Soviet dictatorship, American democracy faces no bitter struggle for power upon the death of a president. In accordance with the provisions of the United States Constitution, the vice president assumes the office of president.)

Khrushchev's removal in 1964 was probably engineered by a small group of Communist leaders, headed by Khrushchev's deputy in the Secretariat—Leonid Brezhnev.

## ECONOMIC SYSTEM OF COMMUNIST RUSSIA

1. **War Communism (1917–1921).** Immediately upon seizing power, the Communists sought to transform Russia's economic system from capitalism to communism. While fighting civil war and foreign intervention, the government nationalized mines, factories, railroads, and land, and prohibited most private ownership—a program called *War Communism*.

War Communism proved a failure. Many factories and farms had been damaged during wartime; government officials lacked economic management skills; factory workers failed to maintain production schedules; and farmers curtailed output because the state seized their surplus crops without payment. With manufactured goods scarce, foodstuffs lacking, and famine widespread, Russia by 1921 was in economic chaos.

2. **New Economic Policy (1921–1928).** To restore Russia's economic health and safeguard Communist rule, Lenin in 1921 announced the *New Economic Policy (NEP)*. This *temporary retreat* from communism *(a)* permitted private owners to operate retail stores and small factories for profit, *(b)* allowed farmers to sell surplus crops in the open market, *(c)* encouraged foreign capitalists to invest in Russia, and *(d)* attracted foreign engineers and technicians to work in Russia by offering liberal salaries. These represented only small concessions to capitalism, since over 80 percent of Russia's economy—including railroads, iron and steel mills, coal mines, banks, and public utilities—remained in government hands.

The NEP, operating in peacetime, revived Russia's economy. By 1928 agricultural and industrial output had reached pre-World War I levels.

3. **Centralized Economic Planning: The Five-Year Plans.** In 1928 Stalin began Russia's five-year programs of centralized economic planning. Russia has completed ten such plans and is now engaged in its eleventh Five-Year Plan.

*a. Overall Objectives.* The Five-Year Plans called for rapid and sustained economic growth. Although they sought increased agricultural output, the plans placed major emphasis upon expanding *heavy industry*, such as iron and steel, aluminum, chemicals, electric power, and machinery. Heavy industry received top priority in order to produce weapons and thereby strengthen the country militarily.

The plans gave low priority to *light industry*, or consumer goods—just enough to provide the people with minimal living conditions. The Communists viewed a higher standard of living as an ultimate, not an immediate, goal. Unlike the American economy, which is consumer-oriented, the Russian economy under the Five-Year Plans has been geared to the needs of the state.

*Dowling in The Kansas City Star*

**"I'd like to fry an egg."**

Which figure—military or consumer—is saying "I'd like to fry an egg"? Does the statement refer only to eggs or to other goods as well? If other goods, what ones? Why is the military shown at the stove whereas the consumer is in the background?

*b. Special Objectives.* The first Five-Year Plan (1928–1932) also called for the elimination of the remnants of capitalism—namely, the owners of private stores and factories *(nepmen)* and the well-to-do peasants *(kulaks)*. The fourth Five-Year Plan (1946–1950) repaired the destruction wrought by the German invasion during World War II. The fifth Five-Year Plan (1951–1955) provided for Russian economic aid to Communist-bloc and underdeveloped nations. The sixth Five-Year Plan (1956–1960) was burdened by the economic demands resulting from the 1956 uprisings in the Soviet satellite nations of Poland and Hungary (check the Index). This sixth plan was scrapped as a failure two years before its end and replaced by a one-time Seven-Year Plan (1958–1965). The ninth Five-Year Plan (1971–1975) sought to modernize the Soviet economy through imports from capitalist nations of Western technology and production facilities.

*c. Industry.* The *State Planning Commission (Gosplan),* composed of trained economists, established master plans for each industry and factory. The planners determined all economic matters such as the wages and hours of workers, the kind and location of new factories, the type and amount of goods to be produced, and the allocation of investment capital between and within industries.

To achieve ever-increasing production goals, the Communists (1) employed propaganda, stressing the needs of the country and the promise of a better life in days to come, (2) rewarded outstanding workers with pay differentials and social approval, and (3) punished unsuccessful plant managers by demotion and sometimes arrest as saboteurs.

*d. Agriculture.* Russia's farmland is divided approximately as follows: (1) 30 percent is in *state farms,* vast agricultural factories that pay their workers fixed wages. (2) 65 percent is in *collectives,* compulsory farm communities that pay their peasant members in produce and in money. (In many ways the collectives resemble the Czarist mirs.) (3) 5 percent is in *garden plots,* essentially private-enterprise farms permitted industrial workers and collective farmers, as a sideline, to raise food for family use and for sale in the open market. Although the garden plots utilize less than 5 percent of the farmland, they are most carefully cultivated and account for 25 percent of the nation's agricultural production.

During the first Five-Year Plan, collectives arose as the government forced farmers to pool their land, livestock, and equipment and to work the total area together. However, members of collectives are permitted small garden plots. The collectives pay the government a portion of the harvest as land taxes and for government services: bank credit, rental of farm machinery, and technical help. The collectives must sell a portion of the harvest to the government at low government-set prices and may sell the remainder on the open market. The collectives make possible large-scale production and strict government control over farming.

During the first Five-Year Plan the kulaks, or prosperous farmers, slaughtered their livestock and wrecked their equipment rather than join collectives. They received harsh treatment from the Communist regime; they were driven from their lands and starved to death, sentenced to forced labor, or killed. By 1932 the kulaks as a class had been eliminated at the cost of several million lives.

*e. Accomplishments.* The Five-Year Plans transformed Russia from an agricultural into a leading manufacturing nation. Russian industrial output increased more than twentyfold. The Communists created new industrial centers deep in Siberia and central Asia. During World War II, when the Germans occupied large portions of European Russia, these new centers helped sustain the economy and the war effort.

Russia developed a pool of skilled technicians and engineers and produced the most complex space vehicles and the most modern military equipment. It became the world's second largest industrial power, surpassed only by the United States. As measured in *gross national product (GNP)*—the money value of all goods and services—since 1950, the Soviet economy has grown from 30 percent to somewhat less than 60 percent of the American economy. (Although the Soviets talk of "overtaking and surpassing" the United States, Western economists believe that, from its larger current economic base, Russia will find it much more difficult to achieve further percentage gains in relation to the American economy.)

Compared to Czarist days, the Russian people enjoy improved living standards. These standards, however, remain below those of most Central and West European nations and far below those of the United States.

### f. Weaknesses

(1) *In Industry.* Centralized planning and management have resulted in bureaucracy, waste, and error. Costs of production have been high. Goods often have been of poor quality. Consumer goods have been scarce, and a housing shortage has existed. Investment capital has not been sufficient for the needs of industry. Soviet labor productivity has been low—one-half that of American industrial workers.

(2) *In Agriculture.* Although Russia has employed 30 percent of its labor force in agriculture, the increase in food output has barely kept up with the increase in population. By contrast the United States, with 5 percent of its workers in agriculture, has produced huge surpluses. Soviet farm labor productivity has been less than one-fifth that of American farmers. Stated differently—whereas one Soviet farm worker has produced enough to feed seven persons, one American farm worker has produced enough to feed 46.

Some problems of Soviet agriculture, in addition to poor weather conditions, have been crude farm equipment, meager irrigation facilities, shortages of fertilizers, outmoded production methods, lack of adequate storage and transport facilities, and peasant misuse and abuse of farm machinery. Serious food shortages have occurred periodically. The peasants have resented collectivization. Whenever possible they have neglected work on the land of the collectives and have devoted their energies to their own small garden plots. Agriculture has been the weakest link in the Russian economy.

### 4. Remedial Economic Measures: Already Undertaken

*a. For Agriculture.* (1) In disastrous crop years the Soviets have bought substantial quantities of grain from capitalist nations, especially Canada, Australia, and the United States. (2) The Soviets have increased capital investment in agriculture to provide additional irrigated lands, mineral fertilizers, and farm machines. (3) The Soviets have offered farm workers "bread and butter" incentives: raising prices paid by the government for compulsory grain deliveries, lowering prices on manufactured goods sold in rural areas, and lowering taxes on collective farms so as to leave more income for collective farm members. (Farmers, however, have had little use for additional money income as long as consumer goods remain in short supply.)

*b. For Labor.* To increase the labor force, the Soviets have permitted only 20 percent of high school graduates to go on to colleges and universities. The remaining 80 percent must go to work in industry or agriculture.

*c. For Industry.* (1) The Soviets have frequently revised economic goals downward by cutting back on projected growth rates. (2) The Soviets have granted some factory managers in consumer goods industries greater freedom to improve production and quality. They would receive bonuses based upon their ability to satisfy consumer wants. (3) The Soviets have moved to buy the latest technology and production facilities from the West. (For Soviet efforts to increase trade with the United States, check "trade" in the Index.)

**5. The Five-Year Plan for 1976–1980.** Since the previous plan had not achieved its projected growth goals, this plan set more moderate goals. *(a) For Heavy Industry.* The plan continued the Soviet emphasis on heavy industry. It called for a five-year growth rate of 38 to 42 percent on the relatively large heavy industry base. *(b) For Consumers.* Although the plan declared the economy's main task to raise the material standards of the people, it projected a five-year growth rate of 30 to 32 percent on the much smaller consumer industry base. *(c) For Agriculture.* Because of previous disastrous crop years, the plan gave considerable emphasis to agriculture. It called for a five-year increase in food output of 26 to 28 percent. It substantially raised capital investment in agriculture—for irrigation, fertilizer, and farm machinery. The plan demanded increased efficiency on state farms and collectives. *(d) For Workers.* The plan pledged moderate wage gains but demanded sharply increased labor productivity—for industrial workers, an increase of 30 to 40 percent; for farm workers, an increase of 27 to 30 percent. *(e) For Foreign Trade.* The plan called for increased imports of the latest Western technology and for agreements with Western corporations to build fertilizer, plastics, computer, and other factories in the Soviet Union— all designed to modernize Soviet industry and to develop Siberian oil, gas, and mineral resources. The plan envisioned payment for these imports by Soviet exports of raw materials—minerals, crude oil, and fur—and by loans from the Western nations.

OBSERVATIONS BY WESTERN ECONOMISTS: (1) Although the Soviet GNP was less than 60 percent of the American GNP, the Russians were spending as much as, if not more than, the United States on the heavy industry military sector. This meant that a far greater proportion of Soviet output was devoted to military purposes. (2) Consequently the average Soviet citizen had a per capita consumption of material goods that was far below—perhaps only one-third—that of the average American citizen. (3) This plan faced problems—not enough workers and investment capital, an unfavorable balance of trade, and poor labor productivity. The plan did not provide for basic reforms: less bureaucratic control, greater authority for lower-ranking managers, and material incentives for workers and managers.

1980 RESULTS: Soviet data showed that industrial growth was 3.6 percent—a respectable figure—but far below the moderate plan goal of 4.5 percent. The Soviet economy fulfilled its 1980 plan in tableware, farm equipment, computers, and natural gas. The plan failed to reach its goals as follows: (1) Farm output fell sharply—as the country experienced its third consecutive poor harvest. (2) Oil production rose only 3 percent, far below plan goals—as older oil fields were being depleted while the development of Siberian fields was slowed by the region's remoteness, the harsh environment, and the lack of equipment, capital, roads, and labor. (3) Coal production declined compared with the previous year's output. (4) Fertilizer, freight car, truck, and cement output did not reach plan goals.

**6. The Five-Year Plan for 1981–1985.** Because of previous disappointing results, this plan set moderate goals: *(a)* Overall industrial output was to rise by 26 to 28 percent, far below the targets set in the previous plan. *(b)* Modest increases were set for oil production, livestock output, and grain harvests. *(c)* Farm and industrial workers were exhorted to increase labor productivity, but the plan did not offer to remedy any of the system's inherent weaknesses, thus discouraging such improvement.

## THE WORKING CLASS IN COMMUNIST RUSSIA

The Communists boast that Russia is the "workers' state" and that its government is a Communist party-led "dictatorship of the proletariat." The Soviet Constitution guarantees to each worker the right to (1) employment, (2) leisure time, including annual paid vacations, and (3) social security, including old-age, accident, and sickness insurance, as well as medical and hospital care. Soviet workers, however, are normally subjected to working conditions far less desirable than those of most American workers.

### 1. Labor Conditions

*a. Choice of Employment.* The Soviet government denies most beginning workers any choice of occupation and channels them into those jobs considered essential to the state.

*b. Labor Discipline.* The state requires industrial workers to have official *workbooks*, also known as *internal passports*. The passport contains the owner's name, birth date, residence, nationality, educational achievement, and employment record. It is used to identify the worker, to keep the person from frequent job changes, and to control the person's movements within the country.

Under Stalin workers guilty of unexcused lateness and absence, or leaving a job without approval, could be heavily fined or even sent to a slave labor camp. Under Khrushchev lateness and absence penalties were lightened, and most workers were permitted to leave their jobs without approval. Brezhnev restored stricter labor discipline. (In 1976 farm workers became eligible for internal passports—previously denied, so as to keep them on the farms.)

*c. Factory Conditions.* Although the newer plants generally provide good working conditions, the older plants remain substandard, having poor lighting, insufficient ventilation, and inadequate protection against accidents.

Since 1958 the factory workweek has decreased from 45 hours in six days to 41 hours in five days.

## Cost of Selected Items Affecting Living Standards in Washington, D.C., and Moscow

| Item | Washington, D.C. (worktime) | Moscow (worktime) | Item | Washington, D.C. (worktime) | Moscow (worktime) |
|---|---|---|---|---|---|
| Beef (1 lb., .45 kilo) | 30 min. | 65 min. | Man's Haircut | 51 min. | 36 min. |
| Milk, fresh (1 qt., .95 liter) | 7 min. | 21 min. | Lipstick | 31 min. | 469 min. |
| Eggs (1 doz. large) | 12 min. | 116 min. | Color TV | 86 hr. | 780 hr. |
| White Bread (1 lb., .45 kilo) | 10 min. | 9 min. | Refrigerator (4.8 cu. ft., .14 cu. meters) | 47 hr. | 168 hr. |
| Toilet Soap (large bar) | 5 min. | 72 min. | Apartment Rent, Monthly (small, 3 rooms, unfurnished) | 46 hrs. | 10 hrs. |

Source: Radio Liberty

Costs are expressed in worktime spent by an average industrial worker. Figures reflect differences in take-home pay and prices between the two cities but do not reflect differences in quality of items.

*d. Wages.* The state determines pay scales. These vary greatly according to the importance of the industry to the state, the worker's possession or lack of skill, and the worker's output, or productivity. Wherever possible the pay is based on piecework, which compels the worker to speed up production in order to earn a better living. For most workers wages remain low. In 1972 the minimum wage was $85 per month; in 1976 the average pay of an industrial worker was $215 per month. In contrast, American workers in 1972 had a minimum wage of over $300 per month and in 1976 earned an average industrial wage of over $800 per month.

These dollar wage figures do not measure exactly the relative economic status of American and Russian workers. The wage comparisons neglect the differences in living costs between the two countries and do not reflect the broad range of welfare services available to Russian workers. These services—at low cost or free—include rents, basic utilities, medical care, sickness and accident insurance, old-age pensions, and union-subsidized vacations. Certain of these welfare services are also available to American workers.

Although Russian workers have a higher standard of living than in Czarist times, it remains low by American and even by Central and West European standards. After World War II, as the Russian people became aware of their lagging living standards, their dissatisfaction—although muted—was obvious and constituted a steady pressure on Soviet leaders for economic improvement.

In 1980 unconfirmed reports circulated that 250,000 auto workers staged a two-day strike protesting food shortages. The reports were denied by Soviet officials.

**2. Labor Unions.** Russian workers belong to large labor unions under Communist party domination. The unions administer welfare programs and promote social and cultural activities: health resorts, libraries, theaters, sports, and dances. The unions' chief function, however, is to serve the state by spurring the workers to greater productivity. Unlike American labor organizations, Russian unions have no say in determining wages and no right to strike.

**3. Slave Labor.** Stalinist Russia utilized a large labor force, estimated in the millions, consisting of persons arbitrarily arrested by the secret police as enemies of the state. Political prisoners, as well as ordinary criminals, were sentenced to *corrective labor camps*, located in desolate and inhospitable regions, especially northern European Russia and Siberia. As *forced*, or *slave*, *laborers*, they were harshly treated and assigned to backbreaking work in mines and forests and on construction projects. Many did not survive.

The Khrushchev regime ended mass political arrests, freed most political prisoners, and abolished many corrective labor camps. It retained some camps as penal work colonies for ordinary criminals. The Brezhnev regime persecuted dissenters, sending some outspoken intellectuals to labor camps.

(A vivid exposé of the Soviet slave labor camps was provided by the dissident Russian writer, Alexander Solzhenitsyn, in his work *The Gulag Archipelago*.)

## SOCIAL AND CULTURAL CONDITIONS IN COMMUNIST RUSSIA

**1. Status of Women.** The Soviet government grants women full legal equality with men, including equal access to schools, jobs, and promotions. Few women, however, have achieved top industry, government, or party positions.

The Communist regime fosters community kitchens, laundries, and nurseries so as to free women from household tasks and enable them to enter the labor force. Women work as doctors, teachers, clerks, and factory hands; many even perform hard manual labor as construction workers and tractor drivers. Women comprise half the total Soviet labor force.

Although women are encouraged to work outside the home, the Soviet state, by means of bonuses and medals, also encourages them to raise large families. The 1977 Constitution called for "paid maternity leaves" and proposed the "gradual reduction of working hours for women with small children."

**2. Education.** The Communist government uses education to fashion loyal

Soviet citizens and to train individuals for industrial and scientific tasks. Under the 1975 educational revision, students receive free, compulsory schooling for ten years. Then most students must find employment—in factory or on farm—although some may first attend technical or vocational schools. About 20 percent of the high school graduates—the most capable—are permitted to go on to colleges and universities. At these higher levels, students usually receive government salaries and are exempt from military service.

In the primary and secondary schools, Soviet children study *(a)* Russian language and literature; *(b)* Russian and world history as viewed by Marxist-Leninist theory—condemning capitalism, praising the Communist party, and glorifying Russia; *(c)* a foreign language, most often English; *(d)* mathematics; and *(e)* science—biology, chemistry, and physics. Compared with Americans, Russian students receive much more rigorous schooling: longer hours, more schooldays, more homework, and far greater stress on foreign languages, mathematics, and science.

The Communist educational system has practically wiped out illiteracy. Because the emphasis is on science rather than on the humanities, the Communist system graduates many more engineers and technicians than does the American school system. These graduates, in part, help explain Russia's tremendous strides in missile and space developments.

Communist education aims primarily at developing specialists. In the humanities Russian students are not trained to think and decide for themselves but must give unquestioning acceptance to the "party line."

**3. Religion.** At first the Communists considered the Russian Orthodox Church a Czarist agent, ended its control over education and marriage, seized its buildings and lands, and persecuted its leaders. In World War II, however, the government used the Orthodox Church to arouse the people in defense of "Mother Russia." Since then the regime has tolerated the Orthodox Church but strictly limits its activities. Minority religious groups—especially Jews, Roman Catholics, and Moslems—have been special targets for Soviet propaganda. All three have been charged with having loyalties outside the Soviet Union and have been subjected to varying degrees of oppression.

Officially the Soviet constitution permits both freedom of religious worship and freedom of antireligious propaganda. However, the regime actively supports antireligious museums, demonstrations, and publications. The "party line" proclaims that no true Communist can be religious and denies the existence of God—a belief called *atheism*. The Communists, nevertheless, have been unable to drive all religious feeling from the Soviet peoples. In 1977 Western church officials estimated that the Russian population contained 30 million Orthodox Church members and 7 million Roman Catholics and Protestants. Although some of these church-minded persons are dissidents, most are well-integrated Soviet citizens, including party members, who are drawn to religion by tradition, aesthetics, a need for moral values, and a search for meaning in life not provided by Communist ideology.

**4. Russian Nationalism and the Treatment of National Minorities.** At first, insisting that all workers are united by common bonds, the Communists gave equal rights to all national groups. Within the Soviet Union the Communist authorities (a) prohibited discrimination against non-Russian peoples and (b) permitted each national group its own culture.

Since the mid-1930's, however, the Soviet government has pursued policies of (a) Russian nationalism—praising Russian heroes, even of Czarist days, and celebrating Russian national holidays—and (b) Russification—requiring all students, regardless of nationality, to study Russian language and history and supplanting native minority cultures by the dominant Russian culture.

**5. Treatment of Jews.** Russian Jews—considered both a national and a religious minority—were subjected to widespread anti-Semitism in Czarist Russia. Following the Communist Revolution, anti-Semitism abated somewhat. However, during Stalin's last years, Russian Jews suffered severely. Jewish newspapers and theaters were closed; Jewish artists, writers, and doctors were arrested and disappeared; the entire Jewish population experienced bitter anti-Semitism. Jews were not allowed to emigrate. Also, the Soviet regime adopted and has maintained a pro-Arab, anti-Israeli foreign policy. Soviet anti-Semitism has continued as the regime keeps most synagogues closed, restricts the supply of prayer books, prohibits teaching the Hebrew language, and spreads anti-Zionist propaganda. The Communists seek to destroy the Jewish cultural and religious heritage.

With the Israeli victory over the Arabs in the 1967 war, Jews in Russia— numbering 2.8 million—felt a surge of ethnic pride. By the thousands, Jews— especially young ones—claimed the right to emigrate to Israel. After applying for visas, they faced considerable harassment: loss of their jobs and apartments; threats of arrest for not working, officially termed "parasitism," while waiting to see if their applications would be approved; and payment of an exit fee of over $1,000 per person. Nevertheless, the number of Jews permitted to leave rose from 2,000 in 1969 to nearly 35,000 in 1973. To stem emigration by Jews—the most highly educated ethnic group in the Soviet Union—the Soviet regime imposed an additional exit fee based on the education received from the state. This "education tax," which could go as high as $50,000 per person, brought protests from organizations and governments throughout the world, especially the United States. The Soviet regime thereafter indefinitely suspended but did not repeal the "education tax."

In 1975 the Soviet regime rejected a Soviet–American trade agreement (check the Index), in part because the American Congress related trade benefits to the easing of Russian policies regarding dissidents and emigration. The Soviets thereafter sharply curtailed emigration—to the despair of 130,000 Soviet Jews who had already applied for exit visas. Moscow also placed a 30 percent tax (in addition to an already existing 30 percent bank handling fee) on moneys received from abroad. This move was viewed as impeding foreign support for Jews who had applied for exit visas and had lost their jobs.

**6. Culture.** The Soviet regime affords the people many cultural opportunities: libraries, theaters, museums, operas, concerts, and ballets. Since literature and art are expected to propagandize for communism, the regime encourages writers and artists by providing them generous pay and granting honors and awards. The Communists demand that literary and artistic works strive for popular appeal and support the Soviet state. Many Soviet cultural works are dull and undistinguished, but they conform to the "party line" and praise life under communism.

Under Stalin, the party ruled the cultural world heavy-handedly; suspected or open dissenters were sent to slave labor camps. Khrushchev slightly relaxed controls, but under Brezhnev the regime reverted to demanding strict conformity to official standards. Defying the authorities, many writers and artists struggle for their right to produce works in freedom. Dissident writers, unable to publish in the Soviet Union, sometimes circulate their writings in typewritten form through an underground network—the *samizdat*.

In 1974 the Soviets forced into exile the famed writer and critic of Soviet society, Alexander Solzhenitsyn. A few other prominent dissenters have also been exiled. Dissenters remaining in the Soviet Union live in apprehension of petty harassment or of being arrested and sentenced to slave labor camps or confined in mental institutions. Despite the 1975 Soviet signature to the Helsinki Pact (check the Index), which indicated agreement in principle to expanding human rights, Soviet dissidents have reported increased intimidation.

## FOREIGN RELATIONS OF COMMUNIST RUSSIA

**1. 1917–1933: Hostility Toward the World.** The Communists resented the Allies aiding counterrevolutionary forces during the Russian civil war. They believed also that capitalist nations would seek to destroy Communist Russia. To promote revolutions in capitalist nations, Russia in 1919 organized the *Third International*, or *Comintern* (see page 298).

**2. 1933–1939: Cooperation with Capitalist Democracies.** After the Nazi party seized power in Germany, the Soviet Union feared Germany as aggressive, warlike, and anti-Communist. In 1934 Russia joined the League of Nations and urged the "peace-loving" nations to protect themselves against aggression by united action, called *collective security*. In 1935 Russia and France joined in a military alliance.

In 1938 Russia bitterly denounced Britain and France for signing the Munich Agreement with Germany without consulting Russia. This pact allowed Hitler to take part of Czechoslovakia (see page 491).

**3. 1939–1941: Nonaggression Pact with Nazi Germany.** Claiming that Britain and France would not help Russia in case of a German attack, the Soviets in 1939 signed a *Nonaggression Pact* with Germany. The pact gave Russia time to strengthen its defenses. It gave Germany protection against a two-front war and served the Nazis as the "go-ahead signal" for aggression against Poland, thus bringing about World War II.

While the West European nations were at war, Russia annexed eastern Poland, part of Finland, and all of Lithuania, Latvia, and Estonia.

**4. 1941–1945: Wartime Alliance with the Democracies.** In June, 1941, Russia was attacked by Germany and forced into World War II. Thereafter, Russia *(a)* received considerable military equipment from the United States, *(b)* abolished the Comintern to show friendship toward its capitalist allies, *(c)* took part in top-level allied conferences to plan military strategy and arrange postwar settlements, and *(d)* helped create the United Nations. In 1945 Russia and its allies achieved complete military victory.

**5. 1945–Present: Expansion and Cold War Era.** As a result of World War II, Russia enlarged its boundaries and helped local Communist parties seize control of countries in Eastern Europe and Asia. This expansion of Communist power angered and frightened the free world nations and led to the *cold war*—a diplomatic, economic, and ideological struggle accompanied by localized military encounters. (For the Cold War Era, check the Index.)

In the early 1970's Soviet and American leaders declared that relations between their countries were ready to move from the confrontation of the cold war era to negotiation in an era of better understanding, or *détente*. In 1979–1980, however, the Soviets invaded Afghanistan—an invasion that reinforced American distrust of the Soviet Union and led to a sharp deterioration in Soviet-American relations—possibly marking the end of efforts at détente. (For a discussion of détente, check the Index.)

## MULTIPLE–CHOICE QUESTIONS

1. In area Russia is (1) equal to (2) smaller than (3) slightly larger than (4) much larger than the United States.
2. Before 1914 Russia's economy was dependent mainly on (1) mining (2) agriculture (3) fishing (4) industry.
3. Russia's international trade has been hampered by the lack of sufficient (1) natural resources (2) number of workers (3) number of ice-free ports (4) agricultural areas.
4. Russia's major seaport on the Pacific Ocean is (1) Tashkent (2) Vladivostok (3) Leningrad (4) Brest-Litovsk.
5. A Russian complaint regarding the seaport of Odessa is that it (1) is icebound part of the year (2) has too shallow a harbor (3) is located on the edge of a desert (4) is not accessible except through the Turkish-controlled Dardanelles.
6. Reformers intended the Duma in Czarist Russia to be most similar to (1) the Estates General in France (2) Parliament in Britain (3) the Vatican in Italy (4) the veto in ancient Rome.

7. The foreign city that most influenced the culture of early Russia was (1) Athens (2) Rome (3) Constantinople (4) Alexandria.

8. Russian serfs were dissatisfied after emancipation in 1861 because they (1) could not move to the city (2) were required to buy their land in one payment (3) could not acquire enough land (4) were required to pay feudal dues to their former lords.

9. A major aim of Russian foreign policy during the 19th century was to (1) strengthen Poland as an ally against Germany (2) expand to the south and east (3) encourage the working peoples of the world to revolt (4) maintain friendship with Turkey.

10. Which factor contributed most to the Revolutions of 1917 in Russia? (1) The Allied powers favored the revolutions. (2) The czar was willing to abdicate. (3) Tolstoi organized the revolt. (4) The Russian people were discouraged with their defeats in World War I.

11. Which of the following did the Bolsheviks in 1917 emphasize *least* in their efforts to win over the Russian people? (1) immediate peace (2) reform of land ownership (3) redistribution of wealth (4) abolition of religion.

12. The Russian peasant supported the Communists in 1917 mainly because they promised to (1) establish agricultural collectives (2) keep agricultural prices low (3) bring electric power to the farms (4) distribute the nobles' estates.

13. In 1917 one reason why the Bolsheviks were able to seize control of Russia was that they (1) were, a well-organized group (2) promised victory in the war against Germany (3) favored large families (4) were a majority elected by the people.

14. The official name of Russia is the Union of Soviet Socialist Republics. *Soviet* means (1) democratic (2) dictatorial (3) a responsible ministry (4) a council.

15. Soviet elections are marked by (1) the campaigning of many political parties (2) restriction of the vote to men only (3) one slate of candidates (4) voting by Communist party members only.

16. The death of Stalin was followed by a(an) (1) period of brief rule by his son (2) immediate outbreak of international conflict (3) bitter struggle for power among his important followers (4) return to the previous form of government.

17. Of the total Russian population, Communist party members number about (1) 90 percent (2) 50 percent (3) 25 percent (4) 6 percent.

18. A Soviet policy *not* found in Czarist Russia was (1) free compulsory education (2) secret police (3) Siberian penal camps (4) Russification of minority groups.

19. About how long does the Supreme Soviet, the chief legislative body of the Soviet Union, remain in session each year? (1) two weeks (2) two months (3) six months (4) twelve months.

20. The Supreme Court of the Soviet Union has (1) defied the secret police by insisting upon writs of habeas corpus (2) declared Soviet laws unconstitutional (3) affirmed Communist party policy (4) voided decisions of the Council of Ministers.

21. One reason why nearly all Soviet citizens vote in elections is the (1) spirited election campaigns (2) pay given each voter (3) fear that nonvoters will be treated as hostile to the regime (4) fear that the Communist party might lose the election.

22. In general the standard of living of the Soviet Union today is low because of the need for capital accumulation. This statement implies that (1) the Communists do not have the means to raise living standards (2) social progress is possible only in a stable economy (3) industrial growth influences the level of living standards (4) military production, by providing work, raises workers' living standards.

23. In the Soviet Union which would an ambitious person consider most essential for a successful career? (1) army service (2) membership in the Communist party (3) a university education (4) experience on a collective farm.

24. The Five-Year Plans have emphasized   (1) investments by foreign capitalists   (2) agriculture over industry   (3) production of household appliances and automobiles   (4) development of steel mills and electric power plants.

25. An important effect of the Five-Year Plans on Russian agriculture was   (1) the establishment of collectives   (2) the growth of privately owned farms   (3) an increase in the number of farm workers   (4) a decrease in farm machinery.

26. Money wages of Russian workers are   (1) set by the *samizdat*   (2) lower than in the United States   (3) set by collective bargaining   (4) tied to the profits of industry.

27. Under Stalin, Russia maintained corrective labor camps as   (1) health centers for workers   (2) schools for learning new technical skills   (3) scientific research centers   (4) work prisons for "enemies of the state."

28. Under both Czarist and Communist regimes, Russian Jews were   (1) given preferential treatment   (2) treated equally with the other Russian peoples   (3) especially singled out for discrimination   (4) denied education.

29. A cultural aspect of Communist Russia has been to   (1) keep women in the home   (2) emphasize literature and art at the expense of physics and chemistry   (3) discourage Russian nationalism   (4) restrict free creative effort by writers and artists.

30. Which right, considered basic by American workers, is denied Soviet workers?   (1) forming unions   (2) striking for higher wages   (3) receiving social security   (4) receiving paid vacations.

31. Soviet education does *not* seek to   (1) glorify Russia   (2) train scientists   (3) encourage critical analysis of the "party line"   (4) praise the Communist party.

32. According to the "party line," a true Communist   (1) must be a member of the Russian Orthodox Church   (2) may be a member of the Russian Orthodox Church   (3) may be a member of any church   (4) must be an atheist.

33. One policy of the Soviet state toward its Jewish minority is to   (1) encourage the use of the Hebrew language   (2) convert Jews to the Orthodox Church   (3) destroy the Jewish cultural and religious heritage in the Soviet Union   (4) expel all Jews.

34. The Soviet regime would most commend a novel that portrayed   (1) farmers in a collective increasing output   (2) a noble of Czarist times aiding the peasants   (3) a Soviet doctor questioning Communist ethics   (4) a Soviet concert artist requesting asylum in a foreign country.

## TRUE–FALSE QUESTIONS

If the statement is correct, write the word *true*. If the statement is incorrect, substitute a word or phrase for the italicized term to make the statement correct.

1. The village communities which owned the land following emancipation of the serfs in 1861 were the *Dumas*.

2. The Revolution of 1905 was an aftermath of the *Crimean* War.

3. The Russians who fought the Communists from 1917 to 1921 were known as *nepmen*.

4. The official Soviet Communist stand on issues is called the *party line*.

5. The signal for the outbreak of World War II was Russia's Nonaggression Pact in 1939 with *Poland*.

6. The moderate Socialist who headed Russia's 1917 provisional government was *Lenin*.

7. To divert the people's attention from bad conditions, the Czarist government inspired anti-Jewish outbursts of violence, called *pogroms*.

8. The last Romanov ruler of Russia was Czar *Alexander II*.

9. The leader who established Communist control over Russia was *Stalin.*
10. The organizer of the Red Army, later compelled to flee from Russia, was *Trotsky.*
11. The leader who introduced the Five-Year Plans and served as Soviet premier during World War II was *Khrushchev.*
12. The most powerful position in the Soviet Communist party is that of party *President.*

## ESSAY QUESTIONS

1. Compare conditions in Russia about 1850 with conditions today in regard to each of the following: (*a*) suffrage (*b*) treatment of dissenters (*c*) education (*d*) status of women (*e*) land ownership (*f*) industry.
2. (*a*) Discuss *two* factors that enabled the Communists to seize power in Russia in 1917. (*b*) Assume that you are going to move to Soviet Russia and become a citizen of that nation. Describe *three* important ways in which your life would be changed from your present way of living in the United States.
3. The progress made by Russia since World War I was largely responsible for Russia's successful resistance in World War II. (*a*) Discuss *two* factors that retarded Russia's progress before World War I. (*b*) Explain *one* way in which the Russians made remarkable progress between 1917 and 1939. (*c*) State *one* reason why Russia is an important factor in world affairs today.
4. The United States has been called a capitalist democracy, Russia a Communist dictatorship. Describe *three* ways in which the political and economic systems of the United States differ from the political and economic systems of Russia.
5. In comparing the 1917 Russian Revolution with the 1789 French Revolution, discuss (*a*) *three* ways in which they were similar (*b*) *two* ways in which they were different. Which of these two revolutions has had a greater impact upon world affairs? Present *one* argument to support your opinion.
6. Compare Metternich's policy in Europe (1815–1848) with the present policy of the Communist government in Russia with regard to each of the following: (*a*) freedom of press and speech (*b*) political parties (*c*) foreign policy.
7. Since 1928 the Soviet Union has managed its industry by centralized economic planning under a series of Five-Year Plans. In regard to the Five-Year Plans (*a*) explain *two* achievements, (*b*) explain *two* weaknesses, (*c*) state *one* basic reform that non-Communist economists believe necessary and explain why the Soviets are unwilling to adopt this reform.
8. Discuss *two* reasons for agreeing or disagreeing with each of the following statements: (*a*) Although geographically part of Europe, Russia until the present century was isolated from the major historical developments affecting Western Europe. (*b*) Soviet Russia has followed domestic policies similar to those of Czarist Russia. (*c*) Geographic factors have influenced Russian foreign policy. (*d*) A Soviet factory worker enjoys as much economic freedom as a factory worker in the United States. (*e*) Communist agricultural policies are largely to blame for the inability of Soviet agriculture to increase its output significantly. (*f*) Soviet women are fortunate to have been freed from drudgery by community kitchens and nurseries. (*g*) The Soviet Union today reflects a conservative, not a revolutionary, society.

# Part 3. Italy: Fascist Dictatorship to Democratic Republic

## FASCISM IN ITALY: BASIC IDEAS

*Benito Mussolini* after World War I organized the *Fascist* movement. He derived the word "Fascist" from the ancient Roman symbol of authority—the *fasces*—a bundle of rods enveloping an ax. Fascism in Italy served as the model for similar movements in other countries, most notably Nazism in Germany. Fascists favored dictatorship and nationalism; they opposed democracy and Marxism.

**1. Against Democracy.** The Fascists *(a)* denounced democratic government as weak and inefficient; *(b)* denied that the people, as a group, possess common sense, mature judgment, and a knowledge of what is best for the country; *(c)* ridiculed the idea that the state exists to serve the people; and *(d)* scoffed at civil liberties and multiparty systems of government.

**2. For Dictatorship.** The Fascists *(a)* advocated Fascist seizure of power by force and violence; *(b)* praised dictatorship as strong and efficient; *(c)* exalted the dictator as all-knowing, all-wise, and all-competent; *(d)* claimed that "the people are nothing; the state is everything"; and *(e)* indicated that, under fascism, the government would control every phase of human activity, thus forming a *totalitarian state.*

**3. For Extreme Nationalism.** The Fascists *(a)* exaggerated the accomplishments of the nation, *(b)* advocated imperialism so that the nation could rule an empire, *(c)* hailed military might as proof of the nation's strength and vitality, and *(d)* glorified war, claiming that it brought out the best qualities in a people and enabled the "superior" nations to rule the world.

**4. Against Marxism.** The Fascists *(a)* opposed the Marxist goal of a socialist economy, *(b)* condemned Marxist ideology that belittled nationalism and urged international working class unity, and *(c)* claimed that only fascism could save a nation from the evils of socialism and communism.

## FACTORS EXPLAINING THE FASCIST RISE TO POWER IN ITALY

**1. Economic Distress.** After World War I the Italian people saw their already low living standards decline further. They suffered from *(a)* ruinous inflation that drove up prices, *(b)* heavy taxes to pay the war cost, and *(c)* widespread unemployment. By promising to improve economic conditions, the Fascists won support among low-paid workers, the unemployed, the impoverished middle class, and landless peasants.

**2. Fear of Communism.** In some areas Italian workers seized factories, and peasants seized lands, in imitation of what was then happening in Russia. To conservative Italians, these seizures foreshadowed a Communist revolution in Italy. By fighting against Italian Socialists and Communists, the Fascists won widespread support of industrialists and land owners. From these wealthy and influential persons, Mussolini secured funds for his party, arms for his private military bands, and jobs for his followers.

**3. Appeal to Nationalism.** Although Italy had received Italia Irredenta (territory containing Italian-speaking people) from Austria following World War I, Italian nationalists were disappointed. They had expected more territory, especially colonies in Africa and the Middle East and Balkan lands that would have permitted Italy to dominate the Adriatic Sea. Fascist boasts to restore the ancient Roman Empire appealed to nationalists: youths, veterans, and professional army officers.

**4. Weak Government.** Because no one political party commanded a majority in Parliament, Italy had a series of bloc, or coalition, governments. Unstable and weak, they proved unable to solve Italy's economic problems, to maintain law and order, and to overcome the threat of fascism.

**5. Lack of Democratic Tradition.** The Italian people, many of them illiterate and poverty-stricken, were primarily occupied with earning a living. They showed little concern for governmental matters and had little training in civic responsibilities. When faced by the threat of a Fascist dictatorship, the people did little to defend their democracy.

**6. Leadership of Mussolini.** Unscrupulous and ambitious, Mussolini changed from Socialist to extreme nationalist during World War I and served in the Italian army. Following the war he created the Fascist party, organized Fascist military groups called *Black Shirts*, and ordered violence and brutality against his opponents.

## FASCISTS SEIZE POWER IN ITALY

The Fascist party quickly attracted considerable support, and the Fascists grew bold. In 1922 Mussolini felt powerful enough to demand control of the government. He threatened to use force and ordered his supporters to *march on Rome*. King Victor Emmanuel III refused to declare martial law and resist the Fascists. Unopposed by the army, Black Shirt bands poured into the capital, and the king requested Mussolini to form a government. Thus, with neither a popular vote nor a parliamentary majority, Mussolini seized power.

## ITALY UNDER FASCISM (1922–1943)

**1. Government.** The Fascists transformed Italy into a totalitarian dictatorship with Mussolini as the leader, *Il Duce*. They permitted the existence of only one political party, the Fascist party, and limited legislative elections to a yes-no vote on a single Fascist-chosen list of candidates. The Fascists denied civil liberties and, to suppress opposition, used secret police, violence, and imprisonment. Mussolini exhorted the people to "*believe, fight, obey.*"

**2. Labor.** The Fascist government strictly controlled the Italian workers. It (*a*) set wages, hours, and working conditions, (*b*) dominated the labor unions, and (*c*) prohibited strikes. In spite of lavish promises, the standard of living of the working class continued to be among the lowest in Western Europe.

**3. Industry.** Although the Fascists left most industry under private ownership, they did not permit genuine free enterprise. To the disappointment of their capitalist supporters, the Fascists strictly regulated economic matters— production, prices, capital investment—to further government objectives. To insure Fascist control, Mussolini organized both industry and labor into a small number of Fascist-led economic associations, called *corporations.* Consequently Fascist Italy became known as a *corporate state.*

The Fascists built hydroelectric plants and armament factories and encouraged industrial development. They boasted that Fascist efficiency made the railroads run on time.

**4. Public Works.** The Fascists relieved unemployment by a program of public works: clearing slums; building roads, bridges, and public buildings; and draining swamplands. The *Pontine Marshes,* south of Rome, were drained and restored to agricultural use, after having been unfarmed for 25 centuries.

**5. Religion.** To end the long dispute over Italy's seizure of Church lands during Italian unification (see pages 255–256), Mussolini and the Catholic Church in 1929 concluded the *Lateran Pacts.* (*a*) Italy recognized the pope as sovereign ruler of Vatican City (located within Rome). (*b*) Italy retained, but made financial payment for, the rest of the Papal States. (*c*) Italy established Catholicism as the state religion. These pacts strengthened Mussolini's influence over Italian Catholics—99 percent of the population.

Following the formation of the Rome-Berlin Axis, Fascist Italy in 1938 began persecuting its small minority of 70,000 Jews. In this way Italy was deprived of the talents of Italian citizens of Jewish faith.

**6. Militarism.** Seeking military grandeur, Mussolini (*a*) expanded Italy's armed forces by conscripting men for four years of military service followed by 11 years in the reserve, (*b*) required military training in Fascist youth groups and in schools, and (*c*) granted bonuses to large families, whose sons would eventually swell the ranks of his armies.

Mussolini's efforts to make Italy a great military power were severely hindered by Italy's lack of essential raw materials: coal, iron, and oil.

**7. Imperialism and War.** To dominate the Adriatic and Mediterranean seas and to acquire colonies, Fascist Italy embarked on a policy of aggression. (*a*) In

1935–1936, despite League of Nations opposition, Italian troops invaded and conquered Ethiopia (see page 490). *(b)* In 1936 Italy and Nazi Germany reached an understanding that soon became a military alliance, the *Rome-Berlin Axis,* later expanded into the *Rome-Berlin-Tokyo Axis. (c)* In 1936, by supplying massive military aid, Italy and Germany enabled Spain's General Francisco Franco to overthrow the republican Spanish government and establish a dictatorial regime (see page 490). *(d)* In 1939 Italy strengthened its position on the Adriatic Sea by invading and conquering Albania. *(e)* In 1940, when France was near military collapse, Italy joined with Germany in World War II against France and Britain. Mussolini expected a quick and easy victory—but he was wrong.

## ITALY AND WORLD WAR II

**1. Overthrow of the Fascist Regime (1943).** Italian armies met with defeat after defeat. Fascist forces were driven back in Greece; they were wiped out in Ethiopia and North Africa; and in 1943 they were routed by Allied armies invading Sicily.

Stunned by military defeat, bombings, and invasion, the Italian people turned against Mussolini and his Fascist regime. In 1943 the king and leading army officers forced Mussolini to resign and arrested him. A non-Fascist government took office and surrendered unconditionally to the Allies. Meanwhile, Mussolini escaped from prison and fled to northern Italy where, protected by German armies, he proclaimed an Italian Fascist Republic. In 1945 Mussolini was captured and executed by Italian anti-Fascists.

**2. The Treaty of Peace with Italy (1947).** Italy *(a)* ceded border areas to France and Yugoslavia, *(b)* ceded the Dodecanese Islands (in the Aegean Sea) to Greece, *(c)* agreed to pay minor reparations and to limit its military forces, *(d)* surrendered its colonies, and *(e)* gave the United Nations the Adriatic seaport of Trieste as a Free Territory (available for Yugoslav use). (In 1954 Italy, by agreeing to permit unrestricted Yugoslav access to the port facilities, regained Trieste.)

## ITALY BECOMES A REPUBLIC AND ADOPTS
## A DEMOCRATIC CONSTITUTION

By referendum in 1946 the Italian people deposed the monarchy that many persons associated with the discredited Fascist regime. Accordingly King Humbert II left the country, and Italy became a republic.

Italy's 1948 constitution provides for (1) a parliament of two houses—Chamber of Deputies and Senate—with equal legislative powers, (2) a premier and cabinet commanding a majority in Parliament, and (3) a president elected by Parliament and serving chiefly as a symbol of unity.

The constitution (1) provides for universal suffrage—male and female—(2) guarantees civil liberties and economic rights, (3) prohibits the reestablishment of the Fascist party, and (4) recognizes the special position of the Catholic

Church by granting state subsidies to the Church and by requiring state-supported schools to provide Catholic religious instruction. (This last provision may be modified if the Italian Parliament ratifies the 1976 Vatican Accord. Check the Index.)

## PROBLEMS FACING THE ITALIAN REPUBLIC

1. **Government Instability.** Since 1948 the Italian government has been controlled chiefly by the *Christian Democratic* (Catholic) *party*. This center party advocates *(a)* further industrialization, *(b)* social and economic reforms to improve living conditions, *(c)* protection of the interests of the Catholic Church, and *(d)* cooperation with the Western democracies against communism.

Since the 1953 elections the Christian Democrats, although Italy's largest political party, have lacked a majority in Parliament. Therefore, they have formed coalition governments with minor center parties—Liberals, Republicans, Social Democrats, and Socialists. Because such center coalitions disagree frequently, Italy has experienced recurrent cabinet crises but remained under Christian Democratic leadership. In 1981, however, the Christian Democrats yielded the premiership to the leader of the small Republican party. (See page 476.)

2. **Communist Movement.** The *Italian Communist party* has considerable influence among anticlerical persons, intellectuals, workers, the unemployed, and peasants. The Communists are Italy's second largest political party. Despite outspoken opposition by the Catholic Church, they consistently poll one out of every three or four votes. The Communists have failed to gain left-wing Socialist support for a Communist-dominated alliance, or *Popular Front.*

In 1976 the Italian Communist party came out for Italy's membership in NATO, liberty in religion and art, and "a pluralistic and democratic system." By thus abandoning Soviet Communist policies, the Italian Communists hope to establish their image as an Italian democratic and nationalist party and to strengthen their voting appeal. Many question the sincerity of the Italian Communist party's new ideology—known as *Eurocommunism.* (Check the Index.)

3. **Revival of Fascism.** Because fascism is outlawed, persons holding Fascist views named their party the *Italian Social Movement.* This *neo-Fascist* group, in national elections, has attracted a popular vote varying from 5 percent to 10 percent. Although still relatively small, the Italian Social Movement constitutes a nucleus for a possible Fascist revival.

4. **Foreign Policy.** Under the Christian Democrats the Italian government follows a strongly pro-Western foreign policy and favors close military and economic cooperation with the other nations of Western Europe. In 1949 Italy joined the Western nations in the North Atlantic Treaty Organization (a military alliance) and contributed troops to the NATO army.

5. **Economic Improvement.** To better living conditions after World War II, the Italian government *(a)* joined the Marshall Plan and received almost $2 billion in

American economic aid; *(b)* began land reform by distributing land from the large estates to the peasants; *(c)* built roads, houses, schools, and other public works; *(d)* joined with other West European nations in programs of economic cooperation, most notably the Common Market (check the Index); and *(e)* promoted tourist trade and encouraged industrial expansion.

Following World War II Italy experienced tremendous economic progress. Once mainly farmers, Italians have become workers overwhelmingly in service occupations, commerce, and industry. Italy's industries have changed from small handicraft shops to mass-production factories. They produce textiles, chemicals, and machinery. The middle class has grown, and workers in the industrial north have enjoyed considerable prosperity. From the end of World War II to the 1970's, Italy's *gross national product (GNP)*—a measure of the money value of goods and services—quadrupled.

Nevertheless, Italy remains a relatively poor country. It is hampered by limited natural resources, high unemployment and labor unrest, inflation, an unfavorable balance of payments, the high cost of oil imposed since 1974 by the OPEC nations, great poverty in the agricultural south, slow progress in land reform, and a wide disparity between rich and poor.

**6. Social Issues:** *(a)* In the 1970's Italians divided sharply regarding a law, narrowly passed, that, under certain stringent conditions, permits divorce. Devout Roman Catholics, whose religious teachings prohibit divorce, oppose the law; anticlerical groups favor it. The opponents of divorce secured signatures to a petition to force a public referendum on the law. Held in 1974, the referendum produced a 3-to-2 vote margin in favor of retaining the divorce law. *(b)* In the 1970's Italy experienced a sharp increase in crime—including ordinary crimes by juvenile offenders and international drug traffic dealers and politically inspired crimes by right-wing and left-wing extremists. The extremists are believed to total between 2,000 and 5,000 active members. *(c)* The *Red Brigades,* an ultra-left urban guerrilla group, appeals to young Italians—some of middle class and university background. The Red Brigades have sought to destroy the present Italian state and society by use of violence and terrorism. The Red Brigades activists have employed bombings of public and private buildings, shoot-outs with the police, and assassinations and kidnappings of business and political leaders. Although some Red Brigades members have been caught and imprisoned, the group continues to terrorize Italian society.

**7. Recent Developments**

*a. The 1976 Elections.* These elections were marked by some violence, by a papal declaration stressing the incompatibility of Catholicism and communism, and by an American warning against having Communists in the government.

The election results were as follows: (1) The Christian Democrats remained the largest party, polling 38.7 percent of the popular vote and winning 263 Chamber of Deputy seats. (2) The Communist party remained the second-largest party, increasing its support by 7 percent by polling 34.2 percent of the popular

Hy Rosen, Albany Times-Union, NY ROTHCO

**There goes Western Europe.**

vote and securing 228 Chamber seats. (3) The minor center parties fell both in popular vote and legislative seats. The Christian Democrats formed a single-party government. Its ability to rule depended upon tacit Communist support —not to vote against the government on major issues.

**b. The 1979 Elections.** In 1979, having been rebuffed in their demands for cabinet positions, the Communists caused the fall of the minority Christian Democratic government. In the resulting elections for the 630-seat Chamber of Deputies, the Communists suffered a major loss, to 30.4 percent of the popular vote and 201 seats; the Christian Democrats dropped slightly, to 38.3 percent and 262 seats. The Christian Democrats, with center-party support, formed a coalition government. The Communists remained in opposition.

**c. The Minor-Party Premier.** In 1981 the Christian Democratic government fell as some of its ministers were linked to a secret Masonic lodge accused of financial wrongdoing. The Christian Democrats yielded the premiership—for the first time in 36 years—to *Giovanni Spadolini*, head of the Republican party that held only 16 legislative seats. Spadolini constructed a five-party coalition— excluding the Communists and the neo-Fascist Social Movement—and his government won legislative approval. Spadolini stated that "this was the first secular government in the history of the republic" and it set the precedent of "rotation of the prime ministership between secular and Catholic forces." (In contrast to the Christian Democrats, the center secular parties are opposed to church influence in Italy's political affairs.) Spadolini pledged to improve economic conditions, especially to reduce the high inflation rate.

**d. A New Vatican Accord.** In 1976 the Italian government and the Vatican announced agreement on major revisions in Church–State relations. The new proposals (1) ended recognition of Catholicism as the state religion and granted equality to all religious faiths, (2) no longer required religious education in state-supported junior and secondary schools but left it available upon request, and (3) contained Vatican concessions regarding marriage and divorce laws. These new proposals, which seem to indicate a weakening of Church power in Italy, were submitted as a treaty for approval by Parliament.

# Part 4. Germany: Nazi Dictatorship

## DEMOCRATIC GERMANY: THE WEIMAR REPUBLIC (1919–1933)

As World War I ended, the German people revolted against Kaiser William II, overthrew his autocratic regime, and established a democratic republic. Its constitution, drawn up at the town of *Weimar*, provided for (1) a weak president elected by popular vote, (2) a two-house legislature, with the Reichstag—the more powerful house—directly elected by the people, (3) a powerful chancellor and cabinet responsible to the Reichstag, (4) a bill of rights, (5) civil and political equality of men and women, and (6) protection of minority groups.

The *Weimar Republic* provided Germany with democratic government from 1919, when it signed the Treaty of Versailles, until 1933, when the Nazis came into power.

## FASCISM APPEARS IN GERMANY: THE NAZI PARTY

Following World War I a small group of political extremists led by Adolf Hitler formed the *National Socialist*, or *Nazi, party*. Like the Fascists in Italy, the Nazis attacked democracy, promised to save Germany from Marxism, advocated extreme nationalism and militarism, and called for a dictatorship. As has been typical of most totalitarian movements, the Nazis belittled the intelligence of the people by offering *simple solutions for complex problems*.

## FACTORS EXPLAINING THE NAZI RISE TO POWER

**1. Economic Distress.** *(a)* Until 1923 the German government, instead of raising taxes, printed excessive quantities of paper money. The purchasing power of the German mark declined to almost nothing. This inflation harmed especially the middle class, which saw its savings accounts, life insurance policies, and pensions become worthless. *(b)* Starting in 1929 the worldwide depression caused business failures, falling wages, and rising unemployment. In 1932 over six million Germans were out of work.

By promising to improve the economy, the Nazis gained a strong following among the middle class, the workers, and the unemployed. Some observers hold that the Nazis rose to power "on the empty stomachs of the German people."

**2. Fear of Communism.** Many Germans, driven by economic distress, supported the German Communist party. In 1930 the Communists polled nearly five million votes, almost 15 percent of the total cast. Conservative groups now feared a Communist revolution. By battling the Communist movement, the Nazis, like the Fascists in Italy, gained the support of property holders, bankers, and industrialists. These people provided the Nazis with money, military equipment, and jobs.

**3. Appeal to Nationalism.** German patriots, who had gloried in the power of Germany before 1914, were emotionally unable to accept defeat in World War I. The Nazis exploited such nationalist feeling. They *(a)* pledged to tear up the Treaty of Versailles and denounced the German war-guilt clause, *(b)* demanded the return of Germany's colonies and European territories, *(c)* defended Germany's right to rearm, and *(d)* claimed that the German armies had been "stabbed in the back," mainly by Jews and Communists, *not* defeated by the Allies. Nazi chauvinism (extreme nationalism) won support of students, veterans, and army officers.

Hitler also proclaimed that the Germans were destined to rule the world because they constituted a "pure Aryan" race, physically and mentally superior to all other people. Although the Nazi doctrine of German racial superiority is contrary to all scientific evidence, many Germans chose to believe that they were the *master race.*

**4. Anti-Semitism: Attack on Jews.** Hitler personally hated Jews, blamed them for Germany's ills, and pledged to drive them from German life. Hitler's anti-Semitic policies won widespread support. *(a)* Prejudice against Jews had always been strong in Germany. In Bismarck's time religious bigots frequently attacked Jews and discriminated against them. *(b)* Many Germans readily accepted Nazi propaganda making Jews the *scapegoats* for Germany's troubles. If Jews were to blame for Germany's military defeat and economic woes, then the German people were not responsible. *(c)* Unprincipled persons looked forward to looting and seizing Jewish businesses and homes.

**5. Weaknesses of the Weimar Government.** Of Germany's several political parties, no single one commanded a Reichstag majority. The leading moderate parties—Catholic Center and Social Democrat—differed on economic and religious matters and did not cooperate effectively. Also, by 1932 the antirepublican extremists—Nazis on the right and Communists on the left—together had more Reichstag votes than the moderate parties working for the republic's survival. Consequently Germany's democratic government was unstable and could not cope with the country's pressing problems.

**6. Lack of a Democratic Tradition.** The main heritage of the German people was not democracy, but autocracy. Under the autocratic leadership of Bismarck and the kaiser, Germany had achieved unification, economic growth, and world power. In contrast, under the democratic Weimar Republic, Germany had accepted the hated Treaty of Versailles and fallen into economic distress. Hence, to many Germans, autocracy meant success and democracy failure. Furthermore, the German people had little experience in the functioning of a democratic government. Many Germans were willing to exchange their freedom for Nazi promises of economic security and nationalist glory.

**7. Leadership of Hitler.** Born in Austria, Adolf Hitler was an unsuccessful artist who served in the German army during World War I. He helped form the Nazi party and rose to leadership by his organizational ability. While briefly imprisoned for an unsuccessful 1923 rebellion, Hitler outlined his plans for a Nazi Germany in the book *Mein Kampf (My Struggle)*. By means of private armies of *Storm Troopers*, violence to terrorize the opposition, spectacular mass rallies, and his oratorical ability to sway German audiences, Hitler led the Nazis to control of Germany.

## THE NAZIS SEIZE POWER IN GERMANY

In 1923 the Nazis, then a small group, joined with other extreme nationalists in Munich in a petty rebellion, or *putsch*. They were easily suppressed, and Hitler was briefly imprisoned.

After 1929, as economic conditions in Germany worsened, the Nazis attracted increasing support. In 1932 they polled nearly 12 million votes—37 percent of the total—and became the largest party in the Reichstag. However, they lacked a majority. In 1933 Hitler was appointed chancellor, after he swore to President Hindenburg that he would maintain the constitution. He immediately called for new elections. In voting marked by intimidation, violence, and deceit, the Nazis and their supporters achieved narrow control of the Reichstag. Thereupon, they ended the Weimar Republic, and Hitler assumed dictatorial powers.

## THE THIRD REICH: NAZISM IN POWER (1933–1945)

1. **Government.** The Nazis transformed Germany into a dictatorship. *(a)* As *Der Führer*, or *The Leader*, Hitler exercised supreme power. The Reichstag was infrequently summoned and was expected only to applaud and approve Hitler's decisions. *(b)* All parties except the Nazi party were outlawed. The Nazis permitted Reichstag elections but limited the choices to a yes-no vote on a single list of Nazi-selected candidates. *(c)* Under *Heinrich Himmler*, the *Gestapo*, or secret police, brutally suppressed all opposition. Anti-Nazis—whether democrat, liberal, Socialist, Communist, Catholic, Jew, or Protestant—suffered unbelievable tortures and death in concentration camps. The Third Reich deprived the individual of both human dignity and civil liberties. *(d)* By extending government control over every aspect of human activity, the Nazis established a totalitarian state.

2. **Propaganda.** *Joseph Goebbels* headed an elaborate Propaganda Ministry that utilized all media of information and education and operated within Germany and throughout the world. Goebbels used the technique of the *big lie*. Nazi propagandists operated on the theory that any lie—if stated authoritatively, repeated incessantly, and guarded from critical analysis—will eventually be accepted by most people.

3. **Education.** The Nazis used the schools to instill blind obedience to the führer. Only Nazis were permitted to teach; the textbooks and courses of study

were adapted to Nazi purposes. On the high school level, chemistry included the making of poison gases; mathematics calculated airplane bombing distances; and social studies stressed the evils of democracy and the "superiority of the Aryan race." Nazi education was described by an anti-Nazi writer as a "school for barbarians."

**4. Science and Culture.** The Nazis harnessed science and culture to serve the state. (a) Scientists worked on weapons of war. (b) Anthropologists attempted to "prove" Aryan supremacy. (c) Writers extolled Hitler and Nazism. (d) Censors held public book-burning ceremonies to destroy works by anti-Nazis. (e) The government banned works by persons of Jewish origin, such as the poetry of Heine and the music of Mendelssohn.

**5. Persecution of Jews.** The Nazi state proceeded with the organized persecution of German Jews—who then numbered 600,000 out of a total German population of some 80 million. Nazi mobs burned Jewish houses of worship, or synagogues, and Nazi officials ousted Jews from jobs, businesses, and homes. In 1935 the Nazi regime announced a series of anti-Semitic decrees known as the "Nuremburg laws." These decrees (a) deprived German Jews of citizenship, (b) defined as Jewish any person with one Jewish grandparent, and (c) prohibited Jews from publishing any written material, acting on stage or screen, teaching, exhibiting artworks, giving concerts, or belonging to professional organizations. Nazi Storm Troopers subjected Jews to physical violence and sent them to forced labor, torture, and starvation in concentration camps. Only a few Jews escaped from Germany and found refuge in other lands.

During World War II, as German armies overran most of Europe, Jews in the conquered lands fell under the Nazi yoke. The Nazis now intensified their anti-Semitic program with a barbarism unmatched in history. They undertook the systematic extermination of an entire people—a policy called *genocide*. Nazi forces herded Jews into infamous concentration camps such as *Buchenwald, Auschwitz,* and *Dachau.* Employing specially constructed gas chambers and crematoria, the Nazis exterminated 6 million men, women, and children. These human beings were murdered not because they had committed any crime but because they were of Jewish faith or origin. This destruction of most of the European Jewry became known as the *Holocaust.*

(In addition to the murder of 6 million Jews, the Nazis used their concentration camps to exterminate some 4 million other peoples. These unfortunates included gypsies, Slavic-speaking peoples—Poles, Czechs, Slovaks, and Russians—whom the Nazis considered "inferior" and treated harshly for resisting German rule, and anti-Nazis of all nationalities.)

**6. Religion.** The Nazis realized that their doctrines were contrary to the ethical concepts of Christianity. Nazi violence and aggression conflicted with the "Golden Rule." Nazi "master race" propaganda conflicted with the "brotherhood of man."

The Nazis consequently sought to control Christianity. Nazi officials directed the activities of the Protestant churches. Those ministers who failed to cooperate were dismissed, and some were sent to concentration camps. Hitler also tried to weaken the Catholic Church. The Nazis discouraged attendance in Catholic schools, tried many priests and nuns on various trumped-up charges, and imprisoned the clergy who challenged Nazi doctrines.

**7. Women.** The Nazis assigned women to an inferior position in German society. Women were excluded from politics and were ordered to devote themselves to kitchen tasks and childbearing. Hitler wanted an increasing population that he could mold to Nazi ideas and draft into his armies.

**8. Labor.** The Nazi regime determined wages, hours, and working conditions, dominated the labor unions, and prohibited strikes. The Nazis almost completely eliminated unemployment by driving anti-Nazis and married women from jobs, furthering public works, spurring the production of armaments, and enlarging the armed forces.

**9. Industry.** The Nazis permitted private ownership of industry subject to strict regulation. Instead of allowing free enterprise, the state controlled prices, production, profits, capital investment, foreign trade, and banking.

In 1936 *Hermann Goering* headed a Nazi Four-Year Plan to prepare the German economy for a war. He sought economic self-sufficiency, or *autarchy*, and emphasized the production of armaments over goods for civilians. Goering's slogan was "guns not butter."

**10. Militarism.** The Nazis *(a)* created a large conscript army and a powerful air force, *(b)* remilitarized the Rhineland, *(c)* shifted German industry into war production, and *(d)* gave military training to children in schools and in Hitler Youth Organizations. By rebuilding Germany's military might, Hitler violated the Treaty of Versailles, but the Allies took no action. Meanwhile, the Nazis sang "Today we rule Germany, tomorrow the world."

**11. Aggression and War.** Hitler planned territorial expansion in Europe, claiming that Germany needed *Lebensraum* (living space). *(a)* In 1936 Germany and Italy reached an understanding that later became a military alliance, the *Rome-Berlin Axis*. *(b)* In 1936 Germany and Italy gave men and equipment to General Franco of Spain, enabling him to overthrow the Spanish republican government and establish a dictatorial regime. *(c)* In 1938, in violation of the World War I peace settlement, Germany invaded and annexed Austria. *(d)* In 1938 Germany, having secured the reluctant approval of Britain and France, seized the *Sudetenland*, the region of Czechoslovakia bordering on Germany and Austria. Hitler's pretext was that the Sudetens were a German-speaking people. Six months later, however, Hitler seized the rest of Czechoslovakia, inhabited by Slavic-speaking peoples. *(e)* In 1939 Hitler demanded the return of Danzig and the Polish Corridor. When Poland, backed by Britain and France, did not yield, Hitler invaded that country, thereby starting World War II. (For details, see Fascist Aggression, pages 490–491).

## WORLD WAR II AND THE COLLAPSE OF THE NAZI REGIME

At first, German armies achieved great triumphs, overrunning most of Poland, Western Europe, and the Balkans. After June, 1941, Nazi armies penetrated deep into Russian territory.

In late 1942 the tide of battle turned against the Nazis. German armies were retreating in North Africa and no longer were advancing in southern Russia. By 1945 German forces had been routed in Russia, wiped out in North Africa, and driven from France, and the Nazis were fighting on German soil. Germany was being invaded from both east and west. German cities, factories, and railroads lay ruined by Allied bombings. In April, 1945, Hitler died in Berlin, apparently by suicide. Shortly thereafter Germany surrendered unconditionally, marking the end of the Nazi regime.

## GERMANY SINCE WORLD WAR II

The Allies divided Germany into four zones, with Russia, Britain, France, and the United States each occupying a zone. By quarreling over Germany's future, the Western powers and Russia soon linked German postwar history to the cold war (check the Index).

## NAZISM IN THE PERSPECTIVE OF WESTERN CIVILIZATION

**An Exaggeration of Certain Trends Discernible in West European History.** Nazi practices and doctrines can be traced back to various developments in Western Europe. (1) Dictatorial government existed under the absolute monarchs of the Age of Transition and later under the first modern dictator, Napoleon Bonaparte. (2) Idealization of the dictator typified the European attitude toward political leaders of the past, such as Julius Caesar, Augustus, Charlemagne in earlier times and Napoleon Bonaparte in modern times. Such idealization was spurred also by the concept that great men, not impersonal economic and social forces, determine the course of history—a concept presented in the writings of the historian Thomas Carlyle. (3) Disregard of moral values and limitless use of violence reflected the Renaissance philosophy of government as described in the book *The Prince* by Machiavelli. (4) Excessive and bigoted nationalism arose during the French Revolutionary Era and prevailed afterwards throughout Western Europe. (5) Various techniques of dictatorial rule—control of education, censorship of press, secret police, arbitrary arrests, mass rallies, and meaningless plebiscites—were employed by Napoleon Bonaparte and his nephew Napoleon III. (6) Anti-Semitism long had been prevalent in Western Europe. Originally growing out of religious matters, anti-Semitism later also reflected economic and other cultural causes. Anti-Semites found Jews to be ideal victims since they were dispersed and defenseless. In the Middle Ages Jews were denied citizenship by the various political entities, were compelled to live in ghetto areas, were prohibited from owning land and entering most professions, and were subjected to many special taxes. Although abating somewhat during the French Revolutionary Era, anti-Semitic prejudice remained a powerful tradition rooted in the minds of the West European peoples. (7) Concepts of "racial superiority" and a "master race" evolved out of European imperialist attitudes toward the so-called backward peoples of Africa and Asia. (8) Glorification of war was an irrational application of Darwin's "survival of the fittest" theory to nations—an example of Social Darwinism.

Democratic observers have concluded that Nazism took the worst of the West European past and upon that foundation built a regressive society of unmatched horror and barbarism.

**A Complete Contradiction of Fundamental Western Values.** Nazism spurned the decent and humane values, painstakingly developed over many centuries, in Western civilization. Nazi practices and doctrines (1) scorned democratic government that originated in the ancient Greek city-states and evolved in recent times in Britain, France, and most West European nations; (2) rejected the democratic belief in the intelligence, decency, and good judgment of the common people; (3) ridiculed the democratic concept that political leaders are servants of the people—not their masters; (4) contradicted basic ethical concepts of Christianity—notably "Do unto others as you would have others do unto you" (the Golden Rule), the brotherhood of all men and the sisterhood of all women, and the worthiness of each individual; (5) denied the Renaissance concept that each individual be free to think, achieve, and contribute to society—in accordance with the individual's potential; (6) rejected the spirit of free inquiry, fundamental to scientific progress, that emerged during the Renaissance; (7) despised the use of reason, logic, and intelligence that had typified the Age of Reason and the Enlightenment; and (8) refused to acknowledge that war degrades the human spirit, destroys human and material resources, and ensures the survival of the fortunate—not necessarily those best qualified to contribute to civilized progress.

## MULTIPLE–CHOICE QUESTIONS

1. In a totalitarian state (1) all industry is owned by the government (2) the state controls every aspect of the lives of its people (3) the state guarantees civil liberties to loyal citizens (4) a complete revolution occurs about every 20 years.
2. In general a dictator (1) furthers critical thinking on political matters by students (2) encourages free labor unions (3) suspends military service (4) controls the means of communication.
3. Dictatorships do *not* accept the principle that (1) might makes right (2) strict censorship is necessary (3) one party should be supreme (4) the state exists for the individual.
4. A major difference between dictatorship and democracy is that a dictatorship does *not* have a (1) multiparty system (2) cabinet (3) parliament (4) written constitution.

5. In seizing and maintaining power in the 20th century, the Communists, Fascists, and Nazis all (1) established good relations with churches (2) respected existing treaties (3) blamed their nations' troubles on scapegoats (4) encouraged private economic enterprise.

6. One reason for Mussolini's rise to power in Italy was that he (1) promoted the annexation of Rome (2) promised Italians a republican form of government (3) conquered Ethiopia (4) had the support of industrial leaders.

7. Mussolini gained control of the Italian government following (1) a national election (2) a majority vote in the Italian legislature (3) his threat to use force (4) the depression of 1929.

8. The Fascist government of Italy was similar to the Communist government of Russia in that it (1) was controlled by the proletariat (2) was democratically elected (3) was controlled by capitalists (4) suppressed opposition.

9. The controversy between Italy and the pope over state seizure of Church lands was settled by the (1) abdication of the Italian king (2) Law of Papal Guarantees (3) Lateran Pacts with the pope (4) elevation of Pope Paul VI.

10. Under fascism workers could *not* (1) belong to labor unions (2) go out on strike (3) vote in national elections (4) belong to the Fascist party.

11. Under fascism industrial prices were generally set by the (1) capitalists (2) state (3) consumers (4) workers.

12. Which was supported by Mussolini? (1) an alliance with Nazi Germany (2) a policy of free trade (3) nonintervention in the Spanish Civil War (4) nationalist movements in Ethiopia and Libya.

13. Mussolini was forced to resign because he (1) denied civil liberties (2) placed the welfare of the state ahead of the welfare of the people (3) extolled imperialism (4) led Italy to defeat in World War II.

14. The 1948 constitution of the Italian Republic did *not* guarantee (1) civil liberties (2) universal suffrage (3) separation of Church and State (4) cabinet responsibility to Parliament.

15. Today the Italian Republic faces the problem of (1) securing workers for new mass-production industries (2) gaining allies in the cold war (3) regaining ownership of Sicily (4) maintaining stable government.

16. In the 1976 elections how did the Italian Communist party rank among Italy's political parties in voting strength? (1) first (2) second (3) third (4) fourth.

17. The greatest poverty in Italy today is to be found in the (1) industrial north (2) agricultural south (3) seaports (4) Rome area.

18. After World War I a constitution for a German republic was drawn up in the city of (1) Berlin (2) Bonn (3) Weimar (4) Munich.

19. For the period 1920–1940, which is considered a result of the other three? (1) rise of the Nazi movement (2) rise of unemployment in Germany (3) German tradition of militarism (4) Treaty of Versailles.

20. A major reason for the failure of democratic government in Germany after World War I was the (1) illiteracy of the masses (2) threat of attack from neighboring nations (3) war destruction of German farms and factories (4) inability of the government to deal with economic distress.

21. The inflation, by which the German mark lost its purchasing power, most hurt (1) workers who lived on wages (2) landlords who collected rents (3) the middle class who had substantial savings in banks and insurance policies (4) factory owners who produced and sold consumer goods.

22. The Nazis blamed Germany's defeat in World War I on   (1) the German General Staff   (2) Allied superiority in troops and equipment   (3) German scientists for failing to develop new weapons   (4) traitors in the German civilian population.

23. In matters of religion the Nazis   (1) permitted freedom of worship   (2) forced all Germans to become Protestants   (3) sought to make the churches serve the nation   (4) made Catholicism the official religion.

24. A policy of Nazi Germany was   (1) self-determination for the peoples of Europe   (2) adoption of laissez-faire   (3) establishment of collective farms   (4) maintenance of concentration camps.

25. German Nazism differed most from Russian Communism with respect to the   (1) ownership of property   (2) existence of secret police   (3) political party system   (4) censorship of newspapers and radio.

26. Hitler's territorial demand immediately preceding the outbreak of World War II was   (1) Alsace-Lorraine   (2) the Sudetenland   (3) the Polish Corridor   (4) Albania.

27. In regard to race the Nazis held that the Germans   (1) were the "master race"   (2) were as good as the British   (3) had been persecuted by the Aryans   (4) should help educate the backward races.

28. Auschwitz and Dachau were Nazi   (1) territorial demands upon Poland   (2) military victories in World War II   (3) concentration camps   (4) generals.

29. Which of the following persons was safe from imprisonment in a Nazi concentration camp?   (1) a Jewish child   (2) a Polish underground fighter   (3) a labor unionist on strike   (4) none of these.

30. Which method did the Nazi regime *not* use to reduce unemployment?   (1) creating a large conscript army   (2) increasing the production of war materials   (3) dismissing married women from jobs   (4) establishing a 30-hour workweek.

## MATCHING QUESTIONS

|  |  |
|---|---|
| *Column A* | *Column B* |
| 1. Leader known as "Il Duce" | a. Joseph Goebbels |
| 2. Minister of Nazi Propaganda | b. Hermann Goering |
| 3. Last kaiser of Germany | c. Heinrich Himmler |
| 4. Head of the Gestapo | d. Adolf Hitler |
| 5. Author of *Mein Kampf* | e. Humbert II |
| 6. Composer whose music was banned in | f. Felix Mendelssohn |
| Nazi Germany | g. Benito Mussolini |
|  | h. William II |

## ESSAY QUESTIONS

1. For either Italy or Germany after World War I, show how each of the following led to the rise of dictatorship: (*a*) economic conditions (*b*) weakness of parliamentary government (*c*) lack of a democratic tradition (*d*) fear of communism (*e*) extreme nationalism.

2. (*a*) Give *two* policies of Germany from 1871 to 1914 that were also policies of Germany from 1933 to 1945. (*b*) Show how one German leader of *each* period attempted to carry out these policies. (*c*) In your opinion, did Bismarck's Germany pave the way for Hitler's Germany? Present *one* argument to support your point of view.

3. Democracies and totalitarian dictatorships differ in their policies of government. Compare a democracy and a totalitarian dictatorship in regard to *each* of the following: *(a)* power of the legislature *(b)* political party system *(c)* education *(d)* treatment of minority groups *(e)* free enterprise *(f)* labor unions.

4. By illustrations drawn from Nazism in Germany, explain the following terms: *(a) Mein Kampf (b)* "master race" *(c)* scapegoat *(d)* totalitarianism *(e)* Gestapo *(f)* school for barbarians *(g)* big lie *(h)* "tomorrow the world" *(i)* concentration camp.

5. Discuss *(a) two* provisions of the Italian peace treaty after World War II, *(b) two* democratic features of the government of the Republic of Italy, and *(c) two* problems facing Italy today.

6. Did Nazism represent *(a)* a logical outcome or *(b)* an aberration (sharp deviation) from West European civilization? Present *two* arguments to support each point of view. In a brief paragraph, explain which point of view you accept and why.

# Part 5. Failure of the Peace Movement and World War II

## THE LEAGUE OF NATIONS

Following World War I humankind hoped for an era of world peace. Woodrow Wilson, wartime American president, believed the League of Nations to be the single most important step toward this goal. At President Wilson's insistence, the League of Nations Covenant (constitution) was made part of the Treaty of Versailles. In 1920 the League started operations; its headquarters were at Geneva, Switzerland.

## PURPOSES OF THE LEAGUE OF NATIONS

The League was a world organization created to (1) eliminate international anarchy, (2) prevent war by encouraging disarmament and by settling international disputes peacefully, and (3) solve economic and social problems through international cooperation.

## ORGANIZATION OF THE LEAGUE OF NATIONS

1. The **Assembly,** consisting of all member nations, discussed international issues and made recommendations by *unanimous* vote.

2. **The Council,** consisting of selected permanent and nonpermanent members, was concerned chiefly with threats to world peace. Its recommendations also required *unanimity.*

**3.** The **World Court** was to settle legal disputes between nations on the basis of international law.

**4.** Specialized **commissions** and **agencies** dealt with economic and social problems. For example, the *Permanent Mandates Commission* supervised colonies held as mandates, the *International Health Organization* combated disease, the *Minorities Commission* sought to protect the rights of minority groups, and the *International Labor Organization (ILO)* gathered labor statistics and worked to improve world labor conditions.

## THE LEAGUE: INTERNATIONAL COOPERATION TO PREVENT WAR

To settle disputes peacefully, League procedures called for (1) arbitration by neutral third parties or (2) judicial decision by the World Court or (3) inquiry and recommendation by the Council.

If an aggressor nation refused to submit to peaceful settlement, the League could advise (but could not force) its member nations to employ coercive measures, called *sanctions.* These might be *diplomatic,* such as withdrawing ambassadors; *economic,* such as halting trade; and, finally, *military.* (The League, in its brief existence, never attempted military sanctions.)

## THE UNITED STATES REFUSES TO JOIN THE LEAGUE

In 1919 President Wilson presented the Treaty of Versailles with its provision for League membership to the Republican-controlled Senate. Leading Republican Senators, favoring isolation and personally hostile to Wilson, a Democrat, led a long, bitter fight against the League. Wilson countered by an extensive speaking tour, but his efforts ended abruptly when he suffered a paralyzing stroke. The Senate decisively rejected the Treaty of Versailles.

The isolationists argued as follows: (1) The League might involve the United States in a war, thereby violating the American Constitution that gives only Congress the power to declare war. (2) The League might interfere in domestic matters, such as tariff and immigration policies. (3) The League would be dominated by Britain and its dominions, which held six Assembly votes. (4) League membership would involve us in the problems of the entire world and thus violate America's traditional policy of isolation.

The United States never joined the League.

## THE UNITED STATES COOPERATES WITH THE LEAGUE

The United States cooperated, in a limited way, with the League by (1) joining the International Labor Organization, (2) working with League agencies to wipe out disease, suppress slavery, and establish standards in communication and transportation, and (3) supporting the League during the crisis over Manchuria (see Stimson Doctrine, page 405).

## LEAGUE SUCCESSES

In the 1920's the League peacefully settled boundary disputes between small nations, such as disputes between Finland and Sweden, Yugoslavia and Albania, and Greece and Bulgaria. Also, the League achieved economic and social progress by aiding nations financially, combating disease, and curtailing opium traffic.

## LEAGUE WEAKNESSES

1. **Membership.** The League did not include all major nations. The United States never joined. Russia entered the League in 1934 but in 1939 was expelled. Germany and Japan withdrew in 1933, and Italy withdrew three years later.

2. **Voting.** League decisions required unanimous votes.

3. **Powers.** The League was an association of independent nations, each retaining complete freedom of action, that is, *national sovereignty*. The League lacked the power to tax, to draft an army, and to enforce its decisions. Although it could request money, men, and support from its members, each state was free to respond according to its own national interests. The League was not a strong world government; rather, it was a very weak *confederation*.

## LEAGUE FAILURES

The League's outstanding failures were its inability to (1) halt the Japanese invasion of Manchuria (1931), (2) halt the Italian conquest of Ethiopia (1935), and (3) prevent Nazi German rearmament and territorial seizures (1935–1938) in violation of the Treaty of Versailles. In 1946 the League voted itself out of existence and transferred its properties to the new world organization, the United Nations.

## NAVAL DISARMAMENT

1. **Early Agreements.** Realizing that the armaments race had helped cause World War I, the naval powers sought disarmament.

*a. Washington Conference (1921–1922).* Britain, the United States, Japan, France, and Italy agreed to stop building capital ships (large warships) for ten years and to maintain capital ships in a ratio of 5:5:3:1.67:1.67, respectively.

*b. London Naval Conference (1930).* Britain, the United States, and Japan agreed to a ratio of 10:10:7, respectively, for five years, for cruisers and destroyers as well as capital ships.

2. **Eventual Failure.** At the *London Conference* (1935), Japan demanded that Britain and the United States accept a 10:10:10 ratio, or *parity*. The democracies

refused on the ground that Japan had no need of such naval power unless for aggression. No agreement was reached; soon afterward Japan started a new naval race.

## INTERNATIONAL PACTS

**1. Nine-Power Treaty at the Washington Conference (1921–1922).** Japan, the United States, Britain, France, and five smaller nations agreed to respect equal trade in and the independence of China. By thus reaffirming the Open Door Policy, these nations hoped to prevent imperialist conflict over China.

**2. Locarno Pacts (1925).** Germany agreed (a) to accept as permanent its western boundaries with Belgium and France, (b) to keep the Rhineland demilitarized as required by the Treaty of Versailles, and (c) to submit to peaceful settlement any disputes concerning its eastern boundaries with Czechoslovakia and Poland. The Locarno Pacts were guaranteed by the nations involved and by Italy and Britain.

**3. Kellogg–Briand Pact (1928).** *Frank Kellogg,* American secretary of state, and *Aristide Briand,* French foreign minister, proposed a pact to settle all disputes peacefully and to outlaw war "as an instrument of national policy." Most nations, including Germany, Japan, and Italy, signed this idealistic statement, also called the *Pact of Paris.*

**4. Failure of International Pacts.** In the 1930's militarist Japan, Fascist Italy, and Nazi Germany began aggressions in defiance of these pacts. When Germany under Hitler first violated the Locarno Pacts, the other signatory powers failed to take effective action, and the Locarno agreements became worthless. The Nine-Power Treaty and the Kellogg-Briand Pact contained no provision for enforcement.

## THE UNITED STATES AND THE PEACE MOVEMENT (1919–1939)

Following World War I the American people desired peace, but they could not decide which policy would best ensure peace: *international cooperation* or *isolation.*

Toward international cooperation, the United States (1) supported certain activities and decisions of the League, (2) joined in naval disarmament, and (3) signed the Nine-Power Treaty and the Kellogg-Briand Pact.

Many Americans, however, still rejected international cooperation and held that we could ensure peace for ourselves only through isolation. Their views dominated American foreign policy in the years between World Wars I and II. Pursuing a policy of isolation, the United States (1) refused to join the League of Nations and the World Court, (2) discouraged international trade by raising tariff barriers, and (3) adopted neutrality legislation.

## AMERICAN NEUTRALITY ACTS (1935, 1937)

Sensing that Europe was again headed toward war, Congress passed two *Neutrality Acts* that (1) prohibited the sale of war implements to belligerents, (2) banned loans to belligerents, (3) prohibited Americans from sailing on ships of belligerents, and (4) forbade American merchant ships to enter war zones. This last provision surrendered traditional American claims to *freedom of the seas*— the right of a neutral nation to trade with belligerents in goods not intended for war use.

Congress hoped that these laws would prevent the economic and emotional entanglements that many believed had involved the United States in World War I. However, these American efforts to assure peace for ourselves weakened the world peace movement and overlooked the fact that aggression elsewhere might endanger our own security.

## FASCIST AGGRESSION (1931–1939)

Japan, Italy, and Germany (1) engaged in one act of aggression after another, thereby violating, without any effective opposition, the major international peace agreements: Treaty of Versailles, Covenant of the League of Nations, Nine-Power Treaty, Locarno Pacts, and Kellogg-Briand Pact; (2) withdrew from membership in the League; and (3) joined together to form a military alliance, the *Rome-Berlin-Tokyo Axis*. The record of aggression follows.

**1. Manchuria.** In 1931–1932 Japan invaded and conquered China's northern province of Manchuria. Japan flouted League of Nations efforts to halt its aggression and thus, for the first time, revealed the League's weaknesses. (For details, see pages 404–405.)

**2. Ethiopia.** In 1935 Fascist Italy invaded Ethiopia. The League of Nations named Italy the aggressor and voted minor economic sanctions but failed to recommend an embargo on Italy's most essential import—oil. Undeterred by such feeble opposition, Mussolini conquered and annexed Ethiopia.

**3. German Remilitarization.** Nazi Germany violated the Treaty of Versailles in 1935 by reintroducing military conscription and in 1936 by remilitarizing the Rhineland. Hitler encountered no serious Allied opposition despite Germany's then limited military strength.

**4. Spain.** In 1936 General *Francisco Franco* began a revolt against the legally elected left-of-center government of Spain. While this Loyalist government received limited aid from Russia, Franco received extensive support of troops and military equipment from Italy and Germany. After three years of civil war, Franco won complete control and established a dictatorship friendly to Germany and Italy.

**5. China.** In 1937 Japanese forces from Manchuria invaded China proper. The Japanese overran China's coastal areas but failed to penetrate far into the interior. The Chinese continued their resistance and received limited aid from Britain and the United States.

**6. Austria.** In 1938 Hitler invaded and annexed Austria on the ground that all German-speaking people belonged within one German nation. *Anschluss* (union) of Germany and Austria violated the World War I peace treaties. Furthermore, Anschluss was never approved by the Austrian people in an honest plebiscite.

**7. Czechoslovakia.** Later in 1938 Hitler demanded the *Sudetenland,* a region in Czechoslovakia bordering on Germany and inhabited by German-speaking people. Although the Sudeten people were not oppressed, Nazi propagandists manufactured stories of "Czech atrocities," and Hitler promised "help." The Czech government, a democracy under President *Eduard Benes,* refused to yield. It counted on its alliance with Russia and France and expected British support. However, Britain and France decided not to risk war but to appease Hitler.

At the *Munich Conference* British Prime Minister *Neville Chamberlain* and French Premier *Edouard Daladier* agreed to let Hitler seize the Sudetenland. Deserted by its friends, Czechoslovakia yielded. Chamberlain returned to Britain and proclaimed that he had preserved "peace in our time." Hitler announced that this was his last European territorial demand.

Six months later, however, Hitler seized the Slavic-inhabited remainder of Czechoslovakia. In Britain the Chamberlain government at last realized that Hitler could not be trusted to keep his promises. Britain and France joined in a military alliance and guaranteed protection to Germany's next probable victim, Poland.

**8. Albania.** In 1939 Mussolini invaded and annexed Albania, giving Italy control of the Adriatic Sea.

**9. Poland.** In 1939 Hitler demanded the return of Danzig and the Polish Corridor on the ground that they were inhabited by German-speaking people.

Before Poland responded, Nazi Germany and Communist Russia announced a ten-year *Nonaggression Pact.* The world was surprised because Hitler had always preached hatred of communism, and Stalin had always condemned fascism. *(a)* The pact **enabled Russia** to avoid (for the time being) involvement in a major war and, by its secret clauses, gave Stalin a free hand over eastern Poland and the Baltic states. *(b)* The pact **protected Germany** against a two-front war and secretly promised Hitler foodstuffs and war supplies from Russia.

On September 1, 1939, German troops invaded Poland; two days later, Britain and France honored their guarantee to Poland and declared war on Germany. World War II had started.

## BASIC CAUSES OF WORLD WAR II: AXIS PHILOSOPHY AND AGGRESSION

**1. Axis Totalitarianism.** With Japan ruled by the military and Germany and Italy each dominated by a Fascist party, the Axis nations were totalitarian dictatorships. They scorned the democratic ideals of civil liberties, of the dignity of the individual, and of world peace, and they openly declared their intent to destroy democracy.

**2. Axis Militarism.** The Axis nations spent vast sums on armaments, devised new weapons and battle techniques, built huge military organizations, and psychologically prepared their peoples for war. They proclaimed war a glorious adventure and death for the Fatherland the highest honor.

**3. Axis Nationalism.** Japanese Shinto teachings, Italian dreams of a revival of the Roman Empire, and German "master race" doctrines all fostered a narrow and bigoted nationalism. The Axis nations considered themselves superior and destined to rule over "lesser peoples."

**4. Axis Imperialism.** The Axis powers embarked upon imperialism with the excuse that they lacked land and resources and were *have-not* nations. Japan expanded into Manchuria and China proper to establish a Japanese-dominated "New Order in Asia." Italy enlarged its African empire and planned to make the Mediterranean an "Italian lake." Germany annexed Austria and Czechoslovakia as first steps toward European domination and eventually, perhaps, world domination.

## SUBSIDIARY CAUSES OF WORLD WAR II

**1. Failure of Appeasement.** Britain and France followed a policy of *appeasement*—that is, making concessions to the dictators in the hope that the dictators would eventually be satisfied and stop their aggressions. Anxious for peace, democratic peoples failed to understand that each concession strengthened the aggressors and emboldened them to make further demands. The chief advocate of appeasement was Neville Chamberlain, and its final application was the transfer of the Sudetenland by the Munich Conference.

**2. Failure of Collective Security.** Peace-loving nations by coordinating their military strength and acting collectively might have protected each other from aggression. The democratic peoples, however, shrank from any kind of military action. The United States was determined to remain neutral; Britain and France delayed the formation of a firm alliance until 1939.

Communist Russia urged collective security because it feared attack by Nazi Germany. Democratic nations, however, were reluctant to enter into collective security pacts with the Soviet Union because they *(a)* did not believe Communist sincerity, *(b)* feared Communist plans for world revolution, and *(c)* were not eager to protect the Soviet Union. Indeed, some people felt that a Russo-

German war would lessen both the Communist and Fascist threats to Western democracy. In 1939, however, Russia saw an opportunity to turn the Nazi war machine against Britain and France. Thereupon, Russia terminated its support of collective security and concluded the Stalin-Hitler Nonaggression Pact.

**3. American Neutrality Legislation.** By prohibiting loans and the sale of war implements to all belligerents, the Neutrality Acts actually favored the well-armed aggressor nations over their ill-equipped victims. Furthermore, these laws implied that Americans would "stay on their side of the street" and would not intervene to check Axis aggression in Asia and Europe.

## THE SECOND WORLD WAR (1939–1945)

### 1. Initial German Successes (1939–1940)

*a. Conquest of Poland.* German armies, employing massive air bombings and tank assaults, unleashed a new "lightning war," or *blitzkrieg.* They speedily rolled across the open plains of Poland and destroyed all resistance. Germany annexed western Poland. (As agreed in the Hitler-Stalin Pact, Russia seized eastern Poland. Russia also annexed the Baltic countries of Estonia, Latvia, and Lithuania and, after a four-month war, secured territory from Finland.)

*b. Conquest of Denmark and Norway.* Nazi armies next overran neutral Denmark and Norway. In Norway Nazi armies received assistance from traitors, called *fifth columnists,* led by *Vidkun Quisling.* Germany thus gained valuable submarine bases on the Atlantic Ocean.

*c. Conquest of France.* Nazi armies invaded northern France in 1940 by going through the plains of neutral Holland and Belgium. The Germans thus bypassed the Franco-German border with its mountainous terrain and French defensive fortifications, the *Maginot Line.* Nazi armies easily defeated the Allied defenders. The British retreated to *Dunkirk* and miraculously evacuated most troops to England. French resistance collapsed, and French forces fled southward. With Mussolini confident that victory was already won, Italy entered the war. As the German forces continued their advance southward, France surrendered.

The Germans occupied over half of France, including the whole Atlantic and English Channel coasts. For unoccupied France, they permitted an antidemocratic government at *Vichy,* headed by Marshal *Henri Pétain.* In Britain General *Charles de Gaulle* proclaimed a *Free French* movement determined to continue the war and liberate France.

### 2. Britain Stands Alone (1940–1941)

*a. Leadership of Churchill. Winston Churchill,* who had repeatedly opposed appeasement of the Nazis, replaced Chamberlain as prime minister. Churchill inspired the British people to courage and determination, as he called upon them

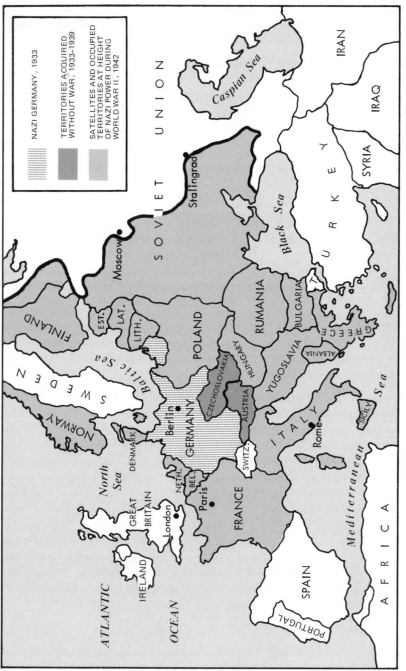

**Nazi German Expansion in Europe (1933–1942)**

NAZI GERMANY, 1933

TERRITORIES ACQUIRED WITHOUT WAR, 1933–1939

SATELLITES AND OCCUPIED TERRITORIES AT HEIGHT OF NAZI POWER DURING WORLD WAR II, 1942

to save the world from the "abyss of a new dark age." "I have nothing to offer," he said, "but blood, toil, tears, and sweat."

*b. Battle of Britain.* Hitler ordered his *Luftwaffe* (air force) to soften Britain for invasion. For three months Britain was subjected to devastating air attacks. The *Royal Air Force (RAF)*, however, drove off the Luftwaffe. By maintaining control of the air lanes, the RAF compelled the Nazis to shelve their plans for an invasion of Britain. Instead, the Nazis turned southward, overrunning the Balkans and placing an army in North Africa to support the Italians.

### 3. American Preparedness and Aid to the Allies (1939–1941)

*a. Neutrality Act of 1939.* Soon after World War II started, President *Franklin D. Roosevelt* requested Congress to pass the Neutrality Act of 1939. This law permitted belligerents to purchase war materials, provided they paid cash and carried the goods away in their own vessels. *Cash and carry* was designed to give limited assistance to the Atlantic sea powers (France and Britain) and, at the same time, maintain American neutrality.

*b. Changes in Public Opinion.* President Roosevelt labored to awaken the American people to the threat to their national security. When France fell in 1940, Americans finally realized that Britain alone stood between them and a hostile Fascist world. For America's self-defense, Congress supported a vast military buildup and aid to Britain by *all measures short of war.*

*c. Military Preparedness.* Congress authorized a two-ocean navy and a huge air force and passed the 1940 *Selective Service Act.* It provided for America's first peacetime conscription (draft).

*d. Destroyer-Naval Base Deal of 1940.* President Roosevelt traded 50 "over-age" destroyers to Britain in exchange for military bases on British territory in the Western Hemisphere from Newfoundland to British Guiana. Britain needed the destroyers to combat German submarines; the United States used the bases as defensive outposts.

*e. Lend-Lease Act of 1941.* Realizing that Britain's cash was almost exhausted, President Roosevelt requested new legislation to maintain the United States as the *"arsenal of democracy."* Congress passed the *Lend-Lease Act* authorizing the president to lend or lease goods to any nation whose defense he deemed necessary for the defense of the United States. Immediately Roosevelt extended substantial aid to Britain. He later gave aid to other Allies, including Russia. (Total lend-lease aid amounted to $50 billion.) Also, Roosevelt ordered that merchant ships carrying lend-lease materials be convoyed by the United States Navy part way across the Atlantic.

*f. Embargo on Strategic Materials to Japan.* As an advocate of the Open Door Policy, the United States opposed Japan's plans for an east Asian empire. In 1940–1941 the United States protested Japanese occupation of French Indo-China. Since protests proved ineffective, President Roosevelt embargoed the sale of aviation gasoline, scrap iron, and other strategic materials to Japan and "froze" Japanese assets in the United States.

## 4. The Axis Makes Two Mistakes (1941)

*a. German Attack on Russia.* Despite the Russo-German Nonaggression Pact, Hitler ordered a blitzkrieg against Russia (June, 1941) to acquire the grain, coal, and iron of the Ukraine and the oil of the Caucasus. Hitler expected a quick victory, but Russia proved to be a formidable foe. Russian armies retreated slowly, "scorching the earth," and Communist guerrilla bands harassed the invaders. The Nazis occupied much territory, stretching their supply lines, but were unable to crush the Soviet armies.

*b. Japanese Attack on the United States.* On December 7, 1941, Japan staged a "sneak attack" upon the American naval base at *Pearl Harbor,* Hawaii, forcing the United States actively into the war. Under General *Hideki Tojo* the Japanese government planned to humble the United States and assure Japanese domination of eastern Asia. Japan's Axis partners—Germany and Italy—immediately declared war on the United States.

Axis strategists hoped that, if they forced the United States into a Pacific war, the United States would be unable to complete its military preparations and would be compelled to curtail lend-lease aid to Britain and Russia. However, the Axis reckoned without the American people. They closed ranks behind President Roosevelt with determination to "win the war and the peace that follows."

## 5. Victory in Europe (1942–1945)

*a. From North Africa to Italy.* In October, 1942, a British army under General *Bernard Montgomery* defeated the Germans and Italians at *El Alamein,* Egypt, and began pursuing them westward. In November, 1942, an Anglo-American army under General *Dwight D. Eisenhower* invaded French North Africa and moved eastward. By thus placing the enemy in a vise, the Allies destroyed the Axis African armies. In 1943 the Allies crossed the Mediterranean and invaded Sicily and southern Italy. Mussolini's Fascist government collapsed, and Italy surrendered unconditionally. To resist the Allied advance northward, Germany rushed troops into Italy.

*b. Russian Counteroffensive.* In early 1943, following a six-month battle, the Russians annihilated a 300,000-man Nazi army deep inside the Soviet Union at *Stalingrad.* Following this great victory Russian armies seized the initiative, materially assisted by huge amounts of American lend-lease, especially motor vehicles and airplanes. The Communists drove the Nazis from Russia and pursued them through Rumania, Bulgaria, Yugoslavia, Hungary, Austria, Czechoslovakia, and Poland. In 1945 the Russians reached eastern Germany and stormed into Berlin.

*c. Anglo-American Invasion of France.* To prepare the way for invasion, American and British airmen bombed Nazi-held Europe, and underground patriots sabotaged Nazi factories and harassed Nazi forces. On June 6, 1944,

American and British forces, commanded by General Eisenhower, crossed the English Channel and landed in *Normandy* in northern France. This greatest waterborne invasion in history established a major *second front.* The invading forces met a powerful German army, which had been kept from the Russian front in anticipation of the attack. Allied forces pushed back the Nazi army and drove the Germans from France.

*d. Surrender of Germany.* In 1945 Anglo-American armies crossed the Rhine River in Germany and continued to the Elbe River. Here they met the Russians driving in from the east. After Hitler committed suicide, Germany surrendered unconditionally.

**6. Victory in the Pacific (1942–1945)**

*a. Initial Japanese Offensive.* In 1942 Japanese forces, pushing southward, overran the Philippines, the Malay States, the Dutch East Indies, and part of New Guinea. Poised just north of Australia, they were halted by American naval victories in the *Coral Sea* and later in the Central Pacific at *Midway.*

*b. Allied Counteroffensive.* In August, 1942, General *Douglas MacArthur* moved the Allied forces (chiefly American) northward in "island-hopping" offensives on the road to Japan. Overcoming fierce resistance, Allied troops seized *Guadalcanal* in the Solomon Islands; the *Gilbert, Marshall,* and *Caroline* islands; and *Guam.* In 1944, while the American navy was winning a decisive victory at *Leyte Gulf,* American forces returned to the Philippines. In early 1945 they also captured *Iwo Jima* and *Okinawa.* From these islands American pilots launched destructive raids upon Japan.

*c. Atom Bomb and the Surrender of Japan.* After Japan belittled the Allied demand to surrender or face "utter destruction," President Truman ordered the air force to use the newly developed atom bomb. Its use, Truman believed, would convince the Japanese military of the hopelessness of their situation, would save an estimated 1 million American casualties (and additional Japanese casualties) that would result from a seaborne invasion of Japan, and would hasten the end of the war.

In August, 1945, the United States dropped a single atom bomb—the first to be used in war—on the Japanese city that contained that nation's army headquarters and munitions factories—the city of *Hiroshima.* The bomb killed or injured 130,000 people. Two days later Russia declared war against Japan and invaded Japanese-held Manchuria. The following day the United States dropped a second atom bomb, this time on the industrial and shipbuilding city of *Nagasaki.* Defenseless against atomic bombings and without allies, Japan surrendered unconditionally.

## SIGNIFICANT FACTS DESCRIBING WORLD WAR II

**1. Total War.** The war was fought not only by armed forces at the battlefront but also by civilians in factories and in the home. Even schoolchildren took part, collecting scrap metal, rubber, and newspapers; helping air-raid wardens; and assisting in War Bond drives.

**2. Global War.** This most extensive war was fought on all major seas and in Africa, Asia, and Europe. It involved almost 60 nations, seven of them on the side of the Axis. To plan global military strategy, top Allied leaders held a series of conferences, such as the ones at Teheran, Yalta, and Potsdam.

**3. Scientific Progress.** Scientists and engineers devised or adapted for war purposes such inventions as radar, guided missiles, jet-propelled planes, magnetic mines, and atom bombs. World War II witnessed the use of blood plasma, penicillin, and sulfa drugs to save lives.

**4. Major Role of the Airplane.** Fleets of airplanes attacked troop and naval units, destroyed railroads and industrial centers, and prepared the way for invasion. Control of the air was essential to offensive action on land or sea.

## RESULTS OF WORLD WAR II

**1. Economic.** (a) The war—the most costly in history—exacted military expenditures of over $1,100 billion and caused property damage of over $230 billion. American military expenditures alone were over $330 billion. (b) European and Asian nations, ravaged by military action, faced difficult problems of economic recovery. (c) The Communist economic system spread from Russia to Eastern and Central Europe, and to several Asian nations.

**2. Social.** (a) The war—the most destructive in history—left over 22 million civilians and service personnel dead and over 34 million wounded. For the United States alone, the dead and wounded totaled over 1 million. (b) Several million *refugees* and *displaced persons,* uprooted by the war, needed assistance to rebuild their shattered lives.

**3. Political.** (a) Germany, Italy, and Japan met complete military defeat, and their totalitarian systems were overthrown. (b) The United States and Russia emerged as the major world powers and soon came into conflict, the *cold war.* (c) Russia acquired an empire of Communist satellite nations. (d) The Asian and African colonial peoples embraced intense nationalism and hastened the downfall of Western imperialism. (e) Great Britain and France declined as world powers and gradually relinquished their empires. (f) The atomic age brought problems of achieving international control of atomic weapons and of delivery systems. (g) To preserve peace, the Allies formed a new international organization, the *United Nations.*

# MULTIPLE–CHOICE QUESTIONS

1. One reason for the failure of the peace movement between World War I and World War II was the (1) absence of an international court of justice (2) weakness of the League of Nations (3) invention of the atomic bomb (4) conflict between the members of the Triple Alliance and the Triple Entente.

2. Between 1919 and 1939 nationalism (1) strengthened the League of Nations (2) weakened the League (3) did not affect the League (4) was greatly lessened by the League.

3. Which nation was *never* a member of the League of Nations? (1) Italy (2) Soviet Russia (3) Germany (4) the United States.

4. The first blow to the prestige of the League of Nations was (1) France's seizure of Syria and Lebanon (2) Italy's conquest of Ethiopia (3) Hitler's occupation of the Sudetenland (4) Japan's invasion of Manchuria.

5. *Not* an accomplishment of the League of Nations was (1) enforcing the disarmament of Germany (2) establishing the World Court (3) curtailing the opium traffic (4) establishing the International Labor Organization.

6. In the Italo-Ethiopian dispute, the League of Nations (1) ineffectively attempted to apply sanctions (2) showed a sympathetic attitude toward Italy (3) refused to take any action (4) brought about a settlement through World Court action.

7. *Not* a concern of the Washington Conference (1921–1922) was (1) the burden of naval armaments (2) the Far Eastern imperialistic ambitions of the great powers (3) Japan's economic penetration into China (4) the Indian nationalist movement.

8. The Kellogg-Briand Pact of 1928 recommended (1) outlawing war (2) settlement of the Allies' war debts (3) nonintervention in the Far East (4) naval disarmament.

9. Which was an important reason for the failure of the peace movement (1919–1939)? (1) lack of an international court (2) general reduction of armaments (3) invention of atomic weapons (4) inadequate treaty enforcement.

10. In the years between World War I and World War II, the United States (1) joined the League of Nations (2) formed an alliance with Britain (3) attempted to return to a policy of isolation (4) agreed to naval parity for Japan.

11. The main purpose of the American Neutrality Act of 1937 was to (1) stay out of war (2) increase foreign trade (3) cooperate more closely with the League of Nations (4) protect the rights of neutrals in wartime.

12. Germany's rearmament, starting in 1935, was (1) essential to the policy of collective security (2) encouraged by France (3) in violation of the Treaty of Versailles (4) a policy of the Weimar Republic.

13. During the Spanish Civil War, General Franco received military aid from (1) Germany and Russia (2) Germany and Italy (3) Italy and France (4) the United States and Britain.

14. Hitler argued that Germany should annex the Sudetenland to (1) protect its German-speaking population (2) reduce French influence in Central Europe (3) gain control of more munitions factories (4) prevent Communist seizure of the area.

15. The Munich Agreement (1938) is significant because it (1) halted Japanese aggression in Manchuria (2) represented the appeasement of the Nazis by Great Britain and France (3) prevented the German annexation of the Sudetenland (4) brought about the creation of the Rome-Berlin Axis.

16. Today the word *Munich* is used to mean (1) a vacation town (2) a successful international conference (3) the surrender of vital interests because of the threat of force (4) a military victory.

17. The Nonaggression Pact of 1939, preceding the outbreak of World War II, was between (1) Germany and Poland (2) Germany and the United States (3) Germany and Russia (4) Britain and the United States.

18. A condition prior to the outbreak of both World War I and World War II was (1) acts of appeasement by Britain (2) a series of international crises (3) the nonexistence of international peace organizations (4) Communist imperialism.

19. What physical feature, which has influenced the history of Poland, was significant in the early months of World War II? (1) many natural seaports (2) an eastern mountain range (3) flat plains (4) large reserves of petroleum.

20. After the fall of France to the Nazis in World War II, a Free French movement was started by (1) Pétain (2) Clemenceau (3) Daladier (4) de Gaulle.

21. In a speech in 1940, the people of Britain were offered nothing but "blood, toil, tears, and sweat" by (1) Churchill (2) Hitler (3) Stalin (4) Roosevelt.

22. The Lend-Lease Act of 1941 provided that the United States could (1) declare war against Germany (2) trade destroyers for British naval bases in the Western Hemisphere (3) supply the countries fighting the Axis nations with the necessary equipment (4) send an expeditionary force to Europe.

23. Hitler invaded the Soviet Union and seized the Ukraine because the Ukraine had (1) Russia's only outlet to the Baltic Sea (2) much fertile land (3) a large supply of oil (4) many large cities, including Moscow.

24. Which represents a similarity in the careers of Napoleon Bonaparte and Adolf Hitler? (1) death in exile (2) an invasion of Russia (3) lasting legal reforms (4) a program of anti-Semitism.

25. The first city in the history of warfare to be atom-bombed was (1) Hiroshima (2) Tokyo (3) Munich (4) Nanking.

26. The two nations that emerged as major world powers following World War II were (1) the United States and Britain (2) the United States and the Soviet Union (3) the Soviet Union and Germany (4) the Soviet Union and China.

## MATCHING QUESTIONS

| *Column A* | *Column B* |
|---|---|
| 1. Confederation | *a.* Nation engaged in war |
| 2. Blitzkrieg | *b.* Solemn agreement |
| 3. Appeasement | *c.* Freedom from external control |
| 4. Covenant | *d.* Consent of all parties concerned |
| 5. Fifth columnist | *e.* Nation that attacks another nation without provocation |
| 6. Aggressor | |
| 7. Sovereignty | *f.* Absence of law and government to regulate conduct of nations |
| 8. Sanction | |
| 9. Belligerent | *g.* Ratio of 10:10:10 |
| 10. International anarchy | *h.* Lightning war |
| | *i.* Coercive measure |
| | *j.* Political organization whose members, not the central body, possess power |
| | *k.* Traitor |
| | *l.* Concession made to powerful nations in the hope of avoiding further trouble |

# ESSAY QUESTIONS

1. The period between World War I and World War II was a period in which democracies and dictatorships were rivals. *(a)* Describe *three* instances of aggression by totalitarian states before World War II. *(b)* Discuss *one* reason why the democracies came to Poland's aid when that country was attacked by Germany. *(c)* Discuss *two* basic causes of World War II.

2. Some writers had been predicting an agreement between Nazi Germany and Communist Russia. Nevertheless, this 1939 Nonaggression Pact surprised most of the world. *(a)* Discuss *one* reason why some writers predicted an agreement between Russia and Germany. *(b)* Discuss *one* reason why the 1939 pact surprised most of the world. *(c)* Give *two* important immediate effects of the 1939 pact.

3. Explain how *each* of the following helped or hindered the peace movement from 1919 to 1939: *(a)* Washington Conference *(b)* Kellogg-Briand Pact *(c)* American neutrality laws *(d)* economic depression of 1929 *(e)* Spanish Civil War *(f)* Rome-Berlin Axis *(g)* Munich Pact *(h)* Russo-German Nonaggression Pact.

4. *(a)* Mention *two* threats to peace with which the League of Nations could not deal successfully. *(b)* Discuss *one* reason for the League's failure in each of these two cases.

5. Show *one* way in which each of the following geographic factors influenced the course of World War II: *(a)* the English Channel *(b)* the plains of Poland *(c)* the vast extent of Russia *(d)* the mountains on the Franco-German border *(e)* the Atlantic coastline of Norway *(f)* the location of Sicily.

6. Discuss *one* similarity and *one* difference for *each* of the following pairs: *(a)* the defeat of France in 1870—the defeat of France in 1940 *(b)* Napoleon's Continental System—Hitler's efforts to blockade Great Britain *(c)* Russia's role in the Napoleonic Wars—Russia's role in World War II.

7. Discuss whether each of the following is true or false, giving *two* reasons to support your point of view: *(a)* Preparedness for war is the best guarantee of peace. *(b)* The United States was right in not joining the League of Nations. *(c)* Appeasement of dictators can preserve the peace. *(d)* The failure of the League proves that wars cannot be prevented by an international organization. *(e)* The causes of World War II were very different from those of World War I. *(f)* The United States was correct in its decision to use the atom bomb against Japan.

# UNIT XIII. THE RECENT PAST— ARE WE BUILDING A BETTER WORLD?

## Part 1. The United Nations

### HOPES FOR A BETTER WORLD

In 1941 President Roosevelt stated that the United States sought a world whose people would enjoy *Four Freedoms:* (a) freedom of speech, (b) freedom of religion, (c) freedom from want, and (d) freedom from fear. To achieve these goals, the Allies moved to create the United Nations.

### STEPS TOWARD THE UNITED NATIONS

**1. The Atlantic Charter (1941).** President Roosevelt and Prime Minister Churchill, meeting on board ship in the Atlantic, issued a statement of principles, the *Atlantic Charter.* Remindful of Wilson's Fourteen Points, this document stated that Britain and the United States (a) desired no territorial gain, (b) respected the right of all peoples to choose their own form of government, (c) hoped that all peoples would live in freedom from fear and want, (d) believed that nations must abandon the use of force, and (e) would seek to establish a "system of general security," implying an international organization.

In 1942 the Allied nations met at Washington, pledged support for the Atlantic Charter, and adopted the name *United Nations (UN).*

**2. Yalta Conference (February, 1945).** The Big Three—President Roosevelt, Prime Minister Churchill, and Premier Stalin—decided upon procedures for voting in the UN Security Council and called on the Allies to send delegates to San Francisco to prepare the UN Charter.

**3. San Francisco Conference (April-June, 1945).** Despite the death of President Roosevelt just before the conference, delegates representing 50 nations met as planned. They completed the UN Charter.

The United States became the first nation to ratify the charter, as the Senate overwhelmingly approved American membership. Also, the United States provided the UN with headquarters located in New York City.

## PURPOSES OF THE UNITED NATIONS

The United Nations proposes to (1) maintain international peace and security, (2) use collective action to remove threats to peace and suppress acts of aggression, (3) develop friendly relations among nations, (4) promote respect for human rights without distinction as to race, sex, language, or religion, and (5) encourage international cooperation to solve economic, social, cultural, and humanitarian problems.

## ORGANIZATION OF THE UNITED NATIONS

### 1. General Assembly: The International Forum

*a. Membership and Voting.* The General Assembly consists of all UN member nations, now totaling about 150, each having one vote. General Assembly decisions on "important questions" require a two-thirds majority.

*b. Powers.* The General Assembly has the power to (1) discuss international problems fully and freely; (2) make recommendations to member nations, to the Economic and Social Council, to the Trusteeship Council, and to the Security Council; (3) elect members of other UN organs; (4) with the prior recommendation of the Security Council suspend or expel any member nation persistently violating UN principles and admit "peace-loving" nations to membership; (5) approve the UN budget and apportion the expenses among the member nations; and (6) propose UN Charter amendments, which come into effect when ratified by two-thirds of the member nations, including all permanent members of the Security Council.

*c. Sessions.* The General Assembly meets in *regular* session annually, for about three months. If necessary, however, the Assembly may be summoned into *special* session.

### 2. Security Council: The Executive Agency

*a. Membership.* The Security Council consists of 15 members: (1) Five are *permanent:* the United States, Great Britain, France, Russia, and China. (Until 1971 China's seat was held by the Nationalist regime, which since 1949 controlled only the island of Taiwan. In 1971, as the United States and Communist China moved toward a better relationship, the General Assembly voted, with American support, to admit Communist China as representative of the Chinese people and, despite American opposition, to expel the Nationalist delegation as representative only of Taiwan.) (2) Ten are *nonpermanent,* each elected for a two-year term by the General Assembly.

*b. Voting.* Decisions by the Security Council on important matters require the affirmative vote of nine members, including the five permanent members. Thus, by a negative vote, any one of the Big Five can defeat a Security Council

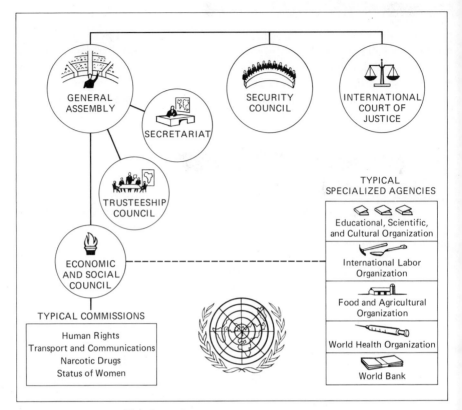

**The Organization of the United Nations**

decision, that is, exercise its *veto power*. Abstention from voting by a permanent member is not considered a veto.

*c. Powers.* The Security Council has the primary responsibility of maintaining international peace and security. It is empowered to (1) investigate disputes that endanger world peace, (2) make recommendations for peaceful settlement, and (3) if necessary, call upon UN member nations to take economic or military action against an aggressor nation.

*d. Sessions.* To be able to deal instantly with any international crisis, the Security Council functions *continuously*.

### 3. Secretariat: The Civil Service

*a. Personnel and Duties.* The Secretariat consists of the *Secretary General* and a staff. They are charged with primary loyalty to the United Nations. The secretary general is appointed (usually for a five-year term) by the General Assembly upon the recommendation of the Security Council. The secretary general selects and directs a staff, numbering several thousand employees, to perform UN clerical and administrative work. In addition the secretary general is authorized to (1) bring to the attention of the Security Council any matter threatening world peace and (2) perform other tasks as requested by major UN organs. Such tasks have included the undertaking of special diplomatic missions and the directing of UN emergency military forces.

*b. Persons Serving as Secretary General.* (1) *Trygve Lie* of Norway (1946–1953), (2) *Dag Hammarskjold* of Sweden (1953–1961), (3) *U Thant* of Burma (1961–1971), (4) *Kurt Waldheim* of Austria (1972–    ).

**4. International Court of Justice: The Court for Nations.** The International Court of Justice consists of 15 judges who decide cases by majority vote. The Court has the power to *(a)* settle legal disputes between nations and *(b)* grant UN organs advisory opinions on legal questions. Nations submitting disputes to the Court agree in advance to accept its decisions.

**5. Trusteeship Council: For Protection of Colonial Peoples**

*a. Membership and Voting.* The Trusteeship Council consists now of the five permanent Security Council members: Four do not administer any trust territories (see pages 328–329); the United States administers the sole remaining trust territory—certain Pacific islands. The council's decisions require a simple majority.

*b. Powers.* The Trusteeship Council was established to supervise trusteeships so as to safeguard colonial peoples. It received power to (1) consider reports from the administering nations, (2) examine petitions from the peoples of the trust territories, (3) with consent of the administering nation, send an investigating committee, and (4) report to the General Assembly. As trust territories gained independence, the work of the Trusteeship Council diminished.

**6. Economic and Social Council (ECOSOC): For Humanity's Welfare**

*a. Membership and Voting.* The Economic and Social Council consists of 27 members, each elected for a three-year term by the General Assembly. Decisions require a simple majority, each member nation having one vote.

*b. Powers.* The Economic and Social Council is concerned with improving economic, social, cultural, educational, and health conditions throughout the world. ECOSOC may conduct studies and make recommendations to UN member nations and to the General Assembly. Through ECOSOC's efforts the UN hopes to eliminate the underlying causes of war.

*c. ECOSOC Commissions and Committees.* To further its objectives, ECOSOC organized (1) the *Commission on Human Rights,* which seeks to encourage respect for human rights and fundamental freedoms for all persons, regardless of race, sex, language, or religion, and (2) other commissions and committees concerned with such problems as control of narcotics, prevention of crime, and the status of women. ECOSOC also receives reports from such UN bodies as the UN Children's Fund and the High Commissioner for Refugees.

## SPECIALIZED AGENCIES

The specialized agencies are independent organizations, some predating the United Nations, that came into existence by intergovernmental agreement. They include most (but not all) nations as members, secure their funds chiefly by voluntary contributions from member nations, directly serve only those nations that request assistance, and they coordinate their efforts with the UN through the Economic and Social Council.

The United States joined all the specialized agencies, actively participated in their work, and provided them with substantial funds. These agencies conduct some of the most important yet least publicized UN activities.

1. The **United Nations Educational, Scientific, and Cultural Organization (UNESCO)** seeks to promote the worldwide exchange of information on education, science, and culture. UNESCO undertakes projects to raise educational standards and to combat ignorance and prejudice. UNESCO contains in its charter the statement: "Since wars begin in the minds of men, it is in the minds of men that the defenses of peace must be constructed."

2. The **International Labor Organization (ILO)** endeavors to improve world labor conditions. ILO defines minimum labor standards and assists countries in formulating labor laws.

3. The **Food and Agriculture Organization (FAO)** Attempts to raise world food and nutrition levels. FAO provides information to improve methods of growing and distributing food.

4. The **World Health Organization (WHO)** seeks to improve world health standards. WHO surveys health conditions, combats mass diseases and epidemics, and helps nations improve public health services.

5. The **International Bank for Reconstruction and Development (World Bank)** encourages economic progress by providing loans to countries for large-scale projects, such as electric power plants and railroads.

6. Other specialized agencies: (a) the **International Civil Aviation Organization (ICAO)** improves civil aviation facilities and standardizes laws regarding use of air lanes; (b) the **Universal Postal Union (UPU)** provides uniform mail procedures; and (c) the **World Meteorological Organization (WMO)** coordinates data on weather and develops weather-forecasting services.

## Major Actions Taken by the United Nations

### ACTIONS PERTAINING TO SOCIAL AND ECONOMIC MATTERS

1. **Children's Fund.** In 1946 the General Assembly created the *United Nations International Children's Emergency Fund (UNICEF)*. It provides food, vita-

mins, and medicine to millions of needy children and trains nurses to help mothers learn proper child care. UNICEF's activities, now permanent, are financed by voluntary contributions of governments and individuals. (American youngsters raise funds for UNICEF by making Halloween "trick or treat" collections and by selling UNICEF greeting cards.)

**2. Declaration of Human Rights.** In 1948 the General Assembly overwhelmingly approved the *Declaration of Human Rights,* drawn up by the ECOSOC Commission on Human Rights. The declaration states that all human beings are born free and equal and are entitled to *(a) civil rights:* life, liberty, freedom of religion, speech, and assembly, and a voice in their government; *(b) legal rights:* freedom from arbitrary arrest and the right to a fair trial; *(c) economic rights:* employment, participation in labor unions, an adequate living standard, private property, and leisure time; and *(d) social rights:* education and a cultural life.

Although these ideals will not soon be realized throughout the world, they provide a "standard of achievement for all peoples and all nations."

**3. Genocide Convention.** In 1948 the General Assembly adopted the *Genocide Convention,* drawn up by the Commission on Human Rights. This convention declares illegal the deliberate extermination of any human group (as the Nazis had attempted with Jews and gypsies) and provides that violators be tried before an international court. The convention, ratified by over 60 nations, represents an attempt to rally world opinion in favor of granting all people freedom from fear.

**4. Technical Assistance.** In 1949 the United Nations and several specialized agencies began the *Expanded Program of Technical Assistance.* This program coordinates efforts to improve social and economic conditions in over 140 underdeveloped territories and countries, chiefly in Africa, Asia, and Latin America. Technical experts have helped underdeveloped peoples increase food production, develop natural resources, build industries, fight disease, and reduce illiteracy. Nationals of underdeveloped areas have received fellowships to study abroad and return to their homelands as technicians and professionals.

## ACTIONS PERTAINING TO INTERNATIONAL DISPUTES

In dealing with international disputes, the UN has compiled a mixed record: in some cases—success; in other cases—inconclusive response; in still others—failure.

**1. Iran.** In 1946 Iran complained that Russia had not withdrawn troops stationed on Iranian soil during World War II. Russia objected to Security Council discussion of the complaint but removed its troops.

**2. Greece.** In 1946 the Greek government charged that three Communist nations—Yugoslavia, Albania, and Bulgaria—were aiding rebel Communist guerrilla bands in northern Greece. The United Nations *(a)* sent an investigating commission, which confirmed the Greek charges, and *(b)* requested the Communist nations to stop supporting the guerrilla bands. Following the split between Yugoslavia and Russia in 1948, Yugoslavia ceased aiding the Greek rebels and the rebellion collapsed. (For American efforts to help Greece, check the Index for the Truman Doctrine.)

**3. Palestine.** In 1947–1948 the General Assembly *(a)* received the Palestine problem from Britain, *(b)* conducted an investigation, and *(c)* approved the partition of Palestine into an Arab state and a Jewish state. The UN decision was defied by the Arab nations, which attacked the new Jewish state, Israel, but without military success. In 1949 *Ralph Bunche*, UN mediator, succeeded in arranging a truce. (Check the Index for Arab-Israeli wars.)

**4. Indonesia.** In 1947–1949 the United Nations *(a)* arranged truces ending hostilities between Dutch and Indonesian forces and *(b)* assisted in negotiations that led to Indonesia's independence. (Check the Index for Indonesia.)

**5. Korea.** After World War II Korea, a former Japanese possession, was divided into American and Russian zones of occupation. In 1948 a UN commission to unify Korea held elections in United States-occupied South Korea but was denied admission into Russian-occupied North Korea.

In 1950 the North Korean Communists invaded South Korea. The Security Council (with Russia absent) called upon the invaders to withdraw and, when that request was ignored, asked UN member nations to provide military aid to South Korea. Sixteen nations sent troops to bolster South Korean forces. This first UN army consisted chiefly of South Koreans and Americans. In 1951, after Communist Chinese forces entered the Korean War, the General Assembly declared China guilty of aggression. In mid-1951 the UN command began negotiations with the Communists and in 1953 achieved a truce. (Check the Index for Korea.)

**6. Kashmir.** Since 1948 the United Nations *(a)* helped end hostilities between India and Pakistan over Kashmir; *(b)* secured agreement of both nations to a UN-supervised plebiscite; *(c)* was defied when India annexed, without any plebiscite, that portion of Kashmir held by Indian troops; and *(d)* declared India's action not binding upon the United Nations.

**7. Hungary.** In 1956 Russian troops suppressed a revolt of the Hungarian people against the Russian-dominated government of their country. The UN General Assembly overwhelmingly condemned Russia and demanded that Russia *(a)* cease its intervention in Hungarian affairs; *(b)* withdraw its military forces from Hungary; and *(c)* admit UN observers into the revolt-torn country. Russia defied the UN by rejecting these demands. (Check the Index for Hungary.)

**8. Egypt: 1956**

    *a. Background.* Check the Index for Egypt, and Suez Canal crisis.

*b. The UN and the Invasion of Egypt.* The General Assembly overwhelmingly condemned the invasion by British, French, and Israeli troops. It passed resolutions demanding a cease-fire and the withdrawal of the invading forces. The resolutions were heeded. The General Assembly then requested member nations (excluding the Big Five) to volunteer troops for an international police force, the *United Nations Emergency Force (UNEF)*. For ten years the UNEF maintained peace in the area.

## 9. The Congo: 1960–1961

*a. Background.* Following independence the Congo experienced widespread disorder, a secessionist movement by Katanga province (now named Shaba), continued occupation by Belgian troops, and cold war rivalries. (For details, check the Index under Zaire.)

*b. The UN and the Congo Crisis.* The UN Security Council (1) called on Belgium to withdraw its troops and (2) authorized Secretary General Hammarskjold to restore order in the Congo by means of a United Nations Emergency Force (UNEF). Under Hammarskjold's direction the UNEF helped prevent bloodshed and violence. Although Russia demanded that he support pro-Communist Premier Lumumba in the Congolese power struggle, Hammarskjold remained neutral.

Meanwhile, Lumumba was removed from office, arrested by the Congo army, and slain by his political foes. Eventually the Congo government passed into anti-Communist hands, Belgium withdrew its troops, and Katanga was brought back under central control.

*c. Dispute Over Hammarskjold and the UN Congo Operation*

(1) *Russia Attacks Hammarskjold.* Enraged by Lumumba's fall from power, Russia blamed Hammarskjold and demanded his resignation. Soviet Premier Khrushchev proposed that the duties of the secretary general be taken over by a "troika," a three-member board of Western, Soviet, and neutralist representatives, each with veto power. (2) *Hammarskjold Receives Support.* With the overwhelming support of the Western and most Afro-Asian nations, Hammarskjold refused to resign. He pointed out that the Soviet Union could prevent the election of a new secretary general and, by insisting upon the creation of a veto-dominated three-member board, would weaken the UN. (3) *Hammarskjold Dies.* After Hammarskjold died on a Congo peace mission, he received worldwide tribute for his devotion to the UN. Thereupon, Russia ceased its demand for a three-member secretary general and agreed to Burma's *U Thant* as Hammarskjold's successor.

10. **Goa.** In 1961 India seized Goa, a tiny Portuguese colony on the Indian coast. At the UN India was defended by most Afro-Asian nations and by Russia, which vetoed a Western resolution urging India to withdraw its troops and negotiate with Portugal. The UN took no other action.

## 11. Cyprus: 1963, 1974

*a. Background.* Check the Index for Cyprus.

*b. UN and the First Cyprus Crisis.* In 1963 Cyprus was torn by civil war between its Greek and Turkish Cypriote peoples. With Greece and Turkey each threatening to intervene militarily, the Security Council authorized a UN peace force that restored order on Cyprus.

*c. UN and the Second Cyprus Crisis.* In 1974 Greek Cypriote forces, led by Greek officers who planned to unite Cyprus with Greece, overthrew the Makarios government. This coup led to renewed civil war between Greek Cypriote and Turkish Cypriote communities and then to an invasion of Cyprus by Turkish troops. Despite Security Council cease-fire calls, the Turkish troops continued to advance, gaining control of 40 percent of the island. Thereafter the fighting ceased, but the problems of Cyprus—aid to war refugees, exchange of prisoners, and a political solution—remained.

## 12. Rhodesia (Zimbabwe): Since 1965

*a. Background.* Check the Index for Rhodesia.

*b. The UN and Rhodesia.* Britain secured a Security Council resolution requesting all UN members to apply economic sanctions against white minority-ruled Rhodesia. This resolution was derided by most African nations, which contended that economic sanctions would not topple the Smith regime and demanded that Britain use military force. In 1970 a Security Council resolution condemning Britain for not using force against Rhodesia was vetoed by Britain and the United States. (In 1980, following an agreement by the interested parties, Britain granted independence to the new nation of Zimbabwe.)

## 13. South-West Africa (Namibia): Since 1966

*a. Background.* Check the Index for South-West Africa.

*b. The UN and Namibia.* In 1966 the General Assembly (1) declared South Africa's mandate over South-West Africa at an end, (2) ordered UN control of the territory, and (3) created a committee to guide South-West Africa to independence. In 1973 the General Assembly declared the "representative of the Namibian people" to be the South-West Africa People's Organization (SWAPO)—a Communist-supported guerrilla group. More recently, South Africa pledged independence for the territory but rejected any role for SWAPO.

**14. Arab-Israeli War of 1967.** Following the outbreak of fighting, the Security Council passed several resolutions calling for a cease-fire. These resolutions, accepted by the victorious Israelis and eventually by the three vanquished Arab states, helped end the hostilities. (Check the Index for Arab-Israeli War of 1967.)

The Soviet Union, in support of the Arab cause, introduced a Security

Council resolution *(a)* condemning Israel as the aggressor and *(b)* demanding the withdrawal of Israeli forces to the 1949 armistice lines. The Soviet resolution was opposed by the United States as a "prescription for renewed hostilities," since it did not link the withdrawal of Israeli forces to steps for a durable peace. The Soviet resolution was overwhelmingly defeated in the Security Council and in an emergency session of the General Assembly. (The General Assembly approved, however, a resolution declaring invalid Israel's unification of Jerusalem.)

The Security Council later adopted an evenhanded statement—Resolution 242—calling for the *(a)* withdrawal of Israeli forces from the occupied territories, *(b)* right of every Middle Eastern state to live in peace within secure boundaries and free from acts of force, *(c)* free navigation of international waterways, and *(d)* just settlement of the refugee problem.

## 15. Indian-Pakistani War of 1971

*a. Background.* Check the Index for Pakistan, war with India.

*b. At the United Nations.* In the Security Council Communist China supported West Pakistan while Russia supported and the United States condemned India. Three Security Council resolutions, calling for a cease-fire and withdrawal of Indian forces, were vetoed by the Soviet Union. Thereupon, the General Assembly considered the issue and voted overwhelmingly for a cease-fire and withdrawal of military forces. India ignored this resolution, and its chief representative called the Assembly "not very realistic." With the war over the Security Council passed a resolution requesting observance of the cease-fire and aid for the Bengali refugees in India. Meanwhile, Pakistani representative *Zulfikar Ali Bhutto*, who was to become the new president of Pakistan, denounced the UN as a "fraud and a farce."

## 16. Arab-Israeli War of 1973

*a. Background.* Check the Index.

*b. The Security Council Cease-fire.* Despite the Arab aggression, Israel did not request a Security Council meeting, asserting that the UN had never stopped any attack on Israel and that, given the size of the Arab, Moslem, and Communist bloc, the Security Council could not achieve a "balanced discussion." The United States requested a Security Council meeting simply for a resolution to halt the hostilities; but with the Arab forces still maintaining their military initiative, the pro-Arab bloc insisted on including a demand that Israel unilaterally withdraw from the 1967-occupied territories. The Security Council remained unable to act. As the Israeli forces turned the tide of battle, the Soviet Union speeded diplomatic moves to protect its Arab "clients." The Soviet Union and the United States jointly secured adoption of an evenhanded Security Council resolution *(a)* calling for an immediate cease-fire, *(b)* reaffirming the 1967 request for an Israeli withdrawal coupled with the 1967 statement that

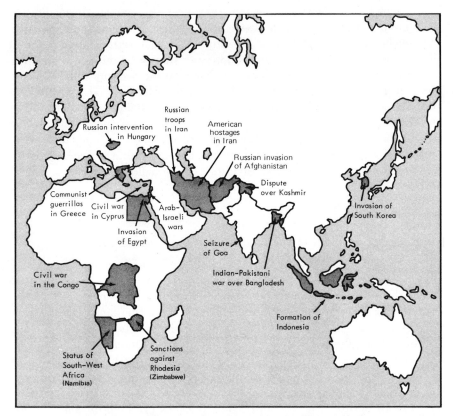

Russian troops in Iran
Russian intervention in Hungary
American hostages in Iran
Russian invasion of Afghanistan
Communist guerrillas in Greece
Civil war in Cyprus
Dispute over Kashmir
Arab-Israeli wars
Invasion of South Korea
Invasion of Egypt
Seizure of Goa
Civil war in the Congo
Indian-Pakistani war over Bangladesh
Formation of Indonesia
Status of South-West Africa (Namibia)
Sanctions against Rhodesia (Zimbabwe)

**International Disputes Considered in the United Nations**

every Mideastern nation has the right to live in peace within secure boundaries, and (c) urging negotiations for a "just and durable peace." The UN cease-fire was accepted by Israel, Egypt, and Syria. The Security Council also approved creation of a UNEF force of 7,000 (excluding troops of the Big Five) to serve as a buffer between the opposing armies.

### c. Subsequent General Assembly Votes:

(1) *On the Palestine Liberation Organization (PLO)*. In 1974 the General Assembly overwhelmingly voted to debate the "Palestine question." It invited the *Palestine Liberation Organization (PLO)*—a coordinating Arab group—to attend as "representative of the Palestinian people," heard *Yasir Arafat* as PLO head demand establishment of a Palestinian state, and then overwhelmingly voted for a resolution declaring the right of the Palestinian people to national independence and sovereignty.

Israel bitterly opposed the General Assembly actions. Israeli officials called the PLO an organization of several thousand terrorists representing only themselves, assailed the demand for a Palestinian state as meaning the destruction of Israel, condemned the resolution for not affirming the right of Israel to exist, and concluded that General Assembly actions would deter progress toward a just and durable Middle East peace. Israel was supported in the General Assembly voting by few nations, the most important one being the United States.

(2) *On Zionism.* Simply stated, Zionism is the Jewish nationalist movement to reestablish and defend a Jewish homeland in Palestine. (See page 382.)

In 1975 the General Assembly approved an Arab-sponsored resolution condemning Zionism as "a form of racism and racial discrimination." In support were 72 nations—mainly Arab, Moslem, and Communist; in opposition were 35 nations—mainly the Western democracies; in abstention were 32 nations.

This resolution against Zionism was part of the Arab diplomatic offensive against Israel. The Israeli delegate at the UN condemned the resolution as reminiscent of Nazi anti-Semitism. *Daniel Moynihan,* the American delegate, expressed his country's outrage at the resolution, warning that the United States "will never acquiesce in this infamous act." UN Secretary General Waldheim deplored the resolution for worsening divisions among nations "at a time when the need for understanding . . . is more than ever necessary."

Knudsen in *The San Diego Union*

**"Ouch!"**

Dennis Renault, *Sacramento Bee (Calif.)*

**"Mirror, mirror, on the wall / Who's the most influential . . . ?"**

**17. Iran.** In 1979 militant Iranians in the capital city of Teheran seized the American embassy and took 50 staff members as hostages. For release of the hostages, the militants demanded that the United States return the deposed Shah to Iran to be punished for his "crimes." The United States refused and demanded the unconditional release of the hostages—a position supported unanimously by the UN Security Council and the World Court. In 1981 Iran reached agreement with the United States and released the hostages. (For details, check the Index.)

**18. Afghanistan.** In 1979–1980 Soviet forces invaded Afghanistan to uphold a pro-Soviet government and to suppress a rebellion by Islamic guerrillas. The Soviets vetoed a UN Security Council resolution calling for "the withdrawal of all foreign troops"; thereafter the General Assembly, by a vote of 104 to 18, passed a similar resolution. The Soviets belittled the General Assembly action and their troops remained in Afghanistan. (For details, check the Index.)

**19. Israeli Raid on the Iraqi Nuclear Facility.** In 1981 the UN Security Council unanimously passed a resolution to "strongly condemn" Israel for this raid and to urge Israel to open its nuclear power plants to inspection by the International Atomic Energy Agency. Israel rejected the resolution as further evidence of the UN's "biased and one-sided" attitude on matters affecting Israel. (For details of the raid, check the Index.)

Scholarship

## AN ANALYSIS OF THE UNITED NATIONS

### 1. An Optimistic View: Effectiveness of the UN

*a. Almost Universal Membership.* The UN is the world's most representative body of nations. It mirrors the hopes and fears of humanity.

*b. Availability of a Forum.* The UN provides a forum where member nations may present their views on world problems.

*c. Uniting for Peace Resolution.* This resolution enables the General Assembly to deal with a threat to world peace if the Security Council fails to act because of a veto. It states that the General Assembly (1) if not in session, may be summoned into emergency session within 24 hours and (2) may recommend, by a two-thirds vote, that UN members take collective action, including the use of armed force. The Uniting for Peace resolution was first invoked during the 1956 Egyptian and Hungarian crises.

*d. Resolving International Problems.* Through the UN many international problems have been solved, brought closer to a solution, or at least kept from erupting into a major war. Examples of UN achievements include (1) independence for Indonesia, (2) the 1948 partition of Palestine, and (3) the 1956 withdrawal of invading forces from Egypt.

*e. UN Military Forces.* The UN has secured the military cooperation of a number of member nations. Examples are (1) the formation of a UN army to repel aggression against South Korea and (2) the creation of UNEF units to preserve peace in the Middle East, the Congo, and Cyprus.

*f. Economic and Social Progress.* The Economic and Social Council and the specialized agencies have worked toward eliminating some economic and social causes of war. The technical assistance program has improved conditions in many underdeveloped countries.

*g. Colonial Independence.* The Trusteeship Council has helped colonial peoples form independent nations, including Cameroon, Togo, Somalia, Tanganyika (now part of Tanzania), Rwanda, and Burundi.

*h. Preventing International Anarchy.* The UN keeps the world from reverting to international anarchy. It serves as a bridge between the opposing sides in the cold war and enables the neutral nations to exert influence.

## 2. A Pessimistic View: Problems Besetting the UN

*a. Blocs Within the UN.* The UN consists of three blocs: (1) The *Western bloc* (about 50 nations) includes the United States, Western Europe, most of Latin America, and some British Commonwealth members. This bloc generally —but not always—supports American leadership. (2) The *Soviet Communist bloc* (about 10 nations) follows Russian policy. (3) The *Afro-Asian,* or *Third World, bloc* (about 85 nations) has grown tremendously and now constitutes a UN majority. The Afro-Asian nations oppose colonialism, and most claim to favor cold war neutrality. Communist China has sought to speak for the Afro-Asian bloc but has had only limited success in securing united Afro-Asian support.

Blocs are a divisive force and tend to aggravate international friction.

*b. Self-serving Use of UN Organs and Specialized Agencies.* UN members often consider international problems on the basis of individual or bloc interests rather than on the basis of UN principles. Most Afro-Asian nations approved India's seizure of Goa, although the UN Charter prohibits the use of force.

In the 1970's Communist and Arab nations with Third World support "politicized" the work of UN specialized agencies. At the ILO the Communist nations secured condemnation of the military regime in Chile for "denying trade union rights." But using a double standard, the ILO has not said a word about the denial of such rights in Communist and many Third World nations. At WHO the Arab nations secured rejection of a report by WHO experts that Israel had improved health conditions of Arab peoples under Israeli control. At UNESCO the Arab nations in 1974 secured condemnation of Israel for archaeological excavations in Jerusalem and achieved UNESCO expulsion of Israel. In 1976, by a technical maneuver, UNESCO readmitted Israel.

Also at UNESCO, Soviet-bloc and Third World nations secured approval for the preparation of a so-called New World Information Order that would empower UNESCO to draw up a code of journalistic ethics, to regulate the flow of

*Crawford. Reprinted by permission of NEA.*

**Bear Market**

"Bear market" is an economics term used to denote values that are sharply falling. What is the cartoonist saying about UN prestige? According to the cartoonist, what has caused this trend in UN prestige? What other factors might be considered? How could the UN reverse this trend?

world news, and to "license" journalists. The Western world's free news organizations viewed these proposals as attempts to justify government censorship over the news media and to restrict Western-type press freedom. In 1981 they vowed to oppose UNESCO's efforts to curtail the "free circulation of news."

In a 1974 speech the chief American representative to the United Nations deplored bloc voting and self-serving use of the UN by Communist, Arab, and other Third World nations. He referred specifically to the majority's decisions in the 1974 General Assembly to exclude South Africa entirely from the meeting and to curb the participation of Israel in the discussion of the "Palestine question." He warned that, by adopting unrealistic, one-sided positions and resolutions, the General Assembly was eroding support for the UN in the American Congress and among the American people. He further declared that "when the rule of the majority becomes the tyranny of the majority, the minority will cease to respect or obey it." The American representative urged the General Assembly to fulfill its true function: "to bridge the differences among its member states."

In 1975, at AFL-CIO and business prodding, the United States gave the required two-year notice of intent to withdraw from the ILO. The United States was particularly incensed that the ILO did not apply its labor standards equally to all nations, including Communist and Third World countries, and that the ILO accepted government delegates as worker representatives from countries that had no free labor unions. In 1977 the United States withdrew, thereby ending its

ILO financial support (about 25 percent of ILO's budget) and expressing American displeasure with the "politicizing" of the UN and the specialized agencies.

(In 1980, as the ILO seemed to be abandoning its "politicizing" activities and returning to its original purpose—improving the condition of workers—the United States rejoined the organization.)

**c. Veto Power.** Russia has used the veto over 100 times, thereby limiting the effectiveness of the Security Council. The United States, Britain, and France each has used the veto only a handful of times.

The initial American vetoes were: (1) In 1970 the United States vetoed a resolution that condemned Britain for not using force to end white rule in Rhodesia. (2) In 1972 the United States vetoed a resolution that condemned Israel for reprisal raids against Palestinian guerrillas in Lebanon without mentioning the provocation—the murder of 11 Israeli athletes at the Munich Olympic Games by Palestinian terrorists. (3) In 1973 the United States vetoed a resolution calling upon it to conclude a new "just and fair treaty" that would assure Panama "effective sovereignty" over the Panama Canal Zone. The resolution made no mention of American efforts to achieve a new treaty and satisfy many Panamanian demands. (4) In 1974 the United States, together with Britain and France, vetoed a resolution to expel South Africa from the United Nations. While deploring South Africa's racial policies, the American delegate asserted that "expulsion would set a shattering precedent," damaging the UN.

**d. Defiance of UN Resolutions.** Some nations have defied UN resolutions, claiming that the issue involved was a domestic matter not subject to UN jurisdiction or insisting that they were protecting their national interests. Examples of defiance of the UN include (1) the 1948 Arab attack on Israel, (2) Russia's refusal to permit UN-supervised elections in North Korea, (3) Russia's suppression of the Hungarian rebellion, (4) India's annexation of part of Kashmir, and (5) South Africa's insistence on apartheid.

**e. Lack of Military Power.** The UN does not have its own military force. It depends on member nations to honor resolutions requesting armed forces. Only 16 nations—at that time constituting about one-fourth of the UN membership—heeded the call for troops to aid South Korea.

**f. Financial Difficulties.** The UN secures funds for its regular budget by assessing member nations according to ability to pay. In 1975 the United States was first, being assessed 25 percent of the UN regular budget; the Soviet Union was second, being assessed 13 percent. In addition the United States has voluntarily contributed up to 45 percent of funds for UN special activities—such as UNICEF, WHO, and technical assistance—whereas the Soviet Union has voluntarily contributed only 1.5 percent.

The UN has been in financial straits because certain nations have been unable or unwilling to pay their regular assessments and to pay special assessments for UNEF peacekeeping operations. For example, Communist and Arab states refused to pay their share of UNEF Middle East expenses.

**g. Bypassing the UN.** The major nations have frequently resorted to direct diplomacy outside the UN. The United States, Russia, and Britain directly negotiated the nuclear test ban treaty. The United States and Russia directly concluded the SALT I missile agreements. The UN loses prestige whenever nations ignore its facilities.

**h. Withdrawal and Return of Indonesia.** In 1965 Indonesia, under the leftist government of President *Sukarno*, resigned from the UN. Sukarno claimed that the world organization was being manipulated by imperialist powers. In 1966 the Indonesian army ended Sukarno's power. Indonesia then returned to the UN, but its withdrawal and return established an unfortunate precedent.

**i. Limited Action Against International Terrorism.** Extremist groups have employed terrorism—deliberate violence against innocent civilians—so as to further the extremists' political goals. Black revolutionaries in the United States hijacked American airplanes to Cuba and Algeria to escape from American authorities and sometimes to secure ransom and the release of other terrorists. Turkish extremists hijacked a Turkish airplane to Bulgaria and demanded that Turkey release three guerrillas sentenced to death for kidnapping and murder. Croatian separatists (opposed to Tito's Yugoslavia) hijacked a Swedish plane to Spain to secure the release of six Croatians imprisoned in Sweden for murder. South Moluccan terrorists in the Netherlands seized Dutch hostages to gain publicity and support for their goal of Moluccan independence from Indonesia.

Palestinian extremist groups seeking to destroy Israel have been the most active terrorists. They have planted bombs to blow up planes of pro-Western nations flying passengers to Israel. Also, they have hijacked pro-Western passenger planes to secure ransom or the release of captured Arab extremists. In recent years Palestinian guerrillas claimed responsibility for several particularly brutal massacres. In 1972 they employed three Japanese left-wing extremists who disembarked at the Israeli airport at Tel Aviv and with machine guns and hand grenades killed 25 persons (including 15 Puerto Ricans on a pilgrimage to the Holy Land) and wounded 77 others. Later, Black September terrorists murdered 11 Israeli athletes at the Munich Olympic Games. In 1973 Black September terrorists coldbloodedly executed three diplomats—two Americans and a Belgian—in the Sudan. In 1974 Arab terrorists seized the school at the Israeli town of Ma'alot and murdered more than 20 schoolchildren.

Secretary General Kurt Waldheim proposed that the General Assembly act to prevent international terrorism. His proposal was defeated in the General Assembly's Legal Committee by a coalition of Arab, Communist, and Third World nations. These nations claimed that terrorism was a legitimate weapon of peoples battling "alien regimes" to secure "self-determination." The United States, Britain, Canada, and other pro-Western nations were disappointed. These nations planned to cooperate in undertaking their own anti-terrorist measures, thereby bypassing the United Nations.

In the mid-1970's, as terrorist attacks continued, many pro-Western nations toughened their stand against terrorists, enforced stringent airport security measures, and trained special commando units to combat airborne terrorism. In 1976, Israeli commandos flew to Entebbe airport in Uganda and rescued 102 Jewish hostages held by pro-Arab terrorists backed up by Ugandan troops. In 1977 West German commandos flew to Somalia and, with the cooperation of the Somali government, rescued 86 hostages, mainly West Germans, held by four Arabic-speaking terrorists. Then the UN General Assembly approved a resolution requesting all member nations to combat air hijackings by strengthening airport security measures and by agreeing to prosecute or extradite hijackers. While some observers hailed this resolution as a significant UN move, others viewed it as a weak response lacking power to diminish airborne terrorism.

In 1981 terrorists attacked three leading world figures. An American terrorist wounded President Reagan; a right-wing Turkish terrorist wounded Pope John Paul II; and Islamic extremists assassinated Egyptian President Sadat.

**3. A Realistic View.** The United Nations is not meant to be a world government; it is a loose confederation whose member states retain their sovereignty. The United Nations is only an instrument available for their use. Although the UN embodies humanity's highest hopes, its strength and influence will reflect the wishes of the world's peoples and governments.

© *Washington Star Syndicate, Inc., permission granted by King Features Syndicate, Inc. 1978*

**The Small Society**

## MULTIPLE–CHOICE QUESTIONS

1. "They hope to see established a peace . . . which will afford assurance that all the men in all the lands may live out their lives in freedom from fear and want" is quoted from the (1) Atlantic Charter (2) Genocide Convention (3) United Nations Charter (4) Lend-Lease Act.

2. According to the UN Charter, each nation's voting strength in the General Assembly is according to (1) size (2) population (3) military strength (4) the principle of one vote per nation.

3. According to the UN Charter, the General Assembly meets (1) in continuous session (2) at least once a year (3) only when called by the secretary general (4) only in time of emergency.

4. Which agency of the UN was given primary responsibility for investigating situations that threaten world peace? (1) the Economic and Social Council (2) the Secretariat (3) the Security Council (4) the Trusteeship Council.

5. The UN Charter gives the Security Council the power to (1) veto decisions of the Assembly (2) cancel treaties made by member nations (3) recommend the use of force to stop aggression (4) elect the secretary general.

6. A resolution proposed in the Security Council may be vetoed by (1) any member of the Security Council (2) the secretary general (3) any permanent member of the Security Council (4) only the Soviet Union and the United States.

7. The distribution of power within the Security Council is based on the principle that (1) neutral nations are an effective power bloc (2) important questions are settled by the International Court of Justice (3) agreement among the major nations is necessary if the organization is to succeed (4) large and small nations have equal influence in decisions about world problems.

8. A *major* criticism of the voting procedure in the Security Council is that (1) the Soviet Union has as much voting power as the United States (2) a veto by any permanent member can prevent or delay action (3) the permanent members have more votes than the nonpermanent members (4) most member nations have no voting power in the Security Council.

9. The nonpermanent members of the Security Council are selected by the (1) General Assembly (2) Economic and Social Council (3) five permanent members of the Council (4) Secretariat.

10. The UN Secretary General is most likely to come from a neutralist nation because (1) of a UN Charter provision (2) the salary is paid by the neutralist bloc (3) the appointment must be recommended by the Security Council (4) of a tradition originating in the League of Nations.

11. One function of the Economic and Social Council is to (1) settle boundary disputes between nations (2) promote respect for human rights (3) direct the economies of underdeveloped nations (4) regulate the use of atomic energy.

12. The specialized agencies connected with the UN raise their funds *chiefly* by (1) voluntary contributions of member nations (2) a worldwide tax on exports (3) charges for services rendered (4) selling stamps, pamphlets, and books.

13. The specialized agency established to promote cultural cooperation and improve understanding among nations is (1) UNICEF (2) the Trusteeship Council (3) WHO (4) UNESCO.

14. A weakness of UNESCO in its effort to foster world understanding is that it (1) must report to ECOSOC (2) is subject to "Big Five" veto power (3) cannot work within a country unless invited (4) selects its personnel chiefly from Communist countries.

15. Since its inception, the United Nations has (1) admitted many new member nations (2) adopted a plan by which nations may withdraw from the UN (3) outlawed atomic weapons (4) established a permanent UN military force.

16. The Genocide Pact was the work of (1) the ILO (2) the Four Freedoms Committee (3) UNESCO (4) the Commission on Human Rights.

17. An accomplishment of the UN has been the (1) abolition of the veto power (2) establishment of a military government in Egypt (3) expansion of technical aid to underdeveloped regions (4) establishment of UN control of atomic energy.

18. The General Assembly resolution urging Russia to cease its interference in the Hungarian revolt of 1956 was (1) unable to secure a majority of the votes (2) defeated by the use of the veto (3) accepted by Russia (4) rejected by Russia.

19. The General Assembly resolution urging Israel, France, and Britain to cease their invasion of Egypt in 1956 was (1) opposed by the United States (2) accepted by Israel but rejected by France and Britain (3) accepted by the three nations concerned (4) opposed by Egypt.

20. "Since wars begin in the minds of men" is a phrase used in the UNESCO Charter to emphasize the need for (1) encouraging regional agreements on trade (2) expanding educational opportunities (3) controlling newspapers that stir up controversies (4) stopping research on atomic weapons.

21. Until 1971 the admission of Communist China to the United Nations had been vigorously opposed by (1) Egypt (2) Russia (3) India (4) the United States.

22. The Secretary General of the United Nations who was attacked by the Soviet Union for his conduct of the UN Congo operation was (1) Trygve Lie (2) Dag Hammarskjold (3) U Thant (4) Kurt Waldheim.

23. The UN finances its activities chiefly by (1) charging admission to visitors (2) assessing member nations (3) placing a tax upon citizens of UN member nations (4) selling UN stamps and souvenirs.

24. In 1950 the Security Council was able to pass a resolution calling upon the North Korean Communists to withdraw from South Korea because (1) Russia approved the resolution (2) Russia was absent from the meeting (3) Russia was prohibited from voting since it was directly concerned with the issue (4) the veto power had not yet gone into effect.

25. Which generalization is *best* supported by the record of UN actions? (1) The big powers are abandoning their nationalistic policies. (2) The spirit of nationalism is being replaced by a spirit of internationalism. (3) All nations are ready to abandon their imperialistic policies. (4) Crises in world trouble spots more often end in deadlocks than in permanent solutions.

26. When the American representative to the UN, in 1974, deplored the "tyranny of the majority," he was referring to (1) Russia's use of the veto (2) Communist China's insistence upon the ousting of Nationalist China (3) the actions of Third World nations in the General Assembly limiting the rights of any nation to which they were opposed (4) the policy of populous nations voting as a bloc.

27. The UN did not take strong action to stem international terrorism because terrorism (1) is declining (2) is better handled by nations acting individually (3) affects only Israel (4) is supported by many Asian, African, and Communist nations if employed for goals of which these nations approve.

28. Which problem has consistently troubled the United Nations? (1) member nations giving consideration only to their national interests (2) a steady decrease in membership of small nations (3) lack of a public forum where any nation may discuss world problems (4) fair distribution of its budgetary surpluses.

# MATCHING QUESTIONS

Column A lists disputes that were brought before the UN. For each dispute in column A, write the letter of the nation or nations in column B that were *directly* involved in that dispute.

| *Column A* | *Column B* |
|---|---|
| 1. Control of the Suez Canal | *a.* Belgium |
| 2. Independence for Indonesia | *b.* India and Portugal |
| 3. Independence for Bangladesh | *c.* India and Pakistan |
| 4. Status of Namibia | *d.* Britain, France, and Egypt |
| 5. Civil war on Cyprus | *e.* Greece and Turkey |
| 6. Foreign troops in the Congo | *f.* Russia |
| 7. Foreign troops in Hungary | *g.* South Africa |
| 8. Possession of Goa | *h.* Communist China and Korea |
| | *i.* The Netherlands |

# ESSAY QUESTIONS

1. The UN represents an effort to solve the problems of international tension in an age of extreme danger. *(a)* Describe *two* ways in which the UN represents an improvement over the League of Nations. *(b)* Discuss *two* different ways in which the UN attempts to maintain world peace. *(c)* Show how the United States has cooperated with the UN in meeting *two* international crises. *(d)* Explain *two* limitations on the ability of the UN to meet world problems.

2. *(a)* State *two* functions of *each* of the following specialized agencies associated with the United Nations: (1) WHO (2) FAO (3) ILO (4) UNESCO. *(b)* Discuss *two* weaknesses that hinder the work of these specialized agencies.

3. Using *two* specific facts, explain why *each* of the following represents a problem for the United Nations: *(a)* use of the veto *(b)* raising funds to finance UN activities *(c)* defiance of UN resolutions *(d)* "politicizing" of UN specialized agencies *(e)* "tyranny of the majority" in the General Assembly.

4. Explain how each of the following has presented a serious problem to the United Nations: *(a)* a divided Korea *(b)* bypassing of UN facilities *(c)* Arab efforts to destroy Israel *(d)* poverty in underdeveloped areas *(e)* communal warfare on Cyprus.

5. At a discussion on the United Nations, the following arguments were given:

| *For the United Nations* | *Against the United Nations* |
|---|---|
| *a.* The United Nations Charter has avoided the weaknesses of the Covenant of the League of Nations. | *a.* Since the United States pays about 25 percent of the cost of running the United Nations, our country might just as well "go it alone." |
| *b.* The war in Korea tested the strength of the United Nations and proved that it can stop aggression. | *b.* The frequent use of the veto power has made the United Nations helpless. |
| *c.* The UN serves as a safety valve where nations may talk out problems rather than resort to war. | *c.* By passing partisan and unrealistic resolutions that nations defy, the General Assembly has destroyed the prestige of the UN. |

Agree or disagree with any *two* of the above arguments, giving *two* specific facts for each to support your point of view.

# Part 2. Adversaries in the Cold War Era

## A. The Cold War: An Overview

### ORIGINS

The "cold war" originated immediately after World War II as a struggle between the free world nations, led by the United States, and the Communist nations, led by the Soviet Union. The American people were alarmed by *(a)* the expressed Soviet aim of communizing the world and *(b)* the expansion of Soviet power into Central Europe and Asia. President Truman began the American policy of keeping Russia from gaining control of any additional territories—a policy called *containment*.

### WEAPONS

The cold war has been fought by means of *(a)* *propaganda*, in newspapers, on radio and television, in street demonstrations, and at the UN; *(b)* *diplomatic moves*, including international conferences and military alliances; *(c)* *scientific competition*, reflected in the development of nuclear weapons and missiles, and in the undertaking of space flights; *(d)* *economic competition*, especially aid to underdeveloped countries; *(e)* *espionage*, conducted by extensive spy rings, by intelligence ships, and by data-gathering vehicles in orbit around the earth; and *(f)* *subversion*, chiefly by local Communist groups that have sought to weaken and overthrow pro-Western governments by demonstrations, strikes, and guerrilla warfare.

The cold war also has been marked by localized military action but not by all-out war. The world has been living under an uneasy armed truce—an absence of total war but also an absence of genuine peace.

### TODAY: A MORE COMPLEX SITUATION

Although the cold war originated in a world generally divided into an American bloc and a Soviet bloc, this simple division no longer exists. Each bloc has experienced strains, and the cold war has become much more complex.

1. **Free World.** The free world nations have become less dependent militarily and economically upon the United States. Some free world nations have disagreed sharply with the United States on foreign policy. France, under President de Gaulle, began to oppose American influence in Europe. De Gaulle

envisioned Europe as a French-led "third force" independent of the United States. Even Britain, our closest ally, diverged from American foreign policy by recognizing Communist China in 1950 and by trading with Communist Cuba.

2. **Communist World.** The Communist world has been troubled by disunity and discontent. Yugoslavia broke sharply with Stalinist Russia and adopted a program of national communism. China has challenged Russia for world Communist leadership and has bitterly disagreed with Soviet foreign policy. (Check the Index for China, Communist, and Soviet Union.)

### A Comparison of the Two Superpowers

| Russia | The United States |
|---|---|
| 1. *Dictatorial* government | 1. *Democratic* government |
| 2. *Communist* economic system | 2. *Capitalist* economic system |
| 3. *Denial* of civil liberties | 3. *Guarantee* of civil liberties |
| 4. *Regimentation* of social and cultural life | 4. *Freedom* in social and cultural life |

## BRIEF HISTORY OF SOVIET-AMERICAN RELATIONS

1. **1917–1941: Unfriendly.** The Communists resented *(a)* American aid to anti-Communist forces following the Russian Revolution and *(b)* America's refusal until 1933 to recognize the Soviet Union.

The United States resented *(a)* Russia's withdrawal from World War I, enabling Germany to concentrate its armies on the western front, *(b)* Russian efforts to spread revolution in non-Communist countries by means of the *Comintern*, and *(c)* Russia's Nonaggression Pact of 1939 with Nazi Germany—an agreement that encouraged Germany to start World War II.

2. **1941–1945: Cooperative.** During World War II Russia and the United States found themselves fighting against a common enemy, Germany. To create amity with its democratic allies, Russia dissolved the Comintern. To assist Russia, the United States *(a)* provided it with $11 billion of lend-lease equipment and *(b)* led the Western Allies in opening second fronts in Europe by invading southern Italy and northern France. Also, Russia, the United States, and Britain coordinated military strategy and made postwar plans at several top-level conferences: *Teheran, Yalta,* and *Potsdam.*

3. **1945–Present: Generally Unfriendly—The Cold War Era.** After World War II, Russia reverted to its prewar hostility toward non-Communist nations, especially the United States. Soviet leaders declared that *(a)* the spread of communism is necessary for the security of the Soviet Union and *(b)* communism must triumph over capitalism throughout the world. Stalin pursued a "hard line" toward the West, but his successors have urged *peaceful coexistence.* They have not, however, abandoned the Soviet goal of communizing the world.

American leaders *(a)* held the expansion of Russian power a threat to the safety of the free world and *(b)* predicted victory for the American way of life in peaceful competition with communism.

**4. Recently: A Search for Détente.** By the early 1970's Soviet and American leaders held that their nations were ready to move from the confrontation of the cold war era to negotiation in an era of better understanding, or *détente*. Détente recognized the basic differences between the two superpowers, but it also recognized their mutual interest in improving relations and avoiding a nuclear war. After several years of détente, the two nations could point to some understandings but also to more disputes that seemed indistinguishable from cold war confrontations. (Check the Index for Détente.)

## B. *The Communist World*

### THE RECORD OF COMMUNIST EXPANSION SINCE 1939

| Outright Annexations | Local Communist Parties Seize Control |
|---|---|
| By Russia<br>1. *Countries:* Estonia, Latvia, Lithuania<br>2. *Territories:* from Czechoslovakia, Finland, Germany, Japan, Poland, Rumania<br><br>By China<br>1. *Country:* Tibet | 1. *In Europe:* Albania, Bulgaria, Czechoslovakia, East Germany, Hungary, Poland, Rumania, Yugoslavia<br>2. *In Asia:* Cambodia, China, Laos, Mongolia, North Korea, South Yemen, Vietnam<br>3. *In America:* Cuba<br>4. *In Africa:* Angola, Ethiopia, Mozambique |

### RUSSIA DOMINATES ITS SATELLITES

**1. Meaning of Satellites.** The *satellites* are the Communist-dominated nations of Eastern and Central Europe: Bulgaria, Czechoslovakia, East-Germany, Hungary, Poland, and Rumania. Mostly they accept Russian authority—somewhat as protectorates submitting to a parent country.

Self-proclaimed *people's republics*, the satellite nations have governments that essentially imitate Russian domestic practices. *(a)* They are dictatorships, each controlled by its own Communist party. *(b)* They have nationalized industry, tried to collectivize agriculture, and adopted master economic plans. *(c)* They have denied many civil liberties and restricted free cultural expression. *(d)* In Poland and Hungary, both predominantly Roman Catholic, the governments have harassed the Catholic Church and at times arrested members of the clergy, most notably Hungary's Cardinal *Mindszenty*.

**2. Establishment of Satellites.** To help local Communist parties take over and maintain control, Russia *(a)* fostered Communist regimes in Eastern and Central

Europe as its armies pursued the retreating Germans in the final phase of World War II, *(b)* trained local Communists in tactics and leadership, *(c)* provided military equipment and advisers for local Communist forces, and *(d)* kept Russian troops in Eastern and Central Europe.

3. **Methods of Russian Control.** *(a)* Russian specialists in political, economic, and military matters "advise" the satellite governments. *(b)* Russia tries to keep the satellite economies tied to its own by trade treaties. *(c)* Russian military forces are stationed in some satellite countries; on occasion they have intervened to compel satellite conformity to Soviet policy. *(d)* Russian generals head a unified military command of Soviet and satellite forces in the *Warsaw Pact.*

## IRON CURTAIN

As part of the cold war, the Communist regimes have kept their peoples from free contact with Western ideas. They have established restrictions on visitors, newspapers, magazines, books, and movies; they have jammed Western radio broadcasts, especially the *Voice of America* and *Radio Free Europe.* Speaking about this barrier between the Communist nations and the West, Winston Churchill used the term "iron curtain."

## TROUBLE BEHIND THE IRON CURTAIN

1. **National Communism in Yugoslavia Since 1945.** *Marshal Tito,* Communist ruler of Yugoslovia, defied Stalinist Russia and pursued nationalist policies. Tito was emboldened to act independently because Yugoslavia was not occupied by Russian troops and does not border Russia. Tito was denounced by world Communist leaders for his "hateful policy" toward the Soviet Union.

Stalinist Russia and the satellites sought to overthrow Tito by economic pressure, propaganda, and subversion within Yugoslavia. These efforts proved unsuccessful. Since Stalin's death, Russia has somewhat repaired relations with Yugoslavia. Nevertheless, Yugoslavia remains free of Russian domination.

The Western democracies were cheered by Tito's independence of Russian control and his advocacy of *national communism.* The democracies hoped that other satellites would follow Yugoslavia's example. To enable Yugoslavia to resist Russian pressure, the democracies extended widespread aid: loans, food, trade treaties, diplomatic support, and military equipment. The West realizes that Yugoslavia is a Communist nation but not a Russian satellite.

Following Tito's death in 1980, the Western nations reaffirmed their support for Yugoslavia's unity, nonalignment, and independence.

2. **Power Struggle Following Stalin's Death in 1953.** The death of Joseph Stalin signaled a bitter struggle for power among the top Russian Communists. *Nikita Khrushchev* became First Secretary of the Communist party, a position that Stalin had used to rise to absolute power. Khrushchev eliminated his chief rivals in Russia. One was executed; others were deposed from positions of importance. In 1958 Khrushchev assumed the premiership of the Soviet Union.

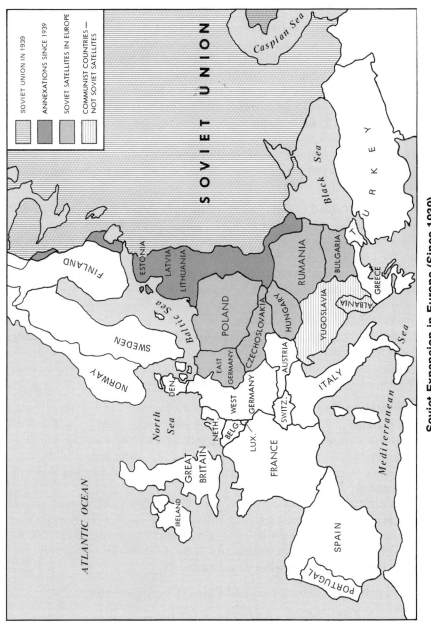

Soviet Expansion in Europe (Since 1939)

SOVIET UNION IN 1939

ANNEXATIONS SINCE 1939

SOVIET SATELLITES IN EUROPE

COMMUNIST COUNTRIES — NOT SOVIET SATELLITES

The struggle for power after Stalin's death gave the world an unusual glimpse of the conflict that can exist within the Russian dictatorship—a conflict that is usually kept well hidden below the surface.

**3. Downgrading of Stalin (1956).** Stalin had used every means of propaganda to encourage hero-worship of himself as a great teacher, leader, and military genius. In 1956 Khrushchev began an all-out attack to downgrade Stalin in the eyes of the Soviet people. Khrushchev condemned Stalin for *(a)* purges of military and political leaders on false charges, *(b)* blunders in foreign affairs, *(c)* terror against innocent Soviet citizens, and *(d)* personal cowardice during World War II. After Khrushchev's denunciation of Stalin, the Communist party spread the new anti-Stalin line.

In the satellite nations the anti-Stalin campaign strengthened the Titoist doctrine of national communism and helped set off upheavals, especially in Poland and Hungary.

**4. Uprising in Poland (1956).** The Polish people engaged in strikes and demonstrations *(a)* to achieve better living conditions and *(b)* to end Russian domination. *Wladyslaw Gomulka,* who had been imprisoned as a Titoist, regained the leadership of the Polish Communist party and announced that Poland would seek its own road to socialism. Khrushchev was alarmed by Poland's trend toward independence, but Gomulka reassured him that Poland would remain Communist and allied with Russia. Khrushchev thereupon pledged not to interfere in Poland's internal affairs.

By this bloodless revolution Poland achieved *(a)* a measure of independence in domestic matters, enabling Gomulka to end the forced collectivization of agriculture, and *(b)* expulsion of Russian agents from positions of authority over the Polish army, economy, and government.

**5. Revolution in Hungary (1956).** The Hungarian people revolted for *(a)* better living conditions, *(b)* the withdrawal of Soviet troops, and *(c)* full national independence. *Imre Nagy,* a Titoist, became head of the government, appointed non-Communists to his cabinet, and demanded the immediate withdrawal of Soviet forces. Nagy announced Hungary's neutrality in the cold war and withdrawal from the Warsaw Pact.

Such anti-Russian moves were more than Khrushchev would permit. Russian troops seized all of Hungary and suppressed the Hungarian *freedom fighters.* Thousands of Hungarians were killed or deported to Siberia; almost 200,000 fled their native land. The Soviets smashed the Nagy government, replacing it with a puppet Hungarian regime under *Janos Kadar.*

**6. Split by 1963 Between Russia and China.** Check the Index.

**7. Removal of Khrushchev (1964).** Check the Index.

**8. Invasion of Czechoslovakia (1968).** *Alexander Dubcek* became head of the Czechoslovak Communist party and pledged a program of "liberalization."

**"Having trouble keeping them in orbit."**

Ellinwood in The Arizona Daily Star, Tucson

Dubcek lifted censorship of press, radio, and television and permitted non-Communists to form political groups. He said that Czechoslovakia would seek trade and loans from the West. To reassure Russia, Dubcek asserted that Czechoslovakia remained Communist and loyal to the Warsaw Pact.

Russian leaders, however, feared that the Czechoslovak reforms might spur similar movements in the other satellite nations. Soviet forces, supported by troops of four Warsaw Pact nations—East Germany, Poland, Hungary, and Bulgaria—occupied Czechoslovakia. The Soviets compelled Czechoslovakia to reestablish censorship, ban non-Communist political groups, accept Soviet advisers, consent to the stationing of Soviet troops, and replace Dubcek as head of the Czechoslovak Communist party with the more amenable *Gustav Husak.*

The Russian invasion of Czechoslovakia, condemned by many Western and neutral nations, was also condemned by three Communist states—Yugoslavia, Rumania, and China—and by West European Communist parties. These Communist groups rejected the Russians' claim to have saved Czechoslovakia from "counterrevolutionary forces." They also rejected the Russian assertion that whenever a Communist nation endangers socialism at home or in other Communist countries, the Soviet Union has the duty to intervene with military force—an assertion termed the *Brezhnev Doctrine.*

### 9. Recurrent Unrest in Poland

*a. 1979–1971.* Polish workers felt their earnings threatened by a new wage incentive system. When the government increased the prices of food, fuel, and clothing, workers in coastal cities began riots and demonstrations. As the rioting spread, Gomulka resigned as head of Poland's Communist party and was replaced by *Edward Gierek*—a change approved by Russia. The Gierek regime quieted discontent by shelving the wage incentive system and revoking the price increases, but it called for "law, order, and discipline."

***b. 1976.*** Polish workers again rioted to protest government increases in food prices—designed to offset internal inflationary costs and higher priced Western food imports. The government rescinded the higher prices, but it also sentenced some riot leaders to prison terms.

***c. 1979.*** Karol Cardinal Wojtyla of Poland was elected as Pope in 1978 and took the name *John Paul II*. He is the first Polish pontiff in the history of the Roman Catholic Church. In 1979, as Pope, he visited his homeland, whose 35 million inhabitants are overwhelmingly Roman Catholic. Warmly and even emotionally received by huge crowds, the Pope spoke out for human rights, religious liberty, and Catholic Church interests; he condemned atheism and questioned Soviet domination of its East European satellites. The visit of this "Slavic Pope" heightened Polish nationalism—to the discomfort of Russia; it also intensified religious fervor and raised expectations of more personal freedom—to the discomfort of Poland's Communist rulers.

***d. 1980–1981.*** Aroused by sharp meat price increases set by the government, workers throughout Poland walked off their jobs. In Gdansk, a Baltic seaport, shipyard workers selected a strike committee headed by *Lech Walesa.* The strikers demanded major reforms—relaxation of censorship; free access for religious and labor groups to the mass media; release from jail of the 1976 riot leaders; wage increases; a reduction in the workweek; and, most important, the right to strike through a free labor union, independent of Communist party and government control. After two months of turmoil, the Gierek regime accepted most of the strikers' demands; in return the labor leaders acknowledged the leading role of Poland's Communist party. Then Gierek, supposedly ill, was removed as Poland's Communist leader.

*Solidarity*—the 10-million-member independent Polish labor union headed by Lech Walesa—represented an unprecedented development in the Communist bloc. It signified a measure of power and authority separate from the Communist party; its existence contradicted Communist ideology requiring complete party supremacy. This situation in Poland was of great concern to Communist leaders in other Soviet-bloc nations and in the Soviet Union.

As the Soviets massed troops along the Polish border, Poland's leaders—party, government, church, and independent union—all urged restraint and voiced Poland's ability itself to solve its internal problems. The Soviet Union also was warned by the United States and other NATO powers that a Soviet invasion of Poland would bring economic and political reprisals and would end any hope of reviving East-West détente. For the time, the Soviets refrained from taking military action.

In 1981 Poland's Communist government was under increasing domestic pressure for further reforms. The government felt compelled to grant (1) private farmers the right to form an independent *Rural Solidarity* union, (2) university students the right to form an independent union with influence to change from compulsory to optional courses in the Russian language and in Marxism-Leninism, and (3) Solidarity access to the mass media and a pledge gradually to reduce the workweek from six to five days. As bitterness between the government and Solidarity mounted, and as the economy worsened and food shortages continued, the situation remained precarious.

## TROUBLE WITH WEST EUROPEAN COMMUNIST PARTIES: EUROCOMMUNISM

In 1976 at Moscow delegates of most world Communist parties attended the 25th Congress of the Soviet party. *Enrico Berlinguer,* head of the Italian Communist party, expressed his party's political differences with and independence of Moscow. Not mentioning Marx, Lenin, or international working class unity, Berlinguer voiced support for a multiparty democratic and nationalist system. *Georges Marchais,* head of the French Communist party, who personally boycotted the congress, had previously denounced Soviet repression of domestic dissent and declared the "dictatorship of the proletariat" doctrine to be obsolete. At the congress the French delegate stated that his party would pursue "a socialism in the colors of France." Other West European Communist leaders expressed similar independent views—all to the displeasure of Soviet leaders.

The ideological changes voiced by the major West European Communist parties were (1) toward democracy—to accept the results of free multiparty elections, guarantee civil liberties, and renounce dictatorship and (2) toward nationalism—to remain independent of Russian domination and consider first the national interests of their respective countries. Denounced by Russia, this West European Communist ideology is known by the term *Eurocommunism.*

# Part 3. Economic and Military Aspects of the Cold War Era

## A. Foreign Aid

### THE TRUMAN DOCTRINE

1. **Purpose.** In 1947 Greece, in economic chaos as a result of Axis occupation in World War II, was under attack from Communist guerrilla bands. Turkey was under pressure from Russia for concessions in the Dardanelles, the straits connecting the Black Sea and the Mediterranean. If successful, these Communist efforts would have expanded Russian influence into the eastern Mediterranean. President Truman therefore announced that "it must be the policy of the

United States to support free peoples" against direct and indirect Communist aggression—the *Truman Doctrine.* Congress overwhelmingly approved economic and military aid for Greece and Turkey.

**2. Effects.** *(a)* With American economic aid, Greece revived its economy. With American military aid, Greece put down Communist guerrilla attacks. Also, Yugoslavia halted aid to the Greek guerrillas following Tito's split with Russia. *(b)* Bolstered by American economic and militiary aid, Turkey withstood Russian demands for control of the Dardanelles.

## THE MARSHALL PLAN

**1. Reasons for Offer.** In 1947 Secretary of State *George C. Marshall* offered American economic aid to *all* European nations (including Russia and its satellites) to enable them to recover from the destruction of World War II. He said, "Our policy is directed not against any country or doctrine but against hunger, poverty, desperation, and chaos." World War II had crippled the economies of European nations, victor and vanquished alike.

The United States wanted to help Europe in order to *(a)* improve European living conditions, *(b)* end the need for continued American relief funds, *(c)* revive a mutually profitable trade between the United States and Europe, and *(d)* lessen the danger of communism in Western Europe.

**2. The European Recovery Program (ERP).** The Marshall Plan, officially the *European Recovery Program,* aided most non-Communist nations of Europe: Great Britain, France, Austria, Belgium, Denmark, Greece, Iceland, Ireland, Italy, Luxembourg, the Netherlands, Norway, Portugal, Sweden, Switzerland, Turkey, and West Germany. These countries cooperated with one another and with the United States to achieve "recovery, not relief." The United States provided $12.5 billion in aid, most of which was spent in this country for foodstuffs, raw materials, and machinery.

**3. Achievements.** During the four years (1948–1951) of its existence, the Marshall Plan helped strengthen Western Europe. It *(a)* promoted strong economic recovery, permitting many countries to surpass prewar levels of production, *(b)* furthered political stability, *(c)* reduced Communist influence, and *(d)* encouraged West European countries to move toward economic unity (check the Index for Inner Six).

**4. Russian Opposition.** Russia condemned the Marshall Plan as an American scheme to gain economic and political control over Europe and opposed the plan. *(a)* Russia and its European satellites refused America's offer of Marshall Plan aid. *(b)* Russia initiated its own economic aid program, the *Council of Mutual Economic Assistance (COMECON).* This program competed with the Marshall Plan by bringing about closer economic relations between Russia and its satellites.

## POINT FOUR PROGRAM

In his 1949 Inaugural Address, President Truman reaffirmed America's opposition to Russian expansion. As *Point Four* in America's effort to contain communism, Truman proposed a "bold new program" to give *technical assistance* to underdeveloped nations.

Under the Point Four Program, Congress has appropriated funds to assist developing nations—in Latin America, the Middle East, Africa, and Asia. The United States has sent technical specialists to help increase agricultural and industrial output, resolve urban problems, improve government administration, promote public health, and advance education.

## EISENHOWER DOCTRINE

In 1957 President Eisenhower warned that, because of economic and political instability, the Middle East was vulnerable to Communist infiltration. Eisenhower offered the Middle East nations (1) economic and military aid and (2) armed assistance, upon request, to repel open Communist aggression. The *Eisenhower Doctrine* was welcomed by Lebanon and Saudi Arabia but was denounced by Egypt and Syria as an American plot to dominate the Arab world. (The Eisenhower Doctrine was used once—in 1958—when the United States sent troops into Lebanon and protected the nation's government against pro-Egyptian rebels.)

## PEACE CORPS

In 1961 President Kennedy inaugurated a new foreign aid agency, the *Peace Corps*. It enrolls idealistic volunteers who receive token pay, work in underdeveloped countries that request aid, and live as the native peoples do. Peace Corps volunteers fill the gap between the highly skilled technical advisers of the Point Four Program and the relatively unskilled local labor. For example, they might follow up a Point Four malaria-control demonstration by remaining with the villagers and assisting in the day-by-day work.

Peace Corps volunteers have performed laudably in about 50 nations and have won friends for the United States.

## AMERICAN FOREIGN AID: AN OVERVIEW

The United States continues to spend substantial sums for foreign aid—annually several billion dollars, an amount that is 3 percent or less of our national budget. Currently military aid is administered by the Defense Department and economic aid by the State Department's *Agency for International Development (AID)*.

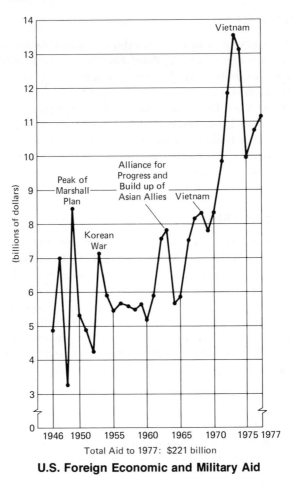

Total Aid to 1977: $221 billion

**U.S. Foreign Economic and Military Aid**

Since 1945 the United States has extended over $220 billion in aid to some 140 countries. Of this total, 34 percent has been for military supplies and services and 66 percent for economic and technical aid. One-third of American aid has been in the form of loans that are repayable; two-thirds has been in the form of grants that are outright gifts.

At first our foreign aid consisted chiefly of economic assistance for Europe, especially Britain, France, Italy, West Germany, and Greece. As Europe recovered from World War II, the United States extended economic and technical aid to the developing nations of the world. As a result of Communist aggression in Korea in 1950, the foreign aid program placed greater emphasis on military aid for the Far East, especially South Korea, Japan, Taiwan, and South Vietnam. In the 1960's the United States also expanded aid to most nations of Latin America.

## CRITICISMS OF OUR FOREIGN AID PROGRAM

Most Americans hold that foreign aid furthers the United States national interest. Nevertheless, a small but vocal minority opposes foreign aid, claiming that it (1) is too great a burden on the American taxpayer, (2) diverts funds that could be used for improvements within the country, (3) is characterized by inefficient administration, waste, and corruption, (4) creates competition for American manufacturers and farmers by building up foreign industry and agriculture, (5) has not won America any appreciation, friendship, or support from recipient nations, and (6) has failed to lessen the danger of communism.

## FOREIGN AID PROGRAMS OF WEST EUROPEAN NATIONS

The United States urged the more prosperous free-world nations—notably Britain, France, and West Germany—to cooperate with us in extending aid to underdeveloped lands. These nations accepted the idea of joint responsibility and initiated their own modest foreign aid programs.

## THE COMMUNIST ECONOMIC OFFENSIVE SINCE 1954

The Russians have boasted that communism will outstrip capitalism in peaceful economic competition. The Communist bloc has challenged the free world by offering economic and military assistance to many underdeveloped nations, both neutral and pro-Western. Communist aid, chiefly loans and skilled personnel, has been accepted by more than 20 countries—notably Argentina, India, Indonesia, Iraq, Syria, and Egypt.

In recent years the Chinese Communists have offered aid to Latin American and Afro-Asian nations in competition with Russian aid programs.

To date American foreign aid remains far greater than that extended by the Communist nations.

## B. West European Economic Unity

### THE INNER SIX

The *Inner Six* West European nations—Belgium, France, Italy, Luxembourg, the Netherlands, and West Germany—having cooperated under the Marshall Plan, moved toward further economic unity.

**1. European Coal and Steel Community.** In 1952 the Inner Six agreed to *(a)* abolish internal tariffs on coal, iron, and steel, *(b)* establish a supranational (above any nation) *High Authority* to administer these resources in the interests of the entire community, and *(c)* grant the High Authority power to control prices, production, wages, and working conditions.

**2. European Atomic Energy Community (Euratom).** In 1957 the Inner Six agreed to form a supranational *European Atomic Energy Commission* to (*a*) coordinate atomic research, (*b*) pool nuclear materials, and (*c*) increase the production of electric power by atomic installations.

**3. European Economic Community (EEC or Common Market).** In 1957 the Inner Six agreed to join in a tariff union. They established a supranational *European Economic Commission* to gradually (*a*) eliminate internal tariff barriers and (*b*) establish a unified tariff system on goods imported from outside the tariff union area. West European leaders envisioned the removal of political barriers to the movement of goods, capital, and labor—that is, a free trade area, or *Common Market.*

**4. Objectives.** West European moves toward economic unity aimed to (*a*) provide more coal, iron, steel, electric power, farm produce, and consumer goods at lower prices, (*b*) raise living standards, (*c*) reduce both domestic and foreign Communist threats, and (*d*) expand foreign trade.

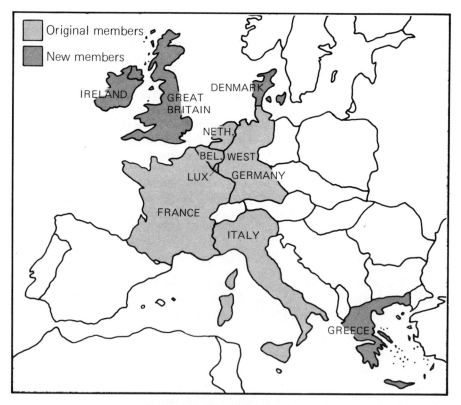

**The Enlarged Common Market**

## AN ENLARGED COMMON MARKET (1973)

Britain twice applied for Common Market membership but each application was vetoed by France under President de Gaulle. He viewed Britain's membership as a threat to his hopes for French leadership in Western Europe. After de Gaulle's retirement, Britain again applied for membership and in 1971 was accepted under these terms: (1) to mid-1977 Britain and the six Common Market members would reciprocally reduce tariffs so as to achieve a customs union and (2) special protection would be provided for dairy products from New Zealand and sugar from other British Commonwealth nations. Also, Britain's entry would be accompanied by membership for Ireland and Denmark. (Norway was also offered membership, but the Norwegians voted narrowly to reject the offer.)

### Comparing the EEC and the Three Major Industrial Nations

|  | Nine-Nation EEC | U.S.A. | U.S.S.R. | Japan |
|---|---|---|---|---|
| Area (square miles) (square kilometers) | 590,000 1,528,000 | 3,600,000 9,363,000 | 8,800,000 22,402,000 | 143,000 370,000 |
| Population (millions) | 258 | 212 | 252 | 110 |
| G.N.P. (billions of dollars) | $918 | $1,118 | $865* | $364 |
| Imports (billions of dollars) | $234 | $80 | $20 | $50 |
| Exports (billions of dollars) | $220 | $78 | $22 | $44 |

Source: Commission of the European Communities (1974 figures)
*1975 estimate

In 1973 Britain, Ireland, and Denmark joined, making a nine-nation Common Market. They also joined the Coal and Steel Community and the Atomic Energy Community. Will the European Community now move toward a common currency and a uniform foreign policy?

In 1981 Greece, a developing eastern Mediterranean European nation, was admitted to the Common Market as its tenth member.

Two West European nations, relatively poor, who seek membership, are Spain and Portugal.

## C. Military Alliances

### THE NORTH ATLANTIC TREATY ORGANIZATION (NATO)

1. **Free-World Fears.** In 1948 the free-world nations were shocked by three Russian-inspired aggressions: (1) a coup d'etat in Czechoslovakia that eliminated democratic leaders—Foreign Minister *Jan Masaryk* was driven to suicide or

murdered, and President *Eduard Benes* resigned—and gave the Communists complete control of the country; (2) pressure upon Finland to accept a mutual assistance pact with the Soviet Union that in effect compelled Finland to adhere to Russian foreign policy; and (3) a Russian attempt to drive the Western powers out of Berlin by a surface route blockade. Made fearful by these Russian moves, the free world nations formed the *North Atlantic Treaty Organization*.

**2. Defensive Military Alliance.** In 1949, 12 nations—Britain, France, Belgium, the Netherlands, Luxembourg, Denmark, Iceland, Italy, Norway, Portugal, Canada, and the United States—signed the *North Atlantic Pact*. They declared that they would *(a)* consider an attack on any one of them as an attack on all and *(b)* come to the defense of the attacked member nation with armed force if necessary.

In 1952 NATO admitted Greece and Turkey and in 1955 West Germany, bringing its total membership to 15 nations.

**3. The NATO Army.** In 1950 the North Atlantic Pact nations further strengthened themselves against Communist aggression by authorizing "an integrated military force adequate for the defense of the freedom of Europe," that is, a NATO army. The head of the NATO army, called the *Supreme Allied Commander in Europe (SACEUR)*, has always been an American general. The first Supreme Commander was Dwight D. Eisenhower. NATO headquarters, located in Belgium, are known as the *Supreme Headquarters of the Allied Powers in Europe (SHAPE)*.

The United States has assigned over 300,000 personnel—army, navy, and air force—to Europe as part of the NATO military establishment and has given billions of dollars in military equipment for NATO use. Other member nations also have assigned personnel and equipment to the NATO command. NATO's military strength, however, remains far less than that of Russia and its European satellites. Nevertheless, NATO hopes that its existence will deter the Communists from undertaking any aggression in Europe.

In 1979 the NATO members, viewing the military buildup of the Communist Warsaw Pact nations, agreed to increase their military defense spending and to accept the stationing in Western Europe of new American nuclear missiles capable of reaching deep into Russia.

**4. Problems Facing NATO**

*a. Nuclear Fears.* Many NATO members, recalling World War II, have been reluctant to equip West German forces in NATO with nuclear weapons. Many NATO members also are fearful that, in case of a Soviet-American conflict, Western Europe would be the nuclear battleground.

*b. French Nationalism and Withdrawal from NATO.* President Charles de Gaulle of France was a French nationalist, ambitious to achieve French leadership of Western Europe and resentful of American influence in NATO. In 1966 de Gaulle claimed that NATO was obsolete because (1) the development of missiles with nuclear warheads had made NATO defenses insignificant and (2)

*Bruce Shanks in The Buffalo Evening News*

the Soviet Union had adopted a policy of peaceful coexistence. Accordingly de Gaulle withdrew all French forces from NATO and demanded the removal of all NATO troops, chiefly American and Canadian, from French soil. De Gaulle, however, pledged that France would remain a member of the North Atlantic Pact. De Gaulle's moves were deplored by the other NATO members, but they yielded to his demands. All NATO troops left French soil, all NATO bases in France were dismantled, and SHAPE headquarters were transferred to Belgium. French presidents following de Gaulle have maintained his NATO policies.

   *c. Hostility Between Greece and Turkey.* Although Greece and Turkey both joined NATO, the two countries have traditionally been enemies and in recent years have clashed bitterly over the island of Cyprus. In 1974 a Greek-backed coup, aimed at uniting Cyprus with Greece, failed and resulted in Turkish armies occupying 40 percent of the island. In Greece the military dictatorship that had planned the coup gave way to civilian and democratic rule. The new Greek government, resenting the lack of NATO support for Greece against Turkey, kept its membership in NATO but withdrew its military forces from the NATO command.

   In the course of the Cyprus dispute, Greece and Turkey both severely criticized the United States. Greece blamed the United States for not preventing the Turkish invasion of Cyprus. Turkey condemned the action of the United States Congress—cutting off military aid to Turkey because "substantial progress" had not been made toward a Cyprus settlement—and ordered American forces out of military installations and intelligence posts in Turkey. (These posts had enabled the United States and NATO to secure considerable information regarding Soviet military activities.)

In 1978 President Carter requested Congress to lift the three-year-old embargo. He pointed out that the embargo had not moved Turkey to make concessions regarding Cyprus, and he feared that Turkey might further weaken its ties to NATO. Congress narrowly approved an end to the ban. Thereafter the United States reached agreement with Turkey to provide military and economic aid in return for American use of Turkish military and intelligence posts "within the NATO framework."

d. *American Disillusionment with NATO.* For years American officials had been unhappy that the NATO powers, economically recovered from World War II, were questioning American leadership and obstructing unified foreign policies. In 1973 American disillusionment became intense as a result of the Arab-Israeli War. The major NATO members, yielding to Arab oil embargo threats, refused permission to the United States to use the facilities on their soil for transporting military equipment to Israel. Their refusal compelled the United States to transport the equipment by a more difficult route. American officials who held that support for Israel was essential to prevent Soviet domination of the Mideast resented the lack of cooperation and began to rethink the value of NATO.

e. *Possibility of Communists in NATO Member Governments.* NATO, formed to defend Western Europe against any Soviet Communist aggression, since the mid-1970's has faced the possibility of Western Communists in the governments of NATO nations. The problem surfaced as follows:

(1) *Portugal.* In 1974 an army coup ended conservative dictatorial rule but plunged Portugal into political chaos. For a time the Portuguese Communist party seemed likely to seize complete control, but that threat disappeared with the suppression of a 1975 attempted leftist coup and with 1976 elections in which the Communists received less than 15 percent of the vote. The Socialists, the largest party, with 35 percent of the vote, formed a minority government committed to democracy, economic reform, and active NATO membership—policies supported by subsequent Portuguese governments.

(2) *Italy.* Following the 1976 parliamentary elections, the Christian Democrats formed a minority government; however, their ability to secure a parliamentary majority depended on tacit Communist cooperation. The Communists indicated that they would accept this arrangement for the time being but that their goal was full membership in an Italian coalition government. If that occurred, Italian Communists might have access to confidential military data regarding NATO—which they now claim to support. Would the Italian Communists refrain from transmitting such NATO data to Moscow?

In 1979 the Communists, having received no cabinet positions, caused the fall of the minority government. After the 1979 elections, Italy was governed by coalition regimes that continued to exclude the Communists. (For details, check the Index under Italy, as a Republic.)

(3) *France.* In 1981 elections, Socialist François Mitterrand was elected president and the Socialist party gained a strong majority in the National As-

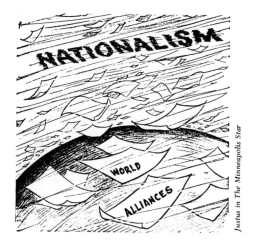

**"Crosscurrents"**

*Justus in The Minneapolis Star*

sembly. Mitterrand, who took a hard line toward the Soviet Union, nevertheless appointed four Communists to his cabinet. He explained that Communist votes had helped the Socialists attain power, that the four Communists were given technical posts—not militarily sensitive—and that the French Communist party had agreed to support the Socialist's anti-Soviet stands. (For details, check the Index.)

The United States voiced grave concern over this development in France as setting an undesirable precedent for other West European countries and threatening the security of NATO.

## SOUTHEAST ASIA TREATY ORGANIZATION (SEATO)

**1. Defensive Military Alliance (1954).** Eight nations—the United States, Britain, France, Australia, New Zealand, Thailand, Pakistan, and the Philippines— established SEATO. Each member nation *(a)* agreed that armed aggression against any other member would "endanger its own peace and safety" and pledged to "meet the common danger in accordance with its constitutional processes," *(b)* recognized that civil wars might involve foreign aggression, and *(c)* offered to aid, upon request, the nonsignatory Southeast Asian states of Cambodia, Laos, and South Vietnam.

**2. Weaknesses of SEATO.** *(a)* SEATO lacked a unified armed force and military command. *(b)* SEATO's main strength came from its non-Asian members. *(c)* Four important Southeast Asian nations—India, Burma, Sri Lanka, and Indonesia—refused to join SEATO. These nations sought neutrality in the cold war. *(d)* France did not actively participate in SEATO. *(e)* Displeased by lack of SEATO support in its quarrels with India, Pakistan in 1972 left SEATO.

**3. End of SEATO (1976).** Following the Communist triumphs in Indo-China, the remaining SEATO members agreed that in view of the "changing circumstances" in Southeast Asia, SEATO should be "phased out."

## ADDITIONAL AMERICAN MILITARY ALLIANCES

Today the United States has military alliances with over 40 nations of the free world. In addition to NATO the United States has entered into the following military commitments:

1. The **Rio Inter-American Defense Treaty** (1947) between the United States and the Latin American nations of the Organization of American States (OAS) provided for the common defense of the Western Hemisphere.

2. The **Anzus Pact** (1951) between Australia, New Zealand, and the United States provided that each nation *(a)* consider an attack upon one of the others as dangerous to its own safety and *(b)* act to meet the common danger.

3. Bilateral **Mutual Defense Treaties** with Japan, the Philippines, and South Korea pledged the United States to consider an attack on any one of these nations as a common danger and to assist the nation attacked.

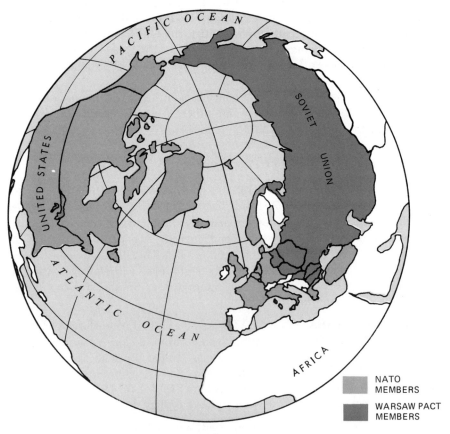

**Opposing Military Alliances**

Also, the United States maintains military bases in Spain.

The United States hopes that its system of military alliances—which provides for over 200 American bases in countries ringing the Soviet bloc—will deter the Communists from further aggression.

## COMMUNIST MILITARY ALLIANCES

1. **Chinese-Soviet Treaty.** In 1950 Soviet Russia and Communist China signed a treaty of "friendship, alliance, and mutual aid" providing for *(a)* mutual military aid in case of attack by Japan or by an ally of Japan (meaning the United States) and *(b)* consultation on all international matters of mutual concern.

Because the Soviet Union and China have been openly hostile toward each other since 1963, many observers doubt that this alliance is valid.

China recently stated that it would not renew this treaty beyond its 1980 expiration date.

2. **Warsaw Pact.** In 1955 Russia and its European satellites formed an alliance providing for a unified Communist military command under a Soviet general. This pact was designed as a counterweight to NATO.

## MULTIPLE–CHOICE QUESTIONS

1. "We must somehow learn to live together in this world, to tolerate one another, or else we cannot survive." The author of this statement would *most* likely support a policy of (1) neutrality (2) coexistence (3) conformity (4) isolation.

2. The cold war era has been marked by all of the following *except* the (1) American policy of containment (2) use of espionage and subversion (3) use of nuclear weapons in localized wars (4) formation of military alliances.

3. Before 1941 relations between the United States and Russia were (1) very friendly (2) based on similar ideals (3) generally unfriendly (4) improved by the Soviet-German Nonaggression Pact of 1939.

4. Which group consists entirely of Russian satellites? (1) Austria, Poland, Turkey (2) Czechoslovakia, Greece, Italy (3) Czechoslovakia, East Germany, Poland (4) Hungary, Israel, Spain.

5. Estonia, Latvia, and Lithuania are (1) islands taken by Russia from Japan (2) territories seized by Communist armies in the Balkans (3) neutralist nations (4) former independent nations now part of the Soviet Union.

6. The Communists seek to keep democratic ideas from their people by means of (1) containment (2) the iron curtain (3) coexistence (4) COMECON.

7. Which European Communist country has most successfully resisted Russian domination? (1) Hungary (2) Yugoslavia (3) Bulgaria (4) Rumania.

8. From events since World War II, which conclusion about communism may *best* be drawn? (1) It has made no headway in Asia. (2) In different nations communism is shaped by national needs and goals. (3) Communist nations have moved closer to the Soviet Union. (4) It was weakened by the Soviet military intervention in Hungary and Czechoslovakia.

9. Under both Czarist and Communist rule, Russia's policy toward Turkey has been influenced by Russia's desire to gain control of (1) the Red Sea (2) Gibraltar (3) the Suez Canal (4) the Dardanelles.

10. The Truman Doctrine was intended to keep Russian influence out of (1) France and Italy (2) Syria and Egypt (3) Greece and Turkey (4) Bulgaria and Poland.

11. The word "underdeveloped" as used in the term *underdeveloped country* refers to a country's lack of (1) a strong government (2) technical know-how (3) a large population (4) natural resources.

12. Originally the Marshall Plan was an offer made to (1) all European nations (2) all UN members (3) only English-speaking nations (4) only anti-Communist nations.

13. An important purpose of the Marshall Plan was to (1) limit European armaments (2) establish a United States of Europe (3) improve economic conditions in European nations (4) prevent Soviet Russia from securing raw materials.

14. The Marshall Plan helped (1) end Communist influence in Italy (2) sharply increase industrial production in Western Europe (3) restore democratic government in Czechoslovakia (4) sharply decrease industrial production in Western Europe.

15. The *primary* purpose of the Point Four Program was to help underdeveloped areas by (1) furnishing technical aid (2) providing food for starving people (3) spreading information concerning the American way of life (4) providing military aid to resist Communist aggression.

16. The Truman and Eisenhower doctrines were *most* similar in that both were designed to (1) reduce tariff barriers (2) end the Korean War (3) resist Communist aggression (4) aid the same nations.

17. A *basic* purpose of the Peace Corps was to provide (1) jobs for unemployed American youths (2) scholarships for Americans to study in foreign countries (3) aid to people in underdeveloped areas (4) relief to Arab refugees in the Middle East.

18. A step already taken toward a united Western Europe has been the (1) selection of Geneva as its capital (2) creation of a common market (3) adoption of a single currency system (4) adoption of a single constitution.

19. In its immediate purpose, the European Common Market most closely resembles the (1) Holy Alliance (2) Hague Court (3) Zollverein of the German states (4) International Red Cross.

20. The Common Market is essentially a (1) military alliance (2) federal form of government (3) tariff union (4) communications corporation.

21. Britain's application for membership in the Common Market was twice vetoed by (1) Russia (2) France (3) West Germany (4) the United States.

22. Which has been a problem for the members of the European Common Market? (1) conflict between national sovereignty and united action (2) active opposition from the United States (3) decline in living standards of West Europeans (4) failure to remove tariff barriers within the union.

23. A major reason for creating the North Atlantic Treaty Organization (NATO) was to (1) supervise the West German government (2) protect member nations against Communist aggression (3) distribute Point Four funds (4) regulate world trade.

24. NATO was weakened when a member nation withdrew all its troops from the integrated military command. This member nation was (1) Italy (2) France (3) West Germany (4) Britain.

25. A major difficulty in providing NATO with nuclear weapons for the defense of Western Europe has been the (1) refusal of the United States to cooperate (2) refusal of West Germany to permit missile bases on its soil (3) reluctance of many

NATO members to give nuclear arms to West German troops   (4) reluctance of Britain to use nuclear weapons even for self-defense.

26. The countries *not* a party to any military pact include   (1) Portugal, Spain, the United Kingdom   (2) Sweden, Switzerland, Yugoslavia   (3) Greece, Italy, the Netherlands   (4) Poland, Rumania, East Germany.

27. Which military alliance is no longer in existence?   (1) NATO   (2) the Warsaw Pact   (3) the Anzus Pact   (4) SEATO.

## TRUE–FALSE QUESTIONS

If the statement is correct, write the word *true*. If the statement is incorrect, substitute a word or phrase for the italicized term to make the statement correct.

1. Soviet armed might in 1968 suppressed a Communist "liberalization" program in *Poland*.

2. The Point Four program of the United States closely parallels the United Nations program of *technical assistance*.

3. In addition to the United States, another North American nation that joined NATO was *Mexico*.

4. Two NATO members, traditional enemies, who have clashed over Cyprus, are *Britain and Italy*.

5. During the 1973 Arab-Israeli War, American efforts to resupply Israel with military equipment were *not supported* by the major NATO powers.

6. The NATO member that borders on the south of the Soviet Union is *Pakistan*.

7. The *Italian* Communist party in 1976 voiced its independence of Soviet domination.

8. The head (SACEUR) of the NATO army has always been a general from *West Germany*.

## ESSAY QUESTIONS

1. The Soviet Union has often claimed that it is a democracy. *(a)* Discuss *two* devices used by the Soviet Union to give the impression that it is democratic. *(b)* Describe *three* democratic features of life in the United States that *do not* exist in the Soviet Union. *(c)* Discuss *two* differences in economic and social life between the United States and the Soviet Union.

2. For success in the cold war, the Western democracies must estimate correctly their own strengths and weaknesses as well as those of Communist Russia and its satellites. *(a)* Describe *one* strength and *one* weakness of the Western democracies. *(b)* Describe *one* strength and *one* weakness of Communist Russia and its satellites. *(c)* Discuss *two* different ways by which the United States has sought success in the cold war.

3. *(a)* Describe *one* way in which the Soviet Union was able to acquire its satellite empire in Europe. *(b)* Describe *two* ways by which the Soviet Union controls its satellites. *(c)* Explain *one* way the satellite nations are an asset to the Soviet Union and *one* way they are a liability.

4. *(a)* Give *two* reasons why the United States has extended military and economic aid to foreign nations since the end of World War II. *(b)* Describe in detail *one* American foreign aid program. *(c)* Explain *one* criticism of American foreign aid. *(d)* Discuss *one* reason why the Communist bloc has undertaken its own foreign aid program.

5. NATO is a defensive military alliance of free nations. (a) Explain one reason why NATO was formed. (b) Discuss two problems facing NATO, showing how each has weakened the organization. (c) In view of these problems, does NATO retain any value as a military alliance today? Give one argument to support your opinion.

6. State whether you agree or disagree with each of the following statements and provide two arguments to support your opinion in each case: (a) The United States has been wasting the taxpayers' money on foreign aid programs. (b) The existence of military alliances in the cold war era has helped to maintain peace. (c) The Italian and French Communist parties are sincere in their declarations of independence from Russian domination. (d) Russia can depend upon the loyalty of its European satellite nations. (e) In the full sense of the word "win," it is impossible for either the United States or the Soviet Union to "win" the cold war.

# Part 4. Crises Throughout the World During the Cold War Era

## A. Germany

### THE ALLIED DECISIONS REGARDING GERMANY (1945)

At the Yalta and Potsdam conferences and in other agreements, the United States, Britain, and Russia made major decisions about Germany.

**1. Territory.** The eastern provinces were detached from Germany with part occupied by Russia but most under Polish control (see map, page 547). The Western powers considered these territorial changes to be temporary, pending a formal peace treaty to set Germany's final boundaries. Russia and Poland considered these changes to be permanent, and in 1975 the Western powers acquiesced by agreeing to the Helsinki Pact (check the Index).

**2. Occupation Zones.** The rest of Germany was divided into four zones, with each of the Big Four powers—Russia, Britain, the United States, and France—governing one zone. Berlin, lying 110 miles (176 kilometers) inside the Russian zone, was likewise divided into four sections, with each of the Big Four controlling one section. The three Western Allies were guaranteed access to Berlin by rail, highway, and air routes across the Russian zone. (See map, page 547.) These divisions of Germany were meant to be temporary, pending a formal peace treaty.

**3. Economy.** The German economy was to be directed toward agriculture and peaceful industries. War industries were barred. Certain German factories and industrial equipment were to be dismantled and removed, chiefly to the Soviet Union, as partial reparation.

**Germany Following World War II**

**4. Disarmament.** Germany was to be thoroughly disarmed so as to render it unable to wage aggressive warfare again.

**5. Education.** German schools were to work for the "development of democratic ideas." The Allies recognized that reeducation of the German people would be a long and difficult task.

**6. Denazification.** Nazism was to be wiped out completely. All Nazi organizations, including the Nazi party, Storm Troopers, and the Gestapo, were dissolved. Active Nazis were not to be allowed to hold public office or other positions of influence. War criminals were to be brought to trial.

## NAZI WAR CRIMES TRIALS

**1. Nuremberg Trials.** An *International Military Tribunal* met at Nuremberg (1945–1946) and tried Hermann Goering and other top Nazi leaders. They were charged with crimes against humanity, violations of international law, and waging aggressive warfare. These trials, it was hoped, would serve to democratize Germany, expose the evils of Nazism, strengthen international law, and discourage future aggressors. The tribunal found 19 of the 22 defendants guilty; it sentenced 12 to death and the others to prison.

**2. In the American Zone.** A special *United States Military Tribunal* tried secondary Nazi leaders. *Alfred Krupp,* head of the Krupp munitions works, was sentenced to prison for exploiting slave labor and plundering Nazi-occupied

Walt Partymiller, The Gazette and Daily, York, PA

**Will we learn the lessons?**

countries. The United States later permitted Western German *denazification courts* to try less important Nazis. These courts were quite lenient, and many former Nazis regained positions of influence.

**3. In the Russian Zone.** At first, the Communists severely punished Nazi war criminals. Soon, however, the Communists abandoned denazification trials and treated former Nazis leniently in order to gain their support.

## THE WEST AND RUSSIA DISAGREE ON GERMANY

After World War II the West and Russia came into conflict over Germany. Western reunification plans that would swing Germany toward the West were rejected by Russia. Soviet reunification plans that would bring Germany into the Communist camp were rejected by the West.

## RUSSIA PROVOKES A CRISIS: BERLIN BLOCKADE (1948–1949)

Under Stalin, Russia tried to drive the Western Allies out of Berlin by blockading the surface routes—roads, rails, and canals—between Berlin and the three western zones of Germany. To thwart this *Berlin Blockade,* the Allies resorted to an *airlift.* For almost a year the airlift supplied more than 2 million West Berliners with food, medicine, and other necessities of life. The Soviets could not halt the airlift except by shooting down Allied planes, a course they were unwilling to take for fear of starting an all-out war. The Russians therefore abandoned the blockade.

# DEVELOPMENTS IN WEST GERMANY

**1. German Federal Republic.** Unable to reach an agreement with Russia for German reunification, the three Western Allies in 1949 combined their zones to form the *Federal Republic of Germany* with its capital at *Bonn*. In 1955 West Germany was granted full sovereignty over domestic and foreign affairs (except for negotiations regarding German reunification and West Berlin) and was admitted to NATO.

West Germany's army, assigned to NATO, was limited to 12 divisions—a force of about 275,000. West Germany also was prohibited from manufacturing atomic, biological, or chemical weapons, guided missiles, or large warships.

**2. Government of West Germany.** The West German constitution provides for a democratic government with *(a)* a guarantee of civil liberties and free elections, *(b)* a two-house Parliament, and *(c)* a chancellor responsible to the Bundestag, the popularly elected lower house of Parliament.

Germany's two major parties are the *Christian Democrats* and the *Social Democrats*. Although they differ on details, both parties support welfare state measures, NATO membership, and a pro-Western foreign policy. The Christian Democrats were for many years the largest party in the Bundestag and controlled the government.

In 1969 elections the Social Democrats in coalition with the minor Free Democratic party secured a narrow legislative majority. *Willy Brandt*, the Social Democratic leader, became chancellor. Brandt pledged to improve relations with East Germany, Poland, and Russia, and to support West European political and economic unity. In 1972 elections Brandt's coalition government won a strong vote of confidence and gained a substantial legislative majority in the Bundestag. In 1974 Brandt, accepting responsibility for failure to detect an East German Communist spy on his staff, resigned as chancellor. Brandt's successor, named by the Social Democratic party, was the former finance minister, *Helmut Schmidt*. Schmidt pledged to continue Brandt's foreign policy, emphasizing the goal of West European political unity in partnership with the United States. In 1976 and again in 1980 parliamentary elections, the Schmidt coalition retained a majority in the Bundestag, and therefore continued to control the government.

# DEVELOPMENTS IN EAST GERMANY

**1. German Democratic Republic.** Russia in 1949 transformed its zone into the *German Democratic Republic* with its capital in *East Berlin*. This state is a Russian satellite occupied by Soviet troops. In addition East Germany maintains its own army with over 100,000 troops.

**2. Government of East Germany.** A self-proclaimed "democratic republic," East Germany is in fact a typical Communist dictatorship with restrictions on civil liberties, a secret police, and only one political party. In 1953 East German riots against the satellite government were suppressed by Soviet tanks and troops. Until the 1970's the Western powers refused to recognize the East German regime.

For 25 years *Walter Ulbricht*, as head of the East German Communist party, exercised tight control over the country. In 1971 Ulbricht resigned because of ill health and old age and was replaced by *Erich Honecker*.

## COMPARISON OF THE TWO GERMANYS

1. **Area.** West Germany comprises 70 percent of the total area of postwar Germany as compared with 30 percent for East Germany.

2. **Population.** West Germany contains over 75 percent of the German people as compared with less than 25 percent for East Germany.

3. **Industrialization.** West Germany, the more industrial of the two Germanys, contains the industrial heart of Europe, the *Ruhr Valley*. The East German economy is more agricultural than that of West Germany.

4. **Economic System.** West Germany has a capitalist economy, typified by private enterprise, free labor unions, and government regulation to prevent economic abuses. East Germany has a Communist economy, typified by government ownership of industry and collectivization of agriculture.

5. **Economic Developments Since World War II.** Aided by Marshall Plan funds, West Germany made a remarkable recovery from the devastation of World War II. Its cities, transportation system, and industry were all rebuilt.

| | Population (millions) | Gross National Product (billions of dollars) | Steel (millions of metric tons) | Cement (millions of metric tons) |
|---|---|---|---|---|
| West Germany | 62 | 348 | 53 | 36 |
| France | 53 | 255 | 27 | 33 |
| Great Britain | 56 | 175 | 22 | 18 |
| Italy | 55 | 138 | 24 | 36 |

*Commission of the European Communities (1974 figures)*

**West Germany Compared with Other Major West European Nations**

Why does West Germany demand greater influence
in West European matters? Do you approve?

Today West Germany is the leading industrial nation of Western Europe and enjoys a high standard of living.

East Germany, in contrast, made a far slower recovery. For years its cities—notably East Berlin—were not rebuilt, and its people suffered serious shortages of food and other consumer goods. In search of better living standards, many East Germans fled to West Germany. To stop this flow, the Communists in 1961 built the *Berlin Wall*. Having thus halted the flight of skilled workers and also having relaxed economic controls, East Germany in the 1960's experienced considerable economic growth, but its living standard—although the highest in the Soviet bloc—remains below that of West Germany.

## CONFLICTING PROPOSALS FOR GERMAN REUNIFICATION

1. **Western Proposals.** The Western nations proposed that the World War II Allies sign a German peace treaty that would *(a)* reunify Germany by UN-supervised elections in both East and West Germany and *(b)* permit reunited Germany to join in any alliance, including NATO. Russia rejected these proposals because *(a)* free elections would probably result in a pro-Western government for all of Germany and *(b)* NATO membership for a reunited Germany would strengthen the military power of the West.

2. **Russian Proposals.** Russia proposed that *(a)* the World War II Allies sign a peace treaty with the two Germanys, thereby enabling East Germany to retain its "socialist gains"; *(b)* the East German and West German governments negotiate with each other regarding reunification; and *(c)* a reunited Germany remain neutral in the cold war. The Western powers rejected these proposals because they would *(a)* perpetuate the East German satellite regime and *(b)* require West Germany to withdraw from NATO.

## RUSSIA PROVOKES ANOTHER CRISIS OVER BERLIN (1958–1961)

1. **The Russian Challenge on Berlin.** In 1958 Soviet Premier Khrushchev announced his determination to drive the Western powers out of West Berlin. If successful, the Soviets probably expected that *(a)* West Berlin would be absorbed by East Germany, thereby expanding Communist rule and closing down a "showcase" of democracy and capitalism behind the Iron Curtain. The freedom and prosperity of West Berlin contrasted sharply with the repression and drabness of East Berlin. *(b)* West Berlin would no longer serve as an escape route for refugees fleeing from Communist East Europe. In 1961 the Communists almost completely closed this escape route by erecting a barbed-wire and concrete barrier, the *Berlin Wall*.

2. **Western Responses to the Soviet Challenge.** The Western nations *(a)* stated their determination to remain in Berlin, *(b)* condemned the Berlin Wall for disrupting the lives of Berlin citizens, and *(c)* indicated willingness to negotiate regarding Berlin. Although negotiations failed, the Soviets did not act to threaten Allied rights in West Berlin.

## STEPS TO REDUCE TENSIONS OVER BERLIN AND GERMANY (SINCE 1970)

**1. West Germany Improves Relations with Communist East Europe (1970–1972).** While affirming West Germany's strong adherence to the Western world, Chancellor Willy Brandt moved in 1970 to "normalize" his country's relations with the Communist nations of Eastern Europe. Brandt traveled to Moscow and later to Warsaw, paying homage to the Soviet Unknown Soldier, the Polish Unknown Soldier, and the Jews who battled in the Warsaw Ghetto uprising—all victims of Nazi aggression in World War II. Brandt signed two separate treaties with the Soviet Union and with Poland. By these treaties *(a)* West Germany accepted the existing Soviet and Polish borders, with the *Oder-Neisse Line* as Poland's western boundary, thereby conceding sizable areas taken from prewar Germany (see map, page 547). *(b)* The signatories also renounced the use of force and agreed to strive for economic, scientific, and cultural cooperation.

These treaties were hailed by Brandt as leading to a new era of peace for Europe, but they were opposed by many Germans for accepting the territorial losses to Poland and Russia. In 1972 the treaties secured a minimal approval in the Bundestag.

**2. The Big Four Reach Another Berlin Agreement (1971).** The Big Four powers reached a new Berlin agreement *(a)* providing for unimpeded road and rail traffic and continued commercial and cultural ties between West Berlin and West Germany; *(b)* permitting personal and business visits by West Berliners to East Germany; *(c)* accepting West German responsibility for, but limiting its political activity in, West Berlin; and *(d)* allowing Russia to open a consular office in West Berlin.

Kuekes. Reprinted by permission of The Plain Dealer, Cleveland, Ohio

**"Maybe there is no solution."**

3. **West Germany and East Germany "Normalize" Their Relations (1972).** West Germany and East Germany signed a treaty that *(a)* confirmed the existence of two Germanys and established formal relations between them; *(b)* allowed additional visits by West Germans to relatives living in East Germany; *(c)* called for the two Germanys to cooperate in such areas as sports, environmental control, airlines, and technical knowledge; *(d)* proposed that both Germanys be admitted to the UN (which was done in 1973); and *(e)* left unanswered the question of German reunification.

4. **Germany Remains Divided.** After East Germany acceded to the 1971 Big Four agreement on Berlin, Britain and France opened diplomatic relations with the Communist regime. Other Western nations did likewise. In 1974 the United States became the last major Western power to establish formal diplomatic relations with East Germany.

Is Germany destined to remain permanently divided?

# B. The Middle East

## EGYPT AND THE COMMUNIST WORLD (1955)

Premier Gamal Abdel Nasser of Egypt failed to secure arms from the United States because he refused to pledge not to use them for aggression. Thereupon, he turned toward the Communist bloc. Egypt concluded an agreement to exchange Egyptian cotton for Communist military equipment and to accept Communist technicians and military personnel. Nasser increasingly became friendly toward the Communist bloc and hostile toward the West.

## EGYPT SEIZES THE SUEZ CANAL (1956)

To increase Egypt's irrigated land area and electric-power facilities, Nasser planned a high dam on the Nile River at *Aswan*. Nasser needed foreign aid, but his anti-Western attitude caused the United States to withdraw its offer of assistance. Thereupon, Nasser proclaimed the nationalization of the Suez Canal Company, owned by British and French stockholders. He explained that the profits from the operation of the canal would be used to build the Aswan Dam. (Subsequently Nasser secured Russian financial and technical aid for construction of the dam.)

Nasser's action was strongly opposed by Britain and France. These two countries depended on the Suez Canal for trade with the Orient and especially for transporting oil from the Middle East to European markets. They therefore wanted to maintain control over the canal.

## THE INVASION OF EGYPT (1956)

Egypt was invaded by Britain and France, which sought to regain control of the Suez Canal, and by Israel, which sought to end Egyptian guerrilla attacks and economic blockades. Most nations condemned the attack. Russia, seeking to extend its influence in the Arab world, denounced the invaders as aggressors and threatened to provide troops for Egypt. President Eisenhower stated that, although Nasser had been guilty of provocation, the invasion had been "taken in error." By taking a stand against the invasion, the United States outraged France and Britain but won the approval of the Afro-Asian bloc, which had rallied to Egypt's support. The crisis ended when the UN General Assembly brought about the withdrawal of the invading forces (check the Index).

**ARAB-ISRAELI WARS (1967 and 1973).** Check the Index.

**RECENT MIDDLE EAST DEVELOPMENTS.** Check the Index.

## FOREIGN INFLUENCE IN THE ARAB WORLD: AN OVERVIEW

1. **Decline of British Influence.** Once predominant in the Arab world, British power dwindled greatly. Britain granted independence to its Arab possessions and yielded the Suez Canal to Egypt.

2. **Factors Aiding Communist Influence.** (a) The Arabs mistrust the West because of past British and French imperialism. (b) Russia supports the Arabs' anti-Israeli stand. (c) The Arab masses subsist close to the poverty level, even in the oil-rich states. Although the ruling classes have amassed great wealth, the people have scarcely benefited. (d) The Communist bloc has extended foreign aid to the Arab states, especially to Syria, Iraq, Libya, and Egypt. In 1960 Communist technicians, working with Egyptian labor, started on the construction of the Aswan High Dam. In 1970 it began full operations.

3. **Factors Opposing Communist Influence.** (a) Moslem leaders realize that communism is antireligious. (b) Arab upper classes fear the loss of their wealth and power. (c) Arab nationalists seek the goal of Arab unity, not the Communist objective of international working class unity. (d) Oil-rich Arab states are economically tied to the West. Saudi Arabia especially reflects a pro-Western orientation. (e) Under President Sadat since 1970, Egypt has moved away from dependence on the Soviet Union and away from a socialist economy. The country has turned toward increased private enterprise and has welcomed Western business executives and investors.

4. **American Policies.** With the decline of British influence, the United States assumed a greater role in the Middle East. American goals are to reduce Communist influence, improve living standards, achieve permanent peace between the Arab states and Israel, and win Arab friendship.

*Reprinted by special permission of Doug Borgstedt and of the Evening and Sunday Bulletin, Philadelphia, PA*

**Pitfalls in the Middle East**

In 1967 America was blamed by the Arabs for their defeat in the war against Israel, and America lost prestige among the Arabs.

As a result of the 1973 Arab-Israeli War, the United States regained some influence in the Arab world, especially in Egypt. While reaffirming support for Israel's right to exist, the United States helped secure an evenhanded UN cease-fire resolution. Also, Secretary of State Kissinger negotiated two Israeli-Egyptian troop disengagement agreements that restored Egyptian control over both sides of the Suez Canal and over Sinai oil fields.

In 1978 President Carter hosted the Israeli-Egyptian summit conference at Camp David; in 1979 he assisted in concluding the Israeli-Egyptian peace treaty. The United States gained prestige in Egypt and moderate Arab states but was denounced by the PLO and radical Arab states.

## C. The Far East

### KOREA

**1. Korea After World War II.** In 1945 Korea (a colony of Japan since 1910) was divided at the 38th parallel: the North occupied by Russian troops, the South by American troops. Russia and the United States failed to agree regarding Korean reunification, and Russia defied UN attempts to unify the country by free elections. In North Korea the Russians established a Communist government led by the Korean Workers Communist party head *Kim Il-Sung*. In South Korea UN-supervised elections established an independent anti-Communist government headed by President *Syngman Rhee*.

2. **Communist Aggression Against South Korea (1950–1953).** In June, 1950, without warning, North Korean Communist forces crossed the 38th parallel and invaded South Korea. The UN Security Council (with Russia absent) promptly recommended that UN members furnish military assistance to South Korea. The UN army consisted chiefly of American and South Korean units, with contingents from 15 other anti-Communist nations. It was headed originally by United States General Douglas MacArthur.

At first the UN forces retreated before the Communist assault. After reinforcements arrived, General MacArthur launched a counterattack that drove the North Korean armies back across the 38th parallel and deep into North Korea close to the Manchurian border. In November, 1950, powerful Communist Chinese armies crossed into North Korea and attacked the UN forces, inflicting heavy losses and compelling MacArthur to retreat. By the summer of 1951 the battle line had become stabilized near the 38th parallel.

Meanwhile, the UN General Assembly voted (with opposition only from the Soviet bloc) to declare Communist China guilty of aggression in Korea and to embargo the shipment of war goods to Communist China.

3. **The MacArthur-Truman Controversy.** In 1951 President Truman, as commander in chief of the American armed forces, dismissed General MacArthur for insubordination. Truman charged that the general had repeatedly disregarded instructions to refrain from making foreign policy statements that criticized government policies.

The two men had disagreed sharply. MacArthur advocated carrying the war to Communist China, especially Manchuria. He urged that the United States fight an all-out war to win complete victory over communism in Asia. Truman feared that an invasion of Manchuria would lead to war with Russia and held that the United States must fight a limited war in Asia so as not to leave Western Europe—the key to American security—defenseless.

4. **Truce in Korea (1953).** Meeting mainly at *Panmunjom*, UN and Communist truce representatives took two years to reach an agreement for halting hostilities. The conference was long deadlocked regarding the return, or *repatriation*, of prisoners. The UN claimed that many of its prisoners did not want to return to their Communist homelands; the Communists insisted upon compulsory repatriation. Finally the conference agreed that prisoners be given freedom of choice. (Eventually two of every five prisoners held by the UN refused to return to Communist rule.)

The truce *(a)* was hailed by the UN as a victory against aggression, *(b)* was criticized by the South Korean government for failing to unify the country under anti-Communist leadership, and *(c)* was greeted by most Americans with relief. The Korean struggle cost the United States $18 billion, 103,000 wounded, and 33,000 killed.

## 5. Korean Developments Since the Truce

*a. Continued American Interest.* In support of South Korea, the United States extended considerable economic and military aid, kept 45,000 troops there, and signed a bilateral Mutual Defense Pact.

In 1977 President Carter, while reaffirming America's commitment to defend South Korea, announced plans for a phased withdrawal by 1982 of 33,000 American ground troops from South Korea. Carter's plans to withdraw these combat units caused concern among South Korean and Japanese leaders.

In 1979, as President Carter became aware of the increased strength of North Korea's armed forces, he suspended the withdrawal of the American ground troops.

*b. Continued Communist Interest.* In 1961 Soviet Russia signed a defense treaty pledging to assist North Korea "with all forces and by every means." China also made a similar defense pledge to North Korea.

*c. Renewed Communist Pressures (1967–1972)*

(1) *On South Korea.* North Korea sent raiding parties into the south to commit sabotage and spread terror. For example, in 1968 North Korean commandoes slipped into the southern capital of Seoul to assassinate President Park, but they were captured before they could carry out their plans.

(2) *On the United States.* In 1968 North Korean patrol boats seized the American intelligence ship *Pueblo*. The Communists claimed that the *Pueblo* had intruded into North Korean waters on a criminal and hostile mission. The United States answered that the *Pueblo* had been in international waters. To secure the release of the *Pueblo* crew, the United States negotiated with the

*Justus in The Minneapolis Star*

"Agonizing Reappraisal"

North Koreans. After almost a year, the chief American negotiator signed a document confessing intrusion into North Korean waters, while publicly repudiating the confession, and North Korea freed the *Pueblo* crew.

### d. Governmental Changes in South Korea

(1) *Rhee Regime (1948–1960)*. In 1960 South Korea was swept by antigovernment riots protesting rigged elections, police terror, corruption, and autocratic rule. Syngman Rhee ended his 12-year presidency by resigning.

(2) *Park Regime (1961–1979)*. In 1961 General *Chung Hee Park*, leading a military junta (council), seized power. Four times thereafter Park was elected president. He improved economic conditions and maintained a pro-American foreign policy. In 1972 Park moved to "reform" South Korea's political structure. He imposed martial law, dissolved the National Assembly, prohibited political activities, and imposed press censorship. Under these conditions Park won a public referendum for a constitution enabling him to remain president for life, to dominate the other branches of government, and to rule dictatorially. Park became increasingly intolerant of dissent.

(3) *American Criticism of the Park Regime*. The United States disapproved of Park's 1972 constitutional changes. Thereafter, the United States criticized the Park regime for its harsh treatment of dissidents, for its use—so it seemed—of campaign contributions and other means to influence American political leaders; and for its unwillingness to cooperate in the investigation of Korean agents presumed to have bribed American officials.

In 1979, after a visit by President Carter to South Korea, the United States—as part of its human rights campaign—asked the Park regime to release over 100 political prisoners held in South Korean jails.

(4) *Assassination of Park (1979)*. Jae Kyn Kim, head of Korea's Central Intelligence Agency, assassinated President Park. Kim's motives were not clearly known—possibly personal quarrels or possibly a policy rift, as Kim felt that Park's repression of opposition threatened the nation's stability. With Park's death South Korea was placed under martial law and faced political instability.

The United States meanwhile warned Communist North Korea not to "attempt to exploit the situation," placed American forces in South Korea on an alert, and sent an American aircraft carrier into South Korean waters.

(5) *Chun Regime (1980–    )*. General *Chun Doo Hwan*, an army strongman, seized control of the Seoul government and became President. Pledging to wipe out corruption and to foster a "democracy suited to our political climate," Chun secured public approval of a new constitution containing many democratic features—guarantees of press freedom and habeas corpus, a ban on forced confessions, and a single seven-year Presidential term. Meanwhile, Chun enforced martial law, strong press censorship, and repression of dissidents.

In early 1981, prior to visiting Washington, Chun ended martial law in South Korea, but his government continued in firm control. In Washington, Chun was reassured by President Reagan that America remained committed to the security of South Korea and would retain there its 39,000 American troops. A State Department official further explained that although "we are for human rights" —which the Carter Administration had emphasized—the Reagan Administration's preeminent concern is for military security.

## COMMUNIST CHINA. (See also pages 400–403.)

### 1. Communist China and the United States: Unfriendly Relations to 1971

*a. Communist China's Policies.* The Communists harshly treated American officials, missionaries, and business people caught in China during the civil war. The Communists directly intervened in the Korean War and fought American troops. They sent military aid to the Communist forces in Vietnam. Communist China remained hostile toward the United States.

*b. America's Policies.* In opposition to Communist China, the United States (1) recognized the Nationalist government on Taiwan as the legal government of China, (2) refused to recognize the Peking regime, (3) opposed Communist China's admission to the UN, (4) maintained an embargo on trade with Communist China, (5) fought to prevent a Communist takeover in South Vietnam, and (6) signed mutual defense treaties to defend South Korea and Taiwan.

### 2. Dispute Over Taiwan (Formosa). 
The United States viewed Taiwan as a vital Pacific military base, the Nationalist army as a dependable anti-Communist force, and the Nationalist government as an ally. Consequently the United States extended economic and military aid to Taiwan and vowed to defend Nationalist-held territory, as agreed in a Mutual Defense Treaty.

Communist China was determined to annex the island and destroy the Nationalist government. The Chinese Communists warned the United States that nothing will deter them from "liberating" Taiwan.

### 3. Chinese-Soviet Split in the Open by 1963. 
Despite their 1950 treaty of alliance, China and Russia gradually became hostile and by 1963 openly disagreed as follows:

*a. Ideological Conflict.* (1) *Russia.* Soviet leaders asserted that world communism can be achieved through *peaceful coexistence.* They claimed that people, impressed by Soviet economic and scientific achievements, will turn to communism. Meanwhile, Communist nations will subject the West to unremitting economic competition, propaganda, subversion, and localized conflict. However, Communists must make every effort to avoid nuclear war. A Communist paradise cannot be built upon millions of corpses. (2) *China.* Mao Tse-tung derided peaceful coexistence as a myth and insisted that Communists support the revolutionary struggles of oppressed peoples even at the risk of nuclear war. If war does come, Mao declared, it will prove the United States to be a "paper tiger," end capitalism, and usher in a glorious Communist future.

*b. Russian Atomic Aid to China.* (1) *Russia.* The Soviets trained Chinese atomic scientists, sent Russian technicians to China, and provided China with an atomic reactor to produce nuclear materials. As the ideological conflict became acute, Russia terminated its aid. (2) *China.* Peking at first complained that Soviet aid was not enough and then deplored its termination.

*c. Chinese-Soviet Borders.* (1) *Russia.* Soviet leaders contended that both Russia and China must respect the 19th-century treaties establishing the borders between them. These treaties provided for Russian annexation of sizable territories, including the Amur River Valley and the port of Vladivostok. (2) *China.* Chinese leaders argued that the treaties were imperialist-imposed and are not valid now. In 1969 Chinese and Russian forces clashed at several border points, most notably north of Vladivostok.

*d. World Communist Leadership.* (1) *Russia.* As the oldest and most advanced Communist nation, Russia claimed the leadership of the Communist bloc. Khrushchev conceded that there are many roads to communism, including

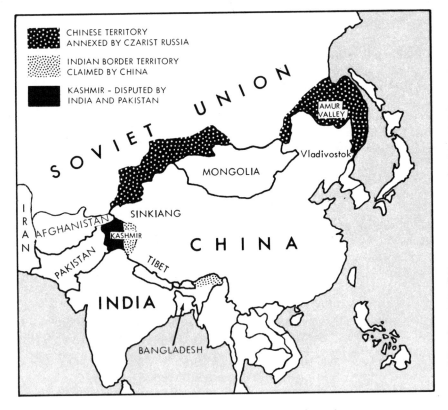

**Border Disputes on the Asian Mainland**

Communist China is said to covet Mongolia and the territory annexed from China by Czarist Russia.

Tito's policies in Yugoslavia. The Soviets condemned Chinese appeals to non-white peoples as containing racial overtones. Russia retained the support of most Communist nations. (2) *China*. The most populous Communist nation, China claimed to be the true interpreter of Marxist-Leninist doctrine and the leader of the Communist world. The Chinese condemned the Yugoslavs as renegades. They also charged that Russia "sold out" the Communist movement in Latin America, Africa, and Asia.

**4. Communist China Develops Nuclear Weapons Since 1964.** In 1964 China set off its first atomic bomb; in 1967 China exploded a hydrogen bomb; and in 1970 China sent up its first earth satellite, indicating sufficient thrust power to launch ICBM's. China's speed in developing nuclear weapons and missiles created a major new world problem. In particular it caused concern in two major Far Eastern nations—India and Japan—whose relations with China had been un-friendly; in the Soviet Union, whose long border with China had been the scene of several armed clashes; and in the United States, whose leaders considered the possibility of a Communist Chinese missile attack.

**5. Recent Developments**

  *a. "Cultural Revolution" (1966–1969).* (1) *Reasons.* Aged and ill, Mao Tse-tung wanted to assure that after his death China would continue his policies: *(a) within the country,* increased collectivization, even over the opposition of the peasants, and *(b) in foreign affairs,* world revolution, even at the risk of war. Mao did not want China to adopt "Soviet revisionism," by which he meant the use of profit as an economic incentive and the loss of revolutionary zeal in foreign affairs. Mao's opponents, holding important positions in the Communist party and the government, considered Mao's views inappropriate for building the nation. (2) *Three Years of Turmoil.* Mao moved to crush his opponents by a "great proletarian cultural revolution." He mobilized millions of youths into *Red Guard* groups that terrorized the opposition. The cultural revolution fragmented the Communist party and undermined production, education, and transport.

  *b. Return to Stability.* By 1970 China returned to stability. The Red Guards were disbanded, and order was restored by realistic army leaders. The govern-ment reflected control of moderate political leaders under Premier Chou En-lai. China then turned from preoccupation with internal matters to a more active foreign role, especially steps to improve Chinese-American relations.

  China arranged a visit by an American table tennis team. Their visit, Premier Chou stated, "opened a new page in the relations of the Chinese and American peoples." President Nixon, who had made several overtures to "normalize" relations, relaxed our trade embargo on exporting nonstrategic goods to China. Thereafter, Chou En-lai invited President Nixon to visit China. Nixon accepted, expressing the hope that this "will become a journey for peace."

  *c. The Nixon Visit to China (1972).* President Nixon visited Communist China. Warmly received, Nixon spent a hectic week that included sightseeing, banquets, a meeting with Mao Tse-tung, and negotiating sessions with Chou

Bruce Shanks in The Buffalo Evening News, May 1, 1971

"They say it shouldn't concern me"

En-lai. The visit concluded with the issuance of the *Shanghai communiqué* in which (1) the United States and China both stated their differences regarding Vietnam, Korea, and Taiwan; (2) the United States agreed that Taiwan is part of China, urged peaceful settlement of the Taiwan issue by the Chinese themselves; and (3) the United States and China agreed to peaceful coexistence and to expand their contacts.

This visit, analysts believed, signified the following: (1) *for China,* realization that the major threat to its national interests comes from the Soviet Union rather than the United States and (2) *for the United States,* less fear that China threatens vital American interests and seeks to dominate Eastern Asia.

Following the Nixon visit, China and the United States encouraged reciprocal visits by scholars, doctors, musicians, and sports figures and also expanded trade. China placed orders for American farm produce and jet planes.

*d. Power Struggle Following the Deaths of China's Leaders (1976).* With the deaths of Premier Chou En-lai and, eight months later, of Chairman Mao Tse-tung, China experienced an open struggle for power between two Communist party factions labeled "radicals" and "moderates." The radicals favored strict adherence to Maoist theories of class warfare, no profit incentives, and "permanent revolution" to prevent backsliding into capitalist ways. The moderates stressed pragmatic goals of economic growth and political stability. The moderates attracted support of the industrial managers, government officials, and army leaders.

*Hua Kuo-feng* (Hua Guofeng), an active party and government figure but little known to the Chinese people was named premier. After Mao's death, Hua was named to the post of Communist party chairman. He then acted swiftly against four top radical leaders, the most notable one being Mao's widow, *Chiang Ching* (Jiang Qing). The radical leaders were purged from their party posts, placed under arrest, and charged with a plot to "usurp party and state power." Hua's action against the "gang of four" was acclaimed by huge demonstrations.

In foreign affairs the new Chinese regime continued Chou's recent policies. China rebuffed Soviet efforts to improve relations and labeled the Soviet Union a "peace swindler and most dangerous source of war today." Also, China indicated a strong desire to improve friendship with the United States.

*e. Full Diplomatic Relations (1979).* The United States and Communist China agreed to establish full diplomatic relations. For the United States, this agreement meant breaking diplomatic ties with Taiwan, withdrawing the American forces on that island, and giving the required one-year notice to end its mutual defense treaty with Taiwan. The United States, however, pledged to maintain cultural and economic ties with Taiwan, to sell Taiwan limited supplies of defensive arms, and to remain interested in the peaceful settlement of the Taiwan issue. For Communist China, the agreement meant an implied promise—but no public statement—not to use force to gain control over Taiwan.

*Teng Hsiao-ping* (Deng Xiaoping), the senior deputy Communist chairman, had spurred the restoration of full diplomatic relations. A pragmatist and a moderate, Teng wanted China to increase trade with and learn from the West so as to hasten China's modernization. Although twice purged during the Mao era, Teng bounced back and became the most influential leader in post-Maoist China.

American skeptics and Taiwanese officials denounced the Sino-American agreement. These people claimed that the United States would lose credibility as to its military defense pledges and its concern for human rights.

President Carter hailed the new Sino-American relationship—economically as furthering trade and politically as "simple reality" that "contributes to the cause of peace." Although the President stated that the normalization of Sino-American relations was not directed against any third nation, the Soviet Union indicated its concern over this development as potentially dangerous to its interests. (In 1981, when the Reagan Administration agreed to sell modern American weapons to China, the Soviets deplored the agreement as "highly dangerous for the cause of peace.")

*f. Mao Downgraded: New Chinese Leaders.* In 1981, the Chinese Communist party gave its official assessment of Mao Tse-tung. Stating that his contributions "far outweigh" his mistakes, the party called Mao a brilliant revolutionary but a blundering national leader. Mao was condemned for the Cultural Revolution that, the party said, "was responsible for the most severe setbacks and the heaviest losses suffered by the party, the state, and the people." Mao was also blamed, in his later years, for being arrogant and arbitrary, for suppressing discussions, and for fostering his own personality cult. In contrast to Mao's "seeking quick results in economic work," the party praised the efforts for orderly economic development by Chou En-lai and Teng Hsiao-ping.

Reflecting this statement of Chinese Communist views, the party made major changes in party and government leaders. Hua Kuo-feng, who was associated with Maoist policies, was replaced as premier and as party chairman by two persons loyal to Teng. Chao Tzu-yang (Zhao Ziyang) became premier and Hu Yaobang (Pinyin spelling) became party chairman. Observers pointed out that Teng—now the most powerful man in China—had arranged an orderly transfer of power to more youthful persons committed to his views.

*g. China vs. Vietnam: Hostility Between Communist Nations.* (Check the Index for Vietnam.)

## JAPAN. (See also pages 405–407.)

### 1. American Friendship for Japan: In the Cold War Era

*a. Reasons.* (1) With the reforms achieved during the American occupation of Japan (check the Index), the United States considers Japan as an Asian "bulwark of democracy." (2) Japan represents a counterbalance to the growth of Communist power in Asia. (3) Japan is a valuable ally because of its industrial capacity, large labor force drawn from a population of 110 million, and strategic location off the Asian continent.

*b. Evidences.* The United States (1) treated Japan generously in the 1952 treaty of peace, (2) extended economic and military aid to Japan, (3) stationed American forces in Japan for the defense of Japan and other free-world nations, (4) developed close commercial and cultural ties with Japan, and (5) in 1972 returned the Ryukyu Islands, including Okinawa, to Japan. (By contrast the Soviet Union has refused to return four small northern islands seized after World War II and repeatedly claimed by Japan.)

### 2. Important Developments

*a. Economic Recovery.* Under its free-enterprise economic system, postwar Japan achieved remarkable economic growth. Industrial production regained prewar levels by 1951 and since then has more than tripled. Japan ranks among the world's top manufacturers of steel, synthetic fibers, electrical products, and cotton yarn and is first in shipbuilding. Japan is the world's third greatest economic power, and its people enjoy a standard of living approaching that of Western Europe. However, with limited farmland and mineral resources, Japan must "export or die."

*b. Trade with the United States.* Japan provides the second largest market for American exports and, in turn, finds the United States its best customer. Americans purchase Japanese textiles, toys, cameras, radios, and television sets. American manufacturers, who complain that Japanese wages are far below those paid American workers, protest this competition and request adequate tariff protection. To quiet these protests, Japan, on several occasions, has voluntarily limited certain exports to the United States.

**INDIA.** (See also pages 410–412.)

**1. Communist Chinese Aggression Affects India (1959–1962).** Prime Minister Nehru's friendship for Communist China was shattered by Chinese actions in Tibet (India's northern neighbor) and along the Indian border.

*a. Tibet.* In 1959, after eight years of Chinese Communist occupation and rule, the Tibetan people revolted. The Chinese Communists (1) suppressed this revolt, taking many Tibetan lives, and (2) accused India of having aided the revolt—a charge which Nehru indignantly denied. Nehru condemned China's brutality in Tibet and granted asylum to thousands of Tibetan refugees, including that country's civil and spiritual head, the *Dalai Lama.* The Indian people were angry at China, especially because Tibet and India have a history of close commercial and spiritual ties.

*b. The Indian Border.* For many years China had disputed its boundary with India. In 1959, following the Tibetan revolt, Communist Chinese troops crossed India's northern frontier, attacked Indian border patrols, and occupied large areas of territory claimed by India. In 1962 the Chinese renewed their attack, overpowered Indian resistance, and occupied additional territory (see map, page 560). Nehru warned that his country would resist Communist aggression. He requested and received military aid from Britain and the United States.

**2. American Relations with India.** The United States hoped that India would side with the free world because India, *(a)* in the words of former Prime Minister Nehru, is "firmly wedded to the democratic way of life," *(b)* had been menaced by Communist China, and *(c)* needs American aid to raise the living standard of its people. India has received billions in American economic aid.

In 1959, during the India-China border dispute, President Eisenhower visited India and received a welcome of a size and enthusiasm unmatched in Indian history. In 1962, when Chinese troops resumed their·attack, President Kennedy airlifted weapons for India's border forces. In 1966 President Johnson authorized large wheat shipments to prevent starvation in India.

In 1971, however, President Nixon condemned India for sending its troops into East Pakistan and forcibly gaining independence for Bangladesh. Nixon also halted most American economic aid programs for India.

**3. Russian Relations with India.** Russia seeks to win India to the Communist side or, at least, to keep it neutral in the cold war. *(a)* Russia granted loans for the development of India's heavy industry. Russia's economic aid to India, however, is far less than that extended by the United States. *(b)* In 1963, as the split between Russia and China widened, Soviet leaders voiced support for India in its border dispute with China. *(c)* In 1966 Russia hosted an Indian-Pakistani conference at the Soviet city of Tashkent in central Asia. India and Pakistan, having recently fought over Kashmir, agreed to observe the UN cease-fire, to restore diplomatic relations, and to settle disputes by peaceful means. *(d)* In 1971 Russia signed a 20-year treaty of friendship with India; thereafter, as the

Indian-Pakistani war started, Russia supported India by vetoing three Security Council resolutions for a cease-fire and withdrawal of Indian forces.

4. **For Nuclear Developments in India, check the Index.**

## THE NATIONS OF INDO-CHINA

1. **For developments in Laos, Cambodia, and Vietnam, check the Index.**

2. **Effects of the Vietnamese War on American Foreign Policy**

*a. The Nixon Doctrine (1969).* President Nixon asserted that the United States would continue to play a major role in the Pacific but would seek to avoid involvement in another war like Vietnam. Nixon told our Asian friends that the United States would honor its treaty commitments, including military and economic aid, but would look to any Asian nation threatened by internal subversion or nonnuclear aggression to provide the armed force for its own defense. This doctrine, said the president, meant a "more responsible role for the Asian nations" and also an American policy that could "be sustained over the long run."

*b. War-Powers Resolution of 1973.* In ordering American forces into combat in Vietnam, three successive presidents—Kennedy, Johnson, and Nixon—had used the presidential power of commander in chief but had not secured a congressional declaration of war. In 1973 Congress moved to limit presidential war-making powers by enacting, over President Nixon's veto, the *War-Powers Resolution*. It provided that (1) if the president commits American troops to combat abroad, the reasons must be presented to Congress within 48 hours; (2) if the president expects to keep American troops in combat abroad for more than 90 days, congressional approval must be secured; (3) if the president does not secure congressional approval, the military action must be terminated; and (4) Congress can order withdrawal of American forces from abroad, before 90 days, by adopting a concurrent resolution not subject to a presidential veto.

President Nixon condemned the resolution as "clearly unconstitutional" and declared that it would "seriously undermine this nation's ability to act decisively . . . in times of international crisis."

*c. Other Effects:* (1) *Thailand.* Now bordered by Communist Laos and Communist Cambodia, and fearful that these regimes might aid Thai guerrilla bands, the Thai government in 1975 moved to reduce the American presence. Thailand requested the United States to close American bases and withdraw American forces from its soil. The United States agreed. (2) *Angola.* After Portugal withdrew in 1975, Angola experienced civil war between pro-Western and pro-Communist groups. When the United States Congress became aware that the Ford administration was sending covert aid to the pro-Western forces, Congress voted overwhelmingly to prohibit such aid. Congress feared that such aid could lead America to involvement in another Vietnam-type situation.

*Bruce Shanks in The Buffalo Evening News, Sept. 30, 1968*

**"Never Again!"**

## AFGHANISTAN

**1. Land and People.** Located in central Asia, Afghanistan is a landlocked country of strategic importance. It is bordered on the north by the Soviet Union, on the west by Iran, on the south by Pakistan, and at its eastern tip by China (see map, page 560). Afghanistan contains some small fertile valleys interspersed among large deserts and extensive mountains. The Khyber Pass, 35 miles (56 kilometers) long, provides a major route through the Hindu Kush Mountains from Afghanistan into Pakistan. Afghanistan's natural resources remain largely untouched except for natural gas fields and coal deposits. Afghanistan is essentially a primitive, underdeveloped country.

The Afghan people, totaling 21 million, are devout Moslems. They belong to a number of different tribes and retain a strong sense of tribal identity and loyalty. They speak Persian or Persian-related languages. Few Afghans are urban dwellers; 90 percent live in rural areas, some working as livestock herders but most as farmers. Their per capita income is slightly above $100 per year, some 90 percent are illiterate, and the average life expectancy is 40 years.

**2. Pro-Soviet Government (1978).** By a 1978 revolution a pro-Marxist party seized control. It established an Afghan regime that signed a treaty of "friendship and cooperation" with the Soviet Union and accepted Soviet military and economic advisers. This pro-Soviet regime aroused strong opposition among the people for being "godless" and anti-Islamic, subservient to the Soviet Union, brutal in its treatment of political prisoners, and a threat to the traditional Afghan way of life. The Communist regime proved unable to suppress the rebellious

Moslem tribal guerrilla bands, and by late 1979 it seemed likely to be overthrown.

**3. Soviet Invasion (1979–1980).** Thereupon the Soviet Union sponsored a coup in Afghanistan, installing a new president—*Babrak Karmal*—in the capital city of Kabul and sending some 50,000 Soviet troops into the country to crush the rebellious tribal guerrillas. Russia claimed that its intervention had been requested by the Afghan authorities. The Soviet forces met resistance from both the Afghan army and the guerrilla units.

This invasion—reminiscent of Soviet actions in 1956 in Hungary and 1968 in Czechoslovakia—was protested by Western and many Third World nations. The United States condemned Russia for "blatant military interference," and President Carter warned of a deterioration of Soviet-American relations. China termed the invasion a threat to Chinese security and warned the Soviets to withdraw. Pakistan, which housed many Afghan refugees, sponsored a letter signed by forty-three Third World and Western nations asking the UN Security Council to consider the situation. The Security Council resolution, calling for the "unconditional withdrawal of all foreign troops from Afghanistan," received 13 out of 15 votes but was defeated by a Soviet veto. Then, under the Uniting for Peace Resolution, the veto-free General Assembly convened in an emergency session to consider the Soviet invasion. By a vote of 104–18 (with 30 not voting), the General Assembly adopted a resolution strongly deploring the armed intervention in Afghanistan and calling for a withdrawal of all foreign troops. The General Assembly action was belittled by the Soviet Union.

## THE CARTER DOCTRINE

In his 1980 State of the Union address, President Carter considered the implications of the Soviet invasion of Afghanistan. That invasion, the President held, threatened the Persian Gulf region, with its oil supplies essential to the Western democracies. Soviet forces now were within 300 miles of the Indian Ocean and close to the major waterway for transporting Persian Gulf oil, the *Strait of Hormuz.* The President therefore issued a warning that any attempt by outside forces "to gain control of the Persian Gulf region will be regarded as an assault" against the United States and "will be repelled by any means necessary, including military force." This warning became known as the *Carter Doctrine.*

The Soviet Union meanwhile denied any designs on Middle East oil or warm-water ports on the Persian Gulf.

To implement the Carter Doctrine, the United States established a small Rapid Deployment Force, sent four radar warning planes to aid a Saudi Arabia fearful of Iranian air attack, promised economic and military aid to Oman in exchange for air and naval bases near the Persian Gulf and to Kenya for bases on the East African coast, and agreed to grant Somalia credits to purchase military equipment in exchange for the use of a Somali naval and air base at Berbera just south of the Red Sea.

# D. Cuba

## CUBAN-AMERICAN RELATIONS UNTIL 1959

The United States has long had a special interest in Cuba, located some 90 miles (144 kilometers) off the Florida coast. By the Spanish-American War in 1898, the United States compelled Spain to free Cuba. In 1901 the United States secured Cuban consent to the *Platt Amendment*. It made Cuba a virtual protectorate by granting the United States (1) the right to intervene militarily in Cuba to preserve Cuban independence and to protect life, liberty, and property and (2) the naval base in eastern Cuba at *Guantanamo Bay*. In 1934, under the *Good Neighbor Policy*, the United States abrogated (abolished) the Platt Amendment but was permitted to retain the Guantanamo base under a lease that could be ended only by mutual consent.

Until 1959 the United States dominated the Cuban economy. American investors placed large sums in Cuban public utilities, iron and nickel mines, and sugar and tobacco plantations. The United States provided the chief market for Cuban agricultural and mineral exports and was the chief source of Cuban imports of manufactured goods. Cuban vacation resorts attracted American tourists. The American people considered Cuba as a friend and ally.

## THE CASTRO REGIME (SINCE 1959)

In 1959 *Fidel Castro*, on the promise to restore democracy, received widespread Cuban support and overthrew the corrupt military dictatorship of *Fulgencio Batista*. Once in power, Castro forbade elections, violated civil liber-

**Russian Proverbs**

*Alexander in the Philadelphia Evening Bulletin*

ties, expropriated American investments without compensation, demanded the return of the Guantanamo naval base, denounced the United States as imperialist, negotiated trade agreements with Communist-bloc nations, and received Communist military equipment for his armed forces. In 1961 Castro admitted being a "Marxist-Leninist" and proclaimed his intention to transform Cuba into a Communist state.

## BAY OF PIGS INVASION (1961)

In 1961 American-trained Cuban exiles launched a small-scale invasion of Cuba at the *Bay of Pigs*. Although easily crushed by Castro's military forces, the invasion sparked a bitter argument between Russia and the United States. Premier Khrushchev demanded that the United States halt the "aggression" against Cuba and warned that the Soviet Union would assist Castro. In reply President Kennedy proclaimed American admiration for the Cuban invaders and warned Russia that the United States would "protect this hemisphere against external aggression."

## SOVIET MISSILE BASES IN CUBA (1962)

**1. The Crisis.** In 1962 President Kennedy disclosed that Russia secretly was constructing offensive bomber and missile bases in Cuba—a threat to the security of the Western Hemisphere. The president ordered a *quarantine* by American naval and air forces on shipments of offensive arms bound for Cuba. He demanded that Russia dismantle the Cuban missile bases and withdraw the bombers and missiles. Furthermore, the president warned that, if any nuclear missiles were launched from Cuba, America would reply with a full retaliatory blow against the Soviet Union. This firm United States stand won the support of our NATO and Latin American allies.

How would Russia respond? At first Russia called the American charges false and labeled the American quarantine "piracy." Then, after several suspenseful days, Khrushchev agreed to dismantle the missile bases and withdraw the offensive weapons. In turn Kennedy agreed to lift the quarantine and pledged that the United States would not invade Cuba. War was averted.

**2. Reactions to the Settlement.** (*a*) President Kennedy considered the settlement an honorable accord, not a victory. The president felt relieved that the Soviet offensive weapons were withdrawn in peace. However, the United States is aware that Cuba remains Communist, heavily armed with defensive weapons, and bolstered by Soviet military and technical personnel. (*b*) Premier Khrushchev called the settlement an example of his policy of "peaceful coexistence." He claimed that the American pledge not to invade Cuba had ended the need for the Soviet missile bases. (*c*) Castro resented the settlement and protested that Cuba had not been consulted.

## COMMUNIST CUBAN TROOPS IN AFRICA: ANGOLA (1975) AND ETHIOPIA (1977)

In 1975 Cuba sent 15,000 troops to Angola, assisting the pro-Soviet MPLA to gain control of the country. (For details on Angola, check the Index.) Thereafter, the question arose whether the Cuban force would be used to further other Communist objectives in Africa.

The United States resented the Cuban intervention in Angola as well as Cuban efforts to spread Communist influence in the Caribbean and Central America, and to stir up an independence movement in Puerto Rico. The United States warned Cuba against further military adventures.

In 1977, despite this warning, the Cuban troops in Africa moved to Ethiopia and went into combat in the Ogaden region. They assisted the pro-Soviet Ethiopian military regime to combat a Somali rebellion. (For details, check the Index for Ethiopia.) President Carter thereafter warned the Soviet Union that its use of Cuban "proxy forces" in Africa endangers Soviet-American cooperation.

**Soviet Combat Force in Cuba (1979).** Check the Index for Cuba.

## MULTIPLE–CHOICE QUESTIONS

1. A major problem in the establishment of peace following World War II was the (1) extreme difficulty in reconciling the goals of the victors (2) refusal of the defeated powers to surrender (3) policies of nonalignment adopted by the emerging nations (4) international agreements that weakened the role of nations.

2. Which was the first major postwar clash between the Western powers and the Soviet Union? (1) the Berlin Blockade (2) the defense of Hong Kong (3) the Hungarian revolt against Soviet Russia's domination (4) the invasion of South Korea.

3. An important similarity between the governments of Great Britain and West Germany in the mid-20th century is that both have (1) a written constitution (2) a king (3) a "responsible" prime minister (4) an elected "upper house."

4. Which was a result of both World War I and World War II? (1) All of Germany was occupied by Allied armies. (2) The United States joined its allies in collecting reparations from Germany. (3) Germany was forced to give up all its African colonies. (4) Germany was forced to transfer territory to Poland.

5. At the Nuremberg trials Nazi leaders were charged with (1) losing the war (2) destroying the German Republic (3) inventing missiles (4) committing crimes against humanity.

6. The United States gave economic aid to West Germany after World War II chiefly to (1) help stop the spread of communism (2) strengthen Germany against French power (3) help Germany socialize its industry (4) raise the German standard of living above the prewar level.

7. The city of Berlin is located (1) within East Germany (2) within West Germany (3) on the border between East Germany and West Germany (4) on the border between East Germany and Poland.

8. The capital of West Germany is (1) Bonn (2) Berlin (3) Nuremberg (4) Strasbourg.

9. The Soviet Union wanted to drive the Western powers from West Berlin because that city was (1) traditionally Communist (2) a valuable seaport (3) NATO headquarters (4) a showcase of democracy and capitalism behind the Iron Curtain.

10. Western determination to remain in West Berlin was based upon  (1) the failure of the airlift of 1948–1949  (2) the friendship given to the Western powers by Berliners throughout the 20th century  (3) an effort to prevent the return of Nazism in West Berlin  (4) the belief that weakness here would encourage further Soviet aggression.

11. Which statement is now true regarding German reunification?  (1) East and West Germans no longer have enough in common to justify reunification.  (2) The International Court of Justice has decided that Germany remain divided.  (3) Russia will permit reunification of Germany but only on Soviet terms.  (4) France has declared itself opposed to German reunification.

12. East Germany erected the Berlin Wall chiefly as a barrier to  (1) trade  (2) Western troops  (3) Western propaganda  (4) refugees seeking to flee Communist rule.

13. Which nation most opposed Egypt's nationalization of the Suez Canal?  (1) Britain  (2) the United States  (3) Israel  (4) Saudi Arabia.

14. Which nation in the Middle East received substantial military aid from the Communist bloc?  (1) Israel  (2) Saudi Arabia  (3) Egypt  (4) Turkey.

15. Which represents the *major* goal of Israeli foreign policy?  (1) ending Communist influence in the Middle East  (2) destroying the Organization of Petroleum Exporting Countries (OPEC)  (3) gaining control of both sides of the Suez Canal  (4) assuring the physical and economic security of Israel.

16. Egypt received foreign aid for construction of the Aswan High Dam chiefly from  (1) the United States  (2) Russia  (3) Communist China  (4) Saudi Arabia.

17. American foreign policy in the Middle East has sought  (1) a confrontation with the Soviet Union  (2) a compromise settlement of Arab-Israeli issues so as to end the recurrent crises  (3) peace in the area enforced by American marines  (4) an end to American investments in Arab countries.

18. Which is a basic cause of unrest today throughout Asia?  (1) complete control by European powers  (2) lack of important natural resources  (3) small population  (4) low standard of living of most people.

19. The Communists have appealed to the people of Southeast Asia by promising to  (1) establish agricultural collectives  (2) distribute land to the peasants  (3) destroy the power of Buddhist monks  (4) hold free elections.

20. The event that occurred *first* in Korea was  (1) North Korea's invasion of South Korea  (2) North Korean seizure of the American intelligence ship *Pueblo*  (3) intervention of Chinese Communist troops in Korea  (4) division of Korea at the 38th parallel.

21. Which issue was the chief cause of delay in negotiating a truce in Korea?  (1) the UN resolution calling Communist China an aggressor  (2) the boundary line between North and South Korea  (3) the exchange of war prisoners  (4) the status of Taiwan.

22. Following the Korean War  (1) Korea was unified  (2) Nationalist China obtained control of Korea  (3) Communist influence in Korea was ended  (4) Korea remained divided in two sections.

23. Which was characteristic of Communist China's foreign policy?  (1) voting with Russia in the UN General Assembly  (2) spreading Communist propaganda in Southeast Asia  (3) offering aid to SEATO  (4) compromising with Nationalist China over control of Taiwan.

24. Which was a *major* point that created disunity between Communist China and Soviet Russia?  (1) Mao Tse-tung's rejection of Marxism  (2) Russia's criticism of India  (3) China's downgrading of Lenin  (4) the borders between China and Russia.

25. The policy of neutralism is best shown in  (1) Japan's economic recovery since 1945  (2) Great Britain's withdrawal from the Suez Canal  (3) the Soviet Union's

attempt to control Yugoslavia   (4) India's stated attitude toward the East-West controversy.

26. Relations between India and Communist China were strained by   (1) China's refusal to provide nuclear weapons to India   (2) India's efforts to spread Hinduism   (3) China's border attacks against India   (4) China's alliance with Sri Lanka.

27. In 1971 India   (1) agreed to divide Kashmir with Pakistan   (2) refused to recognize Communist China   (3) joined SEATO   (4) secured Russian support before waging war for the independence of Bangladesh.

28. Which nation in the Far East has achieved the greatest degree of industrial development?   (1) Burma   (2) India   (3) China   (4) Japan.

29. The *most* important factor in determining United States policy toward Japan and Germany since World War II has been   (1) a need for their raw materials in the United States   (2) the power of the Communist nations   (3) a desire by the United States to fulfill prewar commitments   (4) the effort of the United States to win support in the United Nations.

30. As a result of United States military involvement in Southeast Asia, Congress has   (1) delegated additional powers to the president   (2) placed greater responsibility for foreign policy on the secretary of state   (3) reasserted the role of Congress in foreign policy   (4) eliminated the requirement of a vote of Congress for a declaration of war.

31. An important reason for the quarantine ordered by President Kennedy in the Cuban crisis of 1962 was to   (1) protect refugees escaping from Cuba   (2) protect the security of the United States   (3) prevent a Cuban invasion of the Dominican Republic   (4) prevent Communist China from shipping weapons to Cuba.

32. President Kennedy viewed the settlement of the 1962 missile base crisis over Cuba as a(an)   (1) American victory   (2) Russian victory   (3) honorable accord   (4) proof of the value of the UN.

33. In 1975 Cuban troops were sent to assist a pro-Communist group seize control of   (1) Puerto Rico   (2) West Berlin   (3) Cambodia   (4) Angola.

## MATCHING QUESTIONS

For *each* description in column A, select the letter preceding the name of the person in column B who either once fit or now fits that description.

| Column A | Column B |
|---|---|
| 1. Russian dictator who ordered the Berlin Blockade | a. Fidel Castro |
| | b. Chou En-lai |
| 2. Communist leader of East Germany | c. Hua Kuo-feng |
| 3. Chancellor of West Germany | d. Erich Honecker |
| 4. Egyptian president who nationalized the Suez Canal | e. John F. Kennedy |
| | f. Nikita Khrushchev |
| 5. Communist leader of North Korea | g. Kim Il-sung |
| 6. American president who dismissed an army general for insubordination | h. Gamal Nasser |
| | i. Richard Nixon |
| 7. President of South Korea | j. Chung Hee Park |
| 8. Chairman of Chinese Communist party | k. Anwar Sadat |
| 9. American president who improved relations with China | l. Helmut Schmidt |
| | m. Joseph Stalin |
| 10. Communist leader of Cuba | n. Harry Truman |

# ESSAY QUESTIONS

1. Discuss American foreign policy toward *either* Germany *or* Japan from 1930 to the present. Include in your answer the following topics: *(a) one* cause for ill feeling, during the period from 1930 to 1941, between the United States and the country you have selected, *(b) one* major aim of United States policy toward that country following World War II, *(c) two* specific American attempts to carry out the aim given in your answer to part *(b)*.

2. Under Communist control China has attempted to reassert its historic role as the most important nation in the Far East.
   *(a)* Prove the above statement by describing Communist Chinese policy concerning either the Korean War or the Vietnam War. *(b)* State *one* reason why the United States before 1972 feared Chinese efforts to dominate the Far East. *(c)* State *one* reason why the Soviet Union now is fearful of China's growing power. *(d)* By reference to conditions within China, describe *one* factor aiding and *one* factor hindering Chinese efforts to dominate the Far East.

3. Using *one* specific fact for each, show how geographic location *or* a geographic feature has contributed to making each of the following a "trouble spot" in the 20th century: *(a)* the Dardanelles *(b)* the Gulf of Aqaba *(c)* the Suez Canal *(d)* Belgium *(e)* Poland *(f)* Korea *(g)* Cuba.

4. Agree or disagree with *each* of the following statements and give *two* reasons to support your opinion: *(a)* The dispute between the Soviet Union and Communist China has both ideological and nationalistic roots. *(b)* Korea will remain a divided nation for the foreseeable future. *(c)* The Middle East will have peace only after the Arab nations accept the existence of Israel. *(d)* The Nuremberg trials will serve to deter any future aggressor. *(e)* The unification of East and West Germany would be a threat to world peace. *(f)* From its experiences in Vietnam, the United States should learn many lessons. *(g)* By the mid-1970's the United States was turning away from the role of world police officer.

5. The following paragraph is a model representing events that led to war:

   A long series of minor conflicts strained relations between countries *A* and *B*. Using all means available to them, molders of public opinion on each side aroused hostile feelings. The public on each side was only partially informed. As a result of limited information, each side increased its bitterness toward the other. An event took place that triggered strong emotional reactions and demands for war. Public officials were caught up in the excitement and gave in to demands for military action. War followed.

   *(a)* Select any *one* war since 1945 and, using specific events, discuss the extent to which the model does or does not apply to the war chosen. *(b)* For the war discussed in *(a)*, suggest *two* possible events or actions that might have prevented the war.

# Part 5. Scientific Developments During the Cold War Era

## A. *Nuclear Energy*

### THE ISSUE OF INTERNATIONAL CONTROL

1. **Nations Possessing Nuclear Power.** The United States led the way in developing nuclear energy, exploding the first atomic bomb in 1945. Other nations followed: Russia in 1949, Great Britain in 1952, France in 1960, Communist China in 1964, and India in 1974. A number of other nations, scientists believe, possess the technical know-how to become nuclear powers. (For a discussion of nuclear energy, check the Index.)

The United States and Russia—the two superpowers of today—each has more than enough nuclear weapons and delivery systems to inflict upon the other incredible death and destruction. In former times nations were deterred somewhat from engaging in war because they were uncertain of victory due to a relatively equal "balance of power." In recent times the two superpowers have been deterred somewhat from provoking a major war because they realize that they live in the shadow of a nuclear "balance of terror."

### FIRST EFFORT TO ACHIEVE INTERNATIONAL CONTROL: A FAILURE

1. **United States Proposes the Baruch Plan.** From 1946 to 1949 the United States held a monopoly over nuclear weapons. *Bernard Baruch*, the American representative to the *UN Atomic Energy Commission*, proposed international control of nuclear weapons according to the following generous plan: The United States would destroy its atom bombs and share its technical know-how with other nations on condition that an international authority (1) supervise the use of atomic energy for only peaceful purposes and (2) have the power of unlimited inspection of atomic facilities without the restrictions of the Big Five veto in the UN Security Council.

2. **Russia Rejects the Baruch Plan.** Russia violently criticized the Baruch Plan, especially the proposals to eliminate the veto power and to provide unlimited inspection. In the Security Council in 1948, Russia vetoed the Baruch Plan and thereby halted the work of the UN Atomic Energy Commission. Unrestricted by any international controls, Russia exploded its own atom bomb in 1949 and ended the United States monopoly. Thereafter, both nations continued to develop and test nuclear weapons.

*Yardley Jones, Canada ROTHCO*

**"Who said there was intelligent life on the planet earth . . . ?"**

## EFFORT TO HALT NUCLEAR BOMB TESTS: A PARTIAL SUCCESS

In the mid-1950's the people of the world became increasingly fearful of the rising level of radioactivity resulting from nuclear weapons testing. Their fears moved Russia, the United States, and Great Britain to seek agreement at Geneva (1958 to 1963) for halting nuclear tests.

**1. Conflicting Proposals for Halting Nuclear Tests.** Russia proposed the immediate cessation of nuclear tests without any provision for enforcement. The Western powers rejected an unpoliced ban. Instead they proposed a test ban coupled with a system of inspection and control. Western leaders feared that Russia could violate an unpoliced ban without the free world's knowledge. Russia vehemently rejected the Western proposal as a plot to establish, on Soviet territory, spy rings disguised as inspection stations.

In 1961 the United States proposed a treaty to ban nuclear tests that could be detected without on-site inspection but to exclude underground blasts, since these could be confused with earthquakes and therefore could not be detected from far away. Two years later the Russians agreed to this American proposal.

**2. Limited Nuclear Test Ban Treaty (1963)**

*a. Provisions.* The Big Three powers (1) agreed not to conduct nuclear tests in the atmosphere, in space, and under water (these tests can be detected, by air-sampling and monitoring devices, without on-site inspection), (2) excluded underground tests from the ban but agreed to continue negotiations on this matter, (3) invited all other nations to sign the treaty, and (4) provided an escape clause permitting each signatory to withdraw from the treaty if it feels that the test ban jeopardizes its national interests.

*b. France and Communist China Abstain.* Although about 100 nations joined the Big Three in signing this treaty, two key nations did not. (1) *France.*

President de Gaulle insisted that France continue atmospheric testing and develop its own H-bomb. De Gaulle wanted to restore France to world prestige. (2) *China*. Chinese leaders denounced the treaty as an attempt by a few powers to monopolize nuclear weapons.

## FURTHER EFFORTS TO HALT THE NUCLEAR ARMS RACE

1. **Outlawing Nuclear Weapons in Outer Space.** In 1966 the UN General Assembly approved a treaty on the peaceful uses of outer space. The treaty prohibited any nation from claiming sovereignty over the moon and forbade nations to place nuclear arms or other weapons of mass destruction in outer space or on any heavenly body. In 1967 the treaty went into effect.

2. **Outlawing the Spread of Nuclear Weapons.** The *United Nations Disarmament Committee* sought a treaty to outlaw the spread, or *proliferation*, of nuclear weapons. The committee reasoned that as more nations gain nuclear weapons, the more difficult it will be to prevent their accidental or deliberate use. In 1968 the United States and Russia agreed on a treaty providing that *(a)* nations without nuclear weapons not develop such weapons and accept an international system of inspection, *(b)* the nuclear powers help other nations to develop peaceful uses of atomic energy, and *(c)* the nuclear powers strive to halt the arms race.

The *Nuclear Non-Proliferation Treaty* was overwhelmingly approved by the UN General Assembly. The treaty, however, was viewed with reluctance by some nations without nuclear weapons, including Australia, India, Israel, Japan, and West Germany. They were being asked to forego atomic weapons, which

**Strong Enough?**

*Bruce Shanks in The Buffalo Evening News, June 14, 1968*

could be vital to national defense and prestige. To gain support for the treaty, America, Russia, and Britain each pledged to assist any signatory nation attacked by an aggressor using nuclear weapons. In 1970 the treaty went into effect.

NUCLEAR PROLIFERATION

(1) *Pakistan.* In 1979 the United States ended its economic and military assistance to Pakistan after the Central Intelligence Agency reported that Pakistan secretly was building a plant to produce nuclear weapons. Pakistan denied the report but was unwilling to place its atomic facilities under international safeguards. In 1980, however, as the Soviet invasion of Afghanistan placed Soviet troops at the Pakistani border, President Carter offered to resume American aid. Pakistan rejected the Carter offer as insufficient but in 1981 agreed to a much larger Reagan Administration aid package. The United States explained that this aid was designed—not against India—but against the "serious threat" posed to Pakistan by Soviet troops in Afghanistan. The United States further stated that it was firmly committed to halt the spread of nuclear weapons and warned Pakistan that the aid package would be terminated in the event of a Pakistani nuclear explosion.

(2) *India.* Having refused to sign the Nuclear Nonproliferation Treaty, India in 1974 exploded an underground nuclear device that it claimed was for peaceful purposes. India, however, rejected international safeguards for all its nuclear facilities and refused to rule out production of nuclear weapons.

In 1980 President Carter, citing a 1963 agreement, decided to ship India enriched uranium fuel. Although this fuel was meant for peaceful electric power production, it could be diverted to the making of atomic bombs. The President's decision was political, observers felt, intended to keep India from moving closer to the Soviet Union, but at the sacrifice of America's nonproliferation policy. With majority votes of both Houses of Congress needed to halt the uranium shipment, the House voted against the President, but the Senate, by a two-vote margin, upheld the President's decision.

(3) *Other Third World Nations.* Supposedly for peaceful purposes, other Third World nations that have contracted with industrial powers for nuclear plants, fuel, and technology include Argentina and Brazil with West Germany and Iraq with France. (In 1981, fearing that the Iraqi facility was about to become operational and produce nuclear weapons for use against Israeli targets, Israel bombed and destroyed the Iraqi facility. For details, check the Index.)

**3. Outlawing Nuclear Weapons on the Seabed.** In 1970 the UN General Assembly approved a treaty prohibiting any nation from placing nuclear weapons on the seabed outside its 12-mile limit. In 1972 this treaty went into effect.

**4. Strategic Arms Limitation Talks (SALT).** Check the Index.

# B. Missiles

## TYPES OF MISSILES

Since World War II the United States and Russia have developed rocket-propelled missiles capable of delivering either conventional or nuclear warheads. The smallest are tactical missiles that have a short range and carry warheads of low explosive power. They can be used as battlefield artillery for close support of troops. The largest missiles, for offensive purposes, are the *intermediate range ballistic missile (IRBM)* and the *intercontinental ballistic missile (ICBM)* and, for defense purposes, the *antiballistic missile (ABM)*.

1. **Intermediate Range Ballistic Missile (IRBM).** These missiles soar into space and then descend to earth hitting a target up to 2,500 miles (4,000 kilometers) away from the launching site. The United States has relied chiefly on the *Polaris* and on its newer version, the *Poseidon*. Both missiles can be launched from a surface ship or from a submerged submarine.

Patrolling Norwegian and Mediterranean waters, American missile-carrying submarines are close enough to the Soviet Union to expose Russia's major military targets to IRBM attack. Russia also has IRBM's ready for use *(a)* from land-based sites against our European allies and *(b)* from missile-carrying submarines in the North Atlantic against major American targets.

2. **Intercontinental Ballistic Missile (ICBM).** These missiles soar into space, travel at a speed up to 20,000 miles (32,000 kilometers) per hour, and descend to earth, hitting a target over 6,000 miles (9,600 kilometers) away from the launching site. The earliest ICBM's carried a single warhead. More recent models can carry multiple warheads, with each warhead aimed at a different target. These are named *multiple independently targeted reentry vehicles (MIRV's)*.

The ICBM has been called the "ultimate weapon" because its speed and its nuclear explosive power make any defense against it extremely difficult. The United States relies chiefly on the solid-fuel *Minuteman*. Russia has ICBM's, which can be launched from sites in the Soviet Union to attack targets in the United States. China is working to develop its own ICBM's.

3. **Antiballistic Missile (ABM).** These missiles are designed to destroy offensive missiles in space. When radar indicates that enemy missiles are en route, the ABM's are to be launched to explode in the paths of the approaching missiles and destroy them by explosive force, heat, and radiation.

## EARLIEST ABM DEFENSE SYSTEMS

1. **In the Soviet Union.** By 1967 the Russians had begun installing an antiballistic missile system around Moscow. Western observers surmised that Russian ABM's were meant for defense against American as well as Chinese missiles.

2. **American ABM Plans.** In 1969 President Nixon proposed the *Safeguard* ABM system. Its purpose was to protect, not our cities, but our ICBM launching

sites against any Soviet or Chinese initial attack, or *first strike*, so as to preserve our retaliatory, or *second-strike*, capacity. Nixon won narrow congressional approval for two ABM sites.

## TWO SALT I ACCORDS—SIGNED IN 1972

Two SALT I accords, signed at Moscow by President Nixon and Communist party leader Brezhnev, provided as follows:

1. **The Treaty on ABM's.** The United States and the Soviet Union *(a)* agreed to protect by ABM defense systems only two sites each—the national capital and one ICBM launching site; *(b)* accepted a ceiling of 100 ABM launchers for each site; *(c)* pledged not to build nationwide ABM defense systems; and *(d)* provided that the treaty be of unlimited duration but allowed each nation, upon six months' notice, to withdraw from the treaty. (By a 1974 agreement the number of ABM sites was reduced for each nation from two to one.)

OBSERVATIONS: This treaty *(a)* contained a withdrawal clause in apprehension of Chinese developments and *(b)* reflected the belief that the United States and the Soviet Union each has the ability to absorb a "first strike" and to retaliate powerfully upon the other nation, thereby making a nuclear war between them improbable. This treaty was easily ratified by the United States Senate.

2. **The Interim Agreement on Offensive Missiles.** The United States and the Soviet Union "froze" at the current level their offensive missile systems: *(a)* for the United States—1,054 land-launched ICBM's and 656 submarine-launched missiles—and *(b)* for the Soviet Union—1,618 land-launched ICBM's and 710 submarine-launched missiles. This agreement was to last for five years.

OBSERVATIONS: This agreement *(a)* did *not* cover the number of warheads per missile, thereby giving the United States with its advanced MIRV technology the advantage of 5,700 warheads as compared with 2,500 for the Soviet Union; *(b)* did *not* cover the explosive power of each warhead, thereby giving the Soviet Union with its larger warheads a 3-to-1 lead in explosive power; *(c)* did *not* cover the number of long-range bombers capable of delivering nuclear bombs, thereby giving the United States a lead of 460 strategic bombers to 140 for the Soviets; *(d)* did *not* limit the construction of strategic bombers and did *not* prevent the replacement of existing missiles and submarines by more destructive models; and *(e)* did *not* provide for on-site inspection to prevent violations.

*Supporters* pointed out that the interim agreement *(a)* implied that both nations are roughly equal in offensive missile power, *(b)* may encourage a feeling of friendship and cooperation, and *(c)* may arrest the arms race.

*Critics* pointed out that the interim agreement would *(a)* not reduce the current offensive missile arsenals, *(b)* shift the arms race from competition in missile numbers to competition in technology and in areas not covered by its provisions, and *(c)* make highly improbable any reduction in arms defense spending.

Although the offensive missiles accord was an executive agreement and therefore did not require ratification, it was submitted by Nixon to both houses of Congress and received an overwhelming "concurrence."

## THE SALT II TREATY—SIGNED IN 1979

After seven years of negotiations, the SALT II Treaty was signed at Vienna by President Carter and Soviet leader Brezhnev. It was a technical 100-page document.

1. **Provisions.** (*a*) The United States and the Soviet Union each accepted, as of 1982, an overall ceiling of 2,250 strategic nuclear-delivery vehicles. These included land-based intercontinental ballistic missiles (ICBM's), submarine-launched ballistic missiles (SLBM's), heavy bombers, and air-to-surface ballistic missiles (ASBM's) with a range of over 375 miles (600 kilometers). Within the overall ceiling, the treaty imposed subceilings on these various missile types. It also set limits on the number of MIRV's, or warheads, per missile and the weight per missile. (*b*) The United States and the Soviet Union both agreed to test and deploy no more than one new type of ICBM. (*c*) The treaty placed no limits on Russia's *Backfire* bomber, which the Soviets insisted upon excluding from the treaty. The Soviets held the *Backfire* to be an intermediate-range plane, but Americans considered it to be a strategic long-range bomber. The Soviets pledged not to increase the current rate of *Backfire* production—about 30 per year. (*d*) The treaty limited, until 1982, America's air- or sea-launched cruise missile to a maximum range of 375 miles. (The cruise missile is a low-flying, pilotless vehicle that can be guided to its target.) (*e*) The treaty did not provide for on-site inspection to verify compliance with its terms. Both nations, however, agreed not to conceal missile activities and not to impede verification by "national technical means" (NTM)—such as satellites and intelligence listening posts. (*f*) The SALT II Treaty expires in 1985. Both nations agreed to work for further limitations in nuclear weapons as part of a SALT III treaty.

2. **Arguments for the SALT II Treaty.** (*a*) It furthers the principle of equality in the two superpowers' strategic missile arsenals. (*b*) It requires the Soviets, by 1982, to dismantle over 10 percent of their strategic nuclear missile systems so as to conform to the 2,250 ceiling. Also, by its various other ceilings, the treaty inhibits the growth of Soviet missile power, which without any treaty could expand greatly. (*c*) The restriction to 1982 on America's cruise missile is not vital since the United States could not produce longer-range cruise missiles within that time period. (*d*) President Carter claimed that the treaty "will lessen the danger of nuclear destruction while safeguarding our military security."

3. **Arguments Against the SALT II Treaty.** (*a*) Although the treaty limits both nations equally regarding overall nuclear-delivery vehicles, the Soviets have a major advantage in that their missiles are larger and more destructive than those of the United States. (*b*) By limiting new-type ICBM's to only one, the treaty severely handicaps American efforts to deploy varied mobile missile systems.

These are needed since the existing, fixed, land-based *Minuteman* missiles are vulnerable to a surprise attack by increasingly accurate Soviet missiles. *(c)* The treaty places no limits on the Soviet *Backfire* bomber, which could be used for a one-way attack upon United States targets. *(d)* The United States, having lost its intelligence listening posts in Iran, will be unable to verify Soviet compliance with the treaty. *(e)* By permitting modernization of existing weapons, although limited, the treaty will not halt the nuclear arms race and will not permit any reduction in military spending.

**4. President Carter's Moves to Obtain Senate Ratification.** The SALT II Treaty required a two-thirds vote of the Senate for ratification. A number of Senators feared that the treaty confirmed Soviet nuclear superiority over the United States. To quiet such fears, President Carter agreed to proceed with the *MX mobile missile system.* This system would move more powerful land-based missiles back and forth through 20-mile-long (32-kilometer) trenches to disguise their location from the Soviets. The MX system would be built in sparsely inhabited areas of Nevada and Utah, cost some $30 billion, and be fully operative by 1989.

**5. A Complicating Factor: Soviet Combat Force in Cuba (1979).** American intelligence reported the existence of a Soviet combat brigade, of up to 3,000 men, in Cuba. Although President Carter held that this force posed no direct military threat to the United States, its presence in Cuba raised questions of Soviet motives and intentions. The Carter Administration entered into negotiations with the Soviets, during which the Soviets insisted that the force was a "training center," not a combat unit, but pledged that they would "not change its function or status." President Carter announced countermeasures: increased surveillance of Cuba, a full-time Caribbean military task force headquarters, and more economic assistance for the Caribbean region.

The President urged the Senate to ratify the SALT II Treaty on its own merits. A number of Senators, however, argued that the Soviet combat force in Cuba was an additional reason for rejecting the SALT II Treaty.

**6. A Second Complicating Factor: Soviet Invasion of Afghanistan (1979–1980).** With the Soviet invasion of Afghanistan, President Carter requested the Senate to delay consideration of the SALT II Treaty. While the President still held SALT II to be in the national interest, he concluded that the Soviet invasion made consideration of SALT II at the present time "inappropriate." The United States, however, said that, as long as the Soviets honor the SALT II terms, the United States would do likewise.

**7. Policies of President Reagan.** In his successful 1980 campaign for the Presidency, Ronald Reagan labeled SALT II a "bad treaty" and proposed his policy: to negotiate with the Soviets for a better and more equitable treaty that would achieve a reduction by both sides in nuclear weapons.

In 1981 President Reagan discarded the Carter MX mobile missile system. It was *(a)* opposed by environmentalists and by Nevada and Utah inhabitants, *(b)* costly and would not become operative until 1989, and *(c)* of doubtful military feasibility. Instead, Reagan proposed to *(a)* place 100 MX missiles in existing missile silos, "hardened" to withstand any direct nuclear strike, *(b)* build 100 improved B-1 long-range aircraft bombers (a project canceled by Carter), *(c)* equip existing and new *Trident* submarines with larger, more accurate sea-launched missiles, and *(d)* continue development of the *Stealth* bomber—an aircraft virtually undetectable by radar (the *Stealth* plane is scheduled to replace the B-1 bomber in the 1990's). Reagan explained that his proposals would be less costly, be operative more quickly, and "insure America's national security while vigorously pursuing every path to peace." These Reagan proposals were subjected to much critical analysis.

# C. Satellites and Other Space Vehicles

## RUSSIA LAUNCHES SPUTNIKS

The *International Geophysical Year* (1957–1958) was an international cooperative effort to increase humanity's knowledge of the physical environment. As part of the program, the United States and Soviet Russia each announced plans to place into orbit around the earth data-gathering satellites. The Soviet Union was first to fulfill this promise. In 1957 Russian scientists orbited the first human-made satellite, the 184-pound (82.8-kilogram) *Sputnik I*, and later the 1,120-pound (504-kilogram) *Sputnik II*.

## EFFECT OF RUSSIA'S SATELLITES ON THE UNITED STATES

Russia's initial lead in the space race greatly perturbed the American people. Why had the United States fallen behind? The following explanations were given: (1) As a dictatorship Russia was able to concentrate all necessary resources toward achieving its goals regardless of the low standard of living of the people. As a democracy the United States had to heed the public's demand for consumer goods. (2) Soviet education, critics said, was ahead of that in the United States in science, mathematics, and technical subjects. (3) The Communists channeled their best students into science, mathematics, and engineering. In the United States many capable students selected nontechnical fields.

## THE UNITED STATES SPEEDS UP ITS SPACE PROGRAM

(1) Congress approved additional funds for missile and satellite research, development, and production. (2) Congress passed the *National Defense Education Act* (1958) to improve education, especially in science and mathematics. (3) Congress established a new agency to direct the nonmilitary aspects of space exploration—the *National Aeronautics and Space Administration (NASA)*.

## INITIAL AMERICAN SPACE FLIGHTS

In 1958, from *Cape Canaveral*, Florida, the United States placed into orbit its first satellite, the 18-pound (8-kilogram) *Explorer I*. This achievement came some four months after the Russian launching of Sputnik I. Later in 1958 the United States placed into orbit the three-pound (1.4-kilogram) *Vanguard I* and the 18-pound (8-kilogram) *Explorer III*. Russian Premier Khrushchev gibed at the American satellites, calling them "grapefruits" in relation to the much larger Russian Sputniks.

Thereafter, both nations achieved considerable progress in space.

## MAJOR SOVIET EFFORTS IN SPACE

1. **Unmanned Flights.** *(a) Around the Earth.* The Soviets placed many satellites of their *Cosmos* series into orbit to test equipment for military and peaceful uses, to provide military communications, and to gather weather data. *(b) To the Moon.* The Soviets sent many *Luna* space vehicles to the moon, some reaching its surface and sending back pictures. In 1970 *Luna 17* landed on the moon, carrying a self-propelled vehicle, *Lunokhod 1*. It roamed the lunar surface analyzing lunar soil and relayed the data back to earth. In 1972 *Luna 20* returned to earth with a cargo of moon rocks. (These Soviet unmanned moon explorations contrasted with the American manned moon landings and raised the issue of which method was more advantageous in terms of costs and results.) *(c) To the Planets.* The Soviets sent several spaceships to the planets Mars and Venus and in 1975 achieved two soft landings on Venus. The more recent ships transmitted back scientific data about these planets.

2. **Manned Flights.** The Soviets achieved a number of space firsts. In 1961 *Vostok 1* orbited the earth once, carrying the world's first cosmonaut, *Yuri Gagarin*. In 1963 *Vostok 6* completed a 48-orbit flight carrying the first woman cosmonaut, *Valentina Tereshkova*. In 1964 *Voskhod 1* became history's first multipassenger space capsule. In 1965 a cosmonaut left *Voskhod 2* and achieved the first space walk. In 1971 the Soviets orbited *Salyut 1,* the first space station, and sent a three-man team to live in the station and perform scientific experiments. In 1979 a two-man Soviet team returned to earth after having lived in the *Salyut 6* space station for 175 days.

## MAJOR AMERICAN EFFORTS IN SPACE

1. **Unmanned Flights:** *(a) Around the Earth.* The United States placed many satellites into orbit: the *Explorer* series to increase our scientific knowledge of space; *Transit* satellites to assist airplane and ship pilots in navigation; *Telstar, Early Bird*, and *Intelsat*, all privately financed satellites, to build a global telecommunications system; and the *Tiros* series to gather weather data. *(b) To the Moon.* The United States sent to the moon a number of spacecraft that landed on the lunar surface and sent back thousands of photographs. *(c) To the Planets.* The United States sent to Mars and Venus a number of *Mariner* spaceships that have sent back pictures and scientific data. In 1973 *Pioneer 10* ended a 21-month

journey to Jupiter and provided photographs of that outer planet. Pioneer 10, carrying a pictorial plaque, was expected to escape from our solar system and travel into the Milky Way—where possibly it might be seen by other intelligent beings—if any exist. In 1974 *Mariner 10* reached and photographed Mercury, the planet closest to our sun. In 1976 two *Viking* vehicles reached the vicinity of Mars, and each placed a landing craft on that planet's surface. The Viking landers sent back photographs of the terrain, data regarding the atmosphere, and analyses of the Martian soil. In 1979, after a six-and-a-half-year trip, *Pioneer 11* swept past and sent back data about the rings, moons, and atmosphere of the planet Saturn. In 1981, after a four-year trip, *Voyager 2* sent back pictures and data as it flew by Saturn. The spacecraft then proceeded on a course that by 1986 would enable it to approach the planet Uranus.

**2. Manned Flights.** At first behind, the United States eventually surpassed the Soviets in the number and complexity of manned flights. In 1962 the United States sent *Friendship 7* to circle the earth three times with America's first orbiting astronaut, *John Glenn*. Then the United States orbited many multipassenger space vehicles, and American astronauts practiced spacewalking, then docking (joining together) of spacecraft in orbit, and finally guiding a lunar module, or landing craft, to leave and then return to the command, or "mother," ship.

In 1969, with the 11th flight of the *Project Apollo* series, the United States achieved a historic first. While *Michael Collins* orbited the moon in the command ship *Columbia*, *Neil Armstrong* and *Edwin Aldrin* descended to the moon's surface in the lunar module *Eagle*. Armstrong, the first human to set foot on the moon, spoke the historic words, "That's one small step for a man, one giant leap

**What great discoveries lie ahead?**

R.N. PALMER

*Palmer in The Springfield (MO) Leader & Press*

for mankind." The two astronauts gathered rock samples, set up scientific experiments, stationed a plaque saying "We came in peace for all mankind," and then ascended to the command ship. The three men then returned safely to earth. Five subsequent *Apollo* flights repeated the moon-landing triumph.

In 1973 the United States placed into orbit its first space station, *Skylab*. Successive teams of American astronauts have lived in the space station, performing experiments and gathering data.

### OTHER SPACE EFFORTS

(1) In 1972 President Nixon and Soviet leader Brezhnev agreed to a joint American-Soviet space venture, the *Apollo-Soyuz Test Project*. The project, to link up and exchange crews, took place in 1975 and was successful. (2) Other nations that launched satellites into orbit include Great Britain, France, Italy, Japan, and China. (3) In 1975 ten West European nations, to further space research, established the *European Space Agency (ESA)*.

### FUTURE AMERICAN SPACE GOALS

President Nixon asserted that in the making of space history "this nation means to play a major role." NASA, however, faced a cutback of funds and slowed work on new space projects. Many scientific and technical workers were dismissed, and research teams were broken up. To generate support, NASA advocates pointed out that space exploration—in addition to military uses and to enhanced knowledge of the solar system—benefits our daily lives. Orbiting satellites are used to provide long-distance communications and television broadcasts, to improve weather forecasting, and to map the earth for water and mineral resources. Smoke detectors, now found in many homes, were first developed for use in *Skylab*. Space exploration needs spurred the growth of computer technology.

In 1981 NASA launched the first reusable winged *space shuttle*, the *Columbia*. A manned vehicle carrying two astronauts, it was placed into orbit, circled the earth 36 times, and glided to a safe landing in southern California. Because it can be reused for many trips, the space shuttle will be less costly than previous single-use orbiting vehicles. In late 1981 the *Columbia* was again placed into orbit and, although the flight was cut short because of a faulty fuel cell, the two astronauts on this second flight performed most of the planned experiments and returned safely to earth.

# Part 6. American-Russian Relations Since World War II: A Fluctuating Pattern

Since World War II relations between Russia and the United States have varied from periods of great tension to periods of comparative calm.

## 1947–1953: PERIOD OF TENSION

While Stalin ruled, Russia pursued a "hard line" toward the free world, and the United States responded by its policy of containment. Evidences of tension were the (1) Truman Doctrine (1947), (2) Berlin Blockade (1948–1949), (3) creation of NATO (1949), and (4) Korean War (1950–1953).

## 1954–1959: COMPARATIVE CALM

In the years after Stalin's death, Khrushchev espoused peaceful coexistence, and relations between Russia and the United States improved.

**1. Summit Conference of 1955.** President Eisenhower met at Geneva with the leaders of Great Britain, France, and Russia. They discussed East-West problems in a calm and friendly atmosphere but reached no settlements. Subsequent events indicated that the 1955 summit meeting had failed to resolve any cold war problems.

**2. Scientific and Cultural Exchanges (1958).** The United States and Russia inaugurated a scientific and cultural exchange program. Since then, reciprocal visits have been made by athletes, scholars, concert artists, orchestras, ballet groups, writers, and scientists.

**3. Khrushchev's Visit to the United States (1959).** Khrushchev visited the United States and received a friendly reception. Khrushchev showed great interest in many facets of American life. He met with President Eisenhower, and the two men initiated plans for another summit conference.

## 1960–1962: ANOTHER PERIOD OF TENSION

**1. U-2 Incident and the Summit Conference of 1960.** Two weeks before a new summit conference was to be held in Paris, the Soviets shot down, deep inside Russian territory, an unarmed American U-2 reconnaissance plane. The Soviets, who maintained an extensive espionage system in the West, had known of such U-2 flights but had not previously protested against them. In Paris Khrushchev accused America of aggression, vilified Eisenhower, and demanded an apology. Eisenhower denied the charge of aggression and refused to apologize. The summit meeting was dead.

**2. Building of the Berlin Wall (1961).** (Check the Index.)

**3. Cuban Missile Base Crisis (1962).** (Check the Index.)

## 1963–1968: COMPARATIVE CALM

Following the peaceful settlement of the Cuban crisis and the deepening of the Soviet-Chinese split, Russian-American relations improved.

**1. Limited Nuclear Test Ban Treaty (1963).** The United States and Russia agreed to a ban on all but underground nuclear tests. This was the first agreement to emerge from 18 years of East-West disarmament negotiations.

Reprinted by permission of NEA.

**"It's a good thing we haven't buried capitalism yet
—else what would we do for bread?"**

**2. Hot Line (1963).** Russia and the United States established a "hot line," or emergency communications link, between Washington and Moscow to reduce the risk of war by blunder or miscalculation.

**3. Wheat Sale (1963).** With Russia suffering from a poor grain harvest, the United States sold substantial quantities of wheat to the Soviet Union.

**4. Consular Treaty (1964).** The United States and the Soviet Union signed their first bilateral treaty. It *(a)* granted diplomatic immunity to consular officials and *(b)* required that consular officials be informed of and granted access to any of their country's citizens placed under arrest.

**5. Nuclear Non-Proliferation Treaty (1968).** The United States and Russia agreed to a treaty to outlaw the spread of nuclear weapons.

## 1969–PRESENT: COMPARATIVE CALM AND A SEARCH FOR DÉTENTE

President Nixon, his successor President Ford, and Soviet Communist party chief Brezhnev each voiced support for moving American-Soviet relations into a new era of détente. Secretary of State Kissinger defined détente as the "process of managing relations with a potentially hostile country in order to preserve peace while maintaining our vital interests." A Soviet expert on foreign policy explained that détente "sets limits on what each side can do without risking war and gets officials concerned—Soviet and American—talking with each other."

In 1977 President Carter delivered a major address on Soviet-American relations. While pointing out profound differences between the two societies— in history, values, and concepts of freedom and power—President Carter affirmed the policy of his administration to "enlarge the areas of cooperation between us, on a basis of equality and mutual respect."

# SUCCESSES OF DÉTENTE

1. **Four-Power Agreement on Berlin (1971).** (Check the Index.)

2. **Nixon's Journey to Moscow (1972).** Despite Soviet-American tensions over Vietnam, President Nixon journeyed to Moscow to a summit meeting with Soviet Premier Kosygin and Communist party chief Brezhnev. Nixon received a restrained but correct welcome, and his time was occupied chiefly with businesslike negotiations. Nixon and the Soviet leaders signed a number of significant accords: *(a) on space*—to cooperate in 1975 in a joint Soviet-American docking and flight of manned spacecraft; *(b) on health*—to coordinate Soviet-American research on cancer, heart disease, and public health; *(c) on incidents at sea*—to set rules so that Soviet and American naval vessels operating near each other will avoid collisions; *(d) on environment and technology*—to cooperate in the study of pollution problems and in other scientific research; *(e) on trade*—to establish a joint commission to resolve trade problems so as to increase Soviet-American trade; and *(f) on nuclear arms*—to limit ABM sites and "freeze" current offensive-missile arsenals.

3. **Strategic Arms Limitation Talks; Two SALT I Accords (1972).** (Check the Index.)

4. **Brezhnev's Visit to the United States (1973).** Soviet Communist party chief Brezhnev visited the United States, projected a spirit of friendship, and spoke to the American people via television. He and President Nixon signed a number of accords: to make every effort to avoid a military confrontation, to expand air passenger service between the United States and the Soviet Union, to promote trade, to continue cultural and educational exchanges, and to cooperate in oceanographic, transportation, and agricultural research.

5. **Helsinki Pact (1975).** Leaders of the United States, Canada, and 33 European nations met at Helsinki, Finland, to conclude the *Conference on Security and Cooperation in Europe*. They signed a charter containing two major provisions:

*(a)* Accepting as inviolate the post-World War II boundaries in Europe. By this provision the Western powers held that they were being realistic—acknowledging a situation they could not alter peaceably. Russia was jubilant because this provision formally recognized Soviet territorial gains in Europe, the division of Germany into two nations, and Soviet domination of Eastern Europe. This provision was hailed as a personal triumph for Soviet Communist party head Brezhnev.

*(b)* Agreeing in principle to further human rights. By this provision the Soviet Union and the satellite Communist nations promised to ease the movement of individuals across frontiers, assist in the reunion of separated families, reduce restrictions on journalists, and increase East-West cultural and educational exchanges. Western observers wondered, however, whether these promises would be kept.

**"Détente."**

*Drawing by Richter; © 1974 The New Yorker Magazine, Inc.*

## DISILLUSIONMENT ABOUT DÉTENTE

**1. United States:** (*a*) Members of Congress protested the internal Soviet crackdown on dissident intellectuals and minority groups. Congress members pointed to the forced exile in 1974 of the Russian author and dissenter, *Alexander Solzhenitsyn*. In his book *The Gulag Archipelago,* published only in the West, the famed Nobel Prize winner documented the history of Soviet prison camp tyranny and asserted that tyranny was an integral part of the Soviet system. American Congress members, led by Senator Henry Jackson, also pointed to Soviet harassment of persons, chiefly Jews, seeking to leave the Soviet Union. Would-be emigrants, upon making their intentions known, were fired from their jobs, expelled from their living quarters, kept waiting for months and years enmeshed in bureaucratic red tape, and—if permitted to leave—required to pay exorbitant exit fees. In 1974 Congress approved a trade bill that permitted trade benefits for the Soviets on condition that they allow emigrants to leave the Soviet Union promptly and without harassment.

(*b*) American foreign policy experts concluded that Soviet words and actions in the 1973 Arab-Israeli War were indistinguishable from the bitterest of cold war days.

*(c)* American military leaders pointed out that Russia had accelerated its building of offensive nuclear weapons. Although permitted by the 1972 SALT I accord, these additional offensive nuclear weapons did not indicate peaceful intentions.

*(d)* American critics of détente pointed out that the Soviet Union had provided the massive weapons used by Hanoi to triumph in South Vietnam and by the MPLA and the Cubans to triumph in Angola. They further quoted Brezhnev's statement in 1976 at the 25th Soviet Communist Party Congress that the Soviet Union sees détente as "the way to create more favorable conditions for peaceful socialist and Communist construction" and that détente does not "abolish or alter the laws of class struggle." American critics of détente claimed that it was a "one-way street" benefiting only the Soviet Union.

*(e)* After taking office in 1977, President Carter announced that one aspect of his administration's foreign policy would be concern for human rights. Accordingly the United States charged Czechoslovakia with violating the Helsinki Pact provision on human rights by harassment of Czechoslovak dissidents. Some 300 writers, journalists, scientists, and former political figures had called for internal civil liberties and cultural freedom by signing and publicizing a document called *Charter 77.* The United States also stated that the Soviet Union would be in conflict with "accepted international standards of human rights" by continued

"Don't believe everything you read."

John Knudsen Studios in The Catholic News

efforts to silence the world-renowned dissident: atomic scientist and 1975 Nobel Peace Prize winner *Andrei Sakharov.* (In 1980 the Soviet government, to silence Sakharov, removed him from Moscow and sentenced him to "internal exile" at Gorky, a city closed to foreigners.) The President explained to Moscow that his human rights campaign was not limited to Soviet-bloc nations but was global in scope. It was not intended, said the President, to threaten Soviet interests, nor was it designed to bring back the cold war; rather it was a reaffirmation of fundamental American values.

**2. Soviet Union:**(*a*) Soviet trade experts protested that the American Congress, despite administration promises, had long delayed a sweeping trade agreement. The Soviets wanted substantial American credits and loans with which to purchase American machinery and technology, pay for imports of American grain, and develop Siberian oil and gas resources. The Soviets also wanted the United States to tax Soviet imports at the lowest regular tariff rate—such treatment being known as "most-favored-nation" status. The Soviets resented the 1974 legislation passed by Congress that limited Export-Import Bank loans to Russia and tied trade benefits to the easing of Russian emigration policies. In early 1975 the Soviet Union canceled the 1972 Soviet-American trade accord.

(*b*) Soviet political leaders objected to efforts by American Congress members to change Soviet policies regarding dissident intellectuals and minority groups. These policies, the Russians insisted, dealt with internal Soviet matters beyond the scope of American concern and would be maintained in the interests of the Communist state. The Soviets also expressed resentment against President Carter's human rights campaign as unwarranted interference with internal

*Bruce Shanks in The Buffalo Evening News*

"The course of human events."

Soviet policies. At the 1977–1978 *Belgrade Conference*, held to review compliance with the Helsinki Pact, the Soviet Union warned the United States against raising human rights issues as dangerous to the cause of détente. With unanimous consent required for statements at Belgrade, the Soviet Union was able to omit from the summary communiqué any mention of human rights.

(*c*) Communist foreign policy experts complained that the United States was seeking to erode Soviet influence in the Arab Mideast.

**An End to Détente?** With the Soviet invasion of Afghanistan (1979–1980) and the American responses by the Carter Administration—delaying consideration of the SALT II Treaty, restricting high-technology exports to the Soviet Union, offering substantial military aid to Pakistan, and boycotting the summer Olympic Games at Moscow—observers believed that the two superpowers were abandoning détente and returning to the tensions of the cold war.

Although the Reagan Administration (that took office in 1981) expressed the desire for "fair agreements" with Moscow, the administration held a critical view of Soviet foreign policies. Bluntly, Secretary of State *Alexander Haig* accused the Soviets of (1) responsibility for "international terrorism" by maintaining terrorist training camps in the Soviet Union, in its East European satellites, and in its North African ally Libya, (2) imperialist adventurism to expand Soviet control in the Persian Gulf, South Asia, Africa, and Central America, and (3) posing the "most serious threat to world peace." With vehemence, the Soviets verbally assaulted the Reagan Administration for (1) bringing the "world closer to a nuclear catastrophe" by planning to place American nuclear weapons in Western Europe (where they would face Soviet missiles, already installed, in Eastern Europe) and by deciding to produce the *neutron bomb*—a tactical nuclear weapon designed to produce more radiation but less blast and heat so as to kill soldiers while limiting property damage, (2) "playing the China card" by agreeing to sell China modern American weapons and by jointly operating an intelligence-gathering station in western China to monitor Soviet missile tests, and (3) speeding the arms race by sharp increases in American military spending. With charges and counter-charges flying high, observers foresaw the continued unraveling of détente.

## MULTIPLE–CHOICE QUESTIONS

1. The *least* important factor in explaining the destructiveness of nuclear weapons is their great (1) heat (2) radioactivity (3) blast force (4) weight.
2. The Baruch Plan for international control of atomic energy did *not* propose (1) an international authority in which no nation would have the veto power (2) unlimited inspection (3) stockpiling of atomic bombs (4) sharing American atomic know-how with other nations.
3. The Baruch Plan never went into effect because of (1) the UN's lack of interest in the problem (2) American opposition to international control (3) a Russian veto in the UN Security Council (4) Britain's refusal to cooperate.

4. The *chief* factor that long blocked agreement between Russia and the United States on a nuclear test ban was the dispute regarding (1) admission of Communist China to the test ban conference (2) the war in Vietnam (3) effective measures of inspection and control (4) the building of the Berlin Wall.

5. The 1963 limited nuclear test ban treaty permits testing (1) in the atmosphere (2) in space (3) below ground (4) under water.

6. A leading European nation that refused to sign the limited nuclear test ban treaty was (1) Communist China (2) Czechoslovakia (3) France (4) Italy.

7. The "proliferation" of atomic weapons refers to their (1) spread to many nations (2) complexity (3) radiation (4) use to produce electricity.

8. In regard to the SALT I accords, which statement is *most* valid? (1) They did not provide for limiting ABM systems. (2) They called for on-site inspection to prevent violations. (3) They enabled the United States and Russia to reduce significantly their military defense spending. (4) They did not call for any reduction in existing offensive missile arsenals.

9. The SALT I accords are significant because they (1) provided an example of UN effectiveness (2) provided for joint American-Soviet space flights (3) are a first step toward limiting a nuclear missile arms race (4) ended the cold war.

10. In 1957 the first human-made satellite was placed into orbit around the earth by (1) a UN team of scientists (2) Russia (3) the United States (4) Great Britain.

11. Yuri Gagarin of the Soviet Union was the first person to (1) design a space vehicle (2) achieve a space flight (3) die on a space flight (4) take close-up photographs of the moon.

12. The chief object of Project Apollo was to (1) send space teams to the moon and back (2) gather data about Venus and Mars (3) establish a worldwide telecommunications system (4) improve the forecasting of weather.

13. "We came in peace for all mankind" was said (1) by President Carter and Soviet leader Brezhnev at their 1979 Vienna meeting (2) by American and Soviet negotiators at the SALT II meetings (3) on a plaque left on the moon by the two American astronauts who first set foot on the moon's surface (4) by Alexander Solzhenitsyn, the Russian author and dissenter, who spoke for his family upon being exiled from Russia.

14. The "hot line" and the nuclear test ban treaty are indications that (1) the alliance systems headed by the Soviet Union and the United States are being strengthened (2) to some extent cold war tensions between the United States and the Soviet Union have eased (3) the United States is relying heavily on its policy of containment (4) the great powers are cooperating on the peaceful uses of space.

15. Détente is best explained as (1) an American policy of protection for intellectuals and minority groups (2) a Russian policy of seeking large loans and expanding trade (3) a policy of both the United States and the Soviet Union to reduce tensions and improve relations between the two countries (4) a joint American-Soviet policy to impose peace terms upon the Middle East.

16. Which event indicated a Soviet "hard line" toward the West? (1) establishing the "hot line" communications link (2) signing the limited nuclear test ban treaty (3) placing missiles in Cuba (4) differing with China regarding peaceful coexistence.

17. Russia cancelled the 1972 trade accord with the United States because Russia (1) lacked funds to pay for imports of American grain (2) resented Congress' effort to tie trade to liberalization of Soviet emigration policies (3) had little need of imports from the United States (4) was offered better trade terms by West Germany.

18. In recent years United States involvement in world crises has *most* clearly shown that (1) solutions to major international problems require the cooperation of the major world powers (2) isolation is the only way to assure the safety of the United

States  (3) international affairs have come to be dominated by the small nations  (4) meaningful settlements can come about only through the UN.

19. Based on your knowledge of world history, which prediction would be easiest to defend?  (1) Europe will have a single economic system by 1990.  (2) Unsettled areas of Africa will provide space for the expanding population of Asia.  (3) World problems and the need to solve those problems will grow at an ever-increasing rate.  (4) As more people become literate, conflict among nations will decrease.

## MAP QUESTIONS

For each area described below, write *both* its name and the letter indicating its location on the map.

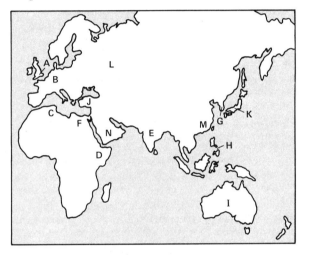

1. During 1962 this country supplied Cuba with missiles and technicians.
2. This populous Asian nation had been engaged in a border war with its Communist neighbor to the north.
3. This divided country containing a divided city has been the scene of many crises between the Communist world and the free world.
4. In the 1950's a United Nations army fought to prevent this country from falling to the Communists.
5. This British Commonwealth nation was a member of both the Anzus Pact and SEATO.
6. This country was conquered by Fascist Italy in 1935–1936 and regained its independence during World War II.
7. This nation, which bombed Pearl Harbor in 1941, now has a military alliance with the United States.
8. From this country the Allied forces launched their invasion of continental Europe in 1944 on D-Day.
9. This Moslem country in Asia has been directly involved in the dispute over Cyprus.
10. This Mideast Arab country, ruled by a conservative monarchy, has been a major source of oil for industrialized nations.

## ESSAY QUESTIONS

1. While we continue to develop peaceful uses for nuclear energy, we must find a way to deal with the problem of more and more countries possessing nuclear weapons. *(a)* Mention *one* military development in nuclear energy since 1945 and *one* development of nuclear energy for a peaceful use. *(b)* Name *two* international agreements regarding nuclear energy or missiles. Evaluate *each* agreement named as a means of reducing the possibility of nuclear warfare.

2. Science has taught us how to put the atom to work, but to make it work for good instead of evil is a problem in human relations. *(a)* Prove briefly that science has "put the atom to work." *(b)* Give *two* facts to show how the atom can "work for good instead of for evil." *(c)* Show why the major world problem today is not progress in science, but the relationship of human beings to one another.

3. Give *two* reasons for agreeing or disagreeing with *each* of the following statements: *(a)* It would have been better for humanity if nuclear energy had never been discovered. *(b)* The development of nuclear energy has increased the military security of the United States. *(c)* The SALT I accords were a major step toward world peace. *(d)* The space age will affect humanity as much as did the 16th-century age of discovery and exploration. *(e)* If détente is to succeed, the United States and the Soviet Union must place the goal of world peace ahead of all other national interests.

4. The cold war has required the Western democracies to estimate correctly their own strengths and weaknesses as well as those of Communist Russia and its satellites. Describe *(a) one* strength and *one* weakness of the Western democracies and *(b) one* strength and *one* weakness of Communist Russia and its satellites. *(c)* State *two* policies of the United States in the cold war and explain, citing evidence, whether each policy was successful or not.

5. United States foreign policy since 1945 has had *three* specific goals: *(a)* defense of the United States against attack *(b)* the maintenance of world peace *(c)* the promotion of economic and social welfare abroad. Discuss *two* specific means used by the United States to accomplish *each* of these goals.

6. To answer this question, refer to the cartoon entitled "The course of human events" on page 592. *(a)* Briefly state the major idea or concept presented in this cartoon. *(b)* Name *two* foreign policy crises of the past and explain how *each* was solved. *(c)* Name *two* foreign policy crises of the present and indicate your ideas of what the solutions might be. *(d)* In your opinion what might be *one* foreign policy crisis in the near future? Discuss *one* reason to support your opinion.

7. Today some of the best minds in our country are giving serious thought to the establishment of permanent world peace. Basing your answer upon your knowledge of modern history, especially since 1914, discuss *three* problems involved in the establishment of a suitable and permanent peace.

# Index

597